THE I TATTI
RENAISSANCE LIBRARY

*James Hankins, General Editor*

NAVAGERO
FLAMINIO

LATIN PASTORAL POETRY

ITRL 101

## THE I TATTI RENAISSANCE LIBRARY

James Hankins, General Editor
Shane Butler, Associate Editor
Leah Whittington, Associate Editor
Patrick Baker, Managing Editor

### Editorial Board

Michael J. B. Allen †
Francesco Bausi
Brian P. Copenhaver
Martin Davies
Vincenzo Fera
Julia Haig Gaisser
Walther Ludwig
Nicholas Mann
Silvia Rizzo †

### Advisory Committee

Alina Payne, Chair

Robert Black
Maurizio Campanelli
Michele Ciliberto
Caroline Elam
Arthur Field
Anthony Grafton
Hanna Holborn Gray
Ralph Hexter
Craig Kallendorf †
Jill Kraye
Marc Laureys
Francesco Lo Monaco

David Marsh
Massimo Miglio
John Monfasani
John O'Malley †
Marianne Pade
David Quint
Christine Smith
Francesco Tateo
Mirko Tavoni
Carlo Vecce
Jan Ziolkowski

# ANDREA NAVAGERO
# MARCANTONIO FLAMINIO
# LATIN PASTORAL POETRY

EDITED AND TRANSLATED BY

ALLAN M. WILSON

THE I TATTI RENAISSANCE LIBRARY

HARVARD UNIVERSITY PRESS

CAMBRIDGE, MASSACHUSETTS

LONDON, ENGLAND

2025

Copyright © 2025 by the President and Fellows of Harvard College
All rights reserved
Printed in the United States of America

Series design by Dean Bornstein

First printing

*Library of Congress Cataloging-in-Publication Data available from*
*The Library of Congress at https://lccn.loc.gov/2024017356*

ISBN 978-0-674-29837-8 (cloth : alk. paper)

# Contents

Introduction   vii

## ANDREA NAVAGERO
*Latin Poems in the 1718 Edition*   2
*Further Poems Ascribed to Navagero*   98

## MARCANTONIO FLAMINIO
*Latin Poems, Book III*   130
*Latin Poems, Book IV*   158

Abbreviations   211

Note on the Texts   213

Notes to the Texts   217

Notes to the Translations   227

Concordances   381

Titles of Poems   385

Manuscripts with Latin Poems of Navagero   395

Handlist of Editions, Translations,
Anthologies, and Further Reading   403

Bibliography   431

Index to Navagero   443

Index to Flaminio   473

# Introduction

❧❧❧

### Andrea Navagero

The humanist scholar, Latin and Italian poet, orator, and diplomat Andrea Navagero or Navagiero, in Latin Andreas Naugerius or Navagerius, was born in Venice in or very close to 1483[1] and died at Blois, France, on May 8, 1529.[2] Of patrician lineage, though his father was not a man of great wealth, he was the son of Bernardo di Andrea Navagero (d. 1517) and Lucrezia Bolani.[3] First educated in his home city by the historian Marcantonio Coccio Sabellico, by his late teens he had moved on to the University of Padua, where a record of 1501/2 describes him as a student of the arts, *Andreas de Naugerio Venetus, artium studens*.[4] Navagero spent several years at Padua, a Venetian possession since 1405, where he was instructed in philosophy by Pietro Pomponazzi and in Greek by Marcus Musurus. He is mentioned in a poem of Pierio Valeriano, *Ad Sodales Patavii Philosophantes* (To Boon Companions Engaged in Philosophy at Padua), as one of eight scholar-poets, including Paolo Canal (30.1n) and Girolamo Borgia (20.69–70n), dining together or participating in a symposium in Padua.[5] Navagero's invocation of the Vanciades, daughters of Vanzo, in poem 31 was presumably written during his time there. In poem 35, probably from just after the 1509 siege, he deplores the damage and disruption inflicted on the city by the emperor Maximilian's heavy bombardment.

Even before he went to Padua, Navagero had begun composing Latin verse. In 1499, when he was around sixteen, he wrote one of two short tributes (poem 48) printed to accompany Bartolomeo Merula's exposition of Ovid's *Tristia*, published in Venice. Those few boyhood lines were fated to be the only example of Navagero's

· INTRODUCTION ·

poetry to appear in print in his lifetime, but their inclusion in such a major academic publication suggests that his youthful promise and aspirations had already been recognized in the scholarly and publishing circles of his native city. Though there is no evidence that Navagero composed verse in Greek, he was clearly proficient in that language and enjoyed reading Greek poetry, for he is said by the printer Aldo Manuzio to have found Pindar's odes so sublime that he sought to commit them all to memory by copying them out many times.[6] A downside to his great dedication to his studies was a period of mental exhaustion in early adulthood.[7]

In 1504, at just over twenty, Navagero was admitted to the Great Council of Venice. In 1510 he was entrusted with the task of composing the formal funeral oration for Caterina Cornaro (1454–1510), the celebrated Venetian one-time queen of Cyprus, and delivering it in tribute to her before the doge and Senate. Caterina Cornaro had been coerced into abdication in 1489 so that Venice could annex her kingdom, but in a gesture of compensation she had been granted for life the town and castle of Asolo in Treviso and had not been required to forfeit the style of queen. Her court was frequented by many men of learning, including Pietro Bembo, whose *Gli Asolani*, published in 1505, was set at Asolo, and Navagero himself, until the emperor's invading forces took control of the town in 1509, ousting Caterina. Navagero's strongly self-critical vein impelled him, when dying in 1529, to destroy the speech for its perceived failings, but his two other great funeral orations — one delivered in 1515 for his friend and patron, the renowned military commander Bartolomeo d'Alviano, the other in 1521 for Doge Leonardo Loredan — survived to be published posthumously in 1530 by his friends along with all that they could gather together of his Latin poetry from copies in their possession.

Navagero was a member of the academy that Alviano set up at Pordenone, about forty miles north-northeast of Venice.[8] He speaks of the local river, the Noncello, in poems 44 (1509) and 20

viii

· INTRODUCTION ·

(1512), and the river god, symbolizing the academy, is pictured on the title page of the 1530 *editio princeps* of Navagero's poems and speeches. Navagero's close relationship with Alviano is particularly apparent from poem 44, a genethliacon, or birthday poem, written to predict a glorious future for Alviano's baby son and to celebrate the father's military successes — ironically, just before his severe defeat and capture by the French at Agnadello on May 14, 1509. Numerous other scholars and literary men were associated with Alviano or his academy. These included Pietro Bembo (addressed in poems 30 and 36), Baldassare Castiglione, Girolamo Borgia (seemingly Damon in poem 20), and Giovanni Cotta, all accomplished Latin poets and friends of Navagero. He was also on good terms with the Ferrara- and Mantua-based Antonio Tebaldeo, as attested by his celebration of that poet's Maltese lapdog Borgetto in poem 43 and by the further tributes in poems 50 and 51, if their ascription to Navagero can be trusted. Further celebrated persons in Navagero's circle included the Ciceronian scholar Christophe de Longueil (Longolius), Gasparo Contarini, Paolo Canal (addressed in poem 30), and the physician Girolamo Fracastoro. Navagero is the eponymous central figure expounding the argument in Fracastoro's prose dialogue *Naugerius, sive De Poetica* (Navagero, or On Poetry, ca. 1540), while the Mantuan citizen Gian Giacomo Bardulone, described as a mathematician and astronomer skilled in both Latin and Greek, is his interlocutor.[9]

Also among Navagero's friends were Bartolomeo Ricci, who wrote on poetic style, and the artists Titian and Raphael. Raphael's 1515/16 portrait of Navagero with Agostino Beazzano shows him, at a little over thirty, as a dark-bearded man of thoughtful and dignified aspect, looking very much the cultured and scholarly patrician. Navagero's epitaph for the poet Ercole Strozzi, murdered in Ferrara in 1508 (poem 54), indicates familiarity with him too. Among grand personages friendly to the arts, Elisabetta Gonzaga, duchess of Urbino (1471–1526), and her sister-in-law Isabella

ix

· INTRODUCTION ·

d'Este, marchioness of Mantua (1474–1539), were both well acquainted with Navagero. He admired but seemingly never met the Naples-based Latin poet and politician Giovanni Gioviano Pontano (1429–1503); in poem 20 Navagero regrets never having been a pupil of "Aegon of the Sebeto." Poem 59, if rightly ascribed to Navagero, seems to show him influenced in style and theme by Pontano.

Navagero's few topical poems mostly belong to the years from 1508/9 to 1512/13, when a formidable combination of hostile powers threatened to wrest Venice's Italian possessions from her by force of arms. Pope Julius II, resentful of Venice holding certain cities in the Romagna that he regarded as rightfully papal, had allied against the Republic with the emperor and the kings of France and Spain in the League of Cambrai. Poem 42, in which Navagero speaks of a crisis for his homeland so great that even unwarlike men like him must take up arms, seems to be from the early part of this period, while in poem 44 (of 1509) he recalls Alviano's victories over the French and the Germans in previous conflicts and predicts that now too he will repel a new French invasion of Italian territory. In the event, however, Alviano was defeated and captured by the French in the Battle of Agnadello, soon followed by the emperor's siege of Padua, described in poem 35. The pope continued to be strongly anti-Venetian until 1510, when changing circumstances led him to transfer his support to his former foe. As a result, the French were forced out of Italy, and in poem 20 (late 1512 or early 1513) Navagero gratefully eulogizes Julius for securing their expulsion. Early in this troubled period Navagero and some of his poet friends, including Borgia and Cotta, had served with Alviano in the field, and two weeks after Agnadello Navagero spoke in his commander's defense before the full *Collegio* in Venice, contending that he bore no personal responsibility for the defeat.[10]

In his youth Navagero explored various humanist poetic genres. As one experiment he wrote a number of *silvae* (miscellaneous

· INTRODUCTION ·

verse essays or occasional poems), but he was so dissatisfied with them that he burned them and gave up writing in that mode (see poem 16n). A great admirer of Vergil, he demonstrated his very different opinion of Martial by carrying out ritual burnings of his epigrams, as Paolo Giovio and Famiano Strada report.[11] In Giovio's version Navagero "was so severe an enemy to Martial that every year, on a set day dedicated to the Muses, he would, with imprecations, devote many volumes of that poet's works to Vulcan as obscene (*improba*)." In his slightly different account Strada says the ceremony took place on Navagero's birthday just after the banquet he shared with friends, a volume of Martial being burned in their presence in tribute to the Muses and the shade of Vergil. Giovanni Matteo Toscano, lauding the moral purity of Navagero's poetry in contrast to Martial's, adopts Giovio's view that Navagero found Martial's crudity objectionable.[12]

The genre now most associated with Navagero is the *lusus pastoralis*. The term (literally, "pastoral amusement") denotes a light epigram, pastoral in character. The use of classicizing personal names and frequent references to pagan deities are among indications that the time setting of such epigrams is ancient. Navagero may have been inspired to write in this mode by his older friend Pietro Bembo's example.[13] Navagero's *lusus pastorales* are brief and eschew overelaboration, largely confining their attention to a particular act or situation in rural life, though sometimes they reveal a little of the background to it. The themes treated often link the natural and divine worlds. In poem 1 country folk dance and prepare to sacrifice and perform libations in honor of Ceres as they call upon her to help the newly-sown seed produce a good harvest. In poem 2 a countryman makes an offering to the breezes to solicit their aid in winnowing. In poem 3 a hunter, no longer young enough to pit himself against a lion or a boar, hangs up a slain deer's antlers to Pan, asking the god to understand the limitations imposed by his age. In poem 4 a vine dresser prays for another

xi

· INTRODUCTION ·

crop as abundant as in previous years. Votive epigrams like these are strongly redolent of comparable pieces found in the *Greek Anthology*. Pagan deities or natural forces are asked for favors in return for offerings made by the suppliant. Poems 11 and 15 are in similar vein, while brave dogs fatally wounded in their master's service are honored with tributes from their owner in poems 8, 10A, and 10B. Some of Navagero's *lusus pastorales* deal with the aspirations and varied fortunes of the characters within them in matters of love and seduction. In poem 6 a young man gives thanks to Venus for at least partial sexual success (three snatched kisses) with a long-desired girl; in poem 7, its sequel, the same speaker rejoices upon having finally achieved full intercourse with her. A clandestine encounter is arranged in poem 12, while poem 13 is a wish that a young couple's faithful devotion may continue to be equally pure and steadfast throughout life. In poem 14 a virgin huntress about to marry and give up both virginity and hunting dedicates her bow and arrows to Diana and prays to be blessed with children in the new life that awaits her. Always succinct in their wording, poems in this mode seek to appeal by their simplicity.

While following to some extent in the whole pastoral tradition of Theocritus' *Idylls* and Vergil's *Eclogues*, the *lusus pastoralis'* chief inspiration lies within the dedicatory poems found in the *Greek Anthology*. Navagero would have known the collection only in the form of the *Planudean Anthology*, first printed in 1494, since the *Palatine Anthology* was not discovered until 1606. If poems 61 through 64 are rightly attributed to Navagero, it appears that he sometimes simply translated, or virtually translated, individual *Greek Anthology* poems by way of an academic exercise, just as he translates comic fragments of Philemon and Menander (poems 45 and 46, respectively). But a *lusus pastoralis* is different from a straight translation. Even if it may sometimes draw upon a *Greek Anthology* model for an element of its inspiration, it is nevertheless

· INTRODUCTION ·

a new poem in its own right composed by its humanist author in the broader spirit of its ancient antecedents. The genre was taken up in Latin by Marcantonio Flaminio in his *lusus pastorales*, and Navagero's pastoral pieces, especially his votive epigrams, were much admired and imitated by vernacular poets in France, Italy, and Spain, most notably Joachim du Bellay.

Navagero's Latin poems other than his *lusus pastorales* fall into various categories and demonstrate a wide range of interests and influences. His deep admiration for Vergil naturally drew him to write pastoral, but he also successfully assayed Horatian ode and Catullan hendecasyllables. He has numerous debts to Ovid, Propertius, and Tibullus and occasionally reflects Lucretius. Navagero can also sometimes follow in the Petrarchan tradition (poems 28 and 38). He displays a fondness for dogs, especially in celebrating the lapdog Borgetto (43, along with 50 and 51 if truly his), and a love of nature (9, 25, 31). There are several amatory poems to or about a Hyella, while other heterosexual pieces ascribed to him include a kiss poem after Pontano's manner (59). One of the two homosexual poems attributed to Navagero (55) treats the poet as impassioned beyond bearing toward a Venetian youth and threatening suicide unless allowed some gratification. Navagero can be restrained in merely hinting at intimacy, as in his handling of covert liaisons (6, 7, 22, 29, 39), but if poems 57 and 65 are correctly ascribed to him, he did not eschew occasionally writing in an explicitly salacious vein. Some poems eulogize individuals, whether honoring the Ovidian scholar Merula (48), the general and patron of poets Alviano (44), Pope Julius II (20), or Navagero's fellow-poet and friend Girolamo Borgia (20).

Navagero's pastoral epigrams are probably quite early compositions. In fact, nearly all of his dateable poems were written before he passed the age of thirty. The earliest, poem 48, is of 1499, when he was sixteen. The poems about Padua (31, 35, and 36), those about service as a soldier (42 and 53, if the latter is truly his), and

xiii

· INTRODUCTION ·

the genethliacon for Alviano's baby son (44) were all written in Navagero's early or mid-twenties, and the eulogy of Pope Julius II (20) is of late 1512 or very early 1513, when Navagero was twenty-nine. As Ercole Strozzi's poem about Tebaldeo's lapdog Borgetto shows that it was killed in or before 1508, when Strozzi was himself murdered, poem 43 and the two other poems about Borgetto attributed to Navagero (50 and 51) must be early. Poem 54, a tribute to Strozzi and his widow ascribed to Navagero, was evidently written shortly after Strozzi's death. All the Hyella poems are also likely to be early. One of them (30) addresses Paolo Canal, who died in 1508. Only two of the Latin poems attributed to Navagero can be dated late. They are 40, of 1526 or very soon after, and 47, of 1528. Some poems cannot be dated. There is also evidence that certain poems were revised after their original composition, as there are credible variants of quite a few lines in the manuscripts (see Notes to the Texts).

Navagero wrote vernacular verse as well as Latin, but his Italian poems (around a score survive) were not so highly regarded or influential, even though, while in Spain, he is said to have played an important part in encouraging Spanish vernacular poets to write in the Italian manner. Some of his Italian poems were published in the edition produced in Padua by the Volpi brothers (Navagero 1718); several more were first printed by Maria Antonietta Benassi in 1940 (see further below). In addition to being a poet in two languages and an orator, Navagero was given the role of censor of all works in the classics by the Council of Ten. In 1516 he was asked by the Venetian Senate to continue, in an official capacity, the history of Venice in Latin prose begun by his former teacher Sabellico (d. 1506). Navagero did not live to finish the history,[14] and in his final illness he burned his manuscript of it, similarly destroying all his other writings that he had taken with him on his embassy to France.[15]

· INTRODUCTION ·

A scholar as well as a poet, Navagero did much work for the Aldine Press, either for Aldo Manuzio (d. 1515) or for his successor, Andrea Torresano, on Quintilian, Vergil, Lucretius, Ovid, Terence, Horace, and Cicero. Navagero's contribution chiefly belongs to the half dozen or so years from about 1513 onward. He included dedicatory letters in the three volumes of his edition of Cicero's speeches, addressing one to Pope Leo X, urging the pontiff to lead a united Christendom against the common Turkish enemy, and others to Bembo and Sadoleto. Early in 1516 he became the librarian of San Marco, assuming responsibility for the numerous manuscripts bequeathed to the Senate of Venice by the great collector Cardinal Bessarion when he died in 1472. The income Navagero enjoyed from the appointment brought him welcome security from financial concerns that may have threatened to make his lifestyle unsustainable a little earlier, as he seems briefly to have thought of taking holy orders around 1513,[16] though, unlike Flaminio, he has left little sign in his Latin poems, other than the hymn to the archangel Gabriel (34), of being particularly religious.

Navagero relinquished the post of librarian when he left Venice for four years as ambassador to Spain with Lorenzo Priuli. His public service as an envoy was to dominate the last part of his life, his early forties. Navagero left a substantial account in Italian prose of this Spanish embassy and subsequent travels in France. While in Spain he met the poet Juan Boscán Almogáver in 1526. Boscán tells of this meeting in the prologue of the second book of his poems, and, importantly for Spanish poetry, Navagero persuaded him to write in Italian meters and verse forms, adopted soon afterward also by Garcilaso de la Vega, a younger friend of Boscán. Before Navagero's intervention there had been only a limited attempt by Spanish poets to compose in this way. From Spain Navagero sent long letters containing much information of botanical, zoological, and wider scientific interest, as well as observations

xv

· INTRODUCTION ·

on geographical and other matters, to the erudite classical scholar and geographer Giovanni Battista Ramusio, a distant relative by marriage as well as Navagero's friend,[17] who, like him, had studied at the University of Padua and worked with the Aldine Press. At the suggestion of Fracastoro, Ramusio was busily amassing material from various sources and scattered correspondents for an ambitious scholarly work on voyages and travels, his celebrated *Delle navigationi et viaggi*, eventually published in stages in the 1550s, and he especially hoped to learn from Navagero of discoveries made during the exploration and colonization of the Americas. Navagero also visited several Spanish cities and Moorish palaces with Castiglione, who was then in Spain on behalf of the pope, and was very taken with the sights of the country, including its gardens, surpassing, in his estimation, those of Italy.[18] Navagero's many official letters sent from Spain to the authorities at Venice show that the fate of the captive Francis I of France, a Spanish prisoner since the Battle of Pavia on February 24, 1525, engaged him early in his embassy. For much of the first part of 1528 Navagero was under detention himself, along with some French diplomats, after Venice joined France and England in declaring war on the emperor, who was then at pains to secure the safe return of his own envoys before he would in reciprocation release Navagero and the others in his custody.

Navagero returned to Italy from Spain via France, where he visited Paris and Lyon, among other places. He wrote poem 47 to express his joy on eventually seeing Venice again, which he did on September 24, 1528. A few days later he took up office as one of the five *savii di terraferma* (ministers with various responsibilities who served for six months). He died the following year of a sudden illness at Blois,[19] soon after having hurried there on another embassy, this time to Francis I, who honored Navagero with a splendid funeral. Quoting Horace, *Odes* 1.24.1–2, the mourning king asked, "What restraint or moderation can there be to regret

xvi

## · INTRODUCTION ·

at the loss of so dear a person?" Navagero's body was sent back to Venice for burial in the church of S. Martino di Murano.

A little under a year after Navagero's death, some of his friends published forty-four of his surviving Latin poems, along with his funeral speeches for Alviano and Doge Loredan, as *Andreae Naugerii Patricii Veneti Orationes Duae Carminaque Nonnulla* (Venice, 1530 = Navagero 1530). The person chiefly responsible for this publication seems to have been Fracastoro. Its preface states that the poems included had either been secretly copied when still rough drafts or taken from provisional versions that Navagero had given only to friends.[20] By the early eighteenth century Navagero's Latin poems had appeared in several further editions and anthologies and had acquired titles, but no real attempt was made to surpass the scope of the *editio princeps* until the Volpi brothers published an edition of Navagero's complete works, titled *Andreae Naugerii, Patricii Veneti . . . Opera Omnia* (Padua, 1718 = Navagero 1718). It included three further Latin poems that had been printed as Navagero's since 1530 (31, 39, and 40) and ambitiously incorporated, in addition to the two orations already published in the *editio princeps*, a wealth of ancillary matter, everything from numerous testimonia and letters to and from Navagero to texts of Fracastoro's dialogue *Naugerius, sive De Poetica* and of Navagero's own *Viaggio in Ispagna* and *Viaggio in Francia*. It was reissued at Venice in 1754 (Navagero 1754). For all his commendable thoroughness in many other respects, however, the editor of the 1718 edition, Giovanni Antonio Volpi, seems not to have considered it worthwhile to look through manuscripts in libraries that might conceivably contain transcripts of poems ascribed to Navagero that had not already been published. He probably thought such a speculative search far too laborious to justify and at great risk of proving futile. Nevertheless, a few additional Latin poems attributed to Navagero were obscurely published from manuscript evidence by others in 1736 (Cinelli Calvoli 1736) and 1786 (Gualtieri 1786), and two twentieth-century

xvii

· INTRODUCTION ·

articles uncovered far more. In 1940 Maria Antonietta Benassi published four previously overlooked poems from manuscript sources (Benassi 1940). In 1976/77 Claudio Griggio added eleven more poems to the list (Griggio 1976–77). In all, we now know of more than a score of Latin poems beyond the 1718 edition's forty-seven attributed to Navagero either in manuscript sources or in obscure places in print, though many of the ascriptions can be regarded as open to question or even probably false.

Apart from its privately produced precursor (Wilson 1997), which it supersedes, the present volume is the first edition to include the Latin text and an English translation of all the poems in Navagero 1718 together with those collected in Benassi 1940 and Griggio 1976–77 from manuscript and early print sources. I present the poems in the following order: (a) Poems in the 1718 edition, numbered 1 to 47; (b) Further poems ascribed to Navagero, numbered 48 to 69. Where Griggio and Benassi number poems differently, that is recorded in the Concordances. For remarks on the textual history of Navagero's poems and details of textual variants, see the Notes to the Texts. For a list of titles given to the poems in various editions, see Titles of Poems. For manuscript sources consulted, with a list of poems included in them, see Manuscripts with Latin Poems of Navagero. For a chronological list of editions and anthologies that include poems by Navagero, see the Handlist of Editions, Translations, Anthologies, and Further Reading.

*Marcantonio Flaminio*

Marcantonio Flaminio (1498–1550)[21] is the best known and most important follower of Navagero in the composition of *lusus pastorales*. His pastoral poems appear in books 3 and 4 of his *Carmina*. The book 3 poems were composed mostly in 1521 and 1526 (with 3.1 and 3.2 added in or just after 1536), and the poems in book 4 were written in 1539/40 (with 4.25 added later). They were for

xviii

· INTRODUCTION ·

him light diversions from worthier pursuits, such as the study of philosophy, astronomy, or, above all, matters of religion, and by his last decade of life he had entirely abandoned their composition, being from about 1540 preoccupied with religious concerns, though he still wrote verse letters to friends. Flaminio draws a distinction between his playful *lusus pastorales* and the serious side of his life in poem 4.25, where *lusus pastorales* are treated as undemanding amusements appropriate only to the gaiety of youth. Having recently passed forty, Flaminio informs his addressee, Francesco della Torre, that it is time now to say farewell to the inconsequential pastoral world and turn to grander themes such as explaining the mysteries of the universe and telling of God and heaven.

In a letter to Gianfrancesco Bini written on February 27, 1540, just after he had finished composing the *lusus pastorales* of book 4, Flaminio describes his periodic urges to write poetry in terms of a recurring malady. He finds it difficult, he says, to break away from his "bad habit" (*cattivo habito*) and "madness" (*pazzia*) of poetry, just as a man is never completely cured of the "French disease" (syphilis), and he jokingly vows in future to take purges and syrups for these "poetic whims" (*capricci poetichi*).[22] That humorous apology for writing poetry treats the activity as a shallow and rather reprehensible self-indulgence that needs checking. He speaks somewhat facetiously, of course, but it is evident that by the early 1540s he had come to see the composition of pagan-rooted light verse as a trivial pastime compared to the real (especially religious) priorities in life. The change in Flaminio's attitude can be seen in his address to Cardinal Alessandro Farnese appended to his paraphrase of certain psalms published in 1546.[23] He speaks of those verses as more wholesome reading for boys and girls than pagan-inspired poems. Why, Flaminio asks, are parents pleased to contaminate their children with "futile trifles" and "shameful song"? By then he seems to have counted *lusus pastorales* among "futile trifles" powerless to raise the soul to heaven.[24]

xix

· INTRODUCTION ·

The poems in this volume present not the serious-minded Flaminio, the fervently pious Christian, but the lighter self he could be when he surrendered to his "bad habit." Flaminio's *lusus pastorales* stand apart from his religious writings. His relationship with God does not figure in them at all till the very last poem, where God and heaven are expressly separate, serious themes to be tackled after leaving forever the play world of rustic deities and bucolic amours. The following short survey of his life gives greater prominence to those aspects that most contribute to understanding him in his lighter role, considering, for instance, what attitude his poems adopt to sexuality rather than examining his theological thinking.

Flaminio was a native of Serravalle,[25] now incorporated in Vittorio Veneto, son of the Imola-born Giovanni Antonio Flaminio, himself a Latin poet and scholar (d. 1536). Giovanni Antonio's real surname was Zarrabini (or Zarrabbini), but he himself tells us that at the academy in Venice, "when barely into his twentieth year," he became known instead as Flaminio. Marcantonio's mother, Veturia (d. 1513), came from a family of some standing in Serravalle. Two older brothers died in childhood, within months of Marcantonio's birth; a sister lived to maturity.[26] In 1509 the Flaminio family's hitherto agreeable life at Serravalle was abruptly destroyed when invading Austrians sacked and burned the town, including their home. This was the same year when imperial forces besieged Padua and caused the destruction lamented in Navagero's poem 35. Left virtually destitute, the elder Flaminio moved back to Imola, where he managed with financial help to recover from this calamity.

Marcantonio, whose early education had been successfully conducted by his father, was already showing great promise when in 1514, aged sixteen, he was sent to Rome with some of Giovanni Antonio's works to try to secure the patronage of the new pope, Leo X (r. 1513–22). When the boy presented these, he also showed

xx

# · INTRODUCTION ·

the pontiff observations he had himself made on certain passages of ancient authors. Much impressed, Leo reportedly applauded Marcantonio's early erudition with Apollo's words hailing the youthful Iulus' valor in Vergil, *Aen.* 9.641: "Bless your young prowess, boy! That is the way to reach the stars" (*Macte nova virtute, puer: sic itur ad astra*). Subsequently pressed by Leo to let his son stay on in Rome, a place of great opportunity for budding scholars but also steeped in moral decadence, the apprehensively protective Giovanni Antonio was at first reluctant, but eventually consented. Young Marcantonio resided with various worthies and diligently pursued his studies, including Greek. In 1514 he met Sannazaro (1458–1530), whom he much admired, on a visit to Naples, and subsequently stayed for a while with Castiglione (1478–1529) at Urbino. Both Sannazaro and Castiglione were friends of his father.

In 1515, when Flaminio was still only around seventeen, a few poems written by him appeared in print, published at Fano with the *Neniae* (Laments) of Michele Marullo (d. 1500). These early poems included an eclogue (2.34), in which Flaminio, as the herdsman Thyrsis, expresses gratitude to his benefactor Castiglione, called Moeris. Some of the poems suggest amorous involvement with several girls, quite possibly more fictitious than real. A letter of Flaminio's father, dated March 15, 1515, warns his son about the bad impression of the youth's morals that could be formed from the lascivious content of one of his odes: after his chaste upbringing, he should avoid seeming to have turned into a debauchee once free of his father's supervision.[27] These early poems are indeed much concerned with love. In poem 2.34 a beautiful girl called Phyllis is madly enamored of Thyrsis (= Flaminio). In 1.28 love for Hierophila is said to preclude grand themes, making Flaminio wretchedly put his neck in an inescapable noose. Having experienced a mistress's severe cruelty, he rids himself of cares with a light lyre.[28] In another poem (App. 1 Scorsone), he says that beau-

xxi

· INTRODUCTION ·

tiful Cynara's "easy love" once used to be for him, and Cupid had joined them in fetters of bronze, but now she cruelly shuns him. In 2.33 Flaminio speaks of suffering the classic symptoms of unhappy love in relation to an unnamed mistress. An address to a Lygda (App. 3 Scorsone) represents her as cruelly and disdainfully rejecting the speaker (i.e., Flaminio), and refusing to talk to him, though he still burns for her.[29] In 1.11 Flaminio asks his addressee to console him with a light lyre, as he grieves over separation from his mistress Chloe and "new battles" with Lygda. In the Catullus-inspired, hendecasyllabic *Ad Septimillam* (App. 4 Scorsone; Maddison 1965, 22–23), the addressee is asked what has become of her former sweet-talk and the passionate embraces she used to indulge in with the poet. Your Flaminio, he tells her, is now returning to Urbino, bringing with him many thousands of kisses and "that elegant sparrow you always longed to hold in your hands," an apparent allusion to one interpretation of Lesbia's pet "sparrow" of Catullus 2 and 3 as his penis.[30] Such poems of youthful passion seem at variance with the general picture of Flaminio's life, at least later, as morally pure.[31] A few were left out by Mancurti in his second edition (Flaminio 1743), though present in his first (Flaminio 1727), perhaps to protect the poet's chaste reputation.[32]

In later 1515 Flaminio moved to Bologna, where he studied philosophy under Navagero's former teacher, Pomponazzi. By 1520, after another brief period in Rome, he moved to study at Padua, where he lived in the household of the protonotary Stefano Sauli of Genoa. During 1520/21 he paid two visits to Venice. In May 1521 Flaminio accompanied Sauli to Genoa, where in the following months he wrote some of the *lusus pastorales* that make up book 3. In composing in this genre he clearly took his chief inspiration from Navagero, whom he knew, though when he returned to it for a final time in 1539, ten years after Navagero's death, Flaminio adopted a new approach. Navagero's pastoral epigrams had largely been unconnected and self-contained, but Flaminio's 1539 poems

xxii

· INTRODUCTION ·

(here book 4) consisted of a series of interrelated pieces about an ultimately tragic love between two fictitious bucolic characters. In spite of the interrelationship of the poems, the reader is not served a continuous and straightforward chronological narrative of the affair but enabled to deduce, little by little and from differing viewpoints, the full story of what unhappily occurred.

During the winter of 1521/22, spent at Padua, Flaminio fell so ill that he wrote[33] of fearing death when, as he puts it, "barely in the first flower of youth" (see 4.7.9n), without a wrinkle on his face or a white hair on his head to mar the black, and guilty of no wickedness. Ill health had troubled him before and would repeatedly trouble him severely at intervals thereafter. It was, in fact, a major factor in his life and figures in much of his verse outside his *lusus pastorales*. Many poems, especially in book 6 of his *Carmina*, speak of symptoms such as fever, sleeplessness, inability to eat, wasting, and pain in the left side. These bouts of illness are often treated as life-threatening. Sometimes medical attention helps (a few poems thank doctors). Sometimes the poet speaks of needing to get away, especially from Rome, to a healthier location (see 2.1, for instance). In 6.20 Flaminio relates how he was restored from a wasted state to health and poetry writing when staying with the count of Caserta in 1539/40. Sometimes he has recourse to prayer. Poem 6.39 (6.40 Scorsone) tells how, in 1549, when doctors' treatments had failed, death threatened, and the last rites were being prepared, the illness passed after Cardinal Carafa said prayers.[34] In 6.59 (6.60 Scorsone) good wine from a friend's vineyard has helped ease the sick poet's half-dead state. Sometimes Flaminio declares his suffering undeserved. For example, in 6.62 (6.63 Scorsone), where Sleep is begged to come (if not, the sleep of death is feared), Flaminio asserts that he has not sullied his life with any foul crime and does not follow the people's ways and practice their wrongdoing but is a priest of the Muses (i.e., a virtuous-living poet and scholar). In 5.49 (5.51 Scorsone), addressing Fracastoro, Flaminio,

xxiii

· INTRODUCTION ·

wasted, sleepless, pale, weary, and fearing death in youth, asks what use it is to have put the Muses before everything and to have lived a pure life. In another address to Fracastoro,[35] appealing for him to come to his aid, Flaminio laments his wasting limbs and "wretched old age in the flower of youth," rebuking the cruel Fates for letting him neither enjoy youth's gifts nor end his lingering pains. Sometimes in his illness he addresses Christ, as in 8.13, where the aging Flaminio is in the fifth month of fever, alternating between a cold tremor shaking his bones and heat burning their marrow, and his body is so wasted that scarcely his shade is left of him. He prays to Christ, not to take the affliction from him, but to give him strength and constancy enough to bear it. Flaminio's last letter[36] speaks of quartan fever — a form of malaria that recurs every third day, gradually fading; the insalubrious neighborhood of Rome was notorious for mosquitoes — and of trouble in the stomach and head.[37]

Whatever the illness that beset Flaminio during the winter of 1521/22, it at last passed. In January he went to Rome with Sauli. There in 1523 he entered the service of Gianmatteo Giberti, bishop of Verona from 1524.[38] After the city had been sacked by imperial forces in 1527, Giberti relocated to his episcopal seat, and Flaminio spent 1528 to 1538 mostly at Verona with him, though he sometimes visited other places, including his native Serravalle, where in 1526, while recovering from another spell of bad health, he added further poems to the *lusus pastorales* that he had composed at Genoa in 1521. Together they make up book 3. In 1529 more of his various other poems were published with Cotta's in the Venice edition of Sannazaro of that year, though as yet none of the *lusus pastorales* appeared in print.

In 1534 Paul III was chosen pope. His teenage grandson and namesake Alessandro Farnese, soon created a cardinal, helped Flaminio out of a distressing situation that had arisen after the death of the poet's elderly father in 1536.[39] Flaminio had hoped to receive

xxiv

# · INTRODUCTION ·

the priory of San Prospero near Faenza, his father's home since 1524, but it had not descended to him. Faced with financial problems, he secured the favor of the Farnese family by writing a lengthy ode (1.8) to celebrate the anniversary of the pope's elevation to his throne, and young Cardinal Farnese saw to it that San Prospero was restored to Flaminio, who expressed deep gratitude in many poems, as this gave him financial security and the leisure to write.[40] Flaminio also received from Giberti the priory of San Colombano on Lake Garda, though it was in a state that called for much costly restoration, and at a later date the abbey of San Fabiano and San Sebastiano in the Lavino valley near Bologna.[41]

In 1538 Flaminio's prose paraphrase of thirty-two of the psalms was published at Venice. That same year he moved for his health from Verona to Naples, but had trouble finding somewhere to live there and so spent the winter of 1538/39 at Sessa with his friend Galeazzo Florimonte, and in July 1539 went to Caserta as the guest of its count, Giovanni Francesco d'Alois. While at Caserta, Flaminio wrote the *lusus pastorales* presented here as book 4, his last revisiting of the genre before putting it permanently behind him. He moved on from Caserta to Naples in early 1540.

At Naples Flaminio encountered the Spaniard Juan de Valdés (d. 1541), an advocate of reform in the Catholic Church, who had fled Spain for Italy after his opinions had made him of interest to the Inquisition. Valdés had come to be a great believer in justification by faith. Even before his exposure to Valdés, Flaminio had already shown sympathy with progressive thinkers in the Catholic Church. In Rome he had attended meetings of the Oratorio del Divino Amore.[42] Flaminio's host of 1539/40 at Caserta was one of those in Valdés' circle; others included Giulia Gonzaga and Vittoria Colonna.

In 1541 Flaminio left Naples. He thereafter became attached to the English prelate Cardinal Reginald Pole (1500–1558), *legato del patrimonio* at Viterbo.[43] A great-nephew of both Edward IV and

· INTRODUCTION ·

Richard III and a second cousin of Henry VIII of England, Pole was later to become the last Catholic archbishop of Canterbury under Mary Tudor. In 1545 Flaminio accompanied Pole, himself a man sympathetic to some reform in the Roman Catholic Church, to the Council of Trent and was there for over a year. During that time, he turned down the opportunity to be Secretary of the Council and could not be induced to accept a bishopric. After much illness in his final years, spent in Rome, Flaminio died there on February 17, 1550, aged fifty-two. He passed away in rather bizarre circumstances in Pole's house, for present at his death was the future pope Paul IV (1555–59), then still Cardinal Carafa (the chief inquisitor), who had strong suspicions that Flaminio held some Lutheran views.[44] Carafa had chanced to encounter the attending priest on his way to administer the last rites to the poet. Entering Pole's house with that priest, Carafa concealed himself behind his back close by Flaminio's deathbed and prompted the priest to test Flaminio's true Catholicism by having him affirm full acceptance of the Catholic faith and recite the Creed, which Flaminio did. Carafa then whispered to the priest to ask Flaminio expressly to use the crucial word *transubstantiatio*. Flaminio did so, and the satisfied Carafa thereupon revealed his presence, sitting supportively by Flaminio till death came.[45] Later, however, as the tyrannical pope Paul IV, fiercely zealous in pursuit of suspected heretics, including several associates of Flaminio, he put all of Flaminio's works on the *Index of Prohibited Books* (1559), though they were removed not long after the pope died.

Although it is beyond the scope of this volume to survey Flaminio's outpourings of Christian piety in his last ten years or so in any detail, two passages illustrate the intensity of his declared devotion to Christ toward the close of his life. In 8.17 he speaks of how, like a stray sheep in danger, he had been rushing blindly through all manner of evils, when the light of the Holy Spirit shone, showing him the way to heaven, and dispelling the dark-

xxvi

· INTRODUCTION ·

ness in his mind. He declares himself ever since then wounded with love for Christ, his mind longing to enjoy Christ's embraces with a yearning greater than that which an impassioned lover feels for an attractive maiden. The imagery of burning adoration there employed is strikingly erotic. Similarly, in 8.20, addressing Christ, Flaminio asks for a lover-to-lover kiss, declaring Christ the "bridegroom" (*sponsus*) of his soul.[46] By that stage of his spiritual development there was no place in his life for shallow flirtations with *lusus pastorales*, however seductive he had once found them.

In 1546 Flaminio's verse paraphrase of thirty psalms had been published in Venice. Within the next few years several publications contained substantial portions of his verse. In 1548 two books of his poems, including the *lusus pastorales* of book 4 here, together with his verse paraphrase of the psalms, were published at Lyon by Cesare Flaminio, his cousin, in a book titled *M. Antonii Flaminii Carminum Libri Duo* (= Flaminio 1548).[47] Flaminio had steadfastly opposed this publication, seeing it as unseemly for a serious-minded man of nearly fifty now engaged in weightier pursuits to take any pleasure in acclaim for juvenile "diversions" (*ludi*) written "to exercise pen and mind" when he was "still young" (*adulescens adhuc*). Poems by Flaminio (including three of the *lusus pastorales* in book 3 and all of those in book 4) were also incorporated in Jean Gagny's collection *Doctissimorum Nostra Aetate Italorum Epigrammata* (Epigrams of the Most Learned Italians of Our Age), published at Paris without date, but probably also in 1548 (= Gagny ca. 1548). Four books of Flaminio's poems, now including all of the *lusus pastorales* in this present volume, appeared in the Venice, 1548 and Florence, 1549 editions of *Carmina Quinque Illustrium Poetarum* (Poems of Five Illustrious Poets), together with the verse paraphrases of the psalms. The third edition of the same work (Florence, 1552) republished what had appeared in the first two and added a fifth book of poems, dedicated to Alessandro Farnese, as well as Flaminio's *Sacrorum Carminum Libellus* (Little

xxvii

· INTRODUCTION ·

Book of Sacred Poems), which had first appeared in print, in a shorter version, at Paris in 1551. The 1552 edition was the fullest and best available for Flaminio's poems in the sixteenth century, but the Padua, 1727 and 1743 editions done by Francesco Maria Mancurti became the principal ones for his verse in the earlier eighteenth (= Flaminio 1727 and 1743). In 1993, Massimo Scorsone printed the Latin text of Flaminio's poems in *Marcantonio Flaminio, Carmina* (= Flaminio 1993), based on Mancurti's 1727 and 1743 editions, and this has been the edition most frequently referred to in modern times.

Whereas I have consulted all the manuscript evidence I could for the poems of Navagero, particularly important for those not in the 1718 edition, and thus produced a detailed apparatus criticus for them in the Notes to the Texts, I have not similarly sought out manuscript evidence for Flaminio's *lusus pastorales*, as there seems to be no reason to doubt the standard printed text in very nearly all places. My text for Flaminio thus scarcely differs, save in some aspects of punctuation and spelling, from Mancurti's in Flaminio 1727, which was followed by the Verona, 1740 edition of the poems of Fracastoro and Flaminio and its derivatives in Verona, 1747; Venice, 1759; and Bassano 1782 (= Fracastoro 1740, 1747, 1759, and 1782). My numbering of the book 3 poems is that of Mancurti in Flaminio 1727, as in his second edition (Flaminio 1743, reprinted in 1831) he chose to omit five poems from that book. Like Scorsone (Flaminio 1993), I have preferred to go back to the earlier Mancurti edition (Flaminio 1727) for the full text of book 3. In citing Flaminio's poems other than those in books 3 and 4, I have generally referred to them as numbered in Flaminio 1743, adding Scorsone's numbering in parentheses if different. Very occasionally I cite a poem attributed to Flaminio that is in neither edition. For differences in the numbering of Flaminio's poems, see the Concordances in this volume.

\*     \*     \*

· INTRODUCTION ·

The texts and translations presented in this volume stem from the edition of Navagero's *Lusus*, with Flaminio's *lusus pastorales* as an unannotated appendix, that I produced privately in a tiny number of copies in the 1990s. The second—revised and improved—version (Wilson 1997) comprised over 1,100 pages. For ITRL, I have greatly abridged, recast, rethought, refined, corrected, and to a very large extent rewritten that work. I express again my gratitude to the many libraries where I consulted early editions of Navagero and Flaminio and other relevant works in the course of my research in the days before easier and less time-consuming accessibility through the Internet became commonly available. I also thank all the numerous institutions that have supplied me with manuscript evidence for the text of Navagero, and I thank Dr. Ornella Rossi for her greatly appreciated help in now obtaining images of manuscript evidence that I did not manage to see in the 1990s, for personally collating on my behalf the text of two poems in manuscripts at the Vatican Library, and for so generously giving much valuable assistance and encouragement besides.[48] I am grateful to Prof. Leah Whittington for making many helpful suggestions for improvements and judicious trimming of notes. I thank Dr. Patrick Baker for his aid in producing this volume and Prof. James Hankins for the opportunity to adapt my original privately produced edition for ITRL and for his support in general.

NOTES

1. There is some uncertainty about the exact date of Navagero's birth. According to Fracastoro 1574, 87v, and the inscription put up for Navagero by two nephews in 1585 (Navagero 1718, viii; Cicogna 1824–53, 6:169 and 216), he died in his forty-sixth year. Paolo Giovio (Navagero 1718, xxxviii) says he died in his forty-seventh; the preface to Navagero 1530, in his forty-fourth. Giovan Mario de' Crescimbeni (Navagero 1718, xlv) states that he died aged forty-four. The year most favored for Navagero's

xxix

## · INTRODUCTION ·

birth in biographical summaries of his life is 1483; see Volpi's *Life* in Navagero 1718, ix–xxvi; Tiraboschi 1795–96, 7:1326; and Cicogna, 1824–53, 6:173 and 6:224n1. Cicogna says that Navagero must have been over twenty when admitted to the Great Council of Venice in 1504 and that his parents' marriage was in 1482, but Melani's entry on Navagero in the *Dizionario biografico degli Italiani* (treating him as born in 1483) calls him the last of their four children. If Cicogna correctly puts Navagero's paternal grandfather's marriage in 1465 and the poet's birth in 1483, he was born when his father was no more than seventeen or eighteen.

2. Fracastoro 1574, 87v, says Navagero's heirs were his brothers Bartolomeo and Pietro, the latter of whom accompanied the poet's remains when they were returned to Venice. Navagero evidently had no issue, having, it seems, never married (see n17 below). The 1585 inscription, put up by Andrea and Bernardo Navagero, sons of his brother Bartolomeo, praised Navagero's diplomatic service to his country "in very difficult times for the state" in both Spain and France, as well as his singular learning and "Roman" eloquence, "at which the whole of Europe marveled." It specifically mentions the great distress of Francis I at Navagero's death on his embassy to France after he had spoken only once or twice to the French king (*semel aut iterum allocutus*).

3. Cicogna 1824–53, 6:224n1, considers Bol(l)ani correct, rather than Polani, as sometimes found. Volpi's *Life* gives the name, in Latin, as Lucretia Polana (Navagero 1718, x); Tiraboschi 1795–96, 7:1326, calls her Lucrezia Polana. The little information that we have of the poet's father is given in Cicogna's same note.

4. Cicogna 1824–53, 6:224n5.

5. The date of Valeriano's poem seems to be 1507/8, as Borgia spent some time at Padua shortly after he came to Venice in 1507, and Canal died on May 16, 1508.

6. So Aldo Manuzio's preface to his 1515 edition of Pindar, addressed to Navagero (see Navagero 1718, 103). Bartolomeo Ricci says that, given a line of Vergil, Horace, Catullus, or Tibullus, Navagero could recite the entire following text from memory (Navagero 1718, 128).

· INTRODUCTION ·

7. Paolo Giovio speaks of serious affliction by "black bile" (melancholy) from chronic lack of sleep through burning the midnight oil; see Giovio 1972, 8:102. Giovio adds that, for the sake of his health, Navagero gave up such diligent studying while with Alviano's forces. He evidently made a good recovery.

8. From an uncertain date Navagero was also, like Bembo and many others, a member of the Hellenist academy at Venice started by Aldo Manuzio in about 1500. Only Greek could be spoken at its gatherings.

9. Fracastoro describes Navagero as a man "of the highest learning and patrician gravity," as well as "very skilled in Greek and Latin" and "an outstanding writer of histories of his time" (see Navagero 1718, 230–31). Portrayed early in the dialogue as suddenly entered by the "spirit" (*manes*) of Vergil beside a fountain, Navagero sweetly reads half of the *Eclogues* aloud from a text kept in his pocket and then casts the text from him with a cry.

10. Girolamo Borgia's *Historiae de Bellis Italicis* says that Alviano had as his "table companions" (*convictores*), both at home and on military service, besides Borgia himself, Giovanni Cotta, Girolamo Aleandro, Girolamo Fracastoro, Andrea Navagero, Aldo Manuzio, and Marcus Musurus, though it seems unlikely that the last two dined with Alviano on a regular basis; see Cotta 1802, 14. Evidence of precisely what part Navagero played in the Agnadello campaign is thin, but his defense of Alviano before the *Collegio* is recorded by Sanudo 1882, col. 325, under May 30, 1509 (see also Cicogna 1824–53, 6:226–27nII, though there Sanudo's text is imperfectly quoted). In Sanudo's account Navagero, called *sier Andrea Navajer di sier Bernardo*, asserts that Alviano fought manfully "like a Hector," overcoming two French squadrons, and lays the blame for the disaster on the lack of support he received from others in the fighting. Navagero's appearance to give evidence implies his presence at Agnadello, and in the same entry Sanudo says that Navagero "was staying with Alviano because his father was bankrupt, and he found himself in arms in the action (*si ritrovò armato nel fatto d'arme*)."

11. Giovio 1972, 8:102 (see also Navagero 1718, xxxviii); Strada 1613, 216.

xxxi

· INTRODUCTION ·

12. Toscano 1576, 195 (see also Navagero 1718, 226). Toscano's poem translates: "Here is the famous Navagero, who hated lascivious Martial's rudeness and his endlessly salacious Muses, for whom all is permissible, their maidenhood lost, no more virgins but shameless wantons. But this Navagero wished his own Muses to be pure and desired them so to sing of love as to revere tender chastity. Therefore, boys and young girls, flock to make him your reading, for he is no less learned than Martial and more decent." The attribution to Navagero of two sexually graphic poems (here numbers 57 and 65) in manuscript sources unknown to Giovio and Toscano is at variance with the once widely accepted view of him as uncompromisingly anti-obscenity. Either the attribution is wrong or the received image of Navagero has to be modified.

13. Before Navagero began composing *lusus pastorales* Bembo penned a handful of what he termed *nugae pastorales* (pastoral trifles) in the 1490s addressed to Faunus/Pan and the like, probably an inspiration to Navagero; see Pecoraro 1959, 120 and 209, for their dating. Bembo's *Iolas ad Faunum* (Bembo 1990, *Carmina* 4) and *Thestylis ad Faunum* (otherwise *Ad Faunum Testilis*; Bembo 1990, *Carmina* 5) seem particularly close to the sort of *Greek Anthology*–inspired *lusus pastoralis* that Navagero wrote.

14. Confusingly, there is an extant history of Venice in Italian from the city's beginnings down to 1498 ascribed to an Andrea Navagero. It is often taken to have been written by an earlier namesake of the poet. Cicogna 1824–53, 6:172–73, thought him the poet's paternal grandfather; another suggestion is that he was the poet's uncle, but Andrea Navagero *il cronista* (the chronicler), as Cicogna calls him, is a very shadowy figure. Ludovico Muratori, who first printed this chronicle, thought the poet its author; see Muratori 1733, cols. 923–1216. Cosenza 1962, the British Library Catalogue, and the National Union Catalog also treat the chronicle as his work. It seems most unlikely to be so.

15. Fracastoro 1574, 87v, particularly regrets the loss of the official history of Venice, covering from the entry into Italy of Charles VIII of France in 1498 to the historian's own times. With it Navagero also destroyed his funeral oration for Caterina Cornaro, a two-book didactic work on hunting in hexameters (*De Venatione*), another such work in the same meter

xxxii

## · INTRODUCTION ·

(*De Situ Orbis*), perhaps a geographical survey of the world, and some shorter poems.

16. See Cicogna 1824–53, 6:173 and 227n13.

17. In 1524 Ramusio (1485–1557) married Francesca or Franceschina Navagero (d. 1536), the daughter of Francesco Navagero, not of Andrea Navagero, as Firmin-Didot 1875, 465, and Cartwright 1908, 2:275, wrongly say. Andrea Navagero never married.

18. Cartwright 1908, 2:274–76, 297–300, and 314, describes the time Navagero spent with Castiglione in Spain.

19. A letter of Gasparo Contarini to the Venetian Council of Ten, written at Rome on May 9, 1529, reported news from France that Navagero was ill with a "very dangerous" fever; see Brown 1871, 209–10. Fracastoro 1574, 87v, thinks the disease must have been contracted in Italy, though it showed itself only at Blois; see also Roscoe 1805, 3:300.

20. Fracastoro 1574, 87v, speaks of the 1530 publication of Navagero's poems that had been secretly or privately copied out, presumably by friends of the poet allowed to see them (who thus preserved them from the very real risk of destruction by their author). See also Fracastoro 2013, 353.

21. On whether Flaminio was born in late 1497 or early 1498, see Cuccoli 1897, 28, and Maddison 1965, 1n. Though his father calls him "only just" (*nunc primum*) sixteen in a letter of April 26, 1514, Flaminio makes himself "barely" or "hardly" (*vix*) eighteen in the dedication of his first published poems, dated September 11, 1515. In a letter of his cousin Cesare Flaminio dated October 13, 1547 (see Flaminio 1548, 4), the poet is reported as describing himself as "almost a quinquagenarian." Like Cuccoli and Maddison, I think 1498 more likely than 1497 as the year of Flaminio's birth. Scorsone (in Flaminio 1993) too gives 1498.

22. See more fully 4.1–4.25n.

23. This poem is 7.36 in Flaminio 1993. Flaminio's words in 2.7, written in late 1538 as he set out from Verona for Naples, already reveal the primacy of religious poetry in his eyes: "It pleases me now to spend my life in shady gardens and to engage in leisure-pursuits worthy of Phoebus

## · INTRODUCTION ·

and the Muses, then to tell the causes and outcomes of things, by what law man should revere the holy names of the gods [or 'saints'], what conduct is proper, what way of life makes one blessed, what truth is distinct from false conceptions. Above all, it pleases me to celebrate with my lyrestrings the Father, of whose creation of all things from nothing the bards sing, whom the denizens of heaven venerate as threefold and as one, who rules the sea, the earth, and the heights above" (lines 49–58). The poem is noticed by Maddison 1965, 96, and by Ferroni 2012, 234–35; a partial text appears in Perosa and Sparrow 1979, 284–86.

24. In 5.51 (5.53 Scorsone) Flaminio asks the poets Lelio and Ippolito Capilupi whether he should abandon writing the poetic trifles that, "letting go more serious study," he sometimes composes, declaring himself uncertain whether to heed approvers or disapprovers of his verse. Significantly, Flaminio would not let his cousin Cesare publish "juvenile" poems of his, though his opposition was eventually disregarded when Cesare brought out two books, including the book 4 *lusus pastorales*, at Lyon in 1548. Flaminio submitted poems to friends for comment. Thus in 6.61 (6.62 Scorsone) Basilio Zanchi (1501–58) is sent a second book of his poems to peruse and criticize or destroy if faults should be found. There, as in 5.23 (5.24 Scorsone), Zanchi is called "frank judge of my poems." In 6.27 Flaminio's book longs to go to Fernando della Torre's house, expecting his usual high praise, but Flaminio playfully invites him to humble its arrogance by deleting all the bad Latin or witless nonsense in it that offends him. Flaminio is several times self-deprecatory about his own poetic ability. For instance, he calls himself a "bad" or "very bad" poet in 5.36.2, 5.50.16, and 6.31.

25. Not of Imola, as sometimes formerly said, though he lived there for part of his boyhood. He is *Forocorneliensis* (of Imola) in, for instance, the caption to the portrait of him, thin-faced and flowing-bearded in his mature years, used as the frontispiece of Flaminio 1727 and 1743. On the family name Zarrab(b)ini and the humanist name Flaminio, see Mancurti's long letter to Gaetano Volpi in Flaminio 1743, 371–83. There Mancurti also rejects the notion that Marcantonio was ever known as Antonio Maria in boyhood. See, however, n29 and n35 below and also 3.15n for the poems ascribed to "Antonio Mario of Imola," seemingly Flaminio.

xxxiv

## · INTRODUCTION ·

26. Flaminio asks his dead mother and brothers in 1.19 to supplicate God to let him die and join them in his grief. His mind, he says, urges him to go to them, but he fears that rejection from heaven by the righteous as a suicide may leave him eternally bereft of them. But for that, he would stab himself. If it seems odd that Flaminio expresses such grief for long-dead brothers he never knew, it was no doubt the loss of his mother in 1513 that chiefly distressed him.

27. In the letter the elder Flaminio approves the ode Marcantonio has sent him in all respects apart from its "subject matter" (*materiam*), which, while permissibly somewhat lighthearted and playful, he would wish *pudentiorem ac minus lascivientem* (more decent and less lascivious). He adds, "For you, who have only just passed boyhood and were brought up no less chastely than a vestal (*non minus pudice quam vestalis*) for as long as you were under your father's eyes and care, should make the greatest effort not to seem, in the few months you have been away from us, to have laid aside the [purity of a] virgin and assumed the ways of a little whore (*deposita virgine mores induisse meretriculae*)." He warns, "It is not fitting that after the upbringing you have had, you should behave foolishly along with the common herd of dissolute young men (*Te sic educatum cum vulgo corruptorum adolescentium ineptire non convenit*)." For the text of the letter, see Flaminio 1743, 195–97. It is part-translated by Maddison 1965, 19, though her version wrongly makes Flaminio's father criticize his son's odes in general rather than one particular ode.

28. Maddison 1965, 14, wonders whether this girl's name (= "Lover of holy things") may be a pseudonym for the beautiful Leucippe of 2.12, "the very pleasing heart-throb of lovers," who joined the Clares as a nun. If so, Hierophila would be a historical person, but such speculation is risky.

29. On Lygda see further note 33, below. Ferroni 2012, 229n13, cites four hendecasyllabic lines of Flaminio's friend Niccolò d'Arco in MS Ashburnham 266 in the Biblioteca Laurenziana in Florence (fol. 53v). There Arco states in coarse terms that "Lygda" will give Flaminio sex (*dabit futu-tiones*) and refers to her versatility, including "playing the male role as rider (*eques*)." Arco is not known ever to have met Flaminio again after their time at Bologna, but he addresses his *Numeri* 2.16, written from

xxxv

# · INTRODUCTION ·

Mantua, to Flaminio, having heard that Flaminio has been living at Verona in the service of its bishop, Giberti. Arco fondly reminisces about the life he and Flaminio led at Bologna, including composing poetry together by the River Reno. An eclogue ascribed to Antonio Mario, i.e., Flaminio (see 3.15n and Maddison 1965, 91; she dates the poem to 1537), recalling earlier days, has Flaminio and Arco as Thyrsis and Alcon, young shepherds singing in turn of their loves by the Reno. Thyrsis sings there of the girls Phyllis and Orithyia, but also of two male beloveds, Iolas and Lycidas, and Alcon too sings of his attraction to both sexes, reflecting the bisexuality of herdsmen and shepherds commonly presumed in ancient bucolic poetry.

30. Poliziano's suggestion, derided by Sannazaro, but accepted by Flaminio's contemporary Benedetto Lampridio. Muret, in his notes on Catullus, rejects the notion, as do modern editors. Maddison 1965, 23, treats this relationship with Septimilla as factual (a view arguably supported by the specific mention of returning to Urbino). Whether or not these early attachments to girls were all real experiences as depicted, the adolescent Flaminio was plainly willing at least to risk being thought to have lost some of his innocence.

31. Flaminio reveals his later condemnatory attitude to sexual dalliance in 2.9.27–30, where young Antonio Giberti, a budding poet, is warned that one who follows Venus is shunned by the Muse. Venus insidiously leads boys to black hell; the pure-white Muse blesses them with heaven.

32. See 3.1–29n. Gagny ca. 1548, fol. 28v, ascribes to Flaminio three short poems not given by Mancurti in Flaminio 1727/43 or by Scorsone in Flaminio 1993; Cuccoli 1897, 154, disproves one ascription (the poem is really Molza's) and doubts the others. In one, the poet, whoever he was, speaks of having been "cured" by kisses of the nectar-sweet lips of a "beautiful goddess." Maddison 1965, 36, incautiously refers this poem specifically to Flaminio's recovery from his serious illness in 1521/22, but the speaker's affliction "cured" by kisses may just have been lovesickness, especially as the addressee is asked why he is not similarly "cured" by like kisses. It is very doubtful whether the poem is Flaminio's.

xxxvi

· INTRODUCTION ·

33. In 2.5, dated January 1522; see Maddison 1965, 34. Fracastoro 2013, 424, takes Flaminio's early 1520s illness to be syphilis, though no evidence is adduced. Maddison does not treat Flaminio's chronic health problems as so caused. See too 4.1–25n for his joking equation of his recurrent urges to write poetry with the French disease — surprising flippancy, were he really himself devastatingly afflicted with it. Scorsone thinks Flaminio very probably suffered intermittently from violent bouts of nephritis; see Flaminio 1993, 315. The exact nature of his malady is unknown. In 2.5 the poet says that, if he must die, he hopes to find Lygda running up to meet him in the next world to give him embraces, kisses, and the joys of a longed-for marriage. If Flaminio had personally experienced the loss of a beloved girl by early death, the tale of Iolas and Hyella in the book 4 poems would gain in poignancy. Laurens 1975, 197, cryptically remarks that the story has an underlying personal relevance to the poet's own life, calling it a "transposition poétique d'une aventure personnelle de l'auteur." It is impossible, however, simply to identify Iolas in book 4 with Flaminio: one obvious difference is that Iolas there was forced by his father to marry against his wishes, whereas Flaminio never married at all; see also Ferroni 2012, 240.

34. See Maddison 1965, 194–95.

35. Ascribed to Flaminio in Gagny ca. 1548, 29v, and to Antonio Mario (i.e., Flaminio) in Ubaldini 1563, 105r–v, and Toscano 1576, 231r. The poem appears in a manuscript at Venice (see Cuccoli 1897, 164). It is noticed by Maddison 1965, 88n1, but does not appear in Flaminio 1727/43 or Flaminio 1993.

36. December 14, 1549, translated by Maddison 1965, 201. For the Italian original, see Atanagi 1554, 157v. Maddison 1965, 19–20, says that the first mention of Flaminio's stomach trouble is in his father's letter to him dated April 13, 1515 (see n. 27 above), but the elder Flaminio there wants to know whether his son is having further trouble with his hands (*an ex manibus labores amplius*), not his stomach.

37. Poems referring to Flaminio's bad health: 1.3; 2.1; 5.7 and 49 (5.51 Scorsone); 6.11, 35 (36 Scorsone), 37–48 (38–49 Scorsone), and 50–59 (51–60 Scorsone); 8.22. There are numerous references in letters too.

xxxvii

· INTRODUCTION ·

38. For a tribute to Giberti as "the model Catholic prelate" and a portrait of him, see Dickens 1968. Giberti was very energetic in reforming his diocese once he took up residence there.

39. Poem 1.36 is a short address to his dying father (d. 1536), recounting the blessings of his good life, a man "neither poor nor rich, erudite enough and eloquent enough, always healthy in body and of sound mind, jovial with friends, and of singular piety." Oddly, Giovanni Antonio is declared to have lived out sixteen lusters well, making him over eighty (a luster being five years), but he is generally taken to have been born ca. 1464 (e.g., Tiraboschi 1795–96, 7:1355) and to have actually been only about seventy-two at death. Flaminio adapted 1.38, originally published in 1515 as a tribute to his father's poetry, into a tribute in death to Navagero.

40. See 3.1.7n and 3.2.5n.

41. Maddison 1965, 90 and 95, describes the situation of the priory and the abbey.

42. See Maddison 1965, 42, for Flaminio's name on a 1524 list of current and former members of this group, which was concerned with matters of theology and possible Church reform, and Maddison 1965, 78, for his membership in the 1530s, when the group met at Venice.

43. Two of Flaminio's best poems (1.35 and 36) concern Pole's lapdog. Compare his sensitive pieces on Hyella's billy goat (4.2 and 4.3).

44. Flaminio had revised for publication (Venice, 1543) the anonymous *Beneficio di Gesù Cristo crocifisso* (The Benefit of Jesus Christ Crucified), in fact by his friend Fra Benedetto of Mantua, which spoke of justification in Lutheran terms. It quickly sold in very great numbers, but the Inquisition condemned it, and every copy found was burned in Rome. See Maddison 1965, 142–46, for a summary of the argument of this work, Flaminio's association with it, and the aftermath of the attack on it by the Inquisition.

45. For this whole episode involving Carafa, see Antonio Carraciolo as cited in Flaminio 1743, 344–45. Maddison 1965, 201–2, includes a translation of Lodovico Beccadelli's version of events.

· INTRODUCTION ·

46. On the eroticism of 8.17 and 8.20, see Maddison 1965, 190–91. The Church was itself regarded as *Christi sponsa* (the bride of Christ). Flaminio sometimes uses erotic imagery elsewhere to express his own strong emotion. In 6.34 his addressee's elevation to cardinal is said to make the poet as delighted as a lover who has "possessed" his girl in chaste marriage. In 5.51 (5.53 Scorsone) he tells the Capilupi brothers that they are loved by their friends "more than lascivious youths love their girls."

47. Cesare describes Marcantonio as his *patruelis* (cousin) in his letter prefixed to Flaminio 1548 and is thus rightly identified as Marcantonio's cousin in Flaminio 1727 and 1743, xxvi; Cuccoli 1897, 153; and Maddison 1965, 151.

48. I also received the assistance of Dottoressa Antonella Imolesi, the director at the Biblioteca Comunale di Forlì, which I gratefully acknowledge on p. 418 below.

# ANDREAE NAUGERII
## CARMINA

## ANDREA NAVAGERO

: I :

Aspice, magna Ceres, tibi quos semente peracta
  ducimus agrestes rustica turba choros.
Tu face ne nimio semen putrescat ab imbre,
  neu sulcos rapido frigore rumpat hiems,
5  neu sterilis surgat silva infelicis avenae
  et quaecumque bonis frugibus herba nocet,
neu terrae prostrata animosi flatibus Euri
  decidat aut densa grandine laesa seges,
neu direpta avidae rapiant frumenta volucres
10  monstrave quae terrae plurima saepe ferunt,
sed quae credidimus bene cultis semina campis
  uberius largo faenore reddat ager.
Sic erit. Interea nivei carchesia lactis
  fundite et annoso mella liquata mero,
15  terque satas circum felix eat hostia fruges
  caesaque mox sanctos corruat ante focos.
Nunc satis haec. Post messem alii reddentur honores,
  et sacras cingent spicea serta comas.

# LATIN POEMS IN THE 1718 EDITION

: 1 :

See, great Ceres, the rustic dances that, on completing our
    sowing,
     we country folk perform in your honor.
For your part, save the seed from rotting through too much rain,
    and do not allow the winter to break up the furrows with
      biting cold
or a barren forest of unfruitful wild oats to spring up        5
    or any other weed harmful to good crops;
and do not let the corn fall to the ground,
    flattened by the raging east wind's blasts or damaged by thick
      hail,
and permit neither greedy birds nor the multitude of pests
    the earth frequently produces to plunder and carry off the    10
      grain,
but make the land pay back more abundantly, with generous
    interest,
    the seeds we have entrusted to the well-tilled soil.
It will be so. Meanwhile, you people, pour out cups of snow-
    white milk
    and honey melted in long-matured unwatered wine,
and let a propitious victim thrice circuit the crops we have sown    15
    and presently fall as a sacrifice before the sacred altar.
These observances suffice for now. After the harvest other honors
    will be paid you,
    and wreaths of wheat spikes will ring your holy hair.

## · ANDREA NAVAGERO ·

### ⁝ 2 ⁝

Aurae, quae levibus percurritis aera pennis
  et strepitis blando per nemora alta sono,
serta dat haec vobis, vobis haec rusticus Idmon
  spargit odorato plena canistra croco.
5  Vos lenite aestum, et paleas seiungite inanes,
  dum medio fruges ventilat ille die.

### ⁝ 3 ⁝

Ille tuus, Pan montivage, venator Iolas
  suetus in audaces comminus ire feras,
a quo et adhuc rictusque suum exuviasque leonum
  sacra tibi, agrestis munera, pinus habet,
5  nunc, iam annis gravis, haec devicti cornua cervi
  dedicat, imbelli congrua dona seni.
Cum tamen Herculeae facta inter fortia clavae
  is quoque sit laudem visus habere labor,
tu, dive, haec inter viridis decora illa iuventae
10  suscipe, neve illis esse minora puta.

### ⁝ 4 ⁝

Hanc vitem, multa quae semper fertilis uva
  haud umquam domini fallere vota solet,

## · LATIN POEMS IN THE 1718 EDITION ·

### : 2 :

Breezes that speed through the air on light wings
    and whistle through the lofty woods with a sweet-sounding
        hum,
the countryman Idmon gives these garlands to you,
    and to you he scatters these baskets filled with fragrant crocus.
In return, ease the heat and separate out the useless chaff     5
    as he winnows his crops at midday.

### : 3 :

Mountain-roaming Pan, that hunter of yours, Iolas,
    accustomed to confront bold beasts at close quarters,
whose countryman's offerings of boars' masks and lion skins
    your sacred pine still bears,
now, burdened with years as he is, dedicates to you these antlers   5
    of a vanquished stag, gifts suited to an old man done with
        fighting.
Yet, since among the valiant exploits of Hercules' club
    that labor too has been considered worthy of praise,
accept these honors, god, among those of green youth,
    and do not deem them inferior to the gifts he made then.     10

### : 4 :

This vine, unfailingly fruitful in its rich yield of grapes
    and never wont to disappoint its owner's prayers,

nunc etiam large florentem consecrat ipse
  vineti cultor Damis, Iacche, tibi.
5 Tu face, dive, tua haec spem non frustretur, et huius
  exemplo fructum vinea tota ferat.


: 5 :


Longius a pecore errantem per devia taurum
  dum sequitur nemorum per iuga longa Lycon,
errantem scopulo capream conspexit ab alto.
  Continuo certo deicit hanc iaculo.
5 Mox etiam catulos sola sub rupe iacentes
  invenit; hos Crocali donat habere suae.
E caprea in viridi statuit convivia luco,
  addidit et veteris pocula multa meri.
Quod reliquum est, Pan semicaper, cum cornibus ipsis
10   suspensum e pinu hac tu tibi tergus habe.


: 6 :


Quod tulit optata tandem de Leucade Thyrsis
  fructum aliquem, has violas dat tibi, sancta Venus.
Post saepem hanc sensim obrepens, tria basia sumpsi.
  Nil ultra potui, nam prope mater erat.

· LATIN POEMS IN THE 1718 EDITION ·

now yet again flowering in great profusion,
    the vine-dresser Damis consecrates to you, Iacchus.
Make this vine of yours, god, fulfill his hopes          5
    and the entire vineyard bear fruit after its example.

: 5 :

While Lycon was on the trail of a bull straying far from the herd
    through out-of-the-way places, pursuing him over far-
        stretching woodland ridges,
from a high rock he saw a she-goat roaming by.
    At once he downed her with his unerring javelin.
By and by he found her kids too lying under a lonely rock.    5
    These he gave to his Crocale to keep.
He made a feast of the goat in a green grove
    and followed it with many cups of old unmixed wine.
As for the hide that is left, have it for yours, half-goat Pan,
    hung up, complete with the horns, on this pine tree.    10

: 6 :

In thanks for having at last reaped some reward from his longed-
        for Leucas,
    Thyrsis presents these violets to you, holy Venus.
Behind this hedge, little by little I crept up to her and took three
        kisses.
    I could go no further, for her mother was nearby.

## · ANDREA NAVAGERO ·

5   Nunc violas, sed, plena feram si vota, dicabo
     inscriptam hoc myrtum carmine, diva, tibi:
*Hanc Veneri myrtum Thyrsis, quod amore potitus,*
*     dedicat atque una seque suosque greges.*

: 7 :

Et quercum et silvam hanc ante omnia Thyrsis amabit
     et certo feret his annua vota die,
dum poterit memor esse quod hac primum ille sub umbra
     ultima de cara Leucade vota tulit.

: 8 :

Venator celerem maerens Augona Melampus,
     confossum rapido dente ferocis apri,
hac illi in ripa tumulum frondente sub umbra
     erigit; hoc ipso concidit ille loco.
5   Non impune quidem praedo sceleratus abivit:
     procubuit iaculis caesus et ore canum.
Tu tamen, e cunctis canibus praestantior Augon,
     fide Augon, silvis qui modo terror eras,
tu, dilecte, iaces; sed ab alta hac fascia pinu
10     millusque et millo vincula iuncta suo,

· LATIN POEMS IN THE 1718 EDITION ·

Now I give violets, but if I achieve my full desires,                    5
    I will dedicate a myrtle to you, goddess, bearing this
        inscription:
*Thyrsis dedicates this myrtle to Venus for having enjoyed his love's favors,*
    *and together with it he dedicates both himself and his sheep.*

: 7 :

Thyrsis will love this oak and this wood above all other things
    and will bring them yearly offerings on a fixed day
as long as he can still remember that it was under this tree
    that he first achieved his fullest desires of dear Leucas.

: 8 :

The huntsman Melampus, grieving for swift Augon,
    gored by the raging tusk of a fierce wild boar,
raises a burial mound for him on this bank, beneath a leafy tree;
    it was in this very place that he fell.
The wicked plunderer did not escape unpunished:                    5
    he met his end dispatched with javelins and by the teeth of
        hounds.
Even so, you, Augon, best of all dogs,
    you, trusty Augon, who lately were the terror of the woods,
you, beloved beast, lie dead; but from this lofty pine let there
        hang in your honor
    your leash, your spiked collar, and your chain, still attached to    10
        its collar,

## · ANDREA NAVAGERO ·

quin decisa feri cervix tibi pendeat hostis,
　　sintque una ex animo signa dolentis eri.

### : 9 :

Et gelidus fons est, et nulla salubrior unda,
　　et molli circum gramine terra viret,
et ramis arcent soles frondentibus alni,
　　et levis in nullo gratior aura loco est,
5　et medio Titan nunc ardentissimus axe est,
　　exustusque gravi sidere fervet ager.
Siste, viator, iter. Nimio iam torridus aestu es;
　　iam nequeunt lassi longius ire pedes.
Accubitu languorem, aestum aura umbraque virenti,
10　　perspicuo poteris fonte levare sitim.

### : 10A :

Ante canes omnes pastori carus Amyntae
　　nuper ab Illyrico litore missus Hylax,
dum solitas agit excubias et saepta tuetur,
　　nec vigilant socii, cetera turba, canes,
5　qua rapidus sese media inter saxa Timavus
　　mergit et inde iterum prosilit amne novo,
ille quidem saeva vitulos tutatus ab ursa est,
　　ipse sed ingenti vulnere caesus obit.

# · LATIN POEMS IN THE 1718 EDITION ·

and along with them the severed head of your savage foe,
    and let them together mark your master's heartfelt sorrow.

## : 9 :

The fountain is cool, no water is more wholesome to drink,
    and the ground round about is green with soft grass;
alders ward off the sun's rays with leafy branches,
    and nowhere is there a light breeze more pleasing.
In midsky the Titan is now beaming down at his fiercest,    5
    and the countryside bakes, scorched by the oppressive star.
Pause in your journey, wayfarer. You are already burning up
    with the excessive heat; your weary feet can now go no further.
You will be able to ease your tiredness with a lie-down, the heat
    with the breeze
    and the green shade, and your thirst with the fountain's clear    10
    water.

## : 10A :

Dear above all other dogs to the herdsman Amyntas,
    Hylax, lately sent from the Illyrian coast,
while keeping his usual watch and guarding the pens
    as the other dogs, his companions, let their vigilance lapse
(it was where the swift Timavo plunges underground amid rocks    5
    and then leaps forth again in a fresh stream),
successfully defended the calves from a savage she-bear
    but was himself ripped open with a massive wound and died.

## · ANDREA NAVAGERO ·

Constituit viridi tumulum de caespite Amyntas;
10    haec voluit raram praemia habere fidem.
Maesta gemunt armenta; mali furesque lupique
    exstincto hoc sibi iam cuncta licere putant.

### : 10B :

Ante canes omnes domino dilectus Hylactor,
    quo custode vagi nil timuere greges,
ille quidem saeva vitulos tutatus ab ursa est,
    ipse sed, ingenti vulnere caesus, obit.
5    Constituit tumulum meritorum haud immemor Almon;
    haec voluit raram praemia habere fidem.
Maesta gemunt armenta; mali furesque lupique
    exstincto hoc sibi iam cuncta licere putant.

### : 11 :

Dat Cereri has Teleson spicas, haec serta Lyaeo,
    haec nivei lactis pocula bina Pali.
Pro quibus arva Ceres, vites fecundet Iacchus,
    sufficiat pecori pabula laeta Pales.

## · LATIN POEMS IN THE 1718 EDITION ·

Amyntas has set up a burial mound of green turf;
   he wanted such seldom-seen faithfulness to have that reward.     10
The cattle low mournfully in their sadness; and wicked robbers
      and wolves
   think they can do as they please, now that the dog is no more.


: 10B :

Hylactor, beloved of his master above all other dogs,
   under whose protection the ranging herds feared nothing,
successfully defended the calves from a savage she-bear
   but was himself ripped open with a massive wound and died.
Almon, not unmindful of his deserts, has set up a burial mound;     5
   he wanted such seldom-seen faithfulness to have that reward.
The cattle low mournfully in their sadness; and wicked robbers
      and wolves
   think they can do as they please, now that the dog is no more.


: 11 :

Teleson gives these ears of corn to Ceres, these garlands to
      Lyaeus,
   and these two cups of snow-white milk to Pales.
In return for them, may Ceres make his fields fruitful, Iacchus
      his vines,
   and may Pales supply rich pasture for his flock.

## · ANDREA NAVAGERO ·

### : 12 :

Cum primum clauso pecus emittetur ovili,
　　urbs, mea Leucippe, cras adeunda mihi est.
Huc ego venalemque agnum centumque, Chariclo
　　ipsa mihi mater quae dedit, ova fero.
5　Afferri tibi vis croceos niveosve cothurnos
　　anne colum qualem nata Lyconis habet?
Ipse feram quae grata tibi; tu basia iunge,
　　gaudia, Leucippe, nec mihi grata nega.
Cras, ubi nox aderit, odiosae elabere matri,
10　　hasque inter corylos ad tua dona veni.

### : 13 :

Illi in amore pares, vicini cultor agelli
　　Thyrsis cumque suo Thyrside fida Nape,
ponimus hos tibi, Cypri, immortales amarantos
　　liliaque, in sacras serta parata comas.
5　Scilicet exemplo hoc, nullo delebilis aevo
　　floreat aeternum fac, dea, noster amor;
sit purus talisque utriusque in pectore candor,
　　in foliis qualem lilia cana ferunt;
utque duo hi flores serto nectuntur in uno,
10　　sic animos nectat una catena duos.

## · LATIN POEMS IN THE 1718 EDITION ·

### : 12 :

Tomorrow, as soon as the flock is sent out from its sheep pen,
    I must go to the city, my Leucippe.
I am taking for sale there a lamb and a hundred eggs
    that my mother Chariclo has given me.
Do you want yellow or snow-white buskins brought back for you    5
    or a distaff such as Lycon's daughter has?
I will bring you whatever pleases you; in return give me kisses,
    and do not deny me, Leucippe, the joys that please me.
Tomorrow, when night comes, slip away from your bothersome
       mother,
    and come and get your gifts amid these hazels.    10

### : 13 :

We, that couple matched in mutual love, the tiller of the
       neighboring plot,
    Thyrsis, and, together with her Thyrsis, faithful Nape,
make an offering to you, Cypris, of these deathless amaranths
    and of these lilies, fashioned into garlands for your holy hair.
Grant that our love, goddess, may follow the example the    5
       amaranths set
    and blossom forever, indestructible for all time to come;
and let us both have such spotless purity within our breasts
    as the white lilies display on their petals;
and, just as these two flowers are woven together in one single
       garland,
    so may one bond entwine together our two hearts.    10

## : 14 :

Candida Niconoe, viduae spes una Terillae,
  montivagas iaculo figere certa feras,
hunc tibi silvipotens arcum Latonia ponit
  atque haec in pharetra condita tela sua.
5 Illam cara parens tenero sociavit Icasto,
  ignotique iubet iura subire tori.
Tu, dea, si silvis aegre discedit ab altis,
  si lacrimans coetus deserit illa tuos,
tu bona sis felixque illi, tu numine dextro
10   optata laetam fac, dea, prole domum.

## : 15 :

Quae duo fert collis fecundi vinitor Acmon
  expressi primum cymbia plena meri,
haec avidis musti satyris mustique parenti
  dat iucunde tibi vitis Iacche sator.
5 Illi illaesa suis linquant vineta rapinis;
  tu tua fac largis auctibus uva fluat.

## · LATIN POEMS IN THE 1718 EDITION ·

### : 14 :

Fair Niconoe, the widow Terilla's only hope,
   sure of aim in piercing mountain-roaming beasts with her
      javelin,
dedicates to you, Latona's daughter, whose dominion is the
      forests,
   this bow and these arrows stored in their quiver.
Her dear mother has pledged her as bride to young Icastus        5
   and bids her submit to the authority of a husband she does
      not know.
If, goddess, she reluctantly quits the lofty forest
   and in tears deserts your band,
be good and kind to her, and through your divine favor
   make her home joyful, goddess, with longed-for offspring.      10

### : 15 :

These two bowls that Acmon, the vine dresser of the fruitful
      hillside,
   brings full of his first-pressed wine
he gives to the satyrs greedy for must and to you, must's father,
   delightful Iacchus, sower of the vine.
May they leave his vineyards undamaged by their plundering,      5
   and for your part make your grapes stream down in
      abundantly swelling clusters.

## · ANDREA NAVAGERO ·

### : 16 :

Has, Vulcane, dicat *silvas* tibi vilicus Acmon;
    tu sacris illas ignibus ure, pater.
Crescebant ducta e Stati propagine *Silvis*,
    iamque erat ipsa bonis frugibus umbra nocens.
5  Ure simul *silvas*, terra simul igne soluta
    fertilior largo faenore messis eat.
Ure istas; Phrygio nuper mihi consita colle
    fac, pater, a flammis tuta sit illa tuis.

### : 17 :

Iam telas calathosque omnesque perosa labores
    quos vitae quaestus pauperioris habet,
Palladio radium cum templo appenderet Euphro
    iamque sequi Venerem constituisset, ait,
5  'Hactenus o mihi culta, vale, dea, et haec tua multi
    instrumenta tibi plena laboris habe.
Iam tua perpessam dudum mala lenis habebit
    adiungetque suo me Cytherea choro.
Nec mirum, quam praetulerit Phryx arbiter, a me
10    si praelata tibi nunc quoque Cypris erit.'

· LATIN POEMS IN THE 1718 EDITION ·

: 16 :

Acmon the steward dedicates these *silvae* to you, Vulcan;
    burn them, father, with your holy fires.
They were growing from a shoot taken from Statius' *Silvae*,
    and their very shade had become harmful to good crops.
Burn the *silvae*, and through the breaking-up of the soil by the    5
    fire
    let the harvest be made richer, with a plentiful yield.
Burn them, but as for my newly planted crop on the Phrygian
    hill,
    keep it safe, father, from your flames.


: 17 :

Now detesting looms, workbaskets, and all the hard effort
    entailed in making a living of great penury,
Euphro, hanging up her shuttle on a wall of Pallas' temple,
    and resolved now to follow Venus, said,
"O goddess whom I have hitherto worshipped, farewell to you,    5
    and have as a gift these tools of yours full of much drudgery.
After all my long endurance of the hardships you impose,
    gentle Cytherea shall have me and add me to her band;
nor is it any wonder, seeing that the Phrygian judge chose her
    over you,
    if now too Cypris will prove my preference."    10

## · ANDREA NAVAGERO ·

### : 18 :

Dum furit Alcippes forma Nonacrius Almo,
    crudeli demum tabe peresus obit,
Almo capripedi non impar arundine Pani,
    quo nullus nymphis gratior Arcas erat.
5  Spargite odorato, pastores, flore sepulcrum,
    et simul infusum lacque merumque fluat.
Non iacet ille sub hac (ut vos male creditis) ulmo;
    in nemus Idalium transtulit alma Venus.
Hic Veneris pascitque greges cantatque; canentis
10    una astant Charites versibus, astat Amor.
Quin etiam hunc Paphii nymphe non ultima coetus
    deperit, et parilis fervor utrumque tenet.
Nimirum felix Almo, modo perfida virgo
    aspera saevitiae det documenta suae.
15  Pastoris pereat succensa informis amore;
    respuat assiduas surdior ille preces.
Praebeat hinc saevis tam dura exempla puellis,
    formosa ut fastus discat habere modum.

### : 19 :

#### *Acon*

Candida nympha olim et Pani dilecta Lycaeo,
    crinibus et culto conspicienda sinu,

## · LATIN POEMS IN THE 1718 EDITION ·

### : 18 :

Nonacrian Almo, maddened by Alcippe's beauty,
   was consumed by cruel wasting till finally he died,
Almo, not inferior to goat-hoofed Pan on the reed pipe,
   and more pleasing to nymphs than any other Arcadian.
Sprinkle his tomb, shepherds, with sweet-scented blooms,   5
   and as you do so, let libations of milk and unwatered wine
      flow.
He does not lie beneath this elm, as you mistakenly believe;
   kindly Venus has transported him to the Idalian wood.
He pastures Venus' sheep and sings; and as he sings,
   the Graces and Love too stand by to hear his verses.   10
Moreover, a nymph, not the least of the Paphian band, is
      enamored of him,
   and a matching passion grips both of them alike.
To crown his bliss, Almo only needs his faithless girl
   to answer for her cruelty with harsh and cautionary
      punishment.
Let her die of desire, inflamed with love for an ugly shepherd;   15
   but let him be quite deaf to her constant pleas and scorn
      them.
Let her thus serve as such a stern warning to hard-hearted girls
   that beautiful maidens may learn to curb their disdain.

### : 19 :

### *Acon*

Once a beautiful nymph and the beloved of Lycaean Pan,
   a glory to behold for your hair and elegant bosom,

## · ANDREA NAVAGERO ·

nunc vox, flebilibus quae semper maesta querelis
    desertos scopulos deviaque antra colis,
5  salve, Echo officiosa. Tibi sub rupe cavata
    ipse ego lanigeri ductor Acon pecoris
constituam umbrosum frondenti ex ilice lucum,
    molliaque ex hedera serta virente feram.
Tu, levibus allecta modis silvestris avenae,
10    excipis e summo carmina nostra iugo.
Tu, quotiens querimur, duros miserata dolores,
    nescio quid tristi flebile voce gemis.
Nec mirum quod tu lacrimis movearis amantum:
    perdidit, infelix, te quoque durus Amor.
15  Ah misera, ipsa quidem et strophio subnectis olenti
    et longa molles excolis arte comas;
ipse puer cultus, ipse omnes odit amores,
    insequiturque vagas per iuga summa feras.
Quin humiles addis voces; et verba precantis
20    effugit, atque omnes neglegit ille preces.
Siste gradum, immitis! Non te violenta leaena,
    non curvo sequitur dente timendus aper,
sed quae candenti facie niveisque papillis
    vel magno possit nympha placere Iovi.
25  Haec aget et celeres tecum per saxa Lacaenas,
    eque suis tendet retia rara plagis.
Siste gradum, immitis, et quas nunc tendis ad undas
    effuge: causa tuae fons erit ille necis.
Heu, miserande puer, tales ten' solvere poenas,
30    ten' decuit tam crudelia fata pati?

## · LATIN POEMS IN THE 1718 EDITION ·

now but a voice, always sad with tearful laments,
    making desolate rocks and lonely caves your abode,
hail, ever-responsive Echo. For you, beneath a hollow crag,     5
    I, Acon, the shepherd of the woolly-coated flock,
will create a shady grove of leafy holm oaks,
    and I will bring you soft wreaths of green ivy.
Drawn to the light strains of my woodland pipe,
    you take up my songs as they resound from the hillcrest.     10
Whenever I complain, in pity for my cruel anguish
    you emit a doleful, sad-voiced groan.
Nor is it any wonder that you should be moved by lovers' tears:
    cruel Love was your undoing too, unhappy one.
Alas, poor girl, you tie up your soft tresses with a fragrant     15
    headband
    and arrange them with long-drawn-out art,
but for his part the adored boy hates all love affairs
    and pursues free-roaming beasts over hilltops.
You go further, appealing to him in humble tones,
    but he flies your imploring words and ignores all your     20
    entreaties.
Stay, hard-hearted youth! It is no fierce lioness,
    no terrifying boar armed with curved tusks that pursues you,
but a nymph who, with her fair face and snowy breasts,
    could be pleasing even to great Jupiter.
She will join you in driving swift Spartan hounds over rocks     25
    and in spreading fine-meshed snares fashioned from her nets.
Stay, hard-hearted youth, and shun the waters for which you now
    are heading:
    that fountain will be the cause of your death.
Alas, pitiable boy, was it right that you should be punished so?
    Was it right that you should suffer so cruel an end?     30

## · ANDREA NAVAGERO ·

Magna parens, quae cuncta leves producis in auras,
  totaque diverso germine picta nites,
quae passim arboribus, passim surgentibus herbis
  sufficis omnifero larga alimenta sinu,
35   excipe languentem puerum moribundaque membra,
  aeternumque tua fac, dea, vivat ope.
Vivet, et ille vetus Zephyro redeunte quotannis
  in niveo candor flore perennis erit.
Tu mecum socias, Echo, coniunge querelas,
40   et percussa novis fletibus antra sonent.

Crudelis Telaira, meos quid spernis amores?
  Quid miseras surda despicis aure preces?
Hei mihi, nulla ovium tangit me cura mearum
  ex quo me iste tuus, perfida, torret amor.
45   It miserum pecus, et seri sub vesperis umbras
  per se ipsi redeunt in sua tecta greges.
Nec mihi iam niveo complent mulctralia lacte,
  densaque promisso vellere terga gerunt.
Quin etiam aucupii studium, quo clarus habebar,
50   languenti penitus excidit ex animo.
Ite leves passim silvis impune volucres:
  cuncta novus nostra e mente fugavit amor.
Otia agunt pedicae et lento lita vimina visco;
  in tenebris amites nexaque lina iacent.

## · LATIN POEMS IN THE 1718 EDITION ·

Great mother, you who bring all things forth into the light air
    and are all-resplendent when painted by your offspring of
        varied hue,
you who supply to the trees and plants that spring up everywhere
    abundant nourishment from your all-providing bosom,
take up the failing boy and his dying body in your embrace,      35
    and through your aid, goddess, make him live forever.
Live he will, and as the west wind returns each year, his white
        beauty of old
    will be perennially seen in a snowy flower.
Come, Echo, join your plaints with mine,
    and let the caverns resound with the reverberations of fresh    40
    weeping.

Cruel Telaira, why do you spurn my love?
    Why do you scorn my piteous prayers with a deaf ear?
Alas, no care for my sheep has touched me
    ever since this love for you, faithless one, has been burning me.
The poor flock goes forth by itself, and, as the late evening    45
        shadows close in,
    the sheep make their own way back to their pen.
They no longer fill my pails with snow-white milk,
    and their backs are thickly covered with unshorn wool.
Even my interest in fowling, for which I was renowned,
    has entirely deserted my languishing heart.    50
Go in safety throughout the woods, you swift-flying birds;
    a new love has driven all other concerns from my mind.
My traps and branches smeared with sticky birdlime now rest
        idle;
    my snare props and plaited nets are left forgotten and disused.

## · ANDREA NAVAGERO ·

## : 20 :

### *Damon*

Vos mecum e vitreis, nymphae Naucelides, antris,
vos mecum viridi paulum considite in herba,
atque hoc quem canimus dignum concedite carmen.
Sic vobis patrias circum vernantia ripas
5   prata, neque hibernis nivibus violata neque aestu,
sufficiant varios in serta nitentia flores.

Quis dolor, o silvae, quae vos, o prata, tenebat
maestities, quanto squalebant omnia luctu,
cum ferus e gelidis descenderet Alpibus hostis,
10   assidue et Latias in praedam verteret oras!
Tum (reor) invita creverunt pabula terra,
invitae e densis ceciderunt frondibus umbrae.
Quippe abigi raptas pecudes passimque videbant
pastorum rapidos tectis involvier ignes.
15   Ipsi etiam hircipedes Fauni Satyrique bicornes,
ipsae etiam in solos nymphae fugere recessus
et sese ignotis occultavere latebris;
et furor is fines prope iam pervaserat omnes,
iamque fugae deerat nobis locus, undique saevos
20   cernere erat latis hostes discurrere campis.
Nulla usquam tam secretis lustra abdita silvis,
nulla aditu est tam difficili, tamque invia rupes,
quo non saepe greges subitis incursibus acti
fessa reclinarint in nudo corpora saxo.

## · LATIN POEMS IN THE 1718 EDITION ·

### : 20 :

### *Damon*

From your glassy caves come sit with me, daughter-nymphs of
 the Noncello,
come sit with me on the green grass for a little while
and grant me a song worthy of him whose praises I sing.
In return, may the meadows that bloom around your father's
 riverbanks
be harmed neither by winter's snows nor heat                    5
but furnish you with flowers of varied hue for gaily-colored
 garlands.

What pain you woods felt, what sadness gripped you meadows,
in what great grief everything languished
when the savage foe descended from the icy Alps,
subjecting the Latin shores to constant depredation!           10
Then (I believe) grass grew from an unwilling earth,
and shade fell unwillingly from the leafy crowns of trees;
for they saw the sheep made plunder and driven off
and consuming fires everywhere engulfing the shepherds' homes.
Even the goat-hoofed fauns and twin-horned satyrs,             15
even the nymphs fled to lonely refuges
and concealed themselves in secret hiding places.
And that fury had now all but overrun our whole land,
and we had no place left to flee to;
the cruel enemy could be seen ranging all over our wide domains.  20
There are no retreats hidden away anywhere in woods so remote,
and there is no crag so inaccessible and so trackless,
that flocks were not many times driven there by sudden raids
and laid their weary bodies down to rest on bare rock.

## · ANDREA NAVAGERO ·

25 Et tamen hinc etiam crebri eiecere tumultus,
insuetaeque maris pecudes (miserabile visu)
qua pelagi mediis iter intercluditur undis
Hadriacos videre sinus, et litore curvo
pro viridi cytiso, pro molli graminis herba,
30 et spinis paliuri et acuta carice pastae
potarunt salsas nitidis pro fontibus undas,
et saepe irati timuerunt murmura ponti.
Quod si non novus ex alto demissus Olympo
hanc cladem nostris deus avertisset ab oris,
35 Ausoniis esset nullus iam pastor in agris;
nos miseri patria extorres, rerum omnium egeni
(ah dolor!), externas longe erraremus ad urbes.
Hic nobis dulces saltus, hic pascua nota
restituit, 'Tuti'-que, inquit, 'iam pascite tauros,
40 iam solitas tuti collo suspendite avenas,
et desueta diu responsent carmina colles.'
Ergo omnes, veluti et Phoebo Panique, quotannis
pastores certis statuent tibi sacra diebus,
Magne Pater, nostrisque diu cantabere silvis.
45 Te rupes, te saxa, cavae te, maxime Iuli,
convalles nemorumque frequens iterabit imago.
At vero nostris quaecumque in saltibus usquam
quercus erit, ut quaeque suos dant tempora flores,
semper erit variis ramos innexa coronis,
50 inscriptumque geret felici nomine truncum.

## · LATIN POEMS IN THE 1718 EDITION ·

Yet the relentless turmoil displaced them even from there,                     25
and (a pitiable spectacle!) sheep that had never before known
        the sea
found their way barred by its open waters
and gazed upon the Adriatic gulf; and on its curving shore,
instead of feeding on green shrubby-clover and on soft shoots
        of grass,
they fed on spines of Christ's thorn and on prickly sedge,                     30
drank sea brine in place of sparkling spring water,
and were many a time terrified by the rumblings of the angry
        deep.
And if a new god sent down from high heaven
had not averted this disaster from our shores,
there would no longer be any shepherd left in the Ausonian                     35
        countryside.
Wretchedly forced from our homeland and destitute of everything
(ah, the pain!), we would be refugees displaced to far-off foreign
        cities.
It was he who restored to us our sweet glades
and familiar pastures, saying, "Now graze your oxen in safety,
now hang your accustomed pipes in safety from your necks,                      40
and let the hills echo songs that have long gone unheard."
And so all the shepherds, just as they do for Phoebus and Pan,
will perform holy rites for you every year on the appointed days,
Great Father, and you will long be celebrated in song in our
        woodlands.
Your name, great Julius, the crags, the rocks, the hollow valleys,             45
and the echoing forests will all ring out again and again.
Truly, every oak that ever stands anywhere in our glades
will, as the successive seasons each bring forth their own flowers,
always have its branches hung with wreaths of varied hue
and boast a trunk carved with your blessed name.                               50

Tum, quotiens pastum expellet pastasve reducet
nostrum aliquis pecudes, totiens, id mente revolvens,
ut liceat, factum esse tuo, Pater Optime, ductu,
nullus erit qui non libet tibi lacte recenti,
55  nullus erit qui non teneros tibi nutriat agnos.
Quin, audire preces nisi dedignabere agrestes,
tu nostra ante deos in vota vocaberis omnes.
Ipse ego bina tibi sollemni altaria ritu
et geminos sacra e quercu lauroque virenti
60  vicino lucos Nauceli in litore ponam.
Hic ripa passim in molli viridante sub umbra,
vere novo dum floret ager, dum germinat arbos,
dum vario resonant volucrum nemora avia cantu,
annua constituam festis convivia ludis.
65  Ductores pecudum hic omnes rurisque coloni
contendent iaculo et rapidi certamine cursus,
horridaque agresti nudabunt membra palaestra.
Ipse pecu et tenero victor donabitur haedo.
Praeterea dulci cantabit harundine Damon
70  carmina quae puerum docuit Sebethius Aegon,
olim cum procul hinc illis habitaret in oris,
scilicet ut quondam Assyrii pastoris amore
capta dea, et caelum et fulgentia sidera linquens,
omnibus his cari praeferret Adonidis ignes.

## · LATIN POEMS IN THE 1718 EDITION ·

Then, whenever any of us drives his sheep out to graze, or after
    grazing
brings them back home again, on each occasion, reflecting in
    his mind
that liberty to do so comes of your leadership, Most Gracious
    Father,
there will be none who will fail to pour you a libation of fresh
    milk,
none who will fail to rear you tender lambs to sacrifice in your    55
    honor.
Furthermore, unless you scorn to listen to the pleas of country
    folk,
you will be called upon in our prayers before all other gods.
I myself with solemn ritual will set you up two altars
and create two groves, of holy oak and green laurel,
on the margin of Noncello's stream close by.    60
Here, everywhere on the soft bank, beneath the green shade,
as the countryside blooms with the new spring, the trees open up
    their buds,
and the trackless woods resound with diverse birdsong,
I will institute a yearly feast with festival games.
Here all the shepherds and husbandmen of the countryside    65
will compete with the javelin and in a fast-run footrace,
and they will bare their rugged bodies in rustic wrestling.
The victor will be presented with a sheep and a young kid.
Furthermore Damon will play on his dulcet reed
the songs that Aegon of the Sebeto taught him as a boy,    70
when in time past he used to live far away from here on those
    shores.
No doubt he will tell how once the goddess, captivated by love
for the Assyrian shepherd, left the sky and gleaming stars behind
and to all of them preferred her passion for her dear Adonis.

## · ANDREA NAVAGERO ·

75  Fortunate puer, tecum formosa Dione
una tondet oves, una ad mulctralia ducit,
atque immunda premit caelestibus ubera palmis.
Dum te complexu teneat, non illa recusat
tecum inter pecudes vili requiescere culmo;
80  at Mars ipse deae cura tabescit inani.
Fortunate puer, mediis pecus errat in agris;
tu, viridi deiectus in umbra, aut carmina cantas,
aut posita in Veneris gremio cervice recumbis.
Illa tibi amplexus molles, illa oscula iungit,
85  caraque odoratis exornat tempora sertis.
Sed tu nimirum, sed felix tu quoque, Damon,
cui licuit totiens Aegonem audire canentem,
divinique senis sacros ediscere cantus.
Quod mihi, Magne Pater, divum si fata dedissent,
90  O quales tibi cantaret mea fistula laudes!
Et quodcumque tamen felix concedet Apollo,
hoc te unum canet, hoc uni tibi serviet omne,
nec quicquam magis optarim quam digna triumphis
posse tuis, videorque, canens tua maxima facta,
95  inferior nullo, non ipso Aegone, futurus.
Ipse suo certet mecum si carmine Daphnis,
ipse suo Daphnis cum carmine victus abibit.
Interea, agrestis dignatus sibila cannae,
dexter ades nobis, et quae facis otia serva.

## · LATIN POEMS IN THE 1718 EDITION ·

Lucky boy, beautiful Dione joins with you in shearing sheep          75
and in leading them to their milking pails
and squeezes their dirty udders with her heavenly hands!
As long as she may hold you in her embrace, she does not refuse
to bed down with you amid your ewes on lowly straw,
as Mars himself pines in fruitless love for the goddess.          80
Lucky boy, your flock ranges out in the fields,
while you, reclining in the green shade, either sing songs
or lie with your head resting on Venus' lap!
She gives you soft embraces and kisses
and decks your dear temples with fragrant garlands.          85
But you were truly, truly lucky too, Damon,
in being allowed so many times to hear Aegon singing
and to learn by heart the divine old man's sacred songs!
Great Father, if the fates had granted that to me,
O what praises my reed pipe would sound in your honor!          90
And yet, whatever skill Apollo of his grace will grant me,
that skill will sing of you alone and be solely at your service,
nor would I desire anything more than to be able to produce
      praises
worthy of your triumphs, and I seem, in singing of your great
      exploits,
sure to be second to none, not even to Aegon.          95
Should Daphnis himself compete against me with his song,
Daphnis himself, along with his song, would surely go away
      defeated.
Till then, deign to accept a rustic pipe's whistlings, favor us
with your propitious presence, and preserve the peace of your
      making.

## · ANDREA NAVAGERO ·

### ⋮ 21 ⋮

Florentes dum forte vagans mea Hyella per hortos
    texit odoratis lilia cana rosis,
ecce, rosas inter latitantem invenit Amorem,
    et simul annexis floribus implicuit.
5  Luctatur primo et, contra nitentibus alis,
    indomitus tentat solvere vincla puer.
Mox, ubi lacteolas et dignas matre papillas
    vidit et ora ipsos nata movere deos,
impositosque comae ambrosios ut sensit odores
10    quosque legit diti messe beatus Arabs,
'I,' dixit, 'mea quaere novum tibi mater Amorem:
    imperio sedes haec erit apta meo.'

### ⋮ 22 ⋮

Nox bona, quae, tacitis terras amplexa tenebris,
    dulcia iucundae furta tegis Veneris,
dum propero in carae amplexus et mollia Hyellae
    oscula, tu nostrae sis comes una viae,
5  neve aliquis nostros possit deprehendere amores,
    aera coge atras densius in nebulas.
Gaudia qui credit cuiquam sua, dignus ut umquam
    dicier illius nulla puella velit.
Non sola occultanda cavis sunt orgia cistis,
10    solave Eleusinae sacra silenda deae;

## · LATIN POEMS IN THE 1718 EDITION ·

### : 21 :

As my Hyella happened to be strolling through flowery gardens,
    weaving white lilies in with sweet-scented roses,
there before her eyes she came upon Love hiding amid the roses
    and bound him up with the intertwined flowers.
At first he struggled, and, beating his wings in an effort to pull     5
    away,
    the indomitable boy tried to break his bonds.
Presently, when he saw milk-white breasts worthy of his mother
    and a face born to move the very gods
and caught the aroma of the ambrosial perfumes applied to
    Hyella's hair,
    scents that the wealthy Arab gathers in his precious harvest,     10
he said, "Go, my mother, and find yourself a new Love:
    this will be the fitting seat for my dominion."

### : 22 :

Kindly Night, you who envelop the world in still darkness
    and hide delightful Venus' sweet intrigues,
as I hurry to enjoy dear Hyella's embraces and soft kisses,
    be you alone the companion of my way,
and, so that no one may be able to discover our love,     5
    condense the air to form a gloomy mist.
The man who confides his pleasures to anyone else
    deserves to find no girl ever willing to be called his.
It is not only mystic symbols that must be hidden in hollow
    chests,
    or only the rites of the goddess of Eleusis that must not be     10
    divulged;

ipse etiam sua celari vult furta Cupido,
    saepius et poenas garrula lingua dedit.
Una meos, quos et miserata est, novit amores
    officiis nutrix cognita fida suis,
15  haec, quae me foribus vigilans exspectat in ipsis,
    inque sinum dominae sedula ducit anus.
Hanc praeter, tu, sancta, latent qua cuncta silentque,
    tu, dea, sis flammae conscia sola meae,
quaeque libens astat nostrorum testis amorum
20  nobiscum tota nocte lucerna vigil.

: 23 :

Oppositae obstabant nostris prius auctibus aedes,
    nec nos caelum ulla solve iuvabat ope.
Disiectis erus his solemque admisit et aura
    concessit nobis liberiore frui.
5  Hinc nos in tenues certatim tollimur auras,
    ornamurque novae frondis honore caput.
At tibi, cui sacris Musarum et Apollinis umbris
    exstructas libuit posthabuisse domos,
perpetuo similes nostris sint frondibus anni,
10  nobiscum augescant et tibi cuncta bona.

## · LATIN POEMS IN THE 1718 EDITION ·

Cupid too wants his intrigues kept secret,
    and a blabbing tongue has often paid for its offense.
The only person who knows of my love — and she has had pity
        on it —
    is a nurse proven trustworthy by her good services,
the old woman who watchfully waits for me right at the door     15
    and carefully conducts me to her mistress's private boudoir.
Her apart, may only you, holy goddess, under whose cover
    everything stays secret and unspoken, may only you be privy to
        my flame,
along with the bedside lamp that is a willing witness of our
        lovemaking
    as it keeps vigil with us all night long.     20

: 23 :

Previously, a house in my way was restricting my growth,
    and no sky or sun was helping me to thrive.
My owner cleared away that obstruction, letting in the sun
    and allowing me to enjoy a more open situation.
As a result I rise eagerly up into the thin air,     5
    and I am crowned on top with the glory of fresh foliage.
As your reward for choosing to rank houses built by man
    second to sacred trees of the Muses and Apollo,
may your years ever be like my leaves,
    and may all your blessings grow along with me.     10

## · ANDREA NAVAGERO ·

### ፥ 24 ፥

Quem totiens vixisse anima redeunte renatum
    mutato fama est corpore Pythagoram
cerne, iterum ut docti caelo generatus Asilae
    vivat, ut antiquum servet in ore decus.
5  Dignum aliquid certe volvit; sic fronte severa est,
    sic in se magno pectore totus abit.
Posset et ille altos animi depromere sensus;
    sed, veteri obstrictus religione, silet.

### ፥ 25 ፥

Iam tristi canos glacie concreta capillos
    afflatu tepidi fugit Hiems zephyri,
iam nitidum os Ver molle auras in luminis audet
    proferre, et teneros ferre per arva pedes,
5  tempora diversis tollens halantia sertis
    purpureo matris Chloridos e gremio.
Summittit varios tellus fecunda colores,
    convertit molles quo puer ipse gradus;
et passim, quacumque vagos deflectit ocellos,
10  diffugiunt toto nubila cuncta polo.
It prope et, incutiens blandas in pectora flammas,
    omnia iucundo accendit amore Venus.
Quam circum vario texunt e flore coronas
    perfusae Assyrio rore comam Charites.

## · LATIN POEMS IN THE 1718 EDITION ·

### ː 24 ː

See how Pythagoras, said to have lived so many times,
    reborn as his soul came back with a change of body,
now lives once more as the offspring of skilled Asilas' chisel,
    and see how he retains on his face his distinguished look of
        old.
He is surely pondering some worthy problem; he has such a     5
    serious expression
    and is so totally immersed in his own great thoughts.
And he might reveal to us the deep reflections of his mind;
    but, restrained by old-time religious scruple, he stays silent.

### ː 25 ː

Now Winter, hoary locks stiff with dismal ice,
    has taken flight at the breath of the warm zephyr,
now gentle Spring ventures to show a bright face to the sunlight
    and trip over the countryside on tender feet,
lifting temples fragrant with garlands of assorted flowers     5
    from Mother Chloris' richly colored bosom.
The fertile earth puts forth her diverse hues
    where the boy directs his gentle steps;
and everywhere he turns his roving gaze,
    all the clouds clear away completely from the sky.     10
Beside him goes Venus, and, stirring pleasant flames in hearts,
    she fires every creature with delightful love.
Around her the Graces weave garlands of many-colored flowers,
    their hair liberally anointed with Assyrian perfume.

· ANDREA NAVAGERO ·

15 Hinc atque hinc mille aligeri pueri assultantes
    coniciunt certa spicula acuta manu.
Concipiunt dulces animalia cuncta calores,
    persultantque vagi pabula laeta greges.
Ipse suam de colle canens Amaryllida pastor
20     pascentes tenui carmine mulcet oves,
percussaeque nova dulcedine corda volucres
    dant laetos passim per nemora alta sonos.
Sola gemit ramoque sedens miserabilis alto
    absumptum mater Thracia plorat Itym.
25 Di bene, quod nostrae tam longe a finibus orae
    exactum hoc dira est in regione scelus.
Heu, puer infelix matri dum bracchia tendit,
    assueto cupiens se implicuisse sinu,
illa, ferox animi caecoque agitata furore,
30     avulsum duro diripit ense caput.
Quid facis, ah demens? Ferro quem perdis iniquo,
    is lac dulce tuis hausit ab uberibus.
Huic tu longinquam votis optare senectam,
    huic solita es teneras dicere blanditias.
35 Heu miserum, genitor nati infelixque sepulcrum,
    ut tibi nunc toto pectore sensus abit,
infandae nosti cum coniugis impia facta
    atque epulas mensis tristibus appositas!
Nempe furis, strictoque ruis violentior ense,
40     sed sublata alis effugit illa novis.

## · LATIN POEMS IN THE 1718 EDITION ·

On this side and that a thousand winged boys launch assaults    15
   and shoot their sharp darts with unerring hands.
All living beasts feel sweet sensations of warmth,
   and the flocks range far and wide and frisk over the lush
      pastures.
The shepherd too, singing of his Amaryllis from the hilltop,
   charms the grazing sheep with light ditties;    20
and, stricken with a new-felt sweetness in their hearts,
   everywhere the birds voice happy songs throughout the lofty
      woods.
Only the Thracian mother mournfully laments,
   and, sitting in sorrow on a high branch, bewails her murdered
      Itys.
It was a blessing from heaven that her crime was committed    25
   so far from the confines of our shore in a hateful land!
Alas, as the hapless boy stretches out his arms to his mother
   in his desire to entwine himself in her familiar embrace,
she, fierce in heart and impassioned by blind fury,
   strikes off his head, severing it with a pitiless sword.    30
What are you doing, mad woman? The boy you murder
   with your iniquitous blade drank sweet milk from your
      breasts.
You prayed for him to be blessed with a life extending long
   into old age; you spoke to him in tender endearments.
Alas for your misery, father and unhappy sepulcher of your son,    35
   how all reason now totally deserts your breast
when you perceive the wicked acts committed by your unutterable
      consort
   and recognize the feast set before you on your grim table!
You naturally rage with fury and charge in a violent onslaught
   with your sword drawn, but, borne away on new-grown wings,    40
      she escapes.

Perpetuum fleat, ut merita est, longisque querelis
    antiqui poenas persoluat sceleris.
Nos, Turri, dum florifero vere omnia rident,
    spirat et e summis gratior aura iugis,
45  nos hic, qua nitida perlucens rivulus unda
    labitur, et leni murmure dulce sonat,
cantemus molles formosae Amathusidos ignes,
    quidque ferox arcu, quid face possit Amor.
Armenias domat hic tigres saevasque leaenas;
50    eripit hic summo, cum libet, arma Iovi.
Hoc duce pallentes umbras Oeagrius Orpheus
    tristiaque horrendi limina regis adit,
nec timuit saevaeve Hecates immania monstra
    armatasve atris Eumenidas facibus.
55  Hoc cogente, omni cum pectore consternatus
    abrupto nollet vivere coniugio,
paulatim Eurydices veterumque oblitus amorum,
    in Calaim tota mente Boreiadem
exarsit, penitusque insano perditus igne
60    sensit ferventes intima ad ossa faces.
Formose o Calai, pulchrae genus Orithyiae,
    te virides silvae, te cava saxa sonant,
in te suspirat, solum te cogitat Orpheus,
    per te sollicito nulla quies animo est.

## · LATIN POEMS IN THE 1718 EDITION ·

May she weep evermore, as she has deserved to do,
    and with long laments pay the penalty for her crime of old.
As for us, della Torre, while all things smile with the flowery
       season of spring,
    and a pleasing breeze blows from the hilltops,
here, where a clear stream glides by with sparkling water     45
    and sweetly babbles with a gentle gurgle,
let us sing of the tender fires of the beautiful goddess of Amathus
    and of the power Love wields, cruel with bow and torch.
He subdues tigresses of Armenia and fierce lionesses;
    he snatches supreme Jupiter's weapons from his hands at will.   50
By his guidance, Oeagrian Orpheus journeyed to the pallid
       shades
    and to the Dread King's dismal threshold,
unafraid of fierce Hecate's frightful monsters
    or of the Eumenides armed with black torches.
Driven by him, though not wanting to live     55
    in his heartbroken distress at the severing of his marriage
       bond,
Orpheus gradually forgot Eurydice and his former love and in his
       thoughts
    became totally inflamed for Calais, the North Wind's son,
and, altogether consumed with an insane fire of passion,
    he felt the burning torches to the very depths of his bones.   60
O beautiful Calais, offspring of fair Orithyia,
    the green woods and hollow rocks echo your name.
It is for you that Orpheus sighs, and he thinks only of you;
    it is because of you that there is no rest for his troubled mind.

## · ANDREA NAVAGERO ·

## : 26 :

Dum te blanda tenent aestivas rura per umbras,
    deliciis nimium rura beata tuis,
ecqua tui, mea lux, tangit te cura poetae,
    an meus e toto pectore cessit amor?
5  Cessit amor certe; soliti cessere calores:
    absentis meminit nulla puella viri.
Non ita concussae versantur in arbore frondes,
    cum gravis adversum verberat aura nemus,
quam facile instabilem permutat femina mentem.
10    Exclusus queritur, qui modo carus erat.
Non sic Penelope, non sic Capaneia coniux
    antiqui meruit temporis esse decus.
Altera, defuncti maerens ad busta mariti,
    noluit abrepto vivere sola viro;
15  altera bis denos potuit durare per annos,
    dum cupidos cauta detinet arte procos.
Femina nunc varias tantum connectere fraudes
    novit et in nulla certa manere fide.
Quid queror haec demens? Durae procul ite querelae!
20    Ite! Decent tristes tristia verba viros.
Laetus ego; hos neque enim sequitur mea Gellia mores,
    mutare incertos nec solet illa toros.
Quin et mansit amor, soliti mansere calores;
    absentis meminit nostra puella viri.

· LATIN POEMS IN THE 1718 EDITION ·

: 26 :

While you stay in your alluring country retreat, seduced by its
    summer shade,
  that country retreat all too favored with your joys,
does any concern for me, your poet, touch you, my light,
  or has love for me completely gone from your heart?
Love has surely gone. The accustomed warmth has gone.      5
  No girl remembers her man in his absence.
The wind-shaken leaves on a tree do not so readily twist and turn
  when a fierce-blowing gale lashes a wood in its path
as a woman changes her fickle mind.
  The man who was lately her beloved is shut out and left    10
    complaining.
Not so did Penelope or Capaneus' wife
  earn her honored place in ancient times.
One, grieving at her dead husband's pyre,
  refused to go on living alone after her man was snatched from
    her;
the other was able to last out twice ten years    15
  of carefully contriving to keep ardent suitors waiting.
Nowadays a woman knows only how to practice deceit in various
    forms
  and how not to keep faith with any man.
Why do I senselessly make these complaints? Away with you,
  harsh complaints! Away! Sad words befit sad men.    20
I am happy; for my Gellia indulges in no such behavior,
  nor is it her way to be inconstant and turn from one lover to
    another.
What is more, her love has not gone; her accustomed warmth is
    still there;
  my girl remembers her man in his absence.

45

· ANDREA NAVAGERO ·

25   Multa tamen timeo; tu multa ignosce timenti.
      Hei mihi, pars nostro nulla timore vacat!
    Ah quotiens vereor, dum picta per arva vagaris,
      dum rutilae texis florida serta comae,
    ne ruat e summis in te Saturnius astris,
30      sisve alii cuivis grata rapina deo!
    Pressit Amymonen mediis Neptunus in arvis,
      dum premeret summum virginis urna caput.
    In mediis Io campis perpessa Tonantem est,
      horridaque hirsuta cornua fronte tulit.
35   Hinc quoque Tartareo raptam Deoida curru
      abstulit Infernus in sua regna Pater.
    Sidonis errabat nitidos Europa per agros,
      cum medium ficto per mare vecta bove est.
    Non tamen hos tantum causantur prata timores.
40      Hei mihi, quam multos dat quoque silva metus!
    Hic habitant Satyrique et agrestia numina Panes
      et timor errantum Faunus Hamadryadum,
    Hic versa in virides Daphne Peneia frondes,
      hic fera mutato Parrhasis ore fuit,
45   hic et semicaper spreta Nonacrius Aegla
      Arcadicae forma virginis incaluit.
    Quod si tecum iisdem pariter versarer in arvis,
      et domus unanimes clauderet una duos,
    non ego caelicolum fraudes, non furta timerem,
50      undique me socio, Gellia, tuta fores.
    Si versa est Daphne, Sicula Proserpina ab Aetna
      si vecta est Stygiis in nova regna rotis,

## · LATIN POEMS IN THE 1718 EDITION ·

Yet I have many fears; pardon me my many fears.                    25
    Alas, nowhere is without worry for me.
Ah, how often I am afraid, as you roam through the bloom-
       painted fields
    and weave flowery garlands for your flaxen hair,
that Saturn's son may descend on you from the stars up above,
    or that you may fall pleasing prey to some other god.         30
Neptune forced himself on Amymone amid plow fields
    as the girl was carrying a pitcher on the top of her head.
Io had to submit to the Thunderer in open pastureland,
    and hideous horns grew from her shaggy temples.
From fields too the Underworld Father snatched Deo's daughter    35
    and carried her off to his realm in his Tartarean chariot.
Sidonian Europa was roaming through the bright countryside
    when she was borne away over the open sea on the feigned
       bull's back.
It is not only meadows, however, that make me feel these
       anxieties.
    Alas, how many fears the forest too stirs in me!               40
Here live satyrs and those rustic gods, the Pans,
    and Faunus, the terror of wandering wood nymphs.
Here Daphne, daughter of Peneus, was turned into green foliage;
    here the Parrhasian was transformed into a beast;
here too the Nonacrian half-goat, spurning Aegle,               45
    was inflamed by the beauty of the Arcadian maiden.
But if I were walking at your side in the same fields,
    and one house were home to the two of us in harmonious
       union,
I would not fear trickery or abduction by gods;
    you would be safe everywhere with me as your companion,       50
       Gellia.
If Daphne was transformed, if Proserpina was carried off
    in the Stygian chariot from Sicilian Etna to her new realm,

## · ANDREA NAVAGERO ·

quid mirum? Facile est deceptas fraude puellas
    fallere, nullius quas tueatur amor.
55 Ipse ego perpetuo tecum, mea vita, manerem,
    sic possem nullos extimuisse deos.
Saepe pererrabat tacitos Atalanta recessus,
    tuta tamen fido Milanione fuit.
Cingeret obsessos seu curva indagine colles,
60     seu cuperet saevas comminus ire feras,
haerebat lateri semper comes ille, nec umquam
    a domina lato longius ungue fuit.
Ergo huic non summi fraudes nocuere Tonantis,
    inque suo nullos sensit amore dolos.
65 Sic ego per silvas tecum et per prata vagarer;
    grata essent sine te gaudia nulla mihi.
Nunc pariter nitida recubare iuvaret in umbra
    et capere in viridi somnia grata toro;
nunc pariter nuda fontes invadere sura,
70     torrida dum siccus finderet arva Canis;
saepius in silvis lepores captare fugaces
    et volucres fictis fallere carminibus;
saepius in denso convivia ducere luco
    et madidas verno flore ligare comas;
75 saepius umbroso choreas ductare sub antro,
    cum daret agrestes tibia pulsa sonos.
Ah quotiens tales inter, mea Gellia, lusus
    inicerem cupidas in tua colla manus
dulciaque e roseis furarer basia labris,
80     basia mi cunctis anteferenda bonis!
O niveam, si qua haec referet mihi gaudia, lucem!
    Gratior optatis non erit ulla meis.

## · LATIN POEMS IN THE 1718 EDITION ·

what wonder? It is easy to practice trickery and deception
    on girls whom no man's love protects.
Were I to stay constantly by your side, my life,     55
    That would embolden me to fear no gods.
Atalanta often used to roam through quiet retreats,
    yet she was safe with her faithful Milanion.
Whether she was encircling penned-off hills with a curved ring of
        nets
    or was eager to confront fierce beasts at close quarters,     60
he always accompanied her, staying close by her side,
    and he was never further from his lady than a fingernail's
        width.
Therefore the supreme Thunderer's deceits did him no harm,
    and he encountered no guile in his love.
So would I roam the woods and meadows with you;     65
    no joys would please me without you.
Now I would delight to lie down with you in lush shade
    and take welcome rest on a green couch,
now to go paddling together barefoot in a spring
    as the dry Dog Star cracked open the parched fields,     70
often to catch swift hares in the woods
    and trick birds by mimicking their songs
or feast long in the dense wood
    and bind our well-oiled hair with spring flowers
or lead dances in a shady cave     75
    as the playing of a flute made rustic music.
Ah, how many times, my Gellia, amid such amusements,
    would I lay desirous hands on your neck
and steal sweet kisses from your rosy lips,
    kisses to be valued more highly than all other joys!     80
O snow-white day, should any restore such delights to me!
    No day will more truly answer my prayers.

· ANDREA NAVAGERO ·

Semper Erythraeis signabitur illa lapillis,
    semper erit sacros inter habenda dies.
85  Nunc, quoniam tecum me non licet esse, caveto
    mutuus exstincto ne cadat igne calor.

: 27 :

### Iolas

Pascite, oves, teneras herbas per pabula laeta,
pascite, nec plenis ignavae parcite campis.
Quantum vos tota minuetis luce, refectum
fecundo tantum per noctem rore resurget.
5  Hinc dulci distenta tumescent ubera lacte,
sufficientque simul fiscellae et mollibus agnis.
Tu vero, vigil atque canum fortissime Teuchon,
dum pascent illae late per prata, luporum
incursus subitos saevasque averte rapinas.
10  Interea hic ego, muscoso prostratus in antro,
ipse meos solus mecum meditabor amores,
atque animi curas dulci solabor avena.

O formosa Amarylli, nihil te absente videtur
dulce mihi. Nunc et nitido vere omnia rident,
15  et vario resonant volucrum nemora avia cantu;

## · LATIN POEMS IN THE 1718 EDITION ·

That day will always be marked with pearls of the Erythraean
    Sea
    and will always be one to be reckoned among holy days.
As it is, since I am not allowed to be with you,         85
    take care that the love we share does not die, its flame
    extinguished.

## : 27 :

### *Iolas*

Graze, my sheep, on the tender grass all over the rich pastures;
graze, and do not hold back and spare the lush fields.
All that you consume throughout the day will grow again
    overnight,
restored with the aid of the nourishing dew.
The grass will make your udders stretch and swell with sweet   5
    milk,
and they will supply plenty for both the cheese form and the soft
    lambs.
For your part, Teuchon, watchful sentinel and bravest of dogs,
as the sheep graze far and wide over the meadows,
ward off sudden raids and savage plundering by wolves.
Meanwhile I will stretch out here in a mossy cave       10
and muse to myself in solitude upon my love,
soothing the cares of my heart with my dulcet reed pipe.

O beautiful Amaryllis, nothing seems sweet to me in your
    absence.
Now everything smiles with the bright sparkle of spring,
and the trackless woods resound with diverse birdsong;     15

## · ANDREA NAVAGERO ·

exsultim virides ludunt armenta per herbas,
lascivique agni, infirmisque artubus haedi
cornigeras matres per florida prata sequuntur.
Non tamen ista magis sine te mihi laeta videntur
20    quam si tristis hiems nimbisque rigentibus horrens
agglomeret gelido canas aquilone pruinas.
Dulce apibus flores, rivi sitientibus herbis,
gramen ovi, caprae cytisus, Amaryllis Iolae.
Non ego opes mihi, non cursu praevertere ventos
25    optarim magis aut pecoris quodcumque per orbem est
quam te, Amarylli, meis vinctam retinere lacertis
et tecum has inter vitam deducere silvas.
Est mihi praeruptis ingens sub rupibus antrum,
quod croceis hederae circum sparsere corymbis,
30    vestibulumque ipsum silvestris obumbrat oliva.
Hanc prope fons, lapide effusus qui desilit alto,
defertur rauco per levia saxa susurro.
Hinc late licet immensi vasta aequora ponti
despicere et longe venientes cernere fluctus.
35    Hoc mecum simul incoleres, Amarylli, simulque
mecum ageres primo pecudes in pascua sole,
mecum, abeunte die, pecudes cava in antra vocares.
Saepe etiam denso in nemore aut convalle virenti,
dum tenue arguta modularer arundine carmen,
40    tu mecum ipsa esses simul, astaresque canenti.
Quin et nunc pariter caneres, nunc dulcia nostro
basiaque et Veneris misceres gaudia cantu.

## · LATIN POEMS IN THE 1718 EDITION ·

the grazing animals caper as they play on the green grass,
and the frisky lambs and the kids on their unsteady legs
follow their horned mothers through the flowery meadows.
Yet without you those sights seem no more joyful to me
than if bleak winter, stiff with freezing showers,                20
were building up layers of hoary frost in the icy north wind.
Flowers are sweet to bees, streams to thirsty plants,
grass to a sheep, shrubby clover to a nanny goat, Amaryllis to
    Iolas.
I would not wish to have riches or to outstrip the winds in
    the race
or to own all the sheep there are in the world                25
more than to hold you, Amaryllis, firmly clasped in my arms
and to spend my life with you in these woods.
I have a huge cave at the foot of sheer crags,
one that the ivies have bedecked round about with clusters of
    yellow berries,
while a woodland olive shades the entrance itself.                30
Near this tree a spring that leaps down as it streams from a high
    rock
flows over the smooth stones with a husky gurgle.
From this spot one can survey far and wide the vast waters
of the boundless sea and watch the waves coming on in the far
    distance.
I wish you would live in this cave together with me, Amaryllis,    35
and together with me drive the flocks to the pastures at sunrise
and, as the day fades away, call them back again into the hollow
    cavern.
Often too, in a thick wood or green valley,
as I play a light ditty on my clear-toned pipe,
you would be there with me and stand by me as I sing.             40
Furthermore, now you would join with me in the music-making,
now mix sweet kisses and Venus' joys with our song.

#### · ANDREA NAVAGERO ·

O solum hoc, superi, misero concedite amanti;
tum licet et rapiantur oves, rapiantur et agni,
45  ipse tamen Croeso mihi ditior esse videbor.
Mollibus in pratis Lycidae, post Daphnidis hortos,
purpureos flores texenda in serta legebas,
cum te succincta tunica fusisque capillis
et vidi simul et totis simul ossibus arsi.
50  Pone sequebatur Gorge soror, et tamen audax
accessi, sumque ipse meos tibi fassus amores.
Risisti, et sertum, nitida quod fronte gerebas,
tamquam ex se cecidisset, humi iecisti abiensque
liquisti. Advertens, collegi protinus ipse
55  servavique et adhuc tamquam tua munera servo;
et, quamvis dudum foliis languentibus aret,
non tamen est serto quicquam mihi carius illo.
Ex illo semperque fui tibi deditus uni,
pulchraque nulla meis oculis te praeter habetur.
60  Saepe mihi Alcippe vicina et munera misit
et dixit, 'Formose puer, quae munera mittit,
mittit et ipsum animum. tu et munera suscipe et illum.'
Sed potius, Amarylli, alio quam tangar amore,
sudabunt humiles flaventia mella genistae,
65  et molles violae dura nascentur in orno,
incultique ferent candentia lilia vepres,
et maestis ululae cedet Philomela querelis.
Quantum ver formosum hieme est iucundius atra,
quantum mite pyrum sorbis est dulcius ipsis,
70  quantum hirsuta capella suo setosior haedo,
quantum nocturnis obscuri vesperis umbris

## · LATIN POEMS IN THE 1718 EDITION ·

Oh, do but grant a poor lover this, gods of heaven,
and then, though my sheep and my lambs too be stolen from me,
I shall still think myself richer than Croesus.                    45
In Lycidas' soft meadows, behind Daphnis' gardens,
you were gathering red flowers to weave garlands
when I saw you with your tunic girt up and your hair flowing,
and at that very same instant I blazed with fire in my every bone.
Your sister Gorge was following behind, and yet I boldly            50
    approached you
and with my own lips declared my love for you.
You smiled and cast the garland you were wearing on your
    radiant brow
to the ground as if it had fallen on its own and left it lying as you
    departed.
I noticed and picked it up at once myself,
and I kept it and still keep it as a gift from you;                55
and, though its flowers have wilted, and it has long been withered,
still there is nothing dearer to me than that garland.
From that moment I have always been devoted to you alone,
and no girl but you is beautiful in my eyes.
Many a time my neighbor Alcippe has sent me gifts and said,       60
"Handsome boy, she who sends you these gifts
sends you her heart too. Accept both the gifts and it."
But before I shall be touched by love for any other, Amaryllis,
lowly brooms will sweat yellow honey,
soft violets will blossom on the hardy mountain ash,              65
wild brambles will bear white lilies,
and in sad laments Philomela will yield place to the screech owl.
As much as the pretty spring is more agreeable than dark winter,
as much as a juicy pear is sweeter than sorb apples,
as much as a shaggy nanny goat is more bristly than her kid,      70
as much as the dawn is brighter at her rosy rising

puniceo exsurgens Aurora nitentior ortu est,
tantum, Amarylli, aliis mihi carior ipsa puellis.
Hae testes mihi sunt silvae, vicinaque silvis
75  populus haec, cuius tale est in cortice carmen:
*Vellera cum setis aries mutarit et hircus*
*velleribus setas, Amaryllida linquet Iolas.*

Sed nos dum longum canimus, iam roscida luna
apparet caelo, et rapidus deferbuit ardor,
80  demerso iam sole; tamen miser ardet Iolas.
Nimirum nostros nequeunt lenire calores
nec quaecumque rigent Rhipaeo in monte pruinae,
nec quaecumque simul gelido durantur in Hebro.
Fors tamen hos illa ipsa, potest quae sola, levabit.
85  Sperando interea duros solabimur ignes.
At vos, ne, sero dum nox insurgit Olympo,
praesidio umbrarum fretus, malus ingruat hostis,
iam pasti, secura, greges, in ovilia abite.

### : 28 :

Quam tibi nunc Iani donamus, Hyella, Kalendis,
  exprimit haec vultus parva tabella meos.
Nulla fuit cuiquam similis mage. Pallet imago;
  assiduus nostro pallor in ore sedet.
5  Est excors; sine corde et ego, quod pectore nostro
  ipse Amor ereptum sub tua iura dedit.

## · LATIN POEMS IN THE 1718 EDITION ·

than the nighttime shadows of gloomy evening,
so much, Amaryllis, are you dearer to me than other girls.
These woods are my witnesses, and the poplar here next to the
      woods,
on whose bark these lines are inscribed:           75
*When the ram has changed his wool for bristles, and the goat*
*his bristles for wool, Iolas will forsake Amaryllis.*

But while I sing so long, already the dewy moon
appears in the sky, and the day's fierce heat has cooled,
with the sun now set; yet poor Iolas burns hot.       80
Without a doubt, my fire cannot be calmed
even by all the ice frozen on a Riphean mountain
or by all that too which hardens over the chilly Hebrus.
Yet perhaps the very girl who alone can ease it will do so.
Till then I shall make the cruel flames more bearable by hoping.   85
But as for you, my sheep, in case, as night draws over the evening
      sky,
a wicked enemy should attack you under cover of darkness,
now that you are fed, away with you to the safety of your sheep
      pens.

:  28  :

This little painting, which I give you now, Hyella,
    on the Kalends of January, is a portrait of me.
No picture was ever more like anyone. The portrait is pale;
    a constant pallor resides on my face.
It has no heart; I too am without a heart, since Love himself     5
    has stolen mine from my breast and given it to you to rule.

## · ANDREA NAVAGERO ·

Non loquitur; mihi sic, tua cum datur ora tueri,
    torpet nescio quo lingua retenta metu.
Unum dissimile est nobis; felicior uno est,
10    tam saeva quod non uritur illa face.
Quod si etiam uretur (tuo enim sub lumine quidquam
    illaesum flammis non licet ire tuis),
non, ut ego, assiduo infelix torrebitur igne;
    in cinerem primo corruet illa foco.

## : 29 :

Beate Somne, nocte qui hesterna mihi
    tot attulisti gaudia,
utinam deorum rector ille caelitum
    te e coetu eorum miserit
5    quae saepius mortalibus vera assolent
    mitti futuri nuntia!
Tu, quae, furenti surdior freto, meas
    superba contemnit preces,
facilem Neaeram praebuisti; quin mihi
10    mille obtulit sponte oscula,
oscula quae Hymetti dulciora sint favis,
    quae suaviora nectare.
Vere beate Somne, quod si saepius
    his, dive, me afficias bonis,
15    felicior caelestibus deis ero,
    summo nec inferior Iove.
At tu, proterva, quolibet fuge; eripe
    complexibus tete meis.

## · LATIN POEMS IN THE 1718 EDITION ·

It does not speak; so too, whenever I am allowed to look on
    your face,
  my tongue goes numb, held in check by some fear.
There is one difference between us; it is luckier in one respect,
  that it is not burned by so cruel a torch.             10
But even if it is burned (for nothing can come under your gaze
  and not be harmed by your flames),
it will not, like me, be unhappily scorched with an unremitting
    fire;
  it will crumble into ash at the first blaze.

### : 29 :

Blessed Sleep, the bringer last night
  of so many joys to me,
how I hope the ruler of the gods of heaven
  sent you as one of those signs
that are often sent to mortals                         5
  in true revelation of what is to come!
Though Neaera haughtily spurns my entreaties,
  deafer to them than the raging sea,
you made her obliging to me; more than that,
  she offered me a thousand kisses of her own accord,     10
kisses to surpass Hymettus' honey in sweetness
  and more delectable than nectar.
Truly blessed Sleep, if you treat me
  to such delights more often, divinity,
I shall be happier than the gods in heaven          15
  and not inferior to supreme Jupiter.
But as for you, impudent girl, run off where you please;
  tear yourself from my embraces.

59

## · ANDREA NAVAGERO ·

Si somnus iste me frequens reviserit,
20  tenebo te, invitam licet.
Quin, dura sis, sis quamlibet ferox, eris
et mitis et facilis tamen.


: 30 :

Canale optime, tuque, Bembe, nostri
amantissimi utrique, amati utrique
a me non minus atque utrique ocelli,
quid rerum geritis? Valetis? Atque
5  absentis memores sodalis estis?
Quid vestrae faciunt bonae Camenae?
Scripseruntne aliquid novi meum post
discessum? Puto; namque quidquid oti
per vestras datur occupationes,
10  id vos in studiis bonis locatis.
Ad me mittite si quid edidistis,
oro, nec socium bonum negate
vestri participem leporis esse.
Sed quid cum Venere ipsa, amoribusque
15  quam vobis bene convenit? Caletis?
Amatisne? Dei deaeque faxint
et feliciter et bene ipsi ametis,
quamque ego leviusque leniusque.
Heu heu me miserum, mei sodales!
20  Quam saevo teneor furore! Quam mi
totus, quam gravis incubat Cupido!
Non quod non amer — intimis medullis
ardet me mea Hyella perditeque,
quantum quid pote perditissimum esse —

## · LATIN POEMS IN THE 1718 EDITION ·

If this dream visits me again regularly,
  I shall hold you in my arms, even against your wishes.          20
What is more, however hard-hearted and cruel you may be,
  you will, for all that, be both gentle and obliging.


:  30  :


Excellent Canal, and you, Bembo,
both friends who love me dearly, and both
no less loved by me than my two eyes,
what sort of things are you getting up to? Are you well?
And do you remember your absent friend?                          5
What are your good Muses doing?
Have they written anything new since my departure?
I imagine so; for whatever free time
the calls of business allow you,
you spend in beneficial studies.                                 10
Send me anything you have produced,
I entreat you, and do not say your good friend
is not a sharer in your wit.
But what is happening as regards Venus,
and how well are things going for you in amours?                 15
Are you afire? Are you in love? May the gods and goddesses
grant you luck and success in your loving
and an easier and gentler time of it than I have!
Alas! Alas! Woe is me, my friends!
What a cruel passion has me in its grip!                         20
How utterly and how grievously Cupid oppresses me!
It is not that I am not loved—in the depths of her marrow
my Hyella burns for me and does so with an intensity
as strong as could possibly be—

61

· ANDREA NAVAGERO ·

25 verum hoc me excruciat magis; potiri
mea nam vetitum mihi puella.
Quod si quando licet, nihil levatur,
sed ferus magis excitatur ardor;
nam, cum nec saturum recedat inde
30 cor mi, nec furor expleatur umquam
caris basiolis papillulisque
atque his qui miserum necant ocellis,
augescit magis et magis. Quid heu heu
adverso paterer deo atque iniquo,
35 si haec incommoda sunt secundo Amore?

: 31 :

Blanda o Naiadum cohors sororum
quae Vanci nitido latetis amne,
fusae colla decentibus capillis,
quos large ambrosii rigant liquores,
5 comptae et carbaseo sinus amictu,
exite e liquidis simul latebris,
in vestros simul hic adeste lusus,
quos large Zephyro favente tellus
vernos florida suggerit per agros.
10 En, scandentibus hinc et hinc flagellis
per flavas salicum comas pererrans
vitis pampineas ministrat umbras,
per quas sibila murmurantis aurae
iucundum tenero strepunt susurro.
15 Hic gemmantibus hinc et hinc rosetis
cultas texere vos licet coronas,
et passim simul omnium colorum

62

## · LATIN POEMS IN THE 1718 EDITION ·

but that tortures me all the more,                                          25
for I am forbidden to enjoy my girl's favors.
Yet if ever I am allowed my way, nothing is eased,
but a fiercer passion is stirred; for, since my heart
does not come away satisfied after such indulgence,
and my raging ardor is never sufficiently appeased                          30
by dear kisses, by fondling her lovely little breasts,
and by those sweet eyes that are the death of me, poor wretch,
my yearning increases more and more. What (alas! alas!)
would I suffer with the god against me and hostile
if these misfortunes happen when Love is on my side?                        35


:   31   :


O charming band of naiad sisters
who lie hidden in Vanzo's sparkling stream,
with your lovely hair, liberally wetted with ambrosial essences,
flowing down over your necks,
and with your bosoms elegantly swathed in fine linen,                        5
emerge from your watery hiding places
and come here to amuse yourselves gathering blooms,
furnished in abundance by the flowery earth with the zephyr's aid
all over the springtime countryside.
See how, as its tendrils climb up this way and that,                        10
the vine rambles through the yellow locks of willows
and provides shade with its shoots,
through which the whistles of the murmuring breeze
hum delightfully with a gentle drone.
Here, from the rose beds that bloom on this side and that,                  15
you can weave elegant garlands
and at the same time pick flowers of every hue from all around

lectos in calathis referre flores,
quis comptas pariter comas revinctae,
20 quis sparsae teretes simul papillas
ductetis pariter choros licentes,
ductetis hilares simul choreas.
Sed quid splendidius nitescit aer?
Quid fragrantius huc feruntur aurae?
25 Rident omnia, et aere in sereno
spirarunt Cyprii Syrique odores.
Agnosco. Resonis strepunt querelis
olores Paphii, Cupidinumque
concussae ex umeris sonant pharetrae.
30 Ad flores properat suos Dione.
30a Nunc vos Vanciades simul sorores
30b instaurate verum novas choreas,
31 nunc vos Vanciades simul sorores
instaurate choros licentiores.
Et novae Venerem decent choreae
et chori Venerem licentiores.
35 Huc mitis, dea, mitiorque semper
adsis muneribus, benigna, nostris,
quae versis tibi fundimus quasillis,
quae pictis tibi teximus coronis.
Tu cultis face Vancium rosetis
40 Paestum vincere floridumque Tibur.
Haec non bruma rigens calorque laedat,
haec non flamina pestilentis Austri,
sed semper tibi cultius nitescant,
sed semper genitalibus Favoni
45 tua in munera mulceantur auris.

## · LATIN POEMS IN THE 1718 EDITION ·

and bring them home in baskets
to serve to adorn and tie back your hair
and to wear festooned across your rounded breasts,                    20
that, so bedecked, you may perform dances free of inhibition
and dances of joyful merriment too.
But why is the air turning brighter?
Why is a balmier fragrance wafting this way on the breezes?
Everything is smiling, and in the clear air                           25
there is an aroma of scents of Cyprus and Syria.
I see why. Swans of Paphos are giving voice
in echoing laments, and from the shoulders of Cupids
the clatter of quivers resounds.
Dione is hastening to her flowers.                                    30
Now, you sister-offspring of the Vanzo,                               30a
begin new dances;                                                     30b
now, you sister-offspring of the Vanzo,                               31
begin also dances of greater abandon.
New dances befit Venus,
as do dances of greater abandon.
Kindly goddess, come hither, and, with a graciousness of heart        35
that waxes ever greater, attend our gifts,
poured out to you from our upturned baskets
and woven for you in colorful garlands.
In return, make Vanzo surpass Pesti
and flower-rich Tivoli in elegant rose beds.                          40
May neither winter's icy cold nor summer's heat harm them,
nor yet the pestilential south wind's blasts,
but may they thrive ever more elegantly for you
and ever be caressed by the west wind's life-giving breezes
into producing gifts with which to honor you.                        45

## · ANDREA NAVAGERO ·

### : 32 :

Quamvis te peream aeque, Hyella, totam,
nec pars sit, mea lux, tui ulla quae me
saevo non penitus perurat igne,
fulgentes tamen illi amabilesque
5  illi sideribus pares ocelli
nostri maxima causa sunt furoris.
O cari nimis, o benigni ocelli,
O dulci mihi melle dulciores,
quando vos misero mihi licebit
10  usque ad milia milies trecenta
aut ultra haec etiam suaviari?
Di, concedite mi hoc misello amanti,
dein nil grave perpeti recuso;
quin, etsi peream, libens peribo.

### : 33 :

Dispeream nisi tu vita mihi carior ipsa
    atque anima atque oculis es, mea Hyella, meis.
Dispeream nisi ego vita tibi carior ipsa
    atque anima atque oculis sum, mea Hyella, tuis.
5  Nec satis hoc. Vellem pote quidquam his esset haberi
    carius, ut posses carior esse mihi.
Tu quoque idem velles, pote quidquam his esset haberi
    carius, ut possem carior esse tibi.

## · LATIN POEMS IN THE 1718 EDITION ·

### : 32 :

Although I love all of you equally, Hyella,
and there is no part of you, my light,
that does not burn me in my depths with a fierce fire,
yet those gleaming and lovable
eyes of yours that match the stars                                     5
are the chief cause of my passion.
O eyes so very dear to me, O kindly eyes,
O eyes sweeter to me than sweet honey,
when shall I be allowed in my wretchedness
to give you up to a thousand times                                    10
three hundred thousand kisses or even more?
Gods, grant me, a poor little lover, this favor,
and then there is no hardship that I refuse to undergo;
indeed, even if I die, I would die gladly.

### : 33 :

May I die, if you are not dearer to me than life itself,
    my soul, and my eyes, my Hyella.
May I die, if I am not dearer to you than life itself,
    your soul, and your eyes, my Hyella.
Nor is that enough. I would wish something might be held     5
        dearer than they,
    so that you might be dearer still to me.
You too would wish the same, that something might be held
        dearer than they,
    so that I might be dearer still to you.

67

· ANDREA NAVAGERO ·

Di, facite haec longos concordia duret in annos,
10     tamque bonos mutent saecula nulla animos.

: 34 :

Iam caeli reserat fores
aurato e thalamo exiens
mater Memnonis et diem
    laeto provocat ore.

5  Nos te, maxime Maximi
minister canimus Patris,
quod nullus qui hominum genus
    tam praesens iuvet usquam est.

Tu, nostras celer ad preces,
10  aures protinus ad deum has
defers nec tenues sinis
    evanescere in auras.

Tu dum fers nova nuntia
Virgini Aetherio Patri
15  dilectae, quibus indicas
    magni vota Tonantis,

nobis fers nova nuntia,
quis e faucibus impii
erepti Hostis in aurea
20    caeli templa vocamur.

·  LATIN POEMS IN THE 1718 EDITION  ·

Gods, make this harmony endure for long years to come,
   and no passage of time change such true devotion.      10

:  34  :

Now Memnon's mother unbars the gates of heaven
as she emerges from her golden bedchamber
and with a joyful face
   calls forth the day.

We hymn you, great servant      5
of the Most Mighty Father,
because there is none anywhere to aid humankind
   with such ready support as you.

You are swift to hear our prayers,
and you immediately pass them on      10
to the ears of the gods and do not let them
   vanish into thin air.

When you brought the tidings
to the Virgin beloved of the Heavenly Father
in which you revealed      15
   the Great Thunderer's will,

you also brought the tidings to us
through which we are snatched from the jaws
of the wicked Enemy and called to enter
   the golden temples of heaven.      20

Adsis, o bone, et in dies
semper nos propius iuva,
nec patrocinio tuo
    umquam mitte tueri.


∴ 35 ∴

Urbs, quam vetusto vectus ab Ilio
post fata Troum tristia, post graves
    tot patriae exhaustos iniquo
    tempore, tot pelago labores,

5  ducente demum Pallade, qua rapax
cultos per agros Medoacus fluit,
    dis fretus Antenor secundis
    condidit Euganeis in oris,

tu, nuper et flos et decus urbium
10  quascumque tellus Itala continet,
    magnas tot artes, tot virorum
    ingenia et studia una alebas,

te septicornis Danubii accola,
te fulva potant flumina qui Tagi
15    longeque semoti Britanni
    cultum animi ad capiendum adibant.

At nunc (acerbi heu saeva necessitas
fati!) severas ut pateris vices!
    Ut te ipse vastatam vel hosti
20    conspicio miserandam iniquo!

## · LATIN POEMS IN THE 1718 EDITION ·

Be with us, good champion, and each day
help us ever more closely
and never fail to guard us
    with your protecting power.


: 35 :

City that, sailing from ancient Ilium
after the Trojans' sad fate, and after suffering so many
    severe hardships during his homeland's misfortune
    and so many borne at sea,

at long last, with Pallas as his guide, and by putting his trust    5
in the aid of the gods, Antenor founded
    where the swift-moving Brenta flows through the farmlands,
    on the Euganean shores,

you, lately the flower and glory of all the cities
in the land of Italy, nurtured together                             10
    so many great arts, so many gifted intellects
    and scholarly studies,

to you came the dweller by the seven-horned Danube,
those who drink the golden waters of the Tagus,
    and the far-removed Britons                                     15
    for the training of their minds.

But now (alas, the cruel necessity of bitter fate!)
how severe a change of fortune you suffer!
    How devastated I see you with my own eyes,
    a sight to arouse pity even in a bitter foe!                    20

## · ANDREA NAVAGERO ·

Quid culta tot pomaria conquerar,
tot pulchra flammis hausta suburbia?
   Quid glande deturbata aena
   moenia praecipitemque saevi

25  Mavortis iram bellaque persequar
horrenda? Squamis ille adamantinis
   ferroque consertam rigenti
   induerat chlamydem trilicem,

fremensque et atrum letifera manu
30  telum coruscans, secum odia et necis
   contemptum et insanos tumultus,
   secum animos rabiemque agebat.

Ille urbe ab imis sedibus eruta
implesset omnes funeribus domos;
35  ·  non ille vel sexu vel ullo
   efferus abstinuisset aevo.

: 36 :

Qui modo ingentes animo parabam,
Bembe, bellorum strepitusque et arma
scribere, hoc vix exiguo male audax
   carmine serpo.

5  Nempe Amor magnos violentus ausus
fregit, iratum velut hic Tonantem
cogit et fulmen trifidum rubenti
   ponere dextra.

## · LATIN POEMS IN THE 1718 EDITION ·

Why should I complain of so many well-tended orchards,
so many beautiful suburbs consumed by flames?
    Why should I tell of walls brought down with brazen shot,
    of the wrathful headlong onslaught

of cruel Mars, and of dreadful wars?                    25
He had donned a triple-linked soldier's tunic
    woven with scales of steel
    and with hard plates of iron,

and, roaring and brandishing a black spear in his death-dealing
        hand,
he was full of thoughts of hatred,                      30
    contempt for death, frenzied turmoil,
    impassioned fury, and mad rage.

He would have destroyed the city from its deepest foundations
and filled every house with corpses;
    he would not in his savagery have spared anyone     35
    of either sex or of whatever age.


                    :  36  :


Lately planning in my mind, Bembo,
to write of warfare's mighty din and arms,
I can only just creep timidly along
    in this trifling little ode.

To be sure, violent Love has shattered my bold ambitions,    5
just as he compels the angry Thunderer
to set down even the three-forked thunderbolt
    from his fiery-red right hand.

Sic eat. Fors et sua laus sequetur
10 candidae vultus Lalages canentem et
purius claro radiantis astro
  frontis honores.

Nota Lesboae lyra blanda Sapphus,
notus Alcaei Lycus, altiori
15 scripserit quamvis animosum Homerus
  pectine Achillem.

: 37 :

Dia Tithoni senioris uxor,
quae diem vultu radiante pandis,
cum genas effers roseas rubenti
  praevia soli,

5 roscidos ut nunc per agros vagari
sub tuo adventu iuvat et recentes
quae tuos semper comitantur axes
  excipere auras!

Sicca iam saevus calor uret arva,
10 iam vagi aurarum levium silescent
spiritus, iam sol rapidus furentes
  exseret ignes.

Dum licet, laeti simul ite amantes,
dum licet, molles pariter puellae
15 ite, flaventes vario capillos
  nectite serto.

· LATIN POEMS IN THE 1718 EDITION ·

So be it. Perhaps acclaim of his own will fall to
one who sings of fair Lalage's face                    10
and of the glories of a brow more purely radiant
    than a bright star.

Lesbian Sappho's charming lyre is well-known,
and Alcaeus' Lycus is well-known too,
for all that Homer wrote the tale of spirited Achilles    15
    with a loftier plectrum.


∶   37   ∶


Divine wife of aged Tithonus,
you who reveal the day with your radiant face
when you display your rosy cheeks
    as the forerunner of the red sun,

how it delights me to stroll through the dewy fields      5
now, just before your coming, and to catch
the fresh breezes that always
    accompany your chariot!

Soon the fierce heat will burn the parched plowlands,
soon the light breezes' roving whispers will fall silent,  10
soon the blazing sun will send out
    his raging fires.

While you may, go, happy lovers,
and, while you may, go, soft maidens too,
and bind your yellow hair with garlands                   15
    of assorted flowers.

## · ANDREA NAVAGERO ·

Nunc simul, telis positis, Amores,
matris haerentes lateri, et decentes
Gratiae plenos referunt resecto
    flore quasillos.

20

Per feros saltus, per iniqua lustra,
undique occultas agitans latebras,
fertur et silvas varia ferarum
    strage cruentat

25   clara Latonae suboles. Nitenti
huic comae in nodum religantur auro,
pendet aurata ex umeris pharetra,
    pendet et arcus.

Circum eunt nymphae simul. Illa cursu
30   gaudet effusos agitare cervos;
hanc iuvat certis iaculis fugaces
    figere lyncas.

Nunc ab umbroso simul aesculeto
Daulias late queritur, querelas
35   consonum circa nemus et iocosa
    reddit imago.

: 38 :

Nil tecum mihi iam, Phoebe, est; nil, Nox, mihi tecum:
    a vobis non est noxve diesve mihi.
Quantum ad me, ut libet, auricomo Sol igneus axe
    exeat Eoae Tethyos e gremio;

## · LATIN POEMS IN THE 1718 EDITION ·

Now the Loves, their weapons laid down,
and clinging to their mother's side,
and the comely Graces with them, bring baskets
    filled with cut flowers.                              20

Through wild glades and steep haunts,
harrying hidden lairs all around,
bloodying the woods with the slaughter
    of beasts of many kinds,

rushes Latona's glorious daughter.                     25
Her hair is bound into a knot with a clasp of gold,
a golden quiver hangs from her shoulders,
    and there too hangs a golden bow.

Around her go attendant nymphs. One delights
in chasing deer as they stream in flight;            30
another's pleasure is to pierce fleeing lynxes
    with unerring javelin casts.

Now from the shady oak forest
the Daulian voices a wide-ranging lament,
and around the reverberating wood a playful echo     35
    returns her plaintive strains.


: 38 :

I have nothing to do with you any more, Phoebus, nor with you,
    Night:
    neither my night nor my day is determined by you.
For all it matters to me, let the fiery Sun in his golden-haired
    chariot
    emerge from eastern Tethys' bosom when it pleases him,

## · ANDREA NAVAGERO ·

5   ut libet, inducat tacitas Nox atra tenebras:
      fert mihi noctem oculis, fert mihi Hyella diem.
   Nam, quotiens a me nitidos avertit ocellos,
      ipsa in luce etiam nox tenebrosa premit;
   at quotiens in me nitidos convertit ocellos,
10     candida et in media fit mihi nocte dies.

## :  39  :

   Iverat ad Philyrem media de nocte Menalcas,
      posset ut ad patrios mane redire greges,
   iamque fores lento religatas vimine pressa
      suspensis manibus solverat ille anima,
5   prospectansque oculis, semiaperta per ostia limen
      protenso poterat transiliisse pede,
   cum sensere canes. Quo murmure victus, ut ira
      ardebat, tales iecit in astra sonos:
   'Cinge triumphali, puer, o tua tempora lauro,
10     qui redis ad patrios tutus, ut ante, greges!'

## :  40  :

   Danubii ad ripas primo rex flore iuventae
      caesus pro patria, cum patria hic iaceo;
   nec queror immiti quod sim prostratus ab hoste,
      sed quod me reges deseruere pii,

## · LATIN POEMS IN THE 1718 EDITION ·

and let black Night bring on the still darkness when it pleases     5
    her:
  Hyella brings the night to my eyes, she brings me my day.
For, whenever she turns her gleaming eyes away from me,
    even in broad daylight dark night oppresses me;
 but whenever she turns her gleaming eyes upon me,
    it becomes bright day for me even at midnight.     10

### :  39  :

Menalcas had gone to visit Philyra in the middle of the night,
    meaning to return early in the morning to his father's flocks,
and with bated breath and light hands he had already undone
    the double doors secured with a pliant withy,
enabling him, while keeping a careful lookout,     5
    to tiptoe across the threshold through the half-open
      entrance —
when the dogs detected him. Foiled by their growling,
    in a blaze of anger he cried out to the stars,
"Oh ring your temples, boy, with triumphal laurel,
    returning safely, as before, to your father's flocks!"     10

### :  40  :

A king cut down by the banks of the Danube in the first flower
    of youth
    for my homeland, with my homeland here I lie;
and I do not complain that I have been laid low by a pitiless foe,
    but that God-fearing kings have forsaken me,

## · ANDREA NAVAGERO ·

5   qui, dum alia ex aliis inter se proelia miscent,
      et me et se rabidis hostibus obiciunt.

: 41 :

Diva, quae has caeli generatim in auras
cuncta producis, cupidumque amorem
undique infundens, facis ut perenne
    saecla propagent,

5   qua nihil laetum sine, amabile est nil
nilque iucundum, sine qua nec ipsae
gratae erunt cuiquam Charites nec ipsa
    blanda Voluptas,

dum tibi laetus reparatur orbis,
10   dum per herbosos pecus omne campos
vim tuam sentit, tibi plaudit omnis,
    diva, volucris,

dum nihil, quamvis rigidum feroxque, est
ossibus quod non penitus sub imis
15   sit tua tactum face, quod tuos non
    sentiat ignes,

una erit flammarum et amoris expers,
una secura his Lalage resistet?
Tange age ultrici, dea, pertinacem
20    tange flagello.

## · LATIN POEMS IN THE 1718 EDITION ·

for, by fighting battle after battle with one another,                    5
    they deliver up both me and themselves to savage enemies.

: 41 :

Goddess, you who bring forth into this air of heaven
all creatures according to their kind and, filling them
on every side with the yearning of love, ensure that
    the generations forever carry on reproducing,

you without whom nothing is joyful, nothing lovable,                    5
and nothing pleasant, without whom not even
the Graces themselves will be agreeable to anyone,
    nor Pleasure herself appealing,

while the happy world is renewed in your honor,
while every beast of the herd grazing over the grassy plains            10
feels your power, and every bird sings
    in approbation of you, goddess,

while there is nothing, no matter how unyielding and fierce,
that has not been touched with your torch
right down to the depths of its bones                                   15
    and does not feel your fires,

shall Lalage alone be exempt from your flames and from love,
shall she alone, unaffected, resist them?
Come, goddess, give the stubborn girl a touch,
    a touch of your avenging whip.                                   20

# · ANDREA NAVAGERO ·

Quod si ita tanges, fera ut obstinatum
applicet nostris animum querelis
nec preces ultra miseras superba
    neglegat aure,

25  conseram laetam tibi, diva, myrtum,
Vancius qua se rosifer revolvit.
Hanc mero supplex, niveo et rigabo
    lacte quotannis;

hanc et immixtae pueris puellae
30  circum agent laetas pariter choreas,
teque prima unam, simul ultima unam
    voce canent te.

Te canent unam volucremque natum,
qui, ferox, duro et similis parenti,
35  acer et flamma est et agente certum
    cuspide vulnus.

Spargam odoratas violas rosasque
ipse ego, votique reus secabo
grata torquatae ante tuas columbae
40    guttura flammas.


: 42 :

Quid magis adversum bello est bellique tumultu
    quam Venus? Ad teneros aptior illa iocos.
Et tamen armatam hanc magni pinxere Lacones,
    imbellique data est bellica parma deae.
5  Quippe erat id signum, forti Lacedaemone natum
    saepe et femineum bella decere genus.

· LATIN POEMS IN THE 1718 EDITION ·

If you touch her so that the cruel creature
directs her unyielding mind to my complaints
and no more ignores my piteous prayers
  with a disdainful ear,

I will plant you a lush myrtle, goddess,                    25
where the rose-lined Vanzo rolls along.
Every year as a suppliant I will give that myrtle a libation
  of wine and snow-white milk;

and around it girls in company with boys
will perform merry dances and hymn you alone              30
with the first words they sing, and with their last too
  they will hymn you alone.

They will hymn you alone and your winged son,
who, so like his hard-hearted father in fierceness,
is cruel with both the firebrand and the arrow            35
  that unerringly inflicts its wound.

For my part, I will scatter fragrant violets and roses,
and, should my prayer be granted, in return
I will cut a ringdove's pleasing throat
  before your altar flames.                                40


: 42 :

What is more opposed to war and war's tumult than Venus?
  She is more suited to the games of love.
And yet the great Laconians painted her in arms,
  and the unwarlike goddess was given a warrior's shield;
for that was a sign that often war was the proper business    5
  even of the women born in brave Lacedaemon.

## · ANDREA NAVAGERO ·

Sic quoque, non quod sim pugna versatus in ulla
　　haec umeris pictor induit arma meis,
verum hoc quod bello, hoc patriae quod tempore iniquo,
10　　ferre vel imbellem quemlibet arma decet.

### ⋮ 43 ⋮

Borgettus lepidus catellus ille,
cuius blanditias proterviores
et lusus erus ipse tantum amabat
quantum tale aliquid potest amari
5　(nec mirum: dominum suum ipse norat,
caram bima velut puella matrem,
et nunc illius in sinu latebat,
nunc blande assiliebat huc et illuc
ludens, atque avido appetebat ore,
10　erectis modo cruribus bipesque
mensae astabat erili, eroque ab ipso
latratu tenero cibum petebat),
nunc, raptus rapido maloque fato,
ad Manes abiit tenebricosos.
15　Miselle o canis, o miser catelle,
nigras parvulus ut timebis umbras,
ut saepe et dominum tuum requires,
cui pro deliciis iocisque longum
heu desiderium tui relinquis!

## · LATIN POEMS IN THE 1718 EDITION ·

So too, it is not because I have taken part in any battle
    that the painter has set armor on my shoulders,
but because in this war, in this time of peril for my homeland,
    it is right that even unwarlike men should all bear arms.    10


⁝ 43 ⁝


That endearing little lapdog Borgetto,
whose cheeky playfulness
and games his master used to love
as much as any such antics can be loved
(and no wonder: he knew his master    5
as a two-year-old girl knows her dear mother,
and now he would hide in a fold of the man's garment,
now jump up appealingly this way and that in his play
and seek to nuzzle his owner with an eager snout,
while at another time he would rear up on his hind legs    10
and stand two-footed at his master's table and beg food
from the man's own hands with a softly pleading bark)—
that Borgetto has now been borne off by a swift and wicked
    death
and has gone to the gloomy world below.
O poor, unfortunate dog, O poor little puppy,    15
how a tiny little thing like you will fear the dark shadows,
and how often you will look about for your master,
with whom, in place of joys and playful fun,
you leave (alas!) an enduring sense of your loss.

## · ANDREA NAVAGERO ·

## ⁚ 44 ⁚

Vos mihi nunc magnos partus ortusque beatos
felicis pueri, quo pinguia culta vetusti
Naonis exsultant, quo Carnia tota superbit,
dicite, Pierides. Vos illum e matre cadentem
5 excepstisque sinu et vestris fovistis in ulnis
et teneram molli cinxistis baccare frontem.
Nec vero vos tantum has accessistis ad oras
nec solae venistis ad haec vos munera, Musae.
Adfuit ipsa etiam pariter spargensque salubres
10 pyxidos arcanae sucos partusque dolores
leniit et matrem fetu Lucina levavit.
Adfuit Idalio veniens e colle Dione,
nectare odorato crines perfusa fluentes,
assuetaeque leves Charites ductare choreas.
15 Hae simul ambrosia puerum lavere liquenti
et parvas tenui cunas stravere ligustro.
Venit et undifluis properans Naucelus ab antris,
quem prope caeruleo e fluctu formosa Metune
ibat. Eos circum violasque rosasque rubentes
20 vimineis nymphae calathis et serta ferebant
purpureo e narcisso eque auricomo chrysantho.
Quae postquam totas passim sparsere per aedes
iucundoque domus late fragravit odore,
protinus ecce Iovis magni de limine Parcae,
25 antiquae Parcae, niveo quis corpora amictu

## · LATIN POEMS IN THE 1718 EDITION ·

### ⋮ 44 ⋮

Tell me now, Pierians, of the noble birth and blessed origins
of a boy favored by fortune, in whom the rich fields
of ancient Pordenone rejoice, and the whole of Carnia takes
    pride.
As he dropped from his mother's womb,
you took him in your embrace and supported him in your arms,    5
and you crowned his baby brow with the soft nard plant.
But it was not only you who visited these shores,
and you did not come alone, Muses, to do the child these
    services.
Lucina herself attended too, and, sprinkling beneficial juices
from her secret box, she eased the pain of the birth    10
and disburdened the mother of her baby.
Dione was there, coming from the Idalian mountain,
her flowing hair wetted with scented nectar,
and so were the Graces accustomed to perform light dances.
They bathed the boy with liquid ambrosia    15
and spread the tiny cradle with fine privet blossom.
Noncello came too, hastening from his watery caverns,
and from her dark-blue stream beautiful Meduna accompanied
    him.
Around them in wicker baskets nymphs carried
violets, red roses, and garlands    20
of bright-colored narcissi and golden-locked marigolds.
After they had sprinkled these flowers here and there throughout
    the house,
and a delightful aroma had pervaded the whole dwelling,
at once down from the threshold of mighty Jupiter the Fates
    appeared,
the ancient Fates, whose bodies are draped in snow-white robes,    25

## · ANDREA NAVAGERO ·

canaque Chaonia velantur tempora quercu.
Hae postquam et matrem complexae et fronte serena
oscula iunxerunt parvo felicia nato,
candida versato torquentes vellera fuso,
30  fatidico tales fuderunt pectore voces:

'O fausto nimium caelo divisque benignis
nate puer, cresce et dulces solare parentes
et fatis laetare tuis. Tuque, optima mater,
tuque, boni genitor pueri, quos omine dextro
35  castus hymen quondam thalamo sociavit in uno,
accipite haec laetis animis neu posse moveri
credite quae vero concordes ore canemus.
Qualis in aprico se tollit amaracus horto
quam, studio sollers omni, formosa puella
40  ipsa suos alit in lusus et lenibus undis
irrigat (illa leves paulatim surgit in auras
pulchrior, et dulcem late diffundit odorem),
sic puer augescens primo se tollet in aevo,
nec se quisquam illi formoso conferet ore.
45  Mox, ubi iam validus teneris excesserit annis,
tunc illum sacras artes doctaeque docebunt
Aonides princepsque chori, formosus Apollo.
Illi et divini latices Aganippidos undae
et virides Haemi saltus Pindique patebunt.
50  Mars quoque bellipotens simul et Tritonia virgo
muneribus bellorum et saevis instruet armis.

## · LATIN POEMS IN THE 1718 EDITION ·

and whose hoary temples are shaded with Chaonian oak leaves.
After embracing the mother and, with serene smiles,
giving propitious kisses to her little son,
as they spun white woolen threads from a rotating spindle,
they poured forth these words from their prophetic breasts:       30

"O boy born with heaven's full favor and the gods' benign
    blessing,
grow and be a comfort to your sweet parents
and rejoice in the destiny that is yours. And you, most excellent
    mother,
and you too, the good boy's father, whom chaste nuptials
once with auspicious omen united in a marriage bond,               35
hear these prophecies with happy hearts, and do not believe
    mutable
the things that we shall with one accord foretell with truthful lips.
As in a sunny garden marjoram grows,
which a beautiful girl, skillfully bestowing on it every care,
rears with her own hands for her enjoyment and gently sprinkles    40
    with water,
(in increasing beauty it rises little by little
into the light air and spreads a sweet aroma far and wide),
so will the boy grow and rise in stature in his childhood,
and none will rival him in beauty of face.
By and by, when, now strong, he has passed beyond his tender      45
    years,
then the skillful Aonians and handsome Apollo,
the leader of their band, will teach him their sacred arts,
and the divine waters of the fount of Aganippe
and the green glades of Haemus and Pindus will lie open to him.
Then too the war-god Mars and with him the Tritonian maiden       50
will instruct the boy in warfare and in cruel arms.

#### · ANDREA NAVAGERO ·

Doctior haud illo quisquam, seu comminus ense,
seu sit opus valida concurrere longius hasta,
sive inflectere equum atque artis compescere habenis,
55  seu libeat laxare et aperto currere campo.
O quotiens medio ferventem in turbine belli
conversae fugient acies! At percitus ille
obvia quaeque metet infesto corpora ferro,
non secus ac praeceps hiberno flumine torrens,
60  cum tumidus late ac pluviis hiemalibus auctus
proluit adversas insano vortice silvas,
obstantesque trahit ripas camposque per omnes
cum sonitu ruit, et rapido rotat omnia fluctu.
Fortunate puer, numquam non victor in hostem
65  bella geres, magnique aequabis facta parentis!
Ille olim magnos Gallorum stravit acervos,
Italaque hostili manarunt arva cruore
tum cum, caesa virum serpens per corpora, Liris
aequoreas cursum vix tandem invenit in undas.
70  Ille idem gelida cum gens immanis ab Arcto
Ausonios passim sese effudisset in agros,
audaces animos ingenti strage repressit
Alpinasque nives Germano sanguine tinxit.
Nunc quoque fallaces abrupto foedere Gallos
75  in Latios iterum fines praedamque ruentes
proteret et victos (divinis credite Parcis)

## · LATIN POEMS IN THE 1718 EDITION ·

There will be none more accomplished than he, whether called
    upon
to fight at close quarters with a sword or at a greater distance
    with a sturdy spear,
and whether he may choose to control and check his horse with
    tight-drawn reins
or to slacken them and speed across the open plain.          55
Oh, how often, as he rages in the thick of the tumultuous fight,
battle lines will turn and flee before him! In impassioned fury,
he will mow down with slashing blade all bodies that bar his way,
just like the charging torrent of a river in its winter sweep,
when, widely swollen, and filled up with the season's rains,     60
it washes away the woods in its path with its mad, swirling waters,
dragging along the banks that obstruct it, rushing over all the
    fields
with a roar, and sending everything spinning in its careering flood.
Lucky boy! You will never make war on a foe without being
    victorious,
and you will equal your great father's deeds.          65
He once laid low great heaps of Frenchmen,
and the fields of Italy ran with enemy blood,
on the day when the Liri, winding its way through the corpses of
    the slain,
only just found a route at long last to reach the waters of the sea.
When a monstrous race from the icy north          70
had everywhere overrun Ausonian territory,
he checked their presumptuous arrogance with huge slaughter
and stained the Alpine snows with German blood.
Now too he will crush the treacherous French, who in violation
of their treaty are again invading Latin territories in quest of     75
    booty,
and he will drive them, vanquished, out of Italy (believe the
    divine Fates)

Italia expellet caeloque aequabit honores.
At tu, si qua tuo restabunt bella parenti,
Ausoniam infenso necdum pacarit ab hoste,
80   ipse, tua fidens animi virtute, subibis
haec primum. Mox, externas egressus in oras,
implebis totum factis audacibus orbem.
Te duce et Ausoniae rursum rediviva resurget
gloria, et antiquum late victricibus armis
85   reddetur Latio imperium. Tua signa timebunt
una omnes passim populi, quaque incidit alto
aequore, et Oceano ferventes abluit axes,
quaque coloratis effert se Phoebus ab Indis.
Tum demum placida contentus pace quiesces,
90   saevaque mitescet posito Discordia ferro.
Aurea tum veniet saeclis melioribus aetas,
felicesque anni et Saturnia regna redibunt.
Tum Pax alma colet terras Astraeaque virgo,
immersumque gemet Stygio scelus omne barathro.
95   Felices, qui tam laeto nascentur in aevo!
Tu vero, ante alias superis gratissima tellus,
quam tanto divum genitor dignatur alumno,
tu nitidas passim fruges arbustaque laeta
sponte tua nulloque hominum cogente labore
100   produces. Humiles sudabunt mella genistae,
incultique ferent candentia lilia vepres.'

Finierant Parcae. Tum Iuppiter aethere ab alto
intonuit laevum, et caeli de parte serena
perspicuus multo fulgor cum lumine fulsit.

## · LATIN POEMS IN THE 1718 EDITION ·

and heap up his honors as high as the heavens.
But as for you, if your father leaves any wars unfinished
and has not yet brought Ausonia peace from an invading foe,
you will deal first with them, confident in your courage of heart.       80
By and by you will venture forth to attack foreign shores,
and you will fill the whole world with your deeds of daring.
Under your leadership the glory of Ausonia will live once more
      and rise again,
and her ancient sway will be restored to Latium
through arms victorious far and wide. All nations alike       85
will everywhere fear your banners, both where Phoebus descends
into the deep sea and bathes his burning chariot in the ocean,
and where he emerges from among the dark-skinned Indians.
Then at last you will rest, content with the calm of peace,
and savage Discord will lay down the sword and turn to gentle       90
      ways.
Then a Golden Age will come, bringing better times,
and years of good fortune and the reign of Saturn will return.
Then kindly Peace and the maiden Astraea will dwell on earth,
and all wickedness will groan, immersed in the Stygian pit.
Lucky the people who will be born in so happy an era!       95
But as for you, land dearer than all others to those on high,
which the Father of the gods deems worthy of so great a nursling,
you will produce glossy fruits and bountiful orchards everywhere
of your own accord and uncoerced by any effort of man.
Humble brooms will sweat honey,       100
and wild briars will bear white lilies."

The Fates had done. Then from the heights of heaven
Jupiter thundered on the left, and from a clear quarter of the sky
a brilliant flash of lightning blazed with a great light.

## · ANDREA NAVAGERO ·

### : 45 :

### *Ex Philemone*

Si quid remedi lacrimae afferrent malis,
minorque semper fieret lugenti dolor,
auro parandae lacrimae nobis forent.
Sed nil, ere, istaec prosunt; res ipsae nihil
5   moventur istis. Sive tu semper fleas
seu numquam, eandem pergere insistent viam.
Quid his iuvamur ergo? [B] nil certe; at dolor,
ut ipsa fructus arbor, sic lacrimas habet.

### : 46 :

### *Ex Menandro*

Nam si te, alumne, genetrix cum peperit tua,
hac sorte es unus omnium in lucem editus,
tibi cuncta ut evenirent quae velles bona,
idque annuit magnorum quispiam deum,
5   iure optimo indignaris; valde enim is tibi
fallax repertus. Quod si eisdem legibus
quibus nos omnes (tragicis ut verbis loquar)
aeque patentem cunctis aerem trahis,
ferenda sunt haec levius, et omnis rectius
10  habenda ratio. Denique haec summa est: puta
hominem esse te, quo nullum animantium omnium

## · LATIN POEMS IN THE 1718 EDITION ·

: 45 :

### From Philemon

If tears brought any cure for troubles,
and a griever's pain were always lessened by them,
tears would be things for us to buy with gold.
But, master, these tears of yours achieve nothing;
events are not affected at all by them. Whether you cry constantly   5
or never, things will still proceed, regardless, on the same course.
What good do tears do us, then? [B] None, to be sure;
but, just as a tree has fruits, pain has tears.

: 46 :

### From Menander

For if, young master, when your mother gave you birth,
you were the only person ever brought forth into the light of day
destined to have every piece of good fortune you'd like come your
    way,
and one of the mighty gods agreed to that arrangement,
you've every right to be aggrieved; for he's very definitely   5
been found false to you. But, if it's on the same terms
as the rest of us that (to speak in the language of tragedy)
you breathe the air common to all alike,
you must take these setbacks less to heart and adopt
an altogether more rational view. In short, this is the sum of it:   10
consider that you're a human being, and there's no other living
    creature

extolli itemque deprimi citius solet.
Ipsumque id haud iniuria. Minimarum enim
id virium est et maximis semper studet,
15  plurimaque secum commoda conterit cadens.
Tu vero et magna non amisisti bona,
et mediocria sunt ipsa ea quae pateris mala.
Ergo et modeste, alumne, quod reliquum est, feras.

: 47 :

Salve, cura deum, mundi felicior ora,
formosae Veneris dulces salvete recessus!
Ut vos post tantos animi mentisque labores
aspicio lustroque libens! Ut munere vestro
5  sollicitas toto depello e pectore curas!
Non aliis Charites perfundunt candida lymphis
corpora; non alios contexunt serta per agros.

# · LATIN POEMS IN THE 1718 EDITION ·

more swiftly raised up and likewise cast down.
And quite rightly too. For the human being's a thing of very little
    strength,
and yet it always concerns itself with the greatest matters,
and when it falls, it brings down with it a multitude of fine          15
    things.
But in your case, you've not only not lost any great benefits,
the actual harm you're experiencing is only moderate.
Therefore, young master, be moderate too in how you take what's
    to come.

:  47  :

Greetings, care of the gods, Earth's most favored shore,
greetings, beautiful Venus' sweet retreat!
After so many toils of soul and mind,
how glad I am to see and survey you! How, thanks to you,
I drive anxious cares completely from my breast!                       5
The Graces bathe their white bodies in no other waters;
they weave garlands in no other fields.

## : 48 :

Dum caderent miserae Neptunia Pergama Troiae,
  et ruerent falsi Laomedontis opes,
ostendit Phrygiae mediis in vallibus Idae
  Dardanidis certas aurea flamma vias.
5  At tu, dum Naso silva foret abditus atra
  atque iterum in Scythicos pulsus ab urbe locos,
traxisti e tenebris vatem silvaque latentem
  qui duce te Latio clarius orbe micat.

## : 49 :

Dum tibi dona parat, dum flavo e vertice vellit
  nos domina atque ipsum hoc daedala texit opus,
flevit, et, 'O,' dixit, 'felices ite capilli!
  Cur mihi nunc crines non licet esse meos?'

## : 50 :

Borgetti hic tumulus canis est: assiste, viator,
  mixtaque purpureis lilia funde rosis.

# FURTHER POEMS ASCRIBED TO NAVAGERO

: 48 :

As unhappy Troy's citadel built by Neptune was falling,
    and false Laomedon's mighty realm was toppling to its ruin,
amid Phrygian Ida's valleys a golden flame
    revealed trustworthy paths to Dardanus' people.
But when Naso was hidden away in a dark forest          5
    and exiled once more from the city to Scythian parts,
you brought the poet, languishing in obscurity, out of the forest's
        darkness
    to shine forth more brightly in Latium through your guidance.

: 49 :

As your lady was preparing her gift for you, plucking us
    from her flaxen crown and skillfully weaving this very work,
she wept and said, "On your way, O lucky strands of hair!
    Why may I not now be my locks?"

: 50 :

This is the tomb of the dog Borgetto: stop here, wayfarer,
    and strew lilies mixed with red roses.

## · ANDREA NAVAGERO ·

Hunc olim Eridani Melite formosa puellis
   munus ab Aeolio miserat usque freto.
5 Protinus in parvum congesta electra monile
   cinxerunt nivei candida colla canis,
inde coronatae bene olenti flore sorores
   portarunt vati munera cara suo.
Ante suos ille hunc semper dilexit ocellos,
10   et memor exstincti nunc quoque nomen amat;
nec mirum est, habeant urbes cum nomina equorum,
   fidi etiam tumulum si meruere canes.

### : 51 :

Et domino fidum et lepidum bellumque catellum
   Borgettum, quo non blandior ullus erat,
quicum animum oblectabat erus curasque levabat,
   eripuere avida Fata proterva manu;
5 eripuere omnes una lususque iocosque,
   eripuere ipsum deliciarum oculum.
Ipse autem, desiderio dum maeret inani
   et queritur duris cuncta licere deis,
ut quodcumque potest tenebroso vindicet Orco,
10   aeternum et tumulo et carmine fecit erus.

· FURTHER POEMS ·

Once beautiful Malta had sent him as a gift to the daughters of
    the Po
     all the way from the Aeolian Sea.
Straightaway gold alloy fashioned into a tiny collar          5
     encircled the snowy dog's white neck,
and then the sisters, crowned with fragrant flowers,
     bore the dear gift to their poet.
He always loved the dog more than his own eyes,
     and, mindful of him in death, now too he loves Borgetto's    10
     name;
nor is it odd, considering that cities have the names of horses,
     if faithful dogs have deserved a burial mound.


: 51 :


Borgetto was a lapdog faithful to his master, charming, fine-
    looking,
     and more endearing than any other,
and his master used to cheer his heart and lighten his cares
    with him,
     but the presumptuous Fates have snatched him away with
     greedy hands,
and with him they have snatched away all the games and fun    5
     and snatched away the very eye of joys.
But his master, as he grieves in empty longing for him
     and complains that hard-hearted deities can do quite what
     they please,
in order to save whatever he can from the dark Underworld,
     has immortalized him with a tomb and an inscription in verse.    10

## · ANDREA NAVAGERO ·

### ⦂ 52 ⦂

Vatum pessimus omnium Secundus,
felicissima Sirmio insularum est.
Hanc laudat numeris tamen trecentis
vatum pessimus omnium Secundus.
5  Iam miserrima Sirmio insularum est.

### ⦂ 53 ⦂

Non ego sum pugnae assuetus nec fortibus armis,
    et tamen audaci pectore bella geram.
Confertas turbabo acies, densosque per hostes
    deferar, et praeceps in media arma ruam.
5  Vivere quippe aliis, Venetis ea denique vere
    vita est, pro patria decubuisse sua.

### ⦂ 54 ⦂

Siste gradum, et sacrum hoc, hospes, venerare sepulcrum:
    contegere huic Strozae est Herculis ossa datum.
Ille quidem maiora sui monumenta reliquit,
    Aonidum et pennis docta per ora volat;
5  ipsa suo posuit coniux Taurella dolori,
    ah misera in viduo sola relicta toro,
scilicet, ut vitae reliquum, quod vivet adempto
    coniuge, sit lacrimas quo ferat illa pias,

## · FURTHER POEMS ·

### : 52 :

Secundus is the worst of all poets,
Sirmione the most blessed of all islands.
Yet Secundus, the worst of all poets,
praises it with three hundred measures.
Now Sirmione is the most wretched of islands. 5

### : 53 :

I am not used to combat or valiant arms,
    and yet I will wage war with a bold heart.
I will break up close-packed lines, charge through massed foes,
    and rush headlong into the thick of the fight.
For to others life is being alive, but to Venetians 5
    true life is falling for their homeland.

### : 54 :

Stay your step, stranger, and venerate this holy tomb:
    it has the honor of housing the bones of Ercole Strozzi.
He in truth has left greater monuments of himself
    and flies on the Aonians' wings where learned lips recite him;
his wife Torelli has put up this memorial to her own grief, 5
    alas poor woman, left alone in an empty bed,
so that, for the rest of the life that she will live bereft of her
      spouse,
    she may have somewhere to bring her loving tears,

postque diem extremum, miseros ubi clauserit annos,
10    tunc saltem hic caro iuncta sit usque viro.


: 55 :

Accipe contempti supremum munus amantis
Pieria de valle fluens, ubi flebile carmen
condimus, et nostri testis Parnassus amoris
saepius audivit praerupta in rupe querelas,
5    et lacrimis crevere meis Libethrides undae.
Omnia iampridem miserae sunt conscia flammae;
antra, nemus, cautes, Helicon, Cadmeia Dirce
carminibus resonant nostris et verba receptant.
Quamquam dura silex docta flectatur ab arte,
10    tu tamen immites, puer unice, despicis ignes,
quique tibi veniunt, mox aspernaris amores.
O silvis, o lacte puer nutrite ferino,
tune illum patiere mori iuvenilibus annis
qui te dilexit, qui te nunc diligit, et qui
15    diliget infelix, tenues dum spiritus artus
servabit, poteroque oculos spectare nitentes?
Ecce vides ut sim macie consumptus inerti,
palleat et vultus, pectus quoque. Squalida tangit
ossa cutis; nullum est consumpto in corpore robur.
20    Sanguis abit fortisque vigor, fugere colores.
Non oculi spectare diem, non sumere dulces
ora cibos possunt, non mens cognoscere rerum
naturas motusque potest, non cernere causas;

## · FURTHER POEMS ·

and after her final day has brought her unhappy years to an end,
   then at least she may here be united evermore with her dear     10
   husband.


: 55 :

Receive a scorned lover's last offering
flowing from the Pierian valley, where I compose my tearful song,
and where Parnassus, witness of my love,
has many a time heard my complaints on its sheer crag,
and Libethra's waters have swollen with my tears.     5
All have long been privy to my passion's unhappy flame;
caves, forest, rocks, Helicon, and Cadmeian Dirce
resound with my songs and hear my words over again.
Though hard flint is made yielding by skilled art,
yet you, matchless boy, scorn cruel fires     10
and are quick to spurn love that comes to you.
O boy suckled in woods and on a wild beast's milk,
will you allow one to die in his years of youth
who has loved you, loves you now, and will love you
in his anguish as long as breath preserves his emaciated frame,     15
and I am able to behold your gleaming eyes?
Look, you can see how I have been consumed with languid
       wasting
and how my face is pale, and my breast too. My haggard skin
touches my bones; there is no strength in my withered body.
My lustiness and sturdy vigor desert me; my color has gone.     20
My eyes cannot look on the daylight; my lips cannot take sweet
       food;
my mind cannot investigate the natural universe,
the motions of planets, or the causes of things.

non iaculum torquere manus, nec tela, nec enses;
25  aegidis impatiens pectus vix sustinet artus.
Aequa mihi nox est, nostrum seu circuit orbem
Phoebus, et oppositae seu praebet lumina genti.
Tanti causa mali Venetus puer, incluta proles,
nobilis et sanguis, verum crudelior urso.
30  Heu morior! Siccis morientem spectat ocellis.
Si facere hoc poteris, si tot patiere dolores,
si facere hoc poteris, iam te genuere leones
aut hominum crudele genus vel inhospita tellus.
Non pater e Latio est, Veneta non sanguis ab urbe;
35  namque procul feritas, procul hinc crudelia facta.
Hic posuit molles arcus pharetramque Cupido;
deliciae Veneris miti dominantur in ora.
Tu solus fera corda geris suffusaque fele
pectora ubi fudit molles Venus aurea mores.
40  O mea spes, mea lux, mea mens, mea vita, meum cor,
respice me miserum finemque impone dolori.
Quod petimus brevis hora dabit, breve tempus amori
sufficiet, dum pauca loquar, dum dulcia carpam
oscula, dumque avidis tangam tua pectora palmis.
45  Quod si forte neges, dabitur mora parva furori,
dextera dum gladium morti vicina recludet
et furibunda suum crudeli vulnere pectus
transfiget cogetque animam miserabile corpus
deserere. Illa volans Stygias properabit ad undas.
50  Credo equidem, ut ferus es, quod te nec dura movebunt
fata, sed obsceno spargetur dextra cruore.

## · FURTHER POEMS ·

My hands have not hurled a javelin or wielded spears or swords;
my chest, too weak for a cuirass, can hardly bear the weight of     25
    my arms.
It is alike night to me, whether Phoebus is traversing our world
or providing light for the people on Earth's other side.
The cause of such great distress is a Venetian boy,
offspring of a distinguished family and of noble blood, but
    crueler than a bear.
Alas, I am dying! With dry eyes he watches me die.     30
If you can do this, if you will let me suffer so many agonies,
if you can do this, then lions were your parents
or else a cruel race of mankind or an inhospitable land.
Your father is not from Latium, your blood not of the city of
    Venice;
for savagery and cruel acts are far removed from here.     35
Here Cupid has installed his tender bow and quiver,
and the delights of Venus hold sway on a kindly shore.
You alone have a cruel heart and a breast pervaded with bile
where golden Venus has diffused her soft ways.
O my hope, my light, my mind, my life, my heart,     40
have pity on me in my misery, and put an end to my pain.
A brief hour will grant what I seek; a short time will suffice to
    satisfy my love,
enough for me to say a few words, snatch sweet kisses,
and touch your breast with eager hands.
But if perchance you refuse, my mad passion will soon see     45
my right hand, near to death, draw my sword,
in its fury pierce its own heart with a cruel wound,
and compel my soul to quit my wretched body.
That soul will hurry away to the waters of Styx.
I believe, as you are so cruel, that not even my grim doom will     50
    move you,
but my right hand will be spattered with foul gore.

## · ANDREA NAVAGERO ·

Quid facis, infelix? Veniet maturior aetas,
qua totidem, quot ego patior, patiere dolores.
Ludere tunc cupies animo, cum fugerit aetas,
55    fugerit et tempus subita velocius aura.
Tunc virides annos solitumque precabere robur,
sed nulli revocare dies datur, idque quod olim
praeteriit semper manet irrevocabile. Perdes
tu quoque (crede mihi) primae lanuginis annos.
60    Propterea, dum fata sinunt, dum postulat aetas,
dum tua labra rosas superant, dum lilia pectus,
dum Ganymedeo certant tua tempora vultu,
iungamus, formose puer, iungamus amores.

## : 56 :

Vos, o vos Paphiae deae ministrae,
quae cultos, Charites, amatis hortos,
dum pictas modo teximus coronas,
et rosis bene olentibus litamus,
5    vos vestris pariter sacris adeste.
Nos rosis bene olentibus litamus,
vos huc ambrosiae liquentis undam,
vos ferte Idalii liquoris haustus.
His vos, his miserum rigate pectus,
10    his pectus miserum, precor, rigate,
quod diris Amor improbus sagittis,

## · FURTHER POEMS ·

What are you doing, unhappy boy? A riper time of life will come
    to you,
when you will suffer as many pains as I endure.
You will long in your heart to dally then, when your youth will
    have passed,
and time will have passed more swiftly than a sudden gust of     55
    wind.
Then you will pray for your green years and your accustomed
    vigor,
but no one is permitted to bring days back, and what has once
    gone by
remains forever beyond recall. You too (believe me)
will lose the years of your first down.
Therefore, while the fates allow, while your youth demands it,    60
while your lips surpass roses, and your breast lilies,
while your looks vie with the face of Ganymede,
let us share, beautiful boy, share love's embraces.

:   56   :

You Graces, O you attendants of the Paphian goddess
who love well-tended gardens,
as now I weave colorful crowns
and make a propitious offering to you of fragrant roses,
do you join me at your sacred rites.     5
I make you an offering of fragrant roses;
do you bring here a wash of liquid ambrosia,
do you bring drafts of Idalian water.
With them, with them wet my poor breast,
with them wet my poor breast, I beg you,     10
which wicked Love inflames with his dreadful arrows,

### · ANDREA NAVAGERO ·

quod torret face fervida Dione.
Sic, cum continuis simul choreis
fessae per teneras iacetis herbas,
15   vos aurae recreent recentiores;
sic, cum in Aonio lavatis amne,
sint puro vada puriora vitro;
sic semper, vario decora fetu,
vobis arva decentius nitescant,
20   nec, mixtae variantibus cyperis,
pallentes violae rosaeque desint;
sic Syros oleant comae liquores
semperque ambrosiam fragrent papillae.

### ∶ 57 ∶

Quidnam pessima, quid fugis puella?
Nostrae pondera num times columnae?
An credor potius parum paratus
et parum tibi mentulatus esse?
5   Ne (certe) fuge, ne, puella, ne, ne!
Namque hic, qui tibi tantulus videtur
languens, pendulus atque araneosus,
idem, si digitis parum titilles,
cristatum caput exseret cucullo,
10   tamque amplo pariter tumore crescet,
rectus turgidulusque ut esse nostri
iam pars non videatur hic, sed huius
me possis potius putare partem.

· FURTHER POEMS ·

and Dione burns with a blazing torch.
For that kindness, when, weary from constant dancing,
you lie down together on the soft grass,
may fresher breezes restore you;                                             15
for that, when you bathe in the Aonian stream,
may the water be clearer than clear glass;
for that, may the fields, pretty with their many-colored blooms,
be ever more charmingly resplendent for you,
and may there be no lack of pale violets and roses                           20
mixed with cyperon blooms of contrasting hue;
for that, may your hair always have the scent of Syrian perfume,
and your breasts the aroma of ambrosia.


: 57 :

O why do you flee from me, wretched girl, O why?
Surely you're not frightened of the size of my column?
Or am I rather thought underequipped
and too poorly endowed for you?
Certainly don't flee from me, don't, girl, don't, don't!                      5
For this very same appendage that seems so tiny to you
when it's languid, drooping, and cobwebby,
will, if you excite it just a little with your fingers,
thrust out a crested head from inside its hood
and at the same time grow with such an ample swelling                        10
that, stiffened and distended,
it will no longer seem to be part of me,
but you might rather suppose me part of it!

## · ANDREA NAVAGERO ·

### : 58A :

Decipitur quicumque hircum te dicit olere,
    Trissine: non tu hircum, te magis hircus olet.

### : 58B :

Mentitur qui, Cadme, hircum te dicit olere:
    non tu, Cadme, hircum, te magis hircus olet.

### : 59 :

Quo, quo, blanda animi mei voluptas,
quo refers nitidos, Lycinna, vultus?
Quo vultus nitidos refers, Lycinna?
Succensesne mihi? Dei volucris
5   iratas mihi sentiam sagittas,
iratam mihi sentiam Dionem,
si prae te tetigit meum cubile,
si prae te ulla mihi, Lycinna, amata est.
Iam semel tibi me Venus dicavit,
10   dicarunt Pueri truces pharetrae,
et natus tibi me ipse et ipsa mater
vinxerunt gravibus simul catenis;
et te plus quam oculos amavi amoque
et te plus quam oculos amo atque amabo,
15   dum mors me in tenuem resolvet umbram.

## · FURTHER POEMS ·

### : 58A :

Anyone who says you smell of a billy goat is mistaken, Trissino:
  you do not smell of a goat, but rather a goat smells of you.

### : 58B :

Anyone who says you smell of a billy goat is lying, Cadmus:
  you do not smell of a goat, Cadmus, but rather a goat smells
    of you.

### : 59 :

Why, O why, dear joy of my heart,
why, Lycinna, do you pull back your radiant face?
Why do you pull back your radiant face, Lycinna?
Are you annoyed with me?
May I feel the wrath of the winged god's arrows,       5
may I feel Dione's wrath against me,
if any girl but you has shared my bed,
if I have ever loved any girl but you, Lycinna!
Now once and for all Venus has dedicated me to you,
as has the Boy's harsh quiver,       10
and the selfsame son and mother
have together fettered me with heavy chains.
I have loved you and love you now more than my eyes,
and I love you now and shall love you more than my eyes
till death turns me into an insubstantial ghost.       15

· ANDREA NAVAGERO ·

At tu irata mihi reflectis ora,
nec vis, improba, basiem hos ocellos,
possunt qui in mediis diem tenebris,
possunt qui in medio die tenebras,
20  nec vis, improba, ut haec labella sugam,
stillant quae Syrios mihi liquores,
stillant quae ambrosiam recensque nectar.
Si non vis, neque basiabo ocellos,
si non vis, neque iam labella sugam,
25  dum nec tu roseam, Lycinna, frontem
avertas mihi candidosque vultus.
Nil (heu!) nil precibus meis movetur,
quin et perstat adhuc Lycinna. Quis nunc
in me, quis rigido feratur ense?
30  Fors tantos nece finiam dolores.
Sed iam maestae abeant procul querelae!
Ira et bella, valete; pax adesto.
Iam pax est mihi cum mea puella.
Ecce, in me nitidos Lycinna vultus,
35  in me sidereos reflexa ocellos,
longas post tenebras diem reduxit.
Sed quid nunc, mea vita, commoramur?
Quin iunctis simul artius labellis
excursent tremulae per ora linguae
40  et sonent querulae osculationes?
Tum morsus leviter genasque et ora
collumque et teretes notent papillas.
Hos inter teneros, Lycinna, lusus,
inter illecebras proterviores,
45  et noctes simul et dies iubemur
ductare. Hoc Paphiae imperant tabellae,
sanxere hanc Charites Amorque legem,
hanc inter pariles Dione amantes.

· FURTHER POEMS ·

But you avert your face from me in anger,
and, wicked girl, you will not let me kiss these eyes
that can make it day in midnight's darkness
and make it darkness at midday,
and, wicked girl, you will not let me suck these lips          20
that drip Syrian perfume for me,
that drip ambrosia and fresh nectar.
If you do not wish it, I will not kiss your eyes, and
if you do not wish it, I will not suck your lips any more,
provided only that you do not turn from me your rosy brow,     25
Lycinna, and your white-skinned face.
Alas, she is not at all moved by my prayers, not at all!
No, Lycinna still persists in her behavior. Would that someone,
someone might now descend upon me with a pitiless sword!
Perhaps I might end such great pain by death.                  30
But away now with sad complaints!
Goodbye to you, anger and wars; let there be peace here.
Now I have peace with my girl.
See, Lycinna, turning round her radiant face
and starlike eyes to look upon me,                             35
has brought back the day after long darkness.
But what are we waiting for now, my life?
Why do our lips not join tightly together,
quivering tongues slip out through our mouths,
and moaning kisses start?                                      40
Then let bites lightly mark cheeks, mouth,
neck, and rounded breasts.
In such tender games, Lycinna,
and in such wanton delights
we are ordered to pass both nights and days.                   45
This the Paphian tablets command;
the Graces, Love, and Dione too
have ordained this law between those who share mutual love.

Quod cum nos pariles, Lycinna, amantes
50  ambo amemus et una amemur ambo,
servanda est Charitum simulque Amoris,
servanda et Veneris iubentis est lex.


## : 60 :

Dum putri tegit arva fimo bene culta ligone
    Simulus, ut segetes laetius uber alat,
suffitus spirare facit de merce Sabaea,
    naribus insinuet ne tibi taeter odor,
5  quos urbe ex multo pauperculus aere paravit,
    dum facilem exoptant nunc sua vota deam.
Nonnulli flores sat erant hunc vincere odorem:
    quippe fimum hic positum tertia vidit hiems.


## : 61 :

Rhetoris aspicio nasum, Menippe, Carini;
    ipsum etiam longe non reor esse procul.
Quamquam etenim multo tractu spatioque feratur,
    non tamen est stadiis longior ille tribus.
5  Quod si vicino hoc tollamur colle, videri
    a nobis forsan rhetor et ipse queat.

· FURTHER POEMS ·

Well then, since we share mutual love, Lycinna,
and are both of us alike its giver and receiver,                    50
we must keep the Graces' law and Love's law too
and that of Venus, who commands our compliance.


: 60 :


As Simulus spreads rotted dung on fields well cultivated with the
        mattock
    so that a fertile soil may more richly feed his crops,
he makes fumigations of Sabaean incense fill the air
    to stop the foul stench from finding its way into your nostrils
(though poor, he has bought it in the city at great expense)        5
    as his prayers now plead for an indulgent goddess.
Some flowers would have sufficed to overcome this smell,
    for the dung spread here is into its third winter.


: 61 :


I see the rhetorician Carinus' nose, Menippus;
    I reckon he too is not far away.
For, though he may be a good distance from here,
    he is still not more than three stades off.
If we climbed up this nearby hill,                                  5
    maybe we could even see the rhetorician himself.

## · ANDREA NAVAGERO ·

### : 62 :

Gallum omnes uno astrologi tamquam ore canebant
    impleturum annis tempora longa suis.
Ante diem solus periturum dixit Olympus,
    sed tum cum in medio iam foret ille rogo.

### : 63 :

Esse atomos celeri tenuissima corpora motu,
    assidue immensum quae per inane meent;
cunctarum hinc visum est Epicuro exordia rerum,
    hinc elementa orbi prima fuisse novo.
5  Scilicet exiguum quoddam minimumque requirens,
    his minus ille atomis credidit esse nihil.
Marce, atomis minor est multoque minutior ipsis
    exilisque magis quam levis umbra Lycus.
Si visus foret hic Epicuro, hinc prima putasset
10    principia, immensum hinc constituisset opus,
ni potius rerum ille atomos primordia, et ipsas
    e multis atomos crederet esse Lycis.

· FURTHER POEMS ·

: 62 :

All the astrologers, as if with one voice, used to predict
   that Gallus would live a long life.
Only Olympus said he would die before his time,
   but said it when Gallus was already on his funeral pyre.

: 63 :

Epicurus claimed that atoms were minute, fast-moving bodies
   constantly passing through the limitless void
and thought that the beginnings of all matter consisted of them,
   and that from them the newly forming world had its first
      elements.
Doubtless, seeking something tiny and minute in the extreme,     5
   he believed there to be nothing smaller than these atoms.
Marcus, there is an entity smaller than atoms, much more
      diminutive than they,
   and slighter than an insubstantial ghost: Lycus.
If Epicurus had set eyes on Lycus, he would have supposed basic
      principles
   made up of him and built up his vast system on him,     10
unless he preferred to believe that atoms were the first principles
      of things,
   and that atoms were themselves composed of many Lycuses.

## · ANDREA NAVAGERO ·

### :  64  :

Vicinos cantor Cinyras male perdidit omnes
    dum pernox tota nocte dieque canit.
Quod solus tamen e cunctis evaserit Aulus
    factum est naturae munere: surdus erat.

### :  65  :

Educens manibus brevem Priapum
tractabat roseus puer natesque
nudabat, gremio meo recumbens.
Dans mi basia melle dulciora,
5  et pulchros leviter movens ocellos,
  †'iam pugnam Veneris hic ineamus,'
dixit; et cruribus nitens, caputque
pronus, excipere ille praeparabat vulnus,
cum (o crudele fatum atque acerbum)†
10  quidam per rimulam ostii videntes
exclamant, 'Facinus!' simulque pulsant.
Quid tum? Quid faceret miser Priapus?
Nec sitim poterat suam replere,
nec desiderium fugare potus.
15  Iam culum puer ille subtrahebat,
maestus et niveas nates tegebat.
Eripi ut sibi quas, cibum paratum,
Hellespontiacus deus resensit,
mollis, languidulus ruberque, tanti
20  testem lacrimulam edidit doloris.

· FURTHER POEMS ·

: 64 :

The singer Cinyras cruelly killed off all his neighbors
   by singing all night long and all day too.
That, alone out of all of them, Aulus nonetheless survived
   was due to a kindness of Nature: he was deaf.

: 65 :

The rosy-faced boy was massaging little Priapus
as he worked to arouse him with his hands
and was baring his buttocks as he reclined in my arms.
Giving me kisses sweeter than honey,
and turning his beautiful little eyes lightly upon me,     5
†he said, "Now let us here join Venus' battle";
and, kneeling and bowing his head down,
he began making ready to receive the wound,
when (O cruel and bitter fate!),†
some people, seeing this through a little gap in the door,     10
cried out, "Wickedness!" and pounded on it as they did so.
What then? What was poor Priapus to do?
He could neither satisfy his thirst
nor free himself of his longing for a drink.
Now the boy was taking his rear away     15
and sadly covering up his snow-white buttocks.
When the Hellespontine god observed that they,
a meal laid out ready, were being snatched from him,
soft, limp, and red, he shed a tiny teardrop
that bore witness to the magnitude of his anguish.     20

## · ANDREA NAVAGERO ·

### : 66 :

Fessus Amor Baiis somnum dum captat et umbram
    ad murmur gelidae prosilientis aquae,
concurrisse ferunt Dryades et fontibus ipsis
    qua laesae fuerant occuluisse facem.
5  Quis credat? Subito mediis innascitur undis
    aestus, et assiduo fervet ab igne liquor.
Inde fluunt calidis haec semper balnea venis,
    flamma etenim gelidam vincit Amoris aquam.

### : 67 :

Dum volui domini iussu perquirere silvas
    ut sequerer timidas cursibus ipse feras,
fortia (me miserum!) letali pectora saxo
    rustica percussit impia, saeva manus.
5  Me precor ut parvo referas, Francisce, sepulcro,
    ne mea sint rapidis viscera praeda lupis.

### : 68 :

Dum videt abscissae miles dispendia dextrae,
    'Sufficiat bello laeva superstes,' ait.
Quam quoque ut iniectat virtus animosa carinae,
    sorte neque alterius territus ille pari est,

· FURTHER POEMS ·

: 66 :

As weary Love was taking a nap at Baiae and enjoying the shade
    beside the gurgle of cool-springing water,
they say that wood nymphs ran up and immersed the torch
    he had used to wound them in the fountain.
Who would believe it? Suddenly heat was generated amid the    5
      waters,
    and the stream boiled with the unremitting fire.
As a result these baths are supplied with a constant hot flow,
    for Love's flame prevails over icy water.

: 67 :

Just as I wanted, at my master's command, to scour the woods
    in order to chase timid beasts in their flight,
to my misfortune a rustic's cruel, wicked hand
    struck my brave chest with a fatal stone.
I beg you, Francesco, to preserve my memory with a small tomb    5
    to save my entrails from being plunder for ravening wolves.

: 68 :

Seeing the loss of his severed right hand, the soldier declared,
    "Let the left I still have suffice to wage war!"
And when the stouthearted hero laid that hand too on the ship
    and was not terrified that it might suffer the same fate as the
      other,

· ANDREA NAVAGERO ·

5   victor adhuc hostem impellens sic intonat ore:
     'Discite quos habeant Caesaris arma viros!
    Nos freta, nos ferrum, nos temnere possumus ignes.
     Vincimus absque manu, vincimus absque anima.'

: 69 :

  Pulcher o sol, qui nitidos dies et
  das et idem subtrahis atque terris
  umidam noctem et placidam quietem
    reddis avaris,

5  aureis caput radiis refulgens
  prome, quis tellus Cereris renidet
  munere et Bacchi; decus o deorum,
    pulchrior exi.

  Namque natalis dominae colendus
10  advenit multis, mihi sanctiorque
  quam meus, qui principium bonorum est
    dulce meorum.

  Transeat clarus sine nube festus
  hic dies nobis, sileantque venti,
15  ponat et saevos placide tumultus
    unda marinos.

  Tu quoque exsurgens manibus decoris
  finge odoratos, mea vita, crines,
  sed prius pura gelidaque lympha
20    discute somnum.

· FURTHER POEMS ·

still victoriously driving the enemy before him, he thundered out   5
    these words:
  "Learn what men Caesar's forces have within them!
We can scorn sea, steel, and fire.
  We win without a hand, we win without life."


: 69 :

O beautiful sun, you who both give us bright days
and take them away, restoring
the dewy night and peaceful repose
  to the eagerly waiting world,

put forth your head gleaming with the golden rays   5
that make the earth resplendent with the gifts
of Ceres and Bacchus; O glory of the gods,
  emerge in full beauty.

For my lady's birthday is dawning,
a day for many to celebrate, and one more sacred   10
to me than my own, the day that is
  the sweet beginning of my joys.

May this festival day go by for us
in cloudless brightness, the winds be silent,
and the sea's waters calmly set at rest   15
  the fierce upheavals of the deep.

You too, my life, rise and arrange
your scented hair with your graceful hands,
but first with pure cold water
  shake off sleep.   20

## · ANDREA NAVAGERO ·

Deinde, dum sertis domus et tapetis
ridet, ac laeti pueri et puellae
cursitant, dulcem thalamum relinque
    cultaque prodi.

25  Prodient tecum Venus et Cupido et
Gratiae nexis manibus, Decorque
cuncta componet, venietque summa
    summus ab arce

Iuppiter, castis precibus vocatus,
30  et tibi quaecumque petes benignus
annuet. Nunc tu pete iam securo
    multa labello

ut tibi duret stabilis iuventa
formaque, et felix habeas quod optas,
35  vivat et multos tibi carus uni
    Trissinus annos,

et senectutem simul et quietum
terminet tecum bene iam peractum
aevum, et ardentem sine fraude amorem
40    saecula laudent.

Spem bonam certamque habeo quod ista
audiet divum pater et vocanti
rite tranquillus faciet quod ipsa
    Fata secundent.

· FURTHER POEMS ·

Then, as the house smiles with wreaths and hangings,
and boys and girls joyfully scurry to and fro,
leave your sweet bedchamber,
    and come forth in your elegance.

With you will come Venus and Cupid                      25
and the Graces, linking hands, and Beauty
will order your whole appearance to perfection,
    and from his citadel on high

will come highest Jupiter, summoned in pious prayers,
and he will benevolently grant whatever you ask.          30
Now ask many things
    with lips free of any fear,

that your youth and beauty may endure without fading,
that you may enjoy the good fortune to have what you wish for,
that your Trissino may live many years               35
    beloved of you alone

and end together old age and a life of peace
spent till then in blissful happiness with you,
and that posterity may praise an ardent love
    free of deceit.                            40

I am confident and firmly hopeful
that the father of the gods will hear those prayers
and will serenely grant you, as you ritually invoke him,
    what the Fates themselves would favor.

# MARCANTONII FLAMINII
## CARMINA

# MARCANTONIO FLAMINIO

# LIBER TERTIUS

### : 1 :

Pan pater et Silvane senex Faunique bicornes
    tuque, pharetratae candida turba deae,
si mea vos dulci delectat fistula cantu,
    si semper vobis annua dona fero,
5  parcite purpureos, quaeso, violare racemos,
    neu tangant avidae lutea pruna manus.
Hunc agrum dat habere mihi Farnesius heros.
    Gratus ego haec illi munera prima dico.

### : 2 :

Cum facies iter hac, Farnesi candide, Iolam
    ne pudeat, quaeso, semper adire tuum.
Te vocat arguto viridissima silva susurro,
    te liquidi fontis garrula lympha vocat.
5  Villula pulchra, tui memorabile munus amoris,
    iamdudum gestit ora videre tua.
Magne puer, ne parva, precor, fuge limina; saepe
    pastorum subiit Iuppiter ipse casas.

# LATIN POEMS, BOOK III

: 1 :

Father Pan, old Silvanus, you two-horned fauns,
  and you beautiful band of the quiver-bearing goddess,
if my pipe delights you with its sweet song,
  and I always bring you yearly gifts,
refrain, I beg you, from plundering my red grapes,          5
  and let no greedy hands touch my honey-colored plums.
The Farnese hero gives me this land to have as mine.
  In gratitude I dedicate these first gifts to him.

: 2 :

Whenever you pass this way, good Farnese,
  do not be ashamed, I beg you, always to come and see your
      Iolas.
The greenest wood calls you with its rustling whisper,
  and a clear stream's babbling water calls you too.
My pretty little country house, the never-to-be-forgotten gift of      5
      your love,
  has long been yearning to see your face.
Great boy, do not, I pray you, shun my modest threshold;
  Jupiter himself has often entered shepherds' cottages.

### · MARCANTONIO FLAMINIO ·

### ∴ 3 ∴

Heu quid ago? Moritur mi animus, mellita Nigella,
    ni tibi quam primum basiolum rapio;
at si basiolum rapio, vereor tibi mecum
    ne sint aeternae post inimicitiae,
5  quae me non morti modo dent, sed post quoque mortem
    perpetuo poenis tristibus excrucient.
Sed rapiam! Immo non! Utrum, o anime, efficiam vis?
    Nescio, sed tantum sentio, quod pereo.

### ∴ 4 ∴

Intonsi colles, et densae in collibus umbrae,
    et qui vos placida fons rigat ortus aqua,
si teneros umquam Fauni celastis amores,
    si vos nympharum dulcia furta iuvant,
5  este boni tutasque mihi praebete latebras,
    dum sedet in gremio cara Nigella meo.

### ∴ 5 ∴

Fugit hiems, nitidis vestitur frondibus arbor,
    iamque novos ducit candida Flora choros.

## · LATIN POEMS, BOOK III ·

### ⦂ 3 ⦂

Alas, what do I do? My heart will surely die, honey-sweet
    Nigella,
  if I do not snatch a little kiss from you this very instant;
but if I do snatch a kiss, I am afraid
  that you may ever after feel such hostility toward me
as would not only be the death of me, but even after death     5
  would still torture me eternally with grievous punishments.
But I will snatch a kiss! No, I will not! Which would you have
    me do, my heart?
  I do not know; I just feel I am dying.

### ⦂ 4 ⦂

Unshorn hills, trees that thickly cover the hills,
  and the spring that rises to water you with its peaceful flow,
if you have ever concealed Faunus' tender loves,
  or if you delight in the sweet intrigues of nymphs,
be kind and furnish me with a safe hiding place     5
  while dear Nigella sits upon my lap.

### ⦂ 5 ⦂

The winter has taken flight, the trees are clothed in gleaming
    foliage,
  and now fair Flora leads new dances.

## · MARCANTONIO FLAMINIO ·

Et cedit Boreas Zephyri genitalibus auris,
    et victum pecori sufficit almus ager.
5  Nunc, Amarylli, gregem secreta pascere silva,
    nunc dabitur Veneris dulcia furta sequi.
Tu venerare deam sertisque recentibus orna,
    illius et sanctos imbuat agna focos,
iucundam ut nobis inter nos ducere vitam
10    annuat et tuto semper amore frui.


: 6 :


Iam fugat umentes formosus Lucifer umbras,
    et dulci Auroram voce salutat avis.
Surge, Amarylli, greges niveos in pascua pelle,
    frigida dum cano gramina rore madent.
5  Ipse meas hodie nemorosa in valle capellas
    pasco, namque hodie maximus aestus erit.
Scisne Menandrei fontem et vineta Galesi
    et quae formosus rura Lycambus habet?
Hos inter colles recubat viridissima silva,
10    quam pulcher liquido Mesulus amne secat.
Nec gelidi fontes absunt nec pabula laeta,
    et varios flores aura benigna parit.
Illic te maneo solus, carissima nympha;
    si tibi sum carus, tu quoque sola veni.

## · LATIN POEMS, BOOK III ·

The north wind yields to the life-giving breezes of the west,
   and the bountiful earth supplies grazing for the flock.
Now, Amaryllis, we shall be able to pasture sheep in a secluded    5
     wood
   and pursue Venus' sweet intrigues.
Venerate the goddess and deck her with fresh garlands,
   and let a lamb's blood stain her holy altar,
that she may allow us to lead a happy life together
   and always enjoy secure love.    10


## : 6 :

Now the beautiful morning star dispels the damp shadows,
   and the birds greet Aurora with sweet voice.
Rise, Amaryllis, and drive your snow-white flocks into the
     pastures
   while the cold grasses are moist with silvery dew.
I am feeding my nanny goats in a wooded valley today,    5
   for today the heat will be very great.
Do you know the spring and vineyards of Menander's son
     Galesus
   and the farm that handsome Lycambus keeps?
Among those hills there nestles the greenest wood,
   which the beautiful Mischio traverses with its flowing stream.    10
There is no lack of either cool springs or rich pastures,
   and a kindly breeze brings forth flowers of varied hue.
There I shall wait for you alone, dearest nymph;
   if I am dear to you, come there too alone.

## · MARCANTONIO FLAMINIO ·

### : 7 :

Dum sonat argutis late vicinia grillis,
    tu, Pholoe, dulci pressa sopore iaces.
Ipse vagor media solus de nocte, tuosque
    ad caros postes florida serta fero,
5  quaeque teris nuda calcando limina planta
    osculor, et lacrimis tristibus illa rigo.
Tu, precor, aut nostri miserere, aut, si tibi tantum
    displiceo, hic animum ponere, dura, iube.

### : 8 :

Et tonat, et vento ingenti nemus omne remugit,
    et cadit effusa plurimus imber aqua,
Noxque, soporiferis alis circumdata, caecam
    horrenti latebra nubis opacat humum;
5  ipse tamen, Veneris crudeli compede vinctus,
    ad dominae cogor pervigilare fores.
Saevit hiems, Auster densissimus aere saevit,
    sed gravius nostro pectore saevit amor.

## · LATIN POEMS, BOOK III ·

### : 7 :

While the neighborhood resounds far and wide with the noisy
    crickets,
  you, Pholoe, lie overcome by sweet sleep.
As for me, I roam abroad alone in the middle of the night,
  bring flowery garlands to your dear doorposts,
kiss the threshold that you wear down with the tread of your     5
    bare feet,
  and dampen it with my sad tears.
I beg you, either pity me, or, if I displease you so much,
  bid me here lay down my life, hard-hearted girl.

### : 8 :

It is thundering, the whole wood moans with the strength of
    the wind,
  rain falls in torrents of streaming water,
and Night, wrapped in sleep-bringing wings,
  enshrouds the hidden earth in a dreadful cover of cloud;
yet I, chained by Venus' cruel fetters,     5
  am compelled to keep vigil all the while at my lady's door.
The wintry storm rages, and the south wind, thick with mist,
    rages too,
  but within my breast love rages more fiercely than they.

## · MARCANTONIO FLAMINIO ·

### ⁝ 9 ⁝

Sic tibi perpetuam donet Venus alma iuventam,
    ne faciem nitidam ruga senilis aret,
post cenam cum matre tua dulcique Lycinna
    ad matrem, Pholoe cara, venito meam.
5  Hic simul ad magnum laeti vigilabimus ignem.
    Candidior pulchra nox erit ista die.
Fabellas vetulae referent, nos laeta canemus
    carmina, castaneas parva Lycinna coquet.
Sic noctem tenerisque iocis risuque trahemus,
10    dum gravet incumbens lumina nostra sopor.

### ⁝ 10 ⁝

Iam rapidus torret mediis sol aestibus agros;
    ad vallem niveum duc, Ligurina, gregem.
Hic avium cantus, hic fons nitidissimus antro
    prosilit, hic densis quercubus umbra cadit.
5  Et circum flores examina laeta susurrant,
    et zephyri blando murmurat aura sono.
Hic laudes, formosa, tuas mea fistula dicet;
    tu Dryadum calamo dulcia furta canes.

## · LATIN POEMS, BOOK III ·

### : 9 :

After dinner, accompanied by your mother and sweet Lycinna,
    come, dear Pholoe, to visit my mother,
and may kindly Venus grant you in return everlasting youth,
    so that no wrinkle of old age may furrow your lovely face.
Here we shall happily sit up together by a big fire.       5
    That night will be brighter than the fair light of day.
The old women will tell their tales, we shall sing happy songs,
    and little Lycinna will cook chestnuts.
Thus we shall draw out the night with tender lightheartedness
      and laughter
    till the onset of sleep weighs down our eyes.       10

### : 10 :

Now the fierce sun scorches the fields with the midday heat;
    bring your snow-white flock to the valley, Ligurina.
Here there is birdsong, here the clearest spring leaps forth from
      a cave,
    here shade is cast by dense oak trees.
Happy swarms of bees buzz about the flowers,       5
    and the west wind's breeze murmurs with a pleasing hum.
Here my pipe will speak your praises, beautiful girl,
    while with your reed you will sing of the sweet intrigues of
      dryads.

· MARCANTONIO FLAMINIO ·

### : 11 :

Nascitur et nostro Vesper crudelis amori
    iam caulis saturas ducere mandat oves.
Deliciae Ligurina meae, te linquere cogor,
    sed tecum remanet mens animusque meus.
5  Quod superest, ubi iam tenebris Aurora fugatis
    in silvam croceo mane reducet oves,
hic illas, mea vita, iterum cogamus in unum,
    hic iterum dulcis me tibi iungat amor.

### : 12 :

Esto magna Ceres et Pan mihi testis, amantum
    et quae firma facit foedera, sancta Venus,
nulla dies, Ligurina, tuo me solvet amore,
    non si me Dryadum sanguinis una petat.
5  Ut rupem hanc validis impellunt flatibus Euri,
    sed nullo rupes verbere pulsa labat,
sic semper mea magna fides immota manebit,
    et mea mens uni serviet usque tibi.
Di faciant in amore pares vivamus, et uno
10    ambos una tegat funeris hora loco.

### : 13 :

Quo te venturam dixti, cum mater ad urbem
    iverit, huc furtim, lux mea, primus eo,

## · LATIN POEMS, BOOK III ·

### : 11 :

The evening star, cruel to our love, is rising
    and now bids us take our sated sheep back to their pens.
Ligurina, my darling, I am forced to leave you,
    but my thoughts and heart stay with you.
One last word: as soon as Aurora dispels the darkness       5
    and in the yellow dawn brings the sheep again to the wood,
let us herd them together here, my life, once more,
    and here let sweet love once more unite me with you.

### : 12 :

Great Ceres and Pan be witness for me,
    and she who makes the bonds of lovers firm, holy Venus,
no day, Ligurina, shall bring an end to the love I feel for you,
    not even if one of dryad blood were to seek my attentions.
Just as the east winds blast this rock with mighty gales,      5
    but it is untoppled by any degree of buffeting,
so will my great faithfulness always remain steadfastly unshaken,
    and my heart will ever serve you alone.
May the gods grant that we live matched in mutual devotion,
    and one hour of death bury us both in one place.      10

### : 13 :

To the place you have said you will come, once your mother is off
    to the city,

## · MARCANTONIO FLAMINIO ·

dumque venis, longo brevis hora videbitur anno
    longior. Ulla igitur si tibi cura mei,
5  tolle moras omnes, timor omnis et absit: amanti
    et comes atque viae dux erit ipsa Venus.


: 14 :

Si Ligurina meos hodie non ludit amores,
    amplexus hodie si petit illa meos,
hoc tibi muscoso laetus, Cytherea, sub antro
    aram de viridi caespite constituam;
5  laetus ego spumante novo tria cymbia lacte,
    et totidem fundam cymbia plena mero;
tum late variis halantem floribus aram
    imbuet effuso lecta cruore bidens;
saltabit Ligurina, tuas mea tibia laudes
10    cantabit, dulces fundere docta modos.
Haec tibi, sancta Venus, sollemnia sacra quotannis
    et faciam, et magno semper honore colam.
Tu fac, diva, tuum supplex dum numen adoro,
    currat in amplexus cara puella meos.

## · LATIN POEMS, BOOK III ·

I stealthily make my way first, light of my life,
and till you come, a brief hour will seem longer than a long year.
If, then, you feel any care for me,
have done with all delays, and be quite free of fear:     5
  in your love, Venus herself will be both your companion and
    guide to the way.


## :  14  :

If Ligurina does not mock my love today,
  if today she seeks my embraces,
I will in my joy set up to you, Cytherea, beneath this mossy
    cavern,
  an altar made of green turf;
and in my joy I will pour out three bowls full of fresh, foaming    5
    milk
  and as many bowls full of wine;
then, as that altar exhales far and wide the aroma of various
    flowers,
  a chosen sheep will stain it with a stream of blood;
Ligurina will dance, and my pipe will sing your praises,
  skilled as it is at pouring out sweet strains.    10
Holy Venus, I will perform these solemn rites for you every year
  and always observe them with great reverence.
 For your part, goddess, as I appeal for your divine aid in
    supplication,
  make my dear girl come running to my arms.

·  MARCANTONIO FLAMINIO  ·

∶  15  ∶

Hos tibi purpureos in serta nitentia flores,
  dum sol exoritur, Thestyli cara, lego,
dumque lego, crebra ingeminans suspiria, dico,
  'O utinam fieri vos, mea dona, queam!'

∶  16  ∶

Thestyli cara, favis Hyblaeis dulcior, ecquid
  munera pulchra vides quae tibi ab urbe fero?
Aspice flaventem pallam roseosque cothurnos
  et mitram et bullis cingula clara suis.
5  Haec ego dum porto, vidit pulcherrima Phyllis
  atque ait, 'Haec dederis si mihi dona, puer,
et Venerem et Cereris sanctissima numina testor,
  te praeter nullus Phyllida habebit amans.'
Ast ego per Phoebum et Musas, mea Thestyli, iuro
10  (si fallo, semper sis inimica mihi),
nulla puella meos te praeter habebit amores;
  dum vivam, semper tu meus ardor eris.

∶  17  ∶

Thestyli, si qua tui superat tibi cura Miconis,
  crastina cum caelo fulserit orta dies,
ad Cereris vallem niveas compelle capellas,
  nec longam pigeat, te precor, ire viam.

## · LATIN POEMS, BOOK III ·

### : 15 :

I gather these red flowers to make a pretty garland for you,
    dear Thestylis, as the sun comes up,
and, as I gather them, sighing again and again, I say,
    "If only I could be you, gifts of mine!"

### : 16 :

Dear Thestylis, sweeter than Hybla's honeycombs,
    do you see the beautiful gifts I bring you from the city?
Look at the yellow robe, the rose-red boots,
    the headband, and the belt gleaming with its studs.
As I was carrying these presents, beautiful Phyllis saw them    5
    and said, "If you give me these gifts, boy,
I call Venus and the most holy divinity of Ceres to witness,
    no lover but you shall have Phyllis."
But I swear by Phoebus and the Muses, my Thestylis
    (if I deceive you, may you always be my enemy),    10
no girl but you shall have my love;
    as long as I live, you will always be the one I burn for.

### : 17 :

Thestylis, if you still have any care for your Micon,
    when tomorrow's day dawns and shines bright in the sky,
drive your snow-white nanny goats to Ceres' valley,
    and do not be averse to making the long journey, I beg you.

145

## · MARCANTONIO FLAMINIO ·

5   Inde, graves aestus ubi sol accenderit, antro
      succede, arbuteis quod tegit umbra comis.
   Huc ego furtivo ingrediar pede munera portans,
      quae iam pridem orat Phyllis habere sibi,
   munera vel nymphis dignissima. Si sapis ergo,
10     ad dulces latebras incomitata veni.

## : 18 :

Dic age, quid tecum faciebat, perfida, Thyrsis,
   sub corylo matrem dum sopor altus habet?
Ah ego te pueri circumdare bracchia collo,
   ah ego te vidi — sed pudet illa loqui.
5   Thestyli, tene meo quemquam praeponere amori?
   Amplexus alii tene dedisse meos?
At neque me Phyllis nec formosissima Gorgo
   nec movit roseis candida Nisa genis.
Ipsa mihi furtiva tulit munuscula saepe,
10    sed lacrimans semper rettulit illa domum.
At tibi cur placuit tantum puer iste? Quid, oro,
   quid tantum egregii possidet iste puer?
Hic domini custodit oves, ego mille capellas
   pasco, quas moriens tradidit ipse pater.
15  Hic Dorylae indocto cessit cantando; peritus
   et voce et calamis cessit Agyrta mihi.
Nec pede nec iaculo valet hic nec viribus; ipse
   audeo vel magnas sollicitare feras.

## · LATIN POEMS, BOOK III ·

Then, when the sun has made it fiercely hot,      5
   come to the cave that a tree shelters with arbute leaves.
There I will come with stealthy step, bringing the gifts
   that Phyllis has long been asking to have for herself,
gifts very worthy even of nymphs. If you are wise, then,
   come all alone to the sweet hiding place.      10

## :  18  :

Come tell me, faithless girl, what was Thyrsis doing with you
   while your mother was in a deep sleep under the hazel?
Ah, I saw you put your arms around the boy's neck;
   ah, I saw you — but I am ashamed to speak of it.
Thestylis, am I to think that you prefer someone else's love      5
     to mine?
   That you have given my embraces to another?
In my own case, neither Phyllis nor beautiful Gorgo
   nor lovely, white-skinned Nisa with her rosy cheeks has
     swayed me.
She has often brought me secret little gifts,
   but she has always taken them back home again in tears.      10
But why has that boy pleased you so much?
   What, I ask you, what does that boy have that is so special?
He guards his master's sheep, while I graze a thousand nanny
     goats
   that my father passed on to me when he died.
He has been defeated by unskilled Dorylas in song;      15
   whereas Agyrta, accomplished with both voice and reed, has
     lost to me.
He is not swift of foot, good with a javelin, or strong,
   while I dare challenge even mighty beasts.

### · MARCANTONIO FLAMINIO ·

Sunt mihi flaventes tenera lanugine malae,
20     sunt nitidi crines, sunt rosea ora mihi.
Ipsa meos oculos tua sidera saepe vocasti;
     ipse tibi quondam pulcher Adonis eram.
Nunc ego despectus, nec te, male sana puella,
     nescio quem prae me Thyrsin amare pudet.
25   Iam fugiat leporem canis, accipiterque columbam,
     incultique ferant dulcia poma rubi!
Iam sperent metuantque simul miseri omnia amantes!
     Credite, nulla fidem servat amica viro.

:  19  :

Huc ades, o mea Lygda; parum decede calori,
     dum medio caeli sol gravis orbe furit.
Nonne vides ut fluas sudoribus utque
     iam lassae nequeant stringere farra manus?
5  Hic patulae ramis sociant umbracula fagi,
     quas circum irriguis Mesulus errat aquis.
Nec salsae desunt oleae, nec olentia caepe,
     nec liba aut veteri cymbia plena mero.
Huc ades; ardenti maneat sub sole Nigella;
10   te molles umbrae, candida nympha, decent.

## · LATIN POEMS, BOOK III ·

My cheeks are yellowed with a youthful down,
　my hair has a fine sheen, my face is of a rose's hue.　　　　20
You yourself have often called my eyes your stars;
　I was once your handsome Adonis.
Now I am despised, and you are not ashamed, foolish girl,
　to love some Thyrsis in preference to me.
Now let the hound flee the hare, and the hawk the dove,　　　25
　and let wild brambles bear sweet apples!
Now let poor lovers alike hope for and fear all reversals of
　　　fortune!
　Believe me, no beloved keeps faith with her man.


: 19 :


Come here, my Lygda; get out of the heat a little
　while in midsky the sun blazes fiercely down with his orb.
Do you not see how you are streaming with sweat,
　and how your hands are now so weary that they cannot reap
　　　the spelt?
Here spreading beeches weave a shady bower with their branches,　5
　and round them the Mischio meanders with its irrigating
　　　waters.
I have salted olives, strong-smelling onions, cakes,
　and bowls brimming with well-matured wine.
Come here; let Nigella stay in the blazing sun;
　gentle shade, fair-skinned nymph, suits you.　　　　10

## · MARCANTONIO FLAMINIO ·

### ⁝ 20 ⁝

Irrigui fontes, et fontibus addita vallis,
    cinctaque piniferis silva cacuminibus,
Phyllis ubi formosa dedit mihi basia prima
    primaque cantando parta corona mihi,
5  vivite felices, nec vobis aut gravis aestas
    aut noceat saevo frigore tristis hiems,
nec lympham quadrupes, nec silvam dura bipennis,
    nec violet teneras hic lupus acer oves,
et nymphae laetis celebrent loca sancta choreis,
10    et Pan Arcadiae praeferat illa suae.

### ⁝ 21 ⁝

Rivule frigidulis nympharum e fontibus orte,
    qui properas liquido per nemora alta pede,
si, formose, venis formosum ad Phyllidis hortum
    arentique levas aurea mala siti,
5  illa tibi centum dabit oscula, quis tua fiet
    dulcior Hyblaeis unda beata favis.

### ⁝ 22 ⁝

Cum ver purpureum tepidi fert aura Favoni,
    ornatur variis floribus almus ager,

## · LATIN POEMS, BOOK III ·

### : 20 :

Watering springs, and valley adjoining the springs,
    and wood girt with pine-covered peaks,
where beautiful Phyllis gave me first kisses
    and where I won my first garland for song,
good fortune attend you, and may neither summer's oppressive    5
      heat
    nor dismal winter with its fierce cold do you harm,
and here may no four-footed beast defile the water,
    cruel ax injure the trees, or fierce wolf attack the tender sheep,
and may nymphs celebrate your holy places with joyful dances,
    and Pan prefer them to his own Arcadia.    10

### : 21 :

Little stream sprung from nymphs' cool fountains,
    you that hurry along on watery foot through lofty woods,
if, pretty rivulet, you come to Phyllis' pretty garden
    and ease her golden apples of their parching thirst,
she will give you a hundred kisses,    5
    making your blessed water sweeter than Hyblaean
    honeycombs.

### : 22 :

When the breeze of the warm west wind brings the bright spring,
    the bountiful earth is bedecked with a variety of flowers,

## · MARCANTONIO FLAMINIO ·

formosae rident silvae, sunt omnia laeta,
  et cantu volucrum dulcia rura sonant.
5  At mihi tristis hiems formosior et mihi vere
  laetior adveniet si, mea Lygda, redis.


:  23  :

Cum Boreas laeto silvam spoliavit honore,
  squalet ager, mixto nix iacet alta gelu,
non liquidi currunt amnes, stat nubibus aer
  obscurus, volucrum garrula turba silet.
5  Tale facis ver cara tuo Ligurina recessu.
  Te sine formosum, te sine dulce nihil.


:  24  :

Ut quondam, nivei correpta cupidine tauri,
  mugitu resonat bucula maesta nemus,
illius caros si forte abducit amores
  pastor — non miseram gramina laeta iuvant,
5  non liquidi fontes — talis mea vita, paterno
  postquam rure procul me sine, Lygda, fugis.


:  25  :

Ut formosa suo felix est bucula tauro,
  nec latos querulis vocibus implet agros,

## · LATIN POEMS, BOOK III ·

the pretty woods smile, everything is joyful,
 and the sweet countryside resounds with the singing of birds.
But to me dismal winter will come prettier and cheerier than   5
  spring
 if you, my Lygda, return.


: 23 :


When the north wind has despoiled the wood of its lush glory,
 the land is left unworked, snow and ice both lie deep,
the clear streams do not flow, the sky is dark with clouds,
 and the chattering throng of birds is silent.
You make spring like that, dear Ligurina, by your departure.   5
 Without you nothing is pretty, without you nothing is sweet.


: 24 :


As sometimes a heifer, seized with longing for a snow-white bull,
 in her sadness makes the wood resound with her lowing
if the herdsman has chanced to take her dear love away—
 no rich grasses can please her in her misery,
nor any clear springs—such is my life, Lygda,   5
 since you have gone far away from your father's farm without
  me.


: 25 :


As a pretty heifer is happy with her bull
 and fills the wide fields with no plaintive lowing

###### · MARCANTONIO FLAMINIO ·

Si dulci reditu caram solatur amantem
    carus amans, talis candida vita mea,
5  meque, prius miserum, fecit Venus alma beatum,
    ex quo restituit te, Ligurina, mihi.

: 26 :

Aspicis ut laeti surgunt per gramina flores,
    explicat ut virides arbor ubique comas,
ut melius fulgent soles, ut nubila caelo
    diffugiunt, terris diffugiuntque nives?
5  Haec facies, haec est Lygdae ridentis imago.
    Tristitiam vultu sic fugat illa suo.

: 27 :

Vidisti nitidas per candida lilia guttas
    ludere, cum tenui decidit imber aqua,
et rorem de puniceis stillare rosetis,
    cum spirat nascens frigora blanda dies?
5  Haec facies, haec est Ligurinae flentis imago.
    Illius lacrimis me ferus urit Amor.

## · LATIN POEMS, BOOK III ·

if her beloved mate consoles his beloved mate
    with his sweet return, such is my happy life,
and kindly Venus has made me blessed instead of wretched     5
    ever since the moment she restored you to me, Ligurina.


: 26 :

Do you see how the flowers spring up joyously throughout the
    meadows,
    the trees everywhere open up their green leaves,
the sunlight gleams more brightly, the clouds vanish from the sky,
    and the snows from the earth?
Such is Lygda's countenance, that is how she looks when she     5
    smiles.
    She chases away sadness with her face in just that way.


: 27 :

Have you seen sparkling droplets play over white lilies
    when a light rain shower falls,
and dew drip off red roses when at its dawning
    the day breathes a pleasing coolness?
Such is Ligurina's countenance, that is how she looks when     5
    she cries.
    Fierce Love burns me with her tears.

## · MARCANTONIO FLAMINIO ·

### : 28 :

Haec, Cytherea, suo dulci cum compare turtur
  caeditur ante tuos victima grata focos.
Unus amor caros felici copula amantes
  iunxerat, unanimos abstulit una dies.
5 Talis amor pulchram tenero cum Daphnide Nisam
  vinciat aeterno foedere, sancta, precor,
et, dum longa dies senio consumpserit ambos,
  alter in alterius corpore vivat amans.

### : 29 :

Luna, decus caeli, astrorum regina bicornis,
  quae medio raptim laberis alta polo,
ad dominam propero, qua nec formosior umquam
  pavit nec pascet ulla puella gregem.
5 Tu, mea ne quisquam valeat deprendere furta,
  conde, precor, lucem, candida diva, tuam.
Sic tibi sit proprio splendescere lumine, sic par
  et magni radiis aemula solis eas.

## · LATIN POEMS, BOOK III ·

### : 28 :

This turtledove, Cytherea, along with her sweet mate,
  is slain before your altar as a sacrifice pleasing to you.
One love had paired the dear doting birds in a happy bond,
  one and the same day has carried them off in mutual devotion.
Holy lady, I beg you to grant that such a love may bind beautiful   5
  Nisa
  with young Daphnis in an everlasting union,
and that till a distant day carries off both from old age,
  each may lovingly live in the other's body.

### : 29 :

Moon, glory of the sky, two-horned queen of the stars,
  you who glide swiftly on high in midheaven,
I am hurrying to my lady, and no prettier girl than she
  has ever grazed a flock or ever will.
So that no one can detect my intrigue,   5
  I pray you, fair goddess, hide your light away.
In return may you have the power to blaze with a brilliance of
    your own,
  and may you be a rival to match even the mighty sun with
    your rays.

# LIBER QUARTUS

: I :

O quae venusta Sirmionis litora
   colis Catulli candida
Musa et beatam citrei silvam doces
   pulchram sonare Lesbiam,
5  et nos Taburni in valle florida tibi
   aram virenti e caespite
et terna melle, terna lacte ponimus
   spumante plena cymbia,
et te vocamus voce supplici, dea,
10   ad sacra parva sed pia,
ut nostram Hyellam fistula dulci canas,
   qua nulla rure pulchrior
vixit, nec ulla vivet ullo tempore
   cani puella dignior.
15  At tu virecta amoena et undas limpidi
   relinque Benaci libens.
Et hic Favoni lenis aura murmurat;
   et hic avium dulci sono
mulcetur aer, prata floribus nitent,
20   purique fontes, vitreis
lymphis decentes, frigerant nemorum deas,
   cum, fessa dammarum nece
et icta luce fervida solis, redit
   pudica Dianae cohors.
25  Quare, o puella candida, huc aditum feras,
   nobisque versus dicito

# LATIN POEMS, BOOK IV

: I :

O radiant Muse of Catullus,
   who dwell on the lovely shores of Sirmione
and teach the blessed citron wood
   to echo beautiful Lesbia's name,
here in the flowery vale of Monte Taburno         5
   I build you an altar of green turf
and on it set three bowls full of honey
   and three more full of foaming milk
and call you with suppliant voice, goddess,
   to small but reverent offerings         10
so that you may sing with sweet pipe of my Hyella,
   for no girl more beautiful than she ever lived in the
      countryside,
nor will there ever live at any time
   one worthier of celebration.
For your part be willing to leave the lovely green pastures    15
   and waters of the clear Lago di Garda.
Here too the west wind's gentle breeze makes its murmur;
   here too the air is charmed with the sweet song of birds,
meadows are bright with flowers,
   and pure springs, pretty with their glassy waters,    20
refresh the goddesses of the woods with their coolness
   when, weary from killing deer
and burned by the sun's hot glare,
   Diana's chaste band returns.
Therefore pray make your way here, beautiful girl,    25
   and inspire me with verses

· MARCANTONIO FLAMINIO ·

per quos Hyella vivat usque dum tua
   formosa vivet Lesbia.


: 2 :


Caper Capella caelitum beatior,
quem tam venusta, tam puella candida,
stipante maximo capellarum grege,
agit per alta montium cacumina,
5   cum sol recludit splendido caelum die,
albentque laeta rore cano gramina!
At cum, furentis excitatus ictibus
solis, siticulosus ignescit calor,
nec aura pulchris arborum instrepit comis,
10  te ducit illa fontis ad lympham sacri,
qui prosilit virente murmurans specu,
domus choreis Naiadum gratissima,
et semicapri dulce lenimen dei,
cum fessus a labore montivago redit.
15  Hinc te reductis vallium cubilibus
sistens, tenello lassulum sinu fovet,
cingitque carum floreis sertis caput,
suadetque blandos sensim inire somnulos,
nunc mollicella barbulam mulcens manu,
20  nunc dulciora melle fundens carmina,
canente garrulo simul avium choro.
Exin cadente sole, cum nox extulit
micantibus stellis coronatum caput,
et prata grillis personant argutulis,
25  te bella Hyella cum tuis uxoribus
domum reducit mollia ad praesaepia,

160

##### · LATIN POEMS, BOOK IV ·

through which Hyella may live on
   for as long as your fair Lesbia lives on.

: 2 :

Billy goat luckier than the Nanny of the gods in heaven,
you that so lovely and beautiful a girl,
with a huge flock of nannies crowding all around,
drives over the high mountain peaks
when the sun opens up the sky with the bright daylight,     5
and the joyful grasses are white with silvery dew!
But when the parched heat produced by the rays
of the blazing sun rises to a burning intensity,
and no breeze rustles in the handsome foliage of the trees,
she leads you to the water of a sacred spring     10
that leaps with a babble from a green cave
to be a delightful home for bands of naiads
and a sweet haven of rest for the half-goat god
when he returns fatigued from his mountain-roaming exertions.
Then she takes you to secluded resting places in the valleys,     15
and, fondling you in her tender lap, as you are a little tired,
she crowns your dear head with a flowery garland
and persuades you to slip gently into an inviting nap,
now stroking your little beard with her soft hand,
now pouring forth songs sweeter than honey     20
as a tuneful chorus of birds adds its strains to hers.
Then, at sunset, when night has raised
her head crowned with gleaming stars,
and the meadows resound with the chirping crickets,
beautiful Hyella leads you back home,     25
along with your wives, to your soft pens

## · MARCANTONIO FLAMINIO ·

vobisque salsas frondium dapes parat.
Cui vita capro contigit iucundior?
Quem capripes Pan aut potens pecorum Pales
30 benigniore vidit umquam lumine,
caper Capella caelitum beatior?


: 3 :

Caper, capellis ire dux ad pascua
suetus, quid aegros ultimus trahis pedes?
Tu primus alta montium cacumina,
cum Sol quadrigis aureis portat diem,
5 primus reposta vallium cubilia,
quo fons loquace limpidus lympha vocat,
primus petebas nocte cum prima domum
magnis capellas antecedens passibus.
Nunc maestus, aeger, ultimus prodis domo.
10 Caper miselle, num requiris candidam
Hyellam, et, illa absente, nec thyma dulcia
nec umbra dulcis nec tibi est dulcis liquor?
Caper miselle, Hyella bella est mortua.
Luge, miselle: bella Hyella est mortua,
15 aliumque valle pascit Elysia gregem,
videtque puro lacte fontes currere,
auraque longe dulciore vescitur.
Neque amplius redire, si velit, huc queat,
neque, si queat, redire iam amplius velit.
20 At tu morere dominamque vise trans Styga,
aut vive posthac omnium miserrimus,
caper miselle, omnium miserrime.

## · LATIN POEMS, BOOK IV ·

and prepares you all a feast of salted leaves.
What goat ever had a happier life
or ever did goat-footed Pan or Pales, goddess of the flocks,
see enjoying a more pampered existence,                                   30
billy goat luckier than the Nanny of the gods in heaven?


: 3 :


Billy goat, accustomed to go at the head of the nannies to the
    pastures,
why do you drag along sorrowful feet in last place?
You used to be the first to make for the lofty mountain peaks
when the Sun with his golden chariot brings the day;
the first to seek the remote resting places in the valleys,                 5
where a clear spring calls you with the babbling of its waters;
the first to make for home on nightfall's first descent,
striding along with great steps in front of the nannies.
Now you come home sad, sick at heart, and last.
Poor little goat, do you miss beautiful Hyella,                             10
and without her is neither thyme
nor shade nor water sweet to you?
Poor little goat, beautiful Hyella is dead.
Grieve, poor beast; beautiful Hyella is dead
and pastures another flock in the vale of Elysium,                         15
seeing streams run with pure milk,
and breathing far sweeter air.
She could neither come back here again if she wanted to,
nor would she now want to come back again, if she could.
You must either die and go and see your mistress beyond the Styx,   20
or live hereafter the most miserable of all creatures,
poor little billy goat, most miserable of all creatures.

## · MARCANTONIO FLAMINIO ·

### ∶ 4 ∶

Adeste, o Satyri bonique Fauni et
quidquid capripedum est ubique divum.
Mecum, numina sancta, lacrimate.
Vestra mortua bella caprimulga est,
5   illa candida, bella caprimulga
quae vobis bona liba factitabat,
quae dulcem mihi caseum premebat,
quae tam carmina bella cantitabat.
Tecum delicias, Hyella, ruris,
10   tecum gaudia ruris abstulisti.
Te formosulus hortus ille quem tu
laetum virginea manu rigabas,
te fons prosiliens specu e virenti
quem illo floridulo ore basiabas,
15   te lugent nemora atque vallis in qua
pascebas niveas tuas capellas,
nunc pictas Dryadis legens corollas,
nunc dulci resonans avena in antro.
At tu, si sapis, o puella Ditis,
20   huic dato nitidas tuas capellas.
Hac pascente, domum tuae capellae
ferent ubera tentiora, lacque
longe dulcius effluet papillis.
Nullam rura tulere doctiorem
25   aut miscere coagula aut decoras
molli texere fiscinas hibisco
aut per florida prata cum puellis
choros ducere, obstupente pago.

## · LATIN POEMS, BOOK IV ·

### ∶ 4 ∶

Come join me, satyrs and good fauns
and all goat-footed gods everywhere,
and weep with me, holy deities.
Your beautiful milkmaid is dead,
that fair and beautiful milkmaid                                    5
who used to make you fine cakes,
press me delicious cheese,
and sing such beautiful songs.
You have taken the delights of the countryside with you, Hyella,
you have taken with you the countryside's joys.                     10
They all grieve for you: the pretty garden that to its bliss
you watered with your maiden's hand,
the spring leaping from a green cave
that you kissed with your rosy lips,
the woods, and the valley in which                                  15
you pastured your snow-white nanny goats,
now picking a dryad's colorful garlands,
now making a cavern resound with your sweet pipe.
But, girl bride of Dis, if you are wise,
entrust your sleek nanny goats to this maid's charge.               20
With her to pasture them, your nannies
will bring home fuller udders,
and milk will flow out far more sweetly from their teats.
The countryside has produced no maid
more skilled at mixing rennet,                                      25
weaving pretty baskets from soft marsh mallow,
or leading dances through flowery meadows with the other girls
as the local folk look on in amazement.

165

## · MARCANTONIO FLAMINIO ·

### ： 5 ：

Cur subito, fons turbidule, tuus umor abundat?
    Dic age, lucidulam quis tibi turbat aquam?
Ah miser, exstinctae turbat te casus Hyellae,
    ipse tuis crescis, perdite, de lacrimis.
5  Infelix, non iam tanges rosea illa labella,
    candida nec liquidis membra lavabis aquis,
non fessam atque tuo crepitanti murmure captam
    aspicies somnos carpere languidulos,
dum niveas inter ludit lasciva papillas,
10    et simul aureolam ventilat aura comam,
ac, leviter motans myrtos superimpendentes,
    spargit odoratos flore cadente sinus.
Ut fulvum nitidumque aurum nitidissimus ipse
    ornat sidereo lumine chrysolithus,
15  ut laurum decorat croceis hedera alba corymbis,
    nectens formosis bracchia bracchiolis,
sic formosa tuas lymphas decorabat imago,
    se vitreo quotiens viderat illa lacu.
Tunc, o frigidule, blando urebaris amore;
20    vos liquidae melius tunc nituistis aquae.
O quotiens, dulci cum vos libaverat ore,
    facta est Hyblaeis dulcior unda favis.
O quotiens vestros requievit carmine cursus,
    cum modulans calamis luderet imparibus,
25  nunc te, sancta Pales, nunc te, Latonia virgo,
    nunc referens laudes, Pan Tegeaee, tuas.
Illa canit, tremula respondent voce capellae,
    saltat et oblitis haedulus uberibus.

· LATIN POEMS, BOOK IV ·

: 5 :

Why, muddied spring, are you suddenly full to overflowing?
　Come, tell me, who troubles your clear waters?
　Ah, poor stream, it is dead Hyella's fate that troubles you;
　you swell, brokenhearted, with your own tears.
Unhappy fount, no more will you touch those sweet, rosy lips　　5
　or bathe her white limbs with your pure waters.
You will not see her, weary and enchanted
　by your babbling murmur, snatch drowsy sleep
as a lascivious breeze plays between her snow-white breasts
　and at the same time ruffles her golden hair,　　10
while, lightly shaking the overhanging myrtles,
　it sprinkles her fragrant bosom with their falling blossoms.
As chrysolite, itself so highly lustrous,
　emblazons tawny, lustrous gold with starlike light,
or as pale ivy beautifies a laurel with its yellow berries,　　15
　entwining the branches with its lovely little stems,
so her lovely image used to beautify your waters
　whenever she saw her own reflection in your glassy pool.
O then, for all your coolness, you used to burn with sweet love;
　you clear waters then sparkled with a brighter gleam.　　20
O how often, when she had touched you with her sweet lips,
　your flow was made sweeter than Hyblaean honey!
O how often she arrested your course with her song
　when she played a tune on her uneven pipes,
now telling of you, holy Pales, now of you, virgin daughter of　　25
　　Latona,
　now recounting your praises, Tegean Pan.
She sang, the nanny goats responded with their tremulous
　　bleating,
　and the tiny kid frisked, his mother's udder all forgotten.

167

## · MARCANTONIO FLAMINIO ·

At circum volitans pictis avium chorus alis
30    discit, et arguto gutture cuncta iterat.
Mirantur Satyri, nymphae mirantur et ipsae,
    et Faunus, ramis abditus arbuteis.
Ipse etiam, vocemque et formosissima mirans
    ora, suas in se vertit Amor faculas.
35    Ardet Amor, pulchrisque genis, roseisque labellis
    incubat, ut myrti floridae avis foliis,
quae solem dulci nascentem voce salutat,
    et patulo rorem lucidulum ore bibit.
Sic Amor ore haurit dulcem dominae halitum hiulco,
40    carmina sic avida candidus aure bibit.
Talia populeis Minci cantabat in umbris,
    dum pascit niveas pulchra Amaryllis oves.
Talia cantabas viridi, Galatea, sub antro,
    formosi recubans Acidis in gremio.
45    Cantabas; puer impatiens saepe intermixtis
    mollia rumpebat carmina basiolis.
Ah miser, ah male caute puer! Tua gaudia Cyclops
    in nebulas iam iam dissipat aerias.
Ille, tuae demens correptus amore puellae,
50    ah! miserum infando perdidit exitio.
Fleverunt nemora et fontes et Oreades altis
    montibus et magni candida turba maris.
Ipsa comas Galatea scidit, maestoque ululatu
    implevit scopulos, caerula Dori, tuos,

## · LATIN POEMS, BOOK IV ·

A chorus of birds with brightly-colored wings, flying round
    above,
  learned and repeated every note with tuneful throat.         30
The satyrs marveled, and the nymphs marveled too,
  and so did Faunus, hidden by the branches of a strawberry
    tree.
Even Love, marveling at her voice and supremely beautiful face,
  turned his little torches on himself.
Love burned with love and settled on her pretty cheeks and rosy   35
    lips,
  as a bird perches on a flowering myrtle's branches,
greeting the rising sun with sweet voice
  and drinking the sparkling dew with open beak.
Just so did radiant Love with mouth agape inhale my mistress's
    sweet breath,
  just so did he drink in her songs with eager ear.         40
Such songs fair Amaryllis sang in the Mincio's poplar shade
  as she grazed her snow-white sheep.
Such songs did you sing, Galatea, under cover of a green grotto
  as you reclined in handsome Acis' arms.
You sang, and often the impatient boy         45
  would interrupt your gentle strains, punctuating them with
    little kisses.
Ah, poor, unwary boy! The Cyclops was at any moment
  about to scatter your joys to the clouds of heaven!
Insanely gripped by passion for your girl,
  alas he murdered you, the hapless victim of his monstrous   50
    crime.
The woods and fountains and the oreads on their lofty peaks
    wept for you,
  and so too did the fair band that dwells within the mighty sea.
Galatea herself tore her hair, filled your reefs,
  sea-blue Doris, with her sad wailing,

· MARCANTONIO FLAMINIO ·

55 optavitque mori subito potuisse suisque
    amissis lucem linquere deliciis.
Non illam sociae longo post tempore nymphae
    viderunt laetis ferre pedem choreis,
non thalamo picta palla procedere cinctam
60    candida puniceis tempora coraliis.
Illa vel undisoni pelagi latet abdita fundo,
    vel repetit furtis litora nota suis;
hic fletum misera ingeminat, fletu omnia complet,
    et verti in fluidas tota cupit lacrimas.
65 Hic miserum querulis compellit vocibus Acin;
    antra sonant *Acin*, caeruleae *Acin* aquae.
Tu quoque, fons miserande, tuae post dura puellae
    fata, tuis numquam pone modum lacrimis.
Quis tibi nunc texet viridanti umbracula myrto?
70    Quis saepem tremulis texet harundinibus?
Quis sparget niveis onerata canistra hyacinthis,
    pictaque purpureis serta papaveribus?
Luge igitur, miser, et, confracta turbidus urna,
    semper cresce novis, fons bone, lacrimulis.
75 Cumque tumens ripa exieris vagus, haud pete florem
    ridentis calthae puniceamve rosam
sed nigras violas et caeruleos hyacinthos;
    ipsa bibat maestam maesta cupressus aquam.
Quod si pulchra puella lavatum huc venerit ulla,
80    candida seu Nais, candida sive Dryas,
dic lacrimans, 'Ne me, quaeso, pulcherrima, tange,
    neve meis corpus commacula lacrimis.
Hae lymphae non sunt lymphae, sed flebilis umor,
    quem carae dominae mittimus inferias.'

## · LATIN POEMS, BOOK IV ·

and longed to be able to die without delay                        55
    and quit life's light, now that her darling boy was lost.
For a long time thereafter her companion nymphs
    did not see her joining in their happy dances
or emerging from her bedchamber clad in a gaily-colored robe,
    her white temples crowned with red-hued coral.          60
She either hid away in the depths of the roaring sea
    or returned to the shores familiar to her from her secret love.
Here she cried and cried again, poor girl, filled everywhere with
      her weeping,
    and longed to be changed entirely into flowing tears.
Here in plaintive tones she called upon poor Acis;              65
    "Acis," the caves echoed, and the blue waters echoed "Acis."
In your sorrow too, poor fountain, after your girl's harsh fate,
    never put an end to your tears.
Who will now weave you a bower of green myrtle?
    Who will weave you a lattice of quivering reeds?          70
Who will scatter baskets laden with snowy hyacinths,
    and garlands painted with crimson poppies?
Grieve then, poor spring, and, muddied from a shattered urn,
    ever swell, good fountain, with fresh-streaming tears.
And when, as your waters rise, you burst your banks and          75
      overflow,
    do not seek the smiling marigold's flower or the red-hued rose
but dark violets and deep blue hyacinths;
    let the sad cypress drink your sad water.
But if any beautiful girl comes here to bathe,
    whether a comely naiad or comely dryad,                  80
tell her with a sob, "Do not touch me, fair nymph, I beg you,
    and do not defile your body with my tears.
These waters are not waters but the flow I weep
    as the tribute I pay in death to my dear mistress."

· MARCANTONIO FLAMINIO ·

: 6 :

Sic tibi perpetuam donet Pomona iuventam,
    hortule, dic, tanti quae tibi causa mali?
Ille tuus decor in tenues evanuit auras,
    ut riget informi cum fera bruma gelu.
5  Non rosa formosum calathi iam pandit honorem,
    non violae ridet purpura lucidulae.
Aruit ille suo viridi cum gramine rivus,
    Daedala nec dulci voce susurrat apis,
quaeque decora albis canebat floribus, ipsa
10    ponit odoratas citrea silva comas.
Ah, nivei subito cur nigrescunt hyacinthi
    atque notis implent flebilibus folia?
Cur vivax apium moritur croceumque papaver
    et panace fusis roscida lacrimulis?
15  Hortule, num luges fatum infelicis Hyellae,
    et piget exstinctam vivere post dominam?
Illa quidem fuerat vivens tibi causa decoris,
    illa tibi moriens abstulit omne decus.

: 7 :

Cum pater invitum Nisae sociasset Iolam,
    venissetque viri iam nova nupta domum,
non potuit tantos pulcherrima Hyella dolores
    ferre nec erepto vivere coniugio;

## · LATIN POEMS, BOOK IV ·

### : 6 :

So may Pomona grant you eternal youth, little garden,
    tell me, what is the cause of your great distress?
The beauty you possessed has vanished into thin air,
    as when the harsh winter is frozen with disfiguring ice.
No more does the rose open the beautiful glory of its cup,    5
    no more does the bright violet's purple smile.
Your stream has dried up along with its green grass,
    the Daedalian bee makes no sweet-voiced hum,
and the citron orchard that was brightly decked with white
        flowers
    is shedding its fragrant foliage.    10
Ah, why are the snowy hyacinths suddenly turning black
    and covering their petals with marks of mourning?
Why is the long-green parsley dying, and the orange poppy,
    and the cure-all, dewy with the shedding of tiny tears?
Little garden, are you grieving for the death of unhappy Hyella,   15
    and have you no will to live after the passing of your mistress?
Indeed, in life she was the cause of your beauty,
    and in dying she has taken all your beauty from you.

### : 7 :

When his father had wedded Iolas to Nisa against the lad's will,
    and the new bride had now come to her husband's home,
beautiful Hyella could not bear such great pain
    or live when the marriage she wanted had been stolen from
        her;

#### · MARCANTONIO FLAMINIO ·

5 sed, veluti flos virgineo decerptus ab ungue,
  cum vita dulcis tabuit ille decor,
tabuit ille decor, quo nil formosius ulla
  aetas, nil umquam vidit amabilius.
Occidis, infelix, primo sub flore iuventae;
10  occidis, heu nullo tempore digna mori.
Sed tua fama superstes erit, quotiensque viator
  praeteriens tumulum viderit et titulum,
ille tuo lecto suspirans nomine dicet,
  'Pulchrior in terris nulla puella fuit.'

: 8 :

Cum pulchra infelicem animam exhalaret Hyella,
  talia cum multis dicta dedit lacrimis:
'Duritia formose puer mihi durior ipsa,
  idem luce mihi carior atque anima,
5 tu licet ipse meam crudeli morte iuventam
  crudelis lympham miseris ad Stygiam,
non tamen ulla mihi vis carum nomen Iolae
  obliviscenti deleat ex animo.
Seu Cytherea meam Campis Lugentibus umbram
10  sistet seu Campis sistet in Elysiis,
semper ero memor ipsa tui, quamvis laticem omnem
  Lethaeum aridulis faucibus ebiberem.
At tu, care puer, pro tanto gratus amore,
  transibis quotiens heu miseros cineres,
15 dic lacrimans, "Heu, cara puella, malus tibi vitam
  abstulit et diro funere mersit amans.

### · LATIN POEMS, BOOK IV ·

but, like a flower snapped off by a maiden's nail,     5
    that sweet beauty of Hyella's wasted away with her life,
 that beauty wasted away, prettier and lovelier
    than anything any age has ever seen.
You died, unhappy girl, in the first flower of your youth;
    you died alas, though you should never have died at any time.   10
But your fame will live on, and, whenever a passing traveler
    sees your tomb and its inscription,
he will read your name and say with a sigh,
    "There has never been any more beautiful girl on earth."

: 8 :

When beautiful Hyella was breathing away her unhappy life,
    with many tears she spoke these words:
"Handsome boy, harsher to me than harshness itself,
    and yet dearer to me than light and life,
though you are the one who, in my youth and by a cruel death,   5
    have cruelly sent me to the waters of Styx,
yet may nothing ever have the power to erase from my mind
    the dear name of Iolas and make me forget you.
Whether Cytherea sets my shade in the Mourning Fields
    or sets it in those of Elysium,   10
I shall always remember you, even should I drink
    all Lethe's waters down my poor, parched throat.
But you, dear boy, in gratitude for such great love,
    whenever (alas!) you pass by my poor ashes,
say with a tear, 'Alas, dear girl, a wicked lover robbed you of   15
    your life
    and brought it to a dreadful end.

· MARCANTONIO FLAMINIO ·

Ah, nunc saltem in morte quiescas." Hoc tibi—Iolae,
    qui potuit miseram perdere—mandat amor.'

: 9 :

Quisquis es, upiliove bonus, bona vel caprimulga,
    siste gregem, et sacro munera fer cineri.
Da violas tumulo, fundat dulcissima vina
    cantharus, et tepido lacte madescat humus.
5  Dehinc lacrimans sic fare: 'Cinis carissime nobis,
    nunc cinis, ast olim candida Hyella, vale.'

: 10 :

Sic Pan bicornis et Pales vitam tuam
    tuumque sospitent gregem,
parum resiste, pastor, et pictis sacrum
    lapidem corona floribus.
5  Hic est Hyella, qua nec ulla pulchrior
    pavit capellas femina,
nec pastor ullus garrulam umquam fistulam
    inflavit ore dulcius.
Nondum misella terna lustra clauserat,
10    cum vidit ultimum diem.
Ut flos apricus, Terra quem Mater sua
    dulci educabat in sinu,

## · LATIN POEMS, BOOK IV ·

Ah, now at least may you have rest in death.' This charge love
    lays upon you—
  upon Iolas, who had the heart to kill a poor girl."


: 9 :


Whoever you are, be it a good shepherd or a good milkmaid
    of goats,
  halt your flock, and bring gifts to these hallowed ashes.
Offer violets to the tomb, let your drinking pot pour out the
    sweetest wine,
  and let the earth be moistened with warm milk.
Then with a tear say this: "Ashes so very dear to me,      5
  now mere ashes, but once beautiful Hyella, fare you well."


: 10 :


So may two-horned Pan and Pales
  preserve your life and your flock,
stay a little while, shepherd, and crown
  this hallowed stone with brightly-colored flowers.
Here is Hyella. Never did a more beautiful woman      5
  than she pasture nanny goats,
nor did any shepherd ever blow
  into a tuneful pipe more sweetly.
The poor young girl had not yet completed three lusters
  when she saw her last day.      10
Like a flower growing out in the sun,
  reared by Mother Earth in her sweet bosom,

## · MARCANTONIO FLAMINIO ·

tunc primum hiare coeperat, cum tabuit
    calore tactus fervido,
15  sic pulchram Hyellam flore sub primo impotens
    amoris aestus perdidit.
At tu, viator, sic faveat amor tibi,
    precare terram ut pulveri
sacro puellae sit levis, dehinc floribus
20    hanc spargito et felix abi.


⁝  II  ⁝


Pastores, teneras procul hinc arcete capellas,
    et sacram nigris spargite humum violis,
neu veteris Bacchi, neu dulcis copia lactis,
    neu desit numeris tibia flebilibus.
5  Hic bona Hyella iacet, pecoris formosa magistra,
    iunctaque cum domina fida capella sua.
Illam saevus amor nimium infelicis Iolae
    perdidit, hanc carae perdit amor dominae;
nam, simul exhalantem animam conspexit Hyellam,
10    ipsius ante pedes concidit exanima.
Fortunata capella, polo fulgere supremo
    dignior Icariae quam canis Erigones,
si tua magna fides dominae comes ire sub umbras
    audet, et ante diem reddere dulcem animam,
15  at florens tua fama viget semperque vigebit
    exemplum sanctae maximum amicitiae,
dum silva gaudebit aper, dum monte capella,
    dum patulis ulmi decidet umbra comis.

## · LATIN POEMS, BOOK IV ·

that had no sooner begun to open than it wasted away,
    withered by the burning heat,
so in her first flower did the fervor of love beyond all bearing     15
    kill beautiful Hyella.
But, traveler (so may love be kind to you),
    pray to the earth to rest lightly on the girl's hallowed ashes,
then sprinkle this spot with flowers,
    and be on your way — and may good luck go with you.     20


: II :


Shepherds, keep your young nanny goats far away from here
    and sprinkle the hallowed ground with dark violets;
let mellow wine and sweet milk flow in abundance,
    and let not the flute with its mournful strains go unheard.
Here lies good Hyella, the beautiful mistress of the herd,     5
    and, along with her mistress, Hyella's faithful she-goat.
It was cruel love for unhappy Iolas that killed the girl,
    and love for her dear mistress that killed the goat;
for, as soon as she saw Hyella breathing out her life,
    she fell dead herself at her mistress's feet.     10
Lucky goat, worthier to shine in the heights of heaven
    than the dog of Icarus' daughter Erigone,
if in your great loyalty you dare accompany your mistress to the
        shades below
    and give up your sweet life before your day,
yet your fame lives strongly on and will always live on     15
    as a very great example of sacred devotion,
as long as the boar delights in the wood, and the she-goat in the
        mountain,
    and as long as the elm's spreading foliage casts its shade.

179

## · MARCANTONIO FLAMINIO ·

### ⦂ 12 ⦂

Deliciae ruris cum pulchra periret Hyella,
    cum domina periit fida capella sua.
Non ipsam violenta lues, non aspera febris,
    sed dominae subita morte peremit amor.
5   I nunc et Pyladas et amoris nomine Orestas
    et iacta fidos, Graecia, Pirithoos.

### ⦂ 13 ⦂

Cum misera ante diem, fida comitata capella,
    iret ad infernas candida Hyella domos,
ille malus saevis redimitus colla colubris
    Cerberus, invisas qui cubat ante fores,
5   non pavidam horribili tremefecit voce puellam,
    nec rabidis illam dentibus appetiit,
sed tremulo blandae gannitu vocis adulans,
    et lingua lambens crura pedesque fera,
aetherias voluisset eam remeare sub auras,
10   et tam formosae virginis ire comes,
quique tot heroum magnas latraverat umbras,
    optavit parvi nunc gregis esse canis.

# · LATIN POEMS, BOOK IV ·

## : 12 :

When beautiful Hyella, the countryside's darling, was dying,
    her faithful nanny goat died along with her mistress.
It was no virulent pestilence or ravaging fever
    but love for her mistress that caused the creature's sudden end.
Go now, Greece, and vaunt as models of devotion        5
    the likes of Pylades, Orestes, and faithful Pirithous.

## : 13 :

When, before her day, accompanied by her faithful nanny goat,
    poor beautiful Hyella was making her way to the abodes
        below,
that cruel creature Cerberus, neck ringed with savage snakes,
    that lies on guard before the hateful gates,
did not make the terrified girl tremble with his dreadful bark,    5
    nor did he attack her with raging teeth,
but, fawning on her with tremulous whimpers in tones of
    affection,
    and licking her legs and feet with his untamed tongue,
he would have been willing to let her return to the air of heaven
    and to accompany so beautiful a maiden himself,    10
and the beast that had barked at so many heroes' great ghosts
    now longed to be the sheepdog of a small-sized flock.

181

## · MARCANTONIO FLAMINIO ·

### : 14 :

Cum nemorum decus et culti solacia ruris
    venit ad Elysias candida Hyella domos,
obstupuere omnes, fixoque in virgine vultu,
    spectabat pro se quisque oculis avidis
5  ardentes oculos surasque umerosque nitentes
    bracchiaque et flavas per rosea ora comas,
atque aliquis iuratus ait, 'Non pulchrior umquam
    venit ad Elysios ulla puella choros.'

### : 15 :

Hanc fistulam, hospes, quam vides pinu sacra
    pendere, Pani Hyella posuit maximo,
cum iam misella, solis aureum iubar
    linquens, beatos ferret ad manes suum.
5  Hac illa pulchra fistula cum luderet,
    nymphas canens et furta earum dulcia,
non aura laetis insonabat frondibus,
    non murmurantes obstrepebant rivuli,
non picta garrulo avis canebat gutture;
10  quin ipse, dulci carminum captus sono,
    inter greges iacebat innocens lupus.
Himella florida, et Taburne pinifer,
    tu testis, ipse es saepe miratus tuas
motare pinus horridas cacumina.
15  Tunc fistula haec beatior calamis fuit
    quicumque labra docta pastorum terunt;

## · LATIN POEMS, BOOK IV ·

### : 14 :

When the glory of the woods and cheerer of the well-tended
    countryside,
  beautiful Hyella, came to Elysium's abodes,
all were astounded, and each fixed his gaze upon the maid
  and stared with avid eyes as intently as he could
at her burning eyes, her calves, her radiant shoulders,     5
  her arms, and the yellow hair that trailed over her rosy face,
and someone avowed, "No more beautiful girl
  has ever come to the bands in Elysium."

### : 15 :

Stranger, this pipe you see hanging on the sacred pine
Hyella dedicated to mighty Pan as the poor girl
was leaving behind the sun's golden radiance
and taking her own to the blessed shades below.
When that beautiful maid used to play on this pipe,     5
singing of nymphs and their sweet intrigues,
no breeze rustled in the trees' joyous crowns,
no gurgle of babbling streams was heard,
no brightly-colored bird sang with chattering throat;
even the wolf, enchanted by the sweetness of her strains,     10
lay down without menace amid the flocks.
Flowery Imella is witness, and you are too, pine-clad Taburno;
you have yourself often marveled to see
your bristling pines sway their heads.
Then this pipe was more blessed than any reeds     15
that rub shepherds' skillful lips;

## · MARCANTONIO FLAMINIO ·

at nunc misella fistula aut semper tacet,
aut, si loquaci ventus illam sibilo
inflavit, usque flebiles edit sonos,
20   acerba dominae fata deplorans suae,
et ore caro basiari expetens,
quo nulla pulchrius neque umquam dulcius
puella gessit os, neque ulla umquam geret.

: 16 :

Quod nulla nec formosior nec fistulam
inflare dulcem doctior niveos greges
umquam Taburni pavit inter horrida
pineta, pastores tuis hunc manibus
5   dicant, Hyella, lucum opacum et hos duos
fontes amoenos, qui levi cum murmure
e rupe muscosa alter, alter e specu
pendente decidunt; at in medio iacens
tua ossa fictilis urna habet, opulentior
10   quam dives Hermus, undaque aurifera Tagi.
Hanc nos quotannis, cum Favoni candida
fert aura ver insigne floreis comis,
dulci Lyaeo et lacte et agni sanguine
rigabimus. Tum virgines circum integrae
15   ducent choreas, et tuas laudes canent.
*Hyella* mons, *Hyella* vallis garrula
sonabit, et cum sol diem face aurea
illustrat, et cum nox polum umbra condidit.
At magnus Alcon fistula quam capripes
20   illi dedit Pan triste carmen ordiens

## · LATIN POEMS, BOOK IV ·

but now the poor pipe is either permanently silent,
or, if the wind has blown into it with a chattering whistle,
it unremittingly emits mournful tones
in lamentation for its mistress's untimely death                    20
and in its longing to be kissed by her dear lips,
the fairest and sweetest lips any girl ever had,
or any ever will have.

:  16  :

Because no more beautiful girl, nor any more skilled
at playing the sweet pipe, ever pastured snowy flocks
amid Taburno's bristling pines,
the shepherds dedicate to your ghost, Hyella,
this shady grove and these two charming springs              5
that tumble with a gentle murmur,
one from a mossy crag, the other from an overhanging cave;
while, lying in the heart of the grove,
an earthenware urn, richer than the wealthy Hermus
and the gold-bearing waters of the Tagus, holds your bones.        10
Every year, when the west wind's cheering breeze
brings spring, brightly decked in flowery foliage,
we shall wet this urn with sweet wine, milk, and the blood of
     a lamb;
and then around it unsullied virgin girls
will lead dances and sing your praises.                          15
Mountain and echoing valley will resound with the name *Hyella*,
both when the sun lights the day with his golden torch,
and when the night has hidden the sky in shadow.
Great Alcon will strike up a sad song
on the pipe goat-footed Pan gave him                             20

· MARCANTONIO FLAMINIO ·

narrabit ut te crinibus passis deae
Oreades defleverint, cum pallidum
videre vultum, ut, arborum tonsis comis,
te silva maesta luxerit, te limpidi
25  fontes, Hyella, te Taburni horridae
flevere cautes; caerula se condidit
sol nube, dira ne videret funera.
Quin saevus ille lacrimis mortalium
gaudens Cupido flexilem arcum et igneas
30  fregit sagittas. Quantum hiems gelu aspero
concreta veri floreo cedit, rubus
quantum virenti acantho, agris tantum omnibus
tibi puellae cesserant. Ut ramulis
in valle myrtus avia nitentibus
35  crescit, quam amico rore fontis educant
nymphae decentes, sic amabilis tua
iuventa surgens enitebat. Nec rosa
rubente mane lucidum calathi sui
pandens honorem est pulchrior, nec pulchrior
40  Aurora, croceo cum gerit diem sinu
coma refulgens aurea. Quis simplices
mores et artes Cypria dignas dea
aequare possit laudibus? Seu fiscinam
virente hibisco texeres, formosius
45  iurabat esse nil Pales; seu duceres
choros sub altis arborum comantium
ramis, Napaeae candidae et Phoebi soror
stabant stupentes; seu levi nemorum deos
calamo canebas, silva dulci carmine
50  gaudebat, ipse Maenalus quantum sui
Fauni sonora fistula. salve, o bona
Hyella, salve, et montibus nostris ades.
Tu Pana maximum et sorores Naidas

## · LATIN POEMS, BOOK IV ·

and tell how, with their hair disheveled,
the oread goddesses wept for you when they saw your pallid face,
and how, with its trees' hair shorn,
the sad wood too grieved for you. The clear springs
and Taburno's rugged crags bewailed you, Hyella; 25
the sun hid in a dark cloud
so as not to see your dreadful death.
Furthermore, that cruel Cupid, who delights in mortals' tears,
broke his pliant bow and fiery arrows.
As much as winter, hard frozen with rough ice, 30
yields place to flowery spring,
and the bramble to green acanthus, so much in every land
had the girls yielded place to you.
As in a trackless valley a glossy-branched myrtle grows
that comely nymphs raise with kindly sprinklings of spring water, 35
so your young loveliness shone brightly forth
as it blossomed. A rose is not more beautiful
as, at the reddening break of dawn,
it opens up the splendid glory of its cup,
nor is Aurora fairer when she brings day in her saffron lap, 40
gleaming brightly with her golden hair.
Who could match with praises your guileless character
and accomplishments worthy of the Cyprian goddess?
If you wove a basket from green marsh-mallow twigs,
Pales vowed that nothing was prettier; 45
or if you led dances beneath the lofty branches of leafy trees,
pretty dell nymphs and Apollo's sister stood amazed;
or if you hymned the woodland gods on a light reed pipe,
the wood delighted as much in your sweet song
as Mount Maenalus itself delights 50
in its own Faunus' tuneful reed.
Hail, good Hyella, hail, and visit our mountains!
Win for your shepherds, blessed one,

## · MARCANTONIO FLAMINIO ·

pastoribus, beata, concilia tuis,
55　morbosque lacrimabiles precibus piis
　　averte, lucum et vise saepius tuum.

### ⁚ 17 ⁚

Dum te flebilibus numeris moriturus Iolas
　　cantat, ades vati, candida Hyella, tuo.
Tale mea carmen moduler tibi harundine, quale
　　deficiens dulci gutture cantat olor,
5　ut tua pastorum volitet vaga fama per ora,
　　dum laetas segetes pinguia rura dabunt,
dum flores apis, et rivos dum gramen amabit,
　　dum metuet celerem tarda capella lupum.
Digna quidem fueras, quam maximus ille Menalcas
10　diceret argutis semper harundinibus
et quam, posthabita Neptunine Galatea,
　　cantaret Siculi clara Thalia senis.
Et facerent, si te natam felicibus annis
　　vidissent oculis, candida nympha, meis.
15　Te iuga Parnasi resonarent, te iuga Pindi,
　　notior Arcadiae nulla puella foret.
Per nemora et silvas incisum cortice levi
　　mille tuum nomen viveret arboribus.
Tu quoque par esses Amphionio Aracyntho
20　et par Maenaliis, care Taburne, iugis.

## · LATIN POEMS, BOOK IV ·

the favor of mighty Pan and the naiad sisters,
and with pious prayers avert the diseases that cause us tears,          55
and many a time come to visit your grove.


: 17 :

As Iolas, soon to die, sings of you in mournful strains,
    come join your bard, fair Hyella.
May I play such a song for you on my reed
    as a dying swan sings with sweet-voiced throat,
so that your wandering fame may fly on shepherds' lips          5
    for as long as fertile country acres furnish joyous crops,
as long as the bee loves flowers, and the grass streams,
    as long as the slow she-goat fears the speedy wolf.
You would truly have been a worthy girl for great Menalcas
        himself
    to celebrate on his ever-tuneful reeds          10
and for the old Sicilian's glorious muse to make his theme
    sooner than Neptune's daughter Galatea;
and they would have done so, had you been born in their blissful
        years,
    and had they beheld you, beautiful nymph, with my eyes.
The ridges of Parnassus would echo your name, and those of          15
        Pindus too,
    and no girl of Arcadia would be more highly famed.
Throughout the woods and forests, inscribed in their smooth
        bark,
    your name would live upon a thousand trees.
You too, dear Taburno, would equal Amphion's Aracynthus
    and match the ridges of Mount Maenalus.          20

189

## · MARCANTONIO FLAMINIO ·

Magne pater, tali fortunatissime alumna,
    tu viridi servas ossa beata sinu,
At misera ante diem, crudeli funere rapta,
    ivit ad infernas, non reditura, domos.
25  O mihi Threiciam citharam si Musa dedisset,
    quae potuit silvas ducere montivagas,
per tenebras Orci, per pallida regna silentum
    quaesissem manes, cara puella, tuos.
Nec me tergemino terreret Cerberus ore,
30    nec torvae anguineis crinibus Eumenides.
Vel mecum vitae repetisses lumina, vel me
    obrueret Stygio mors violenta lacu.
Sed citharae si nil prodessent fila canorae,
    movissem fletu numina dura pio.
35  Vidissent umbrae tenues regemque superbum
    Tisiphonemque malis illacrimare meis.
Sit licet ille fero crudelior angue tyrannus,
    non vacuum blandi pectus amoris habet.
Ipsum etiam, qui cuncta domat, Cythereius ales
40    vicit et invito lenia corda dedit,
tempore quo magnae Cereris pulcherrima nata
    ad nigras Erebi candida venit aquas.
Illa quidem, caris nymphis comitata, legebat
    purpureos flores saltibus, Enna, tuis,
45  iamque parans in lucidulo se fonte lavare,
    traxerat e niveo mollia vincla pede,
cum pavidam et matrem queribunda voce vocantem
    abstulit infernis luridus Orcus equis,

## · LATIN POEMS, BOOK IV ·

Great father, fortunate indeed in such a foster child,
    in your green bosom you keep safe her blessed bones,
though she, poor girl, carried off by a cruel death before her time,
    has gone, never to return, to the abodes of the world below.
O if the Muse had granted me the Thracian lyre       25
    capable of leading the woods from mountain to mountain,
then through Orcus' darkness and the silent ones' pale realms
    I would have sought your ghost, dear girl.
Cerberus would not have frightened me with his threefold jaws,
    nor the forbidding Furies with their snaky hair.       30
Either you would have returned with me to the light of life,
    or violent Death would have overwhelmed me in the Stygian
        lake.
But if my tuneful lyre's strings availed me nothing,
    I would have moved the hard-hearted deities with my devoted
        tears.
The insubstantial ghosts would have seen their haughty king       35
    and Tisiphone too weeping at my woes.
Though that tyrant may be more unpitying than a cruel snake,
    he does not have a breast devoid of tender love.
Cytherea's winged son, who prevails over all things, vanquished
        him too,
    and gave him a gentle heart against his inclination,       40
when great Ceres' supremely beautiful daughter
    came in her white-skinned loveliness to the black waters of
        Erebus.
Accompanied by her dear nymphs,
    she was picking red flowers in your glades, Enna,
and, now making ready to bathe in a clear fountain,       45
    she had slipped off the soft sandals from her snowy feet,
when, terrified and calling for her mother in cries of protest,
    ghastly Orcus bore her away in his infernal chariot

nec veritus natam Iovis est violare supremi,
50     tantum forma potest et violentus amor.
Cur igitur caram mihi non donaret Hyellam?
       Cur lacrimis flecti nollet amantis amans?
O qui pallentes Erebi me ducat ad umbras
       et genibus sistat me, pater Orce, tuis!
55  O quales tibi manarent mea lumina fletus,
       funderet o quantas lingua diserta preces!
Me certe facerent pietasque dolorque disertum,
       verba ministraret dulcia dulcis amor.
Quid loquor infelix? Nulla est revocabilis arte,
60     cum semel exstincto lumine vita fugit.
Non revocat Syringa suam Pan magnus ad auras,
       non Phoebus revocat te, Cyparisse, tuus.
Ipse foret quamvis Cybele gratissimus Attis,
       liquerat infernas non tamen Attis aquas.
65  Ah, quotiens nato mater Berecyntia dixit,
       'Per lac, quod dederunt ubera nostra tibi,
perque uteri tolerata decem fastidia menses,
       redde, oro, puerum Dis mihi care meum.
Non ego, felices superum translatus in oras,
70     Tithoni vivat saecula longa peto—
Aurorae liceat carum servare maritum,
       aequalemque deis reddere caelitibus—
at, mihi cum paucos Attis serviverit annos,
       ad tenebras redeat flebilis umbra tuas.
75  Nunc pia templa colens divis operetur, et omnes
       per populos ritus et mea sacra ferat.

## · LATIN POEMS, BOOK IV ·

and did not fear to violate even supreme Jupiter's daughter,
   so great is the power of beauty and of violent love.      50
Why then would he not give me my dear Hyella?
   Why would he, a lover himself, refuse to be swayed by a
      lover's tears?
O for someone to conduct me to Erebus' pale shadows
   and set me, father Orcus, before your knees!
O what tears my eyes would stream to you,      55
   O what prayers my eloquent tongue would pour forth!
My devotion and pain would surely make me eloquent;
   sweet love would supply me with sweet words.
What am I saying in my unhappy plight? No skill can bring
      life back,
   once it has departed, with its light put out.      60
Mighty Pan cannot bring back his Syrinx to the upper air,
   nor your Phoebus you, Cyparissus.
Though Attis was Cybele's dearest delight,
   yet Attis never left the waters below.
Ah, how many times the Berecyntian mother said to her son,   65
   "By the milk my breasts gave you,
and by the discomfort in my womb that I endured for ten
      months,
   I beg you, dear Dis, give me back my boy.
I do not ask that he be translated to the blessed realms of the
      gods
   and live the long centuries of Tithonus —      70
let Aurora be permitted to preserve her dear husband
   and make him the equal of the gods of heaven —
but, once Attis has served me for a few years,
   let him return to your darkness as a shade I must weep for.
Now let him tend temples of worship and pay the gods honors,   75
   and let him spread my rites and sacrifices throughout all
      nations.

193

## · MARCANTONIO FLAMINIO ·

Dulcia purpureae nunc carpat dona iuventae,
    nunc decoret silvas candida forma meas.
An magnum est, animam si de tot milibus unam
80    des matri, vitam quae dedit ipsa tibi?'
Sic lacrimans ait; ille, suis immanior umbris,
    maternas dura respuit aure preces.
Vix licuit miserae manes descendere ad imos,
    atque umbrae dulci basia vana dare.
85  Crudelis Pluto, nimium crudelia Fata,
    quae vitae nullas heu posuere moras!
Cum silvam glacialis hiems spoliavit honore,
    vere novo silvae laeta iuventa redit.
Occidit Oceani cum sol demersus in undas,
90    nascitur adducto pulchrior ille die.
At nobis nec laeta suo cum vere iuventa,
    nec, mersa immiti funere, vita redit.
Ultima cum Parcae legerunt fila severae,
    urget perpetuus lumina clausa sopor,
95  quem tamen aeterno celebrarint carmine Musae,
    ille vel invita Morte superstes erit.
Sic vivis, vivesque aeternum, pulcher Alexi,
    et tu cum Gallo, nota Lycori, tuo.
Pan, nemorum decus, et Satyri, nymphaeque decentes,
100    quae blando agrestes uritis igne deos,
si formosa pie coluit vos semper Hyella,
    si mea vos semper dulcis avena canit,
vos facite ut longum vivant mea carmina in aevum,
    et cum carminibus candida Hyella meis.

## · LATIN POEMS, BOOK IV ·

Now let him enjoy the sweet gifts of bright-blooming youth,
 now let his beautiful form adorn my woods.
Is it a big matter if you grant your mother,
 who herself gave life to you, one soul out of so many          80
  thousands?"
So she spoke in tears, but he, crueler than his shadows,
 spurned his mother's prayers with an unpitying ear.
Poor Cybele was barely even allowed to go down to the shades
  below
 and give the sweet ghost unavailing kisses.
Cruel Pluto, too cruel Fates,                                   85
 who alas have not granted any clinging on to life!
When icy winter has despoiled the forest of its glory,
 joyous youth returns to it in the new spring.
When the sun sets beneath the waters of Ocean,
 it is born in greater beauty with the renewal of day.          90
But for us neither does joyous youth return with its springtime
 nor does life come back, once submerged in cruel death.
When the stern Fates have gathered in our last threads,
 eternal sleep weighs on our closed eyes;
yet anyone the Muses have celebrated in undying song           95
 will survive, even against the wishes of Death.
So do you live, and will live forever, beautiful Alexis,
 and you, famed Lycoris, along with your Gallus.
Pan, glory of the woodlands, you satyrs, and you comely nymphs
 who burn the rural gods with a delightful fire,              100
if beautiful Hyella has always dutifully worshipped you,
 if my sweet pipe always sings of you,
grant that my songs may live long into time to come,
 and along with my songs lovely Hyella.

## · MARCANTONIO FLAMINIO ·

### : 18 :

Has lacrimas atque haec imo suspiria corde
    tracta gemens libo, candida Hyella, tibi.
Haec tibi nunc, mox vitam ipsam libabo animamque,
    cumque tuis miscebo ossibus ossa mea,
5    quosque maritali non iunxit taeda Hymenaeus,
    funerea iunget Mors violenta face.
Quod si nupta meum conscendit Nisa cubile,
    non tamen umquam animum ceperat illa meum,
sed mea me pietas patri parere coegit
10    impia, me durus perdidit ipse pater.
Si fallo, haud ambo terra tumulemur in una,
    nec tua sit felix manibus umbra meis.

### : 19 :

Cur, ah cur ullo placui tibi tempore, mortis
    si, mea vita, tibi causa futurus eram?
Cur me tam pulchrum cari genuere parentes?
    Cur calamos dono Pan dedit ipse suos,
5    quis ego formosas possem mollire puellas
    cantando et duris lenia corda dare?
Quid formam queror aut calamos nocuisse canoros?
    Perfidia periit cara puella mea.
Ahne meis potui thalamis admittere Nisam?
10    Vimne preces duri tantam habuere patris?

## · LATIN POEMS, BOOK IV ·

### : 18 :

These tears and these sighs drawn from the depths of my heart
   I pour out, sobbing, as an offering to you, beautiful Hyella.
These I offer you now, but soon I will give you my very life and
     soul,
   and I will mingle my bones with your bones,
and those whom Hymen did not join with the wedding torch    5
   violent Death shall join with the funeral brand.
Even though Nisa climbed my bed as my bride,
   for all that she had never won my heart;
but my sense of filial duty cruelly made me obey my father,
   my own father destroyed me in his harshness.    10
If I deceive you, may we not both be buried in the one earth,
   and may your ghost not be kind to mine.

### : 19 :

Why, oh why did I ever please you,
   if, my life, I was to be the cause of your death?
Why did my dear parents produce so handsome a son in me?
   Why did Pan himself make me a gift of his reeds
to enable me to soften beautiful girls with them    5
   and give hard-natured maidens gentle hearts through song?
Why do I complain that my good looks or tuneful reeds did
     me harm?
   It was through my treachery that my dear girl perished.
Was I alas able to admit Nisa to my bedchamber?
   Did my hard-hearted father's entreaties have such great force?    10

· MARCANTONIO FLAMINIO ·

Fugissem durumque patrem patriamque priusque
    fudissem multo sanguine dulcem animam!
Sed fundam, poenasque dabo tibi, candida Hyella.
    O cari manes, o, precor, este boni!
15  Vos puerum vestra linquentem lumina causa
    optatum laeti suscipite in gremium,
et qui me nimio sponsum cupiistis amore,
    iungite nunc dulcis gaudia coniugii.
Sancta veni nostrisque fave Proserpina taedis,
20    faustaque purpureus carmina cantet Hymen,
quique olim valida coniunxit utrumque catena,
    vivat in Elysia valle perennis amor.

: 20 :

Pan Pater et veneranda Pales Faunique, valete,
    tuque, mihi quondam care Taburne, vale.
Vos mihi, vos misero silvae placuistis opacae,
    dum niveum in vobis pavit Hyella gregem,
5  et mecum tenera furtim ludebat in herba
    ludere cum magno digna puella Iove.
Tunc mihi purpureo fulserunt lumine soles,
    tunc fuit heu nimium candida vita mea.
Nunc nemora et fontes et caeli lumen et umbrae,
10    nunc ingrata meis omnia sunt oculis.
Mors mihi sola placet. Mors, o dulcissima rerum,
    huc ades, et vitam, Mors bona, redde mihi.
Illa meam vitam rupes habet, illa sepulcro
    servat delicias terra beata meas.

## · LATIN POEMS, BOOK IV ·

I should have fled from both my cruel father and my homeland
  and sooner have spilled out my sweet life in a pool of blood!
But I will spill it out and answer to you for what I have done,
    beautiful Hyella.
  O dear ghost, O, I beg you, be kind!
Gladly take a boy who leaves life's light on your account          15
  into your yearned-for embrace,
and, after longing with so much love to have me for husband,
  now share with me the joys of a sweet marriage bond.
Holy Proserpina, come and bless our wedding,
  and let rosy-cheeked Hymen sing propitious hymns;               20
and may the love that once united us both with a strong chain
  live eternally in the vale of Elysium.


:  20  :

Father Pan, venerable Pales, and you Fauns, farewell,
  and you, Taburno, once dear to me, farewell.
You shady woods, you pleased me, poor wretch that I am,
  while Hyella grazed her snow-white flock within you,
and a girl worthy to play love's games with great Jupiter         5
  used to play them secretly with me on the soft grass.
Then the sunlight shone for me with beaming brilliance,
  then my life was alas too bright with joy.
Now the woods, the springs, the light of the heavens, the
    shadows —
  now all of them are displeasing to my eyes.                     10
Death alone appeals to me now. Death, O sweetest of all things,
  come here and restore, good Death, my life to me.
Yonder rock has my life within it, that blessed ground
  keeps my darling safe in her tomb.

· MARCANTONIO FLAMINIO ·

15 Pastores, illa dominae me iungite in urna,
    taliaque inscriptis addite verba notis:
*Formosam tuus ardor, Iola, absumpsit Hyellam;*
*te miserum leto perdidit illa suo.*

∴ 21 ∴

Ingrate sol, ortum quid approperas tuum?
Quo lux mihi, si luce non datur frui?
Redisne, grex ut redeat in silvam meus?
At hunc Hyellae mors acerba perdidit.
5 Redis, magis magisque tabescam ut miser,
et te fatigem quaestibus semper novis,
dominae revisens pulverem sacrum meae?
An tu quadrigas aureas tuas refers
ut luminibus aliquam afferas lucem meis?
10 At illa, lacrimis tenebrisque horridis
assueta, lucem odere, nec radiis tuis
imbres suos siccari amant, quibus genas
rigant et ora amoris usta incendio.
Sed fulgeas licebit et radiantibus
15 terras, maria, caelumque lustres ignibus,
tamen omnia tenebris inhorrescunt mihi
ex quo meus sol mihi suam lucem abstulit
deisque manibus occidens eam tulit.

### · LATIN POEMS, BOOK IV ·

Shepherds, unite me with my lady in that urn,     15
 and add these words to the inscription:
*Love for you, Iolas, carried off beautiful Hyella;*
 *in your misery by her death she brought you your end.*

: 21 :

Unwelcome sun, why do you hasten to your rising?
Of what use is daylight to me, if I am not permitted to enjoy
 the day?
Do you return so that my flock may go again to the wood?
But Hyella's untimely death has destroyed me.
Do you return so that I may pine away more and more in my  5
 misery
and constantly weary you with fresh laments
whenever I revisit my lady's sacred dust?
Or do you bring back your golden four-horse chariot
to supply some light to my eyes?
But they are used to tears and dreadful darkness    10
and hate the light, and they do not like your rays
drying their showers, with which they wet my cheeks
and my lips scorched with the flames of love.
But though you may shine and light up
earth, sea, and sky with your beaming fires,     15
yet for me all has been turning to terrible darkness
ever since my sun took away its light from me
and, as it set, bore that light off to the souls below.

## · MARCANTONIO FLAMINIO ·

### : 22 :

Formosa myrte roscido imminens antro,
antrum loquaci suave murmurans fonte,
fons care, fletu facte amare de nostro,
O quam beate viximus quoad vixit
5   Hyella vestra, quoad puella formosa
mecum iacere ista solebat in ripa!
Hic illa cum meo in sinu recumbebat,
mihique in aurem ludibunda cantabat,
tunc, tunc beatam viximus deum vitam,
10  tunc invidebat ipse Iuppiter nobis.
Nunc quis miserior solis aspicit lucem?
Quem saeviore Tartarus premit poena?
Seu vestit alma luce sol agros, seu nox
placida rigat gratis soporibus terras,
15  numquam remittit anxius dolor, numquam
meos ocellos recreat quies dulcis.
Ut pinguem olivam lentus ignis absumit,
sic cor misellum est cura saeva maerorque.
Quo dulcis abiit hei mihi decor vultus?
20  Quo niveus ille purpura color pictus,
Hyella quem suo anteire iurabat?
Iam lacrimae exsangues genas peredere,
modis et ora pallor inficit miris,
et illa pulchrior hyacinthino flore
25  inculta, squalens, hispidula coma horrescit.
Miser, ah miser Iola, tamen mori cessas?
Vitae ac dolori pone iam miser finem,
et illa vise regna quae colunt sancti
manes, ubi beata degitur vita

## · LATIN POEMS, BOOK IV ·

### : 22 :

Beautiful myrtle overhanging a dewy cave,
cave sweetly murmuring with the babble of a stream,
dear stream made bitter from my weeping,
O how happily I lived, as long as your Hyella lived,
as long as that beautiful girl                                      5
reclined with me on your bank!
When she used to lie here in my lap
and sing playfully in my ear,
then, then I lived the blessed life of the gods,
then Jupiter himself was envious of me.                            10
Now what more miserable wretch looks on the sunlight?
On whom does Tartarus inflict a harsher punishment?
Whether the sun clothes the fields with kindly light,
or still night floods the earth with welcome slumbers,
my anxious pain never abates,                                      15
sweet repose never refreshes my eyes.
As a slow fire consumes an oil-rich olive's wood,
so cruel care and sorrow devour my poor heart.
Where alas has my face's sweet beauty gone?
What has become of its snowy whiteness tinged with red            20
that Hyella used to vow surpassed her own?
Now tears have eaten away my bloodless cheeks,
a paleness strangely disfigures my face,
and that hair of mine once more beautiful than the hyacinth's
       flower
has become an unkempt, dirty, bristling shock.                    25
Poor, ah poor Iolas, do you, despite all, hesitate to die?
Put an end now to your life and pain,
and go to the realm where pious shades dwell,
where they live a happy life

· MARCANTONIO FLAMINIO ·

30  sub arborum semper virentium ramis,
    quis insusurrat dulce frigerans aura,
    quam Tethyos circumfluae parit lympha,
    at ipsa passim lucidos parit flores,
    quos lacte puro candidi educant rivi.
35  Illic puellae dulcibus iocis noctem
    diemque cum suis amantibus ducunt
    croceis amictae carbasis, pedes nudae,
    omnesque ramis myrteis coronatae.
    Semper choreis cantibusque iucundis,
40  semper cachinnis tinnulis sonant silvae.
    Has nec protervus Auster, imbribus fetus,
    nec cana nix, nec aestus impotens tangit;
    sed Ver beatas semper incolit sedes,
    flavas corollis mollibus comas cinctum,
45  laetosque Flora cum sua choros ducit,
    ningens rosarum suave olentibus nimbis.
    Huc te vocat puella maximis votis
    tuasque lentas increpat moras saepe.
    Valete, silvae, tuque, fons mihi care,
50  vale; vale, antrum; myrte floridula, salve.
    Moritur Iolas ille notus in silvis,
    peritus ore fistulaque cantare,
    moritur, suoque vos cruore respergit,
    qui lacteo vos ante rore spargebat,
55  qui vos amoenis floribus coronabat,
    docens Hyellam vos sonare formosam.
    At tu, puella, luce carior cara,
    qua mortua misero mihi mori est dulce,
    ades, tuisque manibus meos manes
60  amore iunge, Hyella candida, aeterno.

## · LATIN POEMS, BOOK IV ·

under the branches of trees that are always green,                    30
within which there whispers a pleasantly cooling breeze
produced by the waters of the encircling sea,
while the breeze itself produces bright flowers everywhere,
nourished into growth by streams white with pure milk.
There girls clad in yellow linen,                                     35
barefoot, and crowned with myrtle twigs,
spend night and day
in sweet dalliance with their lovers.
The woods constantly resound with pleasant dances,
singing, and ringing laughter.                                       40
Neither the wanton south wind, laden with rain,
nor white snow nor unbearable heat touches those woods,
but Spring constantly dwells in that blessed abode,
yellow hair ringed with a soft crown,
and, in company with Flora, weaves joyful dances,                    45
snowing fragrant showers of roses.
Here your girl calls you with the most earnest entreaties
and often chides your sluggish delays.
Farewell, woods; and you, spring dear to my heart,
farewell; farewell, cave; flowery myrtle, adieu.                     50
Iolas dies, that well-known figure in the woods,
skilled at rendering a song with lips and pipe.
He dies and sprinkles you with his blood
who formerly would sprinkle you with a milky dew
and crown you with lovely flowers,                                   55
teaching you to echo the name of beautiful Hyella.
But you, girl, dearer than dear life,
after whose death it is sweet to me in my misery to die,
be there to meet me, and join my ghost to yours,
beautiful Hyella, in love everlasting.                               60

## · MARCANTONIO FLAMINIO ·

### : 23 :

Hos calamos, Pan silvipotens, tibi pulcher Iolas,
    saepe quibus cecinit dulcia furta tua,
dum Cytherea potens et cara sinebat Hyella.
    Quae postquam dira tabe peresa iacet,
5  pro dulci Musa, pro carminibus iucundis,
    flebilibus complet vocibus ille nemus,
et, dominam cupiens imas invisere ad umbras,
    non somnos oculis, non capit ore cibum.
At tu, fortunam pueri miseratus acerbam,
10    aeternos pietas si movet ulla deos,
aut misero tantos aufer, bone dive, dolores,
    aut illum silvas transfer in Elysias.
Sed potius longum vivat formosus in aevum,
    et cantet laudes semper, Hyella, tuas.
15  Dignior haud ullus talem celebrare puellam,
    ulla nec est tali dignior ore cani.

### : 24 :

Hanc laurum, formosa, tibi formosus Iolas
    sevit, et hanc madidis irrigat usque genis.
Seu tenebras Vesper, seu lucem portat Eous,
    et laurum lacrimis irrigat et tumulum.
5  Hinc tumulus violas, et laurus protulit umbras;
    umbrae isdem crescunt et violae lacrimis.

## · LATIN POEMS, BOOK IV ·

### : 23 :

To you, Pan, the woodland's lord, handsome Iolas dedicates these
    reeds
  with which he many a time sang of your amorous intrigues
while mighty Cytherea and dear Hyella allowed.
  Now that she is dead, consumed by dreadful wasting,
in place of a sweet Muse, and in place of cheery songs, 5
  he fills the wood with tearful strains,
and, longing to visit the shadows deep below to see his lady,
  he takes no sleep with his eyes, no food with his mouth.
But pity the boy's bitter misfortune,
  if any compassion moves the everlasting gods, 10
and either take such great pain from the poor wretch, kind deity,
  or transport him to the woods of Elysium.
But rather let the handsome youth live a long life
  and ever sing your praises, Hyella.
No other is worthier to celebrate such a girl, 15
  nor is any other girl worthier to be sung by such lips.

### : 24 :

Handsome Iolas planted this laurel, beautiful girl, in your honor
  and constantly waters it with his dripping cheeks.
Whether the evening star brings the darkness, or the morning
    star the light,
  he waters both the laurel and your grave mound with his tears.
The mound has thus put forth violets, and the laurel shady 5
    foliage;
  the foliage and the violets grow with the same tears;

· MARCANTONIO FLAMINIO ·

Cumque umbris violisque amor infelicis Iolae
  crescit, cumque ipso crescit amore dolor.
Hic dolor heu miserum leto dabit, hic, bona Hyella,
  mox pueri apponet ossibus ossa tuis;
et quos felici coniunxit foedere quondam,
  nunc infelici funere iunget amor.

: 25 :

Haec, dulcissime Turriane, lusi
molli carmine nec laborioso,
dum ver florida laetum agebat aetas,
quam iocus decet ac leves cachinni.
Nunc Musas vocor ad severiores,
nunc rerum iuvat explicare causas,
et caelum memorare caelitesque,
et qui caelitibus praeest beatis.
O molles elegi lyraeque dulces,
O et myrtea serta fistulaeque
Faunique Dryadesque, iam valete,
et cum frondiferis Hyella silvis.
At tu, progenies Iovis supremi,
patris deliciae deumque amores,
per quam magna canunt sacri poetae,
felix Uranie, mihi benigno
ades numine, supplicemque tolle
me tuo rutilante curru ad astra.

## · LATIN POEMS, BOOK IV ·

and with the foliage and the violets grows unhappy Iolas' love,
    and with that very love grows his pain.
This pain alas will cause the poor boy's death; this pain, good
      Hyella,
    will soon lay his bones next to yours;          10
and those whom love once united in a happy bond,
    it will now unite in unhappy death.

:  25  :

These poems, sweetest della Torre, I playfully composed
in gentle verse demanding little effort
while flowering youth was in its cheery spring,
a time for gaiety and lighthearted laughter.
Now I am called to more serious themes,          5
now I would explain the causes of things
and tell of heaven, heaven's denizens,
and him who rules over the blessed ones above.
O soft elegies and sweet lyre songs,
O garlands of myrtle, pipes,          10
fauns, and dryads, now farewell,
and Hyella too, along with leafy woods.
Good Urania, supreme Jupiter's daughter,
your father's darling and the love of deities,
you who empower holy poets to sing of great matters,          15
aid me with your kindly divine power,
and raise me, your suppliant,
in your golden chariot to the stars.

# *Abbreviations*

The following abbreviations have been used throughout this volume for ease of reference.

| | |
|---|---|
| F. | Flaminio |
| N. | Navagero |
| Scorsone | Flaminio 1993 |
| | |
| n | note. Thus 32n = headnote to poem 32; 32.3n = note on poem 32, line 3. |

References to the printed texts of Navagero and Flaminio follow Author-Date format, e.g., Navagero 1718 and Flaminio 1727. Full publication details are listed in the Bibliography. Additional bibliographical information for the major editions can be found in the Handlist of Editions, Translations, Anthologies, and Further Reading.

Manuscripts are generally denoted by the abbreviations explained in Manuscripts with Latin Poems of Navagero, e.g., Vat.2 and Mil.3 refer to particular manuscripts at the Vatican Library and in Milan, respectively.

References to ancient Latin or Greek authors and works are generally in abbreviated form following the standards of the *Oxford Classical Dictionary*, such as Ov. = Ovid, Prop. = Propertius, *Aen.* = *Aeneid*, *Met.* = *Metamorphoses*, etc. The author's name and the title of the work cited can be found in full in the appropriate index. The names of Neo-Latin authors other than Navagero and Flaminio are not abbreviated (e.g., Fracastoro, Pontano). Titles of their works are always given in full.

# Note on the Texts

### NAVAGERO

The *editio princeps* (Venice, 1530 = Navagero 1530) printed forty-four of Navagero's poems, those numbered here 1–30, 32–38, and 41–47, titling them collectively *Lusus*, a general term for light verse. As that edition was prepared for publication "by the efforts of friends" (*amicorum cura*), it seems safe to assume that all the poems published in 1530 are genuinely Navagero's. Poems 31, 39, and 40 were not included in Navagero 1530, but were added to the corpus in the Volpi brothers' Padua, 1718 ed. (= Navagero 1718). Of these three poems, 31 had been printed as Navagero's, from a MS now seemingly lost, by Lorenzo Pignoria in *Le origini di Padova* (Padua, 1625 = Pignoria 1625). Poem 39 had been inserted amid the 1530 ed. poems by Gagny in his collection *Doctissimorum Nostra Aetate Italorum Epigrammata* (Paris, ca. 1548 = Gagny ca. 1548), while 40 had been separately printed as Navagero's by Ubaldini in his anthology *Carmina Poetarum Nobilium* (Milan, 1563 = Ubaldini 1563). Both 39 and 40 had been printed unsourced, and neither is found in surviving MSS; their attribution to Navagero depends on trusting Gagny and Ubaldini.

The editor of Navagero 1718, Giovanni Antonio Volpi, seems to have thought it too laborious and perhaps even ultimately futile to search MSS in libraries on the chance that any further Latin poems ascribed to Navagero had survived beyond those already in print. In fact, a considerable number had. A few were obscurely published later in the eighteenth century, but many more were first printed by Maria Antonietta Benassi in 1940 (= Benassi 1940) and Claudio Griggio in 1976–77 (= Griggio 1976–77). I include these additional poems as "Further Poems Ascribed to Navagero," giving them the numbers 48–69. Some of them are uncertainly or even improbably ascribed to him. Only one was printed in Navagero's lifetime: 48, his boyhood tribute to Bartolomeo Merula, which appeared at the end of Merula's exposition of Ovid's *Tristia* (Venice, 1499 = Merula 1499); the poem was further printed anew in 1779. Though it

· NOTE ON THE TEXTS ·

lacks MS evidence, it is certainly by Navagero. Poem 49 was printed unsourced in the Rome 1553 and Basel 1555 eds. of Basilio Zanchi's poems (= Zanchi 1553 and Zanchi 1555); it appeared again in print in Gualtieri 1786 and is also in five MSS. Poems 50–53 were printed as Navagero's, from the MS here called Vat.I, in Giovanni Cinelli Calvoli's *Biblioteca Volante* (= Cinelli Calvoli 1736); all of them appear in four or more MSS. Poems 54 and 55 are extant in four MSS and seem reliably attributed to Navagero, though three of the MSS for 55 weaken their authority by wrongly treating a known poem of Fracastoro as Navagero's. Poem 56 is found in three MSS, 57 in four. Poems 58A–69 have less MS evidence. Poems 58A and 58B survive in just one MS each, as do 59–64 (59 and 60 come from Vat.II; 61–64 from Mil.2). The textually unsatisfactory 65 is also found in just one MS. Navagero, if really its author, cannot have intended it to stand in its present form. In the single MS containing 66 it is not clear that it is actually intended to be taken as Navagero's. Poem 67, an epitaph for a dog, was printed, unsourced, as Navagero's in a Venice, 1826 compilation of verse or prose pieces written by dog lovers (*Rime e prose di alcuni cinofili vicentini e di altri illustri italiani*), but it seems very dubiously ascribed, as it occurs in print in a 1613 compilation of epitaphs (*Flores Illustrium Epitaphiorum*) as anonymous and linked to Siena, and there is no MS evidence for it. It is hard to feel any confidence that 68 is really Navagero's, even though it is ascribed to him in the one MS that includes it; the poem appears in print in several early anthologies from 1560 onward, initially as anonymous, later as Marcantonio Casanova's. One of the two MSS containing 69 attributes it to Navagero, the other to Trissino, making its authorship uncertain, though Trissino probably has the better claim; it was printed from that MS as Trissino's in 1736.

A few other poems are ascribed to Navagero in certain MSS, but the ascriptions are plainly erroneous, as the true authors are known from elsewhere, and the poems are therefore not given in this volume. These include the mistaken ascription, to Navagero himself rather than to Fracastoro, in a MS at Udine of the first interlude sung by a boy at Navagero's bidding in Fracastoro's *Naugerius, sive De Poetica* (see 19.41n). Three MSS wrongly treat a poem of Fracastoro addressed to Julius III (pope

214

## · NOTE ON THE TEXTS ·

long after Navagero died) as Navagero's. A single MS at Venice (Marc. lat. XII 248 = 10625, fol. 132r) erroneously gives an echo poem (*Quae celebrat thermas, etc.*) actually by Evangelista Maddaleni de' Capodiferro, called Fausto, under the heading *Echo Naugerii*. That poem is commonly treated in MSS and early printed anthologies as of uncertain authorship and has also been wrongly ascribed to Pietro Bembo; see Chatfield 2005, 174. It is from Maddaleni's *Thermae* (Baths), its presence in the autograph MS Vat. lat. 3419 (fol. 11r–v) making it clear that it is his.

In preparing the Latin text of Navagero's poems, I have completed a full survey of readings from as many editions and known MSS as possible. For the Navagero poems included in Navagero 1718 (poems 1–47), I have collated the printed versions against available MS versions. In dealing with textual variants, I have generally not rejected the 1718 text in favor of different MS readings unless the latter are clearly preferable, choosing instead merely to record the differences in the apparatus below. Where variants seemed more or less equally credible, I have mostly thought it better to leave the readings of the "traditional" printed text of Navagero's poems unaltered. For poems 48–69 ("Further Poems Ascribed to Navagero"), I have collated all available versions, recording meaningful variants in the apparatus below. Trivial differences and obvious slips of no critical importance are mostly omitted in the survey of readings; a few are recorded either to give a complete picture of the range of variants in a particular line or (selectively) to illustrate just how inept some blunders in these MSS can be. Discrepancies of spelling, including of proper names, are generally not listed unless considered to be particularly noteworthy. A full list of editions is included in the Handlist of Editions, Translations, Anthologies, and Further Reading. A list of MSS consulted appears in Manuscripts with Latin Poems of Navagero. I do not record any different readings in Wilson 1997, as the present volume entirely supersedes that in all textual matters.

### FLAMINIO

The eight books of Flaminio's Latin verse, as we now count them, were published in anthologies and collections before being collected in *Marci Antonii Flaminii Forocorneliensis, Poetae Celeberrimi, Carminum Libri VIII*, ed.

## · NOTE ON THE TEXTS ·

Francesco Maria Mancurti (Padua, 1727 = Flaminio 1727). As there is no reason to doubt the reliability of this edition, I follow its readings. Apart from some adjustments of spelling and punctuation, I depart from the text of Mancurti's text in Flaminio 1727 only once.

A note on numbering: The bk. 3 poems are here numbered as in the first Mancurti ed. (Flaminio 1727) or the 1740 ed. of the poems (Fracastoro 1740) and derived eds. (Fracastoro 1747, 1759, and 1782), which include five poems (here 3.3, 4, 14, 18, and 20) not given by Mancurti in his second ed. (Flaminio 1743). Scorsone, in his 1993 ed. (Flaminio 1993), favors the same numbering; Maddison 1965, however, follows the numbering system in Mancurti's second ed. (Flaminio 1743). In the Notes to the Translations, Flaminio's poems are referred to consistently according to the numbering system in this volume. Thus when Maddison's interpretation of, e.g., F. 3.19, is discussed, the reference is always to 3.19 and not to her numbering of 3.15. When the numbering in Scorsone's ed. (Flaminio 1993) is different, I note this in parentheses, e.g., F. 5.25 (5.26 Scorsone). To assist the reader, I provide a table of parallel numbering systems in the Concordances.

# Notes to the Texts

## NAVAGERO

### LATIN POEMS IN THE 1718 EDITION

2.2. blando strepitis *Vat.1*; strepitis blando *other MSS, eds., Giovio in Tiraboschi 1795–96, 7:1608*

2.3. rusticus haec *at start Flo.ML.*; serta dat haec *other MSS, eds., Giovio in Tiraboschi 1795–96, 7:1608*

2.5. secernite *Ven.2*; seiungite *other MSS, eds., Giovio in Tiraboschi 1795–96, 7:1608*

3.7. quamquam *Bol.U.* (*v. meter*), quamquam etiam *Vat.11*; cum (*or* quum) tamen *other MSS, eds.*

4.3. dedicat *Berg., Mil.1, Wro.*; consecrat *other MSS, eds.*

6.1. qui *Bol.U.*; quod *other MSS, eds.*

6.2. sancta manus *Mil.1* (*ineptly*); sancta Venus *other MSS, eds.*

6.3. mane *Berg., Bol.U., Mil.1, Vat.7 and 8, Wro.* (*and, miscopied as* matre, *Vat.11, which also corrupts* tria *to* tua); sensim *other MSS, eds.*

6.5–6. seretur / incisa hoc myrtus carmine, diva, tibi (*"a myrtle will be planted in your honor inscribed with this poem, goddess"*) *Vat.7* (*and, with trivial slips, Vat.11*); dicabo / inscripta myrtum te, Cytherea, tibi (*"I will dedicate to you, Cytherea, a myrtle with you inscribed upon it"*); dicabo . . . tibi (*as in text*) *other MSS, eds.*

6.7–8. *Bol.U. has this:*

'Hanc myrtum pastor Thyrsis quod amore potitus
datque simul Veneri seque suosque preces [*read* greges].'

(*"This myrtle the shepherd Thyrsis, in thanks for having enjoyed his love's favors, / gives to Venus, and together with it both himself and his prayers [read flocks]"*); *Vat.7 has as Bol.U. in 7, then this in 8:* dedicat et Veneri seque suosque greges; *other MSS and eds. as text*

217

## · NOTES TO THE TEXTS ·

7. *treated as end of 6 Mil.1*

9.3. pendentibus *Si.*; frondentibus *other MSS, eds., Giovio in Tiraboschi 1795–96, 7:1608*

9.4. crebrior *Si., Vat.1 and 11 (all three omit* est; *so too Giovio in Tiraboschi 1795–96, 7:1608), Ven.2, Wro.*; gratior *other MSS, eds.*

9.5. orbe *Si., Vat.1 and 11, Ven.1, Wro., Giovio in Tiraboschi 1795–96, 7:1608*; axe *other MSS, eds.*

9.7–10. *treated as a complete poem in itself Mil.1*

9.9. umbra auraque recenti *Mil.1, Si., Vat.1 (the last with* umbraque *v. meter) and 11, Ven.1, Wro., Giovio in Tiraboschi 1795–96, 7:1608*; aura umbraque virenti *other MSS, eds.*

9.10. perspicuo *MSS, eds.*; exiguo *Giovio in Tiraboschi 1795–96, 7:1608 (a slip?)*

10A.7. ipse *Pignoria 1625*; ille *otherwise*

12.1. ut primum *Duchesne 1560*; cum primum *MSS, other eds.*

12.2. est *om. Berg.*; *present otherwise*

12.5. quid tibi vis referam? *Duchesne 1560*; afferri tibi vis *MSS and other eds.*; niveos croceosve *Berg., Vat.8, Wro., Duchesne 1560*; niveos croceosque *Mil.1*; croceos niveosque *Vat.11, Gagny ca. 1548*; croceos niveosve *Vat.1, most eds. (incl. Navagero 1530)*

13.1. conformes animi cordisque unius amantes *Mil.2*; *other MSS and eds. as text*

13.8. gerunt *Mil.2*; ferunt *other MSS, eds.*

14.2. docta *Vat.1*; certa *other MSS, eds.*

14.9. laevo *Vat.11*; dextro *other MSS, eds.*

15.2. effusi *Vat.7 and 11 (*effussi *Bol.U.)*; expressi *other MSS, eds.*

19.6. Aion *Mil.1 (same error in title)*; Acon *Wro., eds.*

19.11. duros *Wro., eds.*; nostros *Mil.1*

19.13. mirum est *Mil.1, Wro.*; est *om. eds.*

19.15. serto connectis *Mil.1, Wro.*; strophio subnectis *eds.*

## · NOTES TO THE TEXTS ·

19.25. per grandia saxa *Periander 1567*; tecum per saxa *Mil.1, Wro., other eds.*

19.31. alma parens *Mil.1, Wro*; Magna Parens *eds.*

19.41. immitis *Mil.1, Wro.*; crudelis *eds.*

19.44. me tuus hic, scaeva, perurit amor *Mil.1, Wro.*; me iste tuus, perfida, torret amor *eds.*

19.45. umbra *Mil.1*; umbras *Wro., eds.*

19.46. ex se *Mil.1, Wro.*; per se *eds.*

19.47. solito *Mil.1, Wro.*; niveo *eds.*

19.48. promisso *Fracastoro 1759 (perhaps fortuitously)*; permisso *Mil.1, Wro., other eds.*

20.1. undis *Bol.U.*; antris *other MSS, eds.*

20.2. umbra *(miswritten as* umbaa*) Wro.*; herba *other MSS, eds.*

20.5. viduata *eds.*; violata *MSS*

20.10. cottidie *or* quottidie *MSS*; assidue *eds.*

20.11. tunc equidem *Bol.U., Vat.4, Ver.*; tunc reor *Mil.1, Vat.6, Wro.*; tum reor *eds.*

20.15. satyri faunique *Mil.1, Wro.*; fauni satyrique *other MSS, eds.*

20.26. miserabile dictu *MSS*; miserabile visu *eds.*

20.29 and 30. pro . . . paliuri *om. Bol.U., thus following* cytiso *with* et acuta

20.31. liquidis *Vat.6*; nitidis *(slip* nitibus *Mil.1) other MSS, eds.*

20.34–35. hanc Italis cladem *(slip* -vem *Vat.6)* deus avertisset ab agris (oris *Wro.*), / nunc etiam nostros fines (nostros etiam *Ver.*, fines nostros *Mil.1, Wro.*) gens saeva teneret *MSS; eds. as text*

20.38. laeta *replaced by* nota *Wro.*; nota *other MSS, eds.*

20.44. cunctisque *MSS*; nostrisque *eds.*

20.47. umquam *Bol.U.*; usquam *other MSS, eds.*

20.55. teneros qui non *Mil.1*; qui non teneros *other MSS, eds.*

20.61. ripa *and* molli *interchanged Bol.U.; as text other MSS, eds.*

## · NOTES TO THE TEXTS ·

20.63. vario volucrum resonant *Vat.6*; *line om. Mil.1*; *as text other MSS, eds.*

20.65. pecorum *Bol.U., Vat.4 and 6, Ver.*; pecudum *other MSS, eds.*

20.67. palaestra *Wro., eds.*; palaestrae *other MSS*

20.68. pecu *eds.*; pecum *Mil.1*; pedo *other MSS*

20.71. *om. Mil.1*; *present in other MSS, eds.*

20.81. agris *Mil.1 (and with* rv *above Wro.), eds.*; arvis *other MSS*

21.1. mea Hyella (Hiela *Berg.*; Lixella *Bol.U.*; Scylla *Mil.1*) *most MSS, eds.*; Isabella *(without* mea) *Jesi (regular printed text in margin)*

21.2. traxit *Jesi*; texit *other MSS, eds.*; mixta *Vat.1*; plena *Jesi*; cana *other MSS, eds. (Jesi has* texit *and* cana *in margin)*

21.3. vidit *(regular printed text in margin) Jesi*; invenit *other MSS, eds.*

21.9–10. *om. Bel.1, Jesi (added in latter's margin from a printed text)*; *present in other MSS, eds.*

21.11. mea quaere novum tibi *most MSS, eds.*; mea quaere alium tibi *Mil.1, Wro.*; tibi quaere alium, mea *(printed text in margin) Jesi*; mea quaere alium iam *Berg.*

25.46. levi *Mil.3 (v. meter)*; leni *eds.*

26.73. convicia dicere *some eds., incl. Navagero 1530, Gagny ca. 1548, Duchesne 1560, Periander 1567, and Navagero 1718 (and derivatives)*; convivia ducere *Mil.3, other eds., incl. Carmina Quinque Illustrium Poetarum 1548 (and 1549, 1552, and 1558), Toscano 1576, Gruter 1608, and Fracastoro 1740 (and derivatives)*

27.8. pascunt *Mil.1, Vat.11*; pascent *Mil.3, eds.*

27.12. *om. Vat.11, which also omits 66, 68, and 70; all present in other MSS, eds.*

27.16. et passim *Vat.11*; ex(s)ultim *Mil.1 and 3, eds.*

27.17. lascivaeque agnae atque infirmis *Vat.11*; lasivique *(sic)* agni atque infimis *(sic)* artubus haedi *Mil.1*; lascivique agni infirmisque artubus haedi *Mil.3, eds.*

27.31. dum *Mil.1*; quum *Vat.11*; qui *Mil.3, eds.*: imo *Vat.11*; alto *Mil.1 and 3, eds.*

27.32. devia *Mil.1*; levia *Mil.3, Vat.11, eds.*

## · NOTES TO THE TEXTS ·

27.51. meum . . . amorem *Mil.1, Vat.11*; meos . . . amores *Mil.3, eds.*

27.69. pomum *Vat.11 (v. meter)*; pyrum *or* pirum *Mil.1 and 3, eds.*

27.75. his *Mil.1, Vat.11*; haec *Mil.3, eds.*

27.76. mutabit *Vat.11*; mutarit *Mil.1 and 3, eds.*

27.78. nunc *Vat.11*; nos *Mil.1 and 3, eds.*

28.5. nam *Mil.1, Wro.*; quod *Salz., Vat.14, eds.*

28.8. nescio quo torpet *Mil.1*; torpet nescio quo *Salz., Vat.14, Wro., eds.*

28.9. unum dissimilis (*without following* est) *Mil.1*; unum dissimilis *with following* est *deleted Wro.*; unum dissimile est *Salz., Vat.14, eds.*; nobis foelicior *with comma before* nobis *Mil.1*; *with colon instead after* nobis *Salz., Vat.14, eds.*; *with no punctuation Wro.*; *at end* uno est *Salz., Vat.14, Wro., eds.*; nemo est *Mil.1 (ineptly)*

28.11–14. *om. Vat.14; present in other MSS, eds.*

28.11. uretur, qm (*with stroke over;* = quoniam?) sub lumine quaq(ue) *Mil.1 (ineptly)*; *as text Salz., Wro., eds., Wro. with* qsq (= quisque) *deleted before* quicquam (*abbrev.*)

28.12. esse *Mil.1, Wro.*; ire *Salz., eds.*

29.5–6. quae vera nonnumquam assolent mortalibus / mitti futura nuntia *Mil.1, Wro.*; *as text Bol.U., Vat.9, eds.*

29.7. fiet mens *Mil.1 (ineptly)*; freto meas *Bol.U., Vat.9, Wro., eds.*

29.14. afficies *Mil.1, Wro.*; afficias *Bol.U., Vat.9, eds.*

29.21. ut libet (*cf. 38.3 and 5*) *Mil.1, Wro.*; quamlibet *Bol.U., Vat.9, eds.*

30.14. sed quid (*without question mark*) *Vat.9 and 11, Navagero 1530, Carmina Quinque Illustrium Poetarum 1548 and 1549, Fracastoro 1555, Navagero 1718, Carmina Quinque Illustrium Poetarum 1753*; sed quid? (*with question mark*) *Gagny ca. 1548, Duchesne 1560*; sed qui *Carmina Quinque Illustrium Poetarum 1552 and 1558, Toscano 1576, Blijenburgh 1600, Gruter 1608, Carmina Illustrium Poetarum Italorum 1720, Fracastoro 1740 and derivatives*

30.17. beate *Vat.11*; bene ipsi *Vat.9, eds.*

31.29. (h)umeris *Mil.2*; (h)umero *Pignoria 1625, Navagero 1718, etc.*

## · NOTES TO THE TEXTS ·

31.30a and 30b. *present in* Mil.2; *om. Pignoria 1625, Navagero 1718, etc.*

31.33. *lacuna between* Venerem *and* choreae *Pignoria 1625;* decent *(conj. margin Navagero 1718) Mil.2*

31.39. tu cultis *Mil.2;* incultis *Pignoria 1625, Navagero 1718, etc.*

31.42. saevientis *Mil.2 with* pestilentis *in margin;* pestilentis *Pignoria 1625, Navagero 1718, etc.*

33.1. omni *Mil.1, Wro.;* ipsa *(in Vat.8 above deleted* omni*) other MSS, eds.*

33.3. omni *Mil.1, Wro.;* ipsa *other MSS, eds.*

33.5 *and* 7. vellem quicquam his potis esset *Mil.1, Vat.8 and 11, Wro.;* vellem pote quicquam his esset *Salz., Vat.9, eds.*

33.9. duret *all MSS (above deleted* vivat *Vat.8), eds.*

34.7–8. quo *Vat.14, eds.;* quod *is my conjecture*

36.6. iratum *MSS;* iratus *eds.*

36.9. fors *Vat.11, most eds., Navagero 1530 onward;* sors *with comma following, Vat.1;* sors *with colon preceding, Carmina Illustrium Poetarum Italorum 1720;* sors *with comma preceding, Costa 1888*

36.11. clarius puro *MSS;* purius claro *eds.*

37.15. flaventes *most eds., incl. Navagero 1530 (Navagero 1718 and derivatives note* lucentes *in margin);* lucentes *Toscano 1576, Gruter 1608, Anthologia 1684;* fluentes *(v. meter) Carmina Quinque Illustrium Poetarum 1552 (further corrupted to* fluente *in 1558 ed. of same), Periander 1567*

38.4. Tetydos *Mil.3 (slip);* Thethyos *Navagero 1530, Fracastoro 1555;* Thetyos *Navagero 1718, Carmina Quinque Illustrium Poetarum 1753, Navagero 1754, Salz. (from Navagero 1718?);* Tethyos *Gagny ca. 1548, Carmina Quinque Illustrium Poetarum 1548 (and 1549, 1552, and 1558), Periander 1567, Toscano 1576, Blijenburgh 1600, Gruter 1608, Fracastoro 1740, etc.;* Tetyos *Carmina Illustrium Poetarum Italorum 1720, perhaps a misprint*

39.5. semiaperta *Gagny ca. 1548; lacuna (with* semiaperta *noted as unmetrical) Navagero 1718 and derivatives, including Carmina Illustrium Poetarum Italorum 1720*

39.9–10. qui redis ad patrios *Gagny ca. 1548, Navagero 1718 (and 1753, 1754); rewritten as* qui ad patrios tendis *Carmina Illustrium Poetarum Italorum 1720*

222

# · NOTES TO THE TEXTS ·

42.5. id *Vat.14, most eds.*; in *Navagero 1754 (not 1718), an apparent misprint, though adopted in Perosa/Sparrow 1979*

43.1. Borgettus *Navagero 1530, Carmina Quinque Illustrium Poetarum 1548 (and 1549, 1552, and 1558), Fracastoro 1555, Toscano 1576, Gruter 1608, Navagero 1718 and derived eds.*; Borgetus *Gagny ca. 1548, Duchesne 1560, Fracastoro 1740 and derived eds.*

44.61. proruit *eds.*; proluit *in the model (Verg. G. 1.481)*

46.10. ratio habenda *(v. meter) Navagero 1530 and other sixteenth-century texts, Fracastoro 1740 and derivatives, Vat.9*; habenda ratio *Gruter 1608, Navagero 1718 and derivatives*

## Further Poems Ascribed to Navagero

49.1. flavo dum vertice *Mil.1, Wro.*; dum flavo e vertice *other MSS and Zanchi 1553*

50.1. assiste *Mil.2, Vat.1 and 6*; consiste *Ud., Cinelli Calvoli 1736 (Scanzia 22)*

50.4. mimus *Vat.1, Cinelli Calvoli 1736 (ineptly)*; munus *Mil.2, Vat.6 and, corr. from mimus, Ud.*; Illyrico *Mil.2*; Aeolio *other MSS, Cinelli Calvoli 1736*

50.6. nitidi *Mil.2*; nivei *other MSS, Cinelli Calvoli 1736*

50.10. nomen *(in full) Mil.2, Ud., (abbreviated) Vat.1 and 6*; nomine *Cinelli Calvoli 1736 (and Benassi 1940)*

51.3. qui cum *Mil.2*; quocum *other MSS, Cinelli Calvoli 1736*; animum oblectat *Vat.1, Cinelli Calvoli 1736*; animum oblectabat *other MSS*

53.1. non . . . non *Si., Vat.10*; non . . . nec *other MSS, Cinelli Calvoli 1736, Gualtieri 1786*

53.2. gero *Vat.11*; geram *other MSS, Cinelli Calvoli 1736, Gualtieri 1786*

53.3. consertas *Si.*; confertas *other MSS, Cinelli Calvoli 1736, Gualtieri 1786*

53.4. perferar *Si.*; deferar *other MSS, Cinelli Calvoli 1736, Gualtieri 1786*; in media damna *Vat.1 (v. meter)*; in mea damna *Nap., Gualtieri 1786*; in media arma *Si., Ud., Vat.10 and 11, Cinelli Calvoli 1736*

53.5. vere *MSS, Cinelli Calvoli 1736, Gualtieri 1786*; vera *Benassi 1940 (a slip?)*

54.8. pias *Mil.1, Vat.11, Wro.*; suas *Si.*

55.9. nectatur *Trev.1 and 2, Vien.*; flectatur *Lon.*

# · NOTES TO THE TEXTS ·

55.10. immite *Trev.1 and 2, Vien.*; immites *Lon.*

55.11. quaque *Trev.1 and 2, Vien.*; quique *Lon.*

55.18. pangit *Trev.1 and 2, Vien.*; tangit *Lon.*

55.21. oculis *Trev.1 and 2, Vien.*; oculi *Lon.*

55.23. naturam *Trev.1 and 2, Vien.*, naturas *Lon.*

55.30. morior *Trev.1 and 2, Lon.*; moriar *Vien.*

55.33. vel (*altered from* aut) non hospita *Trev.1*; aut inhospita *Trev.2 (all v. meter)*; vel inhospita *Lon., Vien.*

55.37. ora *Trev.1 and 2, Vien.*; ore *Lon.*

55.55. *Lon.*; *om. Trev.1 and 2, Vien.*

56.3. pictas modo teximus coronas *Bol.U., Mil.2*; vernas modo nectimus corollas *Si.*

56.6. nos *Bol.U., Mil.2*; non *Si.*

56.7. hic *Bol.U., Mil.2*; huc *Si.*

56.10. pectus miserum precor *Bol.U., Mil.2*; precor miserum pectus *Si. (v. meter)*

56.11. duris *Bol.U., Mil.2*; diris *Si.*

56.23. *Bol.U. (with* ambrosiae*), Mil.2 (with* ambrosiam*)*; *om. Si.*

57.5. sed certe fuge *Bel.2, Vat.8 (altered in latter from* ne certe fuge*) and 11*; ne recte fuge! *Mil.1*; ne certe fuge *Wro.*

57.11. rectus turgidulusque *Bel.2, Mil.1, Wro.*; rectus rigidusque (*v. meter*) *Vat.11 and (in margin after canceling* rectus turgidulusque*) Vat.8*

59.14. amo atqʼ (= atque) *Vat.11 (not* amo et [*v. meter*], *as Griggio 1976–77*)

59.15. resolvat *Vat.11*; resolvet *Griggio 1976–77*

59.17. iʼproba (= improba) *Vat.11 (as in 20), not* in prata, *as Griggio 1976–77*; basiem ocellos *Vat.11 (v. meter)*; *I add* hos (*cf.* haec *in 20*)

59.28. quis nunc *Vat.11 (not* quis nam, *as Griggio 1976–77*)

59.34. ecce *Vat.11 (not* cur, *as Griggio 1976–77*)

59.37. qʼd (= quid) *Vat.11 (not* quod, *as Griggio 1976–77*)

59.41. leniter *Vat.11 (v. meter)*; leviter *is my correction*

224

## · NOTES TO THE TEXTS ·

59.42. teretes *Vat.11 (not* teneras, *as Griggio 1976–77)*

59.43. tenero *Vat.11;* teneros *corr. Griggio 1976–77*

59.46. ductari *Vat.11;* ductare *corr. Griggio 1976–77*

59.50. amemur ambo *Vat.11 (not* amemus ambo, *as Griggio 1976–77)*

59.51. charitu *(for* Charitum*) Vat.11 (not* caritas, *as Griggio 1976–77)*

60.3. suffirus pirumve *Vat.11;* suffitusve pyramve *Sacré 1987; I suggest* suffitus spirare

60.4. insinuet ve *Vat.11;* insinuet ne *corr. Griggio 1976–77*

60.5. aer *(written* ær*) Vat.11;* aere *Sacré 1987;* tibi *Vat. 11; perhaps consider* sibi

60.6. dum *Vat.11;* diem *Griggio 1976–77;* deum *Sacré 1987; I suggest* deam

63.2. meent *Mil.2 (not* meant, *as Griggio 1976–77, as Sacré 1987 notes)*

65.1. educens *Lon. (not* conducens, *as Griggio 1976–77)*

65.4. *I read* mi *for* mihi *in Lon.*

65.5. *I read* leviter *for unmetrical* leniter *Lon.*

65.6. hic *Lon. (not* sic, *as Griggio 1976–77); slight damage to letter(s) before* eamus, *but* in- *probable (so Griggio 1976–77)*

65.10. hostii *(=* ostii; *not* postis, *as Griggio 1976–77) Lon.*

65.14. *MS damage in Lon. affecting word before* potus, *perhaps* fugare; *extinguere (as in Griggio 1976–77) is too long*

68.4. raptaque magnanimo est altera sorte pari *Duchesne 1560;* sorte nec alterius territus ille pari est *Man., Ubaldini 1563, Toscano 1576, Gruter 1608 (see N. 68.4n)*

68.8. *(after* manu) vivimus *Duchesne 1560, Ubaldini 1563, Toscano 1576, Gruter 1608;* vincimus *Man.*

69.5–8. *stanza accidentally om. Cinelli Calvoli 1736 (Scanzia 22); present in Bol.U., Vat.1*

69.6. pro me *Bol.U.;* prome *Vat.1;* qui *Bol.U.;* quis *Vat.1;* quo *Cinelli Calvoli 1736*

69.8. pulchiore' i *Bol.U.;* pulchrior exi *Vat.1*

225

## · NOTES TO THE TEXTS ·

69.9. tratalis *Bol.U.*; natalis *Vat.1*

69.15. poonat *Bol.U.*; ponat *Vat.1*; scaevos *Bol.U.*; saevos *Vat.1*

69.24. cultamque *Bol.U.*; cultaque *Vat.1*

69.25. proderit *Bol.U.*, *Vat.1*; prodeant *Cinelli Calvoli 1736*; *I conjecture* prodient

69.27. venientque *Bol.U.*; venietque *Vat.1*

69.28. sumus *Bol.U.*; summus *Vat.1*

69.29. precibus *Bol.U.*; manibus *Vat.1*

69.30. petes *Bol. U.*; potest *Vat.1*

69.31. nunc tu *Bol.U.*; i nunc *Vat.1* (*v. meter*); nunc i *Cinelli Calvoli 1736*

69.33. uti tibi divet *Bol.U.*; ut tibi duret *Vat.1*

69.34. formamque *Bol.U.*; formaque *Vat.1*; habeas *Bol.U.*; habens *Vat.1*; optes *Bol.U.*; optas *Vat.1*

69.35. caras *Bol.U.*; carus *Vat.1*

69.41. habeo *Bol.U.*, *Vat.1*; habeas *Cinelli Calvoli 1736*

69.43. ipsa *Bol.U.*, *Cinelli Calvoli 1736*; ipse *or* ipsae *Vat.1*

### FLAMINIO

### Latin Poems, Book III

3.17. hoc *Flaminio 1727 and 1743, and eds. generally from Carmina Quinque Illustrium Poetarum 1548 onward*; huc *is my conjecture*

# Notes to the Translations

🐟🐟🐟

### NAVAGERO

#### LATIN POEMS IN THE 1718 EDITION

I

Inspirations: Verg. G. 1.338–50 (the privately celebrated *Ambarvalia*, de-scribed also in Tib. 2.1.1–26); Ov. *Fast.* 1.658–96, including prayers to Mother Earth and Ceres on *Sementiva Dies*, "Seed-Sowing Day." Closely imitated by Joachim du Bellay (1522–60), *Divers jeux rustiques* 2, where poems 2–13 imitate, in order, Navagero's 1, 2, 11 (twice), 5, 3, 8, 13, 14, 10A, 6, and 28. Du Bellay's Latin eclogue *Votum Rusticum Iolas* (Rustic Vow Iolas) also has debts to this poem and 11. In a letter to Navagero, Bartolo-meo Ricci calls this poem "Ceres"; see Navagero 1718, 127–28. MSS: Salz., Vat.14.

Most of Navagero's poems are, like this one, in elegiac couplets. The exceptions are dactylic hexameters in 20, 27, 44, 47, and 55; Sapphic strophe in 36, 37, 41, and 69; Alcaic strophe in 35; stanzas of three Gly-conics and a Pherecratean in 34; alternating iambic trimeters and dime-ters (iambic strophe) in 29; iambic trimeters (senarii) in 45 and 46; and Phalaecean hendecasyllables in 30–32, 43, 52, 56, 57, 59, and 65.

2. *Rustica turba* (Ov. *Met.* 6.348) is in apposition to the subject ("we") within *ducimus*. The expression is in several other Neo-Latin poets, e.g., Pontano, *Eridanus* 1.36.36; Sannazaro, *Elegies* 2.8.20.

5. *Silva* ("forest") of weeds: Verg. G. 1.152; wild oats (*avenae*) are *steriles* in Verg. *Ecl.* 5.37 and G. 1.154; similarly Ov. *Fast.* 1.692.

7. The last three words combine Verg. G. 2.339 (*flatibus Euri*) and 441 (*animosi Euri*).

8. Ends as Ov. *Fast.* 5.322.

227

## · NOTES TO THE TRANSLATIONS ·

9–10. *Avidae . . . volucres* ("greedy birds") reflects Ov. *Met.* 5.484. Line 10 is after Verg. G. 1.184–85. *Monstra* need not imply great size. Both here and in the Vergilian source the context suggests that insect pests are meant; the gadfly is a *monstrum* in G. 3.152.

11–12. Common imagery from usury (cf. 16.6). The seed is capital loaned to the earth for greater return. Cf., for example, F. 6.63.21–22 (6.64.21–22 Scorsone) and lines 6–8 of his paraphrase of Psalm 128 (7.25 Scorsone; trans. McFarlane 1980, 96), as well as "Antonio Mario of Imola" (= Flaminio; see F. 3.15n), *Ad M. Plemmirium*, 21–22. Line 12 ends as Ov. *Rem. am.* 174 and *Fast.* 1.694 (cf. *Pont.* 1.5.26); Tib. 2.6.22.

13–14. Honeyed milk and wine offered to Ceres: Verg. G. 1.344. Ovidian echoes in *carchesia lactis* (*Met.* 7.247) and *annoso mella liquata mero*, combining *Fast.* 1.152 (*mella liquata*) and *Ars am.* 2.418 (*annoso . . . mero*). Milk is commonly called "snow-white" (Ov. *Met.* 13.829; *Fast.* 4.151 and 780). Cf. 11.2, 19.47 (variant *solito*), and 41.27–28.

15–16. Threefold circumambulation of the plow fields (*arva*) with the victim prior to its sacrifice gave the *Ambarvalia* its name (lit., "Around-the-fields rites"). Line 15 is almost identical to Verg. G. 1.345; line 16 ends almost as Prop. 2.19.14.

18. Ceres garlanded with wheat spikes: Ov. *Fast.* 4.616, *Am.* 3.10.36 (both, like Tib. 1.10.22, end almost as here and 13.4); Tib. 2.1.4.

2

Inspiration: *Anth. Pal.* 6.53 (Bacchylides), thanking the west wind for enabling winnowing. Name *Idmon*: Verg. *Aen.* 12.75; Ov. *Met.* 6.8, *Ib.* 506; etc. Much imitated, most notably by du Bellay, *Divers jeux rustiques*. Hutton 1946, 333–37, analyzes Navagero's poem, its source, and French derivatives; Hutton 1935, 190–91, 315, 354, and 462, notices Italian derivatives of Navagero or his source. What is thought to be a version in Italian by Bargaeus (Pietro Angeli da Barga, 1517–96) is given with others of 6, 7, 13, and 47 in Navagero 1718, 284, where they are all said to derive from the margin of a copy of Navagero 1530, the handwriting being identified by Apostolo Zeno (1669–1750) as that of Bargaeus. Nevertheless, Nava-

· NOTES TO THE TRANSLATIONS ·

gero 1782, an edition of Navagero's Italian verse, prints the same five poems as "commonly attributed" to Navagero himself. Paolo Giovio quotes and praises this present poem and 9 in his *Dialogus de Viris Litteris Illustribus* (Dialogue on Men Distinguished in Letters); see Tiraboschi 1795–96, 7:1608. Wiffen 1823, 385, has a free rendering in verse. Navagero's poem seems the model for that of "Antonio Mario of Imola" (= Flaminio; see F. 3.15n) entitled *Ad Nymphas Bononienses* (To the Nymphs of Bologna), likewise six lines, both in overall structure and especially in line 3, *liba dat haec vobis, vobis haec pulcher Iolas* ("Handsome Iolas gives these cakes to you, and to you he, etc."). MSS: Bel.2, Berg., Bol.U. (x 2), Flo.ML., Flo.Ric.1, Jesi, Man., Mil.1 and 3, Vat.1, 8, 11, and 14, Ven.2, Wro.

2. Cf. F. 3.10.6 for *blando . . . sono* of a breeze/breezes (Ov. *Her.* 16.260 has *blandis . . . sonis*). Pontano has the expression of birdsong in *Tumuli* 2.50.10.

3–4. Scattering flowers from baskets: 31.37–39 (cf. 41.37); F. 4.5.71–72; Pontano, *De Amore Coniugali* 3.3.152. *Croco* is a collective singular for plural.

5. *Vos lenite aestum* also begins F. 2.13.5. Verg. G. 3.134 has *paleae . . . inanes*.

6. Niccolò d'Arco, *Numeri* 1.35.4, is almost identical (*dum medio fruges ventilat aura die*).

### 3

Hanging up animal skins to Pan, sometimes with horns or antlers, figures in many *Anth. Pal.* bk. 6 dedications. Hutton 1935, 463, compares 6.57, where the skin is a lion's. Another common theme is the dedicator's age, often too great for former activities. Apology for a poor offering: *Anth. Pal.* 6.77, 98, and 152. Closely imitated by du Bellay, *Divers jeux rustiques*. Name *Iolas* (also in 27; generally so spelled in Renaissance poetry, as in MSS and eds. here, but anciently *Iollas*): Verg. *Ecl.* 2.57, 3.76, and 3.79; *Aen.* 11.640; also found in the eclogues of Calpurnius Siculus and Nemesianus and in the epigrams of Martial; used by several Neo-Latin and vernacular poets, including Flaminio. MSS: Bol.U. (x2), Mil.1, Vat.1, 8, 11, 12, and 14, Wro.

## · NOTES TO THE TRANSLATIONS ·

1. Pan as *montivagus*: Nemes. *Ecl*. 3.17 (cf. F. 4.2.14). Here the *e* of *montivage* is lengthened *in arsi* (see 20.48n).

2. *Comminus ire feras* (after Ov. *Fast*. 5.176) also ends 26.60, there without *in*.

3–4. *A quo* = "from whom," not "from which time" or "since," which is *ex quo* (cf. 19.44; F. 3.25.6 and 4.17.17; Marullo, *Epigrams* 1.13.4 and 8). *Suum* is gen. pl. of *sus* ("pig"). A boar's head and a stag's antlers are offerings in Verg. *Ecl*. 7.29–30. The pine, once the nymph Pitys, was sacred to Pan (cf. 5.10). *Agrestis* is gen. sing.

7. After Prop. 4.9.39. Hercules' labors included dealing with the Nemean lion, the Erymanthian boar, and the hind of Ceryneia. The club was his regular weapon.

### 4

Name *Damis*: *Anth. Pal*. (several poems). Imitated by du Bellay, *Divers jeux rustiques*. MSS: Berg., Bol.U., Man., Mil.1 and 3, Vat.7, 8, 11, and 14, Wro.

3. Either of the variants *dedicat* or *consecrat* would be satisfactory. For the former cf. 3.6 and 6.8; the latter is not found elsewhere in Navagero's poems, but seven of the ten MSS have it here.

4. Iacchus = Bacchus, as in 11.3.

### 5

Name *Lycon*: Theoc. *Id*. 2.76 and 5.8; *Anth. Pal*. 6.198, 7.112 (there the peripatetic philosopher), and 13.6. The Latin third declension dative *Crocali* (6) may imply a by-form nominative *Crocales*, like *Prognes* for *Progne*, or *Circes* for *Circe*, in some Neo-Latin poets, unclassically substituting Latin third declension forms for Greek first. The usual Greek first declension nominative is *Crocale* (Ov. *Met*. 3.169; *Anth. Pal*. 7.183; Calp. *Ecl*. 2.71 and 73), and the expected Latin first declension dative would be *Crocalae*, but Neo-Latin poets often take unclassical liberties with Greek names, more commonly in the accusative singular, where substitution of

## · NOTES TO THE TRANSLATIONS ·

Latin *m* for Greek final *n* is frequently seen. Cf. *Philyrem*, rather than *Philyren* (or *Philyram*), in 39.1, *Dionem* rather than *Dionen* in the MS text of 59.6, *Itym* for *Ityn* in 25.24, and *Calaim* for *Calain* in 25.58. This poem is imitated by du Bellay, *Divers jeux rustiques*, among others. Benedetto Varchi, *Carmina* 5, owes some inspiration to it. MS: Vat.14.

1–2. Verg. *Aen.* 11.544–45 has *iuga longa . . . nemorum*, suggesting that *nemorum* here should probably be construed with *per iuga longa*, but *devia nemorum* could alternatively go together ("remote forest regions"). T. V. Strozzi, *Erotica* 2.5.11 has *nemorum . . . devia*; Ov. *Met.* 1.479 has *nemorum avia*.

5–6. Young animals as love gifts: Polyphemus intends to give Galatea eleven fawns and four bear cubs in Theoc. *Id.* 11.40–41 (cf. the two bear cubs he has found and will keep for her in Ov. *Met.* 13.834–37); Corydon in Verg. *Ecl.* 2.40–44 keeps two kids found in a valley to give to Alexis. Finding the young under a rock: Ov. *Her.* 5.17–18. Verg. *Ecl.* 10.14 ends almost as 5.

9–10. In Longus, *Daphnis and Chloe* 2.31, a goatskin is hung up "complete with horns" on a pine to Pan (see also 3n). Pan is *semicaper* in Ov. *Met.* 14.515 and *semicaper . . . Nonacrius* in 26.45 below. Cf. *semicapri . . . dei* in F. 4.2.13 (with note there).

6

The name *Thyrsis* is borne by shepherds in Theoc. *Id.* 1 and Verg. *Ecl.* 7. It is also found in *Anth. Pal.* 7.703 and 9.432 and elsewhere. Flaminio (3.18.1) is among the Neo-Latin poets who use the name, including to represent himself in his eclogue *Thyrsis* (2.34); *Tirsi* is found in pastoral works in Italian. I do not find the by-form *Leucas* elsewhere, though Calp. *Ecl.* 1.13 has *Leuce*, and some Neo-Latin poets use that form or *Leucia*. A *Leucippe* occurs in 12. Imitated by du Bellay, *Divers jeux rustiques* 12. An Italian version thought to be by Bargaeus is given in Navagero 1718, 285 (see 2n). Wiffen 1823, 386, has a free translation in verse. MSS: Berg., Bol.U., Mil.1, Par.1, Salz., Vat.7, 8, 11, and 14, Wro. The variant endings of this poem suggest author revision, perhaps more than once.

# · NOTES TO THE TRANSLATIONS ·

2. Ov. *Her.* 17.25 has *non . . . fructum tulit petitum* ("he did not reap the reward sought") of Theseus' failure to get more than kisses by abducting the young Helen.

3. Fewer MSS read *sensim* than *mane*, but "gradually" or "softly" seems to have more point in context than "early in the morning," and *sensim* adds to the alliteration of the line. Both readings look like genuine variants. *Sensim* is used by Pontano (*Parthenopeus* 2.9.69) of the stealthy, tiptoeing approach of Pan to take liberties with a sleeping nymph. It is found in a context of clandestine approach in Tib. 1.8.59. *Sumere* used of taking kisses can have connotations of taking them presumptuously and illicitly, as, for example, in Ov. *Ars am.* 1.664: "Though she does not give them [= 'kisses'], yet take (*sume*) them not given."

4–5. For a girl's protective mother seen as an obstacle to lovemaking to be circumvented, cf. 12.9 and F. 3.13.1 and 3.18.1–2. Pontano, *Parthenopeus* 1.3.43–46, even speaks of frequent furtive entry to a house and sex with a girl in her own bed, her usually watchful mother asleep beside her. For *plena vota* ("full wishes"), cf. especially *plenum votum* in Ov. *Ars am.* 1.671 (and *ultima vota* in 7.4 here); and for *nil ultra* of sexual favors, cf. *ulterius nil* ("nothing more") in Ov. *Her.* 17.28. Promising a deity a better offering later, often for further favor: *Anth. Pal.* 6.41, 152, 190–91, 231, 238, 300, etc.; the theme is also in several Neo-Latin poets.

5–8. See Notes to the Texts for the substantial variants in the MSS here and their translation.

6–8. The myrtle was sacred to Venus; thus 41.25 speaks of planting a myrtle for her. Cf. 19.7, 20.59, and F. 4.24 (all involving planting trees). Carving on trees, whether by lovers, as in 27.74–77, or otherwise, as in 20.50, features quite often in both ancient and Renaissance poetry (as F. 4.17.17–18). Verg. *Ecl.* 10.52–54 and Ov. *Her.* 5.21–30 envisage verses cut into young trees growing with them, while improbably lengthy inscriptions on trees figure in Verg. *Ecl.* 5.20–44 and Calp. *Ecl.* 1.33–88. Line 8 here is echoed in Varchi, *Carmina* 73, where Corydon makes Venus modest gifts after lying once with a girl, but promises dedication of himself and his whole flock if allowed to enjoy her again. For the notion of dedi-

232

## · NOTES TO THE TRANSLATIONS ·

cating oneself to someone in gratitude, cf. also F. 6.42.14–15 (6.43.14–15 Scorsone) and 6.44.9–10 (6.45.9–10 Scorsone). In the latter Flaminio dedicates himself and his Muse in perennial service to his addressee. In 6.51.10–15 (6.52.10–15 Scorsone) Flaminio gratefully dedicates "my life, my whole self, and all mine to the last one" to the doctor who has saved him from death.

7

Sequel to 6. Italian version thought to be by Bargaeus: see 6n (and 2n). A good parallel for the pairing of "vow" poems before and after the granting of a prayer is furnished by Bargaeus in his *Votum Amyllae Nubentis* (The Vow of Amylla on Marrying) and *Persolutio Voti* (The Dischargement of the Vow); see Bargaeus 1568, 389–90. In the first, Amylla sprinkles flowers to the water nymphs and promises them roses every year if she can lose her virginity to her husband without hurt. In the second, having so lost her maidenhood, she gratefully fulfills that vow and further promises a newborn lamb if, whenever she and her husband have intercourse in future, "Iolas is quite unflagging in his vigor." William Drummond of Hawthornden (1585–1649) seems to reflect Navagero here, perhaps through a vernacular intermediary, in *Chlorus to a Grove*, which lauds the shady grove that "crowned" the speaker's desires when a girl lost her virginity to him there; see Drummond 1913, 1:121, and further on 38 and 49. Wiffen 1823, 386, converts the revered spot into the place where Thyrsis "first gained . . . his dear Leuca's marriage vows." Dunlop 1914, 161, dicusses Jean Vauquelin de la Fresnaye's debt to Navagero's poem in *Idillies et pastorales* 2.28. MSS: Berg., Bol.U., Mil.1, Vat.8 and 14, Wro.

3–4. *Quod . . . tulit* is for *se tulisse*, the normal accusative and infinitive construction. *Ultima vota*: 6.4–5n. In Giovanni Battista Pigna's *Ad Hyellam*, a poem seemingly inspired by more than one passage of Navagero, a youth speaks of hoping that night to secure his girlfriend's *ultima munera* (lit., "ultimate gifts") for the first time. The youth promises her presents brought from the city (cf. 12 here) if she will slip away from her sleeping

## · NOTES TO THE TRANSLATIONS ·

mother and meet him by the river now that darkness conceals *Veneris dulcia furta* (cf. 22.2). He speaks of carving an inscription, if successful in seducing her, to declare that riverside location the revered scene of his triumph and warn shepherds driving their flocks there to respect the adjacent waters. See Pigna 1553, 106–7.

8

Many Neo-Latin dog poems are collected in Dornau 1619, including this poem, 10A, and 43. I translate most of the dog poems in that collection along with others in Wilson 1998; the section on Navagero (pp. 40–45) includes this poem, 10A, 43, 50–51, and 67; F. 1.35 and 1.36 are in that volume too (pp. 60–63). See also 67n for this present poem, 10A, and 67 in Canoniero 1613. Navagero's dog poems (including 67, if truly his) are among those collected in Spila 2002. In *Anth. Pal.* 6.168 a vicious boar's hide is hung up to Pan; in 6.34 of the same a boar hunter dedicates to that god his weapons, some boar's feet, and a dog's collar. Many *Greek Anthology* sepulchral epigrams concern the burial of animals. Here Augon is male; *Augo* is a bitch's name in Xen. *Cyn.* 7.3. One Melampus was the mythical physician and soothsayer, but others occur. MS: Vat.14 (part).

2. For *rapido* perhaps read *rabido.* Cf. 67.6.

5. Cf., for example, *Anth. Pal.* 6.263, where a lion has paid with its life for killing a calf, and Verg. *Aen.* 3.628, *haud impune quidem.*

7. *Praestantior* is comparative for superlative (47.1n).

9–10. A *millus,* a hunting dog's collar, had throat-protecting spikes. *Fascia* (9), normally "band" or "bandage," here probably denotes a leash (so Wilson 1973), perhaps one with a girdle that fastens around the dog's body. *Anth. Pal.* 6.35 features the dedication of a "dog-choker for leading" (evidently a collar and leash) and a "throat-fetter." *Anth. Pal.* 6.107 also mentions dedication of dogs' collars.

11. *Cervix* ("neck") = severed head: Luc. 8.12 and 674; Sil. 13.373 (= unsevered head: 20.83 below).

12. A blend of Hor. *Ars poet.* 432 (*dolentibus ex animo*) and Ov. *Rem. am.* 510 (*signa dolentis*).

## · NOTES TO THE TRANSLATIONS ·

### 9

Hutton 1935, 191, compares *Anth. Pal.* 9.374 (a fountain urges thirsty and weary passersby to find rest and shade beside it), but Lei.1 better links Navagero's poem to 16.227, close versions of which by other Neo-Latin poets are also given. There a statue urges the tired wayfarer to rest on green grass by a fountain under a plane tree, so escaping the Dog Star's heat before proceeding. Cf. also 16.228. *Sonetto* 105 of Luigi Tansillo (quoted in Navagero 1718, 288) is an adaptation. Hutton 1935, 191n, notices further Italian versions. Imitated by Philippe Desportes among others; see Desportes 1858, 434. In Flo.NC. Navagero's poem is followed by a version in Italian stated to be by Claudio Tolomei (*Ecco un chiaro rio, pien' eccolo d'acque soavi, etc.*) that is not given in Navagero 1718. For Vincenzo Comaschi's verse paraphrase (Comaschi 1794, 68), see 21n. There are free English verse translations in Greswell 1801, 190, and Wiffen 1823, 388–89. Paolo Giovio quotes and praises this present poem and 2 in his *Dialogus de Viris Litteris Illustribus* (Dialogue on Men Distinguished in Letters); see Tiraboschi 1795–96, 7:1608. Giovio's readings accord with those of Vat.1 and 11. MSS: Flo.NC., Flo.Ric.2, Lei.1, Mil.1 (part), Salz., Si., Vat.1, 11, and 13, Ven.1, Wro.

2. Ends as Ov. *Am.* 2.6.50.

4. The variant *crebrior* would mean "more frequent" (the alternative "more intense" would hardly suit *levis*). *Gratior aura* (cf. 25.44): Hor. *Epist.* 1.10.15.

5. Cf. Verg. *Aen.* 6.536, *medium . . . traiecerat axem* ("had passed the middle of the sky"), and Luc. 3.423, *medio cum Phoebus in axe est* ("when Phoebus [= the sun] is in midsky").

6. Ends as Mart. 4.60.2, where the star meant is Leo. Tolomei here makes it the Dog Star (*l'adusto Cane*), as does Comaschi (*Sirio*), but I think the sun itself is intended. The next four lines are given on their own, as if a separate poem, in Mil.1.

9–10. Easing heat with a breeze: Ov. *Met.* 7.813–15. Cf. 2.5 above. Line 10 ends as Ov. *Tr.* 4.8.26. With the variant reading *umbra auraque recenti*, cf. *recentes . . . auras* in 37.6 and *aurae . . . recentiores* in 56.15. This poem

## · NOTES TO THE TRANSLATIONS ·

seems to have undergone some author modification (cf. the variants in lines 4 and 5).

### 10A

Cf. 8 for the theme. Part-quoted down to the first two words of line 7, there with *ipse quidem*, by Pignoria 1625, 89. Imitated by du Bellay, *Divers jeux rustiques*; French translation in Chamard 1961, 2:215. MSS: Bol.Arch., Salz.

2. *Missus* (lit., "sent") means that the dog was of an imported breed from Illyria, otherwise called Dalmatia, where Venice held territory. Cf. 50.3–4.

4. *Cetera turba* (Verg. *Aen.* 12.607; many times in Ovid) is in apposition to *socii canes. Socius* of an animal (not ancient?): Luigi Alamanni (*Carmina Illustrium Poetarum Italorum* 1:450), *vos socii catuli* ("you fellow little dogs"). Several epitaphs by Heinrich Rantzau for the old hound Vitus, mistaken for a fox and killed by the rest of the pack, have *socii* of his fellows; see Dornau 1619, 1:529 and 532; Wilson 1998, 92–93 and 95–98.

5–6. The Timavo, flowing into the sea northwest of Trieste: Verg. *Aen.* 1.244, *Ecl.* 8.6, G. 3.475. The first passage describes how the sea bursts noisily out from underground through nine mouths and overwhelms the plow fields. Strab. 2.319 cites Posidonius as saying that the Timavo descends from the mountains, plunges down a chasm, and travels underground for 130 stadia (furlongs), re-emerging close to the sea.

9. *Viridi . . . de caespite* ("of green turf"): [Verg.] *Cul.* 393; Ov. *Met.* 13.395; Pontano, *Urania* 1.13; F. 3.14.4 (and cf. 4.1.6).

11–12. Animals, and nature in general, can feel sadness at a death in pastoral poetry (cf. F. 4.16.21–27), as for Daphnis in Theoc. *Id.* 1.71–75. Similarly Verg. *Ecl.* 5.24–28. Cf. also Moschus 3. Line 12 ends as Tib. 1.1.33.

### 10B

A shorter, seemingly earlier, version of 10A, only in Mil.2. See Griggio 1976–77, 92, and Sacré 1987, 297. Lines 3, 4, and 6 are unaltered in the

## · NOTES TO THE TRANSLATIONS ·

expanded 10A. The man's name was originally Almon (so spelled in Mil.2; see 18n); the dog was Hylactor (Ov. *Met.* 3.224). The former was changed to Amyntas (Verg. *Ecl.* 3.66 and 10.38; Theoc. *Id.* 7.2; etc.), the latter to Hylax ("Howler"; Verg. *Ecl.* 8.107).

2. *Vagi . . . greges* ("the ranging herds") occurs also in 25.18.

II

For three offerings to three deities by someone asking an appropriate favor of each, cf. *Anth. Pal.* 6.154 and 158. Name *Teleson* (or *Th-*): *Anth. Pal.* 6.35 and 106. Du Bellay has two versions in *Divers jeux rustiques* (4 and the far freer 5) and debts in *Sonnets divers* 29 and 37 and *Poésies diverses* 28. His *Votum Rusticum Iolas*, with Pales, Ceres, and Bacchus in a refrain, develops this piece, with inspiration also from 1. In a poem in bk. 3 of Baïf's *Passetems*, offerings are hung up to Pan, Ceres, nymphs, and Bacchus, all asked appropriate favors in return; see Baïf 1881–90, 4:362. Bargaeus 1568, 395 (see 2n), has a *lusus pastoralis* entitled *Primitiae* (Firstfruits) addressed to Pan, Ceres, and Bacchus, each given a small offering of firstfruits, but promised an appropriate animal sacrifice if weather, disease, and predators do no harm. MSS: Flo.NC., Mil.3, Salz. In Flo.NC. this poem appears in the left margin alongside Bargaeus' poem with the observation *paulo aliter Naugerius* ("little differently Navagero").

1. Lyaeus, like Iacchus in line 3 (cf. 4.4 and 15.4) = Bacchus.

2. Pales protected shepherds and cattle (also F. 4.2.29). Milk offered her: Ov. *Fast.* 4.746; Tib. 1.1.36; Poliziano, *Silvae* 3.1–5; Sannazaro, *Elegies* 1.1.18; du Bellay, *Votum Rusticum Iolas* 71 (two cups of snow-white milk); Milk "snow-white": 1.13–14n.

4. *Pabula laeta* ("rich pasture"): Verg. G. 3.385; Ov. *Am.* 3.5.28; etc. (see 25.18n).

12

Name *Lycon*: 5n. *Leucippe* occurs in several mythological connections and in *Anth. Pal.* 9.203. Flaminio is among Neo-Latin poets who use the name (2.12). *Leucas* in poem 6 may be intended as another form (not the

237

## · NOTES TO THE TRANSLATIONS ·

same girl). *Chariclo: Anth. Pal.* 5.259 and 288; Ov. *Met.* 2.636. Imitated by Ronsard 1914–75, 6:19, and Jean Vauquelin de la Fresnaye, *Idillies et pastorales* 2.12; see Dunlop 1914, 160–61. Cf. F. 3.16.1–4. Omitted by Duchesne 1560 in its true place, but given (untitled, with variants — or errors?) on fol. 83v. MSS: Berg., Mil.1, Vat.1, 8, and 11, Wro.

5. Depending on which reading is preferred, the buskins are either (a) yellow or white or (b) yellow and white (or white or yellow, or white and yellow). I have settled for the reading of Navagero 1530, supported by Vat.1, though the five other MSS have three different readings between them.

9. See 6.4–5n. The last syllable of *aderit* is lengthened *in arsi* (see 20.48n).

10. *Ad tua dona veni:* Ov. *Fast.* 4.452. See F. 3.16n.

### 13

Name *Thyrsis:* 6n. Name *Nape:* Ov. *Am.* 1.11.2, 1.12.4; *Anth. Pal.* 5.5. French imitations: du Bellay, *Divers jeux rustiques*; Baïf 1881–90, 289; Desportes 1858, 439. Italian versions by Claudio Tolomei (quoted in Navagero 1718) and Bargaeus (see 2n); Cicogna 1824–53, 6:292n311, records another. MSS: Mil.2 and 3, Salz.

1. Cf. *pariles amantes*, 59.48; *in amore pares*, F. 3.12.9. Ov. *Fast.* 5.499 ends *cultor agelli*. In Mil.2's alternative version of this line, *conformes animi cordisque unius amantes* ("lovers in harmony of mind and of one heart"), *conformes animi* is late Latin and was presumably discarded for that reason.

3–4. The name of the fabulous undying amaranth of poetic tradition means "unwithering" in Greek. Its red flowers interwoven with white lilies: [Tib.] 3.4.33–34. *Cypris* of Venus (again 17.10) occurs anciently only in postclassical Latin poetry, such as that of Ausonius, but is in several Neo-Latin poets, e.g., Sannazaro, *Epigrams* 3.2.1; Marullo, *Epigrams* 1.37.4; Valeriano, *Amores* 3.10.9; Angeriano has a number of instances in his *Erotopaegnion. Cypria* is found in [Tib.] 3.3.34. With 4 cf. 1.18.

5. *Exemplo* is used as in 4.6 and Tib. 1.9.40. Mart. 7.84.7 has *nullis delebilis annis* ("destructible by no years"). The spelling out of the significance

· NOTES TO THE TRANSLATIONS ·

of the flowers given is reminiscent of poems like Marullo, *Epigrams* 1.21, where Neaera is warned to infer from Marullo's gift of quickly withering lilies and of violets plucked in their brief spring that her beauty will speedily fade like theirs if she lets her spring go by. Angeriano, *Erotopaegnion* 102, has a similar message.

8. In Ov. *Met.* 13.789 *folium* (usually "leaf") = "petal" or "flower" (perhaps also Verg. *Ecl.* 5.40; Prop. 2.3.12). Cf. 27.56 and F. 4.6.12.

10. Cf. Prop. 2.15.25 (wishing two lovers bound together with a chain never to be undone); [Tib.] 3.11.15–16; Ov. *Met.* 4.677–78. *Nectat* scans with the last syllable lengthened by diastole at the pentameter dieresis (cf. *penitus* in 19.50, *Infernus* in 26.36). The only instances in ancient elegiacs are Prop. 2.8.8 and 2.24.4; Mart. 9.101(102).4 and 14.77.2. Such diastole is common in Landino and seen with varying frequency in other Neo-Latin poets (cf. *pascet* in F. 3.29.4, *apponet* in F. 4.24.10).

14

Imitated by du Bellay, *Divers jeux rustiques*. Name *Niconoe*: *Anth. Pal.* 6.292 and 11.71. I find *Icastus* and *T(h)erilla* nowhere else, though *Iocastus* occurs in Thomas Randolph's *Amyntas*, and *Turilla* in Jean Bonnefons, *Pancharis*, *Basium* 14. MSS: Bol.U., Mil.1, Vat.11, Wro.

1–2. Turnus is his aged mother's "one hope" in Verg. *Aen.* 12.57. Boccaccio calls his deceased daughter *spes unica patris* ("your father's one hope") in *Eclogues* 14.50. Pontano addresses his son as his *spes . . . senectae* ("hope of old age") in *Urania* 2.379. Among ancient authors, only Val. Fl. 1.191 has *certus* or *certior* with an epexegetic infinitive = "(more) unerring at (doing something)." Such an infinitive is common with the variant here, *docta* ("skilled at"). "Mountain-roaming" beasts: Lucr. 2.1081.

3. Diana as Latona's daughter: 37.25–28n. *Silvipotens* is not ancient. In a letter to Basilio Zanchi, Flaminio defends neologisms, including this word, used in F. 4.23.1 after Navagero here, by analogy with some other words ending *potens* (*ignipotens* and *armipotens*) in ancient authors; see Flaminio 1743, 279; Navagero 1718, xxxix; Maddison 1960, 179–82. Navagero uses *bellipotens* ("mighty in war") in 44.50. In Hor. *Carm. saec.* 1

239

## · NOTES TO THE TRANSLATIONS ·

Diana is *silvarum potens* ("mighty over woods"). Cf. 20.8 (*maestities*), 30.31 (the diminutive *papillula*), 35.13 (*septicornis*), 41.26 (*rosifer*), 44.17 (*undifluus*), and 65.18 (*resensit*) for other nonclassical words in Navagero, if 65 is truly his.

4. After Ov. *Fast.* 2.326.

6. Literally, "to submit to the rights (= authority, *iura*; cf. 28.6) of an unknown marriage bed (i.e., of a stranger as husband)." Du Bellay, *Amores* 7.12, has *externi . . . iura subire tori* of marriage to a foreigner; see du Bellay 1918, 1:491.

8. In Ov. *Fast.* 2.173–74, Diana bids pregnant Callisto leave her maiden band (*coetus desere*).

9. Partly after Verg. *Ecl.* 5.65. The variant *laevo* ("propitious") for *dextro* creates wordplay (assonance) with *laetam*, whereas there is alliteration of *d* in the couplet with *dextro*. Diana, whose own concerns included women's welfare, was also sometimes identified with Juno Lucina, the childbirth goddess. Cf. Catull. 34.13; Hor. *Carm. saec.* 14–15.

15

*Anth. Pal.* 6.44 has must-quaffing satyrs and Bacchus as planter of the vine. Name *Acmo(n)*: Verg. *Aen.* 10.128; Ov. *Met.* 14.484, 494, and 497. In 16 (but not here) Acmon denotes Navagero. MSS: Bol.U., Lei.2, 3, and 4, Vat.7 and 11 (x 2).

2. See F. 3.14.5–6n. The variant *effusi* ("poured"), found in some MSS, is closer to the Greek source, where the sense is "first-poured" or "firstflowing," than *expressi* ("pressed"), found in other MSS and eds., though the latter reading arguably enhances the sound of the line.

4. Iacchus/Bacchus (11.1n) was "sower/planter of the vine" (*vitisator*). Cf. Tib. 2.3.63; Ov. *Met.* 4.14.

16

In this poem, Acmon, addressing the fire-god Vulcan, burns off unwanted, detrimental overgrowth from his land. The significance is per-

# · NOTES TO THE TRANSLATIONS ·

haps allegorical, as Famiano Strada (1572–1649) recounts how, every year after his birthday banquet with friends, Navagero would burn a copy of Martial's works before their eyes, declaring that "an offering to the Muses and the shade of Vergil, as he could in no better way show himself to be an imitator and reverencer of Vergil than by ever relentlessly pursuing and destroying worthless poets with water and fire"; see Strada 1631, 216. Strada adds that once, "after Navagero, at a gathering of poets, had in his usual way given a reading of some *silvae* he had composed, and had been told that they seemed to resemble the style of Statius, angry with himself for having, in his desire to fly from Martial, deviated elsewhere from Vergil, as soon as he got home, he immediately set fire to his *silvae*, and, set alight himself by the heat of that fire, poured forth some little verses, almost ex tempore, and at the very next meeting of the same group recited them, employing the guise of the rustic Acmon, and they went like this: [this poem follows]." Paolo Giovio records the story of Navagero's ritual burning of Martial's verses in his *Elogia Virorum Illustrium* (see Giovio 1972, 8:102; quoted in Navagero 1718, xxxviii), and Fracastoro tells us that Navagero burned several of his own works as he was dying. The version of the *silvae* story in the preface of Navagero 1530, reproduced by the Volpi brothers in Navagero 1718, is that "while still a young man, when he was concerned to redirect himself to the imitation of good poets and especially of Vergil (as his epigram to Vulcan bears witness), he burned his *silvae*, composed in imitation of Statius." There follows the alternative suggestion, unsupported and seemingly against the evidence of this poem, that perhaps a friend secretly destroyed the *silvae*. MS: Bol.U.

3. Imagery from layering or taking a cutting, as deliberate acts. Poliziano (1454–94) wrote well-regarded *silvae*.

4. Shade injurious to crops: Verg. *Ecl.* 10.76 and G. 1.121.

5–6. *Soluta* means "made friable." In Verg. G. 1.84–93 burning off stubble can open up soil, enhancing fertility. Usury imagery: 1.11–12n. *Eat* here = *sit*. Cf. 28.12 and 36.9.

7–8. The recent planting "on the Phrygian hill" (Mt. Ida near Troy, "Phrygian Ida" in Verg. G. 4.41; cf. 48.3 here) to be spared seems to al-

# · NOTES TO THE TRANSLATIONS ·

lude to some other poetic work lately begun, somehow related to the story of Troy, perhaps a project never completed. I do not think it can mean Navagero's prose Venetian history, which Wilson 1973 treats as a possibility (what point would "Phrygian hill" then have?). By *istas* understand *silvas*; with *consita* (awkwardly) understand *messis* from 6.

17

In *Anth. Pal.* 6.47 and 6.48 a loom comb is dedicated to Athena (Minerva) by a widow nearly forty resolved to serve Aphrodite (Venus) from then on, i.e., to give up weaving for prostitution. Lei.5, fol. 60v, rightly relates Navagero's present poem to 6.48 (likewise Hutton 1935, 462). Similar too is 6.285, where a woman, speaking scornfully of weaving, burns her shuttle and deserts Athena for Aphrodite. Her future life is seen as one of gaiety, garlands, and music, and she promises Aphrodite a tenth of her takings, asking the goddess to give her work. By contrast, three girls who dedicate weaving and spinning tools in 6.174 have all chosen to live "reproachlessly." In 6.283 a woman of fading charms who once boasted of rich lovers is now reduced to weaving, Athena having won a late victory over Aphrodite. A young widow in Verg. *Aen.* 8.408–15 respectably works long hours at weaving by night "to keep her husband's bed chaste and rear her little children." The name *Euphro* is pointedly chosen from *Anth. Pal.* 5.161 and 6.17 (prostitutes) and 6.39 (weaver). MSS: Lei.5, Mil.2 (part), Salz. Nichols 1998 discusses this poem among others, comparing it to *Anth. Pal.* 6.48.

1. Ov. *Met.* 4.10 has *telasque* (*-que* lengthened) *calathosque.*

2. *Pauperioris* lacks true comparative force and can be seen as a substitute for the positive or superlative adjective. See 8.7n, 22.12n, 25.39n, 29.4–6n, and 47.1n.

6. *Plena laboris* ("full of toil/hardship"): Verg. *Aen.* 1.460.

7. *Iam . . . dudum*: Plaut. *Poen.* 1.2.105 has the same tmesis of *iamdudum.*

8. Cytherea: Venus (F. 3.28.1–2n). Nichols 1998, 448, hesitating to infer prostitution, sees Euphro as literally joining Venus' band of nymphs, but turning from Athena's works to Aphrodite's in classical antecedents regu-

242

## · NOTES TO THE TRANSLATIONS ·

larly implies earning a living wantonly in bed rather than chastely at the loom, and even the name *Euphro* is surely chosen for its connotations of prostitution as well as weaving.

9–10. In the Judgment of Paris, Aphrodite (Venus) defeated both Athena (Minerva) and Hera (Juno). Phrygian: Trojan.

### 18

Name *Alcippe* (or *Alcippa*): Theoc. *Id.* 5.132; Verg. *Ecl.* 7.14; Calp. *Ecl.* 3.31 and 33; *Anth. Pal.* 5.127. *Almo* (sometimes *Almon* in editions of Navagero): Verg. *Aen.* 7.532 and 575; see 10Bn. MS: Bol.U.

1–2. Nonacrian (cf. 26.45): Arcadian, from a mountain and city in Arcadia. *Crudeli . . . tabe peresus* is after Verg. *Aen.* 6.442.

3–4. *Capripes* of Pans or other "goat-footed" rural deities: Prop. 3.17.34 and see 20.15n. Greek equivalent, of Pan: *Anth. Pal.* 6.57. Of Pan also in, e.g., F. 4.2.29 and 4.16.19.

5–6. Offerings of milk and honey (and wine) were regular at ancient Roman tombs, as was sprinkling with flowers (cf. 50.2), frequently mentioned in Neo-Latin epitaphs too.

7. *Frondenti ex ilice* is found in Verg. *Aen.* 5.129.

8. For transportation to Mt. Idalium (in Cyprus, sacred to Venus; see 56.7–8n), cf. Verg. *Aen.* 1.680–81 (of Iulus).

11. Paphos, in Cyprus, had a celebrated temple of Venus.

14. Ov. *Met.* 3.579 may have suggested *det documenta*.

18. *Fastus* ("disdain") or *superbia* ("haughtiness") as the failing of the beautiful is a commonplace of Latin love poetry. Ov. *Fast.* 1.419: "Disdain is in the fair, and haughtiness is attendant on beauty."

### 19

Soliloquies by tormented lovers in wild, empty places: Verg. *Ecl.* 2.4–5; Nemes. *Ecl.* 4.12–73; Prop. 1.18; etc. In Ov. *Met.* 3.342–510. Echo pined away to nothing but her voice when rejected by Narcissus. He fell in love

### · NOTES TO THE TRANSLATIONS ·

with his reflection in a pool, died by its side, and turned into a flower. The name *Acon*, not in ancient poetry, is in several Neo-Latin poets; e.g., Pontano wrote an *Acon*, his Eclogue 4. The Spanish poet Francisco de la Torre nearly translates this poem, omitting the last eight lines, in his *Eco* (*Egloga* 3), drawing also on 27; see Crawford 1915. Cicogna 1824–53, 6:292n311, records a translation by Paolo Chiappino, who also has versions of 21, 25, and 26. MSS: Mil.1 (with error *Aion* in title and line 6), Wro. (with *Acon*). The regular printed text differs in several places from that in the MSS (most notably in lines 11, 15, 31, 41, 44, and 47), suggesting a degree of author revision, or perhaps some editorial changes were made by another hand prior to publication in Navagero 1530. I have mostly preferred the printed text, though the variants are often credible.

1. Pan was associated with Mt. Lycaeus in Arcadia: cf. Verg. *Aen.* 8.344, Val. Fl. 6.533. Echo is linked to him in *Anth. Pal.* 6.79.5–6: "For here Echo in her delight will celebrate marriage with you [Pan]."

2. Wilson 1973 takes *sinu* as "curl" (of hair, a rare sense), but note the naiads' hair and bosoms (*sinus*) in 31.3–5. Sannazaro, *Eclogues* 2.20, calls a woman "elegant in her bosom (*culta sinu*) and white in her breasts."

5–6. *Officiosa* (lit., "obliging" or "ready to serve") seems to be found of Echo only here, though Fausto Sabeo has the similar *obsequiosa* ("complaisant") of her in line 3 of his epigram *De Echo*, hinting how to interpret *officiosa* here: "For Echo is a chattersome but complaisant girl: if you are silent, she is silent; if you speak, she speaks"; see Sabeo 1556, 7. Pontano, *De Hortis Hesperidum* 1.606–7, describes Echo as *facilis* ("easy" or "obliging") in readily responding (there to singing). *Sub rupe cavata*: Verg. *Aen.* 1.310 and 3.229. *Lanigeri . . . pecoris*: Ov. *Fast.* 1.384, 2.681, 4.715.

7–8. See 6.6–8n.

9. The last syllable of *levibus* is lengthened. Cf., for example, Verg. *Aen.* 4.64 (*pectoribus*) and see 20.48n.

11–12. *Nescio quid . . . flebile* (internal accusative with *gemis*) is after Ov. *Met.* 11.52–53. *Tristi voce* is instrumental ablative.

13. Printed texts omit *est* after *mirum*, though both Mil.1 and Wro. have it. The line is credible either way. For inclusion cf. 50.11, for exclusion 17.9.

244

# · NOTES TO THE TRANSLATIONS ·

15–18. Vivid historic present tenses are employed here and in the following passage. The boy in 17 is Narcissus. *Cultus* (17) may be acc. pl. and, like *amores*, object of *odit*, but it is probably better to take it as nom. sing. of the past participle of *colo* (with *us* lengthened *in arsi*; see 20.48n). *Strophium* of a garland: [Verg.] *Copa* 32.

21–22. *Siste gradum* (again 54.1): Verg. *Aen.* 6.465; Ov. *Her.* 13.102; etc. Line 22 ends as Ov. *Her.* 4.104. Cf. Ov. *Met.* 1.504–5 and Hor. *Odes* 1.23.9–10 for assurance that fleeing like prey from a predator is needless.

24. Neo-Latin love poets often declare a girl beautiful enough to stir gods (cf. 21.8), sometimes specifically Jupiter (cf. [Verg.] *Lydia* 26). So, e.g., F. 4.20.6; Pontano, *Eridanus* 2.11.12 ("a prize to be sought by Jupiter"); Marullo, *Epigrams* 2.12.4. Here Ov. *Her.* 14.88 seems partly reflected.

25. Laconian (Spartan) hound: Xen. *Cyn.* 10.4; Verg. G. 3.44, 3.345, and 3.405; Hor. *Epod.* 6.5; etc.

26. Verg. *Aen.* 4.131 begins *retia rara, plagae.*

29. *Heu miserande puer* begins Verg. *Aen.* 6.882.

31. *Magna Parens* ("Great Mother"): Earth/Cybele, not Venus, as Wilson 1973 here argues, influenced by 25. Cf. *Magna Parens* in Ov. *Ib.* 455 and *Met.* 1.393 (and, e.g., Marullo, *Hymni Naturales* 4.5.3–4), more commonly *Magna Mater*. Both MSS have the also credible *alma parens* ("kindly mother"), which Johannes Secundus too has of Earth in *Silvae* 1.76, *alma* being the epithet of Mother Earth in Lucr. 2.992–93, *alma . . . mater . . . Terra*. Pontano, *Urania* 1.904, speaks of all the colors that the kindly earth (*tellus . . . alma*) brings forth in the new spring. Lines 31–38 are quoted and translated by Symonds 1897, 354.

32. Earth painted with flowers (cf. 26.27): Lucr. 5.1396; Ov. *Fast.* 4.430; [Verg.] *Cul.* 69, *Dirae* 21; etc.

33–34. *Sinu* (ablative) = Mother Earth's "bosom" (see 25.6n). *Omnifer* ("all-bearing"): Ov. *Met.* 2.275 (dubious), of her face. Verg. *Aen.* 6.595; Lucr. 2.706, 5.259; and others call her *omniparens* ("parent to all things, all-producing"). Marullo, *Hymni Naturales* 1.5.14, has *omniferens* of her, and she is *omnipara . . . mater* ("the all-producing mother") in 4.5.29 of the same. Milton, *Elegiae* 5.58, speaks of Earth's *omniferos . . . sinus.*

245

### · NOTES TO THE TRANSLATIONS ·

38. Cf. Ov. *Met.* 3.422–24 (Narcissus' whiteness of skin).

40. Cf. Prop. 4.1.120.

41. The name *Telaira* (so MSS here and *Carmina Illustrium Poetarum Italorum*), otherwise *Telayra* (so nearly all eds. here from 1530 on) or *Thelayra* (four syllables) is from Prop. 1.2.16. The accepted reading now is *Hilaira* (Greek spelling *Hilaeira* in Apollod. *Bibl.* 3.10.3; she and her sister Phoebe, daughters of Leucippus, were carried off by Castor and Pollux), but the Aldine editions (Venice, 1502 and 1515) have *Thelayra* (so also the Junta text of 1503), obviously the reading Navagero and his circle knew. The name is significantly found also in two interludes that Navagero bids a boy sing in Fracastoro's dialogues *Naugerius, sive De Poetica* (Navagero, or On Poetry, of ca. 1540) and *Turrius, sive De Intellectione* (Della Torre, or On Intellection); see Fracastoro 2005; Fracastoro 2013, 282–87. The first, savoring of Navagero's pastoral poems, is actually misascribed to him in Ms. 45 (pp. 77–78) at the Biblioteca Comunale in Udine. *Thelayra* occurs also as a rustic singer's "flame" in Fracastoro, *Carmina* 51.7, 193, 284, and 319; see Fracastoro 2013, 316–41. *Crudelis Telaira*, if read here (both MSS have the credible variant *immitis*, "harsh"), probably reflects *o crudelis Alexi* in Verg. *Ecl.* 2.6.

42. After Prop. 2.16.48.

43. Cf. Nemes. *Ecl.* 2.49.

44. Mil.1 and Wro. give an alternative version of this line, *ex quo me tuus hic, scaeva, perurit amor* ("ever since this love for you, perverse girl, has been burning me up"). *Perurere* used as there: 32.3. *Scaeva* of a woman: Apul. *Met.* 9.14. *Scaevus* is a rare word, though Cupid is *scaevus deus* in Bembo, *Carmina* 12.46 (*Ad Lucretiam Borgiam*).

45–46. *It = exit.* Cf. 20.51–52. With 46 cf. Verg. G. 3.316 (of goats returning home on their own). Neglecting duties and activities in love despondency (also 55.21–27): Theoc. *Id.* 10.14 and 11.12–18, in the latter of which passages the Cyclops leaves his sheep to return on their own; Verg. *Ecl.* 2.70 and [Verg.] *Ciris* 177–79; Nemes. *Ecl.* 2.20–52; etc. In Mantuan, *Eclogues* 1.13–35, Faustus has lost interest in all his regular activities, such as singing, piping, hunting, fowling, and fishing. Sannazaro, *Eclogues* 3.82–85, is a comparable passage in a piscatory setting.

## · NOTES TO THE TRANSLATIONS ·

47. The MSS have *solito* ("accustomed"), the printed texts *niveo* ("snow-white"; 1.13–14n), both credible readings, the latter as a general epithet, the former as sufficiently appropriate in this particular context.

48. *Promisso* (only in Fracastoro 1759, perhaps fortuitously), not *permisso*, is appropriate of wool left unshorn. Cf., for example, Verg. *Ecl.* 8.34; Ov. *Tr.* 4.2.34.

50. The last syllable of *penitus* is lengthened at the dieresis (13.10n).

51. Line 5 of Giovanni Battista·Amalteo's *Piscatoris Anathema* (A Fisherman's Dedication) seems to echo this line: *Ite impune leves . . . pisces* ("Go in safety . . . swift-moving fishes"). Amalteo's poem appears in Sannazaro 1728, 450.

53–54. The fowler's equipment, listed in *Anth. Pal.* 6.109, included twigs smeared with birdlime (53) and nets supported with poles (54). In 54, *in tenebris . . . iacent* (lit., "lie in darkness") is figurative (= "are left neglected").

### 20

Discussed by Grant 1965, 332–35, with a loose verse translation. Grant 1957, 85, remarks on the date and historical circumstances. Symonds 1897, 361–62, cites and translates lines 42–60. Kuhn 1914, 311–16, considers allusions in Ronsard's First Eclogue, as does Chamard 1961, 3:47–48. For debts in Rémy Belleau's *Chant pastoral de la paix*, see Chamard 1961, 2:300. Cicogna 1824–53, 6:292n311, mentions an Italian version. The poem celebrates the French expulsion from Italy by the Holy League organized in October 1511 by Pope Julius II (1503–13). The Venetians and Spanish (then ruling Naples) were his initial supporters; Henry VIII of England joined them. The French won a victory at Ravenna on April 11, 1512, but were then forced out of Italy after the emperor Maximilian and the Swiss also sided with the League. As Julius died on February 21, 1513, this poem is of later 1512 or very early 1513. Name *Damon: Anth. Pal.* 7.548, 11.125, 12.35 and 87; Verg. *Ecl.* 3.17 and 8.1, 5, 16, and 62. Bartolomeo Ricci calls the present poem *Damon* in bk. 2 of his *De Imitatione* (quoted in Navagero 1718, xxxv) and remarks that, among other debts to

## · NOTES TO THE TRANSLATIONS ·

Vergil in this poem, "a large part" of it reflects his *Gallus* (*Ecl.* 10), which seems a great overstatement, though lines 4–8 here may weakly recall aspects of lines 4–10 of that eclogue. J. C. Scaliger, in bk. 6 of his *Poetices Libri Septem* (quoted in Navagero 1718, xlii), modifies his general praise of Navagero's style as "noble" by saying that his eclogue to Pope Julius, meaning this poem, is "less sweet, for it offers nothing new to stir one." MSS: Bol.U., Mil.1, Vat.4 and 6, Ver., Wro. In a few places the regular printed text is at variance with most or all of these six MSS. Probably Navagero himself slightly modified this poem at some stage or stages. I have mainly kept to the printed version.

1. The Noncello (*Naucelus*, also 44.17), passing just south of Pordenone (under Venetian rule from 1508), is a tributary of the Meduna (*Metune* 44.18), which joins the Livenza, flowing into the Gulf of Venice. Bartolomeo d'Alviano (1455–1515; see 44n) had set up his Academy, to which Navagero belonged, at Pordenone. In Zanchi, Eclogue 2.5–6 (*Myrtilus, sive Andreas Naugerius*), Iolas has wept for the dead Myrtilus (Navagero) on the Noncello's "curved shore"; see Zanchi 1555, 169. The *Naucelides*, the river god's daughters, are here invoked like local Muses. In Verg. *Ecl.* 10.9–10 the Muses are identified with *puellae Naides*, "naiad girls," just as they are *sorores Naides*, "naiad sisters," in [Verg.] *Cul.* 18. Cf. *Vanciades* in 31.31 and *Eridani . . . puellae* in 50.3. Pontano, *Lyra* 6.7, similarly speaks of the daughter-nymphs of the Sebeto as *Sebethiadum sororum*. Both variants for the final word of this line are credible, as either waves or caves can be "glassy": for *undis* cf. Verg. *Aen.* 7.759; for *antris*, which has the stronger authority here, cf. Stat. *Silv.* 2.2.16.

2. Ov. *Met.* 3.502 has *viridi . . . in herba*, the regular reading here, while the variant *viridi . . . in umbra* (Wro.) recurs in line 82 (cf. also line 61 and 9.9). Pontano, *Parthenopeus* 2.14.7, has *virides . . . umbras*.

4. Cf. 56.13, 16, 18, and 22, and see F. 3.9.1–4n for *sic* here.

5. *Viduata* ("bereft," i.e., of flowers) is read in editions, but all the MSS have *violata* ("harmed"). Verg. *G.* 4.518 and Hor. *Odes* 2.9.8 illustrate *viduari* used figuratively with an ablative. The former is *arva . . . numquam viduata pruinis* ("fields never bereft of frost"); the latter, *foliis viduantur orni* ("ashes are bereft of leaves"). Other instances too show that the ablative

248

## · NOTES TO THE TRANSLATIONS ·

with *viduari* regularly means "of." Here, however, if *viduata* is right, *hibernis nivibus* and *aestu* have to be ablatives of the agent ("by"). Furthermore, I note that Molza describes meadows (*prata*) as *hiberna . . . violata nive* in his poem *Ad Beatricem Hispanam* (Molza 1747–54, 1:230).

8. *Maestities* (= *maestitia*) is not ancient. See 14.3n.

9. "Icy" Alps: Luc. 1.183.

10. The variant *cottidie/quottidie* ("every day," all MSS) has the second syllable shortened. Cf. F. 5.22.11 (5.23.11 Scorsone); Mantuan, *Eclogues* 1.120; Varchi, *Carmina* 1.34 and 42.6. *Assidue* ("constantly," eds.) removes the questionable prosody. "Latin shores" (i.e., "land") = Italy in general. "Latium" and "Latin" are so used also in 44.75 and 85, 48.8, and 55.34.

11–12. *Invita* is probably ablative with *terra*, not nominative with *pabula*. Cf. Verg. *Ecl.* 6.86 ("the evening star came forth in an unwilling sky"). Vergil has *invitae . . . terrae* in *G.* 1.224. For horror in nature at the invasion, cf. the sorrow in 10A.11–12n.

14. *Involvier* = *involvi*, present passive infinitive. See 22.7–8n.

15. Both satyrs and fauns were goat-footed and two-horned and are indiscriminately described with either epithet by a number of Neo-Latin poets. Ov. *Her.* 4.49 ends *Faunique bicornes* like the variant in Wro. (cf. F. 3.1.1), but in most MSS and eds. it is the satyrs who are two-horned. *Hircipes* (= *capripes*, 18.3–4n) occurs in an ancient author only in Martianus Capella, of Pan, but Lucr. 4.580, Hor. *Odes* 2.19.4, and several Neo-Latin poets have *capripedes* of satyrs. The eclogue *Thyrsis* of "Antonio Mario of Imola" (= Flaminio; see F. 3.15n) has *hircipedes Fauni* in line 28 and *Satyri bicornes* in line 35. F. 4.10.1 has *Pan bicornis*.

21–32. With the flight of the flocks to inaccessible forests and heights and to the shore of the sea, cf. Longus, *Daphnis and Chloe* 1.22, where terrified sheep and goats flee, some to crags, some to the seashore.

24. Cf. Verg. *G.* 3.230, where an exiled bull lies "all night long amid hard rocks on an unspread bed" (see 20.29–30n).

26. *Miserabile visu* ("pitiable to see," eds.): Verg. *Aen.* 1.111 (similarly, *visu miserabile*, 9.465); Ov. *Met.* 13.421; Stat. *Silv.* 5.3.70 (there not parenthetical). *Miserabile dictu* ("pitiable to tell," all MSS here) seems not to occur in

249

## · NOTES TO THE TRANSLATIONS ·

an ancient poet, though in Neo-Latin Lorenzo Adriani (d. 1707) has it in a poem in *Carmina Illustrium Poetarum Italorum* 1:12. Vergil has *mirabile dictu* (marvelous to tell) numerous times.

27. *Qua* is literally "where." *Mediis . . . undis* (lit., "mid waters") probably imitates *medium . . . mare* (mid sea) in Verg. *Ecl.* 8.58, where "mid" has been interpreted as "deep" or "deepest." Navagero has *medium . . . per mare* in 26.38.

29–30. Green shrubby-clover (shrub trefoil) was considered good animal feed: Verg. *Ecl.* 1.78, 2.64, 9.31; G. 3.394–95; Theoc. *Id.* 5.128 and 10.30. The prickly weed Christ's thorn (Verg. *Ecl.* 5.39) overgrows a tomb in *Anth. Pal.* 7.656. The driven-out bull in Verg. *G.* 3.231 (see 20.24n) eats the sedge's sharp-edged leaves (cf. Calp. *Ecl.* 3.94). *Graminis herba*: Verg. *Ecl.* 5.26. Cf. *graminis herbae*, Ov. *Met.* 10.87.

33–34. In Verg. *Ecl.* 1.6 Octavian is the "god" who has brought peace, words echoed in 99 here. Lucr. 5.8 declares the philosopher Epicurus "a god," and there are several other instances of a revered man (deified emperors apart) as *deus* in classical Latin literature. As for referring here to Pope Julius as "a new god" and treating him in 42–68 like a pagan deity to be venerated by shepherds with sacred rites on set days, there are many cases of similar quasi-deification (including of popes and cardinals) by Renaissance Latin and vernacular eulogists. For example, acclaiming Borso d'Este, T. V. Strozzi calls him a "new god" in *Erotica* 4.10.14 and declares in 4.12.41–42, "As much as is lawful on earth, we revere the divinity of Borso, and we will now give you your own designated temples, unless you refuse," and in 4.14.5–8, "But since . . . your glory far surpasses the human lot, should you tolerate divine honors, we will readily give them, and we will consecrate well-deserved altars to you." Sometimes fellow poets receive such extravagant veneration. Anisio's eclogue *Melisaeus* includes talk of setting up an altar to the living poet Giovanni Cotta and worshipping him "as a god after Pan," and Pontano is treated as having become a god after his death; see Cotta 1802, 51–56. Several poets speak of the person celebrated as "being sent down from heaven" (Olympus in 33 here is for heaven, as often). Thus Peregrino Agli or Allio (*Carmina Illustrium Poetarum Italorum* 1:125) speaks of Cosimo de' Medici (d. 1464) as "a god sent down from the starry heaven." Popes are

#### · NOTES TO THE TRANSLATIONS ·

so described in a number of eulogies. In a letter to Leo X (quoted in Navagero 1718, 65–78) calling on him to lead the Christian powers against the Turks, Navagero talks of a day "when all Italy, all the world may revere you as a god come down from heaven to ease our troubles." In a poem of 1513, Giano Vitale welcomes Leo's pontificate so: "The Earth did not bear him, no parents born of the human race produced him, such a being came down from heaven; we are permitted to see immortal good, holy and venerable divinity, in the clothing of humankind"; see Roscoe 1805, vol. 2, App. 71, and see also 44.94n. Symonds 1897, 360–62, notes extreme flattery of various popes in very pagan terms in poets such as Poliziano, Fracastoro, and Castiglione. Zanchi, Eclogue 2.28–31 (*Myrtilus, sive Andreas Naugerius*), has the shepherd Iolas say of Myrtilus (the dead Navagero), "He was like a god of high heaven to me. Often I used to call him to come and receive my supplicatory offerings, often a victim of mine stained his altars," and Myrtilus is described in 49–50 there as "sent down from high heaven"; see Zanchi 1555, 170 and 171. See further 20.42–43n and 20.58–70n (and 34.10n).

35. Ausonian: Italian. A totally different line from the text in eds. is found (with some variation of word order) in all the MSS, *nunc etiam nostros fines* [*nostros etiam* Ver., *fines nostros* Mil.1, Wro.] *gens saeva teneret* ("even now a savage race would hold our territories"), following a slightly different 34, *hanc Italis cladem deus avertisset ab agris* [*oris* Wro.], further evidence of adjustments to this poem.

36. Cf. Verg. *Aen.* 1.599 *omnium egenos* (of the refugees from Troy with Aeneas).

38. The general reading *nota* ("familiar") suits the context of restoration better than the canceled stock epithet *laeta* ("joyous" or "fertile") in Wro.; cf. [Verg.] *Cul.* 381; Juv. 12.13.

39–41. Cf. Octavian's message in Verg. *Ecl.* 1.45 ("Graze your cattle as before"). Lines 3–4 of Girolamo Amalteo's eclogue *Iolas* bid, "O with me hang reeds from your rustic necks, forgetting cares"; see Sannazarro 1728, 334.

42–43. In Fracastoro, *Carmina* 51.148–49, *annua sacra* will be performed for the "god" Bishop Gian Matteo Giberti, and in 69–70, 156–57, and

## · NOTES TO THE TRANSLATIONS ·

224–25 of the same poem, farmers are urged to perform them for the "god" Clement VII.

44. Again the MSS (all reading *cunctisque*) differ from the printed text (*nostrisque*), indicating revision. The sense is either "and you will long be sung in all the woods" or "in our woods."

45. *Iuli* (here voc.) may scan as two syllables or three.

48. The oak was the family emblem of Julius II (Giuliano della Rovere). *Erit* has the last syllable lengthened *in arsi*, a practice seen in over fifty lines of Vergil, who lengthens the *it* of *erit* in *Ecl.* 3.97 and *Aen.* 12.883. Here cf. 3.1, 12.9, 19.9, 27.23 and 63, and (if *immite* be read) 55.10.

50. See 6.6–8n. Anisio's *Melisaeus* 122 speaks of carving all of Cotta's sixty-four-line lament for Pontano on a beech; see Cotta 1802, 56.

57. Calling gods *in vota*: Verg. *Aen.* 5.234 and 7.471.

58–70. The laurel (59) symbolizes victory. Kuhn 1914, 315–16, sees imitation of these lines in Ronsard's Second Eclogue, a dirge after Verg. *Ecl.* 5 for Henry II of France. There a shepherd will set up a fine temple on the banks of the Loire, with yearly rustic competitions. For setting up altars to revered figures, see 20.33–34n, and further compare Fracastoro, *Carmina* 5.1, where, addressing Giovanni Matteo Giberti, bishop of Verona, he describes himself as "that friend of yours who set up holy altars to you." To Cardinal Alessandro Farnese, Pope Paul III's grandson, Fracastoro declares (*Carmina* 10.64–70), "Since you will always be held divine in my eyes, I will set up holy altars to you," adding, "I will dedicate a holy day to you and instigate sacred rites to be celebrated anew each year, rites ever called by your name." Hutton 1980, 236, quotes 58–64, pointing out Vergilian antecedents, such as the two altars for Daphnis in Verg. *Ecl.* 5.66 and the talk of setting up a temple to Octavian by the Mincio in G. 3.13–15. He notes the great popularity of Navagero's *Damon* with sixteenth-century French poets, mentioning Rémy Belleau in particular.

62. The opening of the line combines *vere novo* from Verg. G. 1.43 with *floret ager* from 2.6 there.

63. Almost identical to 27.15. *Nemora avia* occurs in several ancient poets, including Lucr. 2.144 and 346 (cf. 5.1386, *avia per nemora*); Verg. *Aen.* 7.580; Ov. *Met.* 1.479.

## · NOTES TO THE TRANSLATIONS ·

66. Rustic javelin contest: Verg. *G.* 2.530. *Certamine cursus* ends Catull. 64.340. *Rapidi* is genitive.

67. After Verg. *G.* 2.531 ("they bare their sturdy bodies in [or *for*] rustic wrestling"), where editors have also read the variants *palaestra* (abl.) or *palaestrae* (dat.). Tib. 2.3.75 has *horrida corpora* of a rustic torso.

68. *Pedo* ("a shepherd's crook," a valued gift in Verg. *Ecl.* 5.88) is the perfectly acceptable reading of most MSS, but *pecu* ("sheep," abl.), also good sense, is favored in eds.

69–70. *Sebethos* = the Sebeto or Maddalona, flowing through Naples. *Sebeth-* is regularly two long syllables in Pontano, Sannazaro, and elsewhere in Neo-Latin (cf. *Sebethos alumna* and *Sebethide nympha*, ending hexameters in Stat. *Silv.* 1.2.263 and Verg. *Aen.* 7.734, respectively). Here, however, Navagero would have to scan the unclassical adjective *Sebetheius* (the general reading here in eds. and also in Wro.), if correct, as two shorts, a long, and two shorts. The alternative reading *Sebethius*, found in Bol.U., Mil.1, Vat.4, and Vat.6, *Carmina Quinque Illustrium Poetarum* (all eds. between 1548 and 1558), and Toscano 1576, far more credibly scans as two longs and two shorts. Aegon stands for Giovanni Gioviano Pontano. Grant 1965, 333 (followed by Wilson 1973), says Damon is Baldassare Castiglione, offering no justification, but perhaps because Zanchi's Third Eclogue (*Damon*) has the alternative title *Baltazar Castalio* (see Zanchi 1555, 174). That need not mean, however, that *Damon* here is Castiglione, who unlike "Damon" never studied under Pontano or resided in Naples. I think Damon is Pontano's former student (and Navagero's friend) Girolamo Borgia (1475–1550), noted as a poet of encomia, including of Bartolomeo d'Alviano; see 44.70–73n. He came to Venice ca. 1507, studied Greek at Padua under Marcus Musurus, and became associated with Alviano's academy at Pordenone; he also served in arms with Alviano. He seems to have returned to Naples after a few years, perhaps by 1513. Kidwell 1991, 399n77, has a few remarks on him. The introduction to Borgia 1666 makes much of how Pontano taught him poetry as a boy while his family were resident in Naples following the death of his father, Antonio Borgia. In *Eridanus* 2.20 Pontano addresses Girolamo Borgia, who subsequently spent time at the papal court in Rome at the invitation of his close friend and distant relative Juan Borgia, illegitimate son of

## · NOTES TO THE TRANSLATIONS ·

Pope Alexander VI, but fled Italy to spend many years in France and Germany after Juan was murdered, reputedly by his brother Cesare, in 1497. Girolamo was eventually made bishop of Massa Lubrense, near Capri, by Paul III in 1544. See further 42n for Girolamo Borgia and Navagero. Name *Aegon*: Verg. *Ecl.* 3 and 5 (in 5.72 a Cretan from whom Menalcas hopes to get songs at the festival of Daphnis); Calp. *Ecl.* 6.84; Theoc. *Id.* 4.2 and 26; *Anth. Pal.* 11.247. The name is used by several other Neo-Latin poets, often denoting some revered teacher, master poet, or similar.

72–74. The goddess in 73 is Venus (= Dione in 75; see 31.30n). Adonis' father was once a king in Assyria. In Ov. *Met.* 10.529–32 Venus "absents herself even from heaven," and "Adonis is preferred to heaven." In Pontano's *De Amore Coniugali* 2.4.63–64, "Venus . . . preferred the earth and the boy [Adonis] to the sky." With 74 cf. Catull. 64.120.

75 and 81. *Fortunate puer* begins Verg. *Ecl.* 5.49.

76–85. Stone 1981 finds debts to this passage in Ronsard's *Adonis* of 1563. Navagero owes something to Ov. *Met.* 10.554–59, where Venus lies on turf with Adonis. In 80 the neglect of Mars, Venus' paramour, for Adonis, may symbolize war rejected for idyllic peace, as Wilson 1973 suggests.

81. Cf. 26.31 for the variant *mediis . . . in arvis* (lit., "in the midst of plow fields"), seen in Ov. *Met.* 15.554.

83. *Cervice* in 83 means "head," as in 8.11.

85. *Odoratis . . . tempora sertis*: Ov. *Tr.* 5.3.3.

96–97. Daphnis, Mercury's son, invented pastoral song (Theoc. *Id.* 1). Cf. Verg. *Ecl.* 4.58–59: were very Pan to compete with the poet, even with Pan's own Arcadia as judge, Pan would have to admit himself defeated. For the syntax see 32.14n.

99. Ov. *Fast.* 1.67–70 twice has *dexter ades* ("be propitiously present") to Janus in a context of peace (*otia*). Verg. *Ecl.* 1.6 says of Octavian that "a god has created this peace (*otia*) for us." Navagero here equates Julius II with Octavian. F. 2.4.3 says *dexter facis otia* to Cardinal Alessandro Farnese.

254

· NOTES TO THE TRANSLATIONS ·

21

*Anacreontea* 6 (= *Anth. Pal.* 16.388) tells of Love found amid roses by a man weaving a garland, who immerses him in wine and drinks him. Cf. also *Anacreontea* 13 and 33. A girl comes across Cupid hiding among flowers in Angeriano, *Erotopaegnion* 121. Fucilla 1938 traces many early debts to Navagero's poem in Italian, Spanish, French, and English and notes several English versions, including those of the poet Thomas Moore (1779–1852) and the translator of Tasso, Jeremiah Holmes Wiffen (1792–1836). Scott 1926 considers Thomas Lodge's 1593 adaptation (*Phillis* 39). The adaptation by Ludovico Dolce (1508–66) was particularly influential; see Fucilla 1938, 289. Cicogna 1824–53, 6:292n3n, records that version and two others, one by Paolo Chiappino. Cristóbal de Castillejo's *Al Amor preso* reflects Navagero here; see Crawford 1915, 214–15n5. Castillejo died in 1550. See Pellini 1911 for a literal translation of this poem and notice of some renderings in Italian verse, including a paraphrase by Vincenzo Comaschi (1750–1817); see Comaschi 1794, 66 and 68 (paraphrase of poem 9). The name *Hyella* (also in 22, 28, 30, 32, 33, and 38 and F.'s *lusus pastorales*), unattested in ancient literature, occurs in Pontano, *Hendecasyllabi* 2.30.5, and in poems of the brothers Girolamo, Giovanni Battista, and Cornelio Amalteo, e.g., Cornelio's simplification of Navagero here: "As Hyella chanced to be gathering red roses, Love sped into the chaste maiden's bosom. Then he declared, 'Find yourself another boy, mother, find one; for from now on this girl will be mother to me'"; see Sannazaro 1728, 483. The name is also found in the *Pastoralis Lusus* of J. C. Scaliger, the *Ocelli* of Jean Leernout (Lernutius, 1545–1619), the *Erotopaegnion* of the younger Janus Dousa (Jan van der Doës), and elsewhere in Neo-Latin poetry. Of Navagero's *Hyella* poems, only 30 (not after early 1508) suggests that the girl was real rather than just a literary fiction. MSS: Bel.1, Berg., Bol.U., Jesi, Man., Mil.1 and 3, Par.1, Vat.1, 9, and 11, Ven.3, Wro. Cf. 66 (if truly Navagero's).

2. The two variants agreeing with *lilia* are both credible: cf. 13.8 (*cana*) and 50.2 (*mixta*).

4. I take *simul* (plus ablative) as "together with" (cf. Hor. *Sat.* 1.10.86; Ov. *Tr.* 5.10.29), as Grilli 1898 seems to do. Ciaffi (in Muscetta/Ponchiroli

255

## · NOTES TO THE TRANSLATIONS ·

1959), Wilson 1973, and McFarlane 1980 make the sense "forthwith/at once" or "suddenly," which is another possibility.

5. *Nitentibus* is from *nitor* ("strive" or "strain"), not *niteo* ("shine"), as the long first *i* shows. After Ov. *Met.* 4.361, *nitentem contra elabique volentem* ("struggling to pull away and wanting to slip free").

6. *Indomitus* of Love is not ancient but is found in several Neo-Latin poets, including Pontano, *De Amore Coniugali* 1.1.131; Ugolino Verino, *Flammetta* 2.22.45–46; Johannes Secundus, *Epistles* 2.6.47 (*Veneris puer indomitus*); and Bonnefons, *Pancharis*, Basium 6.1.

7. I take "milky" here as "milk-white" (so Catull. 55.17 and many times in Pontano), stressing the attractive color of the breasts, rather than, as sometimes, "lactifluous," though Ciaffi (in Muscetta/Ponchiroli 1959) renders *gonfi di latte* ("swollen with milk"), while in Lodge's 1593 adaptation Cupid actually suckles. Girolamo Amalteo's *De Lycoride* 5–6, probably with debts to Navagero here, reads: "Sucking these nipples, Love declares, *Farewell, my mother's breasts; a sweeter nectar drips from these* [Lycoris']"; see Sannazaro 1728, 369. Unless a recent mother, Hyella would have no milk. Castillejo's version clearly takes *lacteolas* as I do: *Pero viendo la blancura / que sus tetas descubrian / como leche fresca y pura* ("But, seeing the whiteness that her breasts displayed, like fresh pure milk"). *Dignas matre papillas* is also in Johannes Secundus, *Basia* 15.5, where Love is overwhelmed by the sight of Neaera's beauty and rushes to kiss her a thousand times.

8. See 19.24n. Girls to stir even gods: cf. Pontano, *Hendecasyllabi* 2.16.6–7, *Eridanus* 1.17.54 and 2.11.8.

9–10. Cf. 31.4. Arabian fragrances: Ov. *Her.* 1.15.76 ("my hair has on it no gifts of the Arabs"); Prop. 3.13.8; Tib. 2.2.3–4; [Tib.] 3.8.18. *Ambrosius* of delightful or sweet-smelling hair: Verg. *Aen.* 1.403; Stat. *Theb.* 9.731. Castillejo does not translate this couplet, omitted in the Jesi and Belluno MSS.

11. Four versions of this Ovid-inspired line are found in the MSS (see Notes to the Texts). Ov. *Am.* 3.11.28 has *quaere alium*; 3.15.1 of the same, *quaere novum*; Ov. *Fast.* 2.249 begins 'i, mea,' dixit. Castillejo's version (with *un nuevo Amor par ti*) translates the reading *novum tibi*. Cf. Baïf, *Les*

256

*amours de Francine* 72.12–14, where Cupid, hiding in Francine's bosom, tells Venus to find another child, as Francine will be his mother now.

12. The idea of Love resident in a person's eyes, hair, etc., already in the *Greek Anthology* (e.g., 5.26), is common in Renaissance Latin and vernacular poetry. Navagero's Italian poem 1 (see Navagero 1718, 275) begins, "Beautiful eyes where Love reigns," and in his Italian poem 6, cited by Benassi 1940, Love makes his lady's eyes his nest. In Petrarch, *Rime sparse* 39 and 151.7–8, Love is in Laura's eyes. In Pontano, *Hendecasyllabi* 2.16.13, he has his kingdom in Focilla's, and in *Hendecasyllabi* 1.19.3 he has set up home (*sedem*) in a girl's eyes. In Fabio Segni's poem *On Neaera's Eyes* (*Carmina Illustrium Poetarum Italorum* 9:24), Venus declares, "Farewell, Idalium, and farewell, Cythera. My son, our home will permanently be here." Cf. also Marullo, *Epigrams* 2.32.81–88.

22

Hyella: 21n. Mention of the nurse suggests Hyella is an unmarried girl. F. 3.29 is worth comparing. So too Ippolito Capilupi's *To the Moon* (Capilupi 1590, 127), asking the Moon not to shine but to grant a cover of thick darkness as the speaker silently makes his way to Pholoe's blessed abode. See also Fausto Sabeo, *To Night* (Sabeo 1556, 127); Toscano, *To the Moon, a Prayer on Behalf of Iolas* (*Carmina Illustrium Poetarum Italorum* 9:370). Ronsard's *Hinne* [*Hymne*] *a la nuit* is thought to draw on this poem and Pontano's *Hymnus in Noctem* (Hymn to Night). MSS: Mil.3, Vat.9.

2. *Dulcia . . . furta*: F. 3.4.4n.

4. Cf., for example, Ov. *Ib.* 630, *comites . . . viae*. Pontano, *De Amore Coniugali* 1.7.3, calls Love *viae . . . duxque comesque* ("both guide and companion of your way"), imitated in F. 3.13.6. Ov. *Tr.* 4.10.119 has *tu dux et comes es*.

5. *Deprehendere* scans by syncopation as if *deprendere*, which could be read.

6. Venus surrounds Aeneas and his two companions in mist to enable them to enter Carthage undetected in Verg. *Aen.* 1.411–12. T. V. Strozzi alludes to that in *Erotica* 4.8.111–14, telling Sylvia that Venus will likewise

## · NOTES TO THE TRANSLATIONS ·

cloak her in a dark shadow of thick mist (*densi . . . aeris*). Hor. *Odes* 2.7.14 has *denso . . . aere* of mist.

7–8. Understand *est* with *dignus*. *Dicier* (= *dici*, "to be called") is present passive infinitive, like *involvier* in 20.14. In mythology, Anchises was punished for divulging his lovemaking with Venus.

9–12. Goddess of Eleusis (in Attica): Demeter/Ceres. With 9 cf. Catull. 64.259–60, where devotees of Bacchus throng round "dark mysteries in hollow caskets (*cavis . . . orgia cistis*)"; Tib. 1.7.48; Ov. *Ars am.* 2.609 (601–40 speaks of keeping secret Venus' mysteries, as initiates must keep secret those of Ceres; Tantalus is mentioned in 606 as punished for disclosures). In Tib. 1.2.34 Venus wants her intrigues kept hidden (*celari vult sua furta Venus*).

12. *Saepius* lacks real comparative force; cf. 26.71, 73, and 75. *Garrula lingua:* Ov. *Am.* 2.2.44 (of Tantalus' indiscreet tongue); [Tib.] 3.19.20. Tib. 1.2.39–40 threatens that Venus will punish any observer who tells about a clandestine meeting of the poet and his lady.

13–16. The old nurse is the classic confidante and go-between, as in Euripides' *Phaedra* and many other places, e.g., Ov. *Met.* 10.382–468. Navagero's *cognita fida* (14) reflects Ov. *Am.* 1.11.3–6, where a go-between maid is *cognita utilis* ("known of service") and *fida reperta* ("found trusty"). Other passages to compare for go-betweens include Tib. 1.2.94; Ov. *Am.* 2.19.41 and 3.1.56, *Ars am.* 1.351–98 and 3.621–24, *Rem. am.* 639–40; [Verg.] *Ciris* 220–82; and Theoc. *Id.* 2.94–101. An old woman waits by the door and brings the lover to the girl in Tib. 1.6.57–62, though there she is the girl's mother. In T. V. Strozzi's *He Boasts after Enjoying His Lady* (*Erotica* 1.6.6), an old woman leads the poet to his mistress after he has climbed over the rooftop while the moon is obscured, so evading the doorkeeper. Pontano in *Parthenopeus* 1.3.23–30 pleads for Fannia's trusted maid to open the door for him. *Sedula . . . anus* is after Tib. 1.3.84.

16. *Dominae* may be "her mistress" (so Wilson 1973 and McFarlane 1980) or "my mistress" (so Nichols 1998). In Tac. *Ann.* 13.13 *suum cubiculum ac sinum* = "her bedchamber and private space." *Sinum* probably has that sense here (so Wilson 1973 and McFarlane 1980), though *in sinus* in Ov. *Ars am.* 2.458 means "into the embrace(s)."

258

# · NOTES TO THE TRANSLATIONS ·

19–20. The lamp as a discreet witness to lovemaking: *Anth. Pal.* 5.4, 5, 8, 128, 165, 166, and 197, 6.162, 7.219; Mart. 10.38, 11.104, 14.39. Lamps are "watchful" (i.e., burn all night) in Hor. *Odes* 3.8.14.

### 23

The titles in Gagny ca. 1548, Duchesne 1560, Toscano 1576, and Navagero 1718 presume that only one laurel is involved and see the plurals in the poem as poetic. That view seems correct. As Apollo's laurel often symbolizes poetic excellence, the poem possibly has allegorical significance. No manuscript evidence, as for 37, 39, 40, 41, 44, 48, and 67.

4. *Aura . . . liberiore* is literally "freer air." Cf. Ov. *Met.* 15.301, *liberiore frui caelo* ("to enjoy freer sky"), said of winds. In Zanchi, *Poemata* 6.4.48, a soaring bird "enjoys ever freer sky" (*fruitur semper liberiore polo*); see Zanchi 1555, 195. In Pontano, *Eridanus* 1.34.10, Ovid's words are applied to palm trees growing taller.

6. Ov. *Met.* 1.564–65 *frondis honores* is used of the laurel's foliage.

7. The laurel, once the nymph Daphne, was above all associated with Apollo, her would-be lover, and so with the Muses. See Ov. *Met.* 1.452–567 for her story and 1.558–67 for the laurel as Apollo's tree.

9. Ov. *Tr.* 3.1.45 talks of Augustus' house having never-failing glory like the evergreen laurel.

### 24

Pythagoras, the ancient Greek philosopher, believed in reincarnation and was thought many times reincarnated himself. Cf. *Anth. Pal.* 2.120–24 (Pythagoras' statue looks intent only on measuring the heavens), 16.325 (the sculptor wished to portray him in wise silence), and 16.326 (a lifelike painting of him looking able to speak, "if Pythagoras had been willing to speak"). MSS: Mil.3, Vat.14.

3. The name *Asilas* (or *Asylas*) is that of an Etruscan in Verg. *Aen.* 9.571, 10.175, etc., and occurs otherwise in Latin poems by Boccaccio. I find no sculptor (ancient or later) so named; he and the statue seem imaginary. See 42n.

259

## · NOTES TO THE TRANSLATIONS ·

6. I cannot parallel *in se . . . totus abit* (lit., "he goes off totally into himself") of absorption in one's thoughts.

8. Secrecy on religious matters was observed by Pythagoras and his followers, who extolled silence. Pythagoreans were "the silent ones" (cf. Ov. *Met.* 15.66), as students had to listen in silence to Pythagoras' instruction for five years. He is "the silent elder" in Pannonius, *Epigrams* 22.11.

25

With the opening lines cf. Hor. *Odes* 1.4.1–12 (winter passing, west wind blowing, Venus dancing, flowers appearing), 4.7.1–10; Lucr. 1.6–20, 5.737–40; Catull. 46.1–3; Verg. *G.* 2.315–45; Ov. *Fast.* 1.151–59. Cf. also poem 41 below. Cicogna 1824–53, 6:292n311, records a version by Chiappino (as also of 19, 21, and 26) and mentions two others. Paul Laumonier suggests that lines 21–36 of Ronsard's *Le Narciss* (the coming of spring, the effect on the birds, etc.) are in some general debt to Navagero here; see Ronsard 1914–75, 6:75. Baïf too has a coming-of-spring poem in *Les amours de Francine* (3.11). MS: Mil.3; see also 34n.

1. Winter has white hair in Ov. *Met.* 2.30 and 15.213.

3–4. Though the word *ver* is neuter, the personified Spring here is treated as a boy (*puer ipse* in 8), possibly under the influence of Ov. *Met.* 15.201, where the year in spring is "very like a boy's age," the seasons marking progression from childhood to old age. Bembo, *Carmina* 1.13 (*Pastorum Chorus*), a coming-of-spring poem, echoes Ovid in declaring, "Now the year is a boy" (13). In line 3, *auras* rather than *oras* seems supported by the assonance with *audet* (so Mil.3 and printed texts). In Verg. *G.* 2.47, early editions, including the Aldine, read *luminis auras* (lit., "air of light") rather than *luminis oras* ("shores [i.e., realms, regions] of light"), though the latter image, a borrowing from Ennius, occurs nine times in Lucretius and also in Verg. *Aen.* 7.660 and Valerius Flaccus, prompting some later editors to substitute *oras* for *auras* in the *Georgics* passage. F. 2.9.3 has *oras in luminis*. Pontano has both *in luminis oras* and *in luminis auras* in lines of his *Urania*. For Navagero's use of *proferre* in line 4, cf. *ferre sub auras* in Verg. *Aen.* 2.158.

260

· NOTES TO THE TRANSLATIONS ·

6. Ovid, *Fast.* 5.195–206 treats Chloris as a nymph who became Zephyr's wife Flora after being raped by him. Botticelli's *Primavera* shows Chloris pursued by Zephyr and also in her new role as Flora, who is "mother of flowers" (*mater . . . florum*) in Ov. *Fast.* 5.183; cf. *Flora . . . mater* in Lucr. 5.739. Bernardino Partenio (*Carmina Illustrium Poetarum Italorum* 7:98; see Hutton 1935, 190–91) also has *Chloridos e gremio*, and Zanchi, *Poemata* 6.2.23, has bright Spring raising a pretty head "from Chloris' bosom" (there *sinu de Chloridos*); see Zanchi 1555, 189. So too Flaminio in his Horatian ode 2.33.1–2: "Now Spring puts forth a flowery-haired head from Chloris' richly colored bosom (*puniceo Chloridis ex sinu*)." Cf. the common imagery of the bosom of Mother Earth (Lucr. 1.251 and 2.375; Verg. *Aen.* 3.509; Stat. *Theb.* 4.787), seen in 19.34 here and F. 4.10.11–12. Flora occurs in F. 3.5.2.

7. Cf. Lucr. 1.7–8 (*tellus summittit flores*); Prop. 1.2.9 (*summittat humus . . . colores*).

10. The winds and clouds flee at Venus' approach in Lucr. 1.6.

11–12. Cf. poem 41. Inspired by the opening lines of Lucretius' *De rerum natura*, where Venus makes animals mate, life proliferate, flowers spring up, etc. Pontano, *Eridanus* 1.36.24–38, is another passage with like debts.

14. The Graces were regularly associated with Venus. *Ros* (lit., "dew") of perfume or myrrh: [Tib.] 3.4.28; Ov. *Her.* 15.76 (reading *Arabo . . . rore*). Pontano, *Parthenopeus* 2.14.4. has *Assyrio . . . rore;* so too Molza in line 26 of his elegy *Ad Venerem* (Molza 1747–54, 1:248). Assyrian (i.e., Syrian) fragrances: Catull. 68.144; Verg. *Ecl.* 4.25; Tib. 1.3.7; Hor. *Odes* 2.11.16; Stat. *Silv.* 2.4.34 and 3.3.212. Cf. "Syrian scents" in 31.26. See also 56.22–23n.

15. The winged boys are proliferations of Cupid, the Loves (see 37.17). Spondaic fifth foot (as in line 61 and 44.21).

18. Lucr. 1.14 ends *persultant pabula laeta.* Navagero has *pabula laeta* also in 11.4 and 27.1. *Vagi . . . greges* is also in 10B.2.

19. The name *Amaryllis,* also in 27.13, is found in Verg. *Ecl.* 1, 2, 8, and 9; Calp. *Ecl.* 4.38; Theoc. *Id.* 3 and 4. It is common in Neo-Latin (as in F. 3.5.5, 3.6.3, 4.5.52) and vernacular poetry.

261

· NOTES TO THE TRANSLATIONS ·

20. For *tenui* (also 27.39) cf. Verg. *Ecl.* 1.2 (of a shepherd's pipe). A lyric or elegiac poet might himself be called *tenuis* ("light"), as Catullus is by Mart. 10.103.5.

21. Lucr. 1.12–13 describes the birds as "excited in their hearts (*perculsae corda*)" by Venus' power. *Perculsae* might be read here, though *percussae* ("stricken") also makes sense (cf. Verg. G. 4.357; Lucr. 5.1223).

23–42. In 24 both *Itym* and Greek *Ityn* (*Carmina Illustrium Poetarum Italorum* 6:478; cf. Ov. *Met.* 6.652 and Hor. *Odes* 4.12.6) are legitimate spellings; cf. *Calaim* or *Calain* in 58. As Navagero has Greek forms in lines 6, 19, 47, 53, 54, and 57, *Ityn* is tempting, but note alliteration of *m* in the couplet. In the earlier Greek version of the myth, Progne (or Procne) kills her son Itys and serves him as food to his father, her Thracian husband Tereus, for violating her sister Philomela and cutting out her tongue. When, on learning what he has eaten, the furious Tereus chases the sisters, intent on killing them, all are turned into birds, Philomela becoming a swallow, and Progne a nightingale. In the later Roman version, however, Progne is often the swallow, and Philomela the nightingale. The story becomes inconsistently told. For instance, Pentadius makes Itys' mother Progne in 1.3–4, but Philomela in 2.7–8. Philomela is Itys' mother in Verg. G. 4.511; likewise in Pontano, *Eclogues* 4.127–33; Castiglione, *Alcon* 8; and Pigna's *Carmen ad Albertum Lollium* (Pigna 1553, 36). Here, by "Thracian mother" Navagero ought to mean Progne (Tereus' wife in 37), apparently (as in the Greek version) the nightingale. Nevertheless, in 27.67 Philomela, mentioned for her melodious song, is presumably the nightingale. *Daulias* ("the Daulian") in 37.34 probably means Progne, as in Catull. 65.14 and Ov. *Her.* 15.154, where the Daulian bird mourns Itys after taking dreadful vengeance on her husband. Daulis is the city in Phocis in central Greece where Tereus ruled and Itys was murdered. At least Johannes Secundus' allusion to the myth in *Silva* 5.120–21 is mercifully unequivocal: "Philomela so mourns her young nephew in the woods; her sister, the swallow, so laments her son on roofs." There Philomela is clearly the nightingale, and Progne the swallow and Itys' mother. Chief ancient account: Ov. *Met.* 6.426–674. With *absumptum* (24) cf. Catull. 65.14 *absumpti . . . Ityli* (Itylus is Itys' alternative

262

· NOTES TO THE TRANSLATIONS ·

name); Prop. 3.10.10 (his mother mourns *absumptum . . . Ityn*); Varchi, *Carmina* 6.92, *absumptum deflet Daulias ales Ithim* ("the Daulian bird bewails murdered Itys").

25–26. With *di bene* understand *fecerunt* ("The gods [did] well"); Stat. *Theb.* 9.296. *Dira . . . regione* is after Ov. *Tr.* 3.2.5.

27–28. Cf. Ovid's treatment of the killing of Itys (*Met.* 6.624–45, especially 639–41). With 27 cf. *Met.* 3.723, ending *matri bracchia tendat*.

30. In Ovid's version the boy is stabbed by his mother Progne in the side, and Philomela cuts his throat, the body being then torn apart. Philomela later throws the boy's severed head into his father's face (*Met.* 6.658). Verg. *Aen.* 2.557 has *avulsum . . . caput* of Priam's hacked-off head.

31. First four words as Ov. *Pont.* 4.3.29.

35. Tereus as his eaten son's "tomb": Ov. *Met.* 6.665; the poet Accius had earlier similarly called Thyestes his sons' tomb. Man-eating creatures are likewise their meals' "tombs" in Ennius and Lucr. 5.991. In English literature cf. Spenser, *Faerie Queene* 2.8.16, "To be entombed in the raven or the kight"; Shakespeare, *Macbeth* 3.4.72–73, "our monuments [= tombs] shall be the maws of kites." Some Neo-Latin poets comparably treat human and animal mothers dying in labor as the tombs of their unborn offspring.

39. *Violentior* lacks comparative force and substitutes for the positive or superlative. Tereus' pursuit of the women, who turn into birds: Ov. *Met.* 6.666–74.

43. Giambattista della Torre (*Turrius*), nobleman of Verona, friend of Navagero, and promoter of literature, was himself a member of Alviano's Pordenone Academy. He and his brothers figure in poems of Fracastoro, who named a dialogue after him, and poem 15 of Cotta (himself born near Verona) is addressed to him and Navagero, called *Naugeri optime* ("excellent Navagero"). Cotta bids farewell to his "good boon companions" (*boni mei sodales*) and wishes he could be with them "at your Bembo's colloquies," but harsh necessity forces him to go to other lands. *Florifero vere*: Sen. *Oed.* 649. *Omnia rident* (cf. 27.14 and 31.25) recalls Verg. *Ecl.* 7.55. See F. 4.25n for the nephew of the della Torre addressed here.

263

## · NOTES TO THE TRANSLATIONS ·

47. Venus is *parens Amathusia* ("the Amathusian mother") in Ov. *Am.* 3.15.15 and simply *Amathusia* in Catull. 68.51 and [Verg.] *Ciris* 242. I do not find her called *Amathusis* in any ancient author, but Pontano calls her that in *De Hortis Hesperidum* 1.605. Cf. such forms as *Cypris* and (of Minerva) *Tritonis*, as well as *Parrhasis* in 26.44. Amathus was in Cyprus.

48–49. Construe as "fierce with bow and torch." Cf. 41.35–36; Ov. *Am.* 3.2.55 ("the boys mighty with the bow"); Pontano, *Eclogues* 5.30 ("Love cruel with the bow"); Marullo, *Epigrams* 1.63.10–12 (*Cupido, / acer . . . pharetra, / acer et arcu*). Armenian tigers: Verg. *Ecl.* 5.29; Prop. 1.9.19; and [Tib.] 3.6.15.

50. For Cupid snatching Jupiter's thunderbolts from him, cf. 36.5–8. Angeriano, *Erotopaegnion* 172.8, says Love dares even to snatch his thunderbolts from angry Jupiter; see Wilson 1995. Cf. also Ov. *Am.* 2.5.52 (kisses "such as might have knocked his three-pronged missiles from angry Jupiter's hand"); Petrarch, *Rime sparse* 11.7–8 and 42.5; Sabeo, *De Cupidine* 3 ("you snatch the blazing thunderbolt from Jupiter's angry hands"); see Sabeo 1556, 35. Cupid's power over Jupiter and other deities is quite a common theme in both ancient and Renaissance poetry, e.g., Ov. *Met.* 5.366–84; Ugolino Verino, *Flammetta* 2.2.11–12, where Love alone scorns the Thunderer's fierce thunderbolts.

51–52. Orpheus went alive to the Underworld to plead with Pluto to return his dead wife, Eurydice (Verg. *G.* 4.453–527; Ov. *Met.* 10.1–63). *Oeagrius* may = "Thracian" or "Oeagrius' son," as in Phanocles (see 25.55–64n) and Ap. Rhod. 4.905. Poliziano, *Silvae* 1.72, and Ercole Strozzi, *Amores* 1.117, have *Oeagrius Orpheus*; see Strozzi 1513, 71r. *Pallentes umbras* is found in Verg. *Aen.* 4.26.

53. Hecate: Underworld form of Diana, worshipped at crossroads and often portrayed as three-headed, associated with magic and ghostly things.

54. The Eumenides were the three Furies or Erinyes, with snakes in their hair or around their waists and brandishing torches, who pursued those guilty of especially heinous crimes.

55–64. Verg. *G.* 4.516–27 and Ovid *Met.* 10.83–86 portray the twice-bereft Orpheus as wanting no further relations with the female sex, be-

264

### · NOTES TO THE TRANSLATIONS ·

coming a pederast in Ovid's version and being torn apart for it by the women of Thrace. Only a fragment of Phanocles preserved by Stobaeus (*Ecl.* 20.2.47) makes Orpheus enamored of Calais, the North Wind's son, born to the abducted Orithyia in Thrace. With the beginning of that fragment ("Or as Oeagrius' son, Thracian Orpheus, loved Calais"), cf. *Oeagrius Orpheus* in line 51. Line 57 ends as Verg. *Aen.* 5.334. *Boreiadem* in 58 (five syllables, the *e* being long) represents Phanocles' *Boreïaden*; the patronymic is not attested in classical Latin. For polysyllabic pentameter endings in Navagero's poems, see F. 3.1–4.25n. Navagero has another five-syllable word ending a pentameter at 26.42 (*Hamadryadum*). Both *Calaim* and Greek *Calain* are possible accusative forms of *Calais*. See poem 5n.

60. Cf. 27.49, 30.22, and 41.14. Passion felt in bones: Verg. *Aen.* 1.660 and 4.101; [Verg.] *Ciris* 163–64; Ov. *Met.* 2.410; Stat. *Ach.* 1.303–4. Possibly construe *penitus* with *ferventes* rather than *perditus* (cf. 41.14 and the *Ciris* passage).

61–64. Pointedly after Verg. *G.* 4.464–66, where repeated *te* refers to Eurydice. Cf. also Ov. *Met.* 10.205. *Orithyiae* scans as four long syllables (*yi* is a diphthong), with a fifth foot spondee, as in Verg. *G.* 4.463 and *Aen.* 12.83; Ov. *Met.* 6.683 (and see 25.15n). For *in te suspirat* cf. Ov. *Fast.* 1.417 and Catull. 64.98.

### 26

Prop. 1.11 wonders whether Cynthia, away at Baiae, gives him any thought, or another has prevailed upon her. The poem *Ad Cupidinem* of Gianantonio Taigeto or Taglietti (*Carmina Illustrium Poetarum Italorum* 9:232–33) resembles the first half of this present poem in theme and structure. Cicogna 1824–53, 6:292n311, records a version by Chiappino. MS: Mil.3.

1–2. Saying a place "holds" someone means that the person is staying there. For instance, Tib. 2.3.1 states, *Rura meam . . . tenent villaeque puellam*, "Her country estate and villa hold my girl." Giovanni Battista Amalteo's *Ad Hyellam* begins *Dum te rura tenent cultis formosa viretis* ("While your country retreat, beautiful with its elegant lawns, holds you"); see San-

## · NOTES TO THE TRANSLATIONS ·

nazaro 1728, 444. Prop. 2.15.2, addressing the bed "made blessed with my delights" (*deliciis facte . . . beate meis*), seems the model for line 2. *Aestiva . . . umbra*: Ov. *Met.* 13.793.

3–4. Line 3 ends as Bembo, *Carmina* 4.15 (*Iolas ad Faunum*); cf. Nemes. *Ecl.* 2.49. Line 4: cf. Ov. *Ars am.* 3.56.

6. Cf. F. 3.18.28. T. V. Strozzi, *Erotica* 1.5.37–38, asserts, "A faithful woman is rare indeed, unless her eye feeds her fire." He gives mythological instances of betrayal of absent men by their women, but then, like Navagero here (19–24), recalls his lady's different character, declaring his fears idle. Several Renaissance poets censure women for supposed inconstancy. Among ancient poets, cf. Verg. *Aen.* 4.569, "Woman is ever a fickle and changeable thing"; [Tib.] 3.4.61; Catull. 70. Mantuan's *Eclogues* 4.110–241 is a particularly fierce tirade against all women.

7–10. Leaves turning in the wind are quite often an image of female inconstancy. Prop. 2.9.33–36 is Navagero's chief model here. Among Neo-Latin poets cf. Tebaldeo, *Ad Galateam* 23–26 ("Not so swiftly do trembling leaves change on a tree . . . as shifts a deceitful girl's heart"); see Pasquazi 1957, 158; T. V. Strozzi, *Erotica* 5.2.54 ("you surpass the poplar's leaves in your constant shifting").

10. The shut-out lover is a regular figure in ancient amatory poetry, bewailing his lot or pleading for admission at his lady's door. His song is a paraclausithyron; see Copley 1956. The pattern of the line resembles Ov. *Tr.* 3.7.42, *Irus et est subito, qui modo Croesus erat* ("and he is suddenly Irus [a beggar] who was just lately Croesus [rich]"); Prop. 1.18.7–8, 2.8.6, 2.17.11–12, 4.7.39–40; Ugolino Verino, *Flammetta* 1.25.32 (*servus qui modo victor eras*).

11–16. Cf. Prop. 2.9.3–8. Penelope, faithful wife of the long-absent Ulysses (Odysseus), pressed by suitors to take a new husband, put off any decision by each night undoing her day's work on a shroud, on completion of which she had promised to make her choice. The twenty years in line 15 are the ten of the Trojan War plus the ten of Ulysses' wanderings thereafter. Capaneus' wife, Evadne, threw herself on his funeral pyre (Prop. 1.15.21–22; Ov. *Ars am.* 3.21–22). In *Capaneia coniux* (Stat.

266

· NOTES TO THE TRANSLATIONS ·

*Theb.* 12.545), *Capaneia* is five syllables (*e* long). Penelope and Evadne are coupled as examples of loyalty and devotion in Prop. 3.13.23–24.

20. Cf. Hor. *Ars poet.* 105–6 ("sad words suit a sad face") and *Epist.* 1.7.44.

21. Martial has the name *Gellia* several times; e.g., in 6.90 he lampoons a Gellia for faithfulness to one partner — in addition to her husband!

22. Literally, "nor is she wont to change unfixed beds," i.e., be promiscuous. In Pontano, *Eclogues* 5.98, with Cupid disarmed and restrained, every woman would have *certum . . . torum* ("a fixed bed"; cf. his *Eridanus* 2.20.38).

25–38. Divine molestation of his addressee is similarly feared by Castiglione, *Carmina* 6 (*To a Girl Walking on the Shore*) and 7 (*To the Same*); see Castiglione 1995. In Giovanni Battista Amalteo's *Ad Lygdamum*, the speaker fears that Lygdamus may, like Hylas, be molested by nymphs; see Sannazaro 1728, 420–22. T. V. Strozzi, *Erotica* 1.3.25–36, speaks of fear that his girl may fall victim to the West Wind or Jupiter in bull, gold, or swan form. In *Epigrams* 4.13 Marullo fears an attack by Faunus (Pan) on Alessandra Scala (his eventual wife). In Pontano, *Eridanus* 2 (addressed to his pupil Girolamo Borgia), the aged poet fears that his far-distant young mistress Stella, forgetful of him, may be at risk from the swan's plumage or a shower of gold, as well as from jealous nymphs. Pontano there advises Borgia (for whom see 20.69–70n) to believe there is no faith in love. *Saturnius* ("Saturn's son"): Jupiter. With 26 cf. Ov. *Pont.* 4.15.6 and 4.7.38. Fields painted with flowers: 19.32n.

30. *Grata rapina*: Prop. 2.2.10; Pontano, *De Amore Coniugali* 2.1.28; Marullo, *Tumuli* 1.14.16.

31–32. In Prop. 2.26.47–48 Amymone was attacked by Neptune while fetching water. See 20.81n for *mediis . . . in arvis.*

33–34. Io, priestess of Juno (Hera) at Argos: Ov. *Met.* 1.583–750. Jupiter (Zeus) violated her, then turned her into a heifer (Ov. *Met.* 1.611). Jupiter, the thunder god, is commonly *Tonans* ("the Thunderer"), as in line 63 and 36.6 (of the Christian God in 34.16).

267

· NOTES TO THE TRANSLATIONS ·

35–36. Proserpina, or Persephone, daughter of Ceres, abducted while flower-picking at Enna in Sicily by her uncle Pluto to be the Underworld queen (Ov. *Met.* 5.359–408), was also known as Deous Kore ("Daughter of Deo"), hence *Deois* here (as Ov. *Met.* 6.114). *Infernus Pater* ("the Underworld Father"): Pluto (*Infernus Parens* in Sil. 2.671). The *-us* of *Infernus* is here lengthened at the dieresis (see 13.10n).

37–38. Europa was carried off to sea near Sidon in Phoenicia by Jupiter in the guise of a bull (Ov. *Met.* 2.843–75; "the feigned bull," *Met.* 3.1).

41–42. Pans (plural): Ov. *Met.* 14.638, *Her.* 4.171, *montanaque numina Panes* ("and the Pans, mountain deities"); Prop. 3.17.34. Sannazaro, *Salices* (The Willows) 15–16, has *agrestia Panes numina*. Satyrs, like Pans, were lustful woodland beings. A hamadryad is a wood nymph. Faunus/Pan is "the lover of fleeing nymphs" in Hor. *Odes* 3.18.1. Marullo, *Epigrams* 4.13.1–2, calls him "the terror of the naiad sisters."

43. Daphne, daughter of the River Peneus, was pursued by Apollo and became the laurel (Ov. *Met.* 1.452–567; *Daphne Peneia* with four syllables occurs in line 452).

44. Callisto, a companion of Diana violated by Jupiter, was transformed by Juno into a bear as punishment (Ov. *Met.* 2.405–530). Eventually Jupiter set her in the sky as the Great Bear. Parrhasian = Arcadian, from Parrhasia, a town in Arcadia. *Parrhasis* as a substantive: Ov. *Met.* 2.460.

45–46. Pan as *semicaper*: 5.9–10n. Nonacrian = Arcadian (see 18.1–2n). The "Arcadian maiden" is presumably Syrinx, who became a reed (Ov. *Met.* 1.689–712), though Pan lusted after Echo too, his "neighbor" in Moschus 5.1. Various nymphs called Aegle (or Aegla) occur (e.g., Verg. *Ecl.* 6.20–21, "Aegle, most beautiful of the naiads"), none specifically linked to Pan.

51–52. The allusions of 35–36 and 43 are picked up here. Mt. Etna is the volcano in Sicily.

57–58. Milanion is Atalanta's devoted lover and protector. In Apollod. *Bibl.* 3.9 he wins her by beating her in the famous footrace. In Ov. *Met.* 10.560–680, however, Atalanta is so won by Hippomenes, not Milanion, while Ov. *Ars am.* 2.185–96 and Prop. 1.1.9–16 connect Milanion and Atalanta differently. He occurs also in Ov. *Ars am.* 3.775 and *Am.* 3.2.29.

268

## · NOTES TO THE TRANSLATIONS ·

Mil.3 and the early editions here all give *Mimalione*, which Navagero probably wrote, as *Mimalion* is the spelling adopted in Prop. 1.1.9 in some printed texts of Navagero's day, including the Aldine (Venice, 1502 and 1515). In keeping with my practice of modernizing spellings of names, I have adopted the form now generally favored in texts of Ovid and Propertius.

60. Omission of *in* (cf. 3.2) after *comminus ire:* Prop. 2.19.22.

62. "A wide fingernail" means "a fingernail's width." Plaut. *Aul.* 1.1.17–18: "If you budge a finger's breadth or a nail's width (*unguem latum*)." Cf. F. 5.23.21–22 ("do not withdraw more than a fingernail's width from him"); Bembo, *Carmina* 13.40 ("never further than a fingernail from my side").

65–80. Cf. 27.35–45. Giambattista Pinelli's poem *Ad Lillam*, concerned with a girl's absence in the country, similarly talks of what bliss it would be to hunt beasts with her, confront wild boars, catch wild goats, outspeed stags and hares, fish with her or trap birds, play music as dances are held, etc; see Pinelli 1594, 10–12.

68. "Green couch": Verg. *Aen.* 5.388 similarly has *viridante toro*.

69–70. The Dog Star, Sirius ("dry" in Prop. 2.28.4), was associated with the hottest period of the year. Cf. especially Verg. *G.* 2.353 ("when the heat-bringing Dog Star cracks the gaping fields with thirst").

73. Several editions, including Navagero 1530, Gagny ca. 1548, and Navagero 1718, have *convicia dicere* ("utter cries"; cf. Pontano, *De Amore Coniugali* 2.15.3, of a baby crying), but *convivia ducere* (as in Mil.3) is surely right (= "draw out banquets" in Tib. 1.9.61; perhaps just "hold banquets" here). That reading first appears in printed texts of Navagero in the four editions of *Carmina Quinque Illustrium Poetarum* between 1548 and 1558 and is thus also in Toscano 1576. Ariosto, *Carmina* 4.26, has *ducere convivia*. Cf. *statuit convivia luco* in 5.7 above.

74. *Madidae* of anointed or perfumed hair: Ov. *Her.* 14.30 ("with fresh flowers restraining the dripping hair"), *Met.* 3.555, and *Am.* 1.6.38.

75–76. Tib. 1.1.4 has *classica pulsa* of blown (valveless) trumpets; Lucr. 5.1384 has *tibia . . . digitis pulsata* ("flute beaten with fingers," i.e., as they play on the holes).

269

## · NOTES TO THE TRANSLATIONS ·

78. Navagero combines elements of Ov. *Ars am.* 1.116 and *Am.* 1.4.6. Jean Bonnefons, *Pancharis*, Basium 15.4, fears that fauns *iniciant rapidas in tua colla manus* ("may lay grasping hands on your neck").

79–80. Epanalepsis: 41.33n. Pontano, admired by Navagero, has many instances of similar repetitions in *Tumuli* 1.8 and was notably fond of epanalepsis in general.

81–82. After [Tib.] 3.3.25. A "white" day was a lucky one, perhaps from marking it white in a calendar, though Pliny the Elder claims (*HN* 7.131) that Thracians put a white pebble in a jar if a day had been good, a black one if bad. Thus, by a count at death, a life could be judged good or bad overall. Marullo, *Epigrams* 3.53.2, talks of a happy day "worthy of the Thracian mark." For white = lucky days, cf. Hor. *Odes* 1.36.10 and *Sat.* 2.3.246; Catull. 68.148 and 107.6; Mart. 8.45.2 ("Let a milk-white gemstone mark this day" — see next note) and 9.53.5; Persius 2.1. The usage is often found in Neo-Latin poets.

83–84. *Erythraeis lapillis* refers to pure-white pearls of the Erythraean or "Red" Sea, in ancient times meaning the present-day Arabian Sea; what is now the Red Sea was then called the Arabian Gulf. In Stat. *Silv.* 4.6.18 a happy night is one "to be marked with . . . Erythraean Sea stones (*Erythraeis . . . signanda lapillis*)." See also Mart. 5.37.4 and 9.2.9. Sannazaro, *Elegies* 2.8.13, speaks of a day to be fittingly marked *Erythraeis . . . lapillis*.

85. *Caveto* is second imperative, like *dicito* in F. 4.1.26.

27

The name *Iolas* (see 3n) sometimes denotes the poet himself (e.g., Castiglione in his *Alcon*), but not here. Grant 1965, 141–43, offers a very loose verse translation with comment. Imitated by Baïf 1881–90, 3:36–40, and Ronsard 1914–75, 12:93–108, where Laumonier cites bibliographical references to discussions of debts to Navagero, such as Kuhn 1914, 317–25. See also Mustard 1909 and Eckhardt 1920, 242. Gilroy 1930 gives this poem substantial attention. Mustard 1909, 265, credibly suggests that in one of his *Songes* entitled "A True Love" Nicholas Grimald imitates Theoc. *Id.* 12 through this poem of Navagero. In Francisco de la Torre's *Egloga* 3 (*Eco*),

## · NOTES TO THE TRANSLATIONS ·

lines 1–14 are translated from Navagero's opening here, the rest of the piece being derived from poem 19; see de la Torre 1984, 239. Cicogna 1824–53, 6:292n311, records two Italian versions. MSS: Mil.1 and 3, Vat.11. The meter is dactylic hexameters.

1. *Pabula laeta*: 11.4n, 25.18n.

2–4. After Theoc. *Id.* 8.67–68, where ewes are told not to hesitate to glut themselves on tender grass, as the shoots will regrow, and Verg. *G.* 2.201–2 ("all that the herds will crop during the long days, that much the cool dew will restore in a very brief night").

5–6. Cf. Theoc. *Id.* 8.69–70 ("Feed, feed, and all fill your udders, so that the lambs may have some of the milk, and I may store the rest in cheese baskets"). New-made cheeses were stored in wicker cheese baskets (*fiscellae*) for the whey to drain off. With 5 cf. Verg. *Ecl.* 4.21.

7. Dog's name *Teuchon* (sometimes spelled *Teucon*): Xen. *Cyn.* 7.5. This line is echoed in Zanchi, Eclogue 5.10 (*Phyllis*): *vigil atque canum fortissimus Alcon*; see Zanchi 1555, 182. See further 27.63–67n and 74–77n.

11. Dido "muses on her love" in Verg. *Aen.* 4.171.

12. Love-cares soothed with music: Verg. *G.* 4.464 and *Aen.* 10.191; Stat. *Ach.* 1.186, *Silv.* 5.3.31, and *Theb.* 9.603; [Tib.] 3.4.71; and above all Theoc. *Id.* 11.17–82 (of the Cyclops Polyphemus), a poem that seems Navagero's inspiration in the description of the cave in 28–34 and in other respects.

13. Name *Amaryllis*: 25.19n. That nothing is sweet without someone: Verg. *Aen.* 12.882–83; Claud. *In Rufin.* 2.268.

15. Almost identical to 20.63.

16. After Verg. *G.* 3.162 and Hor. *Odes* 3.11.10, the latter of which contains the only ancient instance of *exsultim* ("friskily").

17. Cf. Lucr. 1.260. The regular text here has hiatus at the principal caesura, not so uncommon in ancient dactylic hexameters but only here in Navagero's verses in that meter.

18. *Cornigeras matres* ("horned mothers") of she-goats: Lucr. 2.368.

22–23. Cf. Verg. *Ecl.* 3.82–83: "Moisture is sweet to newly sown crops, the arbutus to kids after weaning, the pliant willow to the mother goat

## · NOTES TO THE TRANSLATIONS ·

with young, but only Amyntas to me"). Various things are described as sweet in Theoc. *Id.* 8.76–80 (*Id.* 8.57–59 lists grim things). Cf. also *Id.* 9.31–36 and 10.30–31, while Navagero's lines 68–73 are in some debt to *Id.* 12.3–9. Nemes. *Ecl.* 2.50–52 is another passage to notice. Similar analogies with a piscatory emphasis: Sannazaro, *Eclogues* 3.70–78 and 86–93. See further 27.68–73n. *Cytisus* has its last syllable lengthened *in arsi* (see 20.48n).

24–27. In Theoc. *Id.* 8.53–56, the land of Pelops, wealth, and the speed of the wind are rejected for sitting beneath a rock with the beloved and looking out on the sea. Cf. also Verg. *Aen.* 7.807 for outstripping the wind, and similarly *Aen.* 1.317 and 12.345. In 27, *deducere* for *ducere* (or *producere*) = "spend" (life) is not ancient.

28–34. The cave here is not that in 10, though Ronsard's eclogue *Les Pasteurs* (91–100) makes it so. Cf. Theoc. *Id.* 11.45–48 (the Cyclops' cave); see also Verg. *Ecl.* 9.39–43 and Hom. *Od.* 9.183–87; cf. too Calypso's cave in *Od.* 5.58–74. Verg. *Ecl.* 5.6–7 is another cave description. Paul Laumonier see debts to this poem of Navagero in Ronsard's *Eclogue du Thier* (see Ronsard 1914–75, 19:122), as well as to Verg. *Ecl.* 5.6–7 and Sannazaro.

32. *Rauco . . . susurro:* Calp. *Ecl.* 1.3 (of fermenting wine). In Verg. *G.* 1.109 a torrent "causes a hoarse murmur (*raucum . . . murmur;* cf. [Verg.] *Copa* 12) flowing over smooth rocks (*levia saxa*)." In Giovanni Battista Amalteo, Eclogue 2.55 (*Acon*), a fountain *vix fertur tenui per levia saxa susurro* ("barely trickles with a faint gurgle over the smooth rocks"); see Sannazaro 1728, 381.

33. *Aequora ponti:* Verg. *G.* 1.469; Lucr. 1.8, 2.772 and 6.440; [Tib.] 3.4.85.

34. "Oncoming" water: Ov. *Met.* 15.182; Lucr. 1.285. Cf. also Verg. *G.* 2.108 and perhaps Theoc. *Id.* 11.17–18, where the Cyclops sits on a rock and looks out to sea.

35–36. Cf. Theoc. *Id.* 11.63–66, where the Cyclops wishes (in present optatives) that Galatea might live with him, feed his sheep and milk his ewes with him, and help him make cheeses; Verg. *Ecl.* 2.28–55, where the shepherd Corydon wishes (in the present subjunctive) that the youth

272

## · NOTES TO THE TRANSLATIONS ·

Alexis would live with him. In Pontano, *Parthenopeus* 2.2.63–74, a youth pictures living happily in an idyllic setting with a girl.

39. [Verg.] *Cul.* 100 and Ov. *Rem. am.* 181 both end *modulatur arundine carmen*. *Tenue*: 25.20n. *Arguta* of a musical instrument: Verg. *Ecl.* 7.24; [Verg.] *Ciris* 178.

41–42. In Stat. *Ach.* 1.575, Achilles kisses Deidamia as she sings and plays the cithara. Cf. F. 4.5.45–46.

43. For *misero amanti* cf. Ov. *Her.* 18.171 and *Am.* 1.9.28, and note *misello amanti* in 32.12.

45. Croesus, king of Lydia, was proverbially rich.

46. Lycidas and Daphnis are imagined rustics here. See 20.96–97n for the most famous Daphnis. The name *Lycidas* is found in Theoc. *Id.* 7.13 (and passim) and 27.42; Bion 2.1.5 and 2.6.10; and Verg. *Ecl.* 7.67 and 9.2. It is also in the eclogues of Calpurnius Siculus and Nemesianus. Iolas' first meeting with Amaryllis is based on Theoc. *Id.* 11.25–28, where the youthful Polyphemus instantly fell in love with Galatea, who was picking hyacinths with his mother, and on Vergil's imitation in *Ecl.* 8.37–41.

48–49. See 25.60n. Love (or lust) at first sight: Verg. *Ecl.* 8.41; Theoc. *Id.* 2.82, 3.42, and 11.25–29; Ov. *Met.* 2.409–10; and commonly in Neo-Latin love poetry, e.g., Marullo, *Epigrams* 1.13.4 and 8.

50. One *Gorge* was Meleager's sister (Ov. *Met.* 8.543). *Gorgo* is a woman's name in Theoc. *Id.* 15 and *Anth. Pal.* 7.647 and 9.309; cf. F. 3.18.7.

51. Two of the three MSS have the singular *meum . . . amorem* (cf. *fatenti amorem*, Ov. *Met.* 9.561), though printed texts and Mil.3 (possibly derived from Toscano 1576) have the plural *meos . . . amores* (cf. *fateamur amores*, Ov. *Met.* 9.519). Either reading is credible.

53. The sense seems to justify treating the feminine caesura before *humi* as dominant over the masculine caesura after that word and grouping *humi* with *iecisti* rather than with *cecidisset*.

56. See 13.8n.

60–62. *Alcippe*: see 18n. A rival girl's attempted seduction of a youth resisted by him: F. 3.16.5–12 (cf. 3.17.8) and 3.18.9–10 (and see F. 3.16n).

## · NOTES TO THE TRANSLATIONS ·

René Rapin (1621–87) echoes 61–62 in his *Sacred Eclogues* 3.110–11: "Virgin, he who sends quinces sends his heart too; accept both the gift and him." For Rapin in debt to Navagero, see also 44.19–21n. Nichols 1998, 57, describes Alcippe as an "older woman," but the address "handsome boy" (line 61 here) need not come from someone older: in F. 4.8.3 the same address is used by a girl not yet fifteen.

63–67. Adynata ("impossibilities") signify "never" in such contexts as Verg. *Ecl.* 1.59–63; [Verg.] *Dirae* 4–7 and 98–101; Ov. *Met.* 14.37–39; and Prop. 2.15.31–36. Among several passages of adynata so used in Neo-Latin are T. V. Strozzi, *Erotica* 1.3.43–46 and 5.3.210–15; Giovanni Battista Amalteo, *Lycidas* 72–74 (see Sannazaro 1728, 377); and George Buchanan, *Silvae* 3 (*Desiderium Lutetiae*), last eleven lines. Zanchi has *alio quam tangar amore* (63) in Eclogue 5.22 (*Phyllis*); see Zanchi 1555, 182. *Potius* in 63 has the last syllable lengthened (see 20.48n). Line 64 is almost the same as 44.100, while 66 is identical to 44.101. In 67 *Philomela* is the nightingale (cf. Verg. *G.* 4.511); see 25.23–42n. For *sudabunt . . . mella* (64) cf. Verg. *Ecl.* 4.30. "Lowly" brooms (64): Verg. *G.* 2.434. "Soft" violet (65): Verg. *Aen.* 11.69 and *Ecl.* 5.38.

68–73. See 27.22–23n. Winter is *atra* in Verg. *Aen.* 7.214. Sorb apples, fruit of the wild service tree, are "bitter" in Verg. *G.* 3.380. Cf. Theoc. *Id.* 12.3–11: "As much as spring is sweeter than winter, as much as an apple than a sloe, as much as a ewe is shaggier than a lamb, etc." Comparison of daylight/night and spring/winter: Theoc. *Id.* 18.26–28 (corrupt).

73. *Ipsa* here serves for *tu*. Cf. 43.5, where *ipse* = *ille*, and 12.7, where *ipse* virtually = *ego*.

74–77. Paris carves a declaration of constant love on a tree, with adynata, in Ov. *Her.* 5.29–30. For inscribing trees cf. 6.6 and 20.50. Zanchi exactly reproduces 76 and the first half of 77 in his Eclogue 3.56–57 (*Damon*); see Zanchi 1555, 176. The alternative reading *his* for *haec* in 75 gives the sense "and the poplar next to these woods."

78–83. Line 78 ends as Verg. *G.* 3.337. The Riphean Mountains (82) were in northern Scythia (cf. Verg. *G.* 4.518 for the frosts), far above the Black Sea. The Hebrus ("icy" in Verg. *Aen.* 12.331) is the Maritsa, forming most of the present boundary between Greece and Turkey.

· NOTES TO THE TRANSLATIONS ·

87. Cf. "wicked" of thieves and wolves threatening livestock in 10.11.

88. The coming of darkness ends Verg. *Ecl.* 6 and 10; Calp. *Ecl.* 5; Nemes. *Ecl.* 2.

28

Hyella: 21n and 30n. Imitated by du Bellay (see 1n) and Baïf, *Les amours de Francine* 81. In Angeriano, *Erotopaegnion* 36, the poet compares himself to his portrait; in *Erotopaegnion* 58 he sends his portrait to the girl and asks it to plead for him, but fears that, if she touches it, it will, like him, be burned up. In the following century Giambattista Marino has a comparable poem (*Rime amorose* 10); see Marino 1987, 53, for antecedents, including this poem of Navagero and some vernacular sonnets by Serafino d'Aquila. Marullo's *Epigrams* 3.31 is another portrait poem. There the poet kisses a miniature of his beloved, and the fire of his passion burns the image. MSS: Mil.1, Salz., Vat.14 (lines 1–10 only), Wro.

1. The Kalends were the first day of each month. The two-faced god Janus gave his name to January. For *Iani Kalendis* (lit., "on the Kalends of Janus"), cf. Ov. *Ib.* 63. For New Year presents in Neo-Latin poets, cf. Pannonius, *Epigrams* 10.75, and especially T. V. Strozzi, *Erotica* 5.3.

3–4. Paleness of the lover is a commonplace in classical and Renaissance literature. Ov. *Ars am.* 1.729 declares, "Let everyone in love be pale; that is the proper color for a lover." Cf. also Hor. *Odes* 3.10.14; Prop. 1.1.22, 1.5.21, 1.9.17; [Verg.] *Ciris* 225.

5–6. A lover's absent heart, in his beloved's keeping, is a frequent theme in Neo-Latin and vernacular love poets. With that of the absent soul, it is well represented in Petrarch's *Rime sparse*, e.g., 17, 173, 242.13–14, 249.2–3, 256, 268, and Angeriano's *Erotopaegnion*. In *Epigrams* 1.61.9 Marullo bids Neaera return his stolen heart (*remitte cor*). For the sense of *sub tua iura*, cf. 14.6. *Ego* has the *o* long (as in 30.18, 33.3, and 41.38), against the regular quantity in the major classical Latin poets, though that prosody can be found in the post-Augustan period.

7–8. For *torpet . . . lingua* cf. Catull. 51.9; Ov. *Am.* 1.7.20 and *Her.* 11.82 ("my tongue had gone numb, held back by icy fear"). Speechlessness also

275

# · NOTES TO THE TRANSLATIONS ·

figures in Lucr. 3.152–60 (from fear) and Theoc. *Id.* 2.108–9 (in the presence of a beloved). The end of 7 is after Verg. *Aen.* 6.688.

### 29

Written as if in Navagero's persona, this poem draws on many antecedent dreams of intimacy: Theoc. *Id.* 11.22–23 (Galatea visits Polyphemus in his dreams); Hor. *Odes* 4.1.37–40 (homosexual), *Sat.* 1.5.82–85 (causing a nocturnal emission); Ov. *Met.* 9.470 (incestuous); *Anth. Pal.* 5.2 (a poor man's dreams allow free sex with a costly prostitute), 5.243 (no fulfillment, as the dreamer wakes up), 12.125 (pederastic); Longus, *Daphnis and Chloe,* 2.38–39. Many Neo-Latin poems have the theme, such as Angeriano, *Erotopaegnion* 131. A poem to Sleep by Giovanni Battista Amalteo speaks, as here, of a girl made *facilis* ("easy/obliging") in dreams (lines 5–6); see Sannazaro 1728, 439. Sabeo tells of a dream about his unyielding beloved; see Sabeo 1556, 855–56. Kisses were freely exchanged, but when he tried for the rest, she vanished. In Johannes Secundus' *Elegiae* 1.10 (*Somnium*), the poet wishes no one to wake him from a dream of his beloved Julia that grants delightful private access to her without her mother (or anyone else) there to inhibit his words and preclude intimate physical contact. Théodore de Bèze (Beza), *Epigrams* 19 (*De Candida*), and Muret, *Epigrams* 20 (*Somnium*), also speak of erotic dreams (the dreamer cheated of the desired consummation); see Beza 1879, 180, and Muret 1834, 2:273. Vernacular poets too take up this theme, including several writing in English, as well as Ronsard in France; see Ronsard 1914–75, 4:33, for some references. Navagero's poem is noticed by Maddison 1960, 98–99. Cicogna 1824–53, 6:292n311, records an Italian version. *Neaera*: Lygdamus' mistress in [Tib.] bk. 3; Hor. *Odes* 3.14.21, *Epod.* 15; Verg. *Ecl.* 3.3; Hom. *Od.* 12.133; Ov. *Am.* 3.6.28; etc.; also widely used by other Neo-Latin poets, e.g., Marullo, Johannes Secundus, George Buchanan, and John Milton. MSS: Bol.U., Mil.1, Vat.9, Wro. The meter is iambic strophe, alternating iambic trimeters and dimeters, as in Hor. *Epod.* 1–10.

1–2. In debt to Tib. 2.1.12 (Venus having brought her joys last night). In this poem *somnus* means both "sleep" and "dream."

## · NOTES TO THE TRANSLATIONS ·

4–6. Cf. Verg. *Aen.* 6.893–99 for true and false dreams. In Moschus 2.5, Ov. *Her.* 19.196, and Hor. *Sat.* 1.10.33 dreams after a particular time of night are generally true. In the variant text of 5–6 in Mil.1 and Wro., the future participle *futura* could denote purpose ("to be true messengers") or be a slip for the objective genitive *futuri*. [Tib.] 3.4.5, *venturae nuntia sortis* ("messengers of fate to come"), supports *futuri*. Otherwise, the difference from the standard text is the word order and *nonnumquam* ("sometimes") for *saepius* ("often," without comparative force).

7. "Deafer than the sea": Ov. *Her.* 8.9 and *Met.* 14.711 (cf. *Met.* 13.804).

11–12. Hymettus is the mountain, famous for bees, in Attica. Johannes Secundus similarly describes Neaera's kisses in terms of nectar and honey of Hymettus; see 59.21–22n.

15–16. For being more fortunate than the gods, a god in one's bliss, or of surpassing Jupiter in happiness, cf. Catull. 51 (after Sappho); Prop. 2.15.39–40; Plaut. *Curc.* 1.3.11; Ter. *Hec.* 5.4.3; Theoc. *Id.* 29.7–8; *Anth. Pal.* 5.55, 5.94, 12.177. Angeriano, *Erotopaegnion* 113.12 ("I will be a god"), Pontano, *Hendecasyllabi* 1.16.13 and 29, and Johannes Secundus, *Basia* 4.9–10, are among several comparable passages in Neo-Latin poets.

20. *Tenebo* scans with the last syllable shortened; cf. *puto* in 30.8.

### 30

Hyella: 21n. This poem was written at the latest in 1508, when Canal died, and probably not after 1506, when Bembo began living mostly at Urbino rather than at Venice and Ferrara. It is not clear where Navagero has gone. One possibility is Padua, where Navagero is attested as a student as early as 1501/2. Aquiles Estaço (Achilles Statius) concludes a letter of July 1555 to Marc-Antoine Muret and Paolo Manuzio with an imitation in Latin of Navagero's lines here, also in hendecasyllables and Catullan in spirit (see Gaisser 1993, 169). MSS: Vat.9 and 11. Meter: Phalaecean hendecasyllables, especially associated with Catullus among Roman poets. A manuscript version by Francesco Negri is mentioned by Cicogna 1824–53, 6:292n311.

## · NOTES TO THE TRANSLATIONS ·

1. The wellborn Venetian Paolo Canal (ca. 1481–1508) had connections with the publisher Aldo Manuzio from about 1500, working on Greek texts. In April 1508 he entered the monastery of San Michele di Murano but succumbed to illness only weeks later. Two poems by Valeriano compliment Canal in life. One, *De Paulo Canali* (Valeriano 1550, 123v), playfully treats Canal as Apollo's earthly brother and lauds his proficiency as a Latin, Greek, and Italian poet. In the other, *To Boon-Companions Engaged in Philosophy at Padua* (Valeriano 1550, 126v), eight scholars are briefly eulogized as "poets of sweet speech" and "emulators of Socrates." Canal is there "the supreme glory of the lyre"; Navagero is called *cultus* ("polished"), as Tibullus is by Ovid in *Am.* 1.15.28, "elegant," and "melodious." Valeriano 1550, 129v, has a further tribute to Canal in death. Pietro Bembo (1470–1547), also Venetian and wellborn, was a pupil of Constantine Lascaris at Messina between 1492 and 1494 and studied philosophy at Padua and Ferrara. In 1501 and 1502 he did editions of Petrarch and Dante for the Aldine Press. He and Canal were close; they visited Rome together in 1505. Bembo left Venice in 1506 for the court of Urbino, largely remaining there till 1512, when he went to Rome, being appointed secretary to Leo X. After Leo's death in 1521, Bembo left Rome for Padua, where many of his Latin and vernacular works were published. In 1539 he returned to Rome and was made a cardinal by Paul III. In 1530, a year after Navagero's death, Bembo succeeded him as the librarian of San Marco and historian of the Venetian Republic. In his youth Bembo had a Platonic affair with Lucrezia Borgia, wife of Alfonso d'Este, at Ferrara. He figures in Castiglione's *Il cortegiano*. On Bembo's life and writing, see Kidwell 2004. He also appears in poem 36.2.

2–3. The idea of loving someone or valuing something more than one's eyes (cf. 33.1–4, 50.9, and 59.13–14) is most associated with Catullus (3.5, 14A.1, 82, 104.2). For *minus atque* cf. Hor. *Sat.* 2.7.96.

4. *Quid rerum geritis?* (lit., "What sort of things are you doing?") amounts to "How are you?" The expression is found in Catull. 28.4. Cf. *Quid rerum geris?* in F. 5.30.1 (5.32.1 Scorsone). *Quid* with a following genitive ("What sort of, etc.?") is found in Roman comedy, and Catullus is fond of genitives in indefinite expressions. Cf. *aliquid novi* in 7 and especially *quicquid oti* in 8; similar expressions occur in Catull. 30.13 and 37.4.

278

### · NOTES TO THE TRANSLATIONS ·

6. *Camenae*: Muses.

8. The *o* of *puto* is here counted short (cf. *tenebo* in 29.20) by a license, especially seen with disyllabic verbs forming a natural iambus, as often in Neo-Latin poets (among classical ones, especially in Martial). For the genitive form *oti* rather than *otii*, cf. Verg. G. 4.564. Note also *Favoni* in 31.44 below.

12–13. With the accusative *socium bonum*, the strict meaning is "do not say that your good friend is not a sharer," but Navagero seems to intend to imply the sense "do not refuse to let your good friend be a sharer."

14. *Sed qui*, found first in *Carmina Quinque Illustrium Poetarum* 1552, is probably just a misprint there, though adopted in several later texts. *Sed quid*, the reading in Navagero 1530, seems right, though there is some doubt as to how to punctuate. I think the best way is to put a comma after *ipsa* (as in Navagero 1530) and have no further punctuation till the question mark after *convenit* in 15. For the elliptical *Sed quid cum?* (lit., "But what [dealings] with?"), cf. *nil tecum* (lit., "nothing [to do] with you") in 38.1.

16. *Faxint* (from *facere*) is a conjunctive form chiefly seen in Roman comedy, but also occasionally in Vergil, Horace, Ovid, and elsewhere. *Dei deaeque* in a wish: Catull. 28.14; cf. Ter. *Hec.* 102.

17. The variant *beate* ("happily") for *bene ipsi* ("well yourselves") may have arisen from a desire to avoid a further *bene* after that in 15. The combination *et bene et feliciter* occurs in Cic. *Phil.* 5.15.40.

18. For the scansion of *ego* see 28.5–6n.

19. The double *heu*, seen again in 33 below and in such ancient passages as Verg. *Ecl.* 2.58 and 3.100 and Plaut. *Pseud.* 1.3.26, is much favored by Pontano among Neo-Latin poets.

22–25. In 24 *pote* is for *potest*: cf. Catull. 45.5. That poem has *perdite* in line 3 (cf. 23 here and Catull. 104.3) and *ardet in medullis* in line 16 (cf. 22–23 here). For *potiri* cf. 6.7.

26. *Mea puella*: Catull. 2.1, 11.15, 13.11, 36.2. Understand *est*, or else read it at the end with Vat.11.

279

## · NOTES TO THE TRANSLATIONS ·

31–32. Catullus' liking for diminutives is imitated here. Double diminutive *papillula*, not ancient: Pontano, *Hendecasyllabi* 1.1.29, 1.23.3 and 11, *Parthenopeus* 1.29.23; Augurelli, *Iambici Libri* 1.12.25 (*Faunus*); Cotta, *Carmina* 9.18. The idea of being slain by someone or something sexually exciting is well attested in Renaissance verse both Latin and vernacular. Cf., for example, Angeriano, *Erotopaegnion* 105.30 and 177.10.

34–35. Cf. Prop. 1.14.15, *adverso . . . Amore* ("with Love against one"); Ov. *Her.* 18.3 ("if the gods are . . . on my side in love [*in amore secundi*]"). Ugolino Verino, *Flammetta* 1.9.5, has *sine Amore secundo* ("without Love on one's side"), while *adverso . . . Amore* is found in 1.14.16, 1.23.6, and 2.22.2.

31

In Navagero 1718, 1753, and 1754, and in *Carmina Illustrium Poetarum Italorum* 1720 the title is followed by the observation *carmen a Laurentio Pignorio primum editum in calce libri 'Originum Patavii'* ("a poem first published by Lorenzo Pignoria at the end of the book *The Origins of Padua*"; see Pignoria 1625). Pignoria's text of the poem is reprinted in Orsato 1678, 208–9. The poem is not in Navagero 1530 or any other edition prior to Navagero 1718. It is not in eighteenth-century publications other than those mentioned above apart from Pope 1740, 2:76, with the note on the provenance omitted. Maddison 1960, 99–100, discusses this poem, applauding Navagero as an observer of nature. Ferroni 2012, 81–83, offers substantial comment, considering this poem in conjunction with 41, the other "Vanzo" poem. MS: Mil.2 (lines 23–45 only). Meter: Phalaecean hendecasyllables. The poem must presumably date from Navagero's time as a student at Padua during the first decade of the sixteenth century.

1–9. Cf. start of 20. Wilson 1973 makes *Vancius* the River Piave, over thirty miles northeast of Padua, flowing into the Gulf of Venice, or a branch thereof, but Pignoria 1625, 174, says, before quoting Navagero's verses, "They are composed on a very beautiful region of our city, which we call, by a name going back six hundred years, *Vanzo*. They have never been printed as far as I am aware, and I publish them still with some defects, as they stand in a manuscript of mine, which I have not wished to alter." *Vancius*, or Vanzo, is the quarter of Padua that is marked on a

280

### · NOTES TO THE TRANSLATIONS ·

plan of Padua in 1320 in Hyde 1966, 36, south-southwest of the city center, bordering on a branch of the River Bacchiglione as it flowed then. That is presumably "Vanzo's stream" in line 2, from which the *Vanciades sorores* (31) are invited to emerge. Navagero seems to call both the stream and the quarter *Vancius*. Cf. 41.26. The Brenta, another nearby river, is *Medoacus* (35.6). "Naiad sisters" (1): [Verg.] *Cul.* 18, there of the Muses; F. 4.16.53; Marullo, *Epigrams* 4.13.1–2.

3–5. *Ambrosii liquores* denotes perfume or oil, as in Pontano, *Hendecasyllabi* 2.38.15. For oiled hair cf. 21.9, 25.14, and 26.74. See further on 25–26. *Sinus* ("bosoms"): 19.2n.

6–7. *In vestros lusus*, lit. = "for your amusements" (flowers). *Simul . . . simul* = "both . . . and" (cf. 30a and 31), as *pariter . . . simul* twice signifies in 19–22; cf. also *simul . . . pariter* in 37.13–14. In such use of *simul* and *pariter* Navagero seems to imitate Pontano. Cf. Pontano, *Hendecasyllabi* 1.1 (in several places) and 2.37.49–54 for his fondness for both *simul* and *pariter*.

10–12. Vines were often grown up trees. With 12 cf. Verg. *Ecl.* 7.58; [Verg.] *Cop.* 31; Ov. *Tr.* 3.10.71.

18. See 37.17–19n.

19–22. *Quis* = *quibus* (abl., antecedent *flores*). *Teretes . . . papillas* occurs again in 59.42. Repetition of the opening word or words in successive hendecasyllabic lines (five times in this poem) is a feature of Pontano's poems in Catullan style. See 59.1–3n.

25–26. Cyprus was Venus' sacred isle. Syrian fragrances: [Tib.] 3.4.28, 3.6.63; Prop. 2.13.30; and cf. "Assyrian" (see 25.14n). Pontano often refers to Syrian, Cyprian, or Assyrian fragrances and likes using *spirare* intransitively, with Syrian *odores* as subject in *Hendecasyllabi* 2.19.3–4. Mil.2's *spirantur* (present passive, "are breathed") may seem better here than Pignoria's *spirarunt* (syncopated perfect active, "have breathed"), as the neighboring verbs are all presents, but I cannot cite an ancient instance, or find one in Pontano, of *spirare* used passively, though *inspirare* can be.

27. Cf. Ov. *Rem. am.* 705–6, where Phoebus' arrival is recognized by the sound of lyres and his rattling quiver.

281

## · NOTES TO THE TRANSLATIONS ·

28–29. Swans (proverbial singers) pull Venus' chariot in Hor. *Odes* 3.28.15 and 4.1.10; Ov. *Met.* 10.708–9 and 718; Stat. *Silv.* 1.2.142 and 3.4.22.

30. *Dione* here, as in 20.75, 44.12, 56.12, 59.6, and 59.48 = Venus, a usage familiar from Ovid (e.g., *Fast.* 2.461 and 5.309, *Am.* 1.14.33) and seen in Neo-Latin poets, e.g., Sannazaro, *Epigrams* 2.12.1, 2.15.1 and 5; Fracastoro, *Carmina* 10.59, 35.6. Following this verse Mil.2 preserves two lines not in printed versions; line 33 clearly looks back to line 30b, just as line 34 does to line 32. For *simul . . . simul* (30a and 31), see on 6–7.

31. *Vanciades* is like *Naucelides* in 20.1.

33. Pontano's *Hendecasyllabi* 1.12.28 ends *decent choreae*, as does this line in Mil.2, *decent* being absent in Pignoria 1625.

39–40. Paestum (now Pesti), in Campania south of Naples, was anciently renowned for its twice-blooming roses. Tibur = Tivoli, seventeen miles northeast of Rome. Reading *incultis* ("uncultivated") in 39 with Pignoria 1625 makes Vanzo's rose gardens wild, unlike those at Paestum and Tivoli; but with Mil.2's more credible *tu cultis*, Venus is asked to make Vanzo surpass those places in elegant rose gardens (note *cultius* in 43). For *tu . . . face* cf. 1.3, 4.5.

42. Mil.2 has *saevientis*, but *pestilentis* (Pignoria's reading followed in printed texts) is noted in the margin. I find neither description of the south wind (*Auster*) in an ancient poet, though Ov. *Met.* 7.532 speaks of the deadly blasts of the south winds (there *Austri*) in connection with a plague, perhaps suggesting *pestilentis* here. Horace calls the southwest wind *Africus pestilens* in *Odes* 3.23.5. Marullo, *Hymni Naturales* 1.2.3–4, treats *Auster* as disease bringing.

43. *Nitescere* of a plant is taken to mean "thrive" in Pliny the Elder, *HN* 12.112.

44. Cf. Lucr. 1.11, *genitabilis aura Favoni* ("the breeze of the generative west wind"); F. 3.5.3. Pontano has *genitalis et aura Favonii* in *De Hortis Hesperidum* 1.12; Johannes Secundus has *Favoni . . . genitalis aura* in *Odes* 12.6–7. For *Favoni* = *Favonii* cf. *oti* in 30.8.

45. Cf. Pontano, *De Amore Coniugali* 3.4.44 (flowers *in tua dona*, "as gifts to you").

282

## · NOTES TO THE TRANSLATIONS ·

### 32

Hyella: 21n. Catullan in style. Treated as wrongly ascribed to Navagero and actually by Giovanni Cotta in Zanchi 1553 and Zanchi 1555, to which a few poems by various others are appended. In Zanchi 1555, 280, the poem is headed *Ioannis Cottae Veronensis, falso Andreae Naugerio ascriptum*. It is thus given as doubtfully Cotta's in Cotta 1802, 43, with a claim in a footnote that Gaetano Volpi had thought of excluding it from a planned new edition of Navagero's poems to follow that of 1718. See, however, Cicogna 1824–53, 6:304n341. Mistruzzi 1924, 72, firmly rejects notions of Cotta's authorship, as the girl in his few surviving poems is Lycoris, not Hyella. Omitted in Duchesne 1560, perhaps as not truly by Navagero or perhaps by accident; Duchesne follows 30 with 34, 31 being unknown to him and 33 being wrongly given as Flaminio's in volume 1 (Duchesne 1555), fol. 99. In some confusion, Periander 1567, 8r, gives the full poem as Cotta's, but just lines 1–7 of it as Navagero's on 248r. Cicogna 1824–53, 6:292n311, mentions a version by Francesco Negri. MSS: Bol.U., Vat.5 and 9. Meter: Phalaecean hendecasyllables.

5–6. Eyes are likened to stars (as in 59.35) in, e.g., Ov. *Am.* 2.16.44 and 3.3.9, *Met.* 1.499; Prop. 2.3.14; Mart. 4.42.7. The comparison is common in Neo-Latin poets (e.g., F. 3.18.21), as is the theme of the power of the eyes to stir passion. *Causa furoris*: Ov. *Met.* 14.16, *Fast.* 4.246; Pontano, *Parthenopeus* 1.10.10.

8. Cf. 65.4. Catull. 48.1 describes the youth Juventius' eyes as "honied" in a context of kissing them; Ovid calls his addressee sweeter than Attic honey in *Tr.* 5.4.

10. Cf. Catull. 5.7–9 and especially 48.3: there a mere three hundred thousand kisses, here three hundred million.

12. Cf. *misero . . . amanti* in 27.43. *Misellus* is several times in Catullus. Pontano has *amans misellus* in *Hendecasyllabi* 1.27.8 and *miselli amantes* in *Hendecasyllabi* 1.3.10.

14. The mixing of a present subjunctive in the protasis with a vivid future indicative in the apodosis (stressing the certainty of the action) is seen also in 20.96–97.

## · NOTES TO THE TRANSLATIONS ·

### 33

Hyella: 21n. Debts to Catullus. Duchesne 1560 misascribes this poem to Flaminio. See 32n. A version by Claudio Tolomei makes the young man *Tirsi* (see poems 6, 7, and 13); see Navagero 1718, 287. Cicogna 1824–53, 6:292n311, mentions a version by Francesco Negri. MSS: Mil.1, Salz., Vat.8, 9, and 11, Wro.

1 and 3. Cf. Catull. 92.2 and 4, and see 30.2–3n. For being dearer than what is dearer than the eyes, cf. Catull. 82; and for the typically Catullan expression "or whatever is more . . . than," see also his 13.10, 22.13, and 42.14. For being dearer than life and soul, cf. Catull. 68A.66 (68.106 in some texts). The former comparison is also in 65.10, in Verg. *Aen.* 5.724, and elsewhere. Scansion of *ego* (3): 28.5–6n. Mil.1 and Wro. have *omni* for *ipsa* in both lines, but "than all life" seems inferior to "than life itself." A poem addressed to Fracastoro by "Antonio Mario of Imola" (i.e., Flaminio; see F. 3.15n) calls him *anima mihi carior ipsa* (Ubaldini 1563, 105r); Varchi, *Carmina* 3.46, calls an addressee *oculis carior atque anima*.

2 and 4. Four elisions in each line (and 49.2 has three). See further on line 10.

9. Cf. Catull. 109.3, *di magni, facite.* Sannazaro, *Elegies* 1.3.57, has *Di, facite haec longos maneat spes certa per annos* ("Gods, grant that this hope remain sure through long years to come").

10. Elision in the final dactyl of the pentameter is seen also in 39.4, 51.6, and 68.8. Elision occurs otherwise in the second half of the pentameter in 9.4\*, 12.2\*, 19.4 and 34, 25.16, 22, 60, and 64\*, 26.38\*, 33.2 and 4, 38.6, 53.4, and 68.4\* (where asterisked, the elision involves a final *est*). Such elision is rare in classical elegiacs, though it is seen more in Catullus than in Ovid, which suits the Catullan style of this poem.

### 34

This hymn to the archangel Gabriel has substantial pagan coloring. Cf., for instance, how language appropriate to Mercury is employed in the hymn to Gabriel by Giano Vitale of Palermo (ca. 1485–1560) given in

284

## · NOTES TO THE TRANSLATIONS ·

*Poematia Aliquot Insignia Illustrium Poetarum Recentiorum* (Basel, 1544). MS: Vat.14. Cicogna 1824–53, 6:292n311, records a version by Francesco Negri. The meter is three Glyconics and a final Pherecratean to each stanza, as in Catull. 34; Catull. 61 has four Glyconics and a Pherecratean to each stanza. Marullo's *Hymni Naturales* 2.5 is in the same meter.

1–4. Mother of Memnon: Aurora, the dawn goddess (also in 37); cf. Ov. *Fast.* 4.714 and *Pont.* 1.4.57; similarly *Am.* 1.8.4–5 and 3.9.1. Aurora throws open the gates of heaven in Ov. *Met.* 2.112–13. *Diem . . . provocat:* Ov. *Pont.* 1.4.58. Vulcan and Venus have a golden bedchamber in Verg. *Aen.* 8.372.

7–8. *Quo* ("than whom"), the general reading (Vat.14 and eds.), cannot mean "as whom." Reading *quod* ("because") restores grammar. *Nullus* is for *nemo*, as in a tiny number of ancient passages, e.g., Plaut. *Bacch.* 2.2.12; Suet. *Calig.* 35. *Praesens* is commonly found in contexts of requesting or receiving a deity's supportive presence, ready and powerful aid, etc. Ancient passages include Verg. *Aen.* 9.404; Ov. *Met.* 7.178; Hor. *Odes* 1.35.2.

10. Neo-Latin poets often use "gods" of the denizens of the Christian heaven, including angels and saints.

11. Vanishing into thin air: Verg. *Aen.* 4.278; Ov. *Fast.* 2.509. Air is commonly "thin" elsewhere in those poets, among others.

13–16. Gabriel announced to Mary the "Thunderer's will" that she would bear Jesus; cf. Luke 1:26–38. *Tonans* ("the Thunderer"), an epithet of Jupiter (cf. 26.33 and 36.6), had by Navagero's time long been applied to the Christian God. *Fers* (13) and *indicas* (15) can be seen as historic presents; so too *fers* in the next stanza, though *vocamur* in 20 seems better taken as a true present.

18–20. "The Enemy": Satan, as in Matthew 18:39; Luke 10:19; 1 Peter 5:8. Snatching someone or something from the jaws of an enemy is common imagery; in Livy 26.2.10 cities are snatched "from the jaws of Hannibal." F. 6.50.7 (6.51.7 Scorsone) speaks of a doctor as rescuing him from the jaws of Orcus (i.e., death), and a poem of Girolamo Borgia rejoices that a sick friend has been similarly saved; see Borgia 1666, 160. *Quis* = the ablative *quibus*. *Caeli templa:* Lucr. 6.1228.

285

## · NOTES TO THE TRANSLATIONS ·

### 35

The poem concerns the siege of Padua by the emperor Maximilian I in 1509 and seems written soon after. By agreement at Cambrai in 1508, the pope (Julius II), the emperor, and the kings of Spain (Ferdinand) and France (Louis XII) had united against Venice. When the French marched into her territory, the republic's forces under Alviano were badly defeated at Agnadello on May 14, 1509, and Venice's threatened subject cities were given discretion to surrender to the invaders. Padua did so, but on July 17, declared again for Venice and was sent nearly two hundred young Venetian noblemen, probably including Navagero, to stiffen resistance to Maximilian's impending attack. His cannon breached the walls, but assaults were repulsed, and the siege had been given up by early October. A 1509 Latin poem of Antonio Francesco Rainerio (*Carmina Illustrium Poetarum Italorum* 8:59) refers to Maximilian's attack on Padua, "when the mightiest of foes was pounding the famous city of Padua to great destruction with his thunder-flashes [of cannon-fire]." The present poem is briefly discussed by Maddison 1960, 102–3. It appears in Scardeone 1560, 34–35, in a chapter on the 1509 siege of Padua; see also Navagero 1718, xli. The first two stanzas are quoted by Pignoria 1625, 19. MS: Vat.14. Meter: Alcaic strophe, employed many times in Horace's *Odes*.

1–8. The Trojan Antenor was spared when the Greeks took Troy, either because he had advocated Helen's return to them, or because he had opened the city gates and given the Greeks the palladium that protected Troy. Roman tradition said that when he settled in Venetia and founded Patavium, or Padua (Livy 1.1.1–3), the Eneti from Paphlagonia came with him.

2–4. *Troum* is genitive plural. Lucr. 1.41 and 42.9 below show that *patriae* goes with *tempore iniquo*.

5. Pallas = Minerva. *Demum* ("at long last") goes with *condidit* ("founded") in 8.

6. The *Medoacus* is the Medoaco or Brenta.

8. The Euganei lived in northeast Italy. The *Colli Euganei*, hills near Padua, preserve the name.

286

## · NOTES TO THE TRANSLATIONS ·

9. For *flos* ("flower") of a place, cf. Cic. *Phil.* 3.5.13, "the province of [Cisalpine] Gaul . . . that flower of Italy."

13. *Septicornis*, not ancient (see 14.3n), = "seven-horned," i.e., "seven-branched," just as Ovid speaks of seven "horns" of the Nile in *Met.* 9.774. For the formation cf. *bicornis* ("two-horned") and *septicollis* ("seven-hilled").

14–16. The Tagus, a river of Spain and Portugal, was celebrated for its golden sands. The expression "those who drink the waters of the yellow Tagus," meaning dwellers by it, is inspired by such passages as Verg. *Aen.* 7.715; Hor. *Odes* 3.10.1 and 4.15.21; Luc. 8.213; Mart. 7.88.6.

17. Cf. *saeva Necessitas*, one reading in Hor. *Odes* 1.35.17. Inexorable Necessity is *dira* ("dreadful") in Hor. *Odes* 3.24.6 and *dura* ("harsh") in Cotta, *Carmina* 15.12, and Pigna's poem *Ad Sebastianum Monfalcum* (Pigna 1553, 38).

20. Pitiable even to an enemy: Ov. *Met.* 6.276 and 9.178; Ugolino Verino, *Flammetta* 2.54.7.

22. *Suburbium* is found in an ancient author only in Cic. *Phil.* 12.10.24.

23. *Glans* ("acorn"), found of slingshot in ancient writers, here denotes shot of another kind, cannonballs. Padua's walls were heavily bombarded for two weeks during the siege; cf. Ariosto, *Orlando furioso* canto 16.27. Neo-Latin poets use *glans* also to denote a musket ball, as Fracastoro, *Syphilis* 3.165, in a context of shooting birds. For brazen shot, as opposed to shot of lead, iron, or stone, cf. Niccolò d'Arco, *Numeri* 1.15.23–24, *letiferi glandis aheneae nimbi* ("death-dealing clouds of brazen shot"); and Giannantonio Taigeto, *Ecloga Nautica (Idmon)*, describing the 1571 Battle of Lepanto: "They powerfully hurl brazen shot (*aeratas . . . glandes*) with sulfurous fire"; see *Carmina Illustrium Poetarum Italorum* 9:217.

25–28. *Chlamys*, generally a Greek military cloak, here, it seems, means a leather tunic reinforced with chain mail (*squamis adamantinis*) and solid plate armor (*ferro rigenti*). Cf. Verg. *Aen.* 3.467, *loricam consertam hamis auroque trilicem* ("a leather cuirass woven with hooked scales and triple-linked with gold"), and the very similar 5.259–60 (and also 7.639). In 25 *Mavortis* (= Mars) collectively denotes the emperor's "soldiery." Verg. *Aen.* 8.676 has *instructo Marte* (lit., "with drawn-up Mars") of troops deployed

287

· NOTES TO THE TRANSLATIONS ·

for battle. Mars is clad in a *tunica . . . adamantina* ("a tunic of steel," i.e., a coat of mail) in Hor. *Odes* 1.6.13.

29. *Letifer* ("death-dealing") of the right hand: Ov. *Met.* 12.606.

33. Cf. Verg. *Aen.* 2.612–13.

36

Pietro Bembo: 30n. Lalage (cf. 41.18) is a name from Horace (*Odes* 1.22.10 and 23 and 2.5.16) used by some other Neo-Latin poets. This poem is briefly noticed by Maddison 1960, 103, with reference to *Anacreontea* 23, where the poet would tell of Atreus' sons and Cadmus, but his lyre will sing only of love. Cicogna 1824–53, 6:292n311, records a version by Francesco Negri. MSS: Vat.I and II. Meter: Sapphic strophe (as for 37, 41, and 69), common in Horace's *Odes*, including the first of his Lalage poems. Observe, however, that line 3 lacks the caesura that regularly follows the fifth syllable in Horace's lesser Sapphic lines but often does not in those of Catullus (cf. his 11.6, 7, 13, and 23, 51.3 and 13). See 41.37–40n and 69.2n.

1–4. In *Am.* 1.1.1–2, reflected here in *parabam* and *arma*, Ovid is making ready to write in hexameters of arms and war, but Cupid forces him to write elegiac couplets. There are several other passages where a poet or a singer is made to turn from martial, epic, or otherwise lofty themes to lighter verse, including Verg. *Ecl.* 6.3–5; Hor. *Odes* 4.15.1–4; Prop. 3.3; Angeriano, *Erotopaegnion* 3 and 185; Ugolino Verino, *Flammetta* 2.1.

3–4. *Male negates audax.* Similarly F. 3.18.23, *male sana puella* ("foolish girl"), and 4.5.47, *male caute puer* ("unwary boy"). In Hor. *Ars poet.* 28, a poet who does not dare attempt anything lofty "creeps [*serpit*] along the ground," and in *Epist.* 2.1.250–59 Horace contrasts his *sermones* (there = satires and epistles) "that crawl along the ground" with grander poetry. Whether Navagero ever seriously contemplated writing epic poetry is very doubtful. Nevertheless, Achille Bocchi (1486–1562), in a lyric tribute to Navagero preserved in the Vatican Library's Cod. Vat. lat. 5793, fol. 27v, between equating Navagero as an elegiac poet with Philetas of Cos or Tibullus, and as a bucolic poet with Theocritus, observes, "If you un-

## · NOTES TO THE TRANSLATIONS ·

dertake to sing of cruel battles . . . or of the praises of kings, or bestow on famous Alviano [see on 44] the gift . . . of a blessed song, you equal the lights of Dircaean [Boeotian] Pindar, the Muse of godlike Maro [Vergil], and the buskin of the man of Colophon [Homer]." Bocchi seems there to mean that Navagero could rise at will to grand verse.

5–6. Cf. Ov. *Am.* 2.18.4 ("and tender Love dashes my plans when about to venture on grand enterprises"). Ov. *Met.* 2.328 has *magnis . . . ausis* (from *ausum*), but here *ausus* is acc. pl. of the very rare fourth declension noun *ausus*, used in verse only in Petron. 123.184. The Thunderer: Jupiter (see 26.33–34n). *Iratum* is the reading of both MSS. The regular printed text has *iratus*, making Love "angry," but "angry Jupiter" is imagined as having his thunderbolts dashed from his hand by kisses in Ov. *Am.* 2.5.52 (see 25.50n). *Rubenti* means "fiery-red," as in Hor. *Odes* 1.2.2. Love is "violent" also in F. 4.17.50.

9. *Eat* (normally, "let it go") substitutes for *sit* ("let it be"), as in 16.6. Cf., for instance, Luc. 5.297, *sic eat, o superi!* ("So be it, gods above!"). *Fors et:* Prop. 2.9.1; Hor. *Odes* 1.28.31; Verg. *Aen.* 2.139 and 11.50.

11–12. The phrase *frontis honos* occurs elsewhere in Renaissance poets, e.g., in Pontano, *Parthenopeus* 1.10.139 ("Will gray hair mar this glory of your brow/face?"). *Clarius puro* (MSS) and *purius claro* (eds.) are both credible readings in 11. In Hor. *Odes* 1.19.6, Glycera shines *purius* ("with a whiter gleam") than Parian marble.

13–16. Cf. Hor. *Odes* 4.9.5–12 for Homer holding highest place, but other poets of archaic Greece having conferred immortality too. Sappho and Alcaeus were from Lesbos. Lycus was traditionally Alcaeus' beloved (Hor. *Odes* 1.32.11). Achilles is *animosus* (= "spirited" or "fiery") in Hor. *Sat.* 1.7.12, and in Ov. *Her.* 8.1 Achilles' son Pyrrhus is said to be "*animosus* like his father." Homer's *Iliad* has Achilles' wrath as its theme.

### 37

Aurora: 34.1–4n. Discussed approvingly by Maddison 1960, 100–102, with opening stanzas translated and comparison made to Pseudo-Ausonius, *De rosis nascentibus* (On Budding Roses), once attributed to

· NOTES TO THE TRANSLATIONS ·

Vergil, which advises young maidens to "pluck the flower," as their beauty, like the rose's, is brief. The second stanza here has some resemblance in theme to the early part of that poem, which speaks of walking abroad and surveying the plants at dawn, but the debt is limited. No MS evidence (see 23n). Meter: Sapphic strophe.

1. Tithonus was the mortal lover for whom Aurora (Eos) begged eternal life from Jupiter/Zeus, but, not granted exemption from aging, with time Tithonus became very decrepit. The goddess rises from his bed to bring the new day already in Hom. *Od.* 5.1. For Tithonus (again in F. 4.17.70), see also Hom. *Il.* 11.1; Verg. G. 1.447, *Aen.* 4.585 and 9.460; Hor. *Odes* 2.16.30 (where his age is in point); Ov. *Fast.* 6.473. Aurora is quite often called "the wife of Tithonus": Ov. *Her.* 18.111, *Fast.* 3.403 and 4.943; etc. *Dia* = *diva* ("divine").

3. Aurora/Eos is regularly associated with rosiness. In Homer she is "rosy-fingered," while in Lucr. 5.656 and Ov. *Ars am.* 3.84 she is "rosy." Cf. also Verg. *Aen.* 7.26; Ov. *Met.* 7.705, *Fast.* 4.714; Tib. 1.3.94.

4. Aurora (Pallantias) is *praevia luci* ("forerunner to the light") in Ov. *Met.* 15.190.

6–8. For *recentes auras* cf. 56.15 (*aurae . . . recentiores*) and the variant in 9.9 (*aura . . . recenti*). Pontano applies *recens* to a breeze several times (= "fresh," implying "clean and sweet" or "invigorating"), but I find no ancient instance. In Pontano, *Hendecasyllabi* 2.22.35–36, a rose in the morning emits its *recentem . . . odorem* ("fresh scent").

15. The correct reading *flaventes* (*a* long) was first corrupted to the unmetrical *fluentes* (*u* short) in the 1552 *Carmina Quinque Illustrium Poetarum*. *Lucentes* (*u* long) then arose from a misguided attempt by Toscano 1576 to correct the meter.

17–19. Venus associated with the Loves and Graces: 25.13–16. Cupid is "the boy ever clinging" to Venus in Hor. *Odes* 1.32.10. Johannes Secundus has Love clinging to her side in *Elegiae* 2.1.9–10. The Graces are *decentes* in Hor. *Odes* 1.4.6. *Referre* is used of gathering flowers also in 31.18 and Zanchi, *Poemata* 6.4.8: "and often to bring back (*referre*) laps full of flowers"; see Zanchi 1555, 1993.

290

## · NOTES TO THE TRANSLATIONS ·

25–28. *Latonae suboles* ("Latona's daughter"): Diana, goddess of the chase, daughter of Latona (Leto) and Jupiter. In 28 supply *auratus* ("golden") from *aurata* in 27. The threefold emphasis on "gold" or "golden" imitates Verg. *Aen.* 4.138–39 (of Dido). Cf. also Stat. *Theb.* 8.566–68.

31. Lynxes are *fugaces* ("fugitive" or "fleeing") in Hor. *Odes* 4.6.33–34.

34. See 25.23–42n.

35. Construe the delayed *et* before *querelas*. *Iocosa imago* ("playful echo"): Hor. *Odes* 1.12.4 and 1.20.8.

### 38

Hyella: 21n. The theme here is much favored by Petrarchist poets. Petrarch's Laura is seen as a sun in *Rime sparse* 248.1–4, for example, while in 192.12–14 her eyes clear clouds from the sky, and in 156.5–6 they are lights to make the sun envious. Numerous instances in Pontano include *Eridanus* 1.8 (Stella shines by day and night, as morning star and evening star), *Eridanus* 2.2.15–16 (Stella is his sun, moon, morning star, and evening star), *Hendecasyllabi* 2.17 (when a girl's eyes are covered, there is darkness; when uncovered, day and sunlight), *Hendecasyllabi* 1.8 and 1.23, and *Eridanus* 1.10. Several other Neo-Latin poems similarly liken girls to the sun, stars, or the planet Venus in their radiance. In F. 4.21.14–18 the dead beloved has taken her sun away. In Tebaldeo's *In Deliam* (Ubaldini 1563, 26v), when Delia approaches from the west, the poet thinks the sun rising there, but he is plunged into black night when she hides her face. In the elder Janus Dousa's *Epigrams* 2.24 his girl alone makes night and day for him. The last four lines of William Drummond of Hawthornden's *A Lover's Day and Night* closely resemble the conclusion of the present poem, though Drummond probably did not imitate Navagero directly; see Drummond 1913, 1:120. There is a version of Navagero's poem by Claudio Tolomei; see Navagero 1718, 287–88. Mellin de Saint-Gelais' *D'un oeil* has been considered an imitation too, though Donald Stone in Saint-Gelais 1993, 48, refers the resemblances to Petrarchan tradition. MSS: Mil.3, Salz.

1. Cf., for example, Ov. *Am.* 3.2.48: "I have nothing to do with (*nihil mihi cum*) the sea"; Hor. *Sat.* 1.2.57.

## · NOTES TO THE TRANSLATIONS ·

3. Cf. Ov. *Ars am.* 1.744, *quantum ad Pirithoum* ("as far as Pirithous was concerned").

4. Tethys (with long *e*), meant here, was Oceanus' sister and wife; the sea-nymph Thetis (with short *e*) was Achilles' mother. Confusingly, both names sometimes denote the sea in classical poets; e.g., *Tethys* is so used in Ov. *Met.* 2.69 and 509, *Thetis* in Verg. *Ecl.* 4.32. The form of the name here is variously *Thetyos*, *Thethyos*, *Tethyos*, or *Tetyos* in eds. *Tethyos* (transliterating the Greek genitive *Tethuos*) is the spelling rightly favored in modern editions of classical poets (e.g., in Ov. *Fast.* 5.168). I therefore give that spelling here, as I do in F. 4.22.32. Bosom or lap imagery: 19.33–34n and 25.6n, and cf. Claud. *Rapt. Pros.* 3.319–20 (*gremio . . . Tethyos*) and *IV cons. Hon.* 597 (= 8.597, *Tethyos . . . gremium*); Girolamo Amalteo, *Vellus Aureum* 47 (*gremio . . . Tethyos*); Giovanni Battista Amalteo, *In Obitum Fracastorii* 25 (*Tethyos e sinu*); see Fracostoro 1728, 326 and 434. Here, "from eastern Tethys' bosom/lap" means "from the depths of the eastern ocean."

10. Muret, *Epigrams* 34.10, in a context of similar meaning, also ends *in media fit mihi nocte dies*.

### 39

This poem, not in Navagero 1530, is first found in Gagny ca. 1548, simply following what is here designated 38 without any indication of source or justification for the attribution, if we may assume that the poem's insertion where it appears was deliberate and not the result of some oversight. The attribution must therefore be treated with due caution, though the ascription to Navagero does not seem implausible on internal evidence. No other text includes the poem before Navagero 1718 apart from Duchesne 1560. No manuscript evidence (see 23n). In Mantuan, *Eclogues* 1.148–51, the speaker likewise describes a narrow escape from dogs that cuts short an attempt to pay a secret visit to a girl just as he was creeping up to the threshold. In Varchi, *Carmina* 76, a dog is told by a youth not to bark and raise the alarm, as no wolf or robber is coming to harm the flock, but Leuco on his midnight way to enjoy Glycera's embraces. Clandestine undoing of doors at midnight figures in Tib. 1.9(8).59–60, while

· NOTES TO THE TRANSLATIONS ·

Prop. 4.5.73–74 speaks of "the dog that was too wakeful, so as to cause me woes when I had stealthily to undo the bars with my thumb." Other ancient passages concerned with dogs deterring or betraying lovers include Hor. *Odes* 3.16.2 and *Epod.* 5.58. Tib. 2.4.31–34 talks of dogs set to guard thresholds against lovers who do not pay the porter or other slave for admission (similarly *Anth. Pal.* 5.30), while Tib. 1.6.31–32 speaks of a husband's dog threatening him all night while he was pursuing an adulterous liaison with the man's wife. Ov. *Tr.* 2.459–60 alludes to the latter passage; his *Am.* 2.19.40 similarly speaks of causing the dogs to bark during such an adulterous visit of his own. Name *Menalcas*: Verg. *Ecl.* 2.15, 3.13, 5.4 and 90, 9.10 (and passim), and 10.20; Theoc. *Id.* 8, 9, and 27.44. In Verg. *Ecl.* 5 Menalcas has often been felt in the past to represent the poet (see F. 4.17.9n).

1. Philyra in myth was mother of the centaur Chiron by Saturn; she became the linden tree. See poem 5n for the accusative form of the name. *Media de nocte:* Hor. *Epist.* 1.18.91; Suet. *Calig.* 26.

3–4. With *pressa . . . anima* cf. [Verg.] *Ciris* 211, *pressis singultibus* ("with repressed sobs"). Note tiptoeing in line 212 there, as in 6 here. *Suspensus* means "lightly applied" in a few ancient passages. Pontano, *Parthenopeus* 2.9.69–70 (see 6.3n) says of Pan creeping up to take advantage of a sleeping nymph, *Mox sensim summasque pedes suspendit in herba, / et presso nullus redditur ore sonus* (lit., "Soon he softly balances on the tips of his hooves on the grass, / and no sound is emitted from his tight-pressed lips").

5. Gagny ca. 1548's *semiaperta* ("half-open," in classical Latin only in Livy 26.39), like all compounds in *semi* (cf. *semicaper* in 5.9 and 26.45), should have the first syllable long, as in Ugolino Verino, *Paradisus* 142. Here *sem* would be short, the following *ia* counting as one short syllable by synizesis, just as the longer equivalent *semiadaperta* is five syllables in Ov. *Am.* 1.6.4 — a context of a lover wishing to squeeze through a half-opened door to pay a furtive visit to his mistress — and cf. the regular synizesis of *semianimis* in verse. Here Navagero 1718 leaves a lacuna, noting that *semiaperta* is unmetrical. Navagero (if indeed the poet) has apparently admitted a false quantity. Cf. *redis* in line 10 below, *rimulam* in 65.10, and (if read) *cottidie* or *quottidie* in 20.10. For the sense of *prospectans* cf. Plaut.

293

· NOTES TO THE TRANSLATIONS ·

*Miles glor.* 3.1.2 (597), where *prospectare* is one reading (the Loeb prefers *perspectare*).

6. *Transiliisse* = the more common *transiluisse*. *Protenso . . . pede* is literally "with stretched-forth foot," i.e., on tiptoe.

9–10. Giovanni Battista Amalteo, *Ad Sebastianum Venerium* 25 (Sannazaro 1728, 403), and a line in an anonymous poem also on the 1571 Battle of Lepanto (Toscano 1576, 73r) both have the very similar *cinge triumphali victricia tempora lauro* ("Ring your victorious temples with triumphal laurel"). The *i* in *redis* (10) should be long, prompting the editor of *Carmina Illustrium Poetarum Italorum* to rewrite the line. Nevertheless, Landino similarly shortens the *i* in *venis* in *Xandra* 2.16.1, and Bembo, *Carmina* 7.5 (*Galatea*) that in *fugis*. With 9 cf. Prop. 2.16.13, which modern editors seem to punctuate *At tu nunc nostro, Venus, o succurre dolori* ("but oh, aid now my grief, Venus") rather than mark off *Venus o* together.

40

Lajos (or Louis) II, king of Hungary, perished, aged twenty, fighting the invading Turks at Mohacs on August 29, 1526. Though this poem says "cut down," Lajos reportedly drowned while trying to escape from the carnage. His greatly outnumbered army of sixteen thousand was almost annihilated, and two-thirds of Hungary passed under the rule of Sultan Suleiman the Magnificent. This epitaph-style poem laments the lack of aid from other Christian rulers. Some years before, in a letter prefaced to a volume of his edition of speeches of Cicero, Navagero had in vain urged Pope Leo X to lead a united Christendom against the Turks. In Navagero 1718, 1753, and 1754 the poem is stated to be from Ubaldini 1563, where it appears on fol. 25r, ascribed to Navagero without any indication of source or justification for the attribution. It is not in the earliest editions. At the time of Mohacs, Navagero was in Spain as Venice's ambassador. He heard of the battle in November 1526, thus the earliest possible date for this poem, if truly his; see Cicogna 1824–53, 6:289n298. No manuscript evidence (see 23n).

1. See F. 4.7.9n.

294

## · NOTES TO THE TRANSLATIONS ·

2. After Ov. *Her.* 3.106, *qui bene pro patria cum patriaque iacent* ("who lie nobly dead for their homeland and with their homeland"), also reflected in another epitaph for Lajos, by Celio Calcagnini (1479–1541), *Carmina Illustrium Poetarum Italorum* 3:84: "I, Lajos, king of Hungary, met a brave death bravely pressing the king of the Turks and did not think it dreadful, I confess, to fall for my kingdom, but to fall with my kingdom." An anonymous epitaph for Lajos in Canoniero 1613, 351, ends comparably: "I, Lajos, born of the ancient blood of kings, carried Hungary's scepter in my mighty hand. I was killed while protecting my homeland in valiant arms, as the fierce Thracian [i.e., Turk] was laying waste my kingdom. Yet I do not complain that I fell, slain when defeated in battle, but that my homeland too fell with me."

### 41

Debts to Horace in the name *Lalage* (see 36n), the Horatian meter, a little inspiration from *Odes* 4.1, and the reminiscence in 19–20 of *Odes* 3.26.11–12, where Horace begs Venus to give the disdainful Chloe a touch of the whip to make her just once feel love. Navagero's poem owes to Lucretius its portrayal of Venus as the force that enables all living things to propagate. See on poem 25, especially 11–12. Meter: Sapphic strophe, as for 36 and 37. No manuscript evidence (see 23n). The date may be hinted by the mention in line 26 of "rose-bearing Vanzo" (see 31.1–9n), as Navagero spent time studying at Padua in the first decade of the sixteenth century. Briefly discussed by Maddison 1960, 103, and considered Anacreontic in theme.

1–4. *Generatim* is ten times in Lucretius (cf. especially 1.20 and 227). The former passage has the phrase *saecula propagent* (4 here), and Venus imparting love into creatures' breasts to make them reproduce.

5. After Lucr. 1.22–23. Cf. also Hor. *Epist.* 1.6.65–66. For postponed *sine*, cf., for example, Hor. *Sat.* 1.3.68, *vitiis nemo sine nascitur* ("no one is born without faults").

8. *Voluptas* is commonly *blanda*, including five times in Lucretius and Ovid.

## · NOTES TO THE TRANSLATIONS ·

10. After Hor. *Odes* 3.18.9.

11. In Ov. *Met.* 8.238 the lapwing *plausit pennis* ("applauded with its wings").

14. See 25.60n.

20. Pigna in his poem *Ad Amorem* (Pigna 1553, 74) similarly urges Love to give Lygida a touch of the whip (*tange flagello*; see 41n) after complaining that she ignores his arrows, so potently felt by gods, people, and animals.

21. *Ita* scans with lengthening of the final syllable.

25–26. Offering Venus a myrtle: 6.6–8n. For *laetam* cf. 44.98. *Rosifer* is not ancient (14.3n), but many comparable formulations, such as *populifer* ("poplar-bearing," of the Po in Ov. *Am.* 2.17.32), are found in classical poets. *Se . . . revolvit* ("rolls along") suggests that Vanzo is here a river or a stream. See 31.1–9n.

27–28. Milk "snow-white": 1.13–14n.

29–32. Cf. Hor. *Odes* 4.1.25–29; Ov. *Ars am.* 1.217; and perhaps Tib. 1.3.63. *Pariter* is used with *et . . . que* in, e.g., Pontano, *Hendecasyllabi* 2.38.17–18, *sic amando et noctes pariter diesque agatis* ("so may you spend both nights and days alike in loving"). See 31.6–7n. Beginning and ending with someone: Hom. *Il.* 1.97; Theoc. *Id.* 17.1–4; Hor. *Epist.* 1.1.1; Verg. *Ecl.* 8.11.

33. For the epanalepsis cf. 8.8, 18.3, and 26.80. Some similar examples from Pontano (all from Sapphics) are *Lyra* 5.48–49, "brandishing a torch, a torch and those rays"; *Lyra* 8.20–21, "lilies . . . lilies and indestructible amaranth"; *Lyra* 8.40–41, "a breeze, a breeze and spring's beauty." Reordering the words in the repeated phrase (here *canent te / te canent*) is also a mannerism found in Pontano; see 59.1–3n. Cupid is *natum . . . volucrem* in Ov. *Met.* 5.364.

34. Here Navagero treats Mars (*duro . . . parenti*) as Cupid's father; cf. *duri . . . Martis* in Verg. *Ecl.* 10.44. Others sometimes regarded as such include Jupiter (also therefore his maternal grandfather), Vulcan (Venus' husband), and Mercury. *Acer* of *Amor*: Tib. 2.6.15. Instances in Neo-Latin include Pontano, *Hendecasyllabi* 1.24.10–11.

296

· NOTES TO THE TRANSLATIONS ·

35–36. *Cuspis* ("point"), found in classical poets of javelins and spears, is sometimes used of Cupid's arrows in Neo-Latin verse. Cf. Angeriano, *Erotopaegnion* 14.6, and Cornelio Amalteo, *Cupido* 73 (Sannazaro 1728, 463).

37–40. *Voti reus* (38), literally, "answerable for my vow," i.e., liable to make the promised repayment for the favor requested: Verg. *Aen.* 5.237; Varchi, *Carmina* 73.2. Cutting a ringdove's throat before Venus' altar: Prop. 4.5.65–66; cf. the turtledoves in F. 3.28.1–2. Scansion of *ego*: 28.5–6n. In 37 and 38 there is no caesura after the fifth syllable, contrary to the practice of Horace (and in 17 an elision confuses the caesura); see 36n.

42

Navagero's friend Raphael painted a surviving portrait of him with Agostino Beazzano, another Venetian poet, when Navagero visited Rome in 1516. The portrait meant here, however, if real, is otherwise unknown, like the probably fictitious portrait of Navagero in 28 and Asilas' no doubt imaginary statue of Pythagoras in 24. As line 7 says that Navagero has not been involved in any battle, the date here is probably a little before the disastrous defeat of Venice's forces under Alviano at Agnadello on May 14, 1509, for it seems that Navagero was present in that action and may well have helped defend Padua in the siege that followed. Poem 53 probably belongs to about the same period (Ferroni 2012, 75n12, treats the likely date of both poems as around 1509). A poem of Girolamo Borgia (see 20.69–70n) found in a Vatican MS (Barb. lat. 1903, fol. 109v), addressing Navagero, refers to him as both poet and soldier: Minerva has armed his breast with the learned arts; Mars, his hand with the sword. Borgia adds, "You strike your dread foe with a double wound, and you return home worthy of double honor." Borgia's poem is undated, but it confirms that Navagero spent some time in arms and seems to show that he also attacked the enemy meant in verse. There Borgia may refer to 35's denunciation of the emperor's forces besieging Padua in later 1509. MS: Vat.14.

1–6. *Anth. Pal.* 16.176 states that at Sparta Aphrodite was shown armed. Several other poems in that part of bk. 16 play upon the idea of an armed

297

· NOTES TO THE TRANSLATIONS ·

Aphrodite too. See Hutton 1935, 191–92, where this poem is quoted as "an exercise on the theme of" *Anth. Pal.* 16.177.

4. Cf. Ov. *Am.* 1.10.19–20: "Venus is not suited to savage arms, nor is Venus' son; it does not become unwarlke deities (*imbelles deos*) to earn a soldier's pay." *Bellica parma*: Prop. 2.25.8.

5. With *forti Lacedaemone* ("in brave Lacedaemon [i.e., Sparta]," locative) cf. Stat. *Silv.* 5.3.108, where Sparta is *animosa* ("spirited"). For the syntax (*erat id signum* + object clause), cf. Ter. *Haut.* 2.3.57 (= line 298), *magnum hoc quoque signumst dominam esse* ("this too is a big sign that the lady is . . ."), where *hoc* parallels *id* here.

9. See 35.2–4n.

43

This poem is a lament for the poet Tebaldeo's dead lapdog. Borgettus (otherwise Borgiolus, in Italian, Borgetto, "Little Borgia"). Ricci, in his second letter to Navagero (Navagero 1718, 127) and in his 1545 *De Imitatione* (Navagero 1718, xxxv), correctly sees imitation of Catull. 3 (on Lesbia's dead sparrow). Ricci's remarks are discussed by Gaisser 1993, 197. In his letter Ricci calls this poem simply *Borgettus*, which may imply that he did not know 50 and 51 as Navagero's, for they too concern Borgetto and show him honored by his master with a tomb and an inscription (51.10). Their ascription to Navagero is thus open to doubt, as several other poets wrote tributes to Borgetto. A note in Vat.6, following this present poem and before one of Marco Antonio Casanova, also on this dog, states, "On the death of Borgiolus, the puppy of Antonio Tebaldeo, the very famous poet." Ercole Strozzi's *Lament for the Dog Borgetto*, not later than 1508, when Strozzi died (see 54n), reveals that someone killed Tebaldeo's pet with a sword or a dagger; see Strozzi 1513, 46r–49v. In 123–27 Strozzi treats Lucrezia Borgia, resident at Ferrara from early 1502, as having had Borgetto at her table, teasing him with her finger and fondling him inside her fragrant gown. Strozzi describes the dog (130–35) as the gift of Cesare Borgia (*Borges*) to Tebaldeo, who thus named him *Borgettus*. Cesare had acquired the recently born Maltese puppy on a visit

298

## · NOTES TO THE TRANSLATIONS ·

to Venice (not after August 1504, as Cesare was out of Italy from then on). Strozzi represents Borgetto as fine-looking, as white as snow or a swan, playful, good-natured, affectionate, and above all faithful; Tebaldeo greatly loved him. Strozzi adds (161–63), "I recall that often for a joke I tickled provocatively at the top edge of your [Tebaldeo's] garment. Suddenly he [Borgetto] flashed forth to do battle and chased me off with his spirited charge and the threat of his open jaws." With Borgetto's death Tebaldeo's former cheerfulness has turned to desolate grief, and Strozzi speculates (186–92) where the dog may be now, perhaps in Elysium, welcomed by such pets as Lesbia's sparrow and Corinna's parrot (Ov. *Am.* 2.6), or perhaps (193–207) his ghost roams by night the fragrant gardens of Francesco, marquis of Mantua (Gian Francesco II [d. 1519], the Gonzaga husband of Isabella d'Este, Lucrezia Borgia's sister-in-law), and at daybreak returns to his tomb there. The dog's unnamed killer is said (177–85) to have answered for his wrongdoing in an unspecified way, and Strozzi predicts further punishment when the killer comes to the Underworld, and Cerberus there devours him, regurgitates him, and eats him over and over again forever. For a dog's name being a diminutive of a person's, cf. Bembinus (Bembino), honored with an epitaph by his master, Pietro Bembo (*Carmina* 38). Dog poems in general: 8n. Rouget claims slight debts in Olivier Magny's *Sur la mort d'un petit chien* (see Magny 1995, 311–16). MSS: Cam., Vat.1 and 6. Meter: Phalaecean hendecasyllables. Cam. contains several other unattributed epitaphs for Borgetto and also for another lapdog belonging to Tebaldeo, called Tita.

2. *Blanditias proterviores* is also in Jean Bonnefons, *Pervigilium Veneris* 129.

5–9. After Catull. 3.6–8, speaking of Lesbia's sparrow: "For he (Lesbia's sparrow) was honey-sweet and knew his mistress as well as a girl knows her mother, and never used to stir from her lap." The scansion in 7 of *illius* with the *i* short accords with Catullus' general practice with such pronominal genitives.

8–9. Cf. Catull. 2.2, 3, and 9, and 3.9.

10–14. A lapdog's epitaph by Pietro Gherardi (*Carmina Illustrium Poetarum Italorum* 5:291) has (line 5) *mensae astabas erecto crure bipesque* ("you

299

### · NOTES TO THE TRANSLATIONS ·

used to stand by the table raised up on your two hind legs"). *Mensae . . . erili* (11): Verg. *Aen.* 7.490, there of a deer. Pontano, *De Amore Coniugali* 2.35.11, has *mensae assistere erili* of a dog.

15. In balanced expressions of near-identical meaning, in one the adjective is diminutive, in the other the noun. Cf. Pontano, *De Amore Coniugali* 2.19.4 (a lullaby poem), *pupule belle meus, bellule pupe meus* ("my pretty little baby"). Joseph Scaliger's poem on Catherine de Roches' flea begins *pulicelle niger, nigella pulex* ("little black flea"); see Dornau 1619, 1:28. Catull. 3.16 has *vae miselle passer!* ("Poor little sparrow!").

16. Cf. Mart. 5.34.3, *parvula ne nigras horrescat Erotion umbras* ("lest poor little Erotion [a dead girl] shudder at the dark shadows").


#### 44

A genethliacon (birthday poem) in dactylic hexameters in honor of Bartolomeo d'Alviano's baby son. Quite numerous examples of Neo-Latin pieces in this genre include one of 1508 by Navagero's friend Ercole Strozzi in honor of Lucrezia Borgia's son born that year; see Strozzi 1513, 54r–57r. Navagero's poem predicts that Alviano's son will enjoy good looks and greatness in the arts and in war, and bring a new Golden Age of peace and bliss. The baby's warlike but cultured father, a little over fifty at the probable date of this poem (late 1508 or early 1509; see on lines 64–65), was himself physically unimpressive, according to Paolo Giovio. Cicogna 1824–53, 6:289n, mentions two known sons of Alviano, who both died very young, Angelo and Livio Attilio. In Navagero's funeral speech for Alviano (November 10, 1515), Livio Attilio is Alviano's only living son, "not yet two years of age." Cicogna infers that, unless there had been another son unknown to us who died in infancy, Angelo must be meant here. No manuscript evidence; see poem 23n. Laumonier notes debts in Ronsard 1914–75, 6:77; 7:48, 55, 69–70 and 74; 13:80; and 14:201.

2. *Pinguia culta*: Verg. G. 4.372, *Aen.* 8.63 and 10.141.

3. *Naonis* = "of Pordenone," where Alviano's academy was established. *Carnia*, the land of the Carni, who anciently lived east of Aquileia, here seems more widely applied to Venice's territory in northeast Italy.

· NOTES TO THE TRANSLATIONS ·

4–5. *Pierides:* Muses. Alviano's baby son is taken up by them for their special care, to become a poet or a patron of the arts. Poliziano, *Silvae* 1.49, speaks similarly of the baby Vergil, and several other Neo-Latin poets have comparable passages. Flaminio so flatters his addressee Antonio Giberti in 2.9.3–4, as du Bellay does Ronsard in his *Elegies* 7, saying that the chief Muse Calliope took him in her arms at birth (*nascentem . . . excepit in ulnis*); see du Bellay 1918, 1:444. *Matre cadentem* ends Val. Fl. 1.355; Stat. *Theb.* 1.60; Claud. *In Rufin.* 1.92. *Exceptis = excepistis.*

6. In Verg. *Ecl.* 7.27–28. Thyrsis says *baccare frontem / cingite* ("ring my brow with the nard plant," apparently as protection from jealous malice. Cf. Ugolino Verino, *Flammetta* 2.26.1.

9–11. Lucina was goddess of childbirth (see 14.9n). Cf. Verg. *Aen.* 12.418–19 for sprinkling of *salubres sucos.*

12. Idalium was a mountain city in Cyprus associated with Venus (here = Dione; see 31.30n); 56.7–8n. Elias Rivers raises the possibility of a debt to Navagero here in Garcilaso de la Vega's *Eclogues* 2.1295–8; see de la Vega 1981. A close Spanish translation of Navagero's lines by Diego Girón is also cited.

13. *Nectare odorato:* Ov. *Met.* 4.250.

15. I think *simul . . . et* probably means "both . . . and," though *simul* may mean "together."

16. Passages where privet blossom is a type of pure whiteness include Verg. *Ecl.* 2.18; Ov. *Met.* 13.789; Mart. 1.116.3.

17. Naucelus/Noncello: 20.1n. *Undifluus* is found in ancient usage only in Dracont. *Hexaëm.* 1.607.

18. *Metune* is the River Meduna near Pordenone, into which the Noncello flows.

19–21. With 19 cf. Verg. *G.* 4.430. *Vimineis . . . calathis* (20): [Verg.] *Copa* 16. René Rapin's (see 27.60–62n) *Sacred Eclogues* 5.44 is exactly as 20 here. *Chrysantho* (21) = *chrysanthemo* after the now disputed [Verg.] *Cul.* 405. Line 21 has a spondaic fifth foot, like 25.15 and 61.

23. In debt to Catull. 64.284.

301

## · NOTES TO THE TRANSLATIONS ·

24. The *Parcae* (Fates) spun the threads of destiny at one's birth. Verg. *Ecl.* 4.46–47, the so-called "Messianic Eclogue," has them declaring a baby's destiny.

25. *Quis* = *quibus* (dative pl.). The Parcae are old and wear white in Catull. 64.305–10. In that poem, among Navagero's sources of inspiration here, they foretell at length the achievements of the unborn Achilles (338–70).

26. Chaonia was part of Epirus in western Greece. The oak of Dodona at Zeus/Jupiter's oracle there supposedly spoke by the rustling of its leaves.

28. *Oscula iunxerunt . . . felicia* draws on Ov. *Her.* 18.101.

29. *Versato . . . fuso* ("from a rotating spindle"): Ov. *Her.* 19.37.

31–32. Ovid has *cresce, puer* ("grow, boy") in *Met.* 2.643 and elsewhere.

35. Hymen was the marriage god, his name here standing for marriage itself, like *hymenaeus* in Verg. *Aen.* 4.127 and Catull. 66.11.

36–37. Catull. 64.322 stresses, in different words, the immutability of what the Fates sing as destined.

38–44. Navagero's language and imagery recall a common feature of an epithalamium, or marriage poem, the picture of the boy or the girl growing like a lovingly-reared flower till full bloom is achieved. Cf., for instance, Pontano, *De Amore Coniugali* 3.4.115–32 ("Just as a young hyacinth growing in a sunny garden, etc."). *Diffundit odorem* (42) ends Verg. *G.* 4.415. Cf. Catull. 64.343 for 44. In 40–41 "sprinkles with gentle water" seems to mean "sprinkles gently with water."

45–49. *Aonides* (47): Muses. At Aganippe, the Muses' fountain in Aonia/Boeotia, poets could drink and be inspired. *Aganippidos* (48) is Greek genitive of the adjective *Aganippis* ("Aganippean"; Ov. *Fast.* 5.7). Haemus and Pindus, mountains in Thrace and Thessaly, were associated, respectively, with Orpheus and the Muses.

50–51. Mars as *bellipotens*: Verg. *Aen.* 11.8 and several times in Statius and elsewhere. "The Tritonian maiden" (Verg. *Aen.* 11.483 and Statius) is Minerva, goddess of war as well as of the arts and wisdom.

302

# · NOTES TO THE TRANSLATIONS ·

52–55. Understand *erit* ("will be") with *doctior* (52). *Comminus ense* (52): Ov. *Met.* 3.119 and *Pont.* 4.7.44. *Valida hasta* (53): Verg. *Aen.* 10.401 and 12.93. With 54 cf. Tib. 1.4.11.

59–63. For flood imagery cf. Verg. *Aen.* 2.304–8 and 496–99 and 12.523–28; Lucr. 1.282–94; Hom. *Il.* 5.87–94. Line 61 is after Verg. *G.* 1.481 (of the Eridanus) *proluit insano contorquens vertice silvas* ("washes woods away, spinning them in its mad, swirling waters"). *Proluit* is similarly used in *Aen.* 12.686. The editions of Navagero here give *proruit* ("demolishes"), not impossible, but Vergil's *proluit* seems more likely. *Camposque per omnes* (62) ends Verg. *Aen.* 2.498 and *G.* 1.482. *Cum sonitu* (63): Verg. *G.* 1.327 (of a river's roar).

64–65. *Fortunate puer*: Verg. *Ecl.* 5.49. The predicted matching of Alviano's exploits suggests composition before his unmentioned defeat and capture at Agnadello (May 14, 1509), but after his 1508 victory in Friuli (celebrated in 70–73), at a time when the French were again about to cause trouble (74–77). Navagero's poem probably just postdates Girolamo Borgia's encomium of Alviano delivered to the Venetian Senate in July 1508 (see 40.70–73n.).

66–69. In the Battle of the Garigliano (December 29, 1503), Alviano fought with the Spanish against the French. Louis XII of France and the Spanish king, Ferdinand of Aragon, had agreed in 1500 to invade and break up the kingdom of Naples, each taking a share of its territory. Its king (Federigo) soon yielded Naples to the French (1501), but disputes between them and the Spanish led the erstwhile allies to fight each other. After initial French successes, the Spanish cause began to recover under Gonzalo Fernández de Córdoba, *el gran capitan*, who blocked the advance of a stronger French army for some weeks at the Garigliano, then, through Alviano, delivered a victorious surprise attack. By the 1505 Treaty of Blois, the French king resigned his claim to Naples in favor of a female relative, whose marriage to Ferdinand brought Spain Naples as dowry. Navagero describes the action at the Garigliano in his 1515 funeral oration for Alviano; see Navagero 1718, 7.

70. *Gelida . . . ab Arcto* (lit., "from the icy Bear," meaning from the north) recalls the "icy Bears" in Verg. *Aen.* 6.16 and Ov. *Met.* 4.625.

303

# · NOTES TO THE TRANSLATIONS ·

70–73. When the emperor Maximilian I was refused permission to pass through Venetian territory with a large force—ostensibly to secure his coronation in Rome, though the Venetians doubted his intentions—he invaded, marching on Vicenza. Alviano first defeated Maximilian in person and then followed up in early 1508 with a further rout of Austrian troops (meant here) and the occupation of Gorizia, Fiume, and Trieste. Navagero recounts the events in his funeral speech for Alviano; see Navagero 1718, 7–8. Two poems by Cotta, 13 and 14 (the latter an epitaph for Alviano's dog Caparion), also pay tribute to Alviano's victory over the Germans. Girolamo Borgia (see 20.69–70n) composed a celebration of Alviano's same success in 159 hexameters, read to the doge (Leonardo Loredan) and the Venetian Senate on July 7, 1508. Borgia's poem can be found—with textual faults—in Florio 1909, 74–77. His imperfectly preserved hexameter panegyric on Alviano's same victory is on pp. 78–86. Borgia's two-line epitaph for Alviano (Florio 1909, 18) reads, "This urn is that of the general Alviano. The cruel Fates declare him to have been a man, his brave deeds a god" (see 20.33–34n).

74–77. The prediction that Alviano will again defeat the French, once more treacherously invading Italy, or about to do so, fixes the poem to shortly before the Venetian defeat at Agnadello on May 14, 1509, and Alviano's capture by the French. See 35n. The French are similarly called *foedifragi* ("treaty breakers") in Cotta, *Carmina* 14.11. In line 75 Latin = Italian. *Caelo . . . aequabit* is imagery from Verg. *Aen.* 8.99–100.

78–81. *Restabunt* (78) = "are [lit., "will be"] left over from"; cf. Verg. *Aen.* 1.679. *Paca(ve)rit* (79) is future perfect. Some texts have a period at the end of 80, making *haec primum* elliptical ("These things first"), but the words seem better taken with *subibis* (so Wilson 1973). Ausonia is quite often used poetically for Italy; cf. 83 and *Ausonios . . . in agros* in 71.

81–88. Latium in 85 is for Italy. *Coloratis . . . Indis* ("the dark-skinned Indians," 88): Verg. *G.* 4.292, though there Ethiopians; Claud., *In Eutr.* 2.331. *Phoebus* (88) denotes the sun.

89–92. *Placida contentus pace* is literally "content with quiet peace"; cf. Verg. *Aen.* 1.249. *Discordia* personified: Verg. *Aen.* 6.280; Stat. *Theb.* 2.288, 5.74 and 7.50; Petron. 124.27–51. Navagero may owe something to

304

# · NOTES TO THE TRANSLATIONS ·

Calpurnius' idea of the binding and disarming of Bellona, the war goddess, in *Ecl.* 1.47–51, especially as 1.42–44 there speaks, after Verg. *Ecl.* 4.6, of the return of the Golden Age, and 1.52–53 has the idea of wars being banished to a Tartarean prison (cf. 94 here).

91–94. The Golden Age, when Saturn (Greek, Kronos) ruled, was a time of ease, peace, and plenty in classical literature, both Greek and Latin. Here Navagero predicts its return through Alviano's son, just as Vergil does through the birth of the child celebrated in his Fourth ("Messianic") Eclogue, where line 6 declares, "Now the Virgin [Astraea] returns, Saturn's rule returns." Several Neo-Latin poets flatter rulers or popes by linking them with a new Golden Age; cf., for instance, F. 1.8.77–78, speaking of Paul III. Astraea, then the goddess of justice, eventually left the earth (Ov. *Met.* 1.149–50) and became a constellation (Virgo, or some say Libra). Her return is commonly expected with a new Golden Age. Cf., for example, Ugolino Verino, *Flammetta* 2.51.139–40, for Astraea quitting high heaven for earth. In Italian, note Ariosto, *Orlando furioso* cantos 3.51 and 15.25. *Alma* of Peace (93): Tib. 1.10.67 and quite commonly in Neo-Latin poets.

94. Cf. Stat. *Silv.* 5.168–69 ("Death would be groaning, shut in the sightless pit"). *Stygio . . . barathro* is also in Zanchi, Eclogue 2.56 (*Myrtilus*), with dismal winter dispatched thither (see Zanchi 1555, 171); Marullo, *Hymni Naturales* 4.5.15; and line 19 of a poem of Giano Vitale (cited 20.33–34n), where all the horrors of bloodshed, plunder, etc., have, at Leo X's elevation to the papacy, been "hurried off to the Stygian pit." Verg. *Ecl.* 4.13 has the notion of all remaining traces of *scelus nostrum* ("our wrongdoing," perhaps meaning civil war) being banished from earth in the new Golden Age. Cf. also Fracastoro, *Carmina* 16.12–13.

96–101. In 97 *divum genitor* may hint at the Christian God, often equated with Jupiter in Neo-Latin poetry. Cf. 34.10 and 16 and 34.13–16n. Having plenty to eat without human labor is regularly associated with the Golden Age. Cf., for instance, Verg. *G.* 1.125–28; Ov. *Met.* 1.101–12; Tib. 1.3.45–46. Line 100 is almost the same as 27.64; 101 is identical to 27.66.

102–5. Debts to Verg. *Aen.* 2.689–94, where Jupiter confirms the boy Iulus' future greatness by thundering on the left, and a shooting star de-

305

## · NOTES TO THE TRANSLATIONS ·

scends "with much light," and to *Aen.* 9.630, with thunder on the left "from a clear quarter of the sky" (*caeli . . . de parte serena*), as in 103.

### 45

Navagero here translates a fragment of the Greek New Comedy poet Philemon preserved in Plutarch's *Moralia* (*Consolatio ad Apollonium* 105). Quoted also (with some textual differences) by Stob. *Flor.* 108.1 and 122.12, it is designated Philemon fr. 73 in Kock 1880–88 and Edmonds 1957–61, and fr. 77 in Kassel/Austin 1989. The first speaker is a slave; the second is his master, probably a youth. Muret later composed two very free Latin adaptations of this fragment, *Poemata Varia* 60 and 61 (Muret 1834, 2:341), and playfully pretended they were composed by specific ancient playwrights, fooling some contemporary scholars before eventually admitting a hoax. Du Bellay has debts to Navagero's translation of Philemon's lines in *Les regrets* 52, and lines 73–76 of his poem *A Monsieur d'Avanson* reflect lines 7–8 here. MS: Vat.14. The meter is iambic trimeters (*senarii*).

1. *Lacrimae* here has first syllable long; in line 8 it scans short.

3. Line 3 of Muret's second adaptation is only one word different (*contra* for *nobis* here).

### 46

Navagero here translates a fragment of Menander from Plutarch's *Moralia* (*Consolatio ad Apollonium* 103). The precise text and sense of the original are uncertain in places. The fragment is Menander fr. 531 in Kock 1880–88 and Edmonds 1957–61, and fr. 602 in Kassel/Austin 1998. There is a French adaptation by Ronsard in the 1554 *Le bocage* (see Ronsard 1914–75, 6:120–21). Another, by Mellin de Saint-Gelais, is closer to Navagero's Latin; see Saint-Gelais 1873, 1:248–50. MS: Vat.9. Meter as 45.

10. The meter requires the order *habenda ratio*, but the reverse order is found in Navagero 1530 and many other early and some later texts, as well as in Vat.9. The order is corrected in Gruter 1608; Navagero 1718, 1753, and 1754; and *Carmina Illustrium Poetarum Italorum* 1720.

306

## · NOTES TO THE TRANSLATIONS ·

### 47

In dactylic hexameters Navagero greets Venice "on his return from his embassy to Spain," according to Fracastoro 1555 and Gruter 1608. The statement is not in any other edition or collection, including the 1530 *editio princeps*, prior to Navagero 1718. Navagero returned to Venice on September 24, 1528, according to his *Viaggio fatto in Francia* (Navagero 1718, 419). There may be some general inspiration from Petrarch's Latin verses written on his return home to Italy in May 1353 (*Epistolae Metricae* 3.24). Catull. 31 is an ancient homecoming poem. Symonds 1897, 355, quotes and translates this present poem. Wiffen 1823, 387–88, has a very free version. For one in Italian thought to be by Bargaeus (see 2n), see Navagero 1718, 286. MSS: Cam., Vat.3.

1. The first three words are as in [Tib.] 3.4.43. Cf. Ov. *Ars am.* 3.405 and *Am.* 3.9.17 (*divum cura* of poets). *Felicior*, like *praestantior* in 8.7, is comparative for superlative. Cf., for example, Aeneas Silvius Piccolomini (Pope Pius II), *Chrysis* 676, *lenarum omnium quas novi melior* ("best of all the procuresses I know"); Roscoe 1805, vol. 2, App. 66, quotes a poem by Francesco Maria Grapaldi for Julius II: *Parma, ex omnibus una / laetior* ("Parma, of all [places] the happiest").

2. Cf. 55.36–37 for Venice as a place where Cupid and Venus hold sway. In Molza's poem *De Venere, Relicta Cypro, Sedem Venetiis Deligente*, Venus is said to quit Cyprus and choose Venice for her seat (Molza 1747–54, 1:260).

4. *Vos . . . lustro* probably means "I survey you" rather than "I traverse you"; interpretations of *litora lustrat* in Verg. *Aen.* 5.611 vary.

### FURTHER POEMS ASCRIBED TO NAVAGERO

### 48

A tribute printed at the end of Bartolomeo Merula's exposition of Ovid's *Tristia* (Venice, 1499); Navagero was then around sixteen. Reprinted in Mittarelli 1779, 314 (Appendix of Fifteenth-Century Books). See Cicogna 1824–53, 6:288. No manuscript evidence.

### · NOTES TO THE TRANSLATIONS ·

1–4. See Verg. *Aen.* 2.692–98 (esp. 697) for the fire trail following the star sent to guide the fleeing Trojans. Neptune and Apollo traditionally built Troy's walls for its king Laomedon, who cheated them of payment and is thus "deceitful leader" in Hor. *Odes* 3.3.24. Cf. *Neptunia Troia*, Verg. *Aen.* 2.625 and 3.3. The Trojans were sometimes called *Dardanidae*, as Dardanus was an ancestor of their royal house. Pergamum was Troy's citadel. Mt. Ida: 16.7–8n.

5–6. Ovid (Naso) was exiled from Rome ("the city" in 6) to the shores of the Black Sea. His "second" exile to Scythian parts metaphorically refers to neglect of his works.

8. Latium is for Italy (see 20.10n).

### 49

First printed in Zanchi 1553, 117; also in Zanchi 1555, 294. Reprinted (in ignorance of previous publication) from a Vatican MS, evidently Vat.1 as here designated, by Gualtieri 1786, 86 (see Cicogna 1824–53, 6:288). MSS: Mil.1, Nap., Vat.1 and 11, Wro. (the first and the third are detailed by Benassi 1940, 244–45). In the Naples MS this poem appears between 52 and 53, as in Gualtieri 1786, with the same Latin note (see 52n). Hair is a love gift in several vernacular, as well as Neo-Latin, poems. Examples include John Donne, *The Bracelet* (Elegy 11), *The Funeral*, and *The Relic*; William Smith, *Chloris* (1596), Sonnet 29; Thomas Carew, *A Pastoral Dialogue: Celia, Cleon*, 26–48; and Ronsard's poem beginning *Doux cheveux* (Ronsard 1887–93, 1:356). William Drummond of Hawthornden has three versions of Antonio Tebaldeo's Italian poem beginning *O chiome parte de la treccia d'oro* (*Sonetti* 106) about a bracelet of locks of his mistress's hair. Cf. also Drummond's poems *Anthea's Gift* and *A Locke Desired* (Drummond 1913, 1:118 and 2:239). His Sonnet 48 (Drummond 1913, 1:42) speaks of an armlet of a beloved's hair. When Giovanni Cotta (*Carmina* 5) asked of his girl some little reward for his labor to ease his inner fires, she gave him locks of her hair, so inflaming him more, till he privately burned them. See also Robert Burton's *Anatomy of Melancholy* (Burton 1989–2000, 3:177). Here Navagero's lines are written as though

308

## · NOTES TO THE TRANSLATIONS ·

to accompany the gift, the plucked hairs being imagined as addressing the recipient.

1. Both versions of this line scan and make the same sense. *Vellere* ("pluck" or "tear") is found with a simple ablative or with the prepositions *a* or *de* to mean "from." Use with *e* ("out of") would not seem objectionable. For *dum* beginning successive clauses, cf. 55.43–44 (three) and 60–62 (five).

2. *Domina* (here translated "your lady") could alternatively be "our mistress."

3. Cf. Ov. *Her.* 18.15, '*felix i littera!*' *dixi* ("'Go, lucky letter!' I said"), where Leander writes to Hero.

4. Cf. Ov. *Am.* 2.15.9 ("O that I could suddenly be changed into my gift!"), there of a ring sent to the beloved girl; F. 3.15.4 (and headnote to that poem).

50

This poem was printed with other unpublished poems attributed to Navagero (here 51–53) in Cinelli Calvoli 1736, 6–8 (*Scanzia* 22). See Cicogna 1824–53, 6:288; Benassi 1940, 245; Griggio 1976–77, 99. Griggio omits to record 53 as among the poems then first printed. In Cinelli Calvoli 1736 the poems are stated to be taken from a Vatican Library manuscript, meaning Vat.1 (see 69n), as Griggio 1976–77 rightly infers. MSS: Mil.2, Ud., Vat.1 and 6. In all but Vat.1, this poem and 51 are clearly separate. In Vat.1, where a page ends with line 12, there is no mark to indicate that the poem finishes there, though that seems to be the case. Cinelli Calvoli 1736 prints this poem and 51 (lines unnumbered) with the same one-line space between them as is left between 51 and 52 and then between 52 and 53, meaning that this poem and 51 are treated as separate poems, though Cicogna 1824–53, 6:288, wrongly calls *Tumulus Borgetti Catelli* as printed in Cinelli Calvoli 1736 a poem of eleven distichs (the total for this poem and 51 together). Benassi 1940, 248–49, detailing only Vat.1 as a MS source, treats this poem and 51 as one and numbers the lines accordingly, though

### · NOTES TO THE TRANSLATIONS ·

she leaves a one-line gap between her lines 12 and 13. In Navagero 2001, Griggio follows Benassi 1940 in making this poem and 51 a single poem. See 43n for the dog, Antonio Tebaldeo's. Line 1 here is also the first line of one of several unascribed poems on Borgetto in Ms. Lat. 358 (here denoted by Cam.; see 43n) at Harvard University's Houghton Library. That poem is on p. 107 there.

1. An imagined wayfarer (cf. 9.7 and 54.1; F. 4.7.11–14, 4.9, 4.10.3–4 and 17–20, 4.11.1–4) is often asked in epitaphs to stop at a tomb and offer flowers or otherwise pay respects. Either *consiste* ("halt") or *assiste* ("stand by") makes sense, but the latter has better MS authority.

3–4. *Sorores* (7), for which cf. 31.1 and 31, suggests that the girls in 3 are the nymph daughters of the Po (Eridanus; so *Eridani puellae* in Fracastoro, *Syphilis* 1.392 and 410), which flows near Ferrara, where Tebaldeo long resided (see 43n). They are essentially his local Muses (see 20.1n). *Miserat*: 10A.2n. The *Melitaean* small dog is mentioned a number of times in ancient literature, and the *Melite* associated with it is generally taken to be Malta. If *Melite* is Malta here, it could be said to be in the Aeolian Sea, envisaged south of Sicily (Sil. 14.233–34). Nevertheless, Pliny the Elder (*HN* 3.152) briefly states, on the claimed authority of Callim. fr. 579 (Pfeiffer 1949), that the dog really derives its name from another *Melite*, now Meleda off the Dalmatian coast. The variant *Illyrico* ("Illyrian") for *Aeolio* in Mil.2 in fact makes *Melite* not Malta but Meleda. Navagero, if indeed the poet, seems to have rewritten his line on changing his view of where the dogs we call "Maltese" came from. Leitch 1953 not only covers the breed's history but also has many reproductions of its appearances in art, including around Navagero's time. Caius 1570 speaks of the Maltese as especially the plaything and pet of ladies, who carry it in their dress folds, admit it to their beds, and let it rest on their arms when they ride in carriages. William Harrison (1534–93) frowns severely on the pampering of Maltese dogs, even taken to ladies' beds and fed at table (as Tebaldeo fed Borgetto); see Leitch 1953, 24. Cf. also how Lucrezia Borgia treats Borgetto in Ercole Strozzi's poem cited in 43n.

5. *Electra* strictly refers to an amber-colored alloy of silver and gold already used in the ancient world. In Girolamo Aleandro's *Lament for the*

310

## · NOTES TO THE TRANSLATIONS ·

*Lapdog Aldina* (*Carmina Illustrium Poetarum Italorum* 1:109), Aldina's collar (*monilia*) used to gleam "with many a spike of gold."

9. See 30.2–3n.

10. Ov. *Tr.* 3.4.45–46 bids his distant addressee "love your Naso's name" as the only part of him not in exile. Cf. T. V. Strozzi, *Erotica* 2.10.10 ("I began to love your name"). The implausible reading *nomine* ("with a name" or "by name") in Cinelli Calvoli 1736 and in Benassi 1940 misinterprets the abbreviation in Vat.1, by which the scribe surely intends *nomen*, as read in Mil. 2 and Ud.

11. The city of Bucephala bore the name of Alexander the Great's horse Bucephalas after its death.

### 51

See 50n. Some debt to Catull. 2 and 3. MSS: Mil.2, Ud., Vat.1 and 6.

3. *Quicum* (Mil.2) matches the form in Catull. 2.2 and should probably be preferred to *quocum* (other MSS). Benassi 1940 misguidedly conjectures *animos oblectat* for the unmetrical *animum oblectat* in Vat.1; the correct reading, *animum oblectabat* (imperfect), is preserved in the other MSS.

4–6. Ov. *Nux* 116 has *avida . . . proterva manu*. In line 6, *oculus* ("eye") is used figuratively like its diminutive *ocellus* in Catull. 31.1 (there of Sermione, "eye of peninsulas and islands"). Flaminio hails Mantua as *civitatum ocelle* ("eye of states") in 1.30.1.

8. For *cuncta licere* cf. 10.12.

9. *Orcus* = the Underworld.

### 52

Printed in Cinelli Calvoli 1736 and Gualtieri 1786. A long Latin note in both the Naples MS and *verbatim* in Gualtieri 1786 thinks this poem untypical of Navagero and unconvincingly wonders if it is a solitary survival from his youthful *Silvae* (see 16n). The same note argues by contrast that 49 and 53 seem authentic in style. Cicogna 1824–53, 6:288, takes the note to be by the 1786 editor, Gualtieri. Sirmio = Sermione (cf.

311

## · NOTES TO THE TRANSLATIONS ·

F. 4.1), the peninsula by Lago di Garda famously described in Catull. 31. Cicogna 1824–53, 6:289, and Benassi 1940, 243, see *Secundus* as Johannes Secundus (1511–36), an imitator of Catullus, but he lived in the Low Countries and was only eighteen when Navagero died. Furthermore, Johannes Secundus never wrote poetry on Sermione, though the "three hundred" lines (cf. Catull. 12.10) are probably hypothetical. If Navagero is really the author of this poem, I think his choice of *Secundus* as the poet's name must be a coincidence. Secundus, the cognomen of Pliny the Elder and his nephew (a famously bad poet), could even be a pseudonym; cf. Cadmus in 58B. If, however, Johannes Secundus is truly meant, this poem cannot be by Navagero. Catull. 49.5–6 has *pessimus omnium poeta* of himself. For imitation of Catullus in Navagero, cf. 30, 32, and 33. MSS: Nap., Ud., Vat.1 and 11. Meter: Phalaecean hendecasyllables.

### 53

Cf. 42, probably of the same period. Printed in Cinelli Calvoli 1736 and Gualtieri 1786, 86–87. MSS: Nap., Si., Ud., Vat.1, 10, and 11.

1. *Fortibus armis*: Verg. *Aen*. 10.735.

3. Both *confertas* ("compacted") and *consertas* ("closely engaged") make sense with *acies* ("battle lines"), though the former seems better suited to this context of rushing into the thick of the fight.

4. Cf. Verg. *Aen*. 2.353, *in media arma ruamus* ("Let us rush into the midst of arms!").

### 54

The Neo-Latin poet Ercole Strozzi (see 43n) was stabbed to death in a Ferrara street in 1508, aged mid-thirties or younger, just days after marrying the already widowed Barbara Torelli, the recent mother of the latest of his several illegitimate children. His savage murder, in which he sustained twenty-two wounds, went unpunished. See Cartwright 1903, 1:312–13; Monteforte 1899; Wirtz 1906. Bellonci 1953 provides substantial coverage of Strozzi's marriage to Barbara Torelli and his murder. See also Erlanger 1979, 279, on who might have been responsible. One suspect has

## · NOTES TO THE TRANSLATIONS ·

been Alfonso d'Este, duke of Ferrara, Lucrezia Borgia's husband, but Erlanger thinks the Bentivoglio family probably to blame. Barbara Torelli's first husband was Ercole Bentivoglio of Bologna; see Erlanger 1979, 238, for his mistreatment of her. Strozzi's funeral oration was delivered by Celio Calcagnini (see Calcagnini 1544, 505–8). Tebaldeo (*Carmina Illustrium Poetarum Italorum* 9:245) and Ariosto (*Carmina* 59) were among those who wrote epitaphs. Calcagnini calls Strozzi's widow "one of the very distinguished family of the Torelli (*Taurelli*), notable no more for her beauty than for her modesty and outstanding devotion to her husband"; Ariosto calls her "Barbara, a distinguished member of the Torelli house (*Taurellae . . . domus*)"; Tebaldeo, "Barbara, glory of the Torelli family (*Taurellae . . . gentis honor*)," not rich enough to match the tomb built by Mausolus' widow, but her equal in devoted love. In his tribute to Strozzi's widow, Bembo, *Carmina* 30 (*Herculis Strozzae Epitaphium*), portrays her as regretting that she could not live out a sweet life with him, but vowing soon to be embracing him in death. In her own Italian elegy, Barbara Torelli bewails only thirteen days of marriage and wishes she might revive Strozzi, warming his cold ice with her fire, and restoring his dust to new life with her tears, so as to tell his killer, "Such is the power, cruel monster, that love has"; see Catalano 1930, 1:248, and Erlanger 1979, 281. Ms. Lat. 358 at Harvard University's Houghton Library, here denoted as Cam., contains several unascribed epitaphs for Ercole Strozzi, mostly naming his widow. They include Tebaldeo's poem on p. 202, but this present poem is not among them. MSS: Mil.1, Si., Vat.11, Wro. First printed by Benassi 1940.

1. For *siste gradum* see 19.21–22n. See also 50.1n.

3–4. "Greater monuments of himself": Strozzi's writings. *Aonides*: Muses. Verg. G. 3.9 has the notion of flying on the lips of men, after Ennius' self-composed epitaph (cf. F. 4.17.5).

5–6. *Taurella* is wrongly spelled *Taurilla* in Benassi 1940 and Griggio 1976–77, but the MSS here and the tributes of Ariosto and Tebaldeo all have *Taurella*; Calcagnini calls her family the *Taurelli*. *Taurell-* can also be spelled *Torell-* (the Italian form is *Torelli*, as in Ippolita Torelli, Castiglione's wife). For *viduus . . . torus* ("empty bed"), cf. Ov. *Her.* 5.106 and

# · NOTES TO THE TRANSLATIONS ·

10.14, *Am.* 3.5.42, and *Tr.* 5.5.48; Ovid has similar expressions with *lectus* and *cubile.*

9. Literally, "and after her final day, when it [or possibly 'she'] will have ended her unhappy years."

## 55

A supposed last plea to a beautiful, but unyielding, nobly-born adolescent Venetian boy (28–29, 34, 58–63) to allow the love-tormented older speaker limited sexual favors, or else he will commit suicide (45–51). Except in 28–30, the youth is addressed in the second person. Cf. the soliloquy in 19.41–54 to an absent beloved. This poem and the very much cruder 65 are Navagero's only surviving homosexual poems, if both are truly his. Ancient inspirations include Hor. *Odes* 4.10, Tib. 1.1, and Nemes. *Ecl.* 4; see on 40–41, 52–63. [Theoc.] *Id.* 23 (a paraclausithyron) is another influence. There, a spurned older lover begs a hard-hearted youth to yield, but is still rejected and hangs himself. Verg. *Ecl.* 2 similarly deals with a shepherd's unrequited attraction to a boy. Baïf's Latin adaptation of the same pseudo-Theocritean idyll is heterosexual. MSS: Lon., Trev.1 and 2, Vien. Of these, Lon., the best MS here, heads this poem *And: Nauag.* In the other MSS it is merely headed *Eiusdem* ("of the same"), being preceded by Fracastoro's poem to Pope Julius III (*Carmina* 12), wrongly treated as Navagero's. The meter is dactylic hexameters. There are Italian translations by Pierluigi Gallucci of this poem and 65 on Giovanni Dall'Orto's homepage (http://www.giovannidallorto.com/lavori/navagero.html), though I disagree with Gallucci's versions in certain details.

1–8. Pieria in Thessaly (2), Mt. Parnassus and Mt. Helicon in central Greece (3 and 7), the waters of Libethra in Macedonia (5; Verg. *Ecl.* 7.21), and Cadmeian (= Theban or Boeotian) Dirce (7), a fountain in Boeotia (Ov. *Met.* 2.239; Stat. *Silv.* 1.4.21, 2.7.18), all had associations with the Muses. The "last gift" is the despairing, suicidal lover's final address. Cf. especially the spurned Daphnis' *extremum . . . munus morientis* ("dying man's last gift") in Verg. *Ecl.* 8.60; [Verg.] *Cir.* 267 repeats the same

# · NOTES TO THE TRANSLATIONS ·

words. Cf. also (reflecting Vergil) Naldo Naldi, *Eclogues* 8.75 ("Let Amyntas [an admired boy] have this last gift of a dying man"). A gift "flowing from the Pierian valley" is a message in verse; *fluens* has antecedent *munus*. *Flebile carmen* (2): Ov. *Her.* 15.7 and *Tr.* 5.1.5. For *testis . . . amoris* (3) cf., for example, Prop. 1.18.19–22, where the trees that have heard the poet's songs of Cynthia and have had her name cut into their bark will be his witnesses. Waters swollen with tears (5) figure in Cotta, *Carmina* 9.30, where he bids a river tell Rubella that it could often be dried up by the fire of his passion, were it not swollen with his weeping. Pontano, *Eridanus* 1.12, speaks of the poet flooding the Po with his tears; Sannazaro speaks similarly of the Sebeto in his *Epigrams* 2.56.4. The basic image is in Ov. *Met.* 1.584 and 11.47–48, as well as Val. Fl. 6.565–66; cf. also F. 4.5.4.

9. Comparison of a hard heart to rock, especially flint, is common: Tib. 1.1.64; Prop. 1.9.31 and 1.16.29–30; Ov. *Tr.* 1.8.41 and *Met.* 9.613. For the idea of appeals moving hard (i.e., pitiless, unfeeling) rocks, cf., for example, Ov. *Met.* 9.304.

10–11. *Immite* ("harshly" or "cruelly," adverbial, as in Sil. 17.256 or 257, there of stridently whistling ropes), the reading in Trev.1 and 2 and Vien., can scan only by lengthening *in arsi* (see 20.48n), whereas *immites* (Lon.; also independently conjectured by Benassi 1940) scans normally. Contempt for the fires of love: 19.17 (Narcissus). *Puer unice*: Ov. *Met.* 3.454 (Narcissus to himself); the implied equation of the unresponsive scorn of the beautiful boy here with that of Narcissus is no doubt deliberate.

12. Explaining a person's hard nature by supposed rearing in the wild by a lioness, tigress, or the like is familiar imagery in ancient literature and elsewhere, though *lacte . . . nutrite ferino* particularly recalls Verg. *Aen.* 11.571–72, where the rearing of the baby Camilla on a wild mare's milk is in point. The cruel boy in [Theoc.] *Id.* 23 is rebuked as "offspring of an evil lioness" (20).

17–27. The commonly assumed symptoms of unhappy love are described: the lover is wasted, pale, skin and bone, strengthless, and languishing, with his normal interests neglected (cf. 19.43–54) and his regu-

315

· NOTES TO THE TRANSLATIONS ·

lar powers gone. The general theme is very frequently encountered in love poets. For the skin touching the bones from wasting, cf. Prop. 4.5.64 ("my bones were counted through my thin skin"); Ov. *Am.* 2.9.14 (love leaving bones bare); Ugolino Verino, *Flammetta* 1.22.15 (flesh scarcely covering the bones of the lover, whose ribs one could count). *Sanguis* (lit., "blood") in 20 denotes lustiness or vitality; perhaps cf. Verg. *Aen.* 2.639.

22–23. Taken at face value, these lines imply that Navagero, if truly to be regarded as the speaker, saw himself as an active philosopher and scientist. His intellectual interests are made to sound very Lucretian (he edited Lucretius in 1515). With *cernere causas* cf. *cognoscere causas* in Verg. G. 2.490; see more fully F. 4.25.6–8n.

25. Cf. poems 42 and 53 for Navagero as a soldier. *Aegidis* probably means a breastplate rather than a shield; cf. Ov. *Met.* 2.754–55.

28–30. Cf. *causa mali tanti* in Verg. *Aen.* 6.93 and 11.480.

31. The *dolores* are the speaker's. *Patiere* here = "you will allow," not "endure" (contrast line 53).

32–33. More imagery explaining cruelty (cf. lines 12 and 29, as well as 25.49). Lions for parents: Ov. *Met.* 9.614; Catull. 60.1 and 64.154. Line 33 supposes that the tenderhearted Venetians, and gentle Venice, home of Cupid and Venus (see 47.2), cannot have produced this unpitying boy. Cf. Ov. *Tr.* 1.8.37–40. ("I do not think you born in Quirinus' peaceful city [Rome], but of the rocks, etc."). Several images of cruelty follow there, e.g., suckling by a tigress, 43–44. Cf. also *Met.* 8.120 (Europa not mother, but inhospitable Syrtis, Armenian tigresses, and Charybdis). In Hom. *Il.* 16.33 Achilles is told Peleus was not his father, nor Thetis his mother, but the sea and rocks bore him. In Verg. *Aen.* 4.366–67 the Caucasus and tigers are said to have produced Aeneas. Ov. *Her.* 7.39 talks of savage beasts or the sea as parents. Comparable sentiments are found elsewhere, both in ancient verse and in several Neo-Latin poets. *Iam* (32) = "indeed."

34. *Latium* stands for Italy in general (20.10n), as the boy is Venetian.

36–39. *Posuit* (36) virtually = *imposuit*. *Aurea* (39): Venus (Aphrodite) is commonly "golden." Lines 38–39 amount to, "You are the only cruel person in Venice, the city of love."

316

· NOTES TO THE TRANSLATIONS ·

40–41. Of the tender forms of address in line 40, *mea lux* ("my light") and *mea vita* ("my life") are very common, and *spes mea* ("my hope") and *meum cor* ("my heart") are found in Plautus. *Mens* (usually "mind," sometimes "heart" or "soul") is a term of endearment in Théodore de Bèze's *Juvenilia* 67 (Beza 1879, 195) and in the elder Janus Dousa, *Epigrams* 2.19.2 (Dousa 1976, 70), though in both cases with punning on *mentula* ("penis"), not intended here. Du Bellay has all these expressions save *mea mens* in his *Amores* 12.3 (du Bellay 1918, 1:491). Pontano, *Parthenopeus* 1.25.9–14, has a dozen terms of endearment — including *mea lux, mea vita*, and *meum cor* — in six lines. Nemes. *Ecl.* 4.20 has *respice me* in a similar context of a beautiful boy urged to pity an older admirer, as beauty will not last; the youth there is reminded in line 36 that he is already twenty.

42–44. *Carpere* of kisses: Prop. 1.20.27; Ov. *Met.* 4.358; and elsewhere. Fondling a boy's chest: Petron. 86 ("I filled my hands with his milky breasts"). *Brevis hora*: Ov. *Met.* 4.696.

45–49. I know no parallel for *morti vicina* ("close to death") used to mean *moritura* ("about to die"). *Stygias . . . ad undas* (49): Ov. *Met.* 3.272 and *Pont.* 2.3.43. For ancient passages dealing with the suicide of a lover, see Murgatroyd 2001, commenting on Tib. 2.6.19–20.

51. *Obsceno . . . cruore*: Verg. *Aen.* 4.455.

52–63. In several ancient contexts an older would-be seducer warns a resistant beloved that disdainful rejection of love now will be regretted too late, when looks have gone. In [Theoc.] *Id.* 23, after comparison to flowers that bloom and fade, an unyielding boy is told, "boyhood's beauty is a fine thing, but short-lived," and his admirer warns (34–35), "That time will come when you too will love, when, burning in your heart, you will weep salty tears" (cf. 52–63 here). In [Theoc.] *Id.* 29.25–34, an older man seeks to win a lad's acceptance of him by warning of youth's brevity. Cf. also Hor. *Odes* 4.10 (the model for Ugolino Verino, *Flammetta* 2.19), among other ancient antecedents. In a heterosexual context, in Bargaeus, Eclogue 3 (*Glyce*), where Lycidas, in a lonely place, laments Glyce's rejection of him and his gifts, he warns that the day will soon come when she will weep, with her youth's flower gone; then cruel love will burn her, and her pain will punish her for scorning him; see Bargaeus 1568, 226–29.

317

# · NOTES TO THE TRANSLATIONS ·

55. *Velocius aura* ends Ov. *Met.* 3.209. This line, being present only in Lon., is not in Benassi 1940 (and thus Griggio 1976–77), derived from Trev.1 and 2.

56. Instances of youth described as *green* (cf. 3.9) include Verg. *Aen.* 5.295; Ov. *Tr.* 4.10.17; Catull. 17.14 ("a girl married in her greenest flower").

59. Ends as Prop. 3.7.59. *Crede mihi* is a very frequent parenthesis in Ovid.

60–63. Cf. the repeated *dum* in lines of similar meaning in Prop. 4.5.59–60 ("while your blood is in its spring, while your time of life is free of wrinkles, make use of your blessing"). Ganymede was the beautiful Trojan boy carried off to serve as Jupiter's cupbearer. The adjective *Ganymedeus* is several times in Martial. *Tempora* (usually "temples") is here used as a synonym for "face." The phrase *iungere amores* (63) denotes sharing mutual love. The expression (cf. Catull. 64.372 and 78.3) is in Tib. 1.1.69, advice to enjoy love's pleasures *dum fata sinunt* ("while the fates allow," words also in Prop. 2.15.23 in a comparable context), before death makes such joys impossible.

56

First published by Griggio 1976–77. MSS: Bol.U., Mil.2, Si. Meter: Phalaecean hendecasyllables.

1. Paphos in Cyprus had strong associations with Venus, who had a famous temple there. Tac. *Hist.* 2.2 calls her *Paphia Venus*, for example; she could also be called *Paphie*, "the Paphian." *Ministrae* of the Graces: Pontano, *Lyra* 8.1 and 33, *Hendecasyllabi* 1.30.27, 2.24.16 and 37.

2. See 59.47n for the scansion of *Charites*.

3. Both versions of this line in the MSS are credible. That in Si. translates "as we (= I) now weave spring-flower crowns."

7–8. Cf. *ambrosio . . . liquore* in Stat. *Theb.* 9.731, where the liquid protects from any wound. Ambrosia was the gods' unguent (cf. 23 below) as well as food. Idalium in Cyprus (cf. 18.8 and 44.12) was regularly associated with Venus, who is *Idalie* in Ov. *Met.* 14.694; cf. Prop. 4.6.59.

318

### · NOTES TO THE TRANSLATIONS ·

9–10. Cf. 59.2–3.

11–12. Either *duris* ("cruel," Bol.U., Mil.2) or *diris* ("dreadful," Si.) could be read. Pontano, *Parthenopeus* 1.7.7 has *diras sagittas* of Cupid's arrows. *Amor* is *improbus* in Verg. *Aen.* 4.412 and *Ecl.* 8.49; Prop. 1.1.6. Dione = Venus (see 31.30n).

13 (and 16, 18, and 22). Cf. 20.4 and F. 3.9.1–4n for the use of *sic*.

15. Cf. Hor. *Odes* 1.22.18 and 3.20.13 for *recreare* of breezes. See 37.6–8n for *recentiores*.

16. For *Aonian* see 44.45–49n.

20–21. Seemingly influenced by line 4 of verses in Petron. 127.9 ("roses, violets, and soft *cyperon*"), where one interpretation of *cyperon* has been rosemary, another galingale (a sedge). In Greek, *kypeiron* (or *kypeiros*) is seen as galingale in *LSJ* (cf. *OLD* under *cyperos*). As colorful flowers are in point here, *cyperis* may mean gladioli; see *OLD* under *cypiros* for confusion even in ancient times. Verg. *Ecl.* 2.47 has *pallentes* of violets.

22–23. For *Syros liquores* cf. 59.21. Pontano has *Syros liquores* in *Urania* 4.6, *Syrios liquores* in *Eridanus* 1.14.61, and *Syrium . . . liquorem* in *Hendecasyllabi* 1.13.38. See further 25.14n. The sensual fragrance of sweet-smelling breasts is described many times in Pontano, including *Hendecasyllabi* 2.19.3–4 ("Corycian and Syrian scents breathe from your snow-white breasts"; see 31.25–26n). Navagero (if truly the poet) probably intended this poem to savor of Pontano. Line 23 is lost in Si.

## 57

See Adams 1982, 78, for some ancient contexts that show an interest in penis size, e.g., Mart. 10.55. Pontano's hendecasyllabic poem *Parthenopeus* 1.33 complains that his girlfriend publicly calls him "as badly hung (*male . . . mentulatum*) as a dwarf or a three-year-old boy." For Pontano's influential place in the composition of erotic/lewd verse of Catullan inspiration, including hendecasyllables, see Ludwig 1990. Pontano wrote two versions of a lost collection with Catullan debts called *Pruritus, sive De Lascivia* (Lust, or On Lasciviousness) in 1449 and 1451, and imitated Catullus in some of his later works too. The theme of his own penis size

## · NOTES TO THE TRANSLATIONS ·

appealed also to Pacifico Massimi (1400–1500). In his *De Mentula* (On His Penis), given in Saint-Leger 1791, 124, Massimi claims a huge penis, but protests that his girl still mocks it as tiny and puny; a later poem, *De Matrona* (On a Matron; see Saint-Leger 1791, 138–39), admits that his boast was a lie. MSS: Bel.2, where headed *Naugerii Priapus* (Navagero's Priapus), Mil.1, Vat. 8 and 11, Wro. Meter: Phalaecean hendecasyllables.

2. Cf. Petron. 92.9 ("such a weight of genitalia [*inguinum pondus*] that you would think the man himself a part of his penis"), reflected in line 13 here. *Pondus* (lit., "weight," poetic plural *pondera*) can denote the male parts in general or the penis in particular: Catull. 63.5; Mart. 7.35.4 (a circumcised *pondus*). See further Adams 1982, 71. In Andrelini, *Livia, seu Amores* 3.3.28, the poet's erection is "the distended burden (*pondera*) of my swollen penis"; see Andrelini 1982. Examples of *columna* used of the penis include Mart. 6.49.3 and 11.51.1; *Priap.* 10.8; Massimi, *De Mentula* 18; Janus Etruscus in Toscano 1576, 274v, where a woman prays that her man's "column" may stretch tight and stiffen (*rigeat tenta*) like that of Priapus. It is also found in a long list of Latin terms for the penis in Chorier 1885, 28–29. See Adams 1982, 16–17.

3. Ov. *Fast.* 1.437 speaks of Priapus as "only too well equipped (*paratus*) with a lewd part." Cf. *Priap.* 46.7; Petron. 130.4. *Mentulatus* ("well-endowed") is found in ancient usage only in *Priap.* 36.11, declaring no other god *Priapo mentulatior* ("better-endowed than Priapus"), though it is used elsewhere in Neo-Latin poetry, e.g., Pontano, *Parthenopeus* 1.30.5 and 1.33, quoted in my headnote; Poliziano, *Epigrams* 50; Johannes Secundus, *Basia* 12 (twice).

5. For repeated *ne* cf., for example, Verg. *Aen.* 6.832; Stat. *Theb.* 4.512–13. Pontano often repeats *ne* in appeals. Note especially his *Hendecasyllabi* 2.32.23 (four times in one line) and 2.36 (five times in lines 11–15). As for the variants here (see Notes to the Texts), perhaps *recte* could have the colloquial sense of "it's all right" or "all's well" found in Roman comedy (e.g., Ter. *Hec.* 3.2.20, *Recte, mater*), though "Do not—all's well!—flee" remains awkward. If *sed certe* be read, *fuge ne* must unusually = *ne fuge*. I can cite only one parallel for *ne* following its imperative: Pontano, *Lyra* 3.42, has *crede ne* for *ne crede*. At any rate, the general sense of "Certainly do not flee" is plausible.

320

## · NOTES TO THE TRANSLATIONS ·

7. Cf. 65.19, *languidulus*. For *pendulus* cf. Catull. 67.21. *Araneosus* is used in Catull. 25.3, by one interpretation, of an old man's limp penis, "cobwebby" with disuse (*pene languido senis situque araneoso*). Thus Pontano 1948, 452, declares his salacious book enough to excite an old man's penis "or whatever is limper," and talks of wearing out "spiders' webs" with sex.

8. The first syllable of *titilles*, here short, is long in ancient poets. Instances include Lucr. 2.429 and Hor. *Sat.* 2.3.179. The short quantity is seen elsewhere in Neo-Latin, e.g., Bonnefons, *Pancharis*, Basium 32.2.

9–10. The foreskin is treated as a hood. Cf. Adams 1982, 73, for *cucutium* in the same sense. For the *caput* ("head") of a penis, cf., for example, *Priap.* 83.5, 32, and 37; Mart. 11.46.4; Petron. 132.8; and see Adams 1982, 72. Pacifico Massimi so uses *caput* several times, in his *Ad Mentulam* 3 and elsewhere. In Pontano, *Hendecasyllabi* 1.7.18, the "head" of a young man's penis protrudes from its 'red hood' (*cucullo*)." Chorier 1885, 31, has several references to the *caput* of the penis, including "they call the tip of the penis the head." The foreskin is there called a "skullcap" (*pilleolus*), headgear that the haughty penis would scarcely ever doff save to enter his lady's "hall" bare-headed (*aperto . . . capite*). *Crescere* ("grow") of an erection: Apul. *Met.* 3.24. *Tumor* of an erection: *Priap.* 83.42 (Adams 1982, 59). *Pariter* (10) = "at the same time" (as emerging).

11–13. *Turgidulus*, diminutive of *turgidus*, occurs in Catull. 3.18. In Lucr. 4.1034, describing nocturnal emissions in youths, their parts are "swollen (*turgida*) with much seed." Mart. 9.28.12 has *turgidum . . . penem*. For being part of one's own penis, cf. *Priap.* 37.9 (of Priapus) and see on line 2. Catull. 115.7–8 speaks of *Mentula* (i.e., Mamurra) as being not a man, but a giant, menacing penis.

### 58A and 58B

*Trissinus* is presumably Giovanni (or Gian) Giorgio Trissino (b. 1478 at Vicenza, d. 1550), dramatist, poet, and literary figure, who occurs again in 69, ascribed both to Navagero and, more credibly, to Trissino himself. In bk. 24 of his *Italia liberata*, Trissino names Navagero, along with a few other celebrated Neo-Latin writers ("the excellent Pontano, Sannazaro, Sadoleto, and Flaminio; Bembo, Fracastoro, Navagero, Cotta"), and in

## · NOTES TO THE TRANSLATIONS ·

his Latin poem *De Morte Batti* 128 (Trissino 1729, 1:396) he calls Bembo and Navagero "the two lights of our age." 58B (from Mil.2) is almost identical to 58A, but aimed at Cadmus (a name in legend and otherwise), not Trissino. Numerous ancient passages that liken a person's stench to that of the male goat include Catull. 69 and 71; Hor. *Epod.* 12.5, *Epist.* 1.5.29, *Sat.* 1.2.27, 1.4.92; Ov. *Ars am.* 3.193; Mart. 4.4.4 and 6.93.3. MSS: Vat.2 (58A), Mil.2 (58B).

59

First printed in Griggio 1976–77. Meter: Phalaecean hendecasyllables. Lycinna initiated Propertius in lovemaking (Prop. 3.15.6). The name (also in F. 3.9) seems otherwise not to be found in ancient writers, but is used in Neo-Latin by, for example, Pontano, Johannes Secundus, and Giovanni Battista Amalteo. Lines 37–52 are particularly similar in theme and style to some Renaissance *basia*, or kiss poems, in which repetitions are common, and of which Johannes Secundus (52n) is the best-known exponent, imitated by Jean Bonnefons, among others. Pontano has poems with elements of the genre too, e.g., *Eridanus* 1.9, suggesting the form sex with Stella will take when Pontano comes for dinner. Sannazaro, *Epigrams* 1.6, is another kiss poem. MS: Vat.11.

1–3. Pontano uses such frantic, emotional, or excited repetition in many passages, especially in hendecasyllabic verse, after Catullus. Cf., for example, *Parthenopeus* 1.3.17–18, where the shut-out lover (see 26.10n) pleads: "Fannia, open the door, my Fannia, Fannia, I beseech you, open the door, I beseech you, Fannia, open the door." With 2 and 3 here, the same line with the words rearranged, cf. 56.9–10. *Voluptas* ("joy") of a person: Plaut. *Truc.* 2.4.2; Verg. *Aen.* 8.581. Lines 2 and 3 are picked up at 34. *Quo* means "why?" (as sometimes in classical Latin, e.g., Ov. *Am.* 3.4.41; cf. Marullo, *Epigrams* 3.26.1).

4–6. *Volucer* (4) of Cupid: Ov. *Met.* 5.364 and 9.482. Cf. 41.33. *Dione* (6 and 48): Venus (see 31.30n). For the accusative form *Dionem* see poem 5n. *Mihi* has its last syllable long in 4, short in 5 and 6. Classical poets occasionally scan such a variable word differently even in the same line.

322

## · NOTES TO THE TRANSLATIONS ·

7–8. Prop. 3.15.9–10 claims no other woman has won his heart in three years since (*post*) Lycinna. For *prae te* (strictly = "rather than you"), cf. Catull. 72.2 ("to have Jupiter as lover rather than [*prae*] me"); F. 3.18.24 (*prae me*); Pontano, *Parthenopeus* 1.19.13–14 ("if . . . no woman *prae te* has pleased me") and 1.25.14 ("I desire nothing to be mine *prae te*"). For *tetigit* cf. Ov. *Fast.* 1.427 and *Her.* 14.57.

10. Cupid's quiver is *trux* ("harsh") in Pontano, *Eridanus* 2.19.29 and *Hendecasyllabi* 2.37.124.

12. Cf. 13.10 for the common idea of chains of love.

13–14. See 30.2–3n and 33.1 and 3n. Cf. Catull. 45.3–4 for the sentiment.

15. For *tenuis umbra* cf. [Tib.] 3.2.9.

20. *Sugere* ("suck") is much used by Pontano in sensual descriptions of kissing and tongue- and lip-sucking. Among instances in other Neo-Latin poets are Sannazaro, *Epigrams* 1.6.13; Marullo, *Epigrams* 3.31.20; and Johannes Secundus, *Basia* 5.8 and 10.11. Among ancient poets, cf. Novius *Atell.* 16 ("squeezed tongue into mouth and began to suck [*sugere*] the lips"). See further 59.38–42n.

21–22. *Syrios . . . liquores*: see 56.22–23n. Images of honied, ambrosial, and nectar-sweet lips or kisses are common: 29.11–12n. In Catull. 99.2 a kiss stolen from the youth Juventius is sweeter than ambrosia. In Johannes Secundus, *Basia* 4.1–7, Neaera gives not kisses, but nectar, fragrances, and honey; cf. *Basia* 19. Parallels abound in various poets, especially Pontano. In his *Hendecasyllabi* 2.10, for instance, there are bees in lips. Cf. also Sannazaro, *Epigrams* 1.6.17–20. *Stillare* ("drip") is similarly employed many times by Pontano.

27–29. Cf. 55.30–39, censuring the Venetian boy's coldness to his admirer's appeal. *Quis* introduces a virtual wish (lit., "Who now, who might descend upon me . . . ?"), amounting to, "O that someone might descend . . . !" Cf. F. 4.17.53–54 with note on line 53. *Rigido . . . ense*: Verg. *G.* 1.508 and *Aen.* 12.304; Ov. *Met.* 3.118, *Tr.* 3.9.26 and 5.10.43.

30. *Fors* is adverbial, as in 27.84 and 36.9.

35. See 32.5–6n for star-like eyes. *Reflexa* with accusative imitates the Greek middle voice.

323

# · NOTES TO THE TRANSLATIONS ·

38–42. Pontano, *Parthenopeus* 1.24.7, already associates the so-called "French kiss" with sensual France (*mollis Francia*). In Neo-Latin "kiss" poems, the tongue is often "quivering," the lips or mouth "moaning." As for love bites, in Johannes Secundus, *Basia* 10.9–10, marks are inflicted on cheeks, neck, shoulders, and bosom, while *Basia* 8 complains of a bitten tongue. Love-biting (often specifically of tongue, lips, or neck) is notably prominent in Pontano, where numerous examples include *Eridanus* 1.27.37 ("as you rage with your teeth and inflict wounds"). Du Bellay and Muret both refer to love bites and French kissing in their Latin poems, while Ariosto talks of telltale signs from another's teeth on his girl's neck in *Carmina* 7.12. In ancient poets, for French kisses and/or love bites, cf. especially Catull. 8.18; Tib. 1.6.13 and 1.8.37–38; Prop. 3.8.21–22, 4.3.25–26, and 4.5.39–40; Ov. *Am.* 1.7.41–42, 1.8.98, 2.5.23–24 and 57–58, 3.7.9, 3.14.23 and 34, and *Her.* 15.129–30; Hor. *Odes* 1.13.15–16.; *Anth. Pal.* 5.129.7 and 5.244.2. See also Novius as cited on line 20. *Excursare* ("sally forth repeatedly," 39) is rare: Stat. *Theb.* 2.550.

40. *Osculatio* (Catull. 48.5) is found in a number of Neo-Latin poets, e.g., Pontano (*Parthenopeus* 1.26.10, *Hendecasyllabi* 1.16.19, 2.21.12, and 2.37.30), Johannes Secundus (*Basia* 14.4), and Bonnefons *Pancharis*, Basium 3.26, where Catullus is *pater osculationum*, "father of kissing sessions."

42. Cf. 31.20 for *teretes . . . papillas*.

43. For *teneros . . . lusus* cf. Pontano, *Hendecasyllabi* 2.22.17; Sannazaro, *Epigrams* 1.6.15. *Lusus* (cf. 26.77) = "love games, dalliance," as, for example, in Ov. *Am.* 2.3.13 and Prop. 1.10.9.

44. Pontano likes the word *illecebrae*, especially in his hendecasyllables (though it is not in Catullus), e.g., *Hendecasyllabi* 1.18.28, 1.30.22, 2.22.65, 2.24.45, and 2.37.108.

45. For *simul et* cf. Pontano, *Hendecasyllabi* 2.18.8, *et ducit simul et canit* ("she both leads and sings").

46. *Paphiae tabellae* literally = "Paphian tablets," i.e., laws of Venus, from her association with Paphos in Cyprus (see 56.1n). For lovemaking seen as ordained by Venus, Love, and the Graces, cf. Pontano, *Hendecasyllabi* 2.22.88–89, where Pleasure (*Voluptas*), Venus' son, and Venus (as well as

324

· NOTES TO THE TRANSLATIONS ·

free time at midday) command lovemaking. *Ductare* is not used for *ducere* of passing time in any classical author.

47. *Charites*, nom. pl., here has *es* long (as in 56.2), though short in Greek, some cases of the word being conveniently treated by Neo-Latin poets as of the Latin third declension. Thus the genitive plural is commonly *Charitum*, as in line 51, not the Greek *Chariton*. See also 66.3n for *Dryades* as acc. pl.

48–49. Cf. the better-known version of 13.1. *Dione* denotes Venus (see 31.30n).

60

Griggio 1976–77, iii, despairs of restoring the partly corrupt text, obelizing lines 5 and 6, though Sacré 1987 suggests an interpretation and emendations, some of which I have adopted. In places, however, text and sense remain uncertain. Name *Simulus* or *Simylus* (Greek *Simulos*): Ter. *Ad.* 3.4.19; [Verg.] *Moretum* 3, there the name of the main character, the tender of a very small farm; *Anth. Pal.* 5.38 and 11.187 (imitated by Navagero in 64). The spelling is *Simulus* in the only MS, Vat.ii.

3. *Suffitus* ("fumigation"), a word from Pliny the Elder, is found also in Fracastoro, *Syphilis* 2.262. "Sabaean wares" = incense or perfumes, from the regular ancient association, as in Verg. *Aen.* 1.416–17. For *merce Sabaea* cf. Pontano, *De Laudibus Divinis* 7.19 and *Lyra* 9.23–24. For *spirare* (my tentative conjecture for *pirumve* in Vat.ii) cf. 31.26. Sacré 1987's suggestion *suffitusve pyramve* ("either fumigations or a pyre") seems awkward in making a strange distinction.

4–6. The last word in line 6 is corrupted to *dum* in Vat.ii, for which Griggio 1976–77 suggests *diem* ("day") and Sacré 1987 *deum* ("god"). *Facilis* ("easy" or "indulgent") is used of a deity in Hor. *Sat.* 1.1.22. Sacré does not say which god he thinks could be meant in this context. Possibly read *deam* ("goddess"), i.e., Ceres? Sacré also leaves *tibi* in 4 unexplained. If *deam* is read in 6, *tibi* could refer to that deity. Reading *sibi* would make the nostrils Simulus' own. In line 4 Sacré rightly compares Lucr. 6.777–78 for *insinuare* of particles (and thus smells) getting into nostrils. *Quos*

325

## · NOTES TO THE TRANSLATIONS ·

(5) has as antecedent the acc. pl. *suffitus* in 3, though Simulus is thus said to have bought the fumigations rather than the substances to burn, perhaps as a form of metonymy. For *aere paravit* cf. 45.3 (the similar *auro* with *parare*). *Ex* follows its case several times in Lucretius. The diminutive *pauperculus* is in Hor. *Epist.* 1.17.46, as well as in Roman comedy.

7–8. The point is that no expensive incense bought in the city was ever needed, as the dung that Simulus is spreading has already been left a sufficiently long time to rot down, so losing almost all of its stench. Varro 1.13.4 recommends having two heaps or pits, one for fresh dung, one for dung rotting down, as short (rotted) manure is better. For *tertia vidit hiems* (lit., "the third winter has seen"), cf. Ov. *Pont.* 4.13.40 ("the sixth winter sees me exiled").

### 61

This poem, first published in Griggio 1976–77, almost translates *Anth. Pal.* 11.406 by Nicarchus, which (like 11.405) pokes fun at a man's huge nose: "I see the hook-beaked rhetorician's nose, Menippus; and it looks like the man himself is not now far away. At any rate, he will be along, so let us wait all the same; for even if he is a good way off, he is not five stades away from his nose, I suppose. But it, as you see, goes ahead of him; and if we stand on a high hill, we shall see him too." Hutton 1935, 614, lists four other sixteenth-century Latin versions of this poem. Making fun of a big nose: Catull. 43.1; Hor. *Sat.* 1.2.93; Mart. 14.96.2 (in his 6.36 a man with a big nose has a big penis to match); *Anth. Pal.* 11.198–99, 200, 203–4, 267–68, and 405. One *Carinus* (so MS; the Greek form has *Ch-*) was a late Roman emperor, but *C(h)arinus* is also found in *Anth. Pal.* 7.540, 11.126, and, perhaps of the emperor, 11.336, in Plautus' *Mercator*, and in several poems of Martial not concerned with noses (1.77 or 78, 4.39, 5.39, 6.37, 7.34, and 12.89 or 90). Here the name probably puns on the Greek for nose, *rhis*, genitive *rhinos*. MS: Mil.2.

4. A *stade* was an ancient unit of measurement, roughly equivalent to a furlong.

· NOTES TO THE TRANSLATIONS ·

62

First published in Griggio 1976–77, Navagero's poem is based on *Anth. Pal.* 11.159 by Lucilius: "All the astrologers used to prophesy to my father, as with one voice, that his brother would live long. Hermoclides alone predicted that he would die young; but he said it when we were bewailing his dead body within the house." The same epigram was translated or adapted by several other Neo-Latin poets. See Hutton 1935, 597, where three vernacular versions are also noted; Hutton 1946 details another. In *Anth. Pal.* 11.161 and 162 Olympus is a seer. Olympus as a man's name occurs otherwise in Ov. *Met.* 6.393 and *Pont.* 3.3.42 and elsewhere. Gallus is a well-known Roman cognomen. MS: Mil.2.

63

A poem reflecting both Navagero's Lucretian interests (he edited Lucretius for the Aldine Press) and his taste for the *Greek Anthology*. Navagero suggests that Lycus is so tiny that Epicurus might have thought him the smallest thing instead of atoms and built his universal system around Lycuses. The poem, first printed in Griggio 1976–77, adapts *Anth. Pal.* 11.103 by Lucilius: "Epicurus wrote that the whole universe was composed of atoms, Alcimus, thinking that [i.e., an atom] to be the smallest thing. But if Diophantus had been alive then, he would have written that the universe was made up of Diophantus, who is much smaller than the atoms; or he would have written that everything else is made up of atoms, but that the atoms themselves are made up of Diophantus." *Lycus* is the name of several figures in mythology, of a companion of Aeneas in Verg. *Aen.* 1.222, and of the poet Alcaeus' beloved (see 36.14), and occurs also in *Anth. Pal.* 7.272 and 497. Hutton 1935, 593, and Hutton 1946, 750–51, note that Lucilius' original was quite frequently imitated or translated by both Neo-Latin and vernacular poets. MS: Mil.2.

1–4. Understand *visum est Epicuro* (3) with *esse atomos* (1). The Greek philosopher Epicurus' beliefs about the physical universe, including an atomic theory, were expounded and justified by Lucretius. Navagero's

## · NOTES TO THE TRANSLATIONS ·

poem abounds in Lucretian language. *Atomus* is not Lucretian, though Cicero uses the word, as do all the Neo-Latin translators of the Greek source here.

8. *Levis umbra:* Ov. *Fast.* 5.434.

9–10. *Hinc* here = "from him." Cf. Ter. *Ad.* 3.3.7, *hinc scibo* ("I will find out from him").

### 64

First printed in Griggio 1976–77. After *Anth. Pal.* 11.187, attributed to Leonidas of Alexandria: "Simylus the lyre player, playing away all night long, was the death of all his neighbors, save Origenes alone. For Nature had made him deaf, and thus gave him a longer life in place of hearing." Hutton 1935, 599, records five other Latin versions and two Italian; Hutton 1946 lists another seven Latin and one vernacular. *Cinyras* is the name of Adonis' father in mythology but is encountered otherwise (*Anth. Pal.* 6.25 and 26, 7.365, 11.236). *Aulus*, a common Roman praenomen, is also in several *Greek Anthology* poems. MS: Mil.2.

1. *Male perdidit* ("cruelly killed off") reflects Catull. 14.5.

### 65

This textually problematic poem was first published, unemended and with some misreadings, in Griggio 1976–77. The single MS (Lon.), said to be partly in the hand of the younger Aldo Manuzio (1547–97), mostly consists of poems of his close friend Nicolaus Siccus (Niccolò Secchi) but also contains verse and prose pieces by others, including two poems in succession ascribed to Navagero, namely 55 and (on fol. 138v) this present crudely graphic but humorous poem. Meter: Phalaecean hendecasyllables, though the text of lines 6–9 (here obelized) is either seriously corrupt or perhaps only an unfinished rough draft that never did scan, as the meter is so very faulty. See 55n for the online Italian translation by Pierluigi Gallucci.

1. Literally, "Drawing out [my] little Priapus with his hands, the rosy-faced boy was fondling [i.e., masturbating] him [it], etc." *Priapus* here

328

## · NOTES TO THE TRANSLATIONS ·

and in 12 (cf. also 19) = "penis." Adams 1982, 230, calls this sense largely medieval. It is in several Neo-Latin poets, such as Antonio Beccadelli, *Hermaphroditus* 5.1; Pacifico Massimi, *Ad Priapum* 19; and Alessandro Braccesi, *Carmina* App.a 5.15 (Braccesi 1943, 132). Antonio Tebaldeo has it in his *Ad Flaccum*, concerned, like 57, with penis size; see Pasquazi 1966, 64. The boy here seems to be manually exciting the man's penis, initially *brevem* ("short" or "small"), to induce full erection (cf. 57.8–13) prior to inviting penetration. *Tractare* of manual stimulation or fondling of the penis: *Priap.* 80.2; Mart. 11.29.1; Petron. 86.1 and 140.13; Adams 1982, 186 and 208. *Educens* (lit., "drawing out"), the reading in Lon. (not *conducens*, as Griggio 1976–77), may mean "extracting" (from clothing), but more probably means "making erect." In my translation I settle for interpreting *educens* as manually arousing the penis to an erection.

4. After Catull. 5.7. Cf. 32.8 above.

5. *Leniter* ("softly" or "gently," Lon.) does not scan (first syllable unsuitably long). Reading *leviter* ("lightly" or "slightly") restores the meter, but "slightly moving his beautiful eyes" is weak for sense. Moving eyes seems to mean turning them, as in Prop. 2.29.16; Marullo, *Epigrams* 2.2.1–2 (*ocellos in me . . . moves*); Flaminio 1993, App. 1.3. The issue of *leniter* or *leviter* arises also in 59.41.

6. A short syllable suitably making position is lacking in Lon. between *Veneris* and *hic* (not *sic*, as Griggio 1976–77 gives). Indeed, the whole passage 6–9 is textually unsatisfactory, causing me to obelize it. The image of intercourse as a battle or struggle is common (Adams 1982, 158): Prop. 2.1.45 and 2.15.4; Mart. *Epigr.* 10.38.6–7; Tib. 1.3.64 and 1.10.53. Pontano, for instance, has such imagery many times. For *ineamus*, here scanning with synizesis of *ea*, cf. Muret, *Epigrams* 20.7 ("let us . . . join sweet battles").

7–9. Lon.'s *cruribus* ("on his legs") does not scan and makes poorer sense than would the metrically acceptable *genibus* ("on his knees"). *Caput* ("head") is accusative of the part of the body, as in Greek. *Vulnus* ("wound") of anal penetration: Auson. *Epigr.* 77.7 and elsewhere; it is more often found of vaginal penetration, as in deflowering; see Adams 1982, 152. Sexual "wounds" in Neo-Latin: Pontano, *Hendecasyllabi* 1.18.34–

329

### · NOTES TO THE TRANSLATIONS ·

35; Johannes Secundus, *Epithalamium* 122–28; Bonnefons, *Pervigilium Veneris* 122–23. Line 8 in Lon. has two syllables too many (thirteen); line 9 has two syllables too few (nine), as *fatum*, elided, is one long syllable where the meter requires short, long, short. Line 8 scans but does not make sense without *vulnus*. With 9 cf. Cotta, *Carmina* 8.1, *O factum lacrimabile atque acerbum!* ("O tearful and bitter deed!").

10. *Rimulam* will not scan, as (like *rima*) it should begin with a long syllable. The following word in Lon. is *hostii* (= *ostii*), not *postis* as given in Griggio 1976–77.

11. *Facinus* ("wickedness!") as an exclamation usually follows *heu, o, pro,* or *ah*, though Stat. *Theb.* 7.413 has *facinus* alone. Pederastic activity is interrupted in a graveyard by the offended ghost of the active partner's mother, buried there, in Tebaldeo's poem *In Franciscum Alphanum*, a mighty crash making both participants flee, the boy with his rear still bared; see Pasquazi 1957, 57.

12. *Quid tum?* ("What then?") is mostly in Roman comedy, e.g., Plaut. *Asin.* 349; Ter. *Haut.* 718.

13–14. For *replere* = "satisfy" cf. Vulgate, *Psalmi* 102:5, with *desiderium* ("longing") as object, and Sen. *Dial.* 11.18.3. Ov. *Tr.* 3.11.57 has *explere* governing *sitim. Potus* is genitive. The word before *potus* is damaged in the MS. Griggio 1976–77's *extinguere* is much too long for the space. I think the word may be *fugare*. I cannot, however, parallel *desiderium fugare* (lit., "chase away longing") any more closely than *fugat . . . amorem* (of Cupid's leaden arrow that "drives love away") in Ov. *Met.* 1.469.

17. *Quas* refers to *nates* ("buttocks"), with *cibum paratum* in apposition. The image is of laid-out food snatched away from the would-be diner. Edmund Spenser employs similar dining table imagery of a spread of white flesh in *Amoretti* 77. *Ut* = "when."

18. Priapus was thought born at Lampsacus. Cf. Catull. fr. 1.2. He is "the Hellespontine god" in Ov. *Fast.* 1.440 and Petron. 139.2, and *Hellespontiacus Priapus* in Verg. *G.* 4.111. *Resentio* is unknown in classical Latin. Nonclassical words in Navagero: 14.3n.

19–20. *Languidulus* (diminutive; Catull. 64.331; F. 4.5.8; Pontano, *Hendecasyllabi* 1.16.22, etc.) here = "limp." An old man's flaccid penis is *langui-*

330

## · NOTES TO THE TRANSLATIONS ·

*dus* in Catull. 25.3, while in his 67.21 an impotent husband's "dagger" hangs limper (*languidior*) than a tender beetroot. Cf. also Ov. *Am.* 3.7.66; Mart. *Epigr.* 11.29.1. Johannes Secundus, *Epigrammata* 1.24, says a girl calls him *languiduli vatem . . . penis* ("a limp-penised poet"). Statues of Priapus were often painted red (*ruber*), or their phalluses were (*Priap.* 72.2), and "red" is a regular epithet of Priapus, as in Ov. *Fast.* 1.400 and 415, 6.319; Tib. 1.1.17; in *Priap.* 1.5 he is "the red guardian of gardens" (and cf. 26.9 there). *Lacrimula* (diminutive, "little tear") here denotes a drop of semen. The penis metaphorically weeping (discharging semen): Adams 1982, 30. Lucil. 307 speaks of a girl wiping away a penis's "tears."

### 66

This poem was first published in Griggio 1976–77 from the only MS, Flo.ML., where it follows 2, which is headed *Naugerii*. A line is drawn beneath 2, and, at the foot of the page, this poem is squeezed in, without any further heading either to reiterate or to change the ascription, in reduced-size writing, the last two lines to the side of the first six for lack of room. Navagero's authorship must therefore be held in doubt. The poem is after verses of Marianus Scholasticus, of the early Byzantine period, now *Anth. Pal.* 9.627, though in the sixteenth century still only the Planudean Anthology text was known: "Under these plane-trees Love, shackled in soft slumber, was sleeping, having handed his torch over to nymphs to look after. The nymphs said to each other, 'Why do we delay? O if, together with this torch, we could extinguish the fire in mortals' hearts!' But since the torch set even the waters alight, from then on the love nymphs pour out hot bath water." There the location of the thermal baths is not specified, but in variations on the theme a particular spa, such as Baiae (now Baia, near Naples), may be named, as here. Shakespeare's Sonnets 153 and 154 share the same *Greek Anthology* ancestry through an unidentified intermediary; for Latin and vernacular analogues, see Hutton 1941. See also Hutton 1935, 566, and Hutton 1946, 430–32.

1. Baiae (now Baia), anciently a resort famed for its thermal baths on the Bay of Naples, was deserted by 1500 because of malaria. Pontano's two books of *Hendecasyllabi* are much concerned with Baia.

· NOTES TO THE TRANSLATIONS ·

3. *Dryades* (so MS), if right, is a Latin third declension acc. pl. form with long *e*. Possibly read the Greek form *Dryadas* with lengthening of the last syllable at the caesura. Vergil (*Ecl.* 5.59) and Ovid (*Met.* 11.49 and 13.326 and *Fast.* 4.761) use only *Dryadas*. Ovid similarly favors *Hamadryadas* (*Met.* 1.690 and 14.624; *Fast.* 2.155) and *Naidas* (*Met.* 6.453; *Pont.* 4.16.35). Sannazaro (*Epigrams* 1.23.1) and T. V. Strozzi (*Erotica* 4.8.11) have *Dryadas*, and I observe *Hamadryadas* in several Neo-Latin poets. See, however, 59.47n on *Charites*.

67

First published as Navagero's, following citation of 43 and without mention of a source, in *Rime e prose di alcuni cinofili vicentini e di altri illustri italiani* (Venice, 1826), 329 (misprinted as 529), as noted by Cicogna 1824–53, 6:304n341, who doubts the unsupported ascription, and as recorded by Benassi 1940, 246. In fact, I find this poem unascribed and headed simply *Canis* (A Dog's [Epitaph]) among Siena-related epitaphs in Canoniero 1613, 23, though Cicogna 1824–53 and Benassi 1940 evidently did not know of that earlier appearance (Canoniero 1613, 279–80, also has 8 and 10A). No MS evidence (see 23n). The 1826 ascription to Navagero seems likely to be erroneous, though I give the poem here for completeness.

4. The last syllable of *percussit* is lengthened at the dieresis (see 13.10n).

5. The dog's master (Francesco) is unidentified.

68

Benassi 1940, 243, supposes *Caesaris* (6) to mean the Holy Roman Emperor, but Gaius Atilius or Acilius was a soldier of Julius Caesar. Val. Max. 3.2, ex. 22: "When Atilius, a soldier of the Tenth Legion, was fighting on Caesar's side in a sea battle, he had his right hand, which he had laid on a Massilian ship, cut off, but grasped the ship with his left and did not leave off fighting until he had captured the ship and was sinking it in the deep." Plut. *Caes.* 16.2: "Such a man was Acilius, who in the sea action by Massilia had his right hand struck off with a sword after

# · NOTES TO THE TRANSLATIONS ·

boarding an enemy ship, yet did not drop the shield from his left, but, thrusting it into the faces of his foes, turned them all to flight and took control of the vessel." Similarly Suet. *Iul.* 68. Caesar himself does not mention Acilius in either naval action before Massilia (Marseilles) in June and July 49 BCE (*B Civ.* 1.56–58 and 2.4–7). MS: Man., where the poem follows 2, 21, and 4, all correctly ascribed to Navagero, and is headed *Idem de Atilio* (The Same on Atilius). This poem is in several early anthologies, though not ascribed to Navagero. It is in Duchesne 1560, 80r, entitled *Attilius Caesaris* (Caesar's Attilius), within a section headed on fol. 75r *Sumpta ex multis* ("Taken from many"). At the end of that section on fol. 82r Duchesne notes that some think most of the poems in it are by Iacobus Casanova, evidently giving that forename in error. The poem appears again in Ubaldini 1563, 91v–92r, and Toscano 1576, 223r, entitled in both *De Atilio Caesaris Milite* (On Caesar's Soldier Atilius), but expressly attributed to Marco Antonio Casanova (ca. 1477–1528). All subsequent early anthologies that include the poem follow Ubaldini 1563 and Toscano 1576 in treating it as Casanova's. Benassi 1940 and Griggio 1976–77 say nothing of these appearances in print, which cast great doubt on the ascription to Navagero in the Mantua MS. This poem is of an unusual type for him, if really his, whereas it is similar to many short poems about figures in the ancient world ascribed to Casanova by Ubaldini. I think it is Casanova's, not Navagero's.

4. The Mantua MS and all the anthologies noted above except for Duchesne 1560 give this line as in my text, whereas Duchesne has *raptaque magnanimo est altera sorte pari* ("and the greathearted man's other hand was hacked off by a like fate"). Atilius loses only his right hand in the ancient accounts, but Duchesne 1560 makes him lose his left hand too. Even the alternative version of the line, which I adopt, literally "and he was not terrified by the same fate as the other," could imply loss of both hands, but my translation takes the sense to be that Atilius was undaunted by the risk of losing his left hand too, rather than its actual loss.

6. *Arma* (lit., "arms") here means "forces" as in Livy 9.9.

8. After *manu*, where Man. repeats *vincimus* ("we conquer"), Duchesne 1560, Ubaldini 1563, Toscano 1576, Gruter 1608, *Delitiae Delitiarum* 1637,

333

# · NOTES TO THE TRANSLATIONS ·

and *Carmina Illustrium Poetarum Italorum* all have *vivimus* ("we live"), perhaps correctly. *Absque* is not used in ancient verse outside Roman comedy.

### 69

An ode to the sun in Sapphic stanzas (like 36, 37, and 41). The speaker's girl, whose birthday is dawning, is urged to ask of Jupiter (i.e., God) enduring youth and beauty for herself and a long life of true devotion to her for her lover, Trissino (58A and 58Bn). Bol.U., where this poem follows 29, ascribes it to Navagero (*Idem An⟨dreas⟩*, The Same Andrea), but it is ascribed to Trissino in the sixteenth-century Cod. Vat. lat. 2836 (fols. 109r–109a recto), here designated Vat.1. Internal evidence would suggest that it is Trissino's, as he is named in line 36 and speaks in the first person in 9–12 and 41. This poem was first published from Vat.1 as Trissino's in Cinelli Calvoli 1736, *Scanzia* 22, 79–80. It is there taken to be a youthful piece by Trissino (1478–1550), who wrote some Latin verse, though he composed chiefly in Italian. To be really by Navagero, as Bol.U. claims, this poem would have to be written in the persona of another poet. Such compositions are sometimes found. Flaminio writes 1.34 in the name of his friend Achille Bocchi. Pontano writes some of his *Tumuli* in another's persona. For example, *Tumuli* 2.33 is composed as though spoken by his friend the scholar Summonte, named in the text, for a dead girl. In *Hendecasyllabi* 2.19 (headed "Pietro Summonte to Neaera"), Pontano again writes as Summonte. T. V. Strozzi, *Erotica* 3.4, which names Sigismondo Malatesta in line 1, uses the first person, as if Sigismondo were the author, in several lines. This present poem owes debts to Prop. 3.10, a birthday poem for Cynthia. Most clearly, with 13–16 cf. Prop. 3.10.5–6, and with 19–20 cf. Prop. 3.10.13. Note that Propertius uses the third person of himself in line 15 (cf. *Trissinus* in 36 here), after the first person earlier. MSS: Bol.U. (with ascription to Navagero), Vat.1 (with ascription to Trissino). On balance, this poem is far more likely to be Trissino's than Navagero's, but I include it here for completeness, as Griggio 1976–77, following Bol.U., has published it as Navagero's.

334

## · NOTES TO THE TRANSLATIONS ·

1. *Nitidos dies*: Ov. *Met.* 1.603 (*nitido . . . die*), *Tr.* 5.8.32 (*nitidum . . . diem*).

2. No caesura after the fifth syllable (similarly 11, 30, and 41). See 36n and 41.37–40n.

3. Night is "dewy" five times in Vergil and three times in Ovid. *Placidam quietem* ("peaceful repose") is similarly after several instances in both poets.

4. *Avaris* (with *terris*), normally "greedy," here seems merely to signify eager readiness for overnight rest, with no sense of reproach.

17–18. For *mea vita* cf. 26.55, 55.40, and 59.37. Scented hair: 21.9–10n and 31.3–5n.

22–23. The boys and girls are servants, busily making ready for the important day, as in Hor. *Odes* 4.11.9–10 ("All the servants are hurrying; girls mingled with boys are scurrying this way and that"), there speaking of preparations to celebrate Maecenas' birthday.

25. Bol.U. and Vat.1 have *proderit*, future of *prosum* ("will benefit"), though the future of *prodeo* ("will come forth") is clearly required after *prodi*. The normal future *prodibunt* would not scan, but *prodient* would. Cf. *transiet* (= *transibit*), the disputed MS reading in Tib. 1.4.27; see Murgatroyd 2001. Neue 1897, 3:327–28, records the tiny number of claimed ancient instances of such future forms in compounds of *eo* and very many from late Latin. *Prodiet* and *prodient* are among those noted, with examples from St. Augustine's *De civitate Dei* (City of God), St. Jerome's letters, and elsewhere. *Prodient* is noted in Lactantius by Lewis and Short's *Latin Dictionary*. I think *prodient* or *prodiet* should be read here. Cinelli Calvoli 1736's *prodeant* does not accord with the following futures in line 27.

29. Both MS readings (*precibus* Bol.U.; *manibus* Vat.1) scan and make sense. Jupiter could be invoked "in chaste prayers" or "with chaste hands" extended in prayer. Ovid has *castas preces* in *Her.* 6.73, and *casta . . . manu* in *Fast.* 4.260.

30. Bol.U.'s reading *petes* ("you will ask") is arguably better in context (with *pete* following in 31) than Vat.1's *potest* ("he can").

## · NOTES TO THE TRANSLATIONS ·

### FLAMINIO

### LATIN POEMS, BOOK III

3.1–4.25. Meter: All the bk. 3 poems, and fifteen of the twenty-five in bk. 4, are in elegiac couplets (alternating dactylic hexameters and pentameters). There is a very marked difference between the two books in the admission of polysyllabic endings to the pentameters. In bk. 3 there are very few such endings, whereas fifty-seven of the 184 pentameters in bk. 4 end in a polysyllable. For comparison, twenty-two of the 240 pentameters in Navagero's poems 1–47 end so. Ovid avoids such endings completely in his *Amores* and admits them only very rarely in his *Tristia*. Catullus, whose Muse Flaminio invokes in 4.1, and Propertius in his bk. 1, freely allow them.

3.1–29. Flaminio's eighteenth-century editor, Francesco Maria Mancurti, printed all twenty-nine poems in bk. 3 of Flaminio 1727, but for the second edition (Flaminio 1743) he left out five of them (3, 4, 14, 18, and 20). Maddison 1965, 183, thinks this was to avoid impairing Flaminio's reputation for lifelong moral purity. Perhaps so, for all five are first-person poems with a sexual element, though several of those still printed in Flaminio 1743 are that too, and all of the "suppressed" bk. 3 poems are present in Flaminio 1727. As for date, Maddison 1965, 87n32 and 89n4, credibly thinks the poems to Alessandro Farnese, 3.1 and 3.2, were written in 1536/37; they cannot be earlier, and *iamdudum* ("long since") in 3.2.6 may hint at a slightly later date. She considers eleven of the other bk. 3 poems (here 10–14 and 22–27) probably written in 1521 and the remaining sixteen probably in 1526; see Maddison 1965, 29–33, 50–54. While it does seem that Flaminio wrote some of the bk. 3 poems while staying with Stefano Sauli near Genoa in 1521 (see 3.10.2n), and the others (except for 3.1 and 3.2) probably while in Serravalle in 1526, Maddison's suggested assignment of each individual bk. 3 poem to a particular year, though generally plausible, may be too confident and neat. For instance, she assigns all the poems with Nigella (3.3, 3.4, and 3.19) to 1526, and all the poems with Lygda (3.22, 3.24, and 3.26) to 1521, save for 3.19 (treated as of 1526), which has both Lygda and Nigella. Flaminio already

336

## · NOTES TO THE TRANSLATIONS ·

addresses a Lygda in a poem published in 1515 (9.3 Scorsone; Maddison 1965, 18), complaining of her disdainful cruelty, and refers to his love for that Lygda in a letter to Achille Bocchi written that year; see Maddison 1965, 20. In 1.11, published in 1515, Flaminio describes himself (line 28) as sorrowing on account of his break with Chloe, apparently a pseudonym for another early girlfriend, and "new battles" with Lygda. The "mistress" in 3.29, which Maddison assigns to 1526, is not named, though Maddison seems to treat her as Nigella. It is also unclear why 3.13 should be dated 1521 rather than 1526, as it does not expressly relate to any particular girl. Cuccoli 1897, 210–14, surveys selected bk. 3 poems, but he makes no attempt to place individual poems in 1521 or 1526.

### 3.1

Quoted as an example of Flaminio's *lusus pastorales* by Hutton 1935, 225, with references to the *Greek Anthology*, especially its votive inscriptions.

1. *Pan pater* occurs again in 4.20.1. As Faunus is equated with Pan, fauns = Pans. The aged god Silvanus presided over woodland places. *Fauni bicornes*: Ov. *Her.* 4.49; *Fast.* 2.268, 5.99; see N. 20.15n.

2. Quiver-bearing goddess (cf. *pharetrata virgo* in Ov. *Am.* 1.1.10): Diana, regularly attended by a band of chaste nymphs (cf. 4.1.24).

5–6. Cf. N. 15.5 for fear of predation by greedy woodland deities.

7 (and 3.2.1). With *Farnesius heros* (again in the near-identical line 1.21.7 and in 6.9.3; found elsewhere in, e.g., Molza, *Carmina* 11.1), cf. *Laertius heros* ("hero son of Laertes"), Ov. *Tr.* 5.5.3; *Laomedontius heros* ("hero descendant of Laomedon"), Verg. *Aen.* 8.18. Such periphrases are common in Ovid. *Farnesius* is probably adjectival ("hero of Farnese stock"), though *heros* could alternatively be in apposition to it ("the hero Farnese"), as in *Aeneas heros*, Verg. *Aen.* 6.103. In 1.8.13–14 Flaminio has *Farnesius . . . heros* of Pope Paul III, whose name was also Alessandro Farnese. Du Bellay, *Epigrammata* 29.1, similarly calls his cousin Cardinal Jean du Bellay *Bellaius heros*. Among numerous other Neo-Latin parallels, I notice many instances of *heros*, with its connotations of being a demigod, of a cardinal

337

· NOTES TO THE TRANSLATIONS ·

or a pope, though it can be applied to great laymen too. Alessandro Farnese (1520–89) had recently been made a cardinal in his early teens by his nepotistic grandfather (r. 1534–49), on whose right he stands, in red robes and dark-bearded, in Titian's well-known 1545/46 portrait of the pontiff with his two Farnese grandsons. Here Flaminio is grateful for Farnese's restoration to him of the Priory of San Prospero, near Imola, the birthplace and former holding of Flaminio's father, briefly lost to Flaminio when his father died in 1536; see 3.2.5n. That property, including the land meant here and the "little country house" in 3.2.5, is extolled several times elsewhere in Flaminio's poems both for its own appeal and for the financial security it brought. The first ten poems of bk. 6 thank Farnese for the land, house, and consequent leisure to write. They abound in adulation. For instance, in 6.5 "Iolas [= Flaminio], dear to Phoebus and the Muses but poor and always accustomed to graze a master's flock (i.e., unpropertied; cf. 3.18.13), is now made rich in sheep and land by Farnese's gift, and dedicates to the divine young man . . . his very voice, reeds and creative skill." In 6.9 Poverty is told to seek another home, "for the Farnese hero (*Farnesius heros*) does not allow you to be any longer in my house." The poem ends "Great Alessandro . . . will rightly be like a great divinity to me." In 2.8 Flaminio predicts that in maturity Farnese will himself become pope and bring peace to Italy, which will erect a hundred marble temples to him and make him yearly offerings. Farnese served on several missions to foreign courts. A cultured man of splendid lifestyle (he completed the Farnese palace in Rome), he befriended many artists, scholars, and poets. He certainly made a friend of Flaminio, who in 5.1 presents the cardinal with a book of contemporary poets singing his praises. Flaminio's poems lauding Farnese are noticed by Ferroni 2012, 244–51.

3.2

1. Iol(l)as (see N. 3n and 27n) is Flaminio's pastoral pseudonym for himself in four other poems involving Farnese's generosity to him (1.17.23, 1.29.11, 6.5.1, 6.8.3 and 5). In bk. 4 Hyella's lover Iolas is imaginary. "Iolas" in Flaminio's poems need not always denote the poet. In poems addressed to friends, Flaminio salutes several as *candide*, especially in the

338

· NOTES TO THE TRANSLATIONS ·

first line (e.g., Stefano Sauli in 6.3.1). In *Epod.* 14.5 Horace calls his patron *candide Maecenas*.

4. A stream is *garrulus* in Ov. *Fast.* 2.316.

5. *Memorabile munus*: Ov. *Met.* 14.225. Farnese had restored to Flaminio the San Prospero property once Flaminio's father's (see 3.1.7n; Maddison 1965, 86–87). Addressing that "charming little estate (*agellus*) and beautiful little country house (*villula*)" in 1.17, Flaminio tells how another occupant took them over after his father died in 1536, but Farnese's kindness now enables him to see the trees planted by his father's hand and sleep in the old man's bedroom. Flaminio bids the fountains and limpid streams rejoice, as their former owner's son is coming, and will charm them with the pipe "greatest Alcon gave your Iolas (i.e., Flaminio)," so that the naiads and goat-footed Pan may marvel at him singing illustrious Farnese's praises.

7–8. Jupiter disguised as a mortal visits a cottage in, for instance, Ovid's tale of the old couple Baucis and Philemon (*Met.* 8.620–724).

3.3

This poem appears in Sannazaro 1529 and, with 3.4 and 3.21, is one of only three bk. 3 poems in Gagny ca. 1548. Maddison 1965, 51, translates the first couplet. Omitted from Flaminio 1743: see 3.1–3.29n. All four pentameter lines have polysyllabic endings. The only other pentameters ending so in bk. 3 are 3.14.4 and 3.20.2.

1. *Quid ago?* ("What do I do?") here seems equivalent to *Quid agam?* ("What shall I do?"). *Moritur* is present for future. Nigella ("Dusky"), also in 3.4.6 and 3.19.9, is not a pastoral name in ancient verse. Bernardino Rota (1509–75) addresses several poems to a Nigella, as well as, incidentally, some to a Nisa (see 3.18.8n); see Rota 1726. Nigellus was a Roman surname (the feminine Nigella occurs in an inscription).

8. I take this line as the heart's reply. Catull. 85.2 seems weakly reflected. The *o* in *nescio* (as in Catullus' line and in Verg. *Aen.* 3.602) and *sentio* is shortened, as with *audeo* in 3.18.18 and *nescio* in 3.18.24. See N. 29.20n and N. 30.8n, and cf. the prosody of *scio* in Verg. *Ecl.* 8.43.

339

# · NOTES TO THE TRANSLATIONS ·

## 3.4

Appears in Sannazaro 1529. Translated by Maddison 1965, 51. Omitted from Flaminio 1743: 3.1–3.29n.

1. "Unshorn" (= tree-covered): Verg. *Ecl.* 5.63 and *Aen.* 9.681; Stat. *Silv.* 4.7.10. See 4.16.23n. *Intonsi colles* is also in "Antonio Mario of Imola" (= Flaminio; see 3.15n), *Thyrsis* 42 (Ubaldini 1563, 21r–22v).

3 (and 4.5.32). Faunus is Pan (see 3.1.1n).

4. *Dulcia furta* (also 3.5.6, 3.10.8, 4.15.6, 4.23.2; N. 22.2). Verg. G. 4.346.

## 3.5

Name *Amaryllis* (also 3.6 and 4.5.42): N. 25.19n. Italian sonnets by Claudio Tolomei (1492–1555) based on this poem, 3.7, and 3.8 are quoted by Mancurti in Flaminio 1727 and 1743, who also reports his sonnet inspired by 4.9. The sonnets derive from a Venice, 1565 collection of vernacular verse by Tuscan poets made by Dionigi Atanagi. Cuccoli 1897, 256–57, records versions by Tolomei of 3.3, 15, 20, and 29, and a version of 3.7 by Girolamo Orti.

1. *Arbor* ("tree") is singular for plural.

2 (and 4.22.45). Flora, goddess of flowers: N. 25.6n.

3. *Genitalibus auris*: N. 31.44n.

4. *Almus ager* ("bountiful earth"; also 3.22.2): Verg. G. 2.330; Ov. *Met.* 15.204–5.

6. See 3.4.4n.

7. *Recentibus* ("fresh"): N. 37.6–8n. Meadows are *recentia* in F. 1.6.8 and 82.

8. *Focos* ("altars") is probably plural for singular.

## 3.6

Lines 1–6 and 13–14 are translated by Maddison 1965, 51. This poem and the next three, as well as 4.6, are translated by Simon de Troyes 1786, 2:110–14.

340

### · NOTES TO THE TRANSLATIONS ·

2. Aurora: N. 34.1–4n. *Avis* ("bird") is singular for plural.

3. Amaryllis: 3.5n.

7. Name *Galaesus* (*Galesus*), here an imaginary local man, like Lycambus in 8: Verg. *Aen.* 7.535 and 575. *Menandreus* ("Menander's") here refers to Galesus' father. Lycambus seems a by-form of Lycambes. The best-known of that name was driven to suicide by Archilochus' invective. See Hor. *Epod.* 6.13, *Epist.* 1.19.23–25; *Anth. Pal.* 7.69–71 and 7.351.

10 (and 3.19.6). The Mesulus is the Mischio, flowing through Flaminio's birthplace, Serravalle, now within Vittorio Veneto in Treviso. It is similarly called "beautiful" (*formosus*) in 2.7.106 (Perosa/Sparrow 1979, 286) and "delightful" (*amoenus*) in 5.13.3–4. Maddison 1965, 34, describes severe damage done to Serravalle in October 1521 by swelling of the normally innocuous stream. In mention of an earlier disastrous flood there in 2.34.8–13, the Mischio usually flows *placido . . . amne* ("with peaceful stream"). The setting at Serravalle suggests that this poem was written there in 1526; the occurrence of Amaryllis also in 3.5 and further mention of the Mischio in 3.19 presumably date those poems to the same year.

### 3.7

A shut-out lover poem, like the next. See N. 26.10n.

2. The name Pholoe is also in 3.9.4; cf. Verg. *Aen.* 5.285.

4. Garlands left on doorposts by shut-out lovers, often garlanded as revelers: Tib. 1.2.14 (with *florida serta*); Ov. *Met.* 14.708–9 and 733 (Iphis, rejected, hangs himself at his hard-hearted beloved's door), *Ars am.* 2.528; Prop. 1.16.7; Pontano, *Parthenopeus* 1.4.25–26; etc. The *exclusus amator* leaves garlands and kisses the doorposts in Lucr. 4.1177.

### 3.8

Hutton 1935, 225, sees a debt to *Anth. Pal.* 5.168 (cf. also 5.64), where the anonymous poet defies the elements to blast him as they please or sweep him away, as one worn down by desire and overwhelmed by love does not feel even Zeus' thunderbolt. Suffering inflicted on the shut-out lover from the elements figures in several passages on the theme (see N. 26.10n).

341

## · NOTES TO THE TRANSLATIONS ·

1. Ending as Verg. *Aen.* 12.722.

3. Night is *soporifera* ("sleep-bringing") in Sil. 7.287; Petron. 128.6.1. Sleep, accompanying Night, is *furvis circumdatus alis* ("wrapped in dusky wings") in Tib. 2.2.89–90 and was often thought of as winged (e.g., Sil. 10.344 and 355; Stat. *Theb.* 10.148, *Achil.* 1.620), like Night here; cf. Verg. *Aen.* 8.369, where "Night . . . enfolds the earth in her dark wings."

### 3.9

Perosa/Sparrow 1979, 290. Cuccoli 1897, 212, cites N. 12 with this poem, implying a perceived similarity of theme.

1–4. For the construction (*sic* + subjunctive followed by imperative, here *venito*), cf. 4.6.1–2 (4.6.1 is very similar to line 1 here) and 4.10.1–4. Flaminio begins 5.25 (5.26 Scorsone) and 6.26 in the same way. Ancient examples with the *sic* clause first include Verg. *Ecl.* 9.30, 10.4 and Ov. *Met.* 8.857. Cf. 3.29.7–8 and N. 20.4, where the *sic* clause comes second, as in Tib. 2.6.30; Ov. *Met.* 14.762; Sannazaro, *Elegies* 2.5.1–2. Note especially N. 56.13, 16, 18, and 22. *Alma* is especially found of Venus (again 3.25.5; N. 18.8). Imagery of wrinkles furrowing flesh is quite common: e.g., Verg. *Aen.* 7.417; Ov. *Ars am.* 2.118; Hor. *Epod.* 8.4. *Ruga senilis* is from Ov. *Fast.* 5.58. See 4.1.26n for the second imperative *venito*.

3 and 8. Lycinna (name, also found of another in 2.6.1: N. 59n) is apparently Pholoe's little sister.

6. After Ov. *Her.* 16.320.

### 3.10

Translated by Maddison 1965, 30. She discusses and contrasts 3.10–14 and 3.22–27 on p. 33.

2. Ligurina is a shepherdess (named also in 3.11.3, 12.3, 14.1, 23.5, 25.6, and 27.5), seemingly distinct from Lygda (3.19.1, 22.6, 24.6, 26.5). See 3.22n, 3.26n, and 3.27n. The names *Ligurina* and *Lygda* are not in any ancient poet, but the male equivalents are. *Ligurinus* is found in Hor. *Odes* 4.1.33 and 4.10.5 (a desired beautiful boy), and both names occur in Mar-

342

· NOTES TO THE TRANSLATIONS ·

tial. Maddison 1965, 29, thinks that the *lusus pastorales* "about or related to" Ligurina are very likely to have been written when Flaminio was at Stefano Sauli's villa near Genoa in the summer of 1521, as Liguria denotes the region around Genoa, though the poems otherwise show no link to that location. She treats most of the bk. 3 Lygda poems as also of 1521, though she sets 3.19 in 1526 (see 3.1–29n). Flaminio, however, mentions a Lygda outside bk. 3: for instance, an ode addressed to such a girl was among his early poems published at Fano in 1515 (App. 3 [9.3] Scorsone). Note too Flaminio's talk of suffering through his love for that Lygda in his prefatory letter to Achille Bocchi (Maddison 1965, 20). In his elegy 2.5, of early 1522, Flaminio, facing the possibility of his own death in early youth, hopes that Lygda will give him a loving reception if he goes to Elysium (Maddison 1965, 35–36). That seems to show that the Lygda there was already dead in 1522, but, by Maddison's dating, the Lygda in 3.19 is alive in 1526. As for the name, an elegiac kiss poem of uncertain authorship addresses a Lygda (Toscano 1576, 75r, in the appended section), and there is a poem "To Lygda" by Tebaldeo (*Carmina Illustrium Poetarum Italorum* 9:241). Important for Maddison's allocation of many of Flaminio's bk. 3 poems to 1521 is a verse letter in hendecasyllables (5.28; see Perosa/Sparrow 1979, 283) written by Flaminio that summer from Sauli's villa to Christophe de Longueil (Cristoforo Longolio) inviting him to join Sauli, himself, and two other poets already there, Giulio Camillo and Sebastiano Delio. Within the letter (lines 12–17), Flaminio first refers to writing pastoral poetry. I translate the full poem:

> While you, Longueil, are enjoying the company of Navagero and excellent Bembo, and striving to match the praiseworthy achievements of your Tully [Cicero], for my part, where Genoa rises toward the stars with lofty structures, I am hidden away in the lovely little gardens of my friend and yours Stefano [Sauli]. Now I read Aristotle's books, marveling at the man's heavenly wisdom and genius; now I turn back to Catullus' sweet little verses and sing amid tuneful birds as I lie beneath the shade of a laurel-haired tree; now I playfully compose poems of the sort that the Arcadians used to sing in the dark glades of Lycaeus before a fierce race from the shores of uncivilized Scythia [the Turks] put such as Menalcas and Tityrus [bucolic characters in Ver-

343

## · NOTES TO THE TRANSLATIONS ·

gil's *Eclogues*] to far-distant flight. As for Sauli, he works hard at Tully, toiling to follow in your footsteps; he is full of admiration for him alone, and he thinks you, whom kind Jupiter [God] allows to be so close to that outstanding writer, very lucky, Longueil. But when the heat has eased, the trees no longer resound with complaining crickets, and the fiery sun goes away, we make off to the waterline of the nearby coast. Here each of us sits on a rock and catches fish with his rod, and delights to see skiffs speeding along on the deep blue sea. You see, dear friend, what sort of life your Flaminio and your Sauli are having. If it pleases you, come, and complete the bliss your Flaminio and your Sauli are experiencing.

6. See N. 2.2n.

7–8. With 8 cf. Verg. G. 4.346. Dryads are wood nymphs. *Dulcia furta:* 3.4.4n.

### 3.11

Translated by Maddison 1965, 30. Ligurina: 3.10.2n.

5–6. For *quod superest* (lit., "as to what remains"), cf., with some variation of precise meaning, Verg. G. 2.346, 4.51 (*quod superest, ubi,* as here), *Aen.* 5.691 and 796, 9.157, 11.15. The expression is also in Lucretius. *Croceo mane* (here used as a noun): Aurora, the dawn goddess, leaves Tithonus' yellow (or saffron) couch (*croceum . . . cubile*) in Verg. G. 1.447 and *Aen.* 4.585 and 9.460.

7. *Mea vita:* N. 55.40–41n.

### 3.12

Translated by Maddison 1965, 30–31. Ligurina: 3.10.2n.

4. Dryads: 3.10.7–8n.

9–10. Cf. N. 13.1. Lovers sharing the hour of death (like the turtledoves in 3.28): Ov. *Met.* 8.708–10 (Baucis and Philemon); Prop. 2.20.18. For one death meaning two, cf. Prop. 2.28.39–42; [Tib.] 3.10.19–20; Ov. *Am.*

344

## · NOTES TO THE TRANSLATIONS ·

2.13.15–16. For being buried together (also 4.18.3 and 11, 4.20.15–16, 4.24.10), cf. *Anth. Pal.* 7.378 and 551 (brothers); Val. Flacc. 5.56–61 (after cremation, two comrades' bones are united). Flaminio wishes to live and die together with his close friend Stefano Sauli in 5.6.12–13 and 6.12.11.

### 3.13

Translated by Maddison 1965, 31. Circumvention of a girl's mother (as in 3.18.1–2): N. 6.4–5n.

5. *Tolle moras:* Ov. *Met.* 13.556, *Her.* 4.147.

6. Cf. Ov. *Tr.* 4.10.119 (*tu dux et comes es,* "you are guide and companion") and Pontano, *De Amore Coniugali* 1.7.3 (see N. 22.4n).

### 3.14

Translated by Maddison 1965, 32. Omitted from Flaminio 1743. Ligurina: 3.10.2n.

1–2. Tib. 1.2.89 speaks of one who had mocked the unhappy loves of young men (*qui . . . lusisset amores*). *Ludit amores* here may well have merely that sense of deriding, though Maddison's "trifle with my passion" (i.e., play games or toy with it) is quite tempting. *Petit* (lit., "seeks") is said of actively inviting amorous attention.

3–4. Cf. N. 27.10 for the mossy cave, and 4.1.6 below and N. 10A.9 (with note) for the green turf. Altars of turf: Ov. *Met.* 7.240. Cytherea (Aphrodite/Venus): 3.28.1–2n.

5–6. With 5 cf. Verg. *Aen.* 3.66. Line 6 here ends as 3.19.8 below and almost as N. 15.2.

12. The object of *colam* is *sacra* (11). Cf. Ov. *Met.* 4.32 (*sacra colunt,* "they celebrate the rites") and 15.679 (*tua sacra colentes,* "celebrating your rites"). In Verg. *Aen.* 4.458 Dido tended her dead husband's shrine with reverence (*honore colebat*).

13. Cf. Verg. *Aen.* 3.437, *Iunonis . . . prece numen adora* ("supplicate Juno's divinity in prayer").

345

## 3.15

Hutton 1935, 225, sees a debt to "the well-worn conceit" of *Anth. Pal.* 5.83, where the poet wishes he were the wind, to be taken to his lady's bosom. Cf. also *Anth. Pal.* 5.84, where the speaker wishes to be a rose, to be plucked and held to a desired girl's chest, and 15.35, which has a similarly motivated wish to be a lily. Hutton 1946, 598–99, lists many further imitations (Latin and vernacular) by poets in France, the Low Countries, and beyond. A poem attributed to "Antonio Mario of Imola" (= Flaminio) in several anthologies (e.g., Ubaldini 1563, 24r; Toscano 1576, 235r) translates: "When handsome Hylas was sending soft hyacinths and baskets full of various roses to his mistress, with a tear he said, "Go, roses; go, lucky hyacinths: why may I not now be my gifts?" (*Cur nunc dona mihi non licet esse mea?*); see Cuccoli 1897, 161–63; Maddison 1965, 25n4. Cf. N. 49 (especially for line 4 of this "Mario" poem). For "Mario" poems see further 3.4.1n, 3.26n, 3.27n, 4.1.11n, and 4.25.1n.

2. Name *Thestylis* (a goatherd girl, beloved of Micon, also in 3.16.1 and 9, 3.17.1 and 3.18.5): Verg. *Ecl.* 2.10 and 43; Theoc. *Id.* 2. Here (as in 3.16 and 3.18) Micon is the unnamed speaker; he is named in 3.17.1.

## 3.16

Cf. N. 12 for gifts from the city. Unsuccessful tempting by a rival girl: 3.17.7–8 and N. 27.60–67. Another good instance is Bargaeus' pastoral epigram *Ad Amyllam*; see Bargaeus 1568, 384–85. There Amylla's admirer declares he has several gifts for her, including a distaff "such as not even Mopsus' rich daughter has." Another very beautiful girl is said to be demanding all these gifts from him — "And what has she not promised to have them?" He tells Amylla, "But you shall not have them till you leave the mountain and show me how much you value my presents."

1. The Sicilian Mt. Hybla (also 3.21.6; 4.5.22), famed for bees and honey, occurs in several passages with imagery of sweetness. Cf., for example, Pontano, *Eridanus* 1.13.7–8, "Stella sweeter to me than Hybla's honeycombs." Thestylis: 3.15.2n.

346

# · NOTES TO THE TRANSLATIONS ·

5 and 8. Name *Phyllis* (also 3.17.8, 3.18.7, 3.20.3, 3.21.3): Verg. *Ecl.* 3.78, 5.10, 7.14 and 59, 10.37; Ov. *Tr.* 2.537; Hor. *Odes* 4.11.3.

7. The plural *numina* = "divinity," as in Verg. *Aen.* 3.543 (Pallas); Hor. *Epod.* 17.3 (Diana).

12. Cf. Ov. *Met.* 14.682–83 for *ardor* ("passion" or "flame") of a person.

## 3.17

1. Name *Micon*: Verg. *Ecl.* 3.10, 7.30; Calp. 5.1; Theoc. *Id.* 5.112. Thestylis: 3.15.2n.

7. All texts give *hoc* ("with this furtive foot"), but *huc* ("to this place") seems required. Cf. *huc* in 3.13.2.

8. Phyllis: 3.16.5 and 8n. Cf. Verg. *Ecl.* 5.88–90 for unsuccessful efforts by a sexually attractive person (there a youth) to beg from the speaker a present eventually given to another.

## 3.18

1–2. Name *Thyrsis*: N. 6n. Circumvention of girl's mother (as in 3.13): N. 6.4–5n. Omitted from Flaminio 1743: 3.1–3.29n.

5–6. The accusative and infinitive construction is used in an exclamatory question.

7–8. Phyllis: 3.16.5 and 8n. Name *Gorgo*: Theoc. *Id.* 15; *Anth. Pal.* 7.647, 9.309. Name *Nisa* (or *Nysa*): Verg. *Ecl.* 8.18 and 26 (and see 3.3.1n). The girl here eager to win attention from Micon may be the same as in 3.28.5, partnered with Daphnis. Iolas' wife (4.18.7 and 19.9) is clearly another.

9–10. For the loyal youth spurning a rival girl's attempts to seduce him, cf. 3.16.5–12 and N. 27.60–67.

15. Name *Dorylas*, here an unskilled rustic musician: Ov. *Met.* 5.129–30, 12.380.

16. I have not found the name *Agyrta* in an ancient poet or anywhere else.

# · NOTES TO THE TRANSLATIONS ·

18. *Audeo* has the *o* shortened (like *nescio* in 24). See 3.3.8n.

21–22. Likening eyes to stars: N. 32.5–6n. The name of Adonis, the beloved of Venus, is here used to denote an outstandingly handsome youth, as it still often is; see N. 20.72–74n.

23–24. *Male* negates *sana* (N. 36.3–4n). *Nescio quem . . . Thyrsin* is dismissively contemptuous of Thyrsis; cf. Ov. *Met.* 13.844, *nescio quem . . . Iovem. Prae* must mean "in preference to" or "more than." Cf. N. 59.7 and 8.

25–26. For adynata (impossibilities) see N. 27.63–67n. Here things contrary to the order of nature are indignantly pictured as possible, if Thestylis can so unreasonably prefer Thyrsis to the speaker. For such a use of adynata, cf., for example, Verg. *Ecl.* 8.26–28 and 52–56, reflecting Theoc. *Id.* 1.132–36.

27. Cf. Damon's words in Verg. *Ecl.* 8.26 ("Nysa is given to Mopsus. What may we lovers not expect?"). Fifth foot elision.

## 3.19

This poem appears in Sannazaro 1529.

1. Lygda: 3.10.2n.

2. *Orbe* probably = "with his orb/ball" (cf. Verg. *G.* 1.459), though possibly "in his orbit."

5. Cf. 4.5.69 (with note) and *texunt umbracula*, Verg. *Ecl.* 9.42 (woven shade figures also in Theoc. *Id.* 7.7–8). Bushes weave shade (*umbracula texunt*) in T. V. Strozzi, *Erotica* 4.8.82–83. A beech tree is "spreading" (*patula*) in Verg. *Ecl.* 1.1.

6. Mesulus: 3.6.10n.

8. See 3.14.5–6n.

9–10. For the "dark" Nigella see 3.3.1n. Marble complexions were highly prized. *Nympha* is figuratively said.

## 3.20

Translated by McFarlane 1980, 25; Maddison 1965, 52–53. Omitted from Flaminio 1743: 3.1–3.29n.

· NOTES TO THE TRANSLATIONS ·

1. Cf. *irriguum . . . fontem*, Verg. G. 4.32. *Addita* (lit., "added to" or "joined to" the springs) is oddly used. McFarlane 1980, 25, renders "valley associated with these springs"; Maddison 1965, 52, "vale *of* the fountains." Cf. the structure of 3.4.1.

5–6. *Vivite felices* (Verg. Aen. 3.493), lit., "live happ(il)y," is a strange wish to inanimate springs, etc., though addressing them may be felt to half-personify them, and *vivere* sometimes substitutes for *esse* ("be") in Neo-Latin verse. Cf. Verg. G. 2.377 (*gravis . . . aestas*) and 4.135 (*tristis hiems . . . frigore*).

7. *Dura bipennis* is in debt to Verg. Aen. 2.479.

10. Arcadia is the mountainous central district of the Peloponnese, associated with Pan and often seen as the idyllic pastoral setting. Cf. 4.5.26 and 4.17.16.

### 3.21

1. *Frigidulis:* 4.5.19n.

2. For "watery foot" cf. [Verg.] *Cul.* 17.

3. Phyllis: 3.16.5 and 8n.

4. Cf. *arentem . . . sitim*, Ov. Her. 4.174.

5–6. Cf. 4.5.21–22 for Hyblaean "kisses" given to a stream by the drinker. See 3.16.1n.

### 3.22

Parallel to 3.23, just as 3.24 balances 3.25, and 3.26 corresponds to 3.27. See 3.26n and 3.27n for hints that this alternation of "Lygda" poems with balancing "Ligurina" poems owes something to the form of an amoebean bucolic singing competition, where the competitors sing in turn, often about a beloved; cf., for example, Verg. *Ecl.* 3.58–59. Perhaps Flaminio, in these balanced poems, is singing alternately of two different girls then in his life? Maddison 1965, 32–33, notes the Petrarchan flavor and conventional conceits of 3.22–3.27.

349

## · NOTES TO THE TRANSLATIONS ·

1. *Ver purpureum:* Verg. *Ecl.* 9.40.

2. *Almus ager:* See 3.5.4n.

5. *Tristis hiems:* 3.20.5–6n. The theme of the presence or favor of the beautiful beloved turning gloom to brightness, night to day (cf. N. 38), and similar, is a commonplace in Neo-Latin Petrarchist love poetry; so too the converse if the beloved is absent or hostile.

### 3.23

Parallel to 3.22 (but with Ligurina, not Lygda). See 3.22n.

2. Cf. *squalent . . . arva* ("the plow fields are left untilled") in Verg. G. 1.507.

3. *Stat = est.* Parts of *stare* ("stand") can be used for those of *esse* ("be") in Neo-Latin verse, as rarely in ancient.

### 3.24

Parallel to 3.25.

1–4. The image of the heifer sadly missing her mate owes some debt to Verg. *Ecl.* 8.85–88, itself influenced by Lucr. 2.355–65.

5–6. *Liquidi fontes:* Verg. *Ecl.* 2.59. With *paterno . . . rure* cf. *paterna rura* ("paternal lands") in Hor. *Epod.* 2.3. Flaminio may mean "your father's farm," or possibly "your native countryside."

### 3.25

Parallel to 3.24 (but with Ligurina, not Lygda).

5. See 3.9.1–4n.

### 3.26

Parallel to 3.27. Cf. lines 58–61 of the hexameter eclogue *Thyrsis* attributed to "Antonio Mario of Imola," i.e., Flaminio (see 3.15n), in various anthologies (Ubaldini 1563, 21r; Toscano 1576, 232r; etc.), where line 58 is

350

## · NOTES TO THE TRANSLATIONS ·

identical to 1 here, and line 61 differs from 6 here only in having *Lycidae* for *Lygdae*; Lycidas is a beautiful boy in Hor. *Odes* 1.4 and a shepherd in Verg. *Ecl.* 7.67 and 9.12. Thyrsis, representing Flaminio (singing in competition with another boy, Alcon; for the response see 3.27n), employs this simile (I translate 58–61):

> Do you see how the flowers spring up joyously throughout the
>     meadows,
> the air resounds with the varied songs of birds,
> the woods are green, and every tree is budding?
> Such is Lycidas' countenance, that is how he looks when he smiles.

5. See 3.27.5.

### 3.27

Parallel to 3.26 (but with Ligurina, not Lygda). Translated by Maddison 1965, 32. Lilies and roses quite often figure in imagery of a generally white skin with redness in the cheeks (e.g., Verg. *Aen.* 12.68–69; Ov. *Am.* 2.5.37). Ligurina's complexion is here implied to have that admired coloring. There is similarity to lines of the same eclogue of "Antonio Mario of Imola" noticed in 3.26n, in this case to Alcon's words in 62–65, there responding to those of Thyrsis (translated 3.26n) in the singing competition. Line 64 there differs from 3 here only in beginning *aut*, not *et*; 65 there is as 5 here, save for having *Vari lugentis* (making the context homosexual) for *Ligurinae flentis.* I translate 62–65:

> Have you seen, as the light comes up in the yellow sky,
> either ice gleam amid hoary frost
> or dew drip off red roses?
> Such is Varus' countenance, that is how he looks when he grieves.

3. *Puniceis . . . rosetis*: Verg. *Ecl.* 5.17.

### 3.28

The name Daphnis is a traditional one in pastoral (N. 20.96–97n and 27.46n). Nisa: 3.18.7–8n. The unnamed speaker here is some well-wisher of the couple.

· NOTES TO THE TRANSLATIONS ·

1–2. Cytherea denotes Venus, from the Greek island of Cythera's associations with her. Cf. 3.14.3, 4.8.9, 4.23.3; N. 17.8. For turtledoves (a type of devoted love) sacrificed to her, cf. the ringdove in N. 41.39–40 and Propertius as cited in my note there; cf. also the female dove in Ov. *Fast.* 1.451–52. An ass is *victima grata* to Priapus in Ov. *Fast.* 1.439. *Turtur*, here feminine, is generally masculine.

3–4. Lovers dying or wishing to die at the same time: 3.12.9–10n.

### 3.29

Translated by Maddison 1965, 52. See N. 22n.

1. After Hor. *Carm. saec.*, where the new moon is *caeli decus* (2) and *siderum regina bicornis* (35).

3–4. Cf. 4.10.5–6. In 4 *pascet* has its second syllable lengthened at the pentameter dieresis (cf. 4.24.10). See N. 13.10n.

7–8. See 3.9.1–4n.

8. *Eas* (lit., "may you go") virtually = *sis* ("may you be"). Parts of *ire* can sometimes stand for those of *esse* in Neo-Latin verse, as rarely in ancient.

## LATIN POEMS, BOOK IV

4.1–25. Maddison 1965, 98–103, surveys this second book of *lusus pastorales*, seemingly written when Flaminio was at Caserta from July 1539 till early 1540 as the guest of Giovanni Francesco d'Alois, count of Caserta, who was then in his mid-twenties. As a follower of Valdés, Caserta was in 1564 to suffer death under the Inquisition. Maddison dates the composition of the poems to spring 1540. Cuccoli 1897, 72, 215, says 1539; so too Ferroni 2012, 236, specifying between spring and autumn. Cuccoli 1897 sees allusion to these poems in a letter to the poet Gianfrancesco Bini written by Flaminio from Naples on February 27, 1540, after leaving Caserta. There Flaminio speaks of finding it difficult to break away from his "bad habit" (*cattivo habito*) and "madness" of poetry (*pazzia della Poesia*), just as a man is never completely cured of the French disease (syphilis). He jokingly vows in future to take purges and syrups for these poetic

352

## · NOTES TO THE TRANSLATIONS ·

whims (*capricci poetichi*). In 6.20, a later verse letter to the count, Flaminio speaks of how, on an earlier visit to Caserta, seemingly meaning in 1539/40, he recovered his health, and "there the Muse ever favored me with her kindly divine power, so that the dryads marveled at my singing and the satyrs adorned my head with painted (i.e., multicolored) garlands." That bucolic imagery seems likely to refer to these bk. 4 pastoral pieces, making them written in 1539/40. Support for that date may come from 5.8, in which Flaminio invites Galeazzo Florimonte to come from Sessa and join him and his host at Caserta. Flaminio, who had stayed at Sessa with Florimonte in 1538/39, tells him (lines 73–76), "If you come quickly, I will show you a book of poems, on reading which you will suppose yourself feeding on ambrosia and your mouth being filled with nectar." That book of poems may mean the pastoral pieces of the present bk. 4, though Flaminio is normally self-deprecating about his own poetic abilities. In the same poem (lines 67–70), Flaminio jokes that the roses and other flowers are holding back from blooming as they await Florimonte's visit. The bk. 4 poems are a playful and light literary diversion dealing with the imagined love of a handsome youth, the shepherd Iolas, and a beautiful goatherd girl, not yet fifteen, Hyella (names: N. 3n and 21n), both accomplished rustic musicians. Hyella's hopes of marrying Iolas are painfully ended when his father makes him wed another girl, Nisa, against his wishes. Hyella fades away and dies in her distress, blaming Iolas' cruelty for her end. Iolas too wastes in grief and misery over Hyella's fate, and some passages hint contemplation of suicide. He expresses hopes of being buried beside Hyella and becoming her husband in Elysium (Nisa is quite disregarded). In this tale Iolas does not represent Flaminio, who was just over forty at this time and never married, or anyone real. In 5.8.34–37, however, Flaminio interestingly speaks of a Hyella making Florimonte, should he visit Caserta, a gift of fresh cheeses (cf. 4.4.7) and two kids, describing her as "a very beautiful milkmaid of goats (*caprimulga*; cf. 4.4.4–5)" and a match for Pan as singer or piper. He seems there jokingly to allude to these bk. 4 poems, affecting to use his imaginary character's name to denote some real-life local milkmaid and playfully lauding her in much the same terms as his bucolic charac-

353

# · NOTES TO THE TRANSLATIONS ·

ter. Ferroni 2012, 249, takes a similar view of this "real" Hyella. Cuccoli 1897, 216–24, surveys the bk. 4 poems, offering limited comments on some.

### 4.1

Meter: Iambic strophe (alternating trimeter and dimeter, like 4.10), as seen in Hor. *Epod.* 1–10. See 3.1–4.25n for the range of meters used by Flaminio in his *lusus pastorales*. Flaminio uses this meter also in 1.18 and 2.32 and for the majority of his paraphrases of psalms in bk. 7.

2. Catull. 31's celebration of Sirmione: N. 52n. The invocation of Catullus' Muse has only limited significance, as Maddison 1965, 98, observes, in that Flaminio declares a desire to immortalize Hyella as Catullus did Lesbia. In general, the bk. 4 poems do not reflect Catullus' manner or themes, though in respect of meter two (4.4 and 4.25) are in hendecasyllables (a meter especially associated with Catullus), one (4.22) is choliambic (also much favored by Catullus), and those in elegiac couplets have many polysyllabic pentameter endings (following Catullus' practice rather than Ovid's; see 3.1–4.25n). There are also many diminutives, as in Catullus. Like Maddison, I think 4.2 and 4.3 may owe something to Catullus' poem on the death of Lesbia's sparrow (Catull. 2; cf. also his 3), an influence on N. 43. Flaminio thought highly of Catullus. In 5.19, inviting Lodovico Strozzi to visit him at his Priory of San Colombano, Flaminio says, "Here we shall read at leisure your Vergil and my Catullus." In 5.28 Flaminio writes to Longueil that while staying with Stefano Sauli at Genoa in 1521, as well as reading Aristotle and playfully composing pastorals (part of bk. 3), he reads "Catullus' sweet little verses" (see 3.10.2n). In 5.7 he calls Catullus *lepidus* ("charming" or "witty"). In 5.36.8–9 Flaminio deems nothing wittier or more elegant than Catullus.

4 and 28. Lesbia: Catullus' mistress, here treated as immortalized by him.

5. Monte Taburno (or Tavurno, near Benevento) is also named in 4.15.12, 4.16.3 and 25, 4.17.20, and 4.20.2. Flaminio's host in 1539/40, Giovanni Francesco d'Alois, was count of nearby Caserta.

## · NOTES TO THE TRANSLATIONS ·

6. Turf altar: 3.14.3–4n.

11. The name *Hyella* (N. 21n) occurs in one of the poems (*Ad Vesperum*) ascribed in several anthologies (beginning with Ubaldini 1563, 23v–24r) to "Antonio Mario of Imola" (i.e., Flaminio; see 3.15n). That poem, an unnamed lover's plea to the evening star for it to light his way to Hyella's kisses, probably draws the name *Hyella* from Navagero's poem 22, of which it is reminiscent. The lover there declares that no desire for a sinful intrigue or thirst for blood drives him, but Cupid's mighty power fiercely blazing in his breast.

16. Lago di Garda (Latin *Benacus*) is the lake near Verona into which the peninsula of Sirmione projects. Flaminio had been given the benefice of the Priory of San Colombano there by Gianmatteo Giberti, bishop of Verona, in whose service Flaminio was for around fourteen years till 1538; see Maddison 1965, 90–92.

24. For Diana's chaste band see N. 14.8n.

26. *Dicito* is second imperative, like *venito* in 3.9.4, *spargito* in 4.10.20, and *caveto* in N. 26.85.

### 4.2

Maddison 1965, 99, summarizes and comments on this and the following poem. Meter: Iambic trimeters, like 4.3, 4.15, 4.16, and 4.21.

1. In one version of the myth, a she-goat (Amalthea) fed the baby Zeus/ Jupiter with her milk and later became the star Capella. *Caelitum* is literally "of the dwellers in heaven," i.e., the gods.

5. Verg. G. 4.51–52 has, of the sun, *sol . . . caelumque aestiva luce reclusit* ("and has opened the sky with summer light").

12. *Domus* (nom.) agrees in case with *qui* in 11 rather than the genitive *fontis* in 10.

13–14. "Half-goat god": Pan. See N. 5.9 (with note) and 26.45. In Sannazaro, *Elegies* 2.4.28, he is the "half-god goat and half-goat god." The last three syllables of *montivago* (of Pan in N. 3.1) make an anapaest, found only thrice in Horace's iambic trimeters, including, in the fifth foot (as

355

· NOTES TO THE TRANSLATIONS ·

here, in 4.3.18, and in 4.15.15), *Epod.* 2.35 and 11.23. See 4.3.18n, 4.15.15n, 4.16.8–9n, 4.16.38–39n, 4.16.55n, 4.21n, 4.22.24n, 4.22.58n. *Dulce lenimen* ("sweet comfort"): Hor. *Odes* 1.32.15.

15. Cf. 4.3.5. *Reductus* of a valley: Verg. *Aen.* 6.703; Hor. *Odes* 1.17.17, *Epod.* 2.11. *Cubile* ("couch" or "bed") is found in ancient verse of the lairs, nests, or resting places of various creatures (e.g., of a mole, Verg. G. 1.183; of bees, G. 4.243).

16. *Lassulus* (diminutive), found in an ancient author only in Catull. 63.35, is also in Pontano, *De Amore Coniugali* 2.17.21. Flaminio has it again in 6.13.8.

17. After Mart. 8.77, *et cingant florea serta caput* ("and let flowery garlands ring your head"). *Florea serta* is the MSS reading in Tib. 1.1.12 and 1.2.14, though *florida serta* is often preferred in eds. (cf. Ov. *Fast.* 6.312; N. 26.28).

18. The diminutive *somnulus* ("nap," not ancient) is found, for instance, in Pontano, *De Amore Coniugali* 2.8.6 and 2.17.6. In the former line the diminutive *somniculus* also occurs, as again in 2.19.11 of the same work.

19. *Mollicellus* (diminutive): Catull. 25.10 (of hands); Pontano, *Parthenopeus* 1.11.4. The diminutive *barbula* (once in Cicero, and used of plants in Pliny the Elder) is not in ancient verse. Ov. *Fast.* 1.259 has *manu mulcens* of stroking a beard. A goat's enjoyment of having his beard stroked by a naiad is described in *Anth. Pal.* 9.745. Scorsone (Flaminio 1993) suspects a possible reminiscence here, perhaps rightly.

22. Cf. how Autumn has raised his head (*caput . . . extulit*) in Hor. *Epod.* 2.17–18.

24. *Argutulus* (diminutive): Apul. *Met.* 1, p. 117, 20.

25. A billy goat has "wives" (*uxores*) in Hor. *Odes* 1.17.7. He is the "man" (*vir*) of the herd in Verg. *Ecl.* 7.7 (similarly Theoc. *Id.* 8.49).

29. Pales (also 4.5.25, 4.10.1, 4.16.45, and 4.20.1): N. 11.2n. "Goat-footed Pan" (cf. 4.16.19): N. 18.3–4n.

30. *Lumine* = "(light of) life," as in Lucr. 3.1033; Ov. *Tr.* 4.4.25.

31. The last line repeats the first, as in Catull. 16, 36, 52, and 57. In 5.39 Flaminio repeats the opening two lines at the end.

356

## · NOTES TO THE TRANSLATIONS ·

### 4.3

Briefly noticed by Maddison 1965, 99. The billy goat's bliss of 4.2 is destroyed by Hyella's death. Meter: Iambic trimeters.

5. Cf. 4.2.15. *Reposta* (for *reposita*) = "remote." The word is very rare (Verg. *Aen.* 3.364 and 6.59; Sil. 3.325).

6. Hor. *Odes* 3.13.15–16 has *loquaces lymphae* of the babbling water of the *fons Bandusiae*.

11. Goats like thyme in Hor. *Odes* 1.17.6. Thus Bembo, *Carmina* 1.19–20 (*Pastorum chorus*), has "mountain-roaming she-goats crop the new thyme." Shade is *dulcis* in Verg. *Aen.* 1.694 and [Verg.] *Cul.* 121.

15–16. For streams of milk in Elysium, Underworld abode of the virtuous, happy dead, cf. 4.22.34. In 1.8.64 Flaminio bids the Tiber flow with pure milk amid blissful rejoicing on the anniversary of Paul III's becoming pope and bringing back "old Saturn's Golden Age" (77–78 there; see N. 44.91–94n). Rivers of milk (and of nectar) figure in Ovid's description of that Golden Age in *Met.* 1.111; hence in Bembo, *Carmina* 28.6, rivers then flowed with milk, not icy water.

17. "Feeding on" (breathing) air: Verg. *Aen.* 1.546–47; Lucr. 5.857.

18–19. Flaminio 1548 and Gagny ca. 1548 (the latter text taken from the former) give 18 as *Nec, si velit, redire ad haec loca iam queat* ("She could now neither return to these parts, if she wished") and begin 19 with *nec*, not *neque*. The general reading (including in Flaminio 1727 and 1743) is as I print. It is already in *Carmina Quinque Illustrium Poetarum* (all eds. from 1548 to 1558). Fifth foot anapaest with either text (see 4.2.13–14n).

22. Hiatus between *miselle* and *omnium*.

### 4.4

Summarized by Maddison, 1965, 99. Meter: Phalaecean hendecasyllables, as 4.25.

1–2. The genitive after *quidquid*, found several times elsewhere in Flaminio's poems (e.g., 6.22.16, *quidquid est hominum elegantiorum*, "all elegant

## · NOTES TO THE TRANSLATIONS ·

people") smacks of Catullus (31.14, 37.4), whose 3.1–2 seems reflected in the wider structure here.

4. *Caprimulga* (also 4.9.1, 5.8.35 and 36) does not occur in classical Latin, though Catull. 22.10 (imitated in F. 1.26.17) has the masculine equivalent *caprimulgus*.

6. Cakes or pancakes of meal (*liba*) were commonly offered to the gods. Made with milk or oil, they were sweetened with honey; cf. Tib. 1.7.54.

11. *Formosulus* (diminutive) is ante- and postclassical.

14. *Floridulo ore* is after Catull. 61.186, the only ancient passage where the diminutive *floridulus* occurs; Flaminio has it again in 4.22.50. For "kissing" the spring while drinking, cf. 3.21.5 and 4.5.5 and 21–22. Note also the similar "kiss" Hyella's pipe longs for in 4.15.21.

19. Dis (also 4.17.68): Pluto (Orcus). The girl is his niece and wife Persephone (N. 26.35–36n).

28. Hiatus between *ducere* and *obstupente*. Cf. Catull. 3.16 and 38.2 for hiatus at the same point.

### 4.5

Summarized and discussed in detail by Maddison 1965, 99–101. The speaker is presumably to be seen as Iolas (*mihi* in line 7).

1. *Turbidulus* (diminutive, here in pathos) occurs in an ancient author only in Prudent *Apoth.* 276. Flaminio no doubt intends the sense that *turbidus* has of water, i.e., "muddied" or "troubled" (e.g., Verg. *Aen.* 6.296); that meaning is supported by the contrast in line 2 with the stream's normal clearness. Here *turbidule* scans with lengthening of the *e* at the caesura.

2 (and 38; again 4.6.6). *Lucidulus* (diminutive) is not ancient. Flaminio has *fontes luciduli* in 1.12.11 and 1.55.23, and *luciduli . . . fontis* in 2.6.34.

4. See N. 53.5 and N. 55.1–8n for a river or stream swollen with tears.

8. *Languidulus*: N. 65.19–20n. Flaminio has this diminutive also in 5.7.12 and 6.59.11 (6.60.11 Scorsone). Verg. *Aen.* 12.908 has the similar *languida . . . quies* of sleep.

358

## · NOTES TO THE TRANSLATIONS ·

9–10. *Lasciva* personifies the breeze as a caresser (Hor. *Odes* 1.36.20 has the same word of close-clinging ivy), just as the stream's contact with Hyella's person is treated sexually in 5–6 and 19–22. A breeze agitates the "hair" of poplar trees in Ov. *Am.* 1.7.54 (ending *ventilat aura comas*). In Pontano, *Eridanus* 1.36.5, a light breeze furtively bares the sleeping Venus' calves.

11. *Superimpendens* is found in an ancient author only in Catull. 64.286. Spondaic fifth foot (as in 55).

14. *Chrysolithus* (-os) = chrysolite, an olivine, transparent varieties of which can be used as gems (the Greek means "goldstone"); Prop. 2.16.44 (ending, as here, *lumine chrysolithos*); Ov. *Met.* 2.109.

15. For *hedera alba* ("pale ivy") cf. Verg. *Ecl.* 7.38. Ivy is similarly *pallens* in 3.39 of the same. The mention of yellow berries here (cf. N. 27.29) shows that Flaminio is thinking of Hedera Chrysocarpa (the much more common Hedera Helix has black berries).

16. *Bracchiolum* (diminutive): Catull. 61.174.

18. *Viderat* is pluperfect for imperfect.

19. *Frigidulus* (diminutive; also in 3.21.1 and three other lines of Flaminio): Catull. 64.131, as well as in [Verg.] *Cir.* 250 and 347. The notion of cool water burning is Petrarchan.

22. Hyblaean honey: 3.16.1n.

23–40. The theme of someone's song or music charming nature (wildlife, trees, rivers, etc.) is a commonplace, especially associated with Orpheus, but found of others. Here (31–34) the deities too are affected (cf., for example, N. 18.9–10). See 4.15.7–14n.

23. Cf. Verg. *Ecl.* 8.4, where, enchanted by dulcet rustic music, streams *requierunt . . . cursus* ("arrested their course"). In Hor. *Odes* 1.12.9–10 Orpheus' singing halts rivers.

24. By "unequal reeds" (*calamis imparibus*) Flaminio means panpipes. Cf. Verg. *Ecl.* 2.32–33 and 36–37.

25–26. *Latonia virgo* (Verg. *Aen.* 11.557): Latona was the mother of Diana and Apollo (by Jupiter). Pales (also 4.2.29, 4.10.1, 4.16.45, and 4.20.1): N. 11.2n. "Tegean" is for Arcadian, Tegea being a town in Arcadia. Fla-

359

## · NOTES TO THE TRANSLATIONS ·

minio calls Pan *Tegeaeus* again (after Prop. 3.3.30) in 6.10.2 and *Pater Tegeaeus* in 2.7.67.

28. In Verg. *Ecl.* 8.2 a heifer, hearing delightful rustic song, forgets to eat the grass. The diminutive *haedulus* is found in an ancient poet only in Juv. 11.66.

29. Birds are *pictae* (lit., "painted") in Verg. *Aen.* 4.525.

30. In 5.49.36–37 a laurel wood "learns" Apollo's songs. Elision in final dactyl (cf. 4.11.14, 4.19.12).

32. Faunus: Pan (3.1.1n).

33–40. Love (Cupid) is himself in love with Celia in some poems of Angeriano's *Erotopaegnion*.

38. See 4.5.2.

40. For "drinking in" with the ear (of eager listening), cf. Hor. *Odes* 2.13.32; Prop. 3.4.8.

41–42. Amaryllis (another in 3.5 and 3.6; cf. N. 25.19n) is here a shepherdess. The Mincio (also 1.30.8, 2.7.62, and 2.36.1) flows southward out of the Lago di Garda to join the Po ten miles southeast of Mantua, which it surrounds on three sides. The Mincio is called *populifer* ("poplar-lined") in Niccolò d'Arco, *Numeri* 2.16.15, a poem addressed to Flaminio; see d'Arco 1762, 77–78; Flaminio 1743, 348; Maddison 1965, 91. In Verg. *G.* 4.511 a nightingale sings *populea . . . sub umbra* ("under the shade of a poplar").

43. Galatea (also 4.17.11) is the sea nymph who loved the youth Acis and aroused the jealousy of the Cyclops Polyphemus, who killed him (Ov. *Met.* 13.750–897). The episode is here made into something of a short epyllion down to the end of 66.

47. *Male* negates *caute*: N. 36.3–4n.

51. *Oreades* (again 4.16.22) were mountain nymphs. In this Greek nominative the *-es* is short.

54. Doris was Galatea's mother (by Nereus, a sea god).

69. Weaving shade (here an arbor): 3.19.5n. Cf. also Sannazaro, *Elegies* 2.8.19–20, *viridi texant umbracula quercu / . . . Dryades* ("Let dryads weave an arbor from green oak").

360

### · NOTES TO THE TRANSLATIONS ·

71. Scattering baskets full of flowers: N. 2.3–4n.

73. River gods (e.g., Naucelus/Noncello, who is represented in an engraving on the title page of Navagero 1530) were often portrayed leaning on an urn from which their waters flowed.

74. *Lacrimula* ("little tear," also 4.6.14 and N. 65.20) is a diminutive used by Catullus (66.74).

76–77. Cf. 4.9.3–4 for the associations of violets with death. The "hyacinth" (not, however, the flower now known by that name; see further 4.22.24n) supposedly sprang from the blood of the dead youth Hyacinthus, accidentally killed by a discus hurled by his lover Apollo (Ov. *Met.* 10.162–219), and bore on its petals (as Ovid explains in 215–16 there; cf. Moschus 3.6–7) the letters *Ai, Ai,* a Greek cry of lamentation; cf. 4.6.11–12 below. The cypress was sacred to Pluto and used at funerals. Cf., for instance, Verg. *Aen.* 3.64 and 6.216; Ov. *Tr.* 3.13.21. By contrast, the smiling pot marigold and red rose are cheery flowers.

80. A naiad is a water nymph; a dryad, a wood nymph.

83. *Flebilis umor* (lit., "tearful wetness," i.e., tears) seems not to come from an ancient source. Flaminio uses the word *flebilis* in six other lines in this book (4.6.12, 4.11.4, 4.15.19, 4.17.1 and 74, 4.23.6) and several more times elsewhere in his poems.

### 4.6

1–2. Pomona was the goddess of fruit and fruit trees. For the construction see 3.9.1–4n. The words after *dic* could be treated as a direct or an indirect question.

3. Vanishing into thin air: Verg. *Aen.* 4.278; Ov. *Fast.* 2.509; Lucr. 1.1087; etc. (cf. N. 34.11). Air is "thin" many times in Ovid and Vergil; cf. also N. 23.5.

5–6. *Calathus* can mean the "cup" (calyx) of a flower as well as (more commonly) a "flower basket." In 5.8.67–68 Flaminio speaks of roses "not opening their beautiful cups" (*non pandunt . . . rosae . . . formosos calathos*). Cf. 4.16.38–39 (and 2.5.15, *rosa vix laetum calathi pandebat honorem*, "the

361

## · NOTES TO THE TRANSLATIONS ·

rose was barely opening the glory of its cup"). All are after [Auson.] *Id.*
14.31, the poem on budding roses once ascribed to Vergil (see N. 37n),
*ridentis calathi patefecit honorem* ("it opened up the glory of its smiling
cup"). *Lucidulae:* 4.5.2 and 38n.

10. *Silva* here may unusually mean a single tree rather than a wood or
orchard, though perhaps Hyella's garden had room for a group of citron
trees.

11–12. For the sad marks on the hyacinth (Ov. *Met.* 10.206–8), see 4.5.76–
77n. In his poem *De Hercule et Hyla* (2.6), Flaminio has (line 40) *et te fle-
bilibus scriptum, hyacinthe, notis* ("and you, hyacinth, inscribed with marks
of mourning"). *Folia* here = "petals" (N. 13.8n).

13. *Vivax apium* ("long-living parsley"): Hor. *Odes* 1.36.16. I have not
found *croceum* of the poppy in an ancient poet.

14. See 4.5.74n. *Panace* for *panacea* (the mythical "cure-all"), if correct
(*panacea suis* could conceivably be read), must be based on variant forms
of proper names like *Calliopea/Calliope*. In ancient authors, the word is
*panacea* (Verg. *Aen.* 12.419; Luc. 9.918; Greek *panakeia*), *panaces* (Greek
*panakes*, neuter sing.), or *panax* (masc. sing.; *panaces* in Lucr. 4.123 is its
plural).

### 4.7

Poems 7–11 are discussed as a group by Maddison 1965, 101–2. This poem
is included in Canoniero 1613, 465–66 (headed *Hyellae*, [Epitaph] Of
Hyella), followed by 4.9 and 4.11 (both headed, *Eiusdem*, Of the Same),
and then by 4.12 (headed *Capellae Hyellae*, Of Hyella's She-Goat) and
4.24 (headed *Eiusdem*).

5. Perhaps cf. Prop. 1.20.39, where Hylas boyishly plucks lilies "with his
young nail."

9. Stat. *Theb.* 7.301 has *primae . . . in flore iuventae* ("in the flower of first
youth"); Cicero, in fr. 3 of his poems, has *primo . . . a flore iuventae* ("from
the first flower of youth"). Precisely *primo sub flore iuventae* is found in
some other Neo-Latin passages (e.g., Molza, *Varia* 19.70, of the painter
Raphael, dead at thirty-seven, lamented as Daphnis), and several close

## · NOTES TO THE TRANSLATIONS ·

variations are found, such as *aetatis primo sub flore* of Marcantonio della Torre, dead at around thirty, in Fracastoro, *Syphilis* 1.459. Flaminio has *primo vix flore iuventae* ("barely in, etc.") in 2.5.3. Cf. N. 40.1.

11–12. Imagined wayfarer: 4.10.17–20n; N. 50.1n.

### 4.8

4. Elision in last dactyl of pentameter.

5. *Meam . . . iuventam . . . miseris* is literally "have sent my youth."

9–10. In Verg. *Aen.* 6.441 the "Mourning Fields" (*Campi Lugentes*) are the Underworld abode of those who suffered in life from the cruelties of love.

12. Lethe: Underworld River of Forgetfulness, of which, according to believers in reincarnation, souls drank to erase memories of their former life.

16. After Verg. *Aen.* 6.429 and 11.28, *abstulit . . . et funere mersit acerbo* ("bore off . . . and immersed in bitter death," where "bitter" means untimely; see 4.21.4n).

### 4.9

See 4.7n.

1. See 4.4.4n.

3–4. Violets, wine, and milk figure as offerings to the dead also in 4.11.2–3. See also 4.16.13n. For the associations of violets, cf. 4.5.77.

### 4.10

Meter: Iambic strophe (trimeter alternating with dimeter).

1–4. Construction (cf. lines 17–20): 3.9.1–4n. For *bicornis* ("two-horned") in 1, cf. N. 20.15n.

5–6. Cf. 3.29.3–4.

7. Cf. Tib. 2.5.30, *garrula . . . fistula* ("chattersome/vocal pipe").

9–10. A luster was five years. One's third luster would end on reaching fifteen.

363

## · NOTES TO THE TRANSLATIONS ·

11–14. The past tenses can be seen as gnomic.

17–20. For the imagined wayfarer (here the passing shepherd addressed in line 3), see N. 50.1n. A wish or prayer for the earth to lie lightly on a deceased person's body (as Tib. 2.4.50; Prop. 1.17.24; Ov. *Am.* 3.9.68; Mart. 5.34.9–10) is commonly found on tombstones, often as an abbreviation *S.T.T.L.*, for *sit tibi terra levis* ("Be the earth light for you"), and figures in many Neo-Latin passages. Sprinkling flowers on a tomb or grave is also frequently mentioned (e.g., Verg. *Aen.* 5.79, 6.885; N. 18.5; Marullo, *Epigrams* 1.33.5). In view of 4.11.2, with *hanc* (20) understand *terram* rather than *puellam*. *Spargito* in 20 is second imperative (4.1.26n); *precare* (18) and *abi* (20) are first imperatives. For the construction see 3.9.1–4n. A brief epitaph for Euripides in Canoniero 1613, 34–35, ends by bidding the wayfarer *diu felix . . . abi* (lit., "depart long [to be] happy").

### 4.11

See 4.7n. For the devoted nanny goat celebrated here, see also 4.12 and 4.13.1.

2–3. See 4.9.3–4n.

12. After being guided to the body of her murdered father Icarus (or Icarius) by the dog Maera (rewarded by being turned into the Dog Star), Erigone hanged herself in grief.

13–14. Strictly, *tua magna fides* is the subject of *audet* ("If your great loyalty dares"). Elision in final dactyl in 14 (as in 4.5.30, 4.19.12).

### 4.12

Translated by Maddison 1965, 102. See 4.11 and 4.13.1 for the same nanny goat. See also 4.7n.

5–6. Pylades, Orestes, and Pirithous are types of utterly devoted friends in numerous ancient and Neo-Latin passages (e.g., Ov. *Tr.* 1.9.27–28 and 31–32, *Pont.* 2.6.25–26 and 3.2.69–70, *Rem. am.* 589; Cic. *Amic.* 24; Ugolino Verino, *Flammetta* 2.40.11–12 and 2.45.65–66). Pylades eventually married Orestes' sister, Electra. Pirithous supported Theseus in various

364

## · NOTES TO THE TRANSLATIONS ·

adventures, ending up imprisoned in the Underworld for accompanying him there in an attempt to carry off its queen, Proserpina (Persephone). *I nunc (et)* is similarly used several times in Ovid (e.g., *Her.* 3.26, 9.105, 12.204, 17.57; *Ars am.* 2.22; *Pont.* 1.3.61) and elsewhere (e.g., Prop. 2.19.22, 3.18.17) and much imitated in Neo-Latin poets. The sense here is that the goat's devotion eclipses that of these much-talked-of mythical figures (the plurals generalize). *Amoris nomine* is literally "in the name of love" or "on love's account."

### 4.13

Perosa/Sparrow 1979, 289. Briefly noticed by Maddison 1965, 102.

4 (and 4.17.29). Cerberus, the three-headed dog that guarded the entrance to the Underworld, had snakes as a mane ringing his neck (or else snakes as a tail).

### 4.14

1. In Ov. *Fast.* 1.441 birds are *solacia ruris*.

2. For *Elysias domos* cf. Ov. *Met.* 14.111.

4. For *pro se quisque* (lit., "each for himself," i.e., as much or as well as he could), cf., for example, Verg. *Aen.* 12.552; Ov. *Met.* 3.642; Plaut. *Amph.* 231; Ter. *Haut.* 126.

### 4.15

Meter: Iambic trimeters.

1. *Hospes* ("stranger") denotes an imagined wayfarer (N. 50.1n).

2. Fourth foot tribrach.

6. See 3.4.4n.

7–14. The entranced attention of the breeze, streams, birds, wolf, and trees is like that in several passages concerned with Orpheus (e.g., Hor. *Odes* 1.12.7–12; Prop. 3.2.3–4; Ov. *Met.* 11.1–4., *Ars am.* 3.321–22). See 4.5.23–40n, 4.5.23n, 4.17.25n.

365

## · NOTES TO THE TRANSLATIONS ·

12–13. The Himella mentioned in Verg. *Aen.* 7.714 is the River Aia in the Sabine territory, about 160 miles from Monte Taburno (4.1.5n) and far too remote to be meant here. The context implies that Himella must denote a location in the vicinity of Taburno, but I cannot find any such Himella (or Imella) on maps. In Ov. *Tr.* 5.6.38 Mt. Hybla in Attica, famous for bees, is *florida*, an indication that Himella here need not be a stream. Although grammatically the singular *tu* in 13 picks up only *Taburne* from 12, it seems that *tu testis* has to be understood also with the vocative *Himella florida*, otherwise left hanging.

15. Fifth foot anapaest. See 4.2.13–14n.

16. The use of *terunt* ("rub") is after Verg. *Ecl.* 2.34, *calamo trivisse labellum* ("to rub your lip on a reed"), echoed by Pontano in *Eclogues* 1, Pompa 7, line 59. Cf. F. 5.8.37 for another debt to that line of Vergil, *calamo terit labellum* ("rubs her lip on a reed").

20. See 4.8.16n and 4.21.4n.

21. Hiatus between *basiari* and *expetens*, perhaps with correption (shortening) of the unelided *i*. The hiatus could be avoided by reading *illo* between the two words.


### 4.16

Meter: Iambic trimeters.

3. Monte Taburno (called *pinifer* in 4.15.12): 4.1.5n.

8–9. Fifth foot anapaest in 8, third foot anapaest in 9. See 4.2.13–14n.

10. Hermus: the river in Asia Minor that Verg. *G.* 2.137 calls *auro turbidus* ("thick with gold"). It is now the Gediz, flowing into the Gulf of Izmir.

13. For the wine, milk, and blood offering, cf. Verg. *Aen.* 5.76–79. Cf. 4.9.3–4n. Lyaeus = Bacchus (here wine); N. 11.1n.

19. Name *Alcon*: Verg. *Ecl.* 5.11; [Verg.] *Cul.* 67; Ov. *Met.* 13.683. *Capripes* (also 4.2.29, as well as 1.2.13, of Pan, and 1.13.24, of fauns): N. 18.3–4n. In 1.17.23 Iolas' (i.e., Flaminio's) pipe is given him by "greatest Alcon," there seemingly a pseudonym, here perhaps just an imagined rustic musician, unless the same poet is tacitly hinted.

# · NOTES TO THE TRANSLATIONS ·

21–27. For the sympathetic grieving of nature at Hyella's death, cf. N. 10A.11–12n and 20.11–12n.

22. An oread (22) is a mountain nymph (also 4.5.51).

23. The imagery of leaves = "hair" (*coma* or *comae*) of trees is common in ancient and Neo-Latin verse. Just in his *lusus pastorales* Flaminio uses it also in 3.2.9, 3.17.6, 3.26.2, 4.2.9, 4.6.10, 4.11.18, 4.16.12, and 4.16.46 (cf. also the "unshorn" hills in 3.4.1). Here the trees' "hair" (leaves) is "shorn" (shed) in grief, just as human mourners might cut their hair short.

25–26. Cf. Verg. *Aen.* 4.367, *cautibus duris horrens Caucasus* ("Caucasus rugged with hard crags").

28–30. It seems that the normally cruel Cupid (himself in love with Hyella in 4.5.33–38) feels guilt over Hyella's death from a broken heart after her rejection by Iolas, whom Cupid made her love. In Pontano, *Tumuli* 2.56.1–4, Cupid breaks his bow in sorrow at a girl's death.

34. *Amico rore* (lit., "with kindly dew") seems influenced by Verg. G. 4.115, where plants are watered with *amici imbres* ("kindly showers").

38–39. After [Ausonius]; see 4.6.5–6n. *Calathi* makes a fifth foot anapaest (4.2.13–14n).

42. "Skills worthy of the Cyprian goddess" (Venus, whose sacred isle Cyprus was; N. 13.3–4n) may seem to sit awkwardly with praise here of Hyella's *simplices mores* ("guileless character") and the general picture given of her as a virtuous and delightful girl of fourteen, as such "skills" might normally be taken to refer to sexual know-how. Presumably Flaminio here means only that Hyella's (innocent) accomplishments were charming and appealing (*venustae*). Cf. Ov. *Rem. am.* 713 for *mores* coupled with *artes*.

45–46. Pales: 4.2.29n and N. 11.2n. For *comantium* see on line 23.

47. Phoebus' sister: Diana.

48–49. With *levi . . . calamo* ("on a light reed pipe"; again F. 5.37) cf. Verg. *Ecl.* 5.2 and G. 2.358.

50 (and 4.17.20). The Maenalus Mountains in Arcadia were associated with Pan.

367

## · NOTES TO THE TRANSLATIONS ·

53. For "naiad sisters" (water nymphs) cf. N. 31.1 and Marullo, *Epigrams* 4.13.1–2. For such adjectival use, cf. Verg. *Ecl.* 10.10, *puellae Naides* ("naiad girls"), and precisely *sorores Naides* (there of the Muses) in [Verg.] *Cul.* 18. Other nymphs are "sisters" in, e.g., Prop. 2.32.37 (hamadryad sisters); N. 31.31 and 50.7.

55. Fifth foot anapaest. See 4.2.13–14n. Flaminio similarly has *lacrimabiles morbos* in 1.2.122–23.

### 4.17

Maddison 1965, 102–3, briefly summarizes 4.17–4.24, except for 4.20. Gruter 1608 and (in consequence?) *Carmina Illustrium Poetarum Italorum* 4:407 treat 99–104 as a new poem.

5. See N. 54.3–4n. For *vaga fama* cf. Ov. *Her.* 21.233 and *Met.* 8.267.

6. Vergilian epithets: *G.* 1.1 has *laetas segetes* ("joyous crops"), while *pinguia* describes farmlands in several lines of the *Eclogues* and *Georgics*.

9. Menalcas must here denote Vergil, as he is paired with Theocritus (see 4.17.12n), and some (seemingly including Flaminio) have supposed Vergil to mean himself by Menalcas in *Ecl.* 5 and 9, though that view is now disputed. Thus *Menalcas* is used for Vergil in Pontano, *Lyra* 4.12. Vergil is sometimes similarly denoted by *Tityrus* (after *Ecl.* 1), as, for example, Mantuan, *Eclogues* 2.8–9. See further N. 39n for the name *Menalcas*.

11. Galatea was a sea nymph. Verg. *Ecl.* 7.37 calls her *Nerine Galatea* ("Galatea, daughter of Nereus"). Here, however, she is called *Neptunine* ("daughter of Neptune"), used as an ablative with a Greek dative ending. Bembo, *Galatea* 7.13, has (of Galatea), "I love you alone of all the daughters of Neptune (*de cunctis Neptuninis*)." The word *Neptunine* is from Catull. 64.28, where it is one reading found in MSS, describing Achilles' mother, Thetis. Most modern editions of Catullus reject *Neptunine* in favor of *Nereine*, making Thetis "daughter of Nereus." She is *Nereis . . . Thetis*, "the Nereid Thetis," in Tib. 1.5.45–46.

12. Thalia is used for "muse." The "old Sicilian" is Theocritus. The Cyclops Polyphemus sings a song to Galatea in Theoc. *Id.* 11.

368

# · NOTES TO THE TRANSLATIONS ·

15–16. Both the mountains Pindus in Thessaly and Parnassus in central Greece had associations with the Muses or Apollo. Arcadia: 3.20.10n.

17–18. Carving on trees: N. 6.6–8n.

19–20. Amphion's music caused the walls of Thebes to form (Hor. *Odes* 3.11.2). Aracynthus, a mountain between Boeotia and Attica in central Greece, is mentioned in Verg. *Ecl.* 2.24 as once a haunt of Amphion. Hiatus in fifth foot, similar to that in Vergil's line, ending *in Actaeo Aracyntho*. Maenalian (20): 4.16.50n. Monte Taburno ("great father" in 21): 4.1.5n.

25. The Thracian Orpheus' music had the power to draw rocks, trees, and beasts after him. For him see N. 25.51–52n.

27 (48 and 54). Orcus is an alternative name for Pluto or his Underworld domain, where Orpheus went to try to bring back his dead wife, Eurydice. The dead are "the silent ones" (*silentes*) in, e.g., Ov. *Met.* 5.356, 13.25, 15.772 and 797; Val. Flacc. 1.750.

29–30. Cerberus: 4.13.4n. The Eumenides are the Furies, the avenging goddesses (including Tisiphone in line 36) with snakes for hair.

32. See 4.18.5–6n for "violent Death" (or "a violent death"). In Ov. *Met.* 10.697 Cybele thinks of plunging two offenders beneath the waters of Styx, the river that souls of the dead had to cross to enter the Underworld.

36. The accusative of *Tisiphone* should be the Greek first declension form *Tisiphonen*, but *Tisiphonem* is found also in, e.g., Sannazaro, *De Partu Virginis* 1.35. In classical Latin, Greek female names in final eta (e.g., Penelope, Danae, Circe, Daphne) should not have this Latin accusative in *m*, but that form is sometimes found (as well as the true form in *n*) in MSS. Neo-Latin poets seem to have substituted final *m* for *n* quite often in such names.

39. *Cythereius ales* (lit., "the Cytherean bird"), here of Cupid, denotes the dove in Sil. 3.683. Cf. Claud. 33.77, *Cyllenius ales* ("the Cyllenian bird" or "winged Cyllenian") of Mercury.

41–42. Ceres' daughter was Proserpina, also called Persephone (again 4.19.19; N. 26.35–36n). The story of her abduction by her uncle Pluto is

369

## · NOTES TO THE TRANSLATIONS ·

told by Ovid (*Met.* 5.385–424) and Claudian ("Rape of Proserpine"). Erebus: Underworld.

44. Enna (or Henna) in Sicily was where the abduction of Proserpina took place.

46. *Vincla* ("fetters" or "fastenings") means "sandals" here, as in Tib. 1.5.66; Ov. *Fast.* 1.410, 2.324, and 3.823. *Pede* ("foot") is sing. for plural. *Luridus Orcus* (here = Pluto, as in 27 and 54) is from Hor. *Odes* 3.4.74 (where it denotes the Underworld).

50. *Violentus amor* (or possibly *Amor*): N. 36.5 has *Amor . . . violentus*.

53. *O qui* is used as in Verg. *G.* 2.488, *O qui me . . . sistat!* ("O for someone to set me, etc.!"), a virtual wish (cf. N. 59.27–29n).

61. Syrinx: the nymph beloved of Pan who was changed into a reed.

62. Cyparissus, a youth beloved of Apollo, became the cypress when he died of grief after accidentally killing a stag to which he was devoted (Ov. *Met.* 10.121–42).

63–64. The youthful Phrygian shepherd Attis, best known from Catullus 63, was the beloved of the mother-goddess Cybele. In one version of his story he became her priest but broke a vow of chastity and in insanity castrated himself. Cybele's priests were therefore eunuchs. In line 63 most texts have *Cybele*, which could be Greek dative (though that form seems unused by ancient Latin poets) or possibly be used for the Latin dative *Cybelae* (printed in Gagny ca. 1548), which is one reading in Verg. *Aen.* 11.768; *Cybele* is another, though the modern preference is sometimes for *Cybelo*, the name of the mountain used for the goddess. Cf. *Neptunine* in line 11 above for a Greek dative in *e*.

65. Mt. Berecyntus in Phrygia was associated with Cybele, here treated as Pluto's mother, Cybele being identified, as often, with the Cretan mother-goddess Rhea.

67. In 1.2.101–2 Pan's mother gives birth to him "after nine months' *fastidia*." The source is Verg. *Ecl.* 4.61: "Ten months brought long discomfort (*fastidia*) to your mother."

68. Dis (also 4.4.19) = Pluto.

370

# · NOTES TO THE TRANSLATIONS ·

70. Tithonus (and Aurora): N. 37.1n.

74. *Flebilis* (4.5.83n) may mean "lamentable" (i.e., to be wept over) or "tearful" (i.e., in tears). I have preferred the former sense (perhaps supported by 84?), though the ghost could be tearful at having to return to the Underworld.

87. "Glory" here = leaves. See *frondis honore* in N. 23.6. *Glacialis hiems* is after Verg. *Aen.* 3.285.

89–90. The theme of the setting sun returning the next day in contrast with our eternal night of death is probably best known from Catull. 5.4–6. The brevity of life and the irreversibility of inevitable death commonly feature in passages urging enjoyment of life and love while still possible, e.g., Tib. 1.1.69–70; Prop. 2.15.23–24. Horace reflects on the perpetual night of death as (all too soon) the common lot of all in *Odes* 1.4.15–17, 1.28.15–16, and 4.7.13.

92. After Verg. *Aen.* 6.429 (and 11.28), "whom the black day bore off and plunged in bitter death (*funere mersit acerbo*)."

93–94. The Fates gather in a man's last threads in Verg. *Aen.* 10.814–15 (*extrema . . . Parcae fila legunt*). *Ultima fila*: Sil. 4.28. Death as an unending sleep: Catull. 5.6, though Hor. *Odes* 1.24.5–6, *Quintilium perpetuus sopor urget* ("eternal sleep weighs on Q."), is particularly echoed here.

96. The idea of surviving *invita Morte* ("against Death's will") is also in 2.4.14. Immortality conferred by celebration in verse is a common notion. See 4.17.98n for an instance, as well as 4.1.27–28.

97. Alexis is the beautiful youth beloved of Corydon, formerly taken by some to stand for the poet himself (cf., for example, Sannazaro, *Piscatory Eclogues* 4.69) in Verg. *Ecl.* 2 and 7. The context here seems to imply that Flaminio saw Alexis as masking Vergil's own supposed beloved, a slave boy called Alexander. Martial alludes to the tradition in 6.68.5–6 and 8.56 [8.55].12–16.

98. Lycoris was the mistress of the elegiac poet Gaius Cornelius Gallus. Cf. Ov. *Am.* 1.15.29–30 for the preservation of her memory through Gallus' verse, now lost.

371

## · NOTES TO THE TRANSLATIONS ·

### 4.18

1. Cf. Ov. *Met.* 10.402–3, *suspiria duxit ab imo pectore* ("drew [i.e., heaved] sighs from the bottom of her heart").

3–4 and 11–12. Burial of lovers together: 3.12.9–10n. The notion of dead lovers mingling bones (4) is from Prop. 4.7.94, where Cynthia's ghost tells the poet that after his death he will be entirely hers and *mixtis ossibus ossa teram* ("I will grind bones on mingled bones"). In that context intimate ghostly embraces seem probably to be envisaged, though here, in view of line 11, 4.20.15, and 4.24.10, Flaminio appears to be thinking merely of burial in the same grave (some have understood Propertius that way). For what seem Iolas' thoughts of suicide, cf. line 6 here, 4.19.12–14, 4.20.11–12, and 4.22.26–34 and 47–55, though sometimes he speaks of dying otherwise in his misery, while in 4.23.13–14 he wishes rather to live to go on celebrating Hyella.

5–6. Hymen was the marriage god (cf. 4.19.20). "Violent Death" (or "a violent death") may here, as perhaps in 4.17.32, imply thoughts of suicide, though lines of Flaminio's nephew Gabriele ending his poem 9, *Ad Lalagen*, call death *violenta* in a general way; see Flaminio 1743, 471. Death is likewise desribed in Sannazaro, *Elegies* 2.9.24, and Sen. *Troad.* 1172. *Violentus* occurs as an epithet of love (or Love) too (4.17.50 above).

7–8. As far as we are told, Iolas' unloved and discounted wife Nisa is still alive, though he speaks of being buried with Hyella (4 and 11–12 here) and being with her as husband in Elysium (4.19.15–18). For *conscendit . . . cubile* cf. *Iovis . . . ascendere cubile* ("to climb Jupiter's bed") in Verg. *Aen.* 12.144, and *regni scande cubile mei* ("climb the bed of my kingship," i.e., "become my royal consort") in Prop. 4.4.90.

9–10. For Iolas' father's part in his reluctant marriage to Nisa, cf. 4.19.9–10.

12. *Felix* is meant as in Verg. *Ecl.* 5.65 (*sis bonus o felixque tuis*, "O be good and favorable to your own people!") and *Aen.* 1.330 (*sis felix* to the disguised Venus), i.e., "well-disposed" or "kind." Cf. Turnus' plea to the spirits of the dead, the Manes, to be *boni* to him in death, *Aen.* 12.646–47, reflected here in 4.19.14.

## · NOTES TO THE TRANSLATIONS ·

### 4.19

Wrongly run together with the previous and the following poems in Gagny ca. 1548 through confusion caused by the fact that in its source, Flaminio 1548, both 4.18 and this poem end at the foot of a page, and a new poem (unheaded) starts on the next.

3 and 7. Iolas stresses his own physical attractiveness also in 4.22.19–21 (his former white and red complexion and once beautiful hair).

5. *Quis* is ablative plural (= *quibus*).

9. *Ahne* (or *Ah ne*) very awkwardly appends the enclitic interrogative particle *ne* to an interjection, something I cannot parallel. Flaminio perhaps did not see *ne* here as enclitic; in early texts and MSS it would often be separated by a space from the preceding word.

12. Elision in final dactyl of pentameter (as in 4.5.30, 4.11.14).

14. See 4.18.12n.

15 and 17. *Vos* and *qui* take number and gender from *manes* ("ghost," masc. pl. in Latin) in 14.

19–20. Proserpina: 4.17.41–42n. Hymen: 4.18.5n.

21. Imagery of the chains of love is generally of enslavement through abject infatuation, but for the positive notion here of being united by a strong chain in the sense of a faithful bond, cf. Prop. 2.15.25–26.

### 4.20

See 4.19n.

1. Pales: 4.2.29n and N. 11.2n.

2. Monte Taburno: 4.1.5n.

6. Girl worthy of Jupiter: N. 19.24n.

7. *Fulserunt . . . soles* ("sunlight shone") recalls Catull. 8.3 and 8.

11. For *o dulcissima rerum* (lit., "O sweetest of things"), cf. the masculine equivalent, *dulcissime rerum*, in Hor. *Sat.* 1.9.4 and expressions like *o pulcherrime* (or *pulcherrima*) *rerum*, found in Ovid and Vergil, etc.

## · NOTES TO THE TRANSLATIONS ·

12. "My life" (see N. 55.40–41n) here means Hyella, as the next line reveals.

15–16. Burial together: 3.12.9–10n (and 4.18.3–4 and 11–12n). *Urna*, strictly an urn, often seems a convenient synonym for "grave" or "tomb."

### 4.21

Meter: Iambic trimeters. There are seven anapaestic feet (normally rare) in this short poem, in the following lines, with the anapaestic feet indicated in parentheses: 1 (5), 7 (1), 9 (3), 11 (5), 14 (5), 16 (1), and 18 (3). See 4.2.13–14n. Cuccoli 1897, 223, commenting on the Petrarchism discernible in this poem and 4.20 (i.e., the equation of the beloved with the sun), observes that Flaminio here "almost literally translates" *Eclogue* 12.203–13 of Sannazaro's *Arcadia*, which he quotes in his footnote (beginning *Ingrato sol, per cui ti affretti a nascere? / Tua luce a me che val, s'io più non godala?*). I am not aware that Flaminio draws on the *Arcadia* so distinctly and extensively anywhere else in his *lusus pastorales*, which makes his close imitation here the more noteworthy.

4. *Hunc*, literally, "this boy/man," stands for *me*. A "bitter" death (*mors acerba*) often means an untimely one (as in 4.15.20); cf., for example, Verg. *Aen.* 6.429.

16. *Inhorrescunt* here has the rare sense that *horresco* has in Lucr. 6.26.1 and Sil. 1.134 ("become dreadful").

17. The beloved as a metaphorical sun: N. 38n.

### 4.22

Meter: Choliambic (limping iambic), the last foot being a trochee or a spondee instead of an iambus. Catullus and Martial employ this meter frequently. Flaminio employs it also in 1.10 and 1.26.

1–3. The myrtle overhangs the cave like the poplar in Verg. *Ecl.* 9.41–42. *Myrte* is vocative, like *antrum* and *fons* in the next two lines (*antrum* in 2 picking up *antro* in 1, and *fons* in 3 picking up *fonte* in 2). *Loquax* of flowing water ("babbling"): Hor. *Odes* 3.13.15 (*loquaces lymphae*).

## · NOTES TO THE TRANSLATIONS ·

4–5. *Quoad* scans as two syllables in 4, but as one (by synizesis) in 5, as it does in Lucr. 2.849; Hor. *Sat.* 2.3.91.

12. Tartarus was the Underworld place of punishment for the wicked.

13. Light is *alma* in Verg. *Aen.* 1.306, 3.311, 8.455, and 11.182–83; Ov. *Met.* 15.664. For the image of "clothing" with light, cf. Lucr. 2.147–48; Verg. *Aen.* 6.640.

14. Night is *placida* in Verg. *Aen.* 7.427. When *rigare* and *irrigare* are used figuratively of sleep, one construction found involves flooding persons, lands, etc. (acc.) *with* sleep (abl.); the other, flooding or diffusing sleep (acc.) over them (dat.). The former construction is seen here. Cf. Ugolino Verino, *Flammetta* 1.26.11. Verg. *Aen.* 3.511, *fessos sopor irrigat artus* ("sleep floods over weary limbs"), is a variation with sleep the subject. Instances of the alternative construction include F. 5.44.3–4, *quietem dum terris sopor irrigat* ("while sleep diffuses rest over the earth"). A variation is seen in Verg. *Aen.* 1.692–93, *Venus Ascanio placidam per membra quietem / irrigat* ("Venus diffuses peaceful rest over Ascanius' limbs," lit., "over his limbs for Ascanius").

18. *Est* here is from *edere* ("to eat").

20–21. For admired white and red complexions, see 3.18.8 and 3.27.

23. *Modis . . . miris* literally = "in wondrous wise" (a common expression).

24. *Hyacinthino flore* (beginning with a fourth foot anapaest; see 4.2.13–14n) is after *flos hyacinthinus* in Catull. 61.93. The "hyacinth" meant is not ours (see 4.5.76–77n); its color is deep red in Verg. *Ecl.* 3.63, G. 4.183; and Ov. *Met.* 10.213).

25. The diminutive *hispidulus*, not ancient, is found in Poliziano, *In Scabiem* 167.

26–60. From 26–48 Iolas addresses himself, reverting to the first person in 49, then using the third (*Iolas*) in 51, and finally apostrophizing Hyella in 57–60.

31. *Quis* = *quibus*.

32. Literally, "the water of encircling Tethys," where Tethys (see N. 38.4n) = the sea, here pictured as surrounding Elysium. Flaminio may show influence from the description in Hom. *Od.* 4.561–69 of the Isles of

## · NOTES TO THE TRANSLATIONS ·

the Blessed (there set at the world's end rather than in the Underworld), where a cooling breeze from the ocean blows on them.

34. Streams of milk: 4.3.15–16n.

38. Myrtle sacred to Venus: N. 6.6–8n.

43. Here the sex of Spring (grammatically, *ver* is neuter) is not apparent, as in 2.33.1, though Maddison's translation of 2.33 makes it male; see Maddison 1965, 17. See N. 25.3–4n for Spring as a boy.

45. Flora (3.5.2n) is presumably called Spring's as the first appearance of flowers is associated with that season.

46. The image of "snowing" with roses (i.e., scattering them) is from Lucr. 2.628–29.

51 and 53. Does Iolas stab himself at the end of this poem, as 53's mention of staining the woods with his blood might suggest, or just envisage doing so? See 4.18.3–4 and 11–12n. Actual suicide here is possible only if 4.23 and 4.24 (with Iolas still alive in both) are out of chronological sequence. Maddison 1965, 98–103, takes it that Iolas dies, but does not clarify how. Summarizing 4.24, she speaks of Iolas as awaiting death, presumably meaning one from pining away, not suicide. In 4.23.12 Iolas pleads for a natural death, but 4.23.13 asks rather for long life to praise Hyella (oddly said, as he is there giving his pipes to Pan).

54. The "milky dew" would be a libation (3.14.5, 4.1.8, 4.9.4, 4.11.4, 4.16.13).

58. *Misero* makes a third foot anapaest (see 4.2.13–14n).

### 4.23

1. *Silvipotens:* N. 14.3n. The opening sentence here has no verb (understand "dedicates").

2. See 3.4.4n.

3. Cytherea: 3.28.1–2n.

4. After Verg. *Aen.* 6.442 ("those whom harsh love ate away [= consumed] with cruel wasting," *crudeli tabe peredit*), said of the victims of

376

## · NOTES TO THE TRANSLATIONS ·

unhappiness in love (including Dido) in the *Lugentes Campi* ("Mourning Fields") in the Underworld. *Iacet* (lit., "lies") must mean "is dead" in this context.

7. *Invisere* is found with *ad* plus accusative and a further accusative in passages of Roman comedy, e.g., Plaut. *Capt.* 458, *ad fratrem modo captivos alios inviso meos* ("I'll just look in at my brother's to see my other captives"). *Imas . . . ad umbras*: Verg. *Aen.* 6.404.

13. *Formosus* ("handsome") seems odd in this context, but perhaps, in view of *pulcher Iolas* in line 1 and *formosus Iolas* in 4.24.1, "handsome" is almost a stock epithet of Iolas.

### 4.24

See 4.7n.

2. *Madidis . . . genis* takes the epithet from Ov. *Ars am.* 1.660.

3. This line is reused from 2.2.8 (within Flaminio's *Ianthis*, a pastoral poem of twenty-five verses, published in 1529, in which the girl Mopse rejoices at the return of the much-missed young shepherd Ianthis).

5–8. *Umbrae*, basically "shadows," can mean "trees" in verse. Here it has to denote "shading foliage."

10. See 3.12.9–10n. *Apponet* has its last syllable lengthened at the dieresis (cf. 3.29.3–4n). See N. 13.10n.

### 4.25

Meter: Phalaecean hendecasyllables.

1. Flaminio's friend Francesco della Torre of Verona served as secretary of Gianmatteo Giberti, bishop of Verona (4.1.16n), for many years while Flaminio was also in Giberti's household. Della Torre, who died in 1546, was the dedicatee of Flaminio 1548, published at Lyons by the efforts of Flaminio's cousin Cesare Flaminio; see Maddison 1965, 182. Flaminio says (1.1) that no one is worthier than della Torre to receive the little book of poems that the Muses gave him when "as a boy" he dwelt in the Aonian retreats. This present poem was the last of those making up the two

377

## · NOTES TO THE TRANSLATIONS ·

books of *carmina* in Flaminio 1548, in which the second book consisted of what are the bk. 4 poems here (the bk. 3 poems were not included as a group in that publication). The completion of the bk. 4 pastoral poems seems to be mentioned in 5.8, a pastoral elegy of 1539/40 written to Galeazzo Florimonte, another member of Giberti's household, inviting him to Caserta (Maddison 1965, 103; see 4.1–4.25n). Here in 4.25 Flaminio looks back on "these poems" as lighthearted compositions of the springtime of his youth, though by 1539/40 Flaminio was already slightly past forty, saying that now such youthful themes are behind him, and his concern is with more serious things. It would seem that this poem was added to the others in bk. 4 at a rather later stage (just as 3.1 and 3.2 are substantially later than the rest of bk. 3), when Flaminio had decided to dedicate to della Torre the two books of his *carmina* eventually published in Flaminio 1548; see Cuccoli 1897, 224, for this poem being added later. Other mentions of della Torre in Flaminio's poems are as follows. In 5.34 Flaminio writes (in 1527) to della Torre's uncle Raimondo, a bishop, expressing concern that the "boy" della Torre (Flaminio himself was twenty-nine) is in Rome, then in danger of being attacked by imperial forces, through Flaminio's fault. Flaminio declares della Torre a poet likely to equal or surpass Catullus and says (in lines 22–24) that della Torre, like Flaminio, has dedicated himself to Apollo (i.e., poetry) from his first years. In 5.24 della Torre, regarded as a devotee of Cicero and Terence, is invited to leave Giberti's house early and speed on his horse to visit Flaminio for the day. There will be reading of Vergil's *lusus* (i.e., his *Eclogues*) and the pastorals of Theocritus, "than which pastime there is nothing more charming, nothing sweeter, as it seems to me." In a further poem (App. 6 [9.6] Scorsone), Flaminio is overjoyed to be reunited with his dear friend della Torre after a long period away from him. One of the poems ascribed in anthologies to "Antonio Mario of Imola" (= Flaminio; see 3.15n), that addressing Fracastoro (Ubaldini 1563, 105r–v; Toscano 1576, 231r–v), wonders whether he is discussing astronomy with della Torre (lines 10–15). Fracastoro, *Carmina* 8, is addressed to the same Francesco della Torre, who was the nephew of the Giambattista della Torre named in N. 25.43 (see note there).

378

· NOTES TO THE TRANSLATIONS ·

3. After Catullus' statement in 68.15–20 that from first assuming a man's toga (at fifteen or sixteen) he wrote many playful love poems *iucundum cum aetas florida ver ageret* ("when my flowering youth was in its joyous spring"), but his brother's death has changed all that. Varchi, *Carmina* 107.4, borrows Catullus' words in lamenting a boy's death, from a fall, in the early spring of his life. While Catullus' context also implies that he freely indulged in Venus' pleasures at the time, here Flaminio's line 2 makes clear that he means *lusi* (lit., "I played") in 1 only in the sense of writing light verse. In 2.8.23–24 Flaminio looks ahead, in similar figurative language, to the time when his young patron Cardinal Farnese's age (*aetas*) will have moved on and completed its "sweet spring" (*ver dulce*), making a mature man of him. Fracastoro speaks figuratively in *Syphilis* 1.400 of "his bright spring, that flower of youth," and Marullo in *Epigrams* 1.21.5 of the "spring of life."

4. Cf. F. 5.21.20 (5.22.20 Scorsone), *iocos . . . et leves cachinnos.*

6–8. Flaminio's interests did in fact move on from pagan-inspired amatory and pastoral verse, his themes becoming more religious (see Maddison 1965, III). *Rerum causas* (after Verg. G. 2.490, "Blessed is he who has been able to learn the causes of things, *rerum cognoscere causas*") occurs in other poems of Flaminio (and cf. N. 55.22–23). In 1.21.25–26 Flaminio's addressee, a philosopher, is described as blessed in understanding and elegantly explaining *rerum causas*. In 2.1.24 Flaminio's friend Stefano Sauli concerns himself with *occultas rerum causas* (lit., "the hidden causes of things"), as well as astronomy and ethics. *Rerum . . . causas . . . latentes* has the same sense in 2.4.40, while in 2.21.1 a deceased philosopher taught *rerum causas*. The expression is also in 2.7.51 (of autumn 1538), *rerum causas eventaque dicere* ("to tell the causes and effects of things"), in a context summarizing Flaminio's scholarly and poetic interests. There (lines 55–58) he says it particularly pleases him to celebrate God in verse. When Fracastoro invokes Urania in *Syphilis* 1.24, he addresses her as *tu . . . quae rerum causas, quae sidera noscis* ("you who know the causes of things and the stars").

9. *Molles elegi*: Ov. *Pont.* 3.4.85.

379

## · NOTES TO THE TRANSLATIONS ·

13. In spite of the reference to the Christian God in 8, *Iovis* here clearly has pagan reference, Urania (see next note), here addressed, being, like all the Muses, "offspring of Jupiter (*progenies Iovis*)."

16–18. Urania was the Muse of astronomy. In 2.22 she is the inspiration of Pontano's *Urania*, his long poetic work on astronomy and astrology. I do not know of a chariot (18) associated particularly with her elsewhere, but the Muses as a group are sometimes imagined as riding with Apollo in his chariot. *Rutilante* here probably means "golden" in color rather than "having a reddish glow," as the sixth-century Christian poet Venantius has the simile *rutilantior auro* ("more *rutilans* than gold"). In his *Urania* 4.40 Pontano describes a scepter as *rutilantia auro* ("yellow with gold"), and the Golden Fleece is *rutilans* in *Urania* 5.240, though the red planet Mars is *rutilus* in *Urania* 1.768.

# Concordances

## NAVAGERO

| This edition | Griggio | Benassi |
|---|---|---|
| 31 | 49 | |
| 32 | 31 | |
| 33 | 32 | |
| 34 | 33 | |
| 35 | 34 | |
| 36 | 35 | |
| 37 | 36 | |
| 38 | 37 | |
| 39 | 46 | |
| 40 | 48 | |
| 41 | 38 | |
| 42 | 39 | |
| 43 | 40 | |
| 44 | 41 | |
| 45 | 42 | |
| 46 | 43 | |
| 47 | 44 | |
| 48 | 45 | 1 |
| 49 | 47 | 9 |
| 50 | 50.1–12 | 5.1–12 |
| 51 | 50.13–22 | 5.13–22 |
| 52 | 51 | 8 |
| 53 | 52 | 2 |
| 54 | 55 | 4 |
| 55 | 57 | 10 |
| 56 | 58 | |

# · CONCORDANCES ·

| This edition | Griggio | Benassi |
|:---:|:---:|:---:|
| 57 | 60 | |
| 58A | 56 | 7 |
| 58B | 67 | |
| 59 | 61 | |
| 60 | 62 | |
| 61 | 65 | |
| 62 | 66 | |
| 63 | 68 | |
| 64 | 69 | |
| 65 | 64 | |
| 66 | 63 | |
| 67 | 53 | 6 |
| 68 | 54 | 3 |
| 69 | 59 | |

## FLAMINIO

| This edition / Mancurti 1727 / Scorsone | Mancurti 1743 / Maddison* |
|:---:|:---:|
| Book 3 | |
| 1 | 1 |
| 2 | 2 |
| 3 | omitted |
| 4 | omitted |
| 5 | 3 |
| 6 | 4 |
| 7 | 5 |

---

\* Maddison generally cites bk. 3 poems by the numbering of Mancurti 1743. When she cites poems omitted there, she gives sources in her footnotes. All bk. 4 poems are numbered the same in this edition, Mancurti 1727 and 1743, Scorsone, and Maddison.

## · CONCORDANCES ·

| This edition / Mancurti 1727 / Scorsone | Mancurti 1743 / Maddison* |
|---|---|
| 8 | 6 |
| 9 | 7 |
| 10 | 8 |
| 11 | 9 |
| 12 | 10 |
| 13 | 11 |
| 14 | omitted |
| 15 | 12 |
| 16 | 13 |
| 17 | 14 |
| 18 | omitted |
| 19 | 15 |
| 20 | omitted |
| 21 | 16 |
| 22 | 17 |
| 23 | 18 |
| 24 | 19 |
| 25 | 20 |
| 26 | 21 |
| 27 | 22 |
| 28 | 23 |
| 29 | 24 |

# Titles of Poems

## NAVAGERO

The *editio princeps* (Venice, 1530 = Navagero 1530) printed by Giovanni Tacuino has titles only for 19, 20, 27, 45, and 46, as here numbered. Most other early printed texts of Navagero's collected poems have no more, though the first Giunta ed. (Venice, 1555 = Fracastoro 1555) adds headings for 16 and 47. In contrast, Gagny's Paris, ca. 1548 compilation (= Gagny ca. 1548) gives titles to all the poems included. Some of his titles, especially from 32 onward, are clumsy and occasionally even inept. Duchesne 1560 mostly reuses Gagny's titles, and Periander 1567 more or less does the same for the first fourteen of the twenty of Navagero's poems in his anthology but omits titles for the rest. After Gagny ca. 1548 there are essentially only two further attempts to give titles to all of Navagero's poems as then collected: Toscano 1576 and the Volpi brothers' Padua, 1718 ed. (= Navagero 1718). Toscano generally employs shorter titles than Gagny, and Toscano's titles are adopted by Gruter 1608. The Volpi brothers, whose ed. (Navagero 1718) far surpasses all earlier ones, repeat some of the titles favored by Gagny but replace others. The vast anonymously edited *Carmina Illustrium Poetarum Italorum* in its volume 6 (Florence, 1720) takes over the Volpi titles, as does the Bergamo, 1753 *Carmina Quinque Illustrium Poetarum*. The Verona, 1740 ed. (= Fracastoro 1740; further versions appeared in 1747, 1759, and 1782) reverts to giving only the titles seen in Navagero 1530. Titles are occasionally found with Navagero's poems in MSS, though they are generally lacking, or seem copied from a printed edition, especially in eighteenth-century MSS. A few minor variations of titles in relatively unimportant later anthologies are not listed here. Some spellings are adjusted (e.g, *Bacco* to *Baccho*).

In recording the titles given to Navagero's poems, I use the abbreviations listed below. Full descriptions of each item are found in the Handlist of Editions, Translations, Anthologies, and Further Reading. MSS are designated as in Manuscripts with Latin Poems of Navagero.

385

## · TITLES OF POEMS ·

| 1530 | Navagero 1530 (titles only for 19, 20, 27, 45, and 46) |
|------|------|
| ca. 1548 | Gagny ca. 1548 |
| 1560 | Duchesne 1560 (mostly as Gagny ca. 1548) |
| 1567 | Periander 1567 |
| 1576 | Toscano 1576 |
| 1600 | Blijenburgh 1600 |
| 1608 | Gruter 1608 (where noteworthy; generally as Toscano 1576) |
| 1718 | Navagero 1718 (reprinted Venice, 1754) |
| 1738 | Niccoli 1738 |
| 1746 | *Epigrammatum Selectorum Libri Tres* 1746 |
| 1760 | *Epigrammatum Selectorum Libri Tres* 1760 (2nd ed. of above) |
| 1761 | Niccoli 1761 |

1] Vota Cereri pro Terrae Frugibus (Offerings to Ceres for the Fruits of the Earth), *ca. 1548, 1560, 1718*; title *om. 1576*; Vota Cereri, *Salz.*; Ad Cererem (To Ceres), *1608, 1761*; Ad Cererem, Votum Agricolarum (To Ceres, the Offering of Farmers), *1760*

2] Vota ad Auras (Offerings to the Breezes), *ca. 1548, 1560, 1718, Flo.Ric.1*; Ad Auras, Idmonis Votum (To the Breezes, the Offering of Idmon), *1576, 1761, Mil.3*; Ad Auras, Votum Florum (To the Breezes, an Offering of Flowers), *1746, 1760*; Rusticus ad Auras (A Countryman to the Breezes), *Bel.2*; E Graeco (From the Greek), *Jesi*

3] Vota Iolae Pani Agresti Deo (Iolas' Offerings to the Rustic God Pan), *ca. 1548, 1560, 1718*; Ad Pana, Votum Iolae (To Pan, the Offering of Iolas), *1576*; Ad Panem [*sic* = Pana] Deum, Votum Iolae (To the God Pan, etc.), *1761*; Caput Cervi, Votum Pani (A Stag's Head, an Offering to Pan), *1746, 1760*

4] Vota Damidis ad Bacchum pro Vite (Damis' Prayers to Bacchus for a Vine), ca. *1548, 1560, 1718*; Baccho Damidis Votum (Prayer of Damis to Bacchus), *1576, 1761, Mil.3*; De Baccho (On Bacchus), *Bol.U.*; Baccho (To Bacchus), *Vat.7*

5] Lyconis Vota Pani Deo (Lycon's Offerings to the God Pan), *ca. 1548, 1560, 1718*; De Lycone (On Lycon), *1576*; Caprea (A She-Goat), *1746*; De Caprea a Lycone Pastore Iaculo Interempta (On a She-Goat Killed with a Javelin by the Shepherd Lycon), *1760*

386

· TITLES OF POEMS ·

6] Thyrsidis Vota Veneri (Thyrsis' Offerings to Venus), *ca. 1548, 1560, 1567, 1718, Par.1, Salz.*; Ad Venerem Thyrsis (Thyrsis to Venus), *1576*; Veneri (To Venus), *Vat.7 and 11*

7] Thyrsidis Vota Quercui et Silvae (Thyrsis' Offerings to an Oak and a Wood), *ca. 1548, 1560, and, with another* et, *meaning* both, *after* Vota, *1718*; Thyrsis, *1576*

8] Augoni Venatico Cani Epitaphium et Vota (Epitaph and Offerings to the Hunting Dog Augon), *ca. 1548, 1560*; Tumulus Augonis Canis (Burial Mound of the Dog Augon), *1576, 1761*; Augonis Venatici Canis Epitaphium (Epitaph of the Hunting Dog Augon), *1718*; De Augone Cane Venatico ab Apro Interfecto (On the Hunting Dog Augon, Killed by a Boar), *1760*

9] Invitatio [*misprinted* Imit-, *ca. 1548*] ad Amoenum Fontem (Invitation to a Delightful Fountain), *ca. 1548, 1560, 1718, Salz.*; Inscriptio Fontis (A Fountain's Inscription), *1576, 1761* [Ex Graeco (From the Greek), *added in Sannazaro 1590*]; Ad Viatorem Ut Secedat Tantisper de Via (To a Wayfarer, That He Leave the Road for a Short While), *1746*; De Amoeno Secessu, ad Viatorem (On a Delightful Retreat, to a Wayfarer), *1760*; Fons (A Fountain), *Si., Vat.1 and 11*; Epigramma, *Flo.Ric.2*

10A] De Obitu Hylacis Canis Pastorii [Pastorici, *ca. 1548, 1560*] (On the Death of the Herdsman's Dog Hylax), *ca. 1548, 1560, 1718, Salz.*; Tumulus Hylacis Canis (Burial Mound of the Dog Hylax), *1576, 1761, Bol.Arch.*

10B] *Mil.2 (the sole source for this shorter version) gives no title*

11] Vota Telesonis Cereri, Baccho et Pali Deae (Teleson's Offerings to Ceres, Bacchus, and the Goddess Pales), *ca. 1548, 1560, 1718*; Vota Thelesonis, *Salz.*; Votum Telesonis (Offering of Teleson), *1576, 1761, Mil.3*; Rustici Hominis Rusticis Diis Vota et Dona (Offerings and Gifts of a Rustic Man to Rustic Deities), *1738*; Telesonis ad Deos Ruris Votum (Teleson's Offering to the Countryside Deities), *1760*

12] Leucippem [-am, *1567*] Amicam Spe Praemiorum Invitat (He Invites His Girlfriend Leucippe in the Hope of Rewards), *ca. 1548, 1567, 1718; title om. 1560*; Ad Leucippem (To Leucippe), *1576*

## · TITLES OF POEMS ·

13] Vota Veneri ad Felicitandos Amantium Amores (Offerings to Venus to Bless Lovers' Loves), *ca. 1548, 1560, 1567*; Votum Veneri (An Offering to Venus), *1576, Mil.3*; Vota Veneri Ut Amantibus Faveat (Offerings to Venus That She Favor Lovers), *1718*; Vota Veneri, *Salz.*

14] Vota Niconoes ad Dianam (Niconoe's Offerings to Diana), *ca. 1548, 1560, 1718*; Votum Niconoes Dianae (Niconoe's Offering to Diana), *1576*

15] Vota pro Vite Baccho et Satyris (Offerings for a Vine to Bacchus and the Satyrs), *ca. 1548, 1560, 1718*; Baccho Votum Acmonis (Acmon's Offering to Bacchus), *1576, 1761*; Mustum. Votum Baccho et Satyris (Must. An Offering to Bacchus and the Satyrs), *1746*; Acmonis Vinitoris ad Bacchum et Satyros Votum Musti (The Vine-Dresser Acmon's Offering of Must to Bacchus and the Satyrs), *1760*; Baccho (To Bacchus), *Bol.U., Vat.7*

16] Vota Acmonis Vulcano (Acmon's Offerings to Vulcan), *ca. 1548, 1560, 1718*; Ad Vulcanum (To Vulcan), *Fracastoro 1555*; Eiusdem Vulcano ([Offerings] of the Same [i.e., Acmon] to Vulcan), *1576*

17] Defectio Euphronis a Pallade ad Venerem (Euphro's Defection from Pallas to Venus), *ca. 1548, 1560, 1567, 1718*; De Euphrone [Eufrone] (On Euphro), *1576*; Euphro ad Palladem (Euphro to Pallas), *Salz.*

18] In Almonem Alcippes Fastidio Mortuum (On Almo, Dead through Alcippe's Disdain), *ca. 1548, 1560, 1567, 1718*; De Almone (On Almo), *1576*

19] Acon, *1530, 1576, 1718, Wro.*; Aion, *Mil.1 (same inept error in line 6)*; Acon Pastor (Acon the Shepherd), *ca. 1548, 1560, 1567*

20] Damon, *1530, 1576, 1718, Mil.1, Vat.4, Ver.*; Damon Pastor (Damon the Shepherd), *ca. 1548, 1560*; Laus Iulii Secundi Pont. Max. (Praise of Pope Julius II), *Wro.*; Ad Iulium Pont. Max. Damon (To Pope Julius II. Damon), *Vat.6*; Ad Iul. II Pont. Max. Egloga Andr. Nauagerii. Interlocutor Damon (To Pope Julius II. Eclogue of Andrea Navagero. Interlocutor Damon), *Bol.U.*

21] De Cupidine et Hyella (On Cupid and Hyella), *ca. 1548, 1560, 1567, 1718*; De Hyella (On Hyella), *1576, Mil.3*; Cupido et Hyella (Cupid and Hyella), *Par.1*

## · TITLES OF POEMS ·

22] Precatio ad Noctem pro Celandis Amoribus [*misprinted as* moribus, *1560*], Prayer to Night for Concealment of Lovemaking, *ca. 1548, 1560, 1567*; Ad Noctem (To Night), *1576, 1718, Mil.3*

23] In Herum Suum, Qui, Quo Liberiore Ipse Frueretur Aere, Aedes Proprias Disiecit (On Its Master, Who, in Order That It Might Enjoy Freer Air, Demolished His Own House), *ca. 1548, 1560*; Laurus (A Laurel), *1576, 1718*

24] In Quendam Qui, Cum Nihil Sciret, Tacendo Sapiens Videri Volebat (On Someone Who, Although He Knew Nothing, Wished to Seem Wise by Keeping Silent), *ca. 1548, 1560*; De Pythagorae Simulacro (On a Statue of Pythagoras), *1576, 1718, Mil.3*; In Simulacrum Pythagorae (On a Statue of Pythagoras), *1746*; De Simulacro Pythagorae Philosophi ab Asyla Sculpto (On a Statue of the Philosopher Pythagoras Carved by Asylas), *1760*; De Pythagorae Simulacro s(ive) Statua (On an Effigy or Statue of Pythagoras), *1761*

25] Invitatio ad Turrium ad Canendas Amoris [Amorum, *1567*] Vires (Invitation to Della Torre to Sing of the Strength of Love [of Loves, *1567*]), *ca. 1548, 1560, 1567*; Veris Descriptio, ad Turrium (Description of Spring, to Della Torre), *1576, 1718*; Veris Descriptio (Description of Spring), *Mil.3*

26] Anxia pro Gellia Amica Solicitudo (Anxious Concern for His Girlfriend Gellia), *ca. 1548, 1560, 1567*; Ad Amicam Rusticantem (To His Girlfriend When Staying in the Countryside), *1576, Mil.3*; Ad Gelliam Rusticantem (To Gellia When Staying in the Countryside), *1718*

27] Iolas, *1530, 1576, 1718, Mil.1, Mil.3, Vat.11*; Iolas Pastor (Iolas the Shepherd), *ca. 1548, 1560*

28] In Imaginem Sui, Strenarum Loco Hyellae Missam (On a Likeness of Himself, Sent to Hyella as a New Year Present), *ca. 1548, 1560, 1567*; Ad Hyellam (To Hyella), *1576*; Imaginem Sui Hyellae Mittit (He Sends a Likeness of Himself to Hyella), *1718, Salz.*

29] Gratulatio ad Somnum, per Quem Dormiens Potiri Amica Videbatur (Thanks to Sleep, through Whom, as He Slept, He Imagined Him-

# · TITLES OF POEMS ·

self Enjoying His Girlfriend's Favors), *ca. 1548, 1560*; Gratulatio ad Somnum de Amica (Thanks to Sleep Concerning His Girlfriend), *1567*; Ad Somnum (To Sleep), *1576, 1718*

30] Ad Bembum et Canalum (To Bembo and Canal), *ca. 1548, 1560*; Ad Canalum et Petrum Bembum (To Canal and Pietro Bembo), *1567*; Ad Canalem et Bembum (To Canal and Bembo), *1576, 1718*

31] In Vancium, Vicum Patavinum Amoenissimum (On Vanzo, a Very Lovely Quarter of Padua), *1718; untitled when first printed in Pignoria 1625*

32] In Hyellae Oculos (On Hyella's Eyes), *ca. 1548, 1567, 1718; poem om. 1560*; Ad Hyellam (To Hyella), *1576*

33] Ad Hyellam Amicam (To His Girlfriend Hyella), *ca. 1548; title om. 1567*; Ad Eandem [= *Hyellam*] (To the Same [= *Hyella*]), *1576*; Ad Hyellam (To Hyella), *1560, 1718, Salz.*

34] In Gabrielem Archangelum (To the Archangel Gabriel), *ca. 1548*; Ad Gabrielem Archangelum (To the Archangel Gabriel), *1560*; In Angelum Gabrielem Hymnus (Hymn to the Angel Gabriel), *1576*; Hymnus in Gabrielem Archangelum (Hymn to the Archangel Gabriel), *1718*

35] De Patavio a Militibus Vastato [*ungrammatically* Vastata, *1718, 1754, etc.; perhaps* Urbe *was meant to stand before* Patavio] (On Padua Devastated by Soldiers), *ca. 1548, 1560, 1718*; Ad Urbem Patavium (To the City of Padua), *1576*

36] Ad Bembum, Quod ab Armis ad Canendos Amores Sit Conversus (To Bembo, That He Has Turned from Arms to Singing of Love Affairs), *ca. 1548, 1560; title om. 1567*; Ad Bembum (To Bembo), *1576, 1718, Vat.11*

37] In Auroram (On Aurora), *ca. 1548, 1560, 1718; title om. 1567*; Ad Auroram (To Aurora), *1576*

38] Quod Una Sibi pro Die et Nocte sit Hyella (That Hyella Alone Is as Day and Night to Him), *ca. 1548; poem om. 1560; title om. 1567*; De Hyella (On Hyella), *1576, 1718, Mil.3, Salz.*

39] De Menalca ab Accessu Amicae per Canes Excluso (On Menalcas' Exclusion from Access to His Girlfriend by Dogs), *ca. 1548, 1560*; De Menalca (On Menalcas), *1718; poem om. 1576*

390

## · TITLES OF POEMS ·

40] De Lodovico Pannoniae Rege (On Lajos, King of Hungary), *Ubaldini 1563, 1718; not in earlier (and some later) eds.*

41] Precatio ad Venerem Ut Pertinacem Lalagen Molliat (Prayer to Venus That She Make the Stubborn Lalage More Amenable), *ca. 1548, 1560; title om. 1567*; Ad Venerem (To Venus), *1576*; Ad Venerem, ut Pertinacem Lalagem Molliat (To Venus, etc.), *1718*

42] Quod Imbellis Armatus Incedat (That, Though Unwarlike, He Goes Forth in Armor), *ca. 1548, 1560; title om. 1567*; De Sua Pictura (On His Picture), *1576*; De Imagine Sui Armata (On a Portrait of Himself in Armor), *1718*

43] In Obitum Borgeti Lepidi Catelli (On the Death of the Charming Lapdog [or Puppy] Borgetto), *ca. 1548, 1560*; In Obitum Borgetti Catuli (On the Death of the Lapdog Borgetto), *1576, 1718, 1761*

44] Omen Parcarum de Puero Recens Nato (Prophecy of the Fates Concerning a Newborn Boy), *ca. 1548, 1560*; Genethliacon (Birthday Poem), *1576*; Genethliacon Pueri Nobilis (Birthday Poem of a Noble Boy), *1718*

45] Ex Philemone (From Philemon), *1530, ca. 1548, 1560, 1576, 1718; with added title* Ex Lacrimis Non Levari Dolorem (Pain Not Eased by Tears), *1738*

46] Ex Menandro (From Menander), *1530, ca. 1548, 1560, 1576, 1718*

47] Cum ex Hispanica Legatione in Italiam Reverteretur (When He was Returning to Italy from His Embassy to Spain), *Fracastoro 1555, 1608, 1718 (no title 1560, 1576); most eds. from 1530 on note at end* Desunt nonnulla quae erant in litura (Some things are missing that were in an erasure); *ca. 1548 and 1560 instead note at head (without a title)* Imperfecta sunt quae sequuntur (What follows is incomplete).

Poems 48–69 lack titles, except as follows:

50] Tumulus Borgetti [Borgeti, *Vat.6*] Catelli (Burial Mound of the Lapdog [or Puppy] Borgetto), *Ud., Vat.1 and 6, Cinelli Calvoli 1736 (Scanzia 22; from Vat.1)*

52] In Secundum (On Secundus), *Vat.11*

391

## · TITLES OF POEMS ·

54] Tumulus Herculis Strozae (Tomb of Ercole Strozzi), *Wro.*

56] Ad Charites (To the Graces), *Si.*

57] Naugerii Priapus (Navagero's Priapus), *Bel.2*

58A] Ad Trissinum (To Trissino), *Vat.2*

59] Ad Lycinnam (To Lycinna), *Vat.11*

67] Canis (A Dog's [Epitaph]), *Canoniero 1613 and 1627*

68] Attilius Caesaris (Caesar's Attilius), *1560*; De Atilio Caesaris Milite (On Atilius, a Soldier of Caesar), *Ubaldini 1563, 1576*; Atilius, Caesaris Miles (Atilius, a Soldier of Caesar), *1608*; De Atilio (On Atilius), *Man.*


### FLAMINIO

No titles are given in editions to the poems of Flaminio included in this volume except where otherwise stated (I have made no consultation of MSS for Flaminio). See above for abbreviations used, and note that *ca. 1548* (referring to Gagny's *Doctissimorum Nostra Aetate Italorum Epigrammata*) and *Flaminio 1548* (referring to the 1548 ed. of Flaminio) are different publications.

3.1] Ad Deos Agrestes de Villa Sibi ab Alexandro Cardinale Farnesio Donata (To Rustic Gods on the Villa Given Him by Alessandro, Cardinal Farnese), *1746, 1760*

3.3] Ad Nigellam (To Nigella), *ca. 1548*

3.4] Amorum Suorum Furta Celari Optat (He Wishes His Amours' Intrigues Hidden), *ca. 1548*

3.8] De Se Ipso (On Himself), *1600*

3.12] Ad Ligurinam (To Ligurina), *1600*

3.21] Ad Rivulum Ut Phyllidis Hortum Irriget (To a Stream, That It Water Phyllis' Garden), *ca. 1548*

4.1] Vota pro Hyella ad Musam Catulli (Prayers for Hyella to the Muse of Catullus), *ca. 1548*

## · TITLES OF POEMS ·

4.2] Ad Caprum (To a Billy Goat), *Flaminio 1548, ca. 1548*; De Capro (On a Billy Goat), *1600*; Ad Caprum Quem Hyella, Pulcherrima Nympharum, in Deliciis Habuit (To a Billy Goat That Hyella, Most Beautiful of Nymphs, Treated as Her Favorite), *1746, 1760*

4.3] Ad Eundem (To the Same), *Flaminio 1548, ca. 1548*; De Capro (On a Billy Goat), *1600*; Ad Caprum, de Morte Hyellae (To a Billy Goat, on the Death of Hyella), *1746, 1760*

4.4] Ad Satyros et Faunos (To Satyrs and Fauns), *Flaminio 1548, ca. 1548*

4.5] Ad Fontem (To a Fountain), *Flaminio 1548, ca. 1548*; Fonti (To a Fountain), *1600*

4.6] Ad Hortulum (To a Little Garden), *Flaminio 1548*; Ad Hortulum Hyellae Morte Flaccescentem (To a Little Garden Wilting through Hyella's Death), *ca. 1548*; Hortulo (To a Little Garden), *1600*; Ad Hortum, de Morte Hyellae (To a Garden, on the Death of Hyella), *1746, 1760*

4.7] De Morte Hyellae ob Iolam Alteri Sociatam [*read –um*] (On the Death of Hyella Because of Iolas' Marriage to Another), *ca. 1548 (see also 4.7n for this poem, 4.9, 4.11, 4.12, and 4.24)*

4.8] Expostulatio Hyellae Morientis cum Iola (Expostulation of the Dying Hyella with Iolas), *ca. 1548*

4.9] In Hyellae Tumulum (On Hyella's Tomb), *ca. 1548*; Tumulus Hyellae (Hyella's Tomb), *1746, 1760*

4.10] In Eundem (On the Same [i.e., Tomb]), *ca. 1548*

4.11] In Eundem (On the Same [i.e., Tomb]), *ca. 1548*; Ad Pastores, de Morte Hyellae (To Shepherds, on the Death of Hyella), *1746, 1760*

4.12] De Hyella Eiusque Capella (On Hyella and Her Nanny Goat), *ca. 1548*; Capellae cum Domina Mortuae ([Epitaph] of a She-Goat Dead with Her Mistress), *Thesaurus Epitaphiorum 1666 and 1686*

4.13] De Cerbero ad Hyellae Adventum Mansuefacto (On Cerberus Tamed at Hyella's Approach), *ca. 1548*

4.14] Umbrarum Admiratio ad Hyellae Adventum (The Shades' Marveling at Hyella's Arrival), *ca. 1548*

393

## · TITLES OF POEMS ·

4.15] De Hyellae Fistula Pani Consecrata (On Hyella's Pipe Dedicated to Pan), *ca. 1548*

4.16] Vota Pastorum Hyellae Cicata (Shepherds' Offerings Dedicated to Hyella), *ca. 1548*

4.17] Iolas Hyellae Suae Canebat [*error for* Canit?] (Iolas Was Singing [Sings?] to His Hyella), *ca. 1548*

4.18] Iolae Querela de Admissa in Coniugem Nisa (Iolas' Complaint of Having Taken Nisa to Wife), *ca. 1548*

4.21] In Solem, ob Hyellae Mortem Sibi Invisum (To the Sun, Hateful to Him because of Hyella's Death), *ca. 1548*; Ad Solem (To the Sun), *1600*

4.22] Desiderium Amicae Hyellae (Longing for His Girlfriend Hyella), *ca. 1548*

4.23] Pana Orat Ut aut Sui Misereatur aut Hyellae Suae Iunget (He Begs Pan Either to Pity Him or Unite Him with Hyella), *ca. 1548*

4.24] In Hyellae Tumulum (On Hyella's Tomb), *ca. 1548*

4.25] Ad Turrianum (To Della Torre), *ca. 1548*

# Manuscripts with Latin Poems
## of Navagero

☙❧

Abbreviations used to denote MSS are given in square brackets. An asterisk indicates *not in Griggio 1976–77*. A semicolon within a list of poems marks interruption by material unrelated to Navagero in the MS, whereas commas indicate that the Navagero poems listed are in an uninterrupted sequence.

Belluno, Biblioteca Civica

[Bel.1] Cod. 371. Contains 21 with two lines omitted (p. 71). 16th century.

[Bel.2] Cod. 656. Contains 2 (7r); 57 (46v). An unheaded poem follows 2 without either a change of attribution or an indication that it too is to be taken as Navagero's. I suspect that it is not his. 16th century.

Bergamo, Biblioteca Civica Angelo Mai*

[Berg.] Ms. Lambda V 15. Contains 2, 6, 7, 4, 12, 21 (23v–24r). 16th century.

Bologna, Archivio Isolani*

Kristeller 1963–97, 5:509, records three MSS as seemingly having some material by Navagero, but all were fire-damaged through bombing in World War II, and I have not been able to ascertain what precisely they contain (or contained) of Navagero's poems. They are MSS F 11.80.2 (CN 40), F 11.80.6 (CN 40), and F 71.178 (CN 97), fol. 73.

Bologna, Biblioteca Comunale dell'Archiginassio

[Bol.Arch.] Ms. A 392. Contains 10A (58r–v). Early 18th century.

## · MANUSCRIPTS WITH POEMS OF NAVAGERO ·

Bologna, Biblioteca Universitaria

[Bol.U.] Ms. 400. Contains 21 (21r), 3 (21r), 6 (21v), 7 (21v), 56 (21v–22r), 16 (22r), 32 (22r–v), 18 (22v–23r), 29 (23r–v), 69 (23v–24r), 2 (25v), 3 (again, 26v), 14 (26v); 4 (59r), 15 (59v); 2 (again; 65r); 20 (73v–75r). Before 21 the copyist notes it as published (*editum*) and expressly gives the page reference to Navagero 1530 (as also for 2, 3, 6, 7, 16, 29, and 32), though the MS text sometimes differs from that in the 1530 ed. Early 16th century.

Cambridge, Massachusetts, Harvard University, Houghton Library*

[Cam.] Ms. Lat. 358. Contains 43 (p. 290); 47 (p. 328). 16th century.

Florence, Biblioteca Medicea Laurenziana

[Flo.ML.] Ms. Laurenziano Acq. e Doni 81. Contains 2 (30v), 66 (30v). 16th century.

Florence, Biblioteca Nazionale Centrale

[Flo.NC.] Cod. II, III, 284 has 11 (58v); 9 (141v). 16th century.

Florence, Biblioteca Riccardiana

[Flo.Ric.1] Ms. Moreniano 118, collection of epigrams dated 1716. Contains 2 (20r).

[Flo.Ric.2] Ms. Moreniano 255. Contains 9 (31v). 18th century.

Jesi, Biblioteca Comunale Planettiana

[Jesi] Cod. K IX 9 (formerly Ann. 274), dated 1587. Notes in margin emend and supplement the MS from a printed text. Contains 21 (26r); 2 (28r–v). Griggio 1976–77, 103, omits 21.

Leiden, Universiteitsbibliotheek*

[Lei.1] Scal. 23 has 9 (142v) as a version of Greek Anthology 16.227.

[Lei.2] B. P. G. 25 V has 15 (42r) as based on Greek Anthology 6.44.

[Lei.3] B. P. G. 52 II has 15 (28r) as based on Greek Anthology 6.44.

396

## · MANUSCRIPTS WITH POEMS OF NAVAGERO ·

[Lei.4] B. P. G. 52 IV has 15 (35v) as based on Greek Anthology 6.44.

[Lei.5] B. P. G. 52 V has 17 (60v) as a version of Greek Anthology 6.48.

London, British Library

[Lon.] Additional Ms. 12054. Contains 55 (fols. 137r–38r) and 65 (138v). 16th century.

Mantua, Biblioteca dei Marchesi Capilupi di Grado, now at the Archivio di Stato di Mantova

[Man.] Fondo Capilupi, Ms. b 27 vol. 62 has 2 (36v), 21 (37r), 4 (37r), 68 (37v). Formerly known as Ms. LXIX. 16th century. Benassi 1940, 244.

Milan, Biblioteca Ambrosiana

Three MSS each include a substantial number of poems, a few repeated; detailed by Griggio 1976–77, 103–4. See my notes on 2–14, 6, 7, 9–14, 17, 19–22, 24–29, 31, 33, 38, 49–54, 56, 57, 61–64.

[Mil.1] Cod. Ambr. C 112 inf. lat./it. Contains 20 (119v–21r), 6 (121r), 7 (as end of 6, 121r), 3 (121r–v), 14 (121v), 4 (121v), 21 (121v–22r), 12 (122r), 2 (122r), 54 (122v), 49 (122v), 33 (122v), 57 (123r), 28 (123r), 9 [part] (123v), 29 (123v), 19 (124r–v), 27 (124v–25bis r). Early 16th century. Benassi 1940, 244 (for 54, 49, 57). This MS and Vat.4 and Vat.20 share variants for poem 20 in six places.

[Mil.2] Cod. Ambr. J 48 inf. Contains 61 (27r), 62 (27r), 17 [part] (27r), 58B (27r), 63 (27r), 64 (27v), 56 (27v), 50 (27v–28r), 51 (28r), 31 [part] (28r–v), 13 (28v), 10B (28v). 16th century. Navagero is named as the poet only at the very start of this uninterrupted series. Though there is no new heading for the poem that immediately follows 10B on fol. 29r (beginning *Haec ego florentes sophiae digressus in hortos*), it is clearly not Navagero's as it addresses and eulogizes Pope Paul III (1534–49). I have not identified its author.

397

## · MANUSCRIPTS WITH POEMS OF NAVAGERO ·

[Mil.3] Ms. X 14 sup. Contains 13 (p. 108), 11 (p. 108), 4 (p. 108), 2 (pp. 108–9), 21 (p. 109), 22 (p. 109), 24 (p. 110), 25 (pp. 110–12), 26 (pp. 112–14), 27 (pp. 114–16), 38 (p. 117). 18th century. This anthology is stated to have been collected by A. Parravicino and checked with Toscano 1576. The titles of Navagero's poems in this MS are clearly derived from Toscano, and the same laudatory poem by Flaminio as in Toscano 1576 precedes the selection.

Naples, Biblioteca Nazionale

[Nap.] Ms. V E 53 (MS of Nicolaus Roscius) has 52, 49, and 53 (all 28r). 17th/18th century. Benassi 1940, 249 (for 49). The three poems are accompanied by the same Latin note as in Gualtieri 1786 (see 49n), in which they were printed from a Vatican MS (i.e., Vat.1, the only MS there with all three). The shared misguided reading *in mea damna* in 53.4 for Vat.1's unmetrical *in media damna* (the correct reading *in media arma* is preserved elsewhere) further shows the close link between this Naples MS and Gualtieri 1786.

Paris, Bibliothèque Nationale (see Kristeller 1963–97, 3:258a and 284a)*

[Par.1] Nouvelles acquisitions latines 738 (dated 1795, Venice) has in full 6 (72r) and 21 (72r–v).

[Par.2] Ms. latin 14161 includes very brief extracts from Navagero's poems. As these extracts, numbered and given marginal captions, e.g., *metus* (fear) for 26.25, probably derive from a printed text (one with *convivia ducere* in 26.73) and so lack critical value, it is superfluous to detail them, but, for instance, p. 187 has six extracts in order from poem 26, comprising lines 7–8, 13, 19–20, 25, 29, and 73–76, preceded by 25.49–50 (ending an item) and followed by 27.1–5. 17th century.

Salzburg, Universitätsbibliothek*

[Salz.] M I 35. Contains 28 (210r), 1 (210r), 10 (210v), 11 (211r), 9 (211r), 13 (211v), 17 (211v), 33 (212r), 38 (212r), 6 (212v). Seemingly from Navagero 1718 (same text; mostly same titles, sometimes abbreviated). 18th century.

398

· MANUSCRIPTS WITH POEMS OF NAVAGERO ·

Siena, Biblioteca Comunale degli Intronati

[Si.] Ms. K V 30. Contains 60 (29v–30r), 9 (30r–v), 53 (30v), 54 (30v–31r). 16th century.

Treviso, Biblioteca Comunale (Benassi 1940, 245)

[Trev.1] Cod. 585 I has 55 (7v–8v). Griggio 1976–77, 104, incorrectly lists this MS as 385 I. 17th century.

[Trev.2] Cod. 1404 has 55 (151v–52v). 16th century.

In both MSS poem 55, headed *Eiusdem Amatoria Carmina* (Amatory Poems of the Same), follows a poem of Fracastoro to Julius III (*Carmina* 12) wrongly treated as Navagero's (see under "Vienna" below).

Udine, Bibl. Comunale

[Ud.] Ms. Manin. 1333. Contains 50 (74r), 51 (74r), 52 (74v), 53 (74v), all unascribed. A handwritten note inserted above the title of the first poem observes (in Latin) that these are poems of Navagero missing from Navagero 1718, adding, "from a manuscript in the Vatican Library, unless I am mistaken." Only Vat.1 there has all four of the poems. Probably taken (correcting some errors) from the 1736 transcript of Vat.1 (see 50n). 18th century.

Vatican City, Biblioteca Apostolica Vaticana

Detailed by Griggio 1976–77, 101–3. The following poems (as here numbered) are in one or more MSS: 1–9, 12, 14, 15, 20–22, 24, 25, 27–30, 32, 33, 35, 36, 42, 43, 45–47, 49–54, 57, 58A, 59, 60.

[Vat.1] Cod. Vat. lat. 2836. Contains 50 (107v–8r), 51 (108r), 43 (108r); 21 (110r), 2 (110r–v); 9 (110v–11r); 52 (111r), 12 (111r), 49 (111r–v); 36 (111v–12r, interrupted by two extraneous lines); 3 (114v), 14 (115r), 53 (115r). Poem 69 is expressly attributed to Trissino (fol. 109r–109a recto). 16th century. Benassi 1940, 245 (for 52, 49, 50).

[Vat.2] Cod. Vat. lat. 2874 has 58A (110v; 111v Benassi 1940, 245; Griggio 1976–77, 102; and Kristeller 1963–97, 2:355). 15th/16th century.

399

### · MANUSCRIPTS WITH POEMS OF NAVAGERO ·

[Vat.3] Cod. Vat. lat. 3352 has 47 (280r). 16th century. See on Vat.14.

[Vat.4] Cod. Vat. lat. 3388 has 20 (123r–25r). 16th century.

[Vat.5] Cod. Vat. lat. 5182 has 32 (161v). 16th century.

[Vat.6] Cod. Vat. lat. 5225 vol. IV, has 20 (950r–52r); 50 (1009r), 51 (1009r–v), 43 (1009v–10r, full poem, not part, as Griggio 1976–77, 102, says). 16th century.

[Vat.7] Cod. Vat. lat. 5227. Contains 4 (fol. 137r), 6 (137v), 15 (137v). 16th century.

[Vat.8] Cod. Vat. lat. 5383. Contains 33 (167r, *not* 161r, as Griggio 1976–77, 102, says), 57 (167v, *not* 161v, as Griggio 1976–77, 102, says); 2 (183v), 6 (184r), 7 (184r), 4 (184r), 12 (184v), 3 (184v). 16th century.

[Vat.9] Cod. Vat. lat. 5640 has 21 (9r), 22 (9r), 29 (9v), 30 (9v–10r), 32 (10r), 33 (10v); 46 (106r). 16th century. See on Vat.14.

[Vat.10] Cod. Vat. lat. 5892 has 53 (288v). 16th century.

[Vat.11] Cod. Vat. lat. 6250. Contains 9 (41v), 52 (42r), 53 (42r), 54 (42r–v), 12 (42v), 49 (42v–43r), 59 (43r–44r), 36 (44v); 2 (70r–v), 14 (70v), 3 (70v), 4 (71r), 6 (71r), 15 (71r), 21 (71r–v), 60 (71v); 30 (81r–v); 33 (84v), 57 (85r), 21 (85r–v), 27 (85v–88r). 16th century.

[Vat.12] Cod. Barb. lat. 2163. Contains 3 (24r). 16th century.

[Vat.13] Cod. Ottob. lat. 1183. Contains 9 (68v). 16th century.

[Vat.14] Cod. Ottob. lat. 2860. Contains 35 (12r); 45 (116r); 1 (146r), 2 (146r), 3 (146r), 4 (146r), 5 (146v), 6 (146v), 7 (146v), 8 [part] (146v); 24 (158r), 28 [part] (158r), 42 (158r); 34 [*not* 25, as Griggio 1976–77, 102, says] (177r). A marginal note alongside 35.2 gives the reference in Gruter 1608 as *Del. Poet. It. p. 126 vol. 2*. 16th century. Kristeller 1963–97, 2:437, records this MS as made up of poems collected by Angelo Colocci (d. 1549), who knew Navagero's circle; Cod. Vat. lat. 3352 [here Vat.3] and Cod. Vat. lat. 5640 [here Vat.9] are also known or suspected collections of his. I note that in all three MSS Navagero's poems are copied under categories. Thus 35 here is under *Laudes* (Praises); 45 under *Moralia*; 1–8 under *Pastoral(ia)*; 24, 28, and 42 un-

400

### · MANUSCRIPTS WITH POEMS OF NAVAGERO ·

der *Pictura vel imag(o)* (Picture or image); and 34 under *Preces* (Prayers). In what seems the same hand as in Vat.14 in both cases, Vat.3 has 47 under *Genialia* (Joyous themes), while Vat.9 has 21, 22, 29, 30, 32, and 33 under *Amator(ia)* and 46 under *Fortuna*. None of the poems is repeated in either of the other two MSS, there is no poem in them not in Navagero 1530, and there are no variants from its readings, though Vat.14 omits 28.11–14, and its fol. 146v ends with 8.3 followed by the catchword *erigit* (the poem is not continued on the next leaf, where the unrelated writing is in a very different hand). Vat.14 gives 1–8 in the same (uninterrupted) sequence as Navagero 1530, while Vat. 9 gives the six poems on its fols. 9r–10v in the 1530 order.

Venice, Biblioteca Nazionale Marciana*

[Ven.1] Cod. Marc. lat. XII 140 (4022) has 9 (1r). 16th century.

[Ven.2] Cod. Marc. lat. XII 248 (10625). Contains 2 (132v). The echo poem beginning *Quae celebrat thermas Echo et stagna alta Neronis* is misascribed only in this MS to Navagero on 132r (it also appears canceled on 2v); it is in fact by Evangelista Maddaleni de' Capodiferro.

[Ven.3] Cod. Marc. lat. XII 251 (11880) has 21 (26r).

Verona, Biblioteca Civica*

[Ver.] Ms. 81 [419] has 20. 17th century.

Vienna, Österreichische Nationalbibliothek

[Vien.] Cod. 6603 has 55 (6v–7r), headed *Eiusdem Amatoria Carmina* (Amatory Poems of the Same), following a poem of Fracastoro to Julius III (*Carmina* 12) wrongly treated as Navagero's (see under "Treviso" above). 18th century.

Wroclaw, Biblioteka Uniwersytecka*

[Wro.] Ms. 6575 (formerly Mil. [i.e., Milich Collection] IV 17) has 20 (7v–9r), 6 (9r), 7 (9r, run together with 6), 3 (9v), 14 (9v), 4 (9v), 21 (10r), 12 (10r), 2 (10r–v), 54 (10v); 49 (17v); 19 (31r–v); 28 (111v), 33 (112r), 57 (112r); 9 (116v); 29 (168r). 16th century (title 17th). Poems not

401

## · MANUSCRIPTS WITH POEMS OF NAVAGERO ·

in Gruter 1608 are stated in a Latin note on fol. 1r of the MS to have been marked with D (55 and 61 are so marked, but [by oversight] not 49). The first series of ten poems (on 7v–10v) includes the same poems in the same order as Mil.1; the seven other poems listed above are all also in Mil.1, but in a different order; only 27 is in Mil.1 but not in this MS.

# Handlist of Editions, Translations, Anthologies, and Further Reading

### NAVAGERO

#### Texts and Editions

I include here in chronological order the early collections that printed, along with works of other authors, all, or nearly all, of Navagero's Latin poems that had appeared in the 1530 ed. For a helpful survey of many such collections, see Sparrow 1976. Texts of Navagero's speeches or other works where published separately from his Latin poems are not included in this list. Most of the early editions and anthologies can now be perused online via Google Books.

Venice, 1530

*Andreae Naugerii Patricii Veneti Orationes Duae Carminaque Nonnulla* (Two Speeches and Some Poems of Andrea Navagero, Patrician of Venice). Two-page preface. Forty-four poems (unnumbered), i.e., all of 1–47 in the present volume apart from 31, 39, and 40. Titles only for 19, 20, 27, 45, and 46. The poems, beginning on fol. 25r, are headed *Andreae Naugerii Patricii Veneti Lusus* (Light Poems of Andrea Navagero). The colophon states, "Printed in Venice through the efforts of friends (*amicorum cura*) as diligently as could be done, by the press of Giovanni Tacuino, 12 March 1530."

Paris, 1531

*Andreae Naugerii Patricii Veneti Orationes Duae . . . Carmina Item Eiusdem Nonnulla, etc.* (Two Speeches of Andrea Navagero, Patrician of Venice . . . and Also Some Poems of the Same, etc.). The full title details the speeches. Another, less impressive, issue of the Venice, 1530 ed., printed by Jean Petit. Same preface, same forty-four poems (unnumbered), same titles as in 1530 ed.

403

## · EDITIONS, TRANSLATIONS, FURTHER READING ·

Paris, ca. 1548

Jean de Gagny's (or de Gannay's, etc.) compilation *Doctissimorum Nostra Aetate Italorum Epigrammata* (Epigrams of the Most Learned Italians of Our Age), printed by Nicolas Leriche, includes all the poems in the 1530 ed. plus 39, inserted unsourced after 38 (but not poems 31 or 40). All poems are unnumbered and are given titles save for 47, merely noted as incomplete. The poems, beginning on fol. 40r, are not styled *Lusus*, as in the 1530 ed., but headed *Andreae Naugerii Patricii Veneti Epigrammatum Liber Unus* (One Book of Epigrams). Gagny (d. 1549), who was chancellor of the University of Paris, is stated to have included Navagero's poems "since they had not been published separately," i.e., from the speeches.

Venice, 1548 (printer = Valgrisi)
Florence, 1549 and 1552 (printer = Torrentino)
Venice, 1558 (printer = Giglio)

*Carmina Quinque Illustrium Poetarum* (Poems of Five Illustrious Poets), in four eds. Same forty-four poems (unnumbered) and titles as the 1530 ed.; a misreading there in 26.73 is corrected. The poems are called *Lusus*, as they were in 1530. This printing sometimes occurs bound with other works: e.g., one of several copies of Ubaldini's *Carmina Poetarum Nobilium* (Milan, 1563) accessible via Google Books has the 1549 ed. of this collection bound in with it.

Paris, 1550

Griggio 1976–77, 98, records Navagero's poems as bound with Salmon Macrin's *Naeniarum Libri Tres*, printed by Michel de Vascosan (Paris, 1550), pp. 19–56, together with poems of Bembo, Castiglione, and Cotta, all of whom feature in the collection *Carmina Quinque Illustrium Poetarum* above. Pecoraro 1959, 182, notes that the Biblioteca Antoniana di Padova has a copy. I have not had access to one. According to Griggio, the Navagero poems within this publication are from a Giunti ed. of Fracastoro's *Opera Omnia* printed along with Navagero's poems and two orations at Venice in 1550 but missing 23, 24, and 42. Yet James Gardner in Fracastoro 2013, 506, does not list a Venice, 1550 ed. of Fracastoro, and I have not been able to trace a copy. Gardner

404

## · EDITIONS, TRANSLATIONS, FURTHER READING ·

(p. 505) treats two other reported editions of Fracastoro's *Opera Omnia* (Lyons, 1550, and Venice, 1553) as ghosts.

Venice, 1555

Navagero's Latin poems and speeches are included in the Venice, 1555 Giunti ed. of Girolamo Fracastoro's *Opera Omnia* (= Fracastoro 1555), expressly to pair in death two close friends in life (Fracastoro had died in 1553). Preface of 1530 ed. reprinted; poems unnumbered, as there; titles only as there, plus *Ad Vulcanum* (To Vulcan) for 16 and *Cum ex Hispanica Legatione in Italiam Reverteretur* (When He was Returning to Italy from His Embassy to Spain) before 47. Not included: 31, 39, and 40 (as in 1530), plus (omitted in error?) 23, 24, and 42.

Paris, (1555 and) 1560

The anthology *Flores Epigrammatum ex Optimis Quibusque Authoribus Excerpti* (Flowers of Epigrams Drawn from All the Best Authors), compiled by Leodegarius a Quercu, or Léger Duchesne, vol. 1, Paris, 1555, and printed by P. Beguin, underwent a change of title for vol. 2 (Paris, 1560, printed first by Guillaume Cavellat), which included Navagero's poems, beginning on fol. 43v in the Cavellat version. The second volume's long new title begins *Farrago Poematum* (A Medley of Poems). Printings by Jérôme de Marnef, Cavellat's sister's son-in-law, and by Gilles Gorbin or Gourbin (likewise Paris, 1560) are also found. The titles of Navagero's poems and inclusion of 39 imply derivation essentially from the Paris, ca. 1548 text. As there, the poems are not called *Lusus* but treated as epigrams; some mishandling is evident. Poems 12, 32, 33, and 38 are omitted in their expected places (12 appears later, untitled, on fol. 83r with a few nonstandard readings; 33 appears as Flaminio's in vol. 1, fol. 99r; I do not find 32 or 38). Poem 45 appears in vol. 2 as Navagero's, but also in vol. 1 (fol. 99v) as Flaminio's. No 31 or 40. Poem 68 here is given (fol. 80r), but not as Navagero's; see 68n.

Paris, 1576

Vol. 1 of Giovanni Matteo Toscano's *Carmina Illustrium Poetarum Italorum* (Poems of Illustrious Italian Poets) includes all the poems of the

## · EDITIONS, TRANSLATIONS, FURTHER READING ·

1530 ed. (unnumbered). All but 1 and 47 have titles. These are generally different from, and often simpler than, those in the Paris, ca. 1548 collection. Toscano's readings in 26.73 and 30.14 and the absence of 39, present in the Paris, ca. 1548 and Duchesne's 1560 texts (31 and 40 are also absent), show that he took the text from the 1552 or 1558 ed. of *Carmina Quinque Illustrium Poetarum*. Poem 68 is ascribed to Marco Antonio Casanova (fol. 223r); see 68n.

Frankfurt am Main, 1608

All forty-four of the poems in the 1530 ed. (no 31, 39, or 40) are in *Delitiae CC Italorum Poetarum Huius Superiorisque Aevi Illustrium* (Delights of Two Hundred Illustrious Italian Poets of This Period and Earlier), the collection of Jan Gruter (1560–1627), who used the pseudonym Ranutius Gherus, vol. 2, pp. 104–35. Poems unnumbered. Titles and text are essentially as Toscano 1576, though, unlike him, Gruter gives a title for 1 and links 47 to Navagero's return from the Spanish embassy in his heading to it (see above under *Venice, 1555*). Poem 68 is ascribed to Marco Antonio Casanova (1:713); see 68n.

Padua, 1718

*Andreae Naugerii, Patricii Veneti . . . Opera Omnia, etc.* By the Volpi brothers of Padua, Giovanni Antonio (1686–1766; the firm's provider of introductions, lives, notes, and the like) and Gaetano (1689–1761; corrector only). Printed by Giuseppe Comino. Poems 1–47, all with titles, numbered as here, in the order of the forty-four printed in 1530, with 31, 39, and 40 inserted. Poem 39 is placed as in the Paris, ca. 1548 text, while 31 and 40 appear in seemingly arbitrary positions. The 1530 preface is reprinted. There is a Latin life of Navagero by Giovanni Antonio Volpi; also included is a survey of earlier publications of Navagero's works. Reprinted at Venice in 1754 with a few differences, all seemingly mere oversights, such as 41 wrongly numbered as a further 40. By far the fullest and best early edition, incorporating testimonia, letters, Fracastoro's dialogue *Naugerius, sive De Poetica*, Navagero's vernacular accounts of his travels in Spain and France, some of his vernacular poems, and much more, so that Navagero's Latin poems take up less than a tenth of the volume.

406

## · EDITIONS, TRANSLATIONS, FURTHER READING ·

Florence, 1720

*Carmina Illustrium Poetarum Italorum* (Poems of Illustrious Italian Poets), the eleven-volume anthology of Italian Neo-Latin poets anonymously published 1719 to 1726. Some think the editor was Giovanni Gaetano Bottari; Tommaso Buonaventuri has also been suggested. This anthology includes 1–47 in vol. 6, with the same titles as in the 1718 ed. There are a very few differences from the 1718 text, e.g., the editor rewrites 39.10 to remove a perceived metrical error; he favored such action throughout his anthology. Poem 68 is ascribed, as in Toscano 1576 and Gruter 1608, to Marco Antonio Casanova (3:292); see 68n.

Verona, 1740 (and subsequent editions)

*Hieronymi Fracastorii et Marci Antonii Flaminii Carmina, etc.* Navagero's poems are among those appended. Further eds.: Verona, 1747; Venice, 1759; Bassano, 1782. Same forty-four poems and same few titles as in the 1530 ed. (the fuller 1718 ed. being ignored). Source seemingly the 1552 or 1558 ed. of *Carmina Quinque Illustrium Poetarum* as, among other indications, *qui*, first found in the 1552 ed., is read in 30.14. Printed by Pierantonio Berni, for whom see under *Verona, 1732* and *Verona, 1752* in the "Anthologies" section.

Verona, 1747

See *Verona, 1740*.

Bergamo, 1753

Another collection entitled *Carmina Quinque Illustrium Poetarum* (Poems of Five Illustrious Italian Poets), printed by Lancelotti, includes Navagero's Latin poems. While the title is that of the 1548–58 publications, two of the four other poets incorporated are different. Cotta and Flaminio are replaced by Casa and Poliziano; Bembo and Castiglione are retained. Poems unnumbered; titles as 1718 ed.; text essentially the same. Poems 31 and 39 are included, as is 40, though it is placed between 37 and 38.

Venice, 1754

See *Padua, 1718* for this reprint.

407

## · EDITIONS, TRANSLATIONS, FURTHER READING ·

Venice, 1759
See *Verona, 1740*.

Bassano, 1782
See *Verona, 1740*.

1930 (M.A. dissertation)
Ruth Perry Gilroy, "The Latin Poems of Andrea Navagero, Text, Introduction and Notes" (M.A. diss., Johns Hopkins University, Baltimore, Maryland, 1930). Just under a hundred pages. Text (poems 1–47 only) from 1718 ed. No translation or bibliography. Notes cite many ancient passages and several of French imitators of Navagero but seldom explain historical or personal allusions.

1940
Maria Antonietta Benassi's article "Scritti inediti o mal conosciuti di Andrea Navagero" in *Aevum, anno XIV Fasc.* 2–3, April–Sept. 1940 XVIII (pp. 240–54) includes, as well as poems in Italian, several in Latin not found in any edition of the *Lusus*, though a few had been obscurely published and overlooked. Poems 54, 55, 58A, and 68 are first printed. The opening line of 57 is also given (p. 244), but the rest of it is coyly omitted. Benassi details MS sources (as consulted by her) of the poems listed and early publications that included them but were little noticed. She offers a very few observations on the text. For Benassi's numbering of the additional poems in her article, see the Concordances in this volume.

Nieuwkoop, 1973
*Andrea Navagero, Lusus*, ed. Alice E. Wilson (*Bibliotheca Humanistica et Reformatorica*, vol. 9). The 1530 text (with some spelling changes) plus the three further poems in the 1718 ed. The Venice, 1555 ed. was also consulted, but nothing is said of MS evidence or the extra poems in Benassi 1940. Introductory sections, first full translation of poems 1–47, and commentary. Reviewed by Flaminio Joukovsky in *Bibliothèque d'Humanisme et de Renaissance* 36 (1974): 697–98.

1976–77
Claudio Griggio, "Per l'edizione dei *Lusus* del Navagero" in *Atti dell'Istituto Veneto di Scienze, Lettere ed Arti*, vol. 135, pp. 87–113, lists very

408

· EDITIONS, TRANSLATIONS, FURTHER READING ·

many (but not quite all) printed works that include a text of at least some of the Latin poems of Navagero. He records MS sources (as consulted; the list is fuller than that in Benassi 1940) and prints the text of further poems not in Benassi 1940, i.e., 56, 57, 59–66, and 69 here (with 57 first in full). Griggio's numbering system is to reckon the forty-four of the 1530 ed. as 1–44 and then add on poems published elsewhere in the order of their first appearance in print (i.e., as ascribed to Navagero, though see 67n and 68n), then those given from MS sources in Benassi 1940, then those so given in his own article, here described. For Griggio's numbering of the additional poems, see the Concordances in this volume.

Turin, 1991
Navagero's poems 1–47 are given with some very brief biographical and bibliographical notes in Italian, and a few footnotes, along with those of Giovanni Cotta, in Gi. Cotta–Andrea Navagero, Carmina, ed. R. Sodano, Parthenias, Collezione di poesia neolatina 2. Text based on the 1718 ed. Selective bibliography of eds. 1530–1973. No MSS listed. No translation.

Cheadle Hulme, 1997 (in two versions)
Andrea Navagero, Lusus (Playful Compositions), edited and translated with commentary by Allan M. Wilson, privately produced in a tiny number of copies at Cheadle Hulme, Cheadle, Cheshire, England. Preliminary version early 1997 with copies donated to The John Rylands University Library, Deansgate, Manchester, and Biblioteca Nazionale Marciana, Venice. Superseded by the much changed and improved 1102-page version of June 1997 with copies donated to the Katholieke Universiteit, Leuven, and Biblioteca Medicea Laurenziana, Florence. Includes the poems ascribed to Navagero beyond those in the 1718 ed. Flaminio's lusus pastorales (text and translation) form Appendix A. Fifty-page bibliographical survey and word-index of 113 pages for Navagero. The present ITRL volume thoroughly recasts, abridges, refines, corrects, and to a very large extent rewrites this work, incorporating some new material in places. Fuller consultation of MS evidence and of early editions and anthologies has now been possible.

409

# · EDITIONS, TRANSLATIONS, FURTHER READING ·

2001 (Online Database)

For the digital collection *Poeti d'Italia in lingua latina tra Medioevo e Rinascimento*, Claudio Griggio published an online text of Navagero's Latin poems based on the 1530 ed., checked with Alice Wilson's 1973 ed. and the Turin, 1991 ed. listed above. He adds the poems published in Benassi 1940 and in his own Griggio 1976–77. Text only; no translation or notes. The meter of each poem is provided along with proposed scansion.

https://www.poetiditalia.it/texts/NAVAGERO|lusu|001

## ANTHOLOGIES

I note here most collections that include a limited number of Navagero's poems. A few further works are mentioned in the headnotes to a particular poem or poems.

Basel, 1546

Two of Navagero's poems (20, entitled *Damon*, and 27, entitled *Iolas*) are included with over 150 others, both ancient and Neo-Latin, in *En Habes, Lector, Bucolicorum Auctores XXXVIII, etc.* (Behold, Reader, You Have Thirty-Eight Writers of Bucolic Poems, etc.), ed. Joannes Oporinus. Dated March 1546 in the colophon.

Milan, 1563

*Carmina Poetarum Nobilium Io. Pauli Ubaldini Studio Conquisita* (Poems of Noble Poets Sought Out by the Diligent Research of Giovanni Paolo Ubaldini), includes 40, attributed to Navagero, and 68 otherwise.

Frankfurt am Main, 1567

*Horti Tres Amoris Amoenissimi e Praestantissimis Poetis Nostri Saeculi, etc.* (Three Very Delightful Gardens of Love from the Most Outstanding Poets of Our Age, etc.), the anthology of the Brussels-born Aegidius Periander (1543–68, real name possibly Gilles Omma), includes (*Hortus* 1, fols. 240v–50v) 6, 12–13, 17–19, 21–22, 25–26, 28–30, 32 (lines 1–7 only; the complete poem is given as Cotta's on fol. 8r), 33, 36–38, and 41–42. No titles after 32; until then titles mostly as, or nearly as, those in the Paris, ca. 1548 collection, also used by Duchesne 1560, but 29's

410

· EDITIONS, TRANSLATIONS, FURTHER READING ·

title is far briefer. Misprints and other errors abound in this poorly handled work.

Rome, 1590

Bound with the complete Latin works of Sannazaro, *Jacobi Sannazarii Opera Omnia*, is *Carmina Selecta Illustrium Poetarum Italorum ex Primo Tomo Io. Matthaei Toscani* (Selected Poems of Illustrious Italian Poets from the First Book of Giovanni Matteo Toscano). In this abridgement of Toscano's 1576 anthology, Navagero is represented by 1, 9, 10, 24, 34, 35, and 45 (pp. 247–52.).

Dordrecht, 1600

*Veneres Blyenburgicae* (Van Blijenburgh's Venuses), Damas van Blijenburgh's (Blyenburg's, Blyenburgh's) collection of amatory poems by around 150 Neo-Latin poets of various nationalities printed by Isaak Canin, arranged by themes, includes 6 (p. 625), 13 (p. 625), 21 (p. 364), 22 (p. 857), 30 (p. 549), 33 (p. 156), 37 (p. 825), 38 (p. 857), and 41 (p. 623). For some a wrong ascription or title is carelessly implied by failure to record a change from that for the previous poem. Where correctly given, all titles accord with those in Toscano 1576, the probable source.

Cologne, 1605

Poems 20 and 44 appear in Johann Buchler's anthology *Thesaurus Poematum, ex Variis tam Veteribus quam Recentioribus Poetis Desumptus* (A Treasury of Poems, Taken from both Ancient and More Recent Poets) on pp. 128–32 and 132–35, respectively, both ascribed to Navagero. Poems 34 (pp. 391–92) and 45 (p. 392) are misleadingly in a section headed "Taken from Marius Molsa" (i.e., Francesco Maria Molza). Poem 68, titled *Attlius Caesaris*, appears anonymously within a section headed "Taken from Many."

Antwerp, 1613 (also Antwerp, 1627, and Duaci, 1636)

*Flores Illustrium Epitaphiorum, etc.* (Flowers of Distinguished Epitaphs, etc.), compiled by Pietro Andrea Canoniero (Canonherius, 1582–1639), includes 8 and 10 as Navagero's on pp. 279–80. Poem 67 also appears (p. 23), but as anonymous.

411

## · EDITIONS, TRANSLATIONS, FURTHER READING ·

Hanover, 1619

Caspar Dornau's *Amphitheatrum Sapientiae Socraticae Joco-Seriae, etc.* (A Theatre of Mock-Serious Socratic Wisdom, etc.) 1:526 includes 8, 10A, and 43.

Oxford, 1637

*Delitiae Delitiarum, etc.* (Delights of Delights, etc.), ed. Abraham Wright, includes 68 (p. 69), though attributed not to Navagero but to M. A. Casanova.

Paris, 1659 (and many later editions)

*Epigrammatum Delectus ex Omnibus tum Veteribus, tum Recentioribus Poetis Accurate Decerptus* (Anthology of Epigrams Accurately Compiled from All Ancient and More Recent Poets) includes 24 on p. 364. Many subsequent editions were printed, with some variation of content. For example, Navagero's poem is on p. 364 of the London, 1683 ed., and on pp. 186–87 of the London, 1740 11th ed.

Paris, 1666

*Thesaurus Epitaphiorum Veterum ac Recentium Selectorum, etc.* (A Treasury of Select Old and Recent Epitaphs, etc.), ed. Philippe Labbe (or Labbé), includes 8 (pp. 447–48), 43 (p. 450), and 10 (p. 458). Reprint, Paris, 1686.

London, 1684

*Anthologia, seu Selecta Quaedam Poemata Italorum Qui Latine Scripserunt* (Anthology, or Some Selected Poems of Italians Who Wrote in Latin). This anonymously edited precursor of Pope's 1740 collection includes 37 (p. 142), 41 (p. 143), and 32 (p. 156).

Paris, 1686

See *Paris, 1666.*

Verona, 1732

The printer Pierantonio Berni includes about half of Navagero's published poems (1–5, 8–11, 13–16, 23–24, 34–35, 37, 42–47; titles only for 45 and 46) in vol. 1, pp. 12–25 of *Carmina Selecta ex Illustrioribus Poetis Saeculi XV et XVI* (Select Poems from the More Illustrious Fifteenth- and Sixteenth-Century Poets) (Verona, 1732). This collection was offered as morally sound reading for "studious youths." A fuller edition

412

## · EDITIONS, TRANSLATIONS, FURTHER READING ·

was printed at Verona in 1752. In Cotta 1802 (p. viii), Morelli records two reprints of this same title at Verona in 1792 and 1800, and there seems to have been another published by Redmondi (Venice, 1781).

Rovereto, 1736

Poems 50–53 appear on pp. 6–8 of *Scanzia* (*Scansia*) 22 of Giovanni Cinelli Calvoli's *Biblioteca Volante*, which was continued by Dionigi Andrea Sancassani after Cinelli Calvoli died in 1706. Poem 69 is given as Trissino's (*Scanzia* 22, pp. 79–80).

Florence, 1738

*Veterum et Illustriorum Saeculi XVI Poetarum Epigrammata, etc.* (Epigrams of the Ancient and More Illustrious Sixteenth-Century Poets, etc.), edited by Camillo Niccoli "for the use of godly schools." Includes 1, 9, 11, 24, 28 (pp. 171–74), and 45 (p. 220). Titles mainly as 1718 ed., but different for 11 and 45 (see Titles of Poems). See further *Florence, 1761*.

London, 1740

*Selecta Poemata Italorum Qui Latine Scripserunt, Cura Cuiusdam Anonymi Anno 1684 Congesta, Iterum in Lucem Data, Una cum Aliorum Italorum Operibus, Accurante A. Pope* (Selected Poems of Italians Who Wrote in Latin, Collected by the Efforts of an Anonymous Person in the Year 1684, Now Published Anew, Together with Works of Other Italians), ed. Alexander Pope. The content differs somewhat from the 1684 anthology. Vol. 2 includes 21, 22, 26 (all pp. 42–43), 31, 32, 37, 41 (all pp. 76–80). See further *Oxford/London, 1808*.

Bergamo, 1746

*Epigrammatum Selectorum Libri Tres* (Three Books of Select Epigrams), printed by Paolo Lancelotti "especially for the use of schools." Cf. *Bergamo, 1760*, with slightly different content and some variation of titles. Includes 2, 3, 9, 5, 15, 24 on pp. 193–96.

Verona, 1752

This further edition of Verona, 1732 (printed by Pierantonio Berni) includes more of Navagero (pp. 51–87) but has 38 where 6 should be and 34 where 22 should be, 6 and 22 being lost altogether; 31, 39, and 40 are also absent. Titles only for 19, 20, 27, 45, and 46. In places gaps are left in the printed text, the missing lines inserted by hand in the

## · EDITIONS, TRANSLATIONS, FURTHER READING ·

copy at the Österreichische Nationalbibliothek digitized via Google Books.

Bergamo, 1760

*Epigrammatum Selectorum Libri Tres* (Three Books of Select Epigrams). Another printing by Paolo Lancelotti. Cf. *Bergamo, 1746*. Includes 2, 1, 3, 5, 8, 9, 11, 15, 24 on pp. 176–180.

Florence, 1761

Second ed. of the anthology listed under Florence, 1738, now entitled *Epigrammata ad Usum Scholarum a Patre Camillo Nicolio . . . Selecta* (Epigrams for the Use of Schools Selected by Father Camillo Niccoli). Includes 1–4, 8–11, 15, 24, 43 on pp. 81–85. Titles mostly as Paris, 1576, but different for 3 and 24 (see Titles of Poems).

Bologna, 1767

*Carminum Delectus ex Illustribus Poetis tum Aurea Aetate, tum Saeculo XVI Florentibus, etc.* (A Selection of Poems of Illustrious Poets Flourishing both in the Golden Age and in the Sixteenth Century, etc.). Griggio 1976–77, 100, records this work as containing Navagero's poems 2, 8–11, 24, and 43 on pp. 27–30. I have not had access to a copy. I have also been unable to ascertain whether an earlier publication of the same title (Milan, 1746) contains anything by Navagero.

Venice, 1772

*Selectae Historicorum Conciones, et Poetarum tum Veterum, tum Recentiorum Selectissima Carmina* (Select Speeches of Historical Writers, and the Choicest Poems of both Ancient and More Recent Poets) includes 31, 43, 2, 3, 8, 9, 11, 16, 1, and 25 on pp. 254–60.

Naples, 1786

Poems 49, 52, and 53 are printed by Francesco Saverio Gualtieri in his edition of *Viti Mariae Iuvenati Poematum Libellus*, pp. 86–87.

Oxford/London, 1808

*Poemata Selecta Italorum Qui Seculo Decimo Sexto Latine Scripserunt, Nonnullis Annotationibus Illustrata* (Selected Poems of Italians Who Wrote in Latin in the Sixteenth Century, Illuminated with Some Annotations). Printed in Oxford, sold in London. Anonymously edited, this work follows in the tradition of the *London, 1684* and *1740* collections,

· EDITIONS, TRANSLATIONS, FURTHER READING ·

but it is a new compilation. Brief life of Navagero on pp. xix–xx. Includes 1, 2, 4, 8–10, 13, 31, 35, 37, 41, and 44. Titles as 1718 ed. except for 41, headed simply *Ad Venerem* (To Venus).

Lyons, 1808

Jean Brunel, *Le Parnasse latin moderne, etc.*, 2:468–70, has 1 with a French prose translation.

Vienna, 1816

Anton Stein's *Anthologia Epigrammatum Latinorum Recentioris Aevi* (An Anthology of Latin Epigrams of the More Recent Period) includes 13 on p. 207.

Tübingen, 1818

August Friedrich von Pauly, *Anthologia Poematum Latinorum Aevi Recentioris* (An Anthology of Latin poems of the More Recent Period), includes 1, headed *Ad Cererem* (To Ceres), on p. 148.

London, 1823

Jeremiah Holmes Wiffen appends the text and his own (very free) English verse translations of Navagero's poems 6, 7, 47, 9, and 21 to *The Works of Garcilasso de la Vega, etc.*, printed by James Moyes, on pp. 385–90.

Venice, 1826

*Rime e prose di alcuni cinofili vicentini e di altri illustri italiani*, p. 329 (misprinted as 529), following citation of 43, gives 67 as also Navagero's (but see 67n).

Vienna, 1828

Peter Alcantara Budik, *Leben und Wirken der vorzüglichtsen lateinischen Dichter des XV–XVIII Jahrhunderts sammt metrischer Uebersetzung ihrer Besten Gedichte, etc.*, 3:284–311, has a substantial life of Navagero, which quotes 16 in full on p. 300n, followed by four poems with German verse translations. The first, numbered 8, is in fact 9. After giving 13 and 18 correctly, Budik then bizarrely adds, still as Navagero's, a mysterious poem numbered 40, but not his.

Munich, 1835

Johann Georg Krabinger, *Eclogae Illustrium Poetarum Latinorum Recentioris Aevi* (Eclogues of Illustrious Latin Poets of the More Recent Pe-

415

# · EDITIONS, TRANSLATIONS, FURTHER READING ·

riod), has 1, 2, 4, 9, 24, 36, and 43 on pp. 79–82, titles and text from the 1718 ed.

Città di Castello, 1888

Emilio Costa, *Antologia della lirica latina in Italia nei secoli XV e XVI*, includes 21, 22, 29, 32, 33, 36, and 37 on pp. 128–32, without notes or translation.

New York, 1927

*Latin Writings of the Italian Humanists*, selected by Florence A. Gragg. Reprint, New York, 1981. Includes 1, 2, 12–14, 22, 27, 32, 37, 38, and 47 (Latin only; pp. 333–39 in the reprint). Brief remarks on Navagero on p. xix (reprint).

Haarlem, 1947

*Andreae Naugerii Patricii Veneti Lusus; Joachim du Bellay Gentilhomme Angevin Voeux rustiques; Pierre de Ronsard Gentilhomme Vandomois Ode.* A booklet of twenty-three pages, published by Johannes Enschedé en Zonen, giving the Paris, ca. 1548 Latin text of 4, 2, 5, 6, 10, and 12 with the two French poets' versions. Brief introduction in French.

Turin, 1959

*Poesia del Quattrocento e del Cinquecento*, vol. 4, "Parnasso Italiano," ed. Carlo Muscetta and Daniele Ponchiroli, includes the Latin text and an Italian prose translation by R. Ciaffi of 1, 32, 33, 2, 29, and 21 on pp. 715–19.

Leiden, 1975

Pierre Laurens and Claudie Balavoine, *Musae Reduces: Anthologie de la poésie latine dans l'Europe de la Renaissance*, 1:189–94. Short introduction and bibliography. Latin text with French prose translation of 1, 2, 6, 9, 28, and 38.

London, 1979

*Renaissance Latin Verse, An Anthology*, ed. Alessandro Perosa and John Sparrow, pp. 227–32, has Navagero's poems 2, 9, 13, 22, 29, 16, 42, and 24, with a one-page summary of his life and some very brief annotations. Uses the 1530 Latin text and 1718 numbering. No translations.

## · EDITIONS, TRANSLATIONS, FURTHER READING ·

New Haven and London, 1979

Fred Nichols, *An Anthology of Neo-Latin Poetry*, pp. 376–87, gives the Latin text and English prose versions of 1, 2, 6, 9, 10, 12, 13, 22, 27, and 43. Very brief biographical notes on p. 688.

Manchester, 1980

I. D. McFarlane, *Renaissance Latin Poetry*, has the Paris, ca. 1548 Latin text and English versions of 4, 21 (both pp. 28–29), 22 (pp. 50–51), and 37 (pp. 82–83). Very brief notice of Navagero's life on p. 223. Some notes.

Cheadle Hulme, 1998

Allan M. Wilson, *An Anthology of Neo-Latin "Dog" Poems*, pp. 40–45, includes 8, 10A, 43, 50–51, and 67. Latin text and English translation. Privately produced.

Rome, 2002

*Cani di pietra: L'epicedio canino nella poesia del rinascimento*, ed. Cristiano Spila, includes 8, 10A, 43, 50–51, and 67, with Italian translations and brief notes by Spila and Maria Gabriella Critelli, on pp. 45–49.

### Translations

The translations within the editions of Alice E. Wilson (*Nieuwkoop, 1973;* poems 1–47) and Allan M. Wilson (*Cheadle Hulme, 1997;* all poems) are recorded under "Texts and Editions" above. Below I list some translations of selected poems of Navagero. See also the following entries under "Anthologies": *Lyons, 1808; London, 1823; Vienna, 1828; Haarlem, 1947; Turin, 1959; Leiden, 1975; New Haven and London, 1979; Manchester, 1980; Cheadle Hulme, 1998; Rome, 2002.*

London, 1786

Edouard-Thomas Simon de Troyes (1740–1818) translates 21, 29, 38, 22, 32, 33, 6, 13, and 41 (unnumbered and given French titles) in *Choix de poésies* 1:300–309. The translations are sometimes badly flawed.

Città di Castello, 1898

Luigi Grilli, *Versioni poetiche dai lirici latini dei secoli xv e xvi* gives renderings in Italian verse of 37, 9, 21, 23, and 29 (pp. 47–52).

417

## · EDITIONS, TRANSLATIONS, FURTHER READING ·

Città di Castello, 1900

Arnaldo Bonaventura, *La poesia neo-latina in Italia dal secolo xiv al presente*, translates into Italian 37, 13, 21, 33, and 36 (pp. 146–49).

London, (1915 and) 1919

Richard Aldington (1892–1962), *Latin Poems of the Renaissance*, The Poets' Translation Series, Second Set, no. 4, translates, in the 1919 version, 47, 2, 9, 11, 14, 13, 4, 7, 6, 1, and 19.31–38 (pp. 10–13.). Errors and omissions abound.

Chapel Hill, 1965

W. Leonard Grant includes very free English verse translations of 20 and 27 in his wide-ranging major work *Neo-Latin Literature and the Pastoral* (pp. 332–35 and 141–43, respectively), as well as a brief biographical notice of Navagero on pp. 140–41.

There are also numerous adaptations of individual poems (in various languages, such as those in French by du Bellay), some being near-translations, others much freer. They are often cited in my headnotes. Some Italian versions of poems of Navagero are preserved in MSS. For instance, a nineteenth-century MS in the Biblioteca Comunale di Forlì (Ms. Piancastelli, Sala O Ms. V/50) has, opposite the Latin text, Italian versions (on fols. 63–113) of 6, 7, 12–14, 17, 18, 21, 22, 28–30, 32, 38, and 27, as well as versions of poems of Flaminio on fols. 1–61. I am grateful to the director, Dott.ssa Antonella Imolesi, for making a list of the Italian incipits of the Navagero poems translated. See Cicogna 1824–53, 6:292–93n311, for notice of several Italian translators or imitators of various poems of Navagero.

### Biography, Commentary, and Criticism (Selected)

Emmanuele Antonio Cicogna, *Delle inscrizioni veneziane*, Venice, 1853, 6:169–348 (reprinted as *Della vita e delle opere di A. Navagero*, Venice, 1855), is very thorough on most points of evidence for Navagero's life and is, in particular, massively detailed on Navagero's time as an ambassador in Spain and France. There are some comments on certain individual po-

418

· EDITIONS, TRANSLATIONS, FURTHER READING ·

ems. In note 311 on pp. 292–93, Cicogna details a number of very obscure Italian versions of various poems of Navagero, many in highly inaccessible publications, some in MS. A section entitled *Testimonianze illustri e autori che ricordano Andrea Navagero* (pp. 210–23) contains a summary of mostly minor references to Navagero in various later and often obscure works.

The Latin *Life* by Giovanni Antonio Volpi in the 1718 ed., reprinted in the 1754, is by far the most useful biographical summary in the early editions and collections, most of which say little or nothing about Navagero's career and circumstances, though Budik (see *Vienna, 1828,* above), 3:284–304, offers a moderately substantial life of the poet in German. Passages of Paolo Giovio, Girolamo Fracastoro, and other early writers who offer some degree of summary of Navagero's life can mostly be found cited in the 1718 and 1754 eds. or in Cicogna 1824–53.

Among notices of Navagero before modern times are J. P. Niceron, *Mémoires pour servir à l'histoire des hommes illustres dans la république des lettres, etc.* (Paris, 1727–45), 13:361–74 (with a list of Navagero's works); G. Tiraboschi, *Storia della letteratura italiana* (Venice, 1796), vol. 7, pt. 4, sect. 17; and A. Meneghelli, *Elogio di Andrea Navagero* (Venice, 1813), incorporated in *Opere dell'abate Antonio Meneghelli,* vol. 1 (Pavia, 1830), 1:103–47. In his *Alde Minuce et l'hellenisme à Venice* (Paris, 1875), A. Firmin-Didot summarizes Navagero's connection with the Aldine Press on pp. 465–66. William Roscoe, *The Life and Pontificate of Leo the Tenth* (Liverpool, 1805), 3:295–304, has a summary of Navagero's life with citation of his poems 16 (wrongly called 17), 36, and 47; Roscoe also gives an English version of Fracastoro's lengthy tribute to Navagero in describing his death (*De Contagione et Contagiosis Morbis,* bk. 2, ch. 6). W. Parr Greswell has remarks on Navagero in his *Memoirs of Angelus Politianus, etc.* (2nd ed., Manchester, 1805, pp. 474–77; on p. 489 he offers a free rendering in verse of poem 9). All such notices, however, contribute little factual information about Navagero beyond what is found in Volpi's *Life* and in Cicogna 1824–53. E. Lamma, "Andrea Navagero poeta," *Rassegna nazionale,* 160 (1908): 280–96, is an analysis of his poetry.

## · EDITIONS, TRANSLATIONS, FURTHER READING ·

There are summaries of Navagero's life of varying length in modern Neo-Latin anthologies that include some of his poems, as well as in general or specialized biographical works, both old and new. These include *Dizionario critico della letteratura italiana* (2nd. ed., Turin, 1986) and *Dizionario Biografico degli Italiani* vol. 78 (2013). Their useful entries for Navagero by Renzo Cremante and Igor Melani, respectively, include extensive bibliographies, though many of the works recorded in them are of limited direct relevance to Navagero's Latin poetry and/or not easily accessible. P. G. Bietenholz and Thomas B. Deutscher, *Contemporaries of Erasmus* (Toronto, 1985), 3:8–9, has an entry on Navagero.

In my notes the reader will find many references to books and articles of especial relevance to a particular poem or poems. Giovanni Ferroni's recent study, *Dulces Lusus: Lirica pastorale e libri di poesia nel Cinquecento* (Alessandria, 2012), which includes comment on both Navagero and Flaminio, is detailed further at the end of the section on Flaminio below.

### FLAMINIO

For the most complete bibliography of Flaminio's life and works, I refer the reader to Carol Maddison, *Marcantonio Flaminio, Poet, Humanist and Reformer* (London, 1965), 207–14. She notices publication of his *lusus pastorales* on pp. 182–83; see also her p. 206 for some limited remarks on editions. The Mancurti eds. of 1727 and 1743 usefully include a substantial survey of earlier editions of Flaminio (pp. xxxii–xxxviii in both); Cuccoli 1897, 165–66, gives a less ambitious summary. The note "See Handlist N." means "See the Handlist for Navagero," where the citation may be fuller.

### Texts and Editions

The eight books of Flaminio's verse as now reckoned appeared in stages. His *lusus pastorales*, now comprising the third and fourth books, were published as in the list of editions below. I include early collections that printed, along with works of others, all Flaminio's *lusus pastorales* or a high proportion of them. Here and under "Anthologies" I do not list publica-

420

· EDITIONS, TRANSLATIONS, FURTHER READING ·

tions that include only poems of Flaminio other than his *lusus pastorales*. Thus Duchesne's anthology (*Paris, 1560*) does not appear here, though his volume contains very many of Flaminio's other poems (see Handlist N.) Many of these early editions may be found online via Google Books.

Lyons, 1548

> *M. Antonii Flaminii Carminum Libri Duo. Eiusdem Paraphrasis in Triginta Psalmos, Versibus Scripta* (Two Books of Poems of M. Antonio Flaminio. The Same's Paraphrase of Thirty Psalms, Written in Verse), ed. Cesare Flaminio, printed by Sébastien Gryphe. In this volume Flaminio's kinsman Cesare Flaminio published all the *lusus pastorales* in the present bk. 4 (though he called them bk. 2), unnumbered, along with many other poems of Marcantonio. Titles are given for 4.2–4.6. Poems 3.3, 3.4, and 3.21 are also included (without titles) as part of bk. 1 (pp. 40–41). The Paris, ca. 1548 ed., evidently taking its text from this, wrongly prints 4.18–20 as one poem, since 4.18 and 4.19 both end at the foot of a page without indication that a new poem begins on the next page.

Paris, ca. 1548

> See Handlist N. All Flaminio's present-day bk. 4 poems, still called bk. 2 (fols. 16r–27v), are included, though 4.19 and 4.20 are not divided from 4.18, and lack the titles that have been supplied for all the others. Maddison 1965, 183, wrongly says that one of the *lusus pastorales* about the Hyella-Iolas love story is missing. Included within what is called bk. 1, as in the Lyons, 1548 ed., are 3.3, 3.4, and 3.21 (fol. 15v), now with titles. Some further poems (not *lusus pastorales*) are added at the end of bk. 2 as styled in the Lyons, 1548 ed.

Venice, 1548 (printer = Valgrisi)

Florence, 1549 and 1552 (printer = Torrentino)

Venice, 1558 (printer = Giglio)

> *Carmina Quinque Illustrium Poetarum*. See Handlist N. This edition and its reprints include all Flaminio's poems in the present bks. 3 and 4. More of his other poems appear in the expanded 1549 ed.; that of 1552 adds yet more. The substantially different Bergamo, 1753 volume of

## · EDITIONS, TRANSLATIONS, FURTHER READING ·

the same title has no Flaminio component; Maddison 1965, 206, wrongly implies otherwise.

Frankfurt, 1567

Aegidius Periander's poorly produced *Horti Tres Amoris, etc.* (see Handlist N.) gives nearly all Flaminio's *lusus pastorales* (Hortus 1, fols. 154r–68v), omitting only 4.1, 4.22, 4.23, and 4.25. The poems do not have titles. There is often a failure to mark where one poem ends and another begins. A few textual errors are also found, e.g., *puella* (girl) for *capella* (nanny goat) in 4.11.6.

Frankfurt, 1608

Jan Gruter's *Delitiae CC Italorum Poetarum* (see Handlist N.) includes all the bk. 3 and 4 poems (pp. 1009–37). No titles. He makes 4.17.99–104 a separate poem.

Florence, 1719

*Carmina Illustrium Poetarum Italorum* (see Handlist N. under *Florence, 1720*) 4:392–409 includes 3.1–2, 3.7–9, 3.12, 3.15, 3.19, 3.21–24, 3.26–27, 4.1–4, 4.6–14, and 4.16–17 (with 4.17.99–104 treated as a separate poem, as in Gruter's 1608 anthology, the likely source), 4.20–4.21, 4.24–4.25. No titles.

Padua, 1727

*Marci Antonii Flaminii Forocorneliensis, Poetae Celeberrimi, Carminum Libri VIII* (Eight Books of the Poems of the Very Famous Poet Marcantonio Flaminio of Imola), ed. Francesco Maria Mancurti, printed by Giuseppe Comino, includes all the *lusus pastorales* (untitled), even the five bk. 3 poems omitted in the second ed. (*Padua, 1743*), for which see 3.1–3.29n. Mancurti includes useful indexes, testimonia, a substantial Latin *Life* of Flaminio, and a list of earlier editions. Bk. 2 ends with 2.29. Some of the poems reckoned as 2.30–2.42 in the 1743 ed. appear with others, amid some confusion, on pp. 261–64 in this.

Verona, 1740

*Hieronymi Fracastorii et Marci Antonii Flaminii Carmina* (see Handlist N.). All the *lusus pastorales* are present on pp. 183–209. Based on the 1727 Mancurti ed., with the same poems included in bk. 2. Most of

## · EDITIONS, TRANSLATIONS, FURTHER READING ·

the extra poems in Mancurti's 1727 ed., pp. 261–64, are added on pp. 334–36 in this. Flaminio's eclogue *Thyrsis* is given on pp. 436–38. Subsequently reissued in 1747 (Verona), 1759 (Venice), and 1782 (Bassano) without adjustment of the Flaminio component to take account of changes in the second Mancurti ed. of 1743.

Padua, 1743

*Marci Antonii, Joannis Antonii et Gabrielis Flaminiorum Forocorneliensium Carmina* (The Poems of Marcantonio, Giovanni Antonio, and Gabriele Flaminio of Imola), edited by Francesco Maria Mancurti. Second ed., following Mancurti's Padua ed. of 1727, printed by Giuseppe Comino. This volume now incorporates the poems of Marcantonio's relatives, but also omits some of his bk 3 poems, as well as 5.17, 5.31, and 6.35 (see 3.1–3.29n). Bk. 2 is changed from the 1727 ed. to incorporate extra poems as 2.30–2.42. Republished at Prato with the same title and omissions in 1831. Maddison 1965's references are to this edition.

Verona, 1747

See *Verona, 1740*. Maddison 1965, 206, calls this 1747 ed. one of the three major eighteenth-century editions of Flaminio's poems (with Mancurti's two editions of 1727 and 1743), though it is essentially a reissue of the Verona, 1740 ed.

Venice, 1759

See *Verona, 1740*.

Bassano, 1782

See *Verona, 1740*.

Prato, 1831

See *Padua, 1743*. This is a reprint of that second Mancurti ed.

Turin, 1993

*Marcantonio Flaminio, Carmina*, ed. Massimo Scorsone, Edizioni RES; Parthenias 3. Scorsone presents the Latin text with a very few notes, leaving the *lusus pastorales* untitled. The numbering of poems differs in part from that of the 1743 ed. because of the latter edition's exclusion of 3.3, 3.4, 3.14, 3.19, 3.21, 5.17, 5.31, and 6.35 (all present in the 1727

· EDITIONS, TRANSLATIONS, FURTHER READING ·

ed.). The fuller composition of bk. 2 is as in the 1743 ed., not the 1727. Scorscone's text is published digitally as part of the *Poeti d'Italia in lingua latina tra Medioevo e Rinascimento* database.

https://www.poetiditalia.it/texts/FLAMI_MA|carm|001

Cheadle Hulme, 1997 (in two versions)

See Handlist N. Appendix A comprises the Latin text, taken from the Venice, 1759 ed., and translation of all Flaminio's poems of bks. 3 and 4. Superseded by this present volume.

### ANTHOLOGIES

I note here some collections that include a limited number of poems of Flaminio's bks. 3 and 4. I do not record inclusion of his other poems. Several works of only minor importance for Flaminio are omitted here but may be mentioned in the notes on a particular poem or poems.

Dordrecht, 1600

*Veneres Blyenburgicae* (Van Blijenburgh's Venuses; see Handlist N.) includes 3.6 (p. 14), 3.9 (pp. 14–15), 3.7 (pp. 48–49), 3.12 (pp. 157–58), 3.8 (p. 488), 4.2 (pp. 738–39), 4.5 (pp. 794–97), 4.22 (pp. 797–99), 4.6 (pp. 805–6), 4.4 (pp. 819–20), 4.20 (pp. 820–21), 4.21 (pp. 837–38), 3.29 (p. 853).

Antwerp, 1613 (and Antwerp, 1627)

*Flores Illustrium Epitaphiorum* includes 4.7, 4.9, 4.11, 4.12, and 4.24 on pp. 465–68. See Handlist N.

Paris, 1666

*Thesaurus Epitaphiorum, etc.* (see Handlist N.) includes 4.9 (pp. 272–72), 4.4 (p. 273), 4.14 (pp. 273–74), 4.12 (pp. 452–53), 4.11 (p. 453), 4.2 (pp. 453–54), and 4.3 (pp. 454–55). Reprint, Paris, 1686.

London, 1684

*Anthologia, etc.* (see Handlist N.) includes 4.1 (p. 131) and 4.4 (p. 133).

Paris, 1686

See *Paris, 1666.*

Verona, 1732

*Carmina Selecta, etc.* (see Handlist N.) includes 4.25 (vol. 1, p. 51; p. 178 in Verona, 1752 ed.). Printed by Pierantonio Berni.

424

## · EDITIONS, TRANSLATIONS, FURTHER READING ·

Florence, 1738

*Veterum et Illustriorum, etc.* (see Handlist N.) includes 4.3 on pp. 216–17 with the title *Epitaphium Pastorale* (Pastoral Epitaph), 4.6 on pp. 217–18 headed *Eiusdem Prope Argumenti* (Of Almost the Same Purport), and 4.9 on p. 218 with the title *Eiusdem Argumenti* (Of the Same Purport). See further *Florence, 1761*.

London, 1740

Alexander Pope's anthology (see Handlist N.) includes 4.1 (p. 66) and 4.4 (p. 68).

Bergamo, 1746

*Epigrammatum Selectorum Libri Tres* (see Handlist N.) includes 4.9 (p. 197), 4.3 (p. 199), and 4.6 (p. 199–200), all given titles.

Verona, 1752

See *Verona, 1732*.

Bergamo, 1760

*Epigrammatum Selectorum Libri Tres* (see Handlist N.) has 3.1, 3.9, 4.2, 4.3, 4.9, 4.6, and 4.11 on pp. 193–97. All poems are given titles except for 3.9.

Florence, 1761

The second ed. of the work listed under *Florence, 1738* above (with changed title: see Handlist N.) has only 4.6 (p. 89), entitled *Ad Hortum de Morte Dominae* (To a Garden on the Death of Its Mistress).

Venice, 1772

See Handlist N. Includes 3.1, 3.8, and 3.26–27 on pp. 266–67.

Winchester, 1792

*Carmina Quaedam Elegantissima Accedunt Mar[ci] Antonii [Flaminii] Epistolae Quaedam et Lusus Pastorales in Usum Scholae Wintonensis* (Some Very Elegant Poems with Some Letters and *Lusus Pastorales* of Marcantonio Flaminio for the Use of Winchester School). I have not been able to see a copy, but Maddison 1965, 206, reports that twenty-five pastorals are among the works included.

## · EDITIONS, TRANSLATIONS, FURTHER READING ·

Lyons, 1808

Jean Brunel, *Le Parnasse latin moderne, etc.* (see Handlist N.), 1:262–63, has 3.1 with French prose translation.

Vienna, 1816

Anton Stein, *Anthologia Epigrammatum Latinorum, etc.*, includes 4.13 (p. 246). See Handlist N.

Vienna, 1828

P. A. Budik, *Leben und Wirken, etc.* (see Handlist N.), 2:76–135, has a life of Flaminio followed by a few of his poems with German verse translations, including 3.5–8, 3.21–22, 3.26–27, and 4.1.

Liège, 1829

Jean Dominique Fuss gives the text of 3.6–8 and 3.10 on pp. 67–68 of his *Réflexions sur l'usage de latin moderne en poésie et sur le mérite des poètes latins modernes*, a discussion work with substantial citation of certain Neo-Latin poets. Not exactly an anthology, but included here for convenience.

Città di Castello, 1888

Emilio Costa, *Antologia della lirica latina, etc.* (see Handlist N.), pp. 150–62, includes, without notes or translation, 3.5, 3.10, 3.20, 4.11, and 4.19. Brief introductory notice of the poet in general.

Florence, 1927 (2nd ed.)

Ugo Enrico Paoli, *Prose e poesie latine di scrittori italiani*, includes 3.3 and 3.6 on p. 211.

Leiden, 1975

Pierre Laurens and Claudie Balavoine, *Musae Reduces: Anthologie de la poésie latine dans l'Europe de la Renaissance*, 1:197–206. Short introduction and bibliography. Latin text with French prose translation. Poem 4.3 (pp. 204–5) is included. See Handlist N.

New Haven and London, 1979

Fred J. Nichols, *An Anthology of Neo-Latin Poetry*, pp. 418–33, has the Latin text and English prose versions of selected poems of Flaminio, including 3.4, 3.6, 3.16, and 3.17 (pp. 429–31). Brief biographical notes on pp. 691–93. See Handlist N.

· EDITIONS, TRANSLATIONS, FURTHER READING ·

London, 1979
*Renaissance Latin Verse: An Anthology*, ed. Alessandro Perosa and John Sparrow, includes 3.9 (no. 185, p. 290). See Handlist N.

Manchester, 1980
I. D. McFarlane's *Renaissance Latin Poetry* includes the Latin text and an English version of 3.20 (pp. 24–25). Very brief notice of Flaminio's life on p. 222. See Handlist N.

Rednitzhembach, 1994
*Flaminio, Marco Antonio, Gedichte, lateinisch und deutsch.* Übersetzt und erläutert von Heinz Wissmüller. Second, improved version (I have no details of the first), described as *anthologia bilinguis* in *Humanistica Lovaniensia*, vol. 45 (1996): 563. I have not seen this work (of 168 pp.), which may include *lusus pastorales*.

TRANSLATIONS

Full Translations (of Books 3 and 4)

Cheadle Hulme, 1997
See Handlist N. and under "Texts and Editions."

Partial Translations

London, 1786
Simon de Troyes (see Handlist N.), *Choix de poésies* 2:108–14, translates (sometimes freely) 3.6, 3.9, 3.7, 3.8, and 4.6 (unnumbered and given French titles, respectively, *Le rendez-vous, La veillée, L'hommage nocturne, La nuit orageuse, Le jardin*). Before these he translates 2.2 as *Le retour*.

Chester, 1829
*Fifty Select Poems of Marc Antonio Flaminio Imitated by the Late Rev. Edward William Barnard*, ed. by Archdeacon Wrangham (Barnard, 1791–1828, was Francis Wrangham's son-in-law). *Memoir* of Flaminio by Barnard. The poems very loosely "imitated" in English verse include 3.6, 3.20–23, 3.26–28, and 4.1. Phyllis in 3.20 and 3.21 becomes

427

## · EDITIONS, TRANSLATIONS, FURTHER READING ·

Chloe; Lygda and Ligurina in 3.22, 3.23, 3.26 and 3.27 both become Lydia.

Città di Castello, 1900

Arnaldo Bonaventura, *La poesia neo-latina in Italia, etc.* (see Handlist N.), pp. 195–96, translates 3.26, 3.27, and 4.1.

London, 1919

Richard Aldington (1892–1962), *Latin Poems of the Renaissance* (see Handlist N.), has versions of poems of Flaminio on pp. 15–21, including 4.1, 3.1, 3.21, 3.9, 3.7, 3.5, 3.4, 3.8, 3.15, 3.16, 3.26, 3.27, 3.10, 3.12, 3.17, 3.22, and 3.29.

London, 1965

Maddison's study of Flaminio (see below) includes whole or partial versions of some of his *lusus pastorales*. She uses the 1743 ed.'s numbering.

See also the following entries under "Anthologies": *Lyons, 1808; Vienna, 1828; Leiden, 1975; New Haven and London, 1979; Manchester, 1980; Rednitzhembach, 1994.*

### Biography, Commentary, and Criticism (Selected)

The two most important general studies of Flaminio are Ercole Cuccoli, *Marc Antonio Flaminio* (Bologna, 1897), and Carol Maddison, *Marcantonio Flaminio, Poet, Humanist and Reformer* (London, 1965).

As with Navagero, modern Neo-Latin anthologies that include a selection of Flaminio's poems offer useful summaries of his life. Entries on him in general or specialized biographical works are often a valuable starting point too, though they can occasionally include unjustified or inaccurate statements. The entry on Marcantonio Flaminio by Alessandro Pastore in *Dizionario Biografico degli Italiani*, vol. 48 (1997), is particularly substantial and detailed, with an extensive bibliography, though much of it relates primarily to aspects of Flaminio's life other than his Latin poetry and especially distant from his playful ventures into *lusus*

428

· EDITIONS, TRANSLATIONS, FURTHER READING ·

*pastorales.* Pastore is also the author of *Marcantonio Flaminio, Fortune e sfortune di un chierico nell'Italia del Cinquecento* (Milan, 1981). Girolamo Tiraboschi, *Storia della letteratura italiana* (Venice, 1796), vol. 7, pt. 4, sects. 31 and 32, reviews Flaminio's life at some length, and William Roscoe, *The Life and Pontificate of Leo the Tenth* (Liverpool, 1805), 3:304–14, has a summary of Flaminio's life. Giovanni Ferroni, *Dulces Lusus: Lirica pastorale e libri di poesia nel Cinquecento* (Alessandria, 2012), as well as discussing Flaminio's poetry more generally, comments specifically on the bk. 3 pastoral poems (pp. 233–47) and on those in bk. 4 (pp. 248–70). He also makes observations on several of Navagero's poems (pp. 71–93). Also by Ferroni is "A Farewell to Arcadia: Marcantonio Flaminio from Poetry to Faith," in *Allusions and Reflections: Greek and Roman Mythology in Renaissance Europe,* ed. Elizabeth Wåghäll Nivre (Newcastle, 2015), 309–25.

# Bibliography

Adams, J. N. 1982. *The Latin Sexual Vocabulary*. London.

Andrelini, Publio Fausto. 1982. *Publi Fausti Andrelini Amores*. Edited by Godelieve Tournoy-Thoen. Brussels.

Angeriano, Girolamo. 1995. *The Erotopaegnion: A Trifling Book of Love of Girolamo Angeriano*. Edited and translated by Allan M. Wilson. Nieuwkoop.

Anisio, Aulo Giano. 2008. *Melisaeus*. Edited by Micaela Ricci. Foggia.

*Anthologia, seu Selecta Quaedam Poemata Italorum Qui Latine Scripserunt.* 1684. London.

Ariosto, Ludovico. 1938. *Ludovici Areosti Carmina*. Edited by Ezio Bolaffi. 2nd ed. Modena.

Atanagi, Dionigi. 1554. *De le lettere di tredici huomini illustri libri tredici*. Rome.

Baïf, Jean-Antoine de. 1881–90. *Evvres en rime de Ian Antoine de Baif: secrétaire de la chambre du roy, avec une notice biographique et des notes*. Edited by Charles Marty-Laveaux. 5 vols. Paris.

Bargaeus, Petrus Angelius (Pietro Angeli da Barga). 1568. *Petri Angelii Bargaei Poemata Omnia*. Florence.

Bellonci, Maria. 1953. *The Life and Times of Lucrezia Borgia*. Translated by Bernard Wall and Barbara Wall. London.

Bembo, Pietro. 1990. *Carmina*. Edited by Massimo Scorsone. Turin.

———. 2005. *Lyric Poetry, Etna*. Edited and translated by Mary P. Chatfield. Cambridge, MA.

Benassi, Maria Antonietta. 1940. "Scritti inediti o mal conosciuti di Andrea Navagero." *Aevum* 14, no. 2–3: 240–54.

Beza, Theodore (Théodore de Bèze). 1879. *Les juvenilia de Théodore de Bèze*. Edited by Alexandre Machard. Paris.

Bietenholz, Peter G., and Thomas B. Deutscher. 1985–87. *Contemporaries of Erasmus*. 3 vols. Toronto.

Blijenburgh, Damas van. 1600. *Veneres Blyenburgicae*. Dordrecht.

### · BIBLIOGRAPHY ·

Boccaccio, Giovanni. 1964–98. *Bucolicum Carmen*. Edited by G. Bernardi Perini. In *Tutte le opere di Giovanni Boccaccio*, edited by Vittore Branca. 10 vols. Milan.

Bonnefons, Jean. 1720. *Johannis Bonefonii Arverni Carmina*. London.

Borgia, Girolamo. 1666. *Carmina Lyrica et Heroica*. Venice.

Braccesi, Alessandro. 1943. *Alexandri Braccii Carmina*. Edited by Alessandro Perosa. Florence.

Brown, Rawdon, ed. 1871. *Calendar of State Papers Relating to English Affairs in the Archives of Venice*, Vol. 4, *1527–1533*. London.

Budik, Peter Alcantara. 1828. *Leben und Wirken der vorzüglichtsen lateinischen Dichter des XV–XVIII Jahrhunderts sammt metrischer Uebersetzung ihrer Besten Gedichte*. Vienna.

Burton, Robert. 1989–2000. *The Anatomy of Melancholy*. 6 vols. Oxford.

Caius, John. 1570. *De Canibus Britannicis Liber Unus*. London.

Calcagnini, Celio. 1544. *Caelii Calcagnini . . . Opera Aliquot*. Basel.

Canoniero, Pietro Andrea, ed. 1613. *Flores Illustrium Epitaphiorum*. Antwerp. Reprint, Antwerp, 1627.

Capilupi, Ippolito. 1590. *Capiluporum Carmina*. Rome.

*Carmina Illustrium Poetarum Italorum*. 1719–26. 11 vols. Florence. Vol. 6 = 1720.

*Carmina Quinque Illustrium Poetarum*. 1548. Venice. Reprint, Florence, 1549; Florence, 1552; Venice, 1558. New edition with some different poets: Bergamo, 1753.

Cartwright, Julia. 1903. *Isabella d'Este, Marchioness of Mantua, 1474–1539: A Study of the Renaissance*. 2 vols. London.

———. 1908. *The Perfect Courtier: Baldassare Castiglione, His Life and Letters*. 2 vols. London.

Castiglione, Baldassare, Francesco Berni, and Giovanni della Casa. 1995. *Carmina*. Edited by Massimo Scorsone. Turin.

Catalano, Michele. 1930. *Vita di Ludovico Ariosto*. 2 vols. Geneva.

Chamard, Henri. 1961. *Histoire de la Pléiade*. 3 vols. Paris.

Chatfield, Mary P., ed. 2005. *Pietro Bembo: Lyric Poetry, Etna*. Cambridge, MA.

Chorier, Nicolas. 1885. *Aloisiae Sigeae Toletanae Satyra Sotadica de Arcanis Amoris et Veneris*. Paris.

## · BIBLIOGRAPHY ·

Cicogna, Emmanuele Antonio. 1824–53. *Delle inscrizioni veneziane.* 6 vols. Venice.

Cinelli Calvoli, Giovanni, and Dionigi Andrea Sancassani. 1736. *Biblioteca Volante.* 4 vols. Rovereto.

Comaschi, Vincenzo. 1794. *Saggio di poesie di Vincenzo Comaschi parmigiano.* Venice.

Copley, F. O. 1956. *Exclusus Amator: A Study in Latin Love Poetry.* Madison, WI.

Cosenza, Mario Emilio. 1962. *Biographical and Bibliographical Dictionary of the Italian Humanists, and the World of Classical Scholarship in Italy, 1300–1800.* 2nd ed. Boston.

Costa, Emilio. 1888. *Antologia della lirica latina in Italia nei secoli XV e XVI.* Città di Castello.

Cotta, Giovanni. 1802. *Joannis Cottae . . . Carmina Recognita et Aucta.* Edited by Jacopo Morelli. Bassano.

———. 1991a. *Carmina.* Edited by Massimo Scorsone. Turin.

———. 1991b. *Giovanni Cotta–Andrea Navagero, Carmina.* Edited by Rossana Sodano. Turin.

Crawford, J. P. W. 1915. "Sources of an Eclogue of Francisco de la Torre." *Modern Language Notes* 30, no. 7: 214–15.

Cuccoli, Ercole. 1897. *Marc Antonio Flaminio.* Bologna.

D'Arco, Niccolò. 1762. *Nicolai Archii Numerorum Libri IV.* Edited by Zaccaria Betti. Verona.

———. 1996. *I Numeri di Niccolò D'Arco.* Edited by Mariano Welber. Trent.

De La Torre, Francisco. 1984. *Poesía completa.* Edited by Luisa Cerrón Puga. Madrid.

Desportes, Philippe. 1858. *Oeuvres de Desportes.* Paris.

———. 1963. *Diverses amours, et autres oeuvres meslées.* Edited by Victor E. Graham. Geneva.

Dickens, Arthur Geoffrey. 1968. *The Counter Reformation.* London.

Dornau, Caspar. 1619. *Amphitheatrum Sapientiae Socraticae Joco-Seriae.* 2 vols. Hanover.

Dousa, Jan the Elder. 1976. *Iani Douzae a Noortwyck Epigrammatum Libri II.* Edited by Chris L. Heeksakkers. Leiden.

## · BIBLIOGRAPHY ·

Drummond, William. 1913. *The Poetical Works of William Drummond of Hawthornden.* Edited by L. E. Kaster. 2 vols. Manchester.

Du Bellay, Joachim. 1918. *Poésies françaises et latines.* Edited by E. Courbet. 2 vols. Paris.

Duchesne, Léger, ed. 1560. *Flores Epigrammatum ex Optimis Quibusque Authoribus Excerpti.* Vol. 2, *Farrago Poematum, etc.* Paris. Vol. 1 appeared in 1555.

Dunlop, Geoffrey A. 1914. "The Sources of the Idylls of Jean Vauquelin de la Fresnaye." *Modern Philology* 12, no. 3: 133–64.

Eckhardt, Alexandre. 1920. "Ronsard accusé de plagiat: L'invention de l'églogue." *Revue du Seizième Siècle* 7, no. 3–4: 235–47.

Edmonds, J. M., ed. 1957–61. *The Fragments of Attic Comedy.* Leiden.

*Epigrammatum Selectorum Libri Tres.* 1746. Bergamo. 2nd ed., Bergamo, 1760.

Erlanger, Rachel. 1979. *Lucrezia Borgia: A Biography.* London.

Ferroni, Giovanni. 2012. *Dulces Lusus: Lirica pastorale e libri di poesia nel Cinquecento.* Alessandria.

Firmin-Didot, Ambroise. 1875. *Alde Manuce et l'hellénisme à Venise.* Paris.

Flaminio, Giovanni Antonio. 1744. *Joannis Antonii Flaminii Forocorneliensis Epistolae Familiares.* Edited by Domenico Giuseppe Capponi. Bologna.

Flaminio, Marcantonio. 1548. *M. Antonii Flaminii Carminum Libri Duo. Eiusdem Paraphrasis in Triginta Psalmos, Versibus Scripta.* Edited by Cesare Flaminio. Lyons.

———. 1727. *Marci Antonii Flaminii Forocorneliensis, Poetae Celeberrimi, Carminum Libri VIII.* Edited by Francesco Maria Mancurti. Padua.

———. 1743. *Marci Antonii, Joannis Antonii et Gabrielis Flaminiorum Forocorneliensium Carmina.* Edited by Francesco Maria Mancurti. Padua. Reprint, Prato, 1831.

———. 1993. *Marcantonio Flaminio, Carmina.* Edited by Massimo Scorsone. Turin.

Florio, Raffaele di. 1909. *Girolamo Borgia, poeta e storico.* Salerno.

Fracastoro, Girolamo. 1555. *Opera Omnia, in Unum Proxime Post Illius Mortem Collecta . . . Accesserunt Andreae Naugerii Patricii Veneti Orationes Duaeque Carminaque Nonnulla.* Venice.

# · BIBLIOGRAPHY ·

———. 1574. *Opera Omnia, in Unum Proxime Post Illius Mortem Collecta . . .* Venice.

———. 1740. *Hieronymi Fracastorii et Marci Antonii Flaminii Carmina, etc.* Verona. Further eds.: Verona, 1747; Venice, 1759; Bassano, 1782.

———. 2005. *Navagero, Della poetica.* Edited and translated by Enrico Peruzzi. Florence.

———. 2013. *Girolamo Fracastoro, Latin Poetry.* Edited and translated by James Gardner. Cambridge, MA.

Fucilla, Joseph G. 1938. "Navagero's *De Cupidine et Hyella.*" *Philological Quarterly* 17:288–96.

Gagny, Jean de, ed. Ca. 1548. *Doctissimorum Nostra Aetate Italorum Epigrammata.* Paris.

Gaisser, Julia Haig. 1993. *Catullus and His Renaissance Readers.* Oxford.

Gilroy, Ruth Perry. 1930. "The Latin Poems of Andrea Navagero, Text, Introduction and Notes." M.A. diss., Johns Hopkins University.

Giovio, Paolo. 1972. *Pauli Iovii Opera.* Edited by Renzo Meregazzi. 8 vols. Rome.

———. 2013. *Notable Men and Women of Our Time.* Edited and translated by Kenneth Gouwens. Cambridge, MA.

Gragg, Florence A., ed. 1927. *Latin Writings of the Italian Humanists.* New York. Reprint, 1981.

Grant, W. Leonard. 1957. "New Forms of Neo-Latin Pastoral." *Studies in the Renaissance* 4:71–100.

———. 1965. *Neo-Latin Literature and the Pastoral.* Chapel Hill.

Greswell, William Parr. 1801. *Memoirs of Angelus Politianus, Actius Sincerus Sannazarius, Petrus Bembus, Hieronymus Fracastorius, Marcus Antonius Flaminius, and the Amalthei: Translations from Their Poetical Works, and Notes and Observations Concerning Other Literary Characters of the Fifteenth and Sixteenth Centuries.* Manchester.

Griggio, Claudio. 1976–77. "Per l'edizione dei *Lusus* del Navagero." *Atti dell'Istituto Veneto di Scienze, Lettere ed Arti, Classe di scienze morali, lettere ed arti* 135:87–113.

Grilli, Luigi. 1898. *Versioni poetiche dai lirici latini dei secoli XV e XVI.* Città di Castello.

Gruter, Jan. 1608. *Delitiae CC Italorum Poetarum.* Frankfurt am Main.

## · BIBLIOGRAPHY ·

Gualtieri, Francesco Saverio, ed. 1786. *Viti Mariae Iuvenati Poematum Libellus*. Naples.

Hutton, James. 1935. *The Greek Anthology in Italy to the Year 1800*. Ithaca.

——. 1941. "Analogues of Shakespeare's Sonnets 153–54: Contributions to the History of a Theme." *Modern Philology* 38, no. 4: 385–403.

——. 1946. *The Greek Anthology in France and in the Latin Writers of the Netherlands to the Year 1800*. Ithaca.

Hyde, John Kenneth. 1966. *Padua in the Age of Dante*. Manchester.

——. 1980. *Essays on Renaissance Poetry*. Edited by Rita Guerlac. Ithaca and London.

Kassel, Rudolf, and Colin Austin, eds. 1989. *Poetae Comici Graeci*. Berlin.

Kidwell, Carol. 1991. *Pontano: Poet and Prime Minister*. London.

——. 2004. *Pietro Bembo: Lover, Linguist, Cardinal*. Montreal.

Kock, Theodor, ed. 1880–88. *Comicorum Atticorum Fragmenta*. Leipzig.

Kristeller, Paul Oskar. 1963–97. *Iter Italicum: A Finding List of Uncatalogued or Incompletely Catalogued Humanistic Manuscripts of the Renaissance in Italian and Other Libraries*. 7 vols. London and Leiden.

Kuhn, Paul. 1914. "L'influence néo-latine dans les églogues de Ronsard." *Revue d'Histoire Littéraire de la France* 21, no. 2: 309–25.

Lamma, Ernesto. 1908. *Andrea Navagero poeta: con un saggio di traduzione dai Carmina*. Florence.

Landino, Cristoforo. 1939. *Christophori Landini Carmina Omnia*. Edited by Alessandro Perosa. Florence.

Laurens, Pierre, and Claudie Balavoine, eds. and trans. 1975. *Musae Reduces: Anthologie de la poésie latine dans l'Europe de la Renaissance*. 2 vols. Leiden.

Leitch, Virginia T. 1953. *The Maltese Dog*. Riverdale, MD.

Ludwig, Walther. 1990. "The Origin and Development of the Catullan Style in Neo-Latin Poetry." In *Latin Poetry and the Classical Tradition: Essays in Medieval and Renaissance Literature*, edited by Peter Godman and Oswyn Murray, 183–98. Oxford.

Maddison, Carol. 1960. *Apollo and the Nine: A History of the Ode*. Baltimore.

——. 1965. *Marcantonio Flaminio, Poet, Humanist and Reformer*. London.

## · BIBLIOGRAPHY ·

Magny, Olivier de. 1995. *Les trois premiers livres des odes de 1559*. Edited by François Rouget. Geneva.

Mantuanus, Baptista (Battista Spagnoli). 1911. *The Eclogues of Baptista Mantuanus*. Edited by W. P. Mustard. Baltimore. Reprint, London, 2017.

Marino, Giambattista. 1987. *Rime amorose*. Edited by Ottavio Besomi and Alessandro Martini. Ferrara.

Marullo, Michele. 1951. *Michelis Marulli Carmina*. Edited by Alessandro Perosa. Zurich.

——. 2012. *Poems*. Translated by Charles Fantazzi. Cambridge, MA.

McFarlane, I. D. 1980. *Renaissance Latin Poetry*. Manchester.

Merula, Bartolomeo. 1499. *Ovidius de Tristibus cum Commento*. Venice.

Milton, John. 2009. *Complete Shorter Poems*. Edited by Stella P. Revard. Malden, MA.

Mistruzzi, Vittorio. 1924. "Giovanni Cotta." *Giornale storico della letteratura italiana*, suppl. 22–23: 1–131.

Mittarelli, Giovanni-Benedetto. 1779. *Bibliotheca Codicum Manuscriptorum Monasterii S. Michaelis Venetiarum Prope Murianum*. Venice.

Molza, Francesco Maria. 1747–54. *Delle poesie volgari e latine di Francesco Maria Molza*. 3 vols. Bergamo.

——. 1999. *Elegiae et Alia*. Edited by Massimo Scorsone and Rossana Sodano. Turin.

Monteforte, Carmelo. 1899. *Ercole Strozzi poeta ferrarese: La vita, le sue poesie latine e volgari con un sonetto inedito*. Catania.

Muratori, Ludovico Antonio. 1733. *Rerum Italicarum Scriptores ab Anno Aerae Christianae Quingentesimo ad Millesimum Quingentesimum*. Vol. 23. Milan.

Muret, Marc-Antoine. 1834. *M. Antonii Mureti Opera Omnia*. Edited by Karl Heinrich Frotscher. 3 vols. Leipzig.

Murgatroyd, Paul, ed. 2001. *Tibullus 1: A Commentary on the First Book of the Elegies of Albius Tibullus*. Bristol.

Muscetta, Carlo, and Daniele Ponchiroli, eds. 1959. *Poesia del Quattrocento e del Cinquecento*. Turin.

Mustard, Wilfred P. 1909. "Later Echoes of the Greek Bucolic Poets." *American Journal of Philology* 30, no. 3: 245–83.

· BIBLIOGRAPHY ·

Navagero, Andrea. 1530. *Andreae Naugerii Patricii Veneti Orationes Duae Carminaque Nonnulla*. Venice.

———. 1718. *Andreae Naugerii, Patricii Veneti Oratoris et Poetae Clarissimi Opera Omnia*. Edited by Giovanni Antonio Volpi and Gaetano Volpi. Padua. Reprint, Venice, 1754.

———. 1782. *Le rime di Messer Andrea Navagero*. Nice.

———. 1991. *Giovanni Cotta–Andrea Navagero, Carmina*. Edited by Rossana Sodano. Turin.

———. 1997. *Lusus (Playful Compositions)*. Edited by Allan M. Wilson. Cheadle Hulme.

———. 2001. *Lusus*. Edited by Claudio Griggio. In *Poeti d'Italia in lingua latina* online database, https://www.poetiditalia.it/texts/NAVAGERO|lusu|001.

Neue, Friedrich. 1897. *Formenlehre der lateinischen Sprache*. 3 vols. Berlin.

Niccoli, Camillo, ed. 1738. *Veterum et Illustriorum Saeculi XVI Poetarum Epigrammata, etc*. Florence.

———. 1761. *Epigrammata ad Usum Scholarum a Patre Camillo Nicolio . . . Selecta*. Florence.

Nichols, Fred J. 1979. *An Anthology of Neo-Latin Poetry*. New Haven and London.

———. 1998. "Navagero's *Lusus* and the Pastoral Tradition." In *Acta Conventus Neo-Latini Bariensis, Bari, 29 Aug.–3 Sept. 1994*, 445–52. Tempe, AZ.

Nivre, Elizabeth Wåghäll, ed. 2005. *Allusions and Reflections: Greek and Roman Mythology in Renaissance Europe*. Newcastle upon Tyne.

Orsato, Sertorio. 1678. *Historia di Padova*. Padua.

Pannonius, Janus. 1985. *Epigrammata*. Edited and translated by Anthony A. Barrett. Budapest.

Pasquazi, Silvio, ed. 1957. *Rinascimento ferrarese: Tebaldeo, Bendedei, Guarini*. Rome.

———. 1966. *Poeti Estensi del Rinascimento*. Florence.

Pastore, Alessandro. 1981. *Marcantonio Flaminio, Fortune e sfortune di un chierico nell'Italia del Cinquecento*. Milan.

Pecoraro, Marco. 1959. *Per la storia dei carmi del Bembo*. Venice.

Pellini, Silvio. 1911. "Andrea Navagero." *Classici e neolatini* 7, no. 2: 236–52.

## · BIBLIOGRAPHY ·

Periander, Aegidius, ed. 1567. *Horti Tres Amoris Amoenissimi e Praestantissimis Poetis Nostri Saeculi*. Frankfurt.

Perosa, Alessandro, and John Sparrow, eds. 1979. *Renaissance Latin Verse: An Anthology*. London.

Petrarch, Francesco. 1976. *Petrarch's Lyric Poems: The* Rime Sparse *and Other Lyrics*. Edited and translated by Robert M. Durling. New Haven.

Pfeiffer, Rudolph, ed. 1949. *Callimachus*. Oxford.

Pigna, Giovanni Battista. 1553. *Io. Baptistae Pigna Carminum Libri Quatuor, ad Alphonsum Ferrariae Principem*. Venice.

Pignoria, Lorenzo. 1625. *Le origini di Padova*. Padua.

Pinelli, Giovambattista. 1594. *Io. Baptista Pinelli Genuensis Carminum Liber Secundus*. Florence.

*Poematia Aliquot Insignia Illustrium Poetarum Recentiorum*. 1544. Basel.

Poliziano, Angelo. 2004. *Silvae*. Edited and translated by Charles Fantazzi. Cambridge, MA.

Pontano, Giovanni Gioviano. 1501. *De Hortis Hesperidum, sive De Cultu Citriorum*. Venice.

———. 1902–5. *Carmina*. Edited by Benedetto Soldati. 2 vols. Florence.

———. 1948. *Carmina, ecloghe, elegie, liriche*. Edited by Johannes Oeschger. Bari.

———. 2014. *On Married Love, Eridanus*. Translated by Luke Roman. Cambridge, MA.

Pope, Alexander, ed. 1740. *Selecta Poemata Italorum Qui Latine Scripserunt*. 2 vols. London.

Rapin, René. 1672. *Hortorum Libri, Eclogae, Liber de Carmine Pastorali, Odae*. Leiden.

*Rime e prose di alcuni cinofili vicentini e di altri illustri italiani*. 1826. Venice.

Ronsard, Pierre de. 1887–93. *Oeuvres de P. de Ronsard, gentilhomme vandomois*. Edited by Charles Marty-Laveaux. 6 vols. Paris.

———. 1914–75. *Oeuvres complètes de P. de Ronsard*. Edited by Paul Laumonier. 20 vols. Paris.

Roscoe, William. 1805. *The Life and Pontificate of Leo the Tenth*. 4 vols. Liverpool.

Rota, Bernardino. 1726. *Delle poesie del signor Bernardino Rota cavaliere napoletano*. Edited by Scipione Ammirato. Naples.

## · BIBLIOGRAPHY ·

Sabeo, Fausto. 1556. *Epigrammatum Fausti Sabaei Brixiani Custodis Bibliotecae Vaticanae Libri Quinque*. Rome.

Sacré, Dirk. 1987. "Andrea Navagero, *Lusus*: Three Textual Notes." *Humanistica Lovaniensia* 36:296–98.

Saint-Gelais, Mellin de. 1873. *Oeuvres complètes de Melin de Sainct-Gelays*. Edited by Prosper Blanchemain. 3 vols. Paris.

———. 1993. *Oeuvres poétiques françaises*. Edited by Donald Stone, Jr. Paris.

Saint-Leger, Mercier de, ed. 1791. *Quinque Illustrium Poetarum Lusus in Venerem*. Paris.

Sannazaro, Jacopo. 1529. *Odae. Eiusdem Elegia de Malo Punico. Ioannis Cotta Carmina. M. Antonii Flaminii Carmina*. Venice.

———. 1590. *Jacobi Sannazarii Opera Omnia*. Rome.

———. 1728. *Actii Sinceri Sannazarii Patricii Neapolitani Opera Latine Scripta . . . Accedunt . . . Fratrum Amaltheorum Carmina*. Amsterdam.

———. 2009. *Latin Poetry*. Edited and translated by Michael C. J. Putnam. Cambridge, MA.

Sanudo, Marino. 1882. *I diarii di Marino Sanudo*. Edited by Nicolò Barozzi. Vol. 8. Venice.

Scaliger, Julius Caesar. 1994. *Poetices Libri Septem*. Edited by Luc Deitz and Gregor Vogt-Spira. 6 vols. Stuttgart-Bad Cannstatt.

Scardeone, Bernardino. 1560. *De Antiquitate Urbis Patavii . . . Libri Tres*. Basel.

Scorsone, Massimo, ed. 1993. *Marcantonio Flaminio, Carmina*. Turin.

Scott, Janet G. 1926. "Parallels to Three Elizabethan Sonnets." *Modern Language Review* 21, no. 2: 190–92.

Simon de Troyes, Edouard-Thomas, ed. and trans. 1786. *Choix de poésies, traduites du grec, du latin, et de l'italien*. 2 vols. Paris.

Sparrow, John. 1976. "Renaissance Latin Poetry: Some Sixteenth-Century Italian Anthologies." In *Cultural Aspects of the Italian Renaissance*, edited by Cecil H. Clough, 386–405. Manchester.

Spila, Cristiano, ed. 2002. *Cani di pietra: L'epicedio canino nella poesia del rinascimento*. Rome.

Stone, Donald, Jr. 1981. "'L'Adonis' de Ronsard et Andrea Navagero." *Bibliothèque d'Humanisme et Renaissance* 43, no. 1: 155–58.

## · BIBLIOGRAPHY ·

Strada, Famiano. 1631. *Famiani Stradae Romani e Societate Iesu, Prolusiones Academicae.* Oxford.

Strozzi, Ercole. 1513. *Strozii Poetae Pater et Filius.* Venice.

Strozzi, Tito Vespasiano. 1916. *Tito Vespasiano Strozzi: Poesie latine.* Edited by Anita della Guardia. Modena.

Symonds, John Addington. 1897. *The Renaissance in Italy.* Vol. 2, *The Revival of Learning.* 3rd ed. London.

*Thesaurus Epitaphiorum, etc.* 1666. Paris. Reprint, Paris, 1686.

Tiraboschi, Girolamo. 1795–96. *Storia della letteratura italiana.* 9 vols. Venice.

Toscano, Giovanni Matteo, ed. 1576. *Carmina Illustrium Poetarum Italorum.* Vol. 1. Paris.

Trissino, Giovanni Giorgio. 1729. *Tutte le opere di Giovan Giorgio Trissino.* Edited by Scipione Maffei. 2 vols. Verona.

Ubaldini, Giovanni Paolo, ed. 1563. *Carmina Poetarum Nobilium Io. Pauli Ubaldini Studio Conquisita.* Milan.

Valeriano, Giovanni Pierio. 1549. *Pierii Valeriani Amorum Libri V.* Venice.

———. 1550. *Hexametri, Odae, et Epigrammata.* Venice.

Varchi, Benedetto. 1969. *Liber Carminum Benedicti Varchii.* Edited by Aulo Greco. Rome.

Vega, Garcilaso de la. 1981. *Obras completas: con comentario.* Edited by Elias L. Rivers. Madrid.

Wiffen, Jeremiah Holmes, trans. 1823. *The Works of Garcilasso de la Vega.* London.

Wilson, Alice E., ed. and trans. 1973. *Andrea Navagero, Lusus.* Nieuwkoop.

Wilson, Allan M., ed. and trans. 1995. *The Erotopaegnion: A Trifling Book of Love of Girolamo Angeriano.* Nieuwkoop.

———. 1997. *Andrea Navagero, Lusus (Playful Compositions).* Cheadle Hulme.

———. 1998. *An Anthology of Neo-Latin "Dog" Poems.* Cheadle Hulme.

Wirtz, Maria. 1906. *Ercole Strozzi, poeta ferrarese.* Ferrara.

Zanchi, Basilio. 1553. *Basilii Zanchi Poemata.* Rome.

———. 1555. *Basilii Zanchi Bergomatis Poematum Libri VIII.* Basel.

# Index to Navagero

Lowercase Roman numerals refer to page numbers in the Introduction. All other references are to Navagero's poems or to their notes, keyed to poem and, where applicable, line number. Line numbers are given in accordance with the Latin text.

Accius, 25.35n
Achilles, 27.41–42n, 36.13–16n, 36.16, 44.25n, 55.32–33n
Acmon, 15n, 15.1; representing Navagero, 16n, 16.1
Acon, 19n, 19.6
Adonis, 20.72–74n, 20.74, 20.76–85n
Adriani, Lorenzo, 20.26n
Adriatic Sea, 20.28
adynata, 27.63–67n, 27.74–77n
Aegle, 26.45, 26.45–46n
Aegon (seemingly for Pontano), x, 20.69–70n, 20.70, 20.87, 20.95
Aeolian Sea, 50.3–4n, 50.4
Aganippe, 44.45–49n; *Aganippis* (adj.), 44.48
Agli, Peregrino, 20.33–34n
Agnadello (Ghiaradadda), battle of, ix, x, xxxi n10, 35n, 42n, 44.64–65n, 44.74–77n
Alamanni, Luigi, 10A.4n
Alcaeus, 36.13–16n, 36.14, 63n
Alcippe, 18n, 18.1; another, 27.60, 27.60–62n

Aleandro, Girolamo, xxxi n10, 50.5n
Alexander the Great, 50.11n
allegory, 16n, 23n
Almo(n), 10Bn, 10B.5, 18n, 18.1, 18.3, 18.13
Alps/Alpine, 20.9, 20.9n, 44.73
Alviano, Bartolomeo d' (in Latin commonly *Livianus*), 36.3–4n; academy at Pordenone, viii–ix, 20.1n, 25.43n, 44.3n; Agnadello, defeat at, ix, x, xxxi n10, 35n, 42n, 44.64–65n (situation just before, 44.74–77, 44.74–77n); dog Caparion, Cotta's epitaph for, 44.70–73n; Garigliano (Liri), 1503 victory over French at, 44.66–69, 44.66–69n; Gir. Borgia, relations with and tributes of, x, xxxi n10, 20.69–70n, 44.64–65n, 44.70–73n; Maximilian I, victories over, 44.64–65n, 44.70–73, 44.70–73n; Navagero's funeral oration for, x,

443

· INDEX TO NAVAGERO ·

Alviano, Bartolomeo d' (*continued*)
44n, 44.66–69n, 44.70–73n;
sons of, Angelo (prob. sub-
ject of genethliacon, 44) and
Livio Attilio, ix, xiv, 44n,
44.4–5n, 44.91–94n; wife of
(Pantasilea Baglioni), ad-
dressed, 44.33; widowed
wife left with three daugh-
ters and one baby son, 44n
Amalteo, Cornelio, 21n, 41.35–36n
Amalteo, Giovanni Battista,
19.5In, 21n, 26.1–2n, 26.25–
38n, 27.63–67n, 29n, 38.4n,
39.9–10n, 59n; *Eclogues*,
27.32n
Amalteo, Girolamo, 20.39–41n,
21n, 21.7n, 38.4n
amaranth, 13.3, 13.3–4n
Amaryllis, 25.19, 25.19n; another,
27.13, 27.23, 27.26, 27.35,
27.63, 27.73, 27.77
Amathus (and *Amathusis* =
Venus), 25.47, 25.47n
*Ambarvalia*, In, 1.15–16, 1.15–16n
ambrosia, 56.7–8n, 59.21–22n
Amor. *See* Love
Amymone, 26.31, 26.31–32n
Amyntas, 10A.1, 10A.9, 10Bn
Anacreontea, 21n, 36n
Anchises, 22.7–8n
Andrelini, Publio Fausto: *Eclogues*,
27n; *Livia, seu Amores*, 57.2n
Angeriano, Girolamo, 13.3–4n,
13.5n, 21n, 25.50n, 28n, 28.5–
6n, 29n, 29.15–16n, 30.31–
32n, 36.1–4n, 41.35–36n

animals, as love gifts, 5.5–6n
Anisio, Giano (Giovanni Fran-
cesco), 20.33–34n, 20.50n
Antenor, 35.1–8n, 35.7
*Anthologia Palatina. See Greek An-
thology*
Aonia/Aonian, 56.16; *Aonides* of
Muses, 44.45–49n, 44.47,
55.4
Aphrodite, 17n, 17.8n, 17.9–10n,
42.1–6n. *See also* Venus
Apollo/Phoebus, 20.42, 20.91,
23n, 23.7, 23.7n, 26.43n,
31.27n, 44.47, 48.1–4n;
Canal called his earthly
brother, 30.1n; as the sun,
9.5n, 38.1, 44.81–88n, 44.88,
55.27
Apollodorus, 19.41n, 26.57–58n
Apollonius of Rhodes, 25.51–52n
Apuleius, 19.44n, 57.9–10n
Arabia/Arab, 21.9–10n, 21.10
Arcadia/Arcadian, 18.4, 19.1n,
20.96–97n, 26.45–46n,
26.46; Nonacrian (18.1, 18.1–
2n, 26.45) and Parrhasian
(26.44, 26.44n) are substi-
tutes
Arco, Niccolò d', 2.6n, 35.23n
Ariosto, Lodovico: *Carmina*,
26.73n, 54n, 54.5–6n, 59.38–
42n; *Orlando furioso*, 35.23n,
44.91–94n
Armenia/Armenian, 25.48–49n,
25.49
Asilas/Asylas, 24.3, 24.3n, 42n
Asolo, viii

444

## · INDEX TO NAVAGERO ·

Assyria/Assyrian: Assyrian perfumes, 25.14, 25.14n, 31.25–26n; Assyrian shepherd (Adonis), 20.72, 20.72–74n
Astraea, 44.91–94n, 44.93
Atalanta, 26.57, 26.57–58n
Athena, 17n, 17.8n, 17.9–10n. See also Minerva
Atilius/Acilius, Gaius, 68 (unnamed subject), 68n, 68.4n
Augon (dog), 8n, 8.1, 8.7, 8.8
Augurelli, Giovanni Aurelio, 30.31–32n
Augustine (saint), 69.25n
Augustus, 23.9n. See also Octavian
Aulus, 64n, 64.3
Aurora, 27.72; as mother of Memnon, 34.1–4n, 34.3; as wife of Tithonus, 37.1, 37.1n
Ausonia/Ausonian (for Italy/Italian), 20.35, 20.35n, 44.71, 44.78–81n, 44.79, 44.83
Ausonius and [Ausonius], 1.13.3–4n; De rosis nascentibus, 37n; Epigrams, 65.7–9n

Bacchus, 11n, 15n, 22.9–12n, 69.7; as Iacchus, 4.4, 4.4n, 11.3, 15.4, 15.4n; as Lyaeus, 11.1, 11.1n; as sower of the vine, 15.4, 15.4n
Bacchylides, 2n
Baiae, 26n, 66n, 66.1, 66.1n
Baïf, Jean Antoine de, 11n, 13n, 21.11n, 25n, 27n, 28n, 55n
Bardulone, Gian Giacomo, ix
Bargaeus (Pietro Angeli da

Barga): Italian versions of N., 2n, 6n, 13n, 47n; Latin poems cited, 7n, 11n, 55.52–63n
Bear (constellation), for "north," 44.70, 44.70n. See also Callisto
Beazzano, Agostino, ix, 42n
Beccadelli, Antonio (Panormita), 65.1n
Belleau, Rémy, 20.58–70n; Chant pastoral de la paix, 20n
Bellona, 44.89–92n
Bembo, Pietro, viii, ix, xi, xv, xxxi n8, xxxii n13 (his pastoral trifles), 19.44n, 25.3–4n, 25.43n, 26.3–4n, 26.62n, 30n, 30.1 (joint addressee), 36.2 (addressee), 39.9–10n, 43n, 54n, 58A and 58Bn; career of, 30.1n; pet dog of, 43n
Bentivoglio, Ercole, 54n
Bessarion (cardinal), xv
Bèze, Théodore de, 29n, 55.40–41n
biblical references: Luke 1:26, 34.13–16n; Luke 10:19, 34.18–20n; Matthew 18:39, 34.18–20n; 1 Peter 5:8, 34.18–20n; Psalms 102 (Vulgate), 65.13–14n
Bion, 27.46n
Blois, treaty of (1505), 44.66–69n
Boccaccio, Giovanni, 24.3n; Eclogues, 14.1–2n
Bocchi, Achille, 36.3–4n, 69n

445

## · INDEX TO NAVAGERO ·

Bol(l)ani, Lucrezia, vii, vii n3

Bonnefons, Jean, 59n; *Pancharis*, 14n, 21.6n, 26.78n, 57.8n, 59.38–42n, 59.40n; *Pervigilium Veneris* (Vigil of Venus), 43.2n, 65.7–9n

Borgetto (Borgiolus; Maltese dog of Antonio Tebaldeo), ix, xiii, xiv, 43 (named in line 1), 43n, 50, 50n, 51 (named in line 2)

Borgia, Cesare, 20.69–70n; gives Tebaldeo the dog Borgetto, 43n

Borgia, Girolamo, vii, ix, x, xiii, xxx n5, xxxi n10, 34.18–20n; addressee of Pontano, 20.69–70n, 26.25–38n; addresses N. in poem, 42n; v. prob. = Damon, envied pupil of Aegon (Pontano), 20.69, 20.69–70n, 20.86; encomium of Alviano, 44.64–65n, 44.70–73n; epitaph for Alviano, 44.70–73n; verse panegyric lauding Alviano, 44.70–73n

Borgia, Juan, 20.69–70n

Borgia, Lucrezia, 30.1n, 44n; and Tebaldeo's dog Borgetto, 43n, 50.3–4n

Boscán Amolgáver, Juan, xv

Botticelli, Sandro, 25.6n

Braccesi, Alessandro, 65.1n

Brenta (Medoacus; river), 35.6, 35.6n

Britons, 35.15

Bucephala (and Bucephalas), 50.11 (unnamed), 50.11n

Buchanan, George, 29n; *Silvae*, 27.63–67n

Cadmus/Cadmeian (= Theban), 55.1–8n, 55.7

Cadmus (another, imagined), 58B (addressed; named in lines 1 and 2)

Caesar, Julius, 68n, 68.6

Caius, John, 50.3–4n

Calais (son of Boreas), 25.55–64n, 25.58, 25.61

Calcagnini, Celio, 40.2n, 54n, 54.5–6n

Callimachus, 50.3–4n

Calliope, 44.4–5n

Callisto, 14.8n; called Parrhasis, 26.44, 26.44n

Calpurnius Siculus, 3n, 5n, 6n, 6.6–8n, 18n, 20.29–30n, 20.69–70n, 25.19n, 27.32n, 27.46n, 27.60–62n, 27.88n, 44.89–92n

Cambrai, League of, x, 35n

Camenae. *See under* Muses

Canal, Paolo, vii, ix, xiv, xxx n5, 30n, 30.1 (joint addressee), 30.1n

Capaneus' wife. *See* Evadne

Capella, Martianus, 20.15n

Capilupi, Ippolito, 22n

Carew, Thomas, 49n

Carnia, 44.3, 44.3n

446

## · INDEX TO NAVAGERO ·

carving on trees, 6.6–8, 6.6–8n,
    7.3–4n, 20.50, 20.50n,
    27.74–77, 27.74–77n
Casanova, Marcantonio, 43n;
    poem 68 possibly his, 68n
Castiglione, Baldassare, ix, xvi,
    xxi, xxxiii n18, 20.33–34n,
    20.69–70n, 26.25–38n, 54.5–
    6n; *Alcon*, 25.23–42n, 27n; *Il
    cortegiano*, 30.1n
Castillejo, Cristóbal de, 21n, 21.7n,
    21.9–10n, 21.11n
Catullus, xxii, 25.20n, 30n, 30.4n,
    30.31–32n, 31.19–22n, 32n,
    32.12n, 33n, 33.10n, 52n, 57n,
    59.1–3n
    *Carmina* (refs. as in Loeb text):
    **2**, 30.26n, 43.8–9n, 51n,
    51.3n; **3**, 30.2–3n, 43n, 43.5–
    9n, 43.8–9n, 43.15n, 51n,
    57.11–13n; **5**, 32.10n, 65.4n; **8**,
    59.38–42n; **11**, 30.26n, 36n;
    **12**, 52n; **13**, 30.26n, 33.1 and
    3n; **14**, 64.1n; **14A**, 30.2–3n;
    **17**, 55.56n; **22**, 33.1 and 3n;
    **25**, 57.7n, 65.19–20n; **28**,
    30.4n, 30.16n; **30**, 30.4n; **31**,
    47n, 51.4–6n, 52n; **34**, 14.9n,
    34n; **36**, 30.26n; **37**, 30.4n;
    **42**, 33.1 and 3n; **43**, 61n; **45**,
    30.22–25n, 59.13–14n; **46**,
    25n; **48**, 32.8n, 32.10n,
    59.40n; **49**, 52n; **51**, 28.7–8n,
    29.15–16n, 36n; **55**, 21.7n; **60**,
    55.32–33n; **61**, 34n, 43.16n;
    **63**, 57.2n; **64**, 20.66n, 20.72–

    74n, 22.9–12n, 25.61–64n,
    44.23n, 44.25n, 44.36–37n,
    44.38–44n, 55.32–33n,
    55.60–63n, 65.19–20n; **65**,
    25.23–42n, 33.1 and 3n; **66**,
    44.35n; **67**, 57.7n, 65.19–
    20n; **68**, 25.14n, 25.47n,
    26.81–82n; **68A**, 33.1 and 3n;
    **69**, 58A and 58Bn; **70**, 26.6n;
    **71**, 58A and 58Bn; **72**, 59.7–
    8n; **78**, 55.60–63n; **82**, 30.2–
    3n, 33.1 and 3n; **92**, 33.1 and
    3n; **99**, 59.21–22n; **104**, 30.2–
    3n, 30.22–25n; **107**, 26.81–
    82n; **109**, 33.9n; **115**, 57.11–
    13n; ***fr. 2***, 65.18n
Cerberus, 43n
Ceres (Demeter), 1n, 1.1 (ad-
    dressee), 11n, 11.1, 11.3, 60.4–
    6n, 69.6; as Deo, 26.35–36n;
    as goddess of Eleusis, 22.9–
    12n, 22.10; milk and honeyed
    wine offerings, 1.13–14, 1.13–
    14n; wheat spikes as garland,
    1.18, 1.18n
Chaonia/Chaonian, 44.26,
    44.26n
Chariclo, 12n, 12.3
Charinus (or Car-), 61n, 61.1
Charites. *See under* Graces
Chiappino, Paolo, versions of N.'s
    poems by, 19n, 21n, 25n, 26n
Chloris (for Flora), 25.6, 25.6n
Chorier, Nicolas, 57.2n, 57.9–10n
Cicero, Marcus Tullius, 63.1 –4n;
    N.'s edition of speeches of,

## · INDEX TO NAVAGERO ·

Cicero, Marcus Tullius (*continued*)
xv, 40n; *Orationes Philippicae*,
3, 35.9n; 5, 30.17n; 12, 35.22n

Cinyras, 64n, 64.1

Claudian: *De raptu Proserpinae*,
38.4n; *In Eutropium*, 44.81–
88n; *In Rufinum*, 27.13n,
44.4–5n

Clement VII (pope), 20.42–43n

Coccio, Marcantonio. *See* Sabel-
lico, Marcantonio

Comaschi, Vincenzo, 9n, 9.6n,
21n

comparative without comp. force
or for superl., 8.7n, 17.2n,
22.12n, 25.39n, 29.4–6n,
47.1n

Contarini, Gasparo, ix, xxxiii n19

Córdoba, Gonzalo Fernández de,
44.66–69n

Cornaro, Caterina (queen of
Cyprus), viii, xxxii n15

Cotta, Giovanni, ix, x, xxxi n10,
20.33–34n, 20.50n, 25.43n,
30.31–32n, 32n, 35.17n,
44.70–73n, 44.74–77n, 49n,
55.1–8n, 58A and 58Bn,
65.7–9n

Crescimbeni, Giovan Mario, xxix
n1

Crocale, 5n, 5.6

Croesus, 26.10n, 27.45, 27.45n

Cupid. *See* Love

Cybele (Mother Earth, Great
Mother), 19.31, 19.31n

Cypris. *See under* Venus

Cyprus/Cyprian, 31.25–26n, 31.26,

44.12n; annexed by Venice,
viii. *See also* Cornaro,
Caterina; Idalium; Paphos

Cythera, as associated with Venus,
21.12n

Cytherea. *See under* Venus

Damis, 4n, 4.4

Damon, 20n; v. prob. = Girolamo
Borgia, ix, 20.69, 20.69–70n,
20.86

Danube, 35.13, 40.1

Daphne, 23.7n, 26.43, 26.43n,
26.51

Daphnis, 10A.11–12n, 20.96,
20.96–97n, 20.97; another,
27.46, 27.46n

Dardanidae (Trojans), 48.1–4n,
48.4

dating of poems, x, xiii–xiv, 20n,
30n, 31n, 35n, 40n, 41n, 42n,
43n, 44n, 47n, 48n, 54n

Daulian, the, 25.23–42n, 37.34
(there probably Progne)

Decor (Comeliness; personified),
69.26

Deois (Deo's daughter, i.e.,
Proserpina), 26.35, 26.35–
36n

Desportes, Philippe, 9n, 13n

Diana, 14.3n, 14.8n, 14.9n; as
Latona's daughter, 14.3,
37.25, 37.25–28n. *See also*
Hecate; Moon

diminutive adjectives, 43.15n; dou-
ble diminutive adjective,
30.31–32n

448

## · INDEX TO NAVAGERO ·

Dione (used for Venus). *See under* Venus

Dirce, 55.1–8n, 55.7

Discordia (Strife; personified), 44.89–92n, 44.90

Dodona, oak of, 44.26n

dog collars and leashes, 8.9–10, 8.9–10n

dogs and dog poems, xiii; Augon, 8; Borgetto, 43, 50, 51; Hylactor, 10B; Hylax, 10A; Teuchon, 27.7; unnamed dog, 67. *See also notes on those poems, esp.* 8n, 43n, 43.1n, 43.10–14n, 50.3–4n, 67n

Dogstar, 9n, 9.6n, 26.69–70n, 26.70

Dolce, Ludovico, 21n

Donne, John, 49n

Dornau, Caspar, 8n, 10A.4n

Dousa, Janus (Johan van der Does), the Elder, 38n, 55.40–41n

Dousa, Janus (Johan van der Does), the Younger, 21n

Dracontius, 44.17n

dreams of intimacy, 29, 29n; true and false dreams, 29.4–6n

dryads, 66.3, 66.3n

Drummond, William, of Hawthornden: *Chlorus to a Grove*, 7n; *A Lover's Day and Night*, 38n; poems on gifts of hair, 49n

Du Bellay, Joachim, xiii, 59.38–42n

French works: *A Monsieur d'Avanson*, 45n; *Divers jeux rustiques* (*Voeuz rustiques*), 1n, 2n, 3n, 4n, 5n, 6n, 10An, 11n, 13n, 14n, 28n; *Poésies diverses*, 11n; *Les regrets*, 45n; *Sonnets divers*, 11n

Latin works: *Amores*, 14.6n, 55.40–41n; *Elegiae*, 44.4–5n; *Votum Rusticum Iolas*, 1n, 11n, 11.2n

Earth, Mother, 1n, 19.31, 19.31n, 19.33–34n, 25.6n. *See also* Cybele

Echo, 19n, 19.1n, 19.5, 19.5–6n, 19.39, 26.45–46n

Eleusis, goddess of (Demeter/Ceres), 22.9–10n, 22.10

Ennius, 25.3–4n, 25.35n, 54.3–4n

epanalepsis, 26.79–80n, 41.33n

Epicurus, 20.33–34n, 63n, 63.1–4n, 63.3, 63.9

epitaphs: for dogs, 8, 10A, 10B, 43, 43n, 50, 50n, 51, 51n, 67, 67n; for people, 40, 40n, 40.2n, 44.70–73n, 54, 54n, 54.3–4n

epithalamium, 44.38–44n

Eridanus (Po; river), 44.59–63n; daughters of, 50.3, 50.3–4n

Erythraean Sea pearls, 26.83, 26.83–84n

Este, Alfonso I d', 54n

Este, Borso d', 20.33–34n

Este, Isabella d', ix–x, 43n

Etna (mountain), 26.51, 26.51–53n

449

## · INDEX TO NAVAGERO ·

Etruscus, Janus (Alfonso Pazzi),
57.2n
Euganei/Euganean, 35.8, 35.8n
Eumenides (Furies), 25.54, 25.54n
Euphro, 17n, 17.3, 17.8n
Euripides, 22.13–16n
Europa, 26.37, 26.37–38n
Eurydice, 25.51–52n, 25.57, 25.61–
64n
Evadne (called "Capaneus' wife"),
26.11, 26.11–16n

Farnese, Alessandro (cardinal),
20.58–70n, 20.99n
Fates (Parcae), 44.24, 44.24n,
44.25n, 44.36–37n, 51.4,
69.44
fauns, 20.15, 20.15n
Faunus (Pan), xxxii n13, 26.25–
38n, 26.42. *See also under* Pan
Federigo (king of Naples), 44.66–
69n
Ferdinand II (king of Aragon),
35n, 44.66–69n
Flaminio, Marcantonio, 58A and
58Bn; his *lusus pastorales* in
general, xiii, 3n, 21n, 27n;
N.33 wrongly treated as F.'s
by Duchesne, 32n, 33n; neol-
ogisms of, 14.3n; Zanchi,
letter to, 14.3n. *See also*
Mario, Antonio, of Imola
*Carmina* (refs. as 1743 ed., ex-
cept where *Sc.* [= Scorsone]
stated): **1.8**, 44.91–94n; **1.30**,
51.4–6n; **1.34**, 69n; **2.4**,
20.99n; **2.9**, 25.3–4n, 44.4–

5n; **2.12**, 12n; **2.13**, 2.5n; **2.33**,
25.6n; **2.34**, 6n; **3.1**, 20.15n;
**3.5**, 25.6n, 25.19n, 31.44n;
**3.6**, 25.19n; **3.9**, 59n; **3.10**,
2.2n; **3.12**, 13.1n; **3.13**, 6.4–
5n, 22.4n; **3.14**, 10A.9n; **3.15**,
49.4n; **3.16**, 12n, 27.60–62n;
**3.17**, 27.60–62n; **3.18**, 6n,
6.4–5n, 26.6n, 27.50n,
27.60–62n, 32.5–6n, 36.3–
4n, 59.7–8n; **3.25**, 3.3–4n;
**3.28**, 41.37–40n; **3.29**, 13.10n,
22n; **4.1**, 10A.9n, 26.85n,
52n; **4.2**, 3.1n, 5.9–10n, 18.3–
4n; **4.5**, 2.3–4n, 25.19n,
27.41–42n, 36.3–4n, 55.1–8n,
65.19–20n; **4.6**, 13.8n; **4.7**,
50.1n; **4.8**, 27.60–62n; **4.9**,
50.1n; **4.10**, 20.15n, 25.6n,
50.1n; **4.11**, 50.1n; **4.16**,
10A.11–12n, 18.3–4n, 31.1–9n;
**4.17**, 3.3–4n, 6.6–8n, 36.5–
6n, 37.1n, 54.3–4n, 59.27–
29n; **4.20**, 19.24n; **4.21**, 38n;
**4.22**, 38.4n; **4.23**, 14.3n;
**4.24**, 6.6–8n, 13.10n; **5.22**
(5.23 *Sc.*), 20.10n; **5.23** (5.24
*Sc.*), 26.62n; **5.30** (5.32 *Sc.*),
30.4n; **6.42** (6.43 *Sc.*), 6.6–
8n; **6.44** (6.45 *Sc.*), 6.6–8n;
**6.50** (6.51 *Sc.*), 34.18–20n;
**6.51** (6.52 *Sc.*), 6.6–8n; **6.63**
(6.64 *Sc.*), 1.11–12n; *paraphrase
of Psalm 128* (7.25 *Sc.*), 1.11–
12n; *App.* 1 *Sc.*, 65.5n
Flora (Chloris), 25.6, 25.6n
fowling, 19.49–54, 19.53–54n

## · INDEX TO NAVAGERO ·

Fracastoro, Girolamo, ix, xvi, xvii, xxix n1, xxx n2, xxxi n9, xxxi n10, xxxii n15, xxxiii n19, xxxiii n20, 16n, 20.33–34n, 25.43n, 33.1 and 3n, 55n, 58A and 58Bn; *Carmina*, 19.41n, 20.42–43n, 20.58–70n, 25.43n, 31.30n, 44.94n; *Naugerius*, ix, xvii, 19.41n; *Syphilis*, 35.23n, 50.3–4n, 60.3n; *Turrius*, 19.41n, 25.43n

France/French: defeated at the Garigliano, 44.66–69, 44.66–69n; threatening Italy before Agnadello, 44.64–65n, 44.74, 44.74–77n; driven from Italy by Julius II's Holy League, 20, 20n, 42n. *See also* Agnadello; Francis I

Francesco (unidentified), 67.5

Francis I (king of France), xvi, xxx n2

French kissing, 59.38–42, 59.38–42n

Furies. *See* Eumenides

Gabriel (archangel), xv, 34 (addressee), 34n, 34.13–16n

Galatea, 5.5–6n, 27.35–36n, 27.46n, 29n

Gallus, 62n, 62.1

Ganymede/Ganymedean, 55.60–63n, 55.62

Garigliano, battle of the. *See under* Alviano

Gellia, 26.21, 26.21n, 26.50, 26.77

genethliacon, 44, 44n

Germany/German (Austria/Austrian), 44.70–73n, 44.73. *See also* Maximilian I

Gherardi, Pietro, 43.10–14n

Giberti, Antonio, 44.4–5n

Giberti, Gianmatteo, 20.42–43n, 20.58–70n

Giovio, Paolo, xi, xxix n1, xxxi n7, 2n, 9n, 16n, 44n

Girón, Diego, 44.12n

God, 34.13–16n, 34.14, 34.16, 44.96–101n, 44.97

gods, fear of molestation by, 26.25–38n, 26.27–64

Golden Age, 44n, 44.89–92n, 44.91–94n, 44.94n, 44.96–101n

Gonzaga, Elisabetta (duchess of Urbino), ix

Gonzaga, Gian Francesco II (marquis of Mantua), 43n

Gorge (and Gorgo), 27.50, 27.50n

Graces, 25.14n, 37.19, 37.19n, 69.26; as *Charites*, 18.10, 25.14, 41.7, 44.14, 47.6, 56 (addressed; named in line 2), 59 (named in lines 47 and 51); in notes, 56.1n, 59.46n; prosody of *Charites*, 59.47n

*Greek Anthology* (*Anthologia Palatina*), xii, xxxii n13, 2n, 4n. *See also under* Hutton, James Poems: **2.120–24**, 24n; **5.2**, 29n; **5.4**, 22.19–20n; **5.5**, 13n, 22.19–20n; **5.8**, 22.19–20n; **5.26**, 21.12n; **5.30**, 39n; **5.38**,

451

## · INDEX TO NAVAGERO ·

*Greek Anthology (continued)*
60n; **5.55**, 29.15–16n; **5.94**,
29.15–16n; **5.127**, 18n, 27.60–
62n; **5.128**, 22.19–20n; **5.129**,
59.38–42n; **5.161**, 17n; **5.165**,
22.19–20n; **5.166**, 22.19–20n;
**5.197**, 22.19–20n; **5.243**, 29n;
**5.244**, 59.38–42n; **5.259**, 12n;
**5.288**, 12n; **6.17**, 17n; **6.25**,
64n; **6.26**, 64n; **6.34**, 8n;
**6.35**, 8.9–10n, 11n; **6.39**, 17n;
**6.41**, 6.4–5n; **6.44**, 15n; **6.47**,
17n; **6.48**, 17n; **6.53**, 2n; **6.57**,
3n, 18.3–4n; **6.77**, 3n; **6.79**,
19.1n; **6.98**, 3n; **6.106**, 11n;
**6.107**, 8.9–10n; **6.109**, 19.53–
54n; **6.152**, 3n, 6.4–5n;
**6.154**, 11n; **6.158**, 11n; **6.162**,
22.19–20n; **6.168**, 8n; **6.174**,
17n; **6.190**, 6.4–5n; **6.191**,
6.4–5n; **6.198**, 5n; **6.231**,
6.4–5n; **6.238**, 6.4–5n; **6.263**,
8.5n; **6.283**,17n; **6.285**, 17n;
**6.292**, 14n; **6.300**, 6.4–5n;
**7.112**, 5n; **7.183**, 5n; **7.219**,
22.19–20n; **7.272**, 63n; **7.365**,
64n; **7.497**, 63n; **7.540**, 61n;
**7.548**, 20n; **7.647**, 27.50n;
**7.656**, 20.29–30n; **7.703**, 6n;
**9.203**, 12n; **9.309**, 27.50n;
**9.374**, 9n; **9.432**, 6n; **9.627**,
66n; **11.71**, 14n; **11.103**, 63n;
**11.125**, 20n; **11.126**, 61n;
**11.159**, 62n; **11.161**, 62n;
**11.162**, 62n; **11.187**, 60n,
64n; **11.198**, 61n; **11.199**, 61n;
**11.200**, 61n; **11.203**, 61n;

**11.204**, 61n; **11.236**, 64n;
**11.247**, 20.69–70n; **11.267**,
61n; **11.268**, 61n; **11.336**, 61n;
**11.405**, 61n; **11.406**, 61n;
**12.35**, 20n; **12.87**, 20n;
**12.125**, 29n; **12.177**, 29.15–
16n; **13.6**, 5n; **16.176**, 42.1–
6n; **16.177**, 42.1–6n; **16.227**,
9n; **16.228**, 9n; **16.325**, 24n;
**16.326**, 24n; **16.388**, 21n
Grimald, Nicholas, 27n

Haemus (mountain range),
44.45–49n, 44.49
hair as love gift, 49, 49n
hamadryads, 26.41–42n, 26.42
Harrison, William, 50.3–4n
Hebrus (river), 27.78–83n, 27.83
Hecate, 25.53, 25.53n
Helen (of Troy), 6.2n, 35.1–8n
Helicon (mountain), 55.1–8n, 55.7
Henry II (king of France), 20.58–
70n
Henry VIII (king of England),
20n
Hera, 17.9–10n
Hercules, 3.7, 3.7n
Holy League, 20n
Homer, 36.3–4n, 36.13–16n, 37.3n;
*Iliad*, 36.13–16n, 36.15, 37.1n,
41.29–32n, 44.59–63n,
55.32–33n; *Odyssey*, 27.28–
34n, 29n, 37.1n
homosexuality, male, 25.55–64,
25.55–64n, 55, 55n, 65
Horace, xv, xxx n6, 30.16n, 41.37–
40n

452

# · INDEX TO NAVAGERO ·

*Ars poetica*, 8.12n, 26.20n, 36.3–4n

*Carmen saeculare*, 14.3n, 14.9n

*Epistles*: *1.1*, 41.29–32n; *1.5*, 58A and 58Bn; *1.6*, 41.5n; *1.7*, 26.20n; *1.10*, 9.4n; *1.17*, 60.4–6n; *1.18*, 39.1n; *2.1*, 36.3–4n

*Epodes*, 29n; *5*, 39n; *6*, 19.25n; *12*, 58A and 58Bn; *15*, 29n

*Odes*, 35n, 36n; *1.2*, 36.5–6n; *1.4*, 25n, 37.17–19n; *1.6*, 35.25–28n; *1.12*, 37.35n; *1.13*, 59.38–42n; *1.19*, 36.11–12n; *1.20*, 37.35n; *1.22*, 36n, 56.15n; *1.23*, 19.21–22n; *1.24*, xvi; *1.28*, 36.9n; *1.32*, 36.13–16n, 37.17–19n; *1.35*, 34.7–8n, 35.17n; *1.36*, 26.81–82n; *2.5*, 36n; *2.7*, 22.6n; *2.9*, 20.5n; *2.11*, 25.14n; *2.16*, 37.1n; *2.19*, 20.15n; *3.3*, 48.1–4n; *3.8*, 22.19–20n; *3.10*, 28.3–4n, 35.14–16n; *3.11*, 27.16n; *3.14*, 29n; *3.16*, 39n; *3.18*, 26.41–42n, 41.10n; *3.20*, 56.15n; *3.23*, 31.42n; *3.24*, 35.17n; *3.26*, 41n; *3.28*, 31.28–29n; *4.1*, 29n, 31.28–29n, 41n, 41.29–32n; *4.6*, 37.31n; *4.7*, 25n; *4.9*, 36.13–16n; *4.10*, 55n, 55.52–63n; *4.11*, 69.22–23n; *4.12*, 25.23–42n; *4.15*, 35.14–16n, 36.1–4n

*Satires*: *1.1*, 60.4–6n; *1.2*, 38.1n, 58A and 58Bn, 61n; *1.3*, 29n, 41.5n; *1.4*, 58A and 58Bn;
*1.7*, 36.13–16n; *1.10*, 21.4n, 29.4–6n; *2.3*, 26.81–82n, 57.8n; *2.7*, 30.2–3n

Hungary conquered by Turks (1526), 40n

Hutton, James, 66n; *Essays on Renaissance Poetry*, 20.58–70n; *The Greek Anthology in France*, 2n, 62n, 63n, 64n, 66n; *The Greek Anthology in Italy*, 2n, 3n, 9n, 17n, 25.6n, 42.1–6n, 61n, 62n, 63n, 64n, 66n

Hyella (Navagero's), xiii, xiv; addressed, 28, 32, 33; named in text, 21.1, 22.3, 28.1, 30.23, 32.1, 33.2, 33.4, 38.6; in notes, 21n, 21.7n, 22n; nurse of, 22n, 22.13–16n, 22.14

Hylactor (dog), 10Bn, 10B.1, 10B.8

Hylax (dog), 10A.2, 10Bn

Hymen (name used for marriage), 44.35, 44.35n

Hymettus (mountain), 29.11, 29.11–12n

Iacchus. *See under* Bacchus

Icastus, 14n, 14.5

Ida (mountain), 48.3; as "the Phrygian Hill," 16.7, 16.7–8n

Idalium/Idalian, 18.8, 18.8n, 21.12n, 44.12, 44.12n, 56.7–8n, 56.8

Idmon, 2n, 2.3

Illyria/Illyrian, 10A.2, 10A.2n

India/Indians, 44.81–88n, 44.88

Io, 26.33, 26.33–34n

453

## · INDEX TO NAVAGERO ·

Iolas, 3n, 3.1, 27n, 27.23, 27.77, 27.80

Italy/Italian, 35.10, 44.67, 44.77; variant in, 20.34. *See also* Ausonia; Latium

Itys, 25.24, 25.23–42n, 25.27–28n, 25.30n

Janus, 28.1, 28.1n

Jerome (saint), 69.25n

Julius II (pope), x, xiii, xiv, 20 (named in line 45), 20n, 20.33–34n, 20.48n, 20.99n, 35n

Juno Lucina, 14.9n; Hera/Juno, 17.9–10n

Jupiter: as *divum genitor*, 44.97 (there hinting Christian God); Cupid snatching his thunderbolts, 25.50, 25.50n; as Jupiter, 19.24, 25.50, 29.16, 44.24, 44.102, 69.29; as *Saturnius*, 26.29; as *Tonans*, 26.33, 26.63, 34.16 (where = God), 36.6; in notes, 19.24n, 25.50n, 26.25–38n, 26.33–34n, 26.37–38n, 26.44n, 29.15–16n, 34.13–16n, 36.5–6n, 37.1n, 41.34n, 44.26n, 44.96–101n, 44.102–5n, 55.60–63n, 69n

Juvenal, 20.38n

kiss poems, xiii, 59n

Lacedaemon, 42.5, 42.5n. *See also* Sparta

Laconia/Laconians, 42.3; Laconian hounds, 19.25, 19.25n. *See also* Sparta/Spartans

Lactantius, 69.25n

Lajos (Louis) II (king of Hungary), 40, 40n, 40.2n

Lalage, 36n, 36.10, 41n, 41.18

lamp witnessing lovemaking, 22.19–20, 22.19–20n

Landino, Cristoforo, 13.10n; *Xandra*, 39.9–10n

Laomedon, 48.2, 48.1–4n

Lascaris, Constantine, 30.1n

Latium/Latin (for Italy/Italian), 20.10, 20.10n, 44.74–77n, 44.75, 44.81–88n, 44.85, 48.8, 48.8n, 55.34, 57.34n

Latona's daughter. *See under* Diana

Leernout, Jean, 21n

Leo X (pope), xv, 20.33–34n, 30.1n, 40n, 44.94n

Lesbos/Lesbian, 36.13, 36.13–36n

Leucas, 6n, 6.1, 7.4, 12n

Leucippe, 12n, 12.2, 12.8

Libethra, 55.1–8n, 55.5

Liri (river, with ref. to battle of the Garigliano), 44.68. *See also under* Alviano

Livy, 34.18–20n, 35.1–8n, 39.5n, 68.6n

Lodge, Thomas, 21n, 21.7n

Longueil, Christophe de (Longolio), ix

Longus, 5.9–10n, 20.21–32n, 29n

Loredan, Leonardo (doge of Venice), viii, 44.70–73n

454

## · INDEX TO NAVAGERO ·

Louis XII (king of France), 35n, 44.66–69n

Love (Cupid): as the Boy, 21.6, 59.10; as Cupid, 22.11, 30.21, 55.36, 69.25; as Love, 18.10, 19.14, 21.3, 21.11, 25.48, 28.6, 30.35, 36.5, 56.11, 59.47, 59.51, 66.1, 66.8; as Venus' winged son, 41.33; in notes, 19.44n, 21n, 25.48–49n, 25.50n, 26.22n, 36.1–4n, 37.17–19n, 41.8n, 41.20n, 41.33n, 41.35–36n, 47.2n, 55.32–33n, 59.4–6n, 59.46n, 65.13–14n, 66n; found hiding among flowers, 21n; Hyella's bosom to be his seat, 21.7–12; Jupiter, power over, 25.50, 25.50n; Mars his father, 41.34, 41.34n; resident in someone's eyes, 21.12n; torches create thermal baths at Baiae, 66, 66n; as plural, Loves/Cupids, 25.15 (*aligeri pueri*), 25.15n, 31.28, 37.17, 37.17–19n

love at first sight, 27.48–49, 27.48–49n

love bites, 59.38–42n

lover: absent heart of, 28.5–6, 28.5–6n; neglecting duties and activities, 19.43–54, 19.45–46n, 55.22–27; soliloquies in lonely places by, 19 (esp. 41–54), 19n; suicide of, 55.45–48, 55.45–49n; wasted, pale, sleepless, un-

able to eat, etc., 28.3–4n, 28.4, 55.17–27, 55.17–27n. *See also* shut-out lover

Lucan, 8.11n, 9.5n, 20.9n, 35.14–16n, 36.9n

Lucilius, 65.19–20n

Lucina, 14.9n, 44.9–11n, 44.11

Lucretius, xiii, 63n

*De rerum natura*, 25.3–4n, 41n, 41.8n, 63.1–4n; **1**, 25n, 25.6n, 25.7n, 25.10n, 25.11–12n, 25.18n, 25.21n, 27.17n, 27.33n, 27.34n, 31.44n, 35.2–4n, 41.1–4n, 41.5n, 44.59–63n; **2**, 14.1–2n, 19.31n, 19.33–34n, 20.63n, 25.6n, 27.18n, 27.33n, 57.8n; **3**, 28.7–8n; **4**, 20.15n, 57.11–13n; **5**, 19.32n, 19.33–34n, 20.33–34n, 20.63n, 25n, 25.6n, 25.21n, 25.35n, 26.75–76n, 37.3n; **6**, 27.33n, 34.18–20n, 60.4–6n

*lusus pastoralis*, defined, xi

Lyaeus. *See under* Bacchus

Lycaeus/Lycaean (with ref. to Pan), 19.1, 19.1n

Lycidas, 27.46, 27.46n

Lycinna, 59 (addressed; named in lines 2, 3, 8, 25, 28, 34, 43, and 49), 59n, 59.7–8n

Lycon, 5n, 5.2; another, 12.6

Lycus (Alcaeus'), 36.13–16n, 36.14, 63n

Lycus (a tiny man), 63n, 63.8, 63.12

Lygdamus (author of [Tibullus] 3.1–3.6), 29n

455

# · INDEX TO NAVAGERO ·

Maera (dog), 43n

Magny, Olivier de, 43n

Malatesta, Sigismondo (lord of Rimini), 69n

Malta, 50.3, 50.3–4n

Maltese lapdogs, 43n, 50.3–4, 50.3–4n

Manes, 43.14

Mantuan (Battista Spagnuoli), 19.45–46n, 20.10n, 26.6n, 39n

Manuzio, Aldo, the Elder, viii, xv, xxx n6, xxxi n8, xxxi n10, 30.1n

Manuzio, Aldo, the Younger, 65n

Manuzio, Paolo, 30n

Marcus, 63.7

Marino, Giovan Battista (Giambattista), 28n

Mario, Antonio, of Imola (= M. A. Flaminio), *Ad Hieronymum Fracastorium*, 33.1 and 3n; *Ad Marcum Plemmirium*, 1.11–12n; *Ad nymphas Bononienses*, 2n; *Thyrsis*, 20.15n

Mars (Mavors), 20.76–85n, 20.80, 42n, 44.50, 44.50–51n; as Cupid's father, 41.34, 41.34n; denoting "soldiery," 35.25, 35.25–28n

Martial, xi, xxxii n12, 3n, 30.8n, 55.60–63n; his poems burnt by Navagero, 16n
*Epigrams: 1.77* (*78*), 61n; *1.116*, 44.16n; *4.4*, 58A and 58Bn; *4.39*, 61n; *4.42*, 32.5–6n; *4.60*, 9.6n; *5.34*, 43.16n; *5.37*, 26.83–84n; *5.39*, 61n; *6.36*, 61n; *6.37*, 61n; *6.49*, 57.2n; *6.90*, 26.21n; *6.93*, 58A and 58Bn; *7.34*, 61n; *7.35*, 57.2n; *7.84*, 13.5n; *7.88*, 35.14–16n; *8.45*, 26.81–82n; *9.2*, 26.83–84n; *9.28*, 57.11–13n; *9.53*, 26.81–82n; *9.101* (*102*), 13.10n; *10.38*, 22.19–20n, 65.6n; *10.55*, 57n; *10.103*, 25.20n; *11.29*, 65.1n, 65.19–20n; *11.46*, 57.9–10n; *11.51*, 57.2n; *11.104*, 22.19–20n; *12.89*, 61n; *14.39*, 22.19–20n; *14.77*, 13.10n; *14.96*, 61n

Marullo, Michele, 29n; *Epigrams*, *1*, 3.3–4n, 13.3–4n, 13.5n, 25.48–49n, 27.48–49n, 28.5–6n; *2*, 19.24n, 21.12n, 65.5n; *3*, 26.81–82n, 28n, 59.1–3n, 59.20n; *4*, 26.25–38n, 26.41–42n, 31.1–9n; *Hymni Naturales*, 19.31n, 19.33–34n, 31.42n, 34n, 44.94n; *Tumuli*, 26.30n

Massilia (Marseilles), naval action off (49 BCE), 68n

Massimi, Pacifico: *Ad Mentulam*, 57.9–10n; *Ad Priapum*, 65.1n; *De Matrona*, 57n; *De Mentula*, 57n, 57.2n

Maximilian I (Holy Roman Emperor), vii, 20n, 35n, 44.70–73n, 44.74–77n

456

## · INDEX TO NAVAGERO ·

Medici, Cosimo de', 20.33–34n
Medoacus (Medoaco; river). *See*
　Brenta
Meduna (Metune; river), 20.1n;
　personified, 44.18, 44.18n
Melampus, 8n, 8.1
Melite, 50.3, 50.3–4n
Memnon, Aurora as mother of,
　34.1–4n, 34.3
Menalcas, 39n, 39.1
Menander, fragment of, trans-
　lated, xii, 46, 46n
Menippus, 61n, 61.1
Mercury, 41.34n; father of Daph-
　nis, 20.96–97n; Gabriel spo-
　ken of in terms apt for, 34n
Merula, Bartolomeo, vii, xiii, 48
　(addressed unnamed), 48n
meter and prosody, points of:
　meter: hiatus at principal cae-
　　sura of hexameter, 27.17,
　　27.17n; lengthening *in arsi,*
　　especially at main caesura,
　　3.1, 3.1n, 12.9, 12.9n, 19.9,
　　19.9n, possibly 19.17 (19.15–
　　18n), 20.48, 20.48n, 27.22–
　　23n, 27.23, 27.63, 27.63–67n,
　　possibly 55.10 (if *immite* read;
　　55.10–11n); elision in pen-
　　tameters, 33.2 and 4n,
　　33.10n; lengthening at pen-
　　tameter dieresis, 13.10,
　　13.10n, 19.50, 19.50n, 26.36,
　　26.35–36n, 67.4, 67.4n;
　　other lengthening, 41.21,
　　41.21n, cf. 56.2, 56.2n, cf.

59.47, 59.47n; no caesura af-
　ter fifth syllable in Sapphic
　lines, 36n, 41.37–40n, 69.2n;
　spondaic fifth foot in hex-
　ameter, 25.15, 25.15n, 25.61,
　25.61–64n, 44.19–21n, 44.21;
　summary of meters used by
　Navagero, 1n
prosody: false quantities, *cottidie*
　(variant), 20.10, 20.10n,
　*semiaperta,* 39.5, 39.5n, *redis,*
　39.9–10n, 39.10, *titilles,* 57.8,
　57.8n, *rimulam,* 65.10, 65.10n;
　final *o* shortened, *tenebo,*
　29.20, 29.20n, *puto,* 30.8,
　30.8n; last syllable long in
　*ego,* 28.5, 28.5–6n, 30.18,
　30.18n, 33.1 and 3n, 33.3,
　41.37–40n, 41.38; *persoluat*
　four syllables, 25.42, 25.42n;
　variation of prosody of *mihi,*
　59.4–6, 59.4–6n
Metune. *See* Meduna
Milanion (Mimalion), 26.57–58n,
　26.58
Milton, John, 29n; *Elegies,* 19.33–
　34n
Minerva (also = Pallas), 17 (ad-
　dressed), 17n, 35.5, 35.5n,
　42n; as *Tritonia virgo,* 44.50,
　44.50–51n
Mohacs, battle of, 40, 40n
Molza, Francesco Maria, 20.5n,
　25.14n, 47.2n
Moon, addressed, 22n
Moore, Thomas, 21n

457

## · INDEX TO NAVAGERO ·

Moschus, 10A.11–12n, 26.45–46n, 29.4–6n

mother, girl's protective as obstacle to be circumvented, 6.3n, 6.4–5n

Muret, Marc-Antoine, 30n, 59.38–42n; *Epigrams*, 29n, 38.10n, 65.6n; *Poemata Varia*, 45n, 45.3n

Muses, xi, 16n, 23.7n, 44.4–5n, 44.45–49n, 55.1–8n; as *Aonides*, 44.45–49n, 44.47, 54.3–4n, 54.4; as *Camenae*, 30.6, 30.6n; as *Musae*, 23.7, 23.7n, 44.8; as *Pierides*, 44.4, 44.4–5n; the nymphs of the Noncello and Vanzo are treated as local Muses in 20 (see 20.1n) and 31, respectively (cf. also the daughters of Eridanus in 50.3). *See also* Calliope

Musurus, Marcus, vii, xxxi n10, 20.69–70n

naiads, 19.2n, 20.1n, 26.41–42n, 26.45–46n, 31.1 (addressed), 31.1–9n

Naldi, Naldo, 55.1–8n

names, unusual forms of, 5n, 6n, 14n, 19.41n

Nape, 13n, 13.2

Naples, 20.69–70n, 44.66–69n

Narcissus, 19n, 19.15–18n, 19.17–38, 19.38n, 55.10–11n

Naso, 48.5. *See also* Ovid

Navagero, Andrea, *passim*
career: enters Great Council, viii, xxx n1; delivers funeral orations, viii; as soldier, x, xxxi n7, xxxi n10, 42, 42n, 53, 53n; censor, xiv; work for Aldine Press, xv; official historian and Saint Mark's librarian, xv; embassy to Spain, xv–xvi; prisoner in Spain, xvi; travels in France, xvi; return to Venice (1528), xvi, 47n; embassy to France and death at Blois (1529), xvi, xxx n2, xxxiii n19; posthumous publication of poems and speeches (1530), viii, xvii; inscription erected by nephews in 1585, xxix n1, xxx n2

denoted by *Acmon*, 16n (cf. 15n)

friends, vii, ix. *See especially* Alviano; Beazzano; Bembo; Borgia, Girolamo; Boscán; Canal; Castiglione; Contarini; Cotta; Flaminio, Marcantonio; Fracastoro; Longueil; Manuzio, Aldo, the Elder; Ramusio; Raphael; Ricci; Strozzi, Ercole; Tebaldeo; Trissino

imitated or translated by French, Italian, and other vernacular poets, xiii (and for N.'s importance for Spanish verse, xv). *See also*

458

· INDEX TO NAVAGERO ·

Baïf; Bargaeus; Castillejo;
Chiappino; Desportes;
Dolce; Drummond; Du Bel-
lay; Grimald; Lodge;
Magny; Negri; Ronsard;
Saint-Gelais; Tansillo; Tolo-
mei; Torre, Francisco de la;
Vauquelin de la Fresnaye
influence of others: debts to
ancient poets, xiii; Petrar-
chist influence, xiii; Pindar,
admiration for, viii; Ponta-
no's influence, x (in 20.86–
90 N. regrets not having
been Pontano's pupil), xiii;
Vergil, admiration for, xi,
xxxi n9. See also *individual
ancient poets*
interests and likes: dogs, xiii;
gardens and nature, xiii, xvi,
31n; science, etc., xv–xvi. *See
also* dogs and dog poems
Martial and Statius, attitude
to, xi, xxxii n12, 16n
other works: funeral orations,
viii, 44.66–69n, 44.70–73n;
Italian poems, xiv; cited,
21.12n; letter to Leo X, xv,
20.33–34n; prose Venetian
history, xiv, 16.7–8n; *Silvae*,
x–xi, 16n, 52n; work for Al-
dine Press, xv; works burnt
by N., viii, xi, xiv, xxxii n15,
16, 16n
personal details: age at death,
vii n1; birth, vii, xxix n1;

character, xi; education, vii;
memory, powers of, xxx n6;
mental exhaustion, period
of, viii, xxxi n7; nephews,
xxix–xxx nn1–2; parents and
siblings (and paternal
grandfather), vii, xxix n1,
xxx n3; physical appearance
in Raphael's portrait, ix;
Pordenone, member of
Alviano's academy at, viii–
ix; religious attitudes, sparse
evidence for, xv; sexual rela-
tionships, xiii (*for named
girls, real or fictitious, see*
Gellia; Hyella; Lycinna;
Neaera); unmarried, xxx n2,
xxxiii n17
range of themes as Latin poet,
x–xii
topical poems, x
Navagero, Andrea (grandfather of
poet), xxx n1, xxxii n14
Navagero, Andrea (nephew of
poet), xxix–xxx nn1–2
Navagero, Andrea ("the chroni-
cler"), xxxii n14
Navagero, Andrea (uncle of poet),
xxxii n14
Navagero, Bartolomeo (brother
and co-heir of poet), xxx n2
Navagero, Bernardo (father of
poet), vii, xxx n1, xxx n3,
xxxi n10
Navagero, Bernardo (nephew of
poet), xxix–xxx nn1–2

459

# · INDEX TO NAVAGERO ·

Navagero, Francesca (France-schina; wife of Giambattista Ramusio), xxxiii n17

Navagero, Francesco (father-in-law of Giambattista Ramusio), xxxiii n17

Navagero, Pietro (brother and co-heir of poet), xxx n2

Neaera, 29n, 29.9

Negri, Francesco, versions of N.'s poems, 30n, 32n, 33n, 34n, 36n

Nemesianus, 3n, 3.1n, 19n, 19.43n, 19.45–46n, 26.3–4n, 27.22–23n, 27.46n, 27.88n, 55n, 55.40–41n

Neptune, 26.31, 26.31–32n, 48.1, 48.1–4n

New Year presents, 28.1, 28.1n

Niconoe, 14n, 14.1

Night (personified), 38.1, 38.5

Nile (river), 35.13n

Nonacria/Nonacrian, 18.1, 18.1–2n, 26.45

Noncello (river, and daughters), viii, 20.1, 20.1n, 20.60, 44.17, 44.18n

nonclassical words, 14.3n

noses, fun made of big, 61, 61n

Novius, 59.20n, 59.38–42n

nurse as confidante, 22.13–16, 22.13–16n

nymphs, 18.4, 18.11 (*nymphe*, Greek nom.), 19.1, 19.24, 20.1 (*nymphae Naucelides*), 20.16, 37.29, 44.20, 66n. *See also* dryads;

hamadryads; naiads (*and individual nymphs*)

Ocean, 44.87

Octavian, 20.33–34n, 20.39–41n, 20.58–70n, 20.99n; as Augustus, 23.9n

Oeagrian (of Orpheus), 25.51, 25.51–52n

Olympus (an astrologer), 62n, 62.3

Olympus (used for "heaven"), 20.33, 20.33–34n

Orcus (the Underworld), 51.9, 51.9n (and cf. 34.18–20n)

Orithyia, 25.61, 25.61–64n

Orpheus, 25.51, 25.51–52n, 25.55–64n, 25.63, 44.45–49n; in love with Calais after losing Eurydice, 25.55–64, 25.55–64n

Orsato, Sertorio, 31n

Ovid, xiii, 10A.4n, 30.16n, 33.10n, 41.8n, 48.5, 48.5–6n

*Amores*: **1.4**, 26.78n; **1.6**, 26.74n, 39.5n; **1.7**, 28.7–8n, 59.38–42n; **1.8**, 34.1–4n, 59.38–42n; **1.9**, 27.43n; **1.10**, 42.4n; **1.11**, 13n, 22.13–16n; **1.12**, 13n; **1.14**, 31.30n; **1.15**, 30.1n; **2.2**, 22.12n; **2.3**, 59.43n; **2.5**, 25.50n, 36.5–6n, 59.38–42n; **2.6**, 9.2n, 43n; **2.9**, 57.17–27n, **2.15**, 49.4n; **2.16**, 32.5–6n; **2.17**, 41.25–26n; **2.18**, 36.5–6n; **2.19**,

460

## · INDEX TO NAVAGERO ·

22.13–16n, 39n; *3.1*, 22.13–
16n; *3.2*, 25.48–49n, 26.57–
58n, 38.1n; *3.3*, 32.5–6n; *3.4*,
59.1–3n; *3.5*, 11.4n, 54.5–6n;
*3.6*, 29n; *3.7*, 59.38–42n,
65.19–20n; *3.9*, 34.1–4n,
47.1n; *3.10*, 1.18n; *3.11*, 21.11n;
*3.14*, 59.38–42n; *3.15*, 21.11n,
25.47n

*Ars amatoria: 1*, 6.3n, 6.4–5n,
22.13–16n, 26.78n, 28.3–4n,
38.3n, 41.29–32n; *2*, 1.13–14n,
22.9–12n, 22.16n, 26.57–58n;
*3*, 22.13–16n, 26.3–4n, 26.11–
16n, 26.57–58n, 37.3n, 47.1n,
58A and 58Bn

*Epistulae ex Ponto: 1*, 1.11–12n,
34.1–4n; *2*, 57.45–49n; *3*,
62n; *4*, 25.31n, 26.25–38n,
44.52–55n, 60.7–8n, 66.3n

*Fasti: 1*, 1n, 1.5n, 1.11–12n, 1.13–
14n, 18.18n, 19.5–6n, 20.99n,
25n, 25.61–64n, 57.3n, 59.7–
8n, 65.18n, 65.19–20n; *2*,
14.4n, 14.8n, 19.5–6n, 21.11n,
31.30n, 34.11n, 66.3n; *3*,
37.1n; *4*, 1n, 1.13–14n, 1.18n,
11.2n, 12.10n, 19.5–6n, 19.32n,
32.5–6n, 34.1–4n, 37.1n,
37.3n, 66.3n, 69.29n; *5*, 1.8n,
3.2n, 13.1n, 25.6n, 31.30n,
38.4n, 44.45–49n, 63.8n; *6*,
37.1n, 65.19–20n

*Heroides: 1*, 21.9–10n; *3*, 40.2n;
*4*, 19.21–22n, 20.15n, 26.41–
42n; *5*, 5.5–6n, 6.6–8n,

27.74–77n, 54.5–6n; *6*,
69.29n; *7*, 55.32–33n; *8*,
29.7n, 36.13–16n; *10*, 54.5–
6n; *11*, 28.7–8n; *13*, 19.21–
22n; *14*, 19.24n, 26.74n,
59.7–8n; *15*, 25.14n, 25.23–
42n, 55.1–8n, 59.38–42n; *16*,
2.2n; *17*, 6.2n, 6.4–5n; *18*,
27.43n, 30.34–35n, 37.1n,
44.28n, 49.3n; *19*, 29.4–6n,
44.29n

*Ibis*, 2n, 19.31n, 22.4n, 28.1n

*Metamorphoses: 1*, 5.1–2n, 19.21–
22n, 19.31n, 20.63n, 23.6n,
23.7n, 26.33–34n, 26.43n,
26.45–46n, 32.5–6n, 44.91–
94n, 44.96–101n, 55.1–8n,
65.13–14n, 66.3n, 69.1n; *2*,
12n, 19.33–34n, 25.1n, 25.60n,
26.37–38n, 26.44n, 27.48–
49n, 34.1–4n, 36.5–6n,
38.4n, 44.31–32n, 55.1–8n,
55.25n; *3*, 5n, 10Bn, 18.14n,
19n, 19.38n, 20.2n, 25.27–
28n, 26.37–38n, 26.74n,
44.52–55n, 55.10–11n, 55.45–
49n, 55.55n, 59.27–29n; *4*,
13.10n, 15.4n, 17.1n, 21.5n,
44.13n, 44.70n, 55.42–44n;
*5*, 1.9–10n, 25.50n, 26.35–
36n, 41.33n, 59.4–6n; *6*, 1.2n,
2n, 25.23–42n, 25.27–28n,
25.30n, 25.35n, 25.39n,
25.61–64n, 26.35–36n,
35.20n, 62n, 66.3n; *7*, 1.13–
14n, 9.9–10n, 31.42n, 34.7–

## · INDEX TO NAVAGERO ·

Ovid (continued)
  8n, 37.3n; 8, 27.50n, 41.11n,
  55.32–33n; 9, 27.51n, 29n,
  35.13n, 35.20n, 55.9n, 55.32–
  33n, 59.4–6n; 10, 20.29–30n,
  20.72–74n, 20.76–85n,
  22.13–16n, 25.51–52n, 25.55–
  64n, 25.61–64n, 26.57–58n,
  31.28–29n; 11, 19.11–12n,
  55.1–8n, 66.3n; 12, 35.29n;
  13, 1.13–14n, 5.5–6n, 10A.9n,
  13.8n, 20.26n, 26.1–2n,
  29.7n, 44.16n, 66.3n; 14,
  5.9–10n, 15n, 26.41–42n,
  27.63–67n, 29.7n, 32.5–6n,
  56.7–8n, 66.3n; 15, 20.81n,
  23.4n, 24.8n, 25.1n, 25.3–4n,
  27.34n, 37.4n
  Nux, 51.4–6n
  Remedia amoris, 1.11–12n, 8.12n,
  22.13–16n, 27.39n, 31.27n
  Tristia: Merula's exposition of,
  vii, 48n; 1, 55.9n, 55.32–33n;
  2, 39n; 3, 23.9n, 25.25–26n,
  26.10n, 31.10–12n, 50.10n,
  59.27–29n, 65.13–14n; 4, 9.9–
  10n, 19.48n, 57.56n; 5, 1.8n,
  20.85n, 21.4n, 32.8n, 54.5–
  6n, 55.1–8n, 59.27–29n, 69.1n

Padua, vii, x, xiii, xiv, xvi, xxx n5,
  20.69–70n, 30n, 30.1n, 31n,
  31.1–9n, 35 (addressed), 35n,
  35.1–8n, 35.8n, 35.23n, 41n,
  42n
Paestum/Paestan roses, 31.39–
  40n, 31.40

Pales, 11n, 11.2, 11.2n, 11.4
Pallas (Athena). See Minerva
Pan, xxxii n13, 3n, 6.3n, 8n, 11n,
  20.15n, 20.33–34n, 20.42,
  20.96–97n, 26.45–46n, 39.3–
  4n; as capripes, 18.3, 18.3–4n,
  20.15n; as Faunus, 26.42; as
  Lycaean, 19.1, 19.1n; as mon-
  tivagus, 3.1, 3.1n; as semicaper,
  5.9, 5.9–10n, 26.45; and
  Aegle, 26.45; and "the Arca-
  dian maiden" (Syrinx?),
  26.45–46n, 26.46; and Echo,
  19.1, 19.1n; and Pitys (who
  became the pine), 3.4, 3.3–
  4n; Pans, 18.3–4n, 26.41,
  26.41–42n
Pannonius, Janus (Johann
  Cesinge), 24.8n, 28.1n
Paphos/Paphian, 18.11, 18.11n,
  31.28, 56.1 ("Paphian god-
  dess" = Venus), 56.1n, 59.46
Parcae (Fates), 44.24, 44.25,
  44.76, 44.102
Paris (and Judgment of), 17.9,
  17.9–10n, 27.74–77n
Parnassus, 55.1–8n, 55.3
Parrhasian, the. See under Callisto
Partenio, Bernardino, 25.6n
Paul III (pope), 20.69–70n, 30.1n,
  44.91–94n
Pavia, battle of, xvi
Penelope, 26.11, 26.11–16n
Peneus (as father of Daphne),
  26.43, 26.43n
penis size, theme of poet's, 57, 57n
Pentadius, cited, 25.23–42n

## · INDEX TO NAVAGERO ·

Pergamum. *See* Troy
Persephone. *See* Proserpina
Persius, 26.81–82n
Petrarch (Francesco Petrarca), edited by Bembo, 30.1n; *Epistolae Metricae*, 47n; *Rime sparse*, 21.12n, 25.50n, 28.5–6n, 38n
Petrarchism, xiii
Petronius, 36.5–6n, 44.89–92n, 55.42–44n, 56.20–21n, 57.2n, 57.3n, 57.9–10n, 65.1n, 65.18n
Phanocles, 25.51–52n, 25.55–64n
Philemon, fragment of translated, xii, 45, 45n
Philetas of Cos, 36.3–4n
Philomela, 25.23–42n, 25.30n, 27.63–67n, 27.67
Philyra, 39.1, 39.1n
Phoebus. *See* Apollo
Phrygia/Phrygian, 16.7, 16.7–8n, 17.9, 17.9–10n, 48.3
Piave (river), 31.1–9n
Piccolomini, Enea Silvio (Pope Pius II), 47.1n
Pieria/Pierian, 55.1–8n, 55.2; Pierides, 44.4. *See also under* Muses
Pigna, Giovan Battista, 7.3–4n, 25.23–42n, 35.17n, 41.20n
Pignoria, Lorenzo, 10An, 31n, 31.1–9n, 35n
Pindar, viii, 36.3–4n
Pindus, 44.45–49n, 44.49
Pinelli, Giambattista, 26.65–80n
Pitys, 3.3–4n
Plautus, 55.40–41n; *Asinaria*,

65.12n; *Aulularia*, 26.62n; *Bacchides*, 34.7–8n; *Curculio*, 29.15–16n; *Mercator*, 61n; *Miles gloriosus*, 39.5n; *Poenulus*, 17.7n; *Pseudolus*, 30.19n; *Truculentus*, 59.1–3n
Pliny the Elder, 26.81–82n, 31.43n, 50.3–4n, 60.3n
Plutarch: *Consolatio ad Apollonium*, 45n, 46n; *Life of Caesar*, 68n
Pluto: as the Dread King, 25.51–52n, 25.52; as the Underworld Father, 26.35–36n, 26.36
Poliziano (Angelo Ambrogini), 20.33–34n; *Epigrams*, 57.3n; *Silvae*, 11.2n, 16.3n, 25.51–52n, 44.4–5n
Polyphemus (Cyclops), 5.5–6n, 19.45–46n, 27.12n, 27.28–34n, 27.34n, 27.35–36n, 27.46n, 29n
Pomponazzi, Pietro, vii
Pontano, Giovanni Gioviano, x, xiii, 20.33–34n, 20.50n, 20.69–70n, 21.7n, 30.19n, 31.19n, 37.6–8n, 57n, 58A and 58Bn, 59n, 59.20n, 59.38–42n, 65.6n; as Aegon, 20.69–70n, 20.70, 20.87, 20.95; Appendix One, poem 8 (in Pontano 1948, p. 452), 57.7n
*De Amore Coniugali*: **1**, 21.6n, 22.4n; **2**, 20.72–74n, 26.30n, 26.73n, 43.10–14n, 43.15n; **3**, 2.3–4n, 31.45n, 44.38–44n

463

## · INDEX TO NAVAGERO ·

Pontano (*continued*)
    *De Hortis Hesperidum*, 19.5–6n,
      25.47n, 31.44n
    *De Laudibus Divinis*, 60.3n
    *Eclogues*, 19n, 25.23–42n, 25.48–
      49n, 26.22n
    *Eridanus:* **1**, 1.2n, 21.8n, 23.4n,
      25.11–12n, 38n, 55.1–8n,
      56.22–23n, 59n, 59.38–42n;
      **2**, 19.24n, 20.69–70n, 21.8n,
      26.22n, 26.25–38n, 38n,
      56.22–23n, 59.10n
    *Hendecasyllabi:* **1**, 21.12n, 29.15–
      16n, 30.31–32n, 31.3–5n,
      31.6–7n, 31.33n, 32.12n, 38n,
      41.34n, 56.1n, 56.22–23n,
      57.9–10n, 59.40n, 59.44n,
      65.7–9n, 65.19–20n, 66.1n;
      **2**, 21n, 21.8n, 21.12n, 31.3–5n,
      31.6–7n, 31.25–26n, 37.6–8n,
      38n, 41.29–32n, 56.1n, 56.22–
      23n, 57.5n, 59.10n, 59.21–
      22n, 59.40n, 59.43n, 59.44n,
      59.45n, 59.46n, 66.1n, 69n
    *Hymni*, 22n
    *Lyra*, 20.1n, 41.33n, 56.1n, 57.5n,
      60.3n
    *Parthenopeus:* **1**, 6.4–5n, 22.13–
      16n, 30.31–32n, 32.5–6n,
      36.11–12n, 55.40–41n, 56.11–
      12n, 57n, 57.3n, 59.1–3n,
      59.7–8n, 59.38–42n, 59.40n;
      **2**, 6.3n, 20.2n, 25.14n, 27.35–
      36n, 39.3–4n
    *Pruritus, sive De Lascivia*, 57n
    *Tumuli:* **1**, 26.79–80n; **2**, 2.2n,
      29n, 69n

    *Urania*, 10A.9n, 14.1–2n, 19.31n,
      25.3–4n, 56.22–23n
popes. *See* Clement VII; Julius II;
    Leo X; Paul III; Piccolo-
    mini, Enea Silvio (Pope Pius
    II)
popes treated as gods, 20.33–34,
    20.33–34n, 20.54–60
Pordenone (Naone), viii, 20.1n,
    20.69–70n, 25.43n, 44.3,
    44.3n, 44.18n
Posidonius, 10A.5–6n
*Priapea*, 57.2n, 57.3n, 57.9–10n,
    57.11–13n, 65.1n, 65.19–20n
Priapus, 57.2n, 57.3n, 57.11–13n;
    "the Hellespontine god,"
    65.18, 65.18n; = penis, 65.1,
    65.1n, 65.12, 65.19–20n
Priuli, Lorenzo, xv
Progne, 25.23–42, 25.23–42n,
    25.30n. *See also under*
    Daulian, the
Propertius, xiii
    *Elegies* (refs. as in Loeb text):
      **1.1**, 26.57–58n, 28.3–4n,
      56.11 –12n; **1.2**, 19.41n, 25.7n;
      **1.5**, 28.3–4n; **1.9**, 25.48–49n,
      28.3–4n, 55.9n; **1.10**, 59.43n;
      **1.11**, 26n; **1.14**, 30.34–35n;
      **1.15**, 26.11–16n; **1.16**, 55.9n;
      **1.18**, 19n, 26.10n, 55.1–8n;
      **1.20**, 55.42–44n; **2.1**, 65.6n;
      **2.2**, 26.30n; **2.3**, 13.8n, 32.5–
      6n; **2.8**, 13.10n, 26.10n; **2.9**,
      26.7–10n, 26.11–16n, 36.9n;
      **2.13**, 31.25–26n; **2.15**, 13.10n,
      26.1–2n, 27.63–67n, 29.15–

464

## · INDEX TO NAVAGERO ·

16n, 55.60–63n, 65.6n; *2.16*, 19.42n, 39.9–10n; *2.17*, 26.10n; *2.19*, 1.15–16n, 26.60n; *2.24*, 13.10n; *2.25*, 42.4n; *2.26*, 26.31–32n; *2.28*, 26.69–70n; *2.29*, 65.5n; *3.3*, 36.1–4n; *3.7*, 55.59n; *3.8*, 59.38–42n; *3.10*, 25.23–42n, 69n; *3.13*, 21.9–10n, 26.11–16n; *3.15*, 59n, 59.7–8n; *3.17*, 18.3–4n, 26.41–42n; *4.1*, 19.40n; *4.3*, 59.38–42n; *4.5*, 39n, 41.37–40n, 55.17–27n, 55.60–63n, 59.38–42n; *4.6*, 56.7–8n; *4.7*, 26.10n; *4.9*, 3.7n

Proserpina, 26.35–36, 26.35–36n, 26.51

prostitution, 17n, 17.8n

Pythagoras, 24n, 24.2, 24.8n

Rainerio (Rinieri), Antonio Francesco, 35n

Ramusio, Giambattista, xvi, xxxiii n17

Randolph, Thomas, 14n

Rantzau, Heinrich, 10A.4n

Raphael (painter), ix, 42n, 55n

Rapin, René, 27.60–62n, 44.19–21n

revision of poems, xiv, 6n, 10Bn, 19n, 20.44n

R(h)ipaean Mountains, 27.78–83n, 27.82

Ricci, Bartolomeo, ix; *De Imitatione*, 20n, 43n; letters of, xxx n6, 1n, 20n, 43n

Ronsard, Pierre de, 12n, 20n, 20.58–70n, 20.76–85n, 22n, 25n, 27n, 27.28–34n, 29n, 44n, 44.4–5n, 46n, 49n

rustic analogies, 27.22–23, 27.22–23n, 27.68–73, 27.68–73n

Sabaea/Sabaean, 60.3, 60.3n

Sabellico, Marcantonio, vii, xiv

Sabeo, Fausto, 19.5–6n, 22n, 25.50n, 29n

Sadoleto, Giovanni, xv, 58A and 58Bn

Saint-Gelais, Mellin de, 38n, 46n

Sannazaro, Jacopo, 20.69–70n, 27.28–34n, 58A and 58Bn; *Eclogues*, 19.2n, 27.22–23n; *Elegies*, 1.2n, 11.2n, 26.83–84n, 33.9n; *Epigrams*, 13.3–4n, 31.30n, 55.1–8n, 59n, 59.20n, 59.21–22n, 59.43n, 66.3n; *Salices*, 26.41–42n

Sappho, 29.15–16n, 36.13–16n, 36.13

Satan (as "the Enemy"), 34.18–20n, 34.19

Saturn/Saturnian, 26.25–38n, 26.29, 39.1n, 44.91–94n, 44.92

Satyrs, 15n, 15.3, 20.15, 20.15n, 26.41, 26.41–42n

Scaliger, Joseph Justus, 43.15n

Scaliger, Julius Caesar (Giulio Cesare), 20n, 21n

Scardeone, Bernardino, 35n

Scythia/Scythian, 27.78–83n, 48.6

Sebeto (Maddalona; river), x,

## · INDEX TO NAVAGERO ·

Sebeto (*continued*)
20.1n, 20.69–70n, 20.70,
55.1–8n

Secundus, Johannes (Jan Second
Everaerts), 52n; *Basia*, 21.7n,
29.11–12n, 29.15–16n, 57.3n,
59n, 59.20n, 59.21–22n,
59.38–42n, 59.40n; *Elegiae*,
29n, 37.17–19n; *Epigrammata*,
65.19–20n; *Epistulae*, 21.6n;
*Epithalamium*, 65.7–9n; *Odes*,
31.44n; *Silvae*, 19.31n, 25.23–
42n. *See also next entry*

Secundus (seemingly not the
above), 52 (named in lines 1
and 4), 52n

Segni, Fabio, 21.12n

*Sementiva Dies* (Seed-Sowing
Day), 1n

Seneca: *Dialogi*, 65.13–14n; *Oedipus*, 25.43n

Serafino d'Aquila, 28n

Sermione. *See* Sirmio

sexual imagery, 57, 65

Shakespeare, William: *Macbeth*,
25.35n; Sonnets 153 and 154,
66n

shut-out lover (*exclusus amator*),
26.10, 26.10n, 59.1–3n

Siccus, Nicolaus (Niccolò Secchi),
65n

Sicily/Sicilian, 26.51, 26.51–52n

Sidon, 26.37, 26.37–38n

Silius Italicus, 8.11n, 26.35–36n,
50.3–4n, 55.10–11n

Simulus/Simylus, 60 (named in

line 2), 60n, 60.4–6n, 60.7–
8n; another, 64n

Sirmio (Sermione), 51.4–6n, 52n,
52.2, 52.5

Smith, William, 49n

Spain/Spanish, x, xiii, xiv, xv, xvi,
xxv, xxx n2, xxxiii n18, 20n,
44.66–69n, 47n

Sparta/Spartans, 42.1–6n, 42.3,
42.5n. *See also* Lacedaemon;
Laconia/Laconian

Spenser, Edmund: *Amoretti and
Epithalamium*, 65.17n; *Fairie
Queen*, 25.35n

Spring (personified as boy), 25.3,
25.3–4n

Statius, 16n, 16.3, 44.50–51n;
*Achilleid*, 25.60n, 27.12n,
27.41–42n; *Silvae*, 20.1n,
20.26n, 20.69–70n, 25.14n,
26.83–84n, 27.12n, 31.28–
29n, 42.5n, 44n, 44.94n,
55.1–8n; *Thebaid*, 21.9–10n,
25.6n, 25.25–26n, 26.11–16n,
27.12n, 37.25–28n, 44.4–5n,
44.89–92n, 56.7–8n, 57.5n,
59.38–42n, 65.11n

Statius, Achilles (Aquiles Estaço),
30n

Stobaeus: *Eclogae*, 25.55–64; *Florilegium*, 45n

Strabo, *Geography*, 10A.5–6n

Strada, Famiano, xi, 16n

Strozzi, Ercole, ix, xiv, 25.51–52n,
43n, 44n, 50.3–4n, 54
(named in line 2), 54n; Bar-

466

## · INDEX TO NAVAGERO ·

bara Torelli, wife of, 54n, 54.5

Strozzi, Tito Vespasiano, 5.1–2n, 20.33–34n, 22.6n, 22.13–16n, 26.6n, 26.7–10n, 26.25–38n, 27.63–67n, 28.1n, 50.10n, 66.3n, 69n

Styx/Stygian, 26.52, 44.94, 44.94n, 55.49

Suetonius: *Caligula*, 34.7–8n, 39.1n; *Julius Caesar*, 68n

Suleiman the Magnificent (sultan), 40n

Summonte, Pietro, 69n

Sun: addressed, 69.1–8; chariot of, 38.3–4; as Phoebus, 9.5n, 38.1, 44.88, 55.27; as Titan, 9.5

synizesis, 39.5n, 65.6n

Syria/Syrian, 31.25–26n, 31.26, 56.22–23n, 59.21. *See also* Assyria/Assyrian

Syrinx (as "the Arcadian maiden"), 26.45–46n, 26.46

Tacitus: *Annals*, 22.16n; *Histories*, 56.1n

Tagus, 35.14, 35.14–16n

Taigeto (Taglietti), Giannantonio, 26n, 35.23n

Tansillo, Luigi, 9n

Tantalus, 22.9–12n, 22.12n

Tartarus/Tartarean, 26.35

Tebaldeo, Antonio, ix, xiv, 26.7–10n, 38n, 43n, 49n, 50n, 50.3–4n, 51, 54n, 54.5–6n,

65.1n, 65.11n. *See also his pet dog*, Borgetto

Telaira (Telayra, Thelayra, i.e., Hilaira), 19.41, 19.41n

Teleson, 11n, 11.1

Terence: *Adelphi*, 60n, 63.9–10n; *Heautontimorumenos*, 42.5n, 65.12n; *Hecyra*, 29.15–16n, 30.16n, 57.5n

Tereus, 25.23–42n, 25.35n, 25.39n

Terilla, 14n, 14.1

Tethys, 38.4, 38.4n

Teuchon (dog), 27.7, 27.7n

Theocritus and [Theocritus], 36.3–4n

*Idylls*, xii; **1**, 6n, 10A.11–12n, 20.96–97n; **2**, 5n, 22.13–16n, 27.48–49n, 28.7–8n; **3**, 25.19n, 27.48–49n; **4**, 20.69–70n, 25.19n; **5**, 5n, 18n, 20.29–30n; **7**, 10Bn, 27.46n; **8**, 27.2–4n, 27.5–6n, 27.22–23n, 27.24–27n, 39n; **9**, 27.22–23n, 39n; **10**, 19.45–46n, 20.29–30n; **11**, 5.5–6n, 19.45–46n, 27.12n, 27.22–23n, 27.34n, 27.35–36n, 27.46n, 27.48–49n, 29n; **12**, 27n, 27.22–23n, 27.68–73n; **15**, 27.50n; **17**, 41.29–32n; **18**, 27.68–73n; **23**, 55n, 55.12n, 55.52–63n; **27**, 27.46n, 39n; **29**, 29.15–16n, 55.52–63n

Theseus, 6.2n

Thessaly/Thessalian, 44.45–49n

Thetis, 38.4n, 55.32–33n

· INDEX TO NAVAGERO ·

Thrace/Thracian, 25.24, 26.81–
82n, 44.45–49n; Thracian =
Turk, 40.2n. *See also* Orpheus; Tereus
Thyrsis, 6n, 6.1, 6.7, 7.1, 13.2
Tibullus, xiii, 30.1n, 36.3–4n
*Elegies:* **1.1**, 10A.11–12n, 11.2n,
26.75–76n, 55n, 55.9n,
55.60–63n, 65.19–20n; **1.2**,
22.9–12n, 22.12n, 22.13–16n;
**1.3**, 22.13–16n, 25.14n,
37.3n, 41.29–32n, 44.96–
101n, 65.6n; **1.4**, 44.52–55n,
69.25n; **1.6**, 22.13–16n, 39n,
59.38–42n; **1.7**, 22.9–12n;
**1.8**, 6.3n, 59.38–42n; **1.9**,
13.5n, 26.73n, 39n; **1.10**,
1.18n, 44.91–94n, 65.6n;
**2.1**, 1n, 1.18n, 29.1–2n; **2.2**,
21.9–10n; **2.3**, 15.4n,
20.67n, 26.1–2n; **2.4**, 39n;
**2.6**, 1.11–12n, 41.34n, 55.45–
49n
[Tibullus], *Elegies:* **3**, 29n; **3.2**,
59.15n; **3.3**, 13.3–4n, 26.81–
82n; **3.4**, 13.3–4n, 25.14n,
26.6n, 27.12n, 27.33n, 29.4–
6n, 31.25–26n, 47.1n; **3.6**,
25.48–49n, 31.25–26n; **3.8**,
21.9–10n; **3.11**, 13.10n; **3.19**,
22.12n
Tibur (Tivoli), 31.39–40n, 31.40
Timavo (river), 10.5, 10.5–6n
Tita (Tebaldeo's dog), 43n
Titan (of sun), 9.5
Tithonus, 37.1, 37.1n
Titian, ix

Tolomei, Claudio, 9n, 9.6n, 13n,
33n, 38n
Torelli, Barbara, 54n, 54.5; spelling of surname, 54.5–6n
Torre, Francisco de la, 19n, 27n
Torre, Giambattista della, 25.43,
25.43n
Torresano, Andrea, xv
Toscano, Matteo, xi, xxxii n12, 22n
Trissino, Giovanni Giorgio, 58A
(addressed; named in line 2),
58A and 58Bn, 69 (named in
line 36), 69n
Tritonian maiden (Minerva),
44.50, 44.50–51n. *See also
under* Minerva
Troy (Pergamum)/Trojans, 35.1–
8n, 35.2, 48.1, 48.1–4n
Turks, xv, 20.33–34n, 40n, 40.2n

Ulysses (Odysseus), 26.11–16n
usury, imagery from, 1.11–12, 1.11–
12n, 16.6

Valeriano, Giovanni Pierio, vii,
xxx n5, 13.3–4n, 30.1n
Valerius Flaccus, 14.1–2n, 19.1n,
25.3–4n, 44.4–5n, 55.1–8n
Valerius Maximus, 68n
Vanzo (in Padua) and daughters
(Vanciades), vii, 31.1–2, 31.1–
9n, 31.31, 31.39, 41n, 41.25–
26n, 41.26
Varchi, Benedetto, 5n, 6.6–8n,
20.10n, 25.23–42n, 33.1 and
3n, 39n, 41.37–40n
Varro, 60.7–8n

### · INDEX TO NAVAGERO ·

Vauquelin de la Fresnaye, Jean, 7n, 12n

Vega, Garcilaso de la, xv, 44.12n

Venice/Venetian, 53.5, 55.28, 55.34; the chief references in notes to contemporary events include 20n, 35n, 42n, 44.70–73n, 44.74–77n. *See also names of individual Venetians and* Agnadello; Alviano; Cambrai, League of; Cyprus; Holy League; Julius II; *etc.*

Venus: named in text as Venus, 6.2 (addressed), 6.7, (variant in 6.8), 17.4, 18.8, 18.9, 20.83, 22.2, 25.12, 27.42, 30.14, 31.33, 31.34, 42.2, 47.2, 55.37, 55.39, 59.9, 59.52, 65.6, 69.25; addressed but unnamed, 41; linked to Amathus, 25.47 (called Amathusis), 25.47n; to Cyprus, 13.3 (called Cypris), 13.3–4n, 17.10 (called Cypris), 31.25–26n, 47.2n; to Cythera, 6.6 (called Cytherea in variant), 17.8 (called Cytherea), 21.12n; to Idalium, 18.8, 18.8n, 21.12n, 44.12, 44.12n, 56.7–8n, 56.8; to Paphos, 18.11, 18.11n, 56.1, 56.1n, 59.46, 59.46n; to Venice, 47.2n, 55.32–33n, 55.36–37; called Dione, 20.75, 31.30, 31.30n, 44.12, 56.11–12n, 56.12, 59.4–6n, 59.6,

59.48, 59.48–49n; as "mother" (of Love), 21.7, 21.11; and Adonis, 20.72–85, 20.72–74n, 20.76–85n; and Anchises, 22.7–8n; "battle of Venus" of sex, 65.6; makes animals mate, flowers spring up, etc., 25.11–12, 25.11–12n, 25.21n, 41.1–4, 41.1–4n; myrtle sacred to, 6.6–8, 6.6–8n, 41.25; her mysteries (sex), 22.9–12n; portrayed in arms at Sparta, though unwarlike, 42.1–6, 42.1–6n, 42.4n; her swans, 31.28, 31.28–29n, 41.11n; other mentions, 17.8n, 17.9–10n, 21.12n, 22.6n, 22.12n, 25n, 25.10n, 29.1–2n, 31.39–40n, 34.1–4n, 41n, 41.34n, 41.37–40n, 55.36–39n. *See also* Adonis; Anchises; Graces; Love; Mars: as Cupid's father

Vergil, 16n, 30.16n, 36.3–4n, 37n, 44.4–5n

*Aeneid*: **1**, 10A.5–6n, 17.6n, 18.8n, 19.5–6n, 20.26n, 20.36n, 21.9–10n, 22.6n, 25.60n, 27.24–27n, 44.78–81n, 44.89–92n, 60.3n, 63n; **2**, 25.3–4n, 25.30n, 35.33n, 36.9n, 44.59–63n, 44.102–5n, 48.1–4n, 53.4n, 55.17–27n; **3**, 8.5n, 19.5–6n, 25.6n, 35.25–28n, 48.1–4n; **4**, 19.9n, 19.26n, 25.51–52n, 25.60n, 26.6n, 27.11n, 34.11n, 37.1n,

469

## · INDEX TO NAVAGERO ·

Vergil (*continued*)
37.25–28n, 44.35n, 55.32–
33n, 55.51n, 56.11–12n; *5*,
18.7n, 20.57n, 25.55–64n,
26.68n, 33.1 and 3n, 35.25–
28n, 41.37–40n, 47.4n,
55.56n; *6*, 9.5n, 18.1–2n,
19.21–22n, 19.29n, 19.33–34n,
28.7–8n, 29.4–6n, 44.70n,
44.89–92n, 55.28–30n,
57.5n; *7*, 18n, 20.1n, 20.57n,
20.63n, 20.69–70n, 25.3–4n,
27.24–27n, 27.68–73n,
35.14–16n, 35.25–28n, 37.3n,
43.10–14n; *8*, 17n, 19.1n,
34.1–4n, 35.25–28n, 44.2n,
44.74–77n, 59.1–3n; *9*,
20.26n, 24.3n, 34.7–8n,
37.1n, 44.102–5n; *10*, 15n,
27.12n, 44.2n, 44.52–55n,
53.1n; *11*, 3n, 5.1–2n, 27.63–
67n, 36.9n, 44.50–51n,
55.12n, 55.28–30n; *12*, 2n,
10A.4n, 14.1–2n, 20.48n,
25.61–64n, 27.13n, 27.24–
27n, 27.78–83n, 44.9–11n,
44.52–55n, 44.59–63n,
59.27–29n
*Eclogues*, xii, xxxi n9; *1*, 20.29–
30n, 20.33–34n, 20.39–41n,
20.99n, 25.19n, 25.20n,
27.63–67n; *2*, 3n, 5.5–6n,
19n, 19.41n, 19.45–46n,
20.29–30n, 25.19n, 27.35–
36n, 30.19n, 39n, 44.16n,
55n, 56.20–21n; *3*, 3n, 10Bn,
20n, 20.48n, 20.69–70n,

27.22–23n, 29n, 30.19n, 39n;
*4*, 20.96–97n, 25.14n, 27.5–
6n, 27.63–67n, 38.4n,
44.24n, 44.89–92n, 44.91–
94n, 44.94n; *5*, 1.5n, 6.6–8n,
10A.11–12n, 13.8n, 14.9n,
20.29–30n, 20.58–70n,
20.68n, 20.69–70n, 20.75
and 81n, 25.48–49n, 27.28–
34n, 27.63–67n, 39n, 44.64–
65n; *6*, 20.11–12n, 26.45–
46n, 27.88n, 36.1–4n; *7*,
3.3–4n, 6n, 18n, 25.43n,
27.39n, 27.46n, 27.60–62n,
31.10–12n, 44.6n, 55.1–8n; *8*,
10A.5–6n, 10Bn, 19.48n,
20n, 20.27n, 25.19n, 27.46n,
27.48–49n, 41.29–32n, 55.1–
8n, 56.11–12n; *9*, 20.29–30n,
25.19n, 27.28–34n, 27.46n,
39n; *10*, 5.5–6n, 6.6–8n,
10Bn, 16.4n, 20n, 20.1n,
27.88n, 39n, 41.34n
*Georgics*: *1*, 1n, 1.5n, 1.9–10n,
1.13–14n, 1.15–16n, 16.4n,
16.5–6n, 20.11–12n, 20.62n,
27.32n, 27.33n, 37.1n, 44.59–
63n, 44.96–101n, 59.27–29n;
*2*, 1.7n, 20.62n, 20.66n,
20.67n, 25n, 25.3–4n, 26.69–
70n, 27.2–4n, 27.34n, 27.63–
67n, 55.22–23n; *3*, 1.9–10n,
2.5n, 10A.5–6n, 11.4n,
19.25n, 19.45–46n, 20.24n,
20.29–30n, 20.58–70n,
27.16n, 27.68–73n, 27.78–
83n, 54.3–4n; *4*, 16.7–8n,

## · INDEX TO NAVAGERO ·

20.5n, 25.21n, 25.23–42n,
25.51–52n, 25.55–64n, 25.61–
64n, 27.12n, 27.63–67n,
27.78–83n, 30.8n, 44.2n,
44.19–21n, 44.38–44n,
44.81–88n, 65.18n
[Vergil]: *Ciris*, 19.45–46n, 22.13–
16n, 25.47n, 25.60n, 27.39n,
28.3–4n, 39.3–4n, 55.1–8n;
*Copa*, 19.15–18n, 27.32n,
31.10–12n, 44.19–21n; *Culex*,
10A.9n, 19.32n, 20.1n,
20.38n, 27.39n, 31.1–9n,
44.19–21n; *Dirae*, 19.32n,
27.63–67n; *Lydia*, 19.24n;
*Moretum*, 60n. *See also* Ausonius
Verino, Ugolino: *Flammetta*, 21.6n,
25.50n, 26.10n, 30.34–35n,
35.20n, 36.1–4n, 44.6n,
44.91–94n, 55.17–27n,
55.52–63n; *Paradisus*, 39.5n
Virgin Mary, 27.60–62n, 34.13–
16n, 34.14
Vitale, Giano, 20.33–34n, 34n,
44.94n

Volpi, Gaetano, xiv, xvii
Volpi, Giovanni Antonio, xiv, xvii;
*Life of Navagero* (1718), xxx
n1, xxx n3, 16n
Voluptas (Pleasure, personified),
41.8, 41.8n
Vulcan, 16n, 16.1, 34.1–4n, 41.34n

wayfarer, imagined, 9.7, 50.1,
50.1n, 54.1
white days, 26.81–82n
Wiffen, Jeremiah Holmes, 2n, 6n,
7n, 9n, 21n, 47n
Winter (personified), 25.2

Xenophon, 8n, 19.25n, 27.7n

Zanchi, Basilio, 23.4n, 25.6n,
37.17–19n; *Eclogues*, 20.1n,
20.33–34n, 20.69–70n,
27.7n, 27.63–67n, 27.74–
77n, 44.94n; letter of Flaminio to, 14.3n
Zephyr (personified), 25.6n

# Index to Flaminio

Lowercase Roman numerals refer to page numbers in the Introduction. All other references are to Flaminio's poems or to their notes, keyed to poem and, where applicable, line number. Line numbers are given in accordance with the Latin text.

Acis, 4.5.43n, 4.5.44–66
Adonis, 3.18.21–22n, 3.18.22
adynata, 3.18.25–26n
Agyrta, 3.18.16, 3.18.16n
Alcon, 4.16.19, 4.16.19n; others, 3.2.5n, 3.26n, 3.27n
Alexis, 4.17.97, 4.17.97n
Amalthea (Capella), 4.2.1, 4.2.1n, 4.2.31
Amaryllis, 3.5n, 3.5.5, 3.6.3, 3.6.10n; another, 4.5.42, 4.5.41–42n
Amphion, 4.17.19, 4.17.19–20n
Angeriano, Girolamo, 4.5.33–40n
*Anthologia Palatina*. See *Greek Anthology*
Apollo/Phoebus, xxi, xxxiii n23, 3.1.7n, 3.16.9, 4.5.25–26n, 4.5.30n, 4.5.76–77n, 4.16.47, 4.17.15–16n, 4.17.62, 4.17.62n, 4.25.16–18n
Apuleius, 4.2.24n, 4.3.5n
Aracynthus (mountain), 4.17.19, 4.17.19–20n
Arcadia, 3.10.2n, 3.20.10, 3.20.10n, 4.16.50n, 4.17.16. *See also* Tegea/Tegean

Archilochus, 3.6.7n
Arco, Niccolò d', xxxv n29, 4.5.41–42n
Aristotle, 3.10.2n, 4.1.2n
Atanagi, Dionigi, 3.5n
Attis, 4.17.63–64, 4.17.63–64n, 4.17.73
Aurora, 3.6.2, 3.11.5, 3.11.5–6n, 4.16.40, 4.17.71
[Ausonius], 4.6.5–6n, 4.16.38–39n

Bacchus/Lyaeus (= wine), 4.11.3, 4.16.13, 4.16.13n
Bargaeus (Pietro Angeli da Barga), 3.16n
Bembo, Pietro, 3.10.2n, 4.3.11n, 4.3.15–16n, 4.17.11n
Benedetto of Mantua, Fra, xxxviii n44
Berecyntus/Berecyntian, 4.17.65, 4.17.65n
Bini, Gianfrancesco, xix, 4.1–25n
Bocchi, Achille, 3.1–3.29n, 3.10.2n
Boreas (north wind), 3.5.3, 3.23.1
Budik, Peter Alcantara, 3.5n

473

## · INDEX TO FLAMINIO ·

Calpurnius Siculus, 3.17.1n
Camillo, Giulio, 3.10.2n
Capilupi, Ippolito, xxxiv n24, xxxix n46
Capilupi, Lelio, xxxiv n24, xxxix n46
Carafa, Gianpietro (cardinal, later Pope Paul IV), xxiii, xxvi, xxxviii n45
Caserta, xxiii, xxv, 4.1–4.25n
Caserta, Giovanni Francesco d'Alois (count), xxiii, xxv, 4.1–4.25n, 4.1.5n
Castiglione, Baldassare, xxi, xxxiii n18
Catullus, 3.1–4.25n, 3.10.2n, 4.1.2, 4.1.2n, 4.1.4 and 28n, 4.22n, 4.25.1n
    Carmina (refs. as in Loeb text): **2**, xxii, xxxvi n30, 4.1.2n; **3**, xxii, xxxvi n30, 4.1.2n, 4.4.1–2n, 4.4.28n; **5**, 4.17.89–90n, 4.17.93–94n; **8**, 4.20.7n; **16**, 4.2.31n; **22**, 4.4.4n; **25**, 4.2.19n; **31**, 4.1.2n, 4.4.1–2n; **36**, 4.2.31n; **37**, 4.4.1–2n; **38**, 4.4.28n; **52**, 4.2.31n; **57**, 4.2.31n; **61**, 4.4.14n, 4.5.16n, 4.22.24n; **63**, 4.2.16n, 4.17.63–64n; **64**, 4.5.11n, 4.5.19n, 4.17.11n; **66**, 4.5.74n; **68**, 4.25.3n; **85**, 3.3.8n
Cerberus, 4.13.4, 4.13.4n, 4.17.29
Ceres, 3.12.1, 3.16.7, 3.17.3, 4.17.41
Chloe, xxii, 3.1–29n
Christ spoken of in erotic language, xxvii, xxxix n46

Cicero, Marcus Tullius, 3.10.2n, 4.2.19n, 4.25.1n; *De amicitia*, 4.12.5–6n; poem of, 4.7.9n
Claudian, 4.17.39n; *De raptu Proserpinae*, 4.17.41–42n
Colonna, Vittoria, xxv
Cupid. *See under* Love
Cybele, 4.17.32n, 4.17.63–84, 4.17.63–64n; called the Berecyntian Mother (and identified with Rhea as mother of Pluto), 4.17.65, 4.17.65n
Cyclops (Polyphemus), 4.5.43n, 4.5.47, 4.17.12n
Cynara, xxii
Cyparissus, 4.17.62, 4.17.62n
Cypris. *See under* Venus
Cytherea. *See under* Venus
Cytherean bird (= Cupid). *See under* Love

Daphnis, 3.18.7–8n, 3.28n, 3.28.5
dating of poems, xviii–xix, xxi, xxii, xxiv, xxv, xxvii, xxxiii n21, 3.1–29n, 3.6.10n, 3.10.2n, 4.1–25n, 4.25.1n
Death (personified), 4.17.32, 4.17.96, 4.18.5–6n, 4.18.6, 4.20.11–12
Delio, Sebastiano, 3.10.2n
devoted friends in myth, 4.12.5–6, 4.12.5–6n
Diana, 4.1.24; as Latona's daughter, 4.5.25, 4.5.25–26n; as the quivered goddess, 3.1.2, 3.1.2n; as sister of Phoebus, 4.16.47; with attendant band

474

## · INDEX TO FLAMINIO ·

of chaste nymphs, 4.1.24,
4.5.25
diminutives, 4.1.2n; particular in-
stances noted, 4.2.16n,
4.2.18n, 4.2.19n, 4.2.24n,
4.4.11n, 4.4.14n, 4.5.1n,
4.5.2n, 4.5.8n, 4.5.16n,
4.5.19n, 4.5.28n, 4.5.74n,
4.22.25n
Dis. *See under* Pluto
Doris, 4.5.54, 4.5.54n
Dorylas, 3.18.15, 3.18.15n
dryads (wood nymphs), 3.10.7–8n,
3.10.8, 3.12.4, 4.1–25n, 4.4.17,
4.5.80, 4.5.80n, 4.25.11
Du Bellay, Joachim, 3.1.7n

Earth, Mother, 4.10.11. *See also*
Cybele
earth asked to lie lightly on dead,
4.10.17–20n
Elysium/Elysian, 3.10.2n, 4.3.15,
4.3.15–16n, 4.8.10, 4.14.2,
4.14.2n, 4.14.8, 4.18.7–8n,
4.19.22, 4.22.32n, 4.23.12
Enna (Henna), 4.17.44, 4.17.44n
epyllia: Acis and Galatea, 4.5.43–
66; Pluto and Proserpina,
4.17.41–50, 4.17.41–42n
Erebus (Underworld), 4.17.41–
42n, 4.17.42, 4.17.53
Erigone (daughter of Icarus), and
her dog Maera, 4.11.12, 4.11.12n
Eumenides, 4.17.29–30n, 4.17.30.
*See also* Tisiphone
evening star (= Venus), 3.11.1,
4.24.3

Farnese, Alessandro (cardinal), xix,
xxiv, xxv, xxvii, 3.1–29n, 3.1.7,
3.1.7n, 3.2.1 (addressee),
3.2.1n, 3.2.5n, 4.25.3n
Fates, 4.17.85; as Parcae, 4.17.93
fauns (also = Pans), 3.1.1, 3.1.1n,
4.4.1, 4.16.19n, 4.20.1, 4.25.11
Faunus (= Pan), 3.1.1n, 3.4.3,
4.5.32, 4.16.51
Flaminio, Cesare (cousin of Marc-
antonio), xxvii, xxxiii n21,
xxxiv n24, xxxix n47, 4.25.1n
Flaminio, Gabriele (nephew of
Marcantonio), 4.18.5–6n
Flaminio, Giovanni Antonio
(father of Marcantonio), xx
(with wife Veturia), xx–xxi,
xxiv–xxv, xxxiii n21, xxxv
n27, xxxvii n36, xxxviii n39,
3.1.7n, 3.2.5n
Flaminio, Marcantonio:
selected topics: born at Serra-
valle, not Imola, 1497 or
1498, xx, xxxiii n21, xxxiv
n25; celebration of Farnese,
3.1.7n, 3.2.1n, 3.2.5n; death,
xxvi; fondness for *flebilis*,
4.5.83n; frivolous elegies
and pastoral themes ended
for serious matters, xviii–xix,
xxxiii n23, 4.25; ill health,
xxiii, xxiv, xxxvi–xxxvii
nn32–33, xxxvii nn36–37;
Index of Prohibited Books,
works put on by Paul IV,
xxvi; meant by *Iolas* in some
poems, 3.2.1n; metrical prac-

475

# · INDEX TO FLAMINIO ·

Flaminio, Marcantonio (*continued*)
tice, 3.1–4.25n; parents and
siblings, xx, xxxv nn26–27
(*see also* Flaminio, Giovanni
Antonio); poetry-writing a
"bad habit" difficult to be
fully rid of, like syphilis, xix,
4.1–4.25n; publication of
poems, xviii–xix, xxi, xxvii,
xxxiv n24; religious views,
xix, xx, xxv, xxvi, xxvii (incl.
Christ addressed in erotic
language), xxxvii, xxxviii
n44, xxxix n46; reputation
for moral purity, xxii, xxiii,
xxiv, xxxv n27, 3.1–29n; Zar-
rabini real surname, xx,
xxxiv n25

other poems cited (refs. as 1743
ed., except where *Sc.* [=
Scorsone] stated): *1.1*,
4.25.1n; *1.2*, 4.16.19n,
4.16.55n, 4.17.67n; *1.3*, xxxvii
n37; *1.6*, 3.5.7n; *1.8*, xxv,
3.1.7n, 4.3.15–16n; *1.10*,
4.22n; *1.11*, xxii; *1.12*, 4.5.2n;
*1.13*, 4.16.19n; *1.17*, 3.2.1n,
3.2.5n, 4.16.19n; *1.18*, 4.1n;
*1.19*, xxxv n26; *1.21*, 4.25.6–
8n; *1.22*, 3.1.7n; *1.26*, 4.4.4n,
4.22n; *1.28*, xxi; *1.29*, 3.2.1n;
*1.30*, 4.5.41–42n; *1.35*, xxxviii
n43; *1.36*, xxxviii n39, xxxviii
n43; *1.38*, xxxviii n39; *1.55*,
4.5.2n; *2.1*, xxiii, xxxvii n37,
4.25.6–8n; *2.2*, 4.24.3n; *2.4*,
3.1.7n, 4.25.6–8n; *2.5*, xxxvii

n33, 3.10.2n, 4.6.5–6n,
4.7.9n; *2.6*, 3.9.3 and 8n,
4.5.2n, 4.6.11–12n; *2.6–9*,
3.1–4.25n; *2.7*, xxxviii n23,
3.6.10n, 4.5.25–26n, 4.5.41–
42n, 4.25.6–8n; *2.8*, 3.1.7n,
4.25.3n; *2.9*, xxxvi n31; *2.12*,
xxxv n28; *2.21*, 4.25.6–8n;
*2.22*, 4.25.16–18n; *2.32*, 4.1n;
*2.33*, xxii, 4.22.43n; *2.34*, xxi,
3.6.10n; *2.36*, 4.5.41–42n;
*5.1*, 3.1.7n; *5.6*, 3.12.9–10n;
*5.7*, xxxvii n37, 4.1.2n,
4.5.8n; *5.8*, 4.1–4.25n,
4.4.4n, 4.6.5–6n, 4.15.16n,
4.25.1n; *5.13*, 3.6.10n; *5.19*,
4.1.2n; *5.21* (*5.22 Sc.*),
4.25.4n; *5.23* (*5.24 Sc.*), xxxiv
n24; *5.24*, 4.25.1n; *5.25* (*5.26
Sc.*), 3.9.1–4n; *5.28*, 3.2.1n,
3.10.2n, 4.1.2n; *5.34*, 4.25.1n;
*5.36*, xxxiv n24, 4.1.2n; *5.37*,
4.16.48–49n; *5.39*, 4.2.3n;
*5.44*, 4.22.14n; *5.49* (*5.51 Sc.*),
xxiii–xxiv, xxxvii n37, 3.2.1n,
4.5.30n; *5.50*, xxxiv n24; *5.51*
(*5.53 Sc.*), xxxiv n24, xxxix
n46; *6*, xxiii; *6.5*, 3.2.1n; *6.8*,
3.2.1n; *6.9*, 3.1.7n; *6.10*,
4.5.25–26n; *6.11*, xxxvii n37;
*6.12*, 3.12.9–10n; *6.13*,
4.2.16n; *6.20*, xxiii, 4.1–
4.25n; *6.22*, 4.4.1–2n; *6.26*,
3.9.1–4n; *6.27*, xxxiv n24;
*6.31*, xxxiv n24; *6.34*, xxxix
n46; *6.35* (*6.36 Sc.*), xxxvii
n37; *6.37–48* (*6.38–49 Sc.*),

· INDEX TO FLAMINIO ·

xxxvii n37; **6.39** (*6.40 Sc.*),
xxiii; **6.50–59** (*6.51–60 Sc.*),
xxxvii n37; **6.59** (*6.60 Sc.*),
xxiii, 4.5.8n; **6.61** (*6.62 Sc.*),
xxxiv n24; **6.62** (*6.63 Sc.*),
xxiii; **7** (paraphrases of
psalms), xix, xxvii, 4.1n; **7.36
Sc.**, xxxiii n23; **8.13**, xxiv;
**8.17**, xxvi–xxvii, xxxix n46;
**8.20**, xxvii, xxxix n46; **8.22**,
xxxvii n37; ***App. 1** (**9.1**) **Sc.**,
xxi–xxii; ***App. 3** (**9.3**) **Sc.**,
xxii, 3.10.2n; ***App. 4** (**9.4**)
**Sc.**, xxii; ***App. 6** (**9.6**) **Sc.**,
4.25.1n; "Antonio Mario"
poems, xxxiv n25, xxxv n29,
xxxvii n35, 3.2.1n, 3.15n; *Be-
neficio di Gesu Cristo Crocifisso*,
xxxviii n44; further poems
ascribed to F. but not in
1743 ed. or Scorsone, xxxvi
n32; letter to Achille Bocchi,
3.1–29n, 3.10.2n; letter to
Gianfrancesco Bini, xix, 4.1–
4.25n; letter written Dec.
1549, xxiv, xxxvii n36
*See also* Caserta; Farnese; Flo-
rimonte; Saints Fabiano and
Sebastiano; San Colombano;
San Prospero; *and the girls*
Chloe; Cynara; Hierophila;
Hyella; Ligurina; Lygda;
Nigella; Phyllis; Septimilla
Flora, 3.5.2, 3.5.2n, 4.22.45,
4.22.45n
Florimonte, Galeazzo, xxv, 4.1–
25n, 4.25.1n

Fracastoro, Girolamo, xiii, xxiv,
4.1–25n; *Carmina*, 4.1–25n;
*Syphilis*, 4.7.9n, 4.25.3n,
4.25.6–8n
Furies. *See* Eumenides; Tisi-
phone

Gal(a)esus, 3.6.7, 3.6.7n
Galatea, 4.5.43, 4.5.43n, 4.5.53,
4.5.54n, 4.17.11, 4.17.11n,
4.17.12n
Gallus, Gaius Cornelius, 4.17.98,
4.17.98n
Garda (*Benacus*; lake), xxv, 4.1.16,
4.1.16n, 4.5.41–42n
garlands on doorposts, 3.7.4n
Genoa, 3.1–29n, 3.10.2n, 4.1.2n
Giberti, Antonio, xxxvi n31
Giberti, Gianmatteo (bishop of
Verona), xxiv, xxv, xxxvi
n29, xxxviii n38, 4.1.16n,
4.25.1n
God, xix, xx, xxxiv n23, xxxv n26,
4.25.8, 4.25.13n; called Jupi-
ter, 3.10.2n
Golden Age, 4.3.15–16n
Gonzaga, Giulia, xxv
Gorgo, 3.18.7, 3.18.7–8n
Greece, 4.12.6
*Greek Anthology* (*Anthologia Pala-
tina*), 3.1n
Poems: **5.64**, 3.8n; **5.83**, 3.15n;
**5.84**, 3.15n; **5.168**, 3.8n; **7.378**,
3.12.9–10n; **7.551**, 3.12.9–10n;
**7.647**, 3.18.7–8n; **9.309**,
3.18.7–8n; **9.745**, 4.2.19n;
**15.35**, 3.15n

## · INDEX TO FLAMINIO ·

hair of trees, image of in bks. 3 and 4, 4.16.23n

Hermus (river), 4.16.10, 4.16.10n

*heros* (used as in *Farnesius heros*), 3.1.7n

Hierophila, xxi, xxxv n28

Himella, 4.15.12, 4.15.12n

Homer, 4.22.32n

homosexuality, male, xxxvi n29, 3.2.1n, 3.10.2n, 3.26n, 3.27n

Horace:
> *Carmen saeculare*, 3.29.1n
>
> *Epodes: 1–10*, 4.1n; *2*, 3.24.5–6n, 4.2.13–14n, 4.2.15n, 4.2.22n; *8*, 3.9.1–4n; *11*, 4.2.13–14n; *14*, 3.2.1n; *17*, 3.16.7n
>
> *Odes: 1.4*, 3.26n, 4.17.89–90n; *1.12*, 4.5.23n, 4.15.7–14n; *1.17*, 4.2.15n, 4.2.25n, 4.3.11n; *1.24*, 4.17.93–94n; *1.28*, 4.17.89–90n; *1.32*, 4.2.13–14n; *1.36*, 4.5.9–10n, 4.6.13n; *2.13*, 4.5.40n; *3.4*, 4.17.46n; *3.11*, 4.17.19–20n; *3.13*, 4.3.6n, 4.22.1–3n; *4.1*, 3.10.2n; *4.7*, 4.17.89–90n; *4.10*, 3.10.2n; *4.11*, 3.16.5 and 8n
>
> *Satires: 1.9*, 4.20.11n; *1.10*, 3.2.1n; *2.3*, 4.22.4–5n

Hutton, James: *The Greek Anthology in France*, 3.15n; *The Greek Anthology in Italy*, 3.1n, 3.8n, 3.15n

Hyacinthus, 4.5.76–77n

Hybla (mountain)/Hyblaean, 3.16.1, 3.16.1n, 3.21.5–6n, 3.21.6, 4.5.22, 4.15.12–13n

Hyella/Iella, bk. 4 *passim*
> named in text, 4.1.11, 4.1.27, 4.2.25, 4.3.11, 4.3.13, 4.3.14, 4.4.9, 4.5.3, 4.6.15, 4.7.3, 4.8.1, 4.9.6, 4.10.5, 4.10.15, 4.11.5, 4.11.9, 4.12.1, 4.13.2, 4.14.2, 4.15.2, 4.16.5, 4.16.16, 4.16.25, 4.16.52, 4.17.2, 4.17.51, 4.17.101, 4.17.104, 4.18.2, 4.19.13, 4.20.4, 4.20.17, 4.21.4, 4.22.5, 4.22.21, 4.22.56, 4.22.60, 4.23.3, 4.23.14, 4.24.9, 4.25.12
>
> character: called "good Hyella," 4.11.5, 4.16.51–52, 4.24.9; guileless, 4.16.41–42, 4.16.42n; no girl more worthy to be sung, 4.1.13–14
>
> occupation, pastimes, and skills: her fountain and garden, 4.4.11–14 (fountain grieves for her, 4.5; garden grieves, 4.6); maker of cakes and cheeses, skilled at rennet-mixing and basket-weaving, 4.4.6–7, 4.4.25–26, 4.5.69–70, 4.16.43–45; milkmaid and tender of goats, 4.4.4–5, 4.4.16, 4.20.4 (commended as such to Persephone, 4.4.19–28; she and her billy-goat, 4.2, 4.3; she and her devoted nanny-goat, buried with her, 4.11.5–18, 4.12, 4.13.1–2); musician, singer and dancer,

478

### · INDEX TO FLAMINIO ·

4.2.20, 4.4.7, 4.4.18,
4.4.27–28, 4.5.23–40,
4.10.7–8, 4.15 (nature entranced by her music,
4.15.5–14), 4.16.1–2, 4.16.45–51, 4.24.8; skills (accomplishments) worthy of Venus, 4.16.42, 4.16.42n
physical looks, age, etc.: aged not yet fifteen at death, 4.10.9–10 (in first flower of youth, 4.7.9, 4.10.15); beautiful (variously *bella, candida, formosa, pulchra*, etc.), 4.1.11–13, 4.2.2, 4.2.25, 4.3.10, 4.4.4, 4.4.5, 4.4.13, 4.4.14, 4.5.17, 4.5.33, 4.5.35, 4.7.3, 4.7.7–8, 4.7.14, 4.8.1, 4.9.6, 4.10.5–6, 4.10.15, 4.11.5, 4.12.1, 4.13.2, 4.13.10, 4.14, 4.15.5, 4.15.21–22, 4.16.1, 4.16.30–41, 4.16.44–45, 4.17.2, 4.17.14, 4.17.101, 4.18.2, 4.19.13, 4.20.17, 4.22.5, 4.22.56, 4.24.1; beauty affects Cerberus, 4.13, impresses the dead in Elysium, 4.14, and makes Love desire her, 4.5.33–40, 4.5.33–40n, 4.16.28–30n; fair-skinned, 4.5.6, 4.5.9; golden-haired, 4.5.10, 4.14.6; rosy-lipped, 4.4.14, 4.5.5, 4.5.35; worthy of Jupiter as lover, 4.20.6
relationship with Iolas (sum-

marized, 4.1–25n; *see also under* Iolas): played love games with Iolas, 4.20.5; wanted to marry him, 4.7.3–4, 4.19.17–18; broken-hearted at his marriage to Nisa, 4.7; blames his cruelty (but still loves him), 4.8; pines and dies, 4.7, 4.8, 4.11, 4.20.17–18; dying address to Iolas, 4.8; tomb (on Mt. Taburno), 4.7.11–14, 4.8.14, 4.9, 4.10, 4.11, 4.16 (where annually venerated), 4.20.13–18, 4.21.7, 4.24; given grove and two springs, semi-deified, 4.16, esp. 51–56; called Iolas' "sun," 4.21.17
remembered in death: celebration by great Alcon foreseen, 4.16.19–24; celebration by Menalcas (= Vergil) or Theocritus would have been deserved, 4.17.9–14; hoped-for immortality of through F.'s verse, 4.1.27–28 (though poems of her now ended, 4.25.12); nature mourns for her, 4.16.23–27
Hymen/Hymenaeus, 4.18.5, 4.18.5–6n, 4.19.20

Icarus. *See* Erigone
Imola, xx, xxxiv n25
Iolas (= Flaminio), 3.2.1, 3.2.1n
Iolas (lover of Hyella), bk. 4 *passim*

479

## · INDEX TO FLAMINIO ·

Iolas (*continued*)
  named in text, 4.7.1, 4.8.7,
    4.8.17, 4.11.7, 4.17.1, 4.20.17,
    4.22.26, 4.22.51, 4.23.1,
    4.24.1, 4.24.7
  age: called a "boy," 4.8.3, 4.8.13,
    4.19.15, 4.23.9, 4.24.10
  character: dutiful to father,
    4.18.9–10
  occupation (shepherd), 4.21.3
  physical looks and skills: hand-
    some, 4.8.3, 4.19.3, 4.19.3 and
    7n, 4.19.7, 4.22.19–25 (incl.
    hair more beautiful than
    "hyacinth flower," 4.22.24–
    25), 4.23.1, 4.23.13, 4.24.1;
    musician, 4.17.1–4, 4.17.102,
    4.19.4–7, 4.22.51–52, 4.23.1–2
  relationship with Hyella (sum-
    marized, 4.1–25n; *see also un-
    der* Hyella): forced by father
    to marry Nisa, 4.7.1–2,
    4.18.9–10, 4.19.9–12; never
    loved Nisa, 4.18.7–8; regrets
    marrying her, 4.18.7–10,
    4.19.9–12; broken by grief at
    Hyella's death, 4.20–24;
    would have sought like Or-
    pheus to restore her to life,
    4.17.35–38; wishes for own
    death, 4.20.11–12; thoughts
    of suicide, (cf. 4.17.32,
    4.17.32n), 4.18.3–4 and 11–
    12n, 4.18.5–6n, 4.18.6, 4.19.12,
    4.22.26–27, 4.22.51, 4.22.51
    and 53n, 4.22.53; hopes for
    burial beside Hyella,

4.18.3–4 and 11–12n, 4.18.7–
8n, 4.18.11–12, 4.24.9–12; will
be husband to Hyella in af-
terlife, 4.18.5–6, 4.19.15–22;
plants laurel to Hyella, 4.24,
4.24.5–8n; "swan song" to
Hyella, 4.17.1–4; hopes to
make her memory immortal,
4.17.99–104

Jupiter, 3.2.7–8n, 3.2.8, 4.2.1n,
  4.17.49, 4.20.6, 4.22.10,
  4.25.13, 4.25.13n; of God,
  3.10.2n
Juvenal, 4.5.28n

"kissing" water or a reed pipe,
  4.4.14, 4.4.14n, 4.5.5,
  4.15.21–22, 4.15.21n

Lampridio, Benedetto, xxxvi n30
Latona, virgin daughter of. *See
  under* Diana
Leo X (pope), xx–xxi
Lesbia (Catullus'), 4.1.4, 4.1.4 and
  28n, 4.1.28; her sparrow,
  4.1.2n
Lethe, 4.8.12, 4.8.12n
Leucippe, xxxv n28
Ligurina, 3.10.2, 3.10.2n, 3.11.3,
  3.12.3, 3.14.1, 3.14.9, 3.22n,
  3.23.5, 3.25.6, 3.27n, 3.27.5
Longueil (Longolio), Cristophe
  de, 3.10.2n, 4.1.2n
Love (Cupid), xxii, 3.27.6, 4.1.11n,
  4.5.34, 4.5.35, 4.5.39–40,
  4.16.29; called "the Cyther-

## · INDEX TO FLAMINIO ·

ean bird," 4.17.39, 4.17.39n;
Love in love, 4.5.33–40,
4.5.33–40n, 4.16.28–30n

lovers sharing time of death and/
or burial place, 3.12.9–10,
3.12.9–10n, 4.18.3–4,
4.18.11–12, 4.20.15–16,
4.24.9–10

Lucretius, 3.11.5–6n; *De rerum
natura*, **1**, 4.6.3n; **2**, 3.24.1–
4n, 4.22.4–5n, 4.22.13n,
4.22.46n; **3**, 4.2.30n; **4**,
3.7.4n, 4.6.14n; **5**, 4.3.17n;
**6**, 4.21.16n

lusters, 4.10.9–10n

Lyaeus. *See* Bacchus

Lycambes, 3.6.7n

Lycambus, 3.6.7n, 3.6.8

Lycinna, 3.9.3, 3.9.3 and 8n, 3.9.8

Lycoris, 4.17.98, 4.17.98n

Lygda, 3.1–3.29n, 3.10.2n, 3.19.1,
3.22n, 3.22.6, 3.24.6, 3.26.5;
another?, xxii, xxxv n29, 3.1–
3.29n

Maddison, C., *Marcantonio Fla-
minio, Poet, Humanist and Re-
former* (selected refs.), xxxiv
n23, xxxv nn27–28, xxxvi
n30, xxxvi–xxxvii nn32–33,
3.1–3.29n, 3:1.7n, 3.6.10n,
3.10n, 3.10.2n, 3.10.7–8n,
3.14n, 4.1–4.25n, 4.1.2n,
4.22.51 and 53n

Maenalus (mountains)/Maena-
lian, 4.16.50, 4.16.50n,
4.17.20

Maera (dog). *See under* Erigone

Mancurti (Mancurzio), Francesco
Maria, xx, xxviii, xxxiv n25,
xxxvi n32, 3.1–4.25n, 3.1–
3.29n, 3.3n, 3.14n

Mantuan (Battista Spagnuoli),
4.17.9n

Mario, Antonio (= Flaminio),
xxxiv n25, xxxvi n29, xxxvii
n35, 3.2.1n, 3.4.1n, 3.15n,
3.26n, 3.27n, 4.1.11n, 4.25.1n

Martial, 3.10.2n, 4.22n; *Epigrams*,
**5.34**, 4.10.17–20n; **6.68**,
4.17.97n; **8.56**, 4.17.97n;
**8.77**, 4.2.17n

Marullo, Michele, 4.16.53n; *Epi-
grams*, 4.10.17–20n, 4.25.3n;
*Neniae*, xxi

Menalcas (= Vergil), 4.17.9,
4.17.9n

Menander, 3.6.7, 3.6.7n

Mesulus (river). *See* Mischio

meter and prosody, observations
on points of:
Catullan features, 3.1–4.25n,
4.1.2n
choliambic (4.22), 4.22n; ana-
paest in third foot, 4.22.58n
elision in fifth foot of hexame-
ter, 3.18.27n
elision in final dactyl of pen-
tameter, 4.5.30n, 4.11.13–14n,
4.19.12n
hendecasyllables, 4.4, 4.25
hiatus, 4.3.22n, 4.4.28n,
4.15.21n, 4.17.19–20n
iambic strophe (4.1, 4.10), 4.1n

481

## · INDEX TO FLAMINIO ·

meter and prosody (*continued*)
iambic trimeters (4.2, 4.3, 4.15, 4.16, 4.21, 4.22), with anapaest other than in first foot, 4.2.13–14n, 4.3.18–19n, 4.15.15n, 4.16.8–9n, 4.16.38–39n, 4.16.55n, 4.21n, 4.22.24n
lengthening at hexameter caesura, 4.5.1n
lengthening at pentameter dieresis, 3.29.3–4n, 4.24.10n
nonelegiac meters in bk. 4, 3.1–4.25n
polysyllabic pentameter endings, 3.1–4.25n
shortening of final *o*, 3.3.8n, 3.18.18n
varying treatment of same word in successive lines, 4.22.4–5n
Micon, 3.15.2n, 3.17.1, 3.17.1n, 3.18.7–8n
milk, streams of, 4.3.15–16n, 4.3.16, 4.22.34
Mincio (river), 4.5.41, 4.5.41–42n
Mischio (*Mesulus*; river at Serravalle), 3.6.10, 3.6.10n, 3.19.6
Molza, Francesco Maria, xxxvi n32, 3.1.7n, 4.7.9n
Moon (personified), 3.29
morning star: (Lucifer) 3.6.1, (Eous) 4.24.3
Moschus, 4.5.76–77n
mother, girl's watchful, circumvented, 3.13n, 3.13n, 3.18.1–2, 3.18.1–2n
Mourning Fields (in Underworld), 4.8.9–10, 4.8.9–10n

Muret, Marc-Antoine, xxxvi n30
Muses, xxiii, xxxiv n23, 3.1.7n, 3.16.9, 4.1.3, 4.16.53n, 4.17.15–16n, 4.17.25, 4.17.95, 4.23.5, 4.25.13n, 4.25.16–18n. *See also* Thalia; Urania

naiads, 3.2.5n, 4.2.12, 4.5.80, 4.5.80n, 4.16.53, 4.16.53n
*napaeae*, 4.16.47
nature in grief, 4.16.21–27, 4.16.21–27n
Navagero, Andrea, xviii, xxii, xxxviii n39, 3.1–4.25n, 3.10.2n
  *Carmina*: **3**, 4.2.13–14n; **5**, 4.2.13–14n; **10A**, 3.14.3–4n; **12**, 3.9n, 3.16n; **13**, 3.12.9–10n; **15**, 3.1.5–6n, 3.14.5–6n; **17**, 3.28.1–2n; **18**, 3.9.1–4n, 4.5.23–40n, 4.10.17–20n; **20**, 3.9.1–4n; **22**, 3.4.4n; **23**, 4.6.3n, 4.17.87n; **25**, 4.25.1n; **26**, 4.1.26n, 4.2.13–14n, 4.2.17n; **27**, 3.14.3–4n, 3.16n, 3.18.9–10n, 4.5.15n; **31**, 4.16.53n; **34**, 4.6.3n; **35**, xx; **36**, 4.17.50n; **38**, 3.22.5n; **40**, 4.7.9n; **41**, 3.28.1–2n; **43**, 4.1.2n; **49**, 3.15n; **50**, 4.16.53n; **55**, 4.5.4n; **56**, 3.9.1–4n; **59**, 3.18.23–24n
Neptune, 4.17.11, 4.17.11n
Nereus, 4.5.54n, 4.17.11n
Nigella, 3.1–3.29n, 3.3.1, 3.3.1n, 3.4.6, 3.19.9
Night (personified), 3.8.3, 3.8.3n, possibly 4.2.22

482

### · INDEX TO FLAMINIO ·

Nisa (Iolas' wife), 3.18.7–8n, 4.1–
25n, 4.7.1, 4.18.7, 4.18.7–8n,
4.18.9–10n, 4.19.9
Nisa (partnered with Daphnis),
3.18.7–8n, 3.28.5
Nisa (temptress of Micon),
3.18.7–8n, 3.18.8
Noncello (river), 4.5.73n
nymphs, 3.1.2n, 3.4.4, 3.17.9,
3.20.9, 3.21.1, 4.5.31, 4.5.57,
4.15.6, 4.16.36, 4.17.43,
4.17.99; figuratively of beau-
tiful girls, 3.6.13, 3.19.10,
4.17.14. *See also* dryads;
naiads; *napaeae*; oreads;
*and under individual names*

Ocean, 4.17.89
offerings and libations, 3.14.5–6,
4.1.7–8, 4.9.2–4, 4.10.17–
20n, 4.10.19–20n, 4.11.2–3,
4.16.13–14, 4.22.54–55,
4.22.54n
Oratorio del Divino Amore, xxv,
xxxviii n42
Orcus (= Underworld), 4.17.27,
4.17.27n. *For Orcus = Pluto,
see under* Pluto
oreads, 4.5.51, 4.5.51n, 4.16.22,
4.16.22n
Orestes, 4.12.5, 4.12.5–6n
Orpheus, 4.5.23–40n, 4.5.23n,
4.15.7–14n, cf. 4.17.25,
4.17.25n, 4.17.27n
Orti, Girolamo, 3.5n
Ovid, 3.1–4.25n, 4.6.3n, 4.20.11n
*Amores*: **1.1**, 3.1.2n; **1.7**, 4.5.9–

10n; **1.15**, 4.17.98n; **2.5**,
3.27n; **2.13**, 3.12.9–10n; **3.9**,
4.10.17–20n
*Ars amatoria*: **1**, 4.24.2n; **2**,
3.7.4n, 3.9.1–4n, 4.12.5–6n;
**3**, 4.15.7–14n
*Epistolae ex Ponto*: **1.3**, 4.12.5–6n;
**2.6**, 4.12.5–6n; **3.2**, 4.12.5–6n
*Fasti*: **1**, 3.28.1–2n, 4.2.19n,
4.14.1n, 4.17.46n; **2**, 3.1.1n,
3.2.4n, 4.6.3n, 4.17.46n; **3**,
4.17.46n; **5**, 3.1.1n, 3.9.1–4n;
**6**, 4.2.17n
*Heroides*: **3**, 4.12.5–6n; **4**, 3.1.1n,
3.13.5n, 3.21.4n; **9**, 4.12.5–6n;
**12**, 4.12.5–6n; **16**, 3.9.6n; **17**,
4.12.5–6n; **21**, 4.17.5n
*Metamorphoses*: **1**, 4.3.15–16n; **2**,
4.5.14n; **3**, 4.14.4n; **4**,
3.14.12n; **5**, 3.18.15n, 4.17.27n,
4.17.41–42n; **7**, 3.14.3–4n; **8**,
3.2.7–8n, 3.9.1–4n, 3.12.9–
10n, 4.17.5n; **10**, 4.5.76–77n,
4.6.11–12n, 4.17.32n,
4.17.62n, 4.18.1n, 4.22.24n;
**11**, 4.15.7–14n; **12**, 3.18.15n;
**13**, 3.13.5n, 3.18.23–24n,
4.5.43n, 4.16.19n, 4.17.27n;
**14**, 3.2.5n, 3.7.4n, 3.9.1–4n,
3.16.12n, 4.14.2n; **15**, 3.5.4n,
3.14.12n, 4.17.27n, 4.22.13n
*Remedia amoris*, 4.12.5–6n,
4.16.42n
*Tristia*: **1.9**, 4.12.5–6n; **2**, 3.16.5
and 8n; **3.13**, 4.5.76–77n;
**4.4**, 4.2.30n; **4.10**, 3.13.6n;
**5.5**, 3.1.7n; **5.6**, 4.15.12–13n

# · INDEX TO FLAMINIO ·

Pales, 4.2.29, 4.5.25, 4.10.1, 4.16.45, 4.20.1

Pan, 3.12.1, 3.20.10, 4.19.4; called *bicornis* ("two-horned"), 4.10.1; *capripes* ("goat-footed"), 4.2.29, 4.16.19–20; *magnus* ("mighty"), 4.17.61; *maximus* ("most mighty"), 4.15.2, 4.16.53; *nemorum decus* ("glory of the woodlands"), 4.17.99; *pater* ("father"), 3.1.1, 4.20.1; *semicaper deus* ("the half-goat god"), 4.2.13; *silvipotens* ("the woodland's lord"), 4.23.1; *Tegaeus* ("Tegean"), 4.5.26; in notes, 3.1.1n, 3.2.5n, 3.20.10n, 4.2.13–14n, 4.16.19n, 4.16.50n, 4.17.61n, 4.17.67n, 4.22.51 and 53n. *See also* Faunus

Parcae. *See* Fates

Parnassus (mountain), 4.17.15, 4.17.15–16n

Paul III (pope), xxiv–xxv, 3.1.7n

Paul IV (pope). *See* Carafa, Gianpietro

Persephone/Proserpina, 4.12.5–6n; as Ceres' daughter, 4.17.41–50, 4.17.41–42n; as "girl-bride of Dis," 4.4.19, 4.4.19n

Petrarch (Francesco Petrarca)/ Petrarchism, 3.22n, 3.22.5n, 4.5.19n, 4.21n

Petronius, 3.8.3n

Phoebus. *See* Apollo

Pholoe, 3.7.2, 3.7.2n, 3.9.3 and 8n, 3.9.4 (with her unnamed mother)

Phyllis, xxi, 3.16.5, 3.16.5 and 8n, 3.16.8, 3.17.8, 3.18.7, 3.20.3, 3.21.3

Pindar, 3.1.7n

Pindus (mountain), 4.17.15, 4.17.15–16n

Pirithous, 4.12.6, 4.12.5–6n

Plautus: *Amphitryo*, 4.14.4n; *Captivi*, 4.23.7n

Pliny the Elder, 4.2.19n

Pluto, 4.17.85; as Dis, 4.4.19, 4.17.68; as Orcus, 4.17.48, 4.17.54 (Orcus = Underworld, 4.17.27); "haughty king," 4.17.35; "that tyrant," 4.17.37; in notes, 4.4.19n, 4.5.76–77n, 4.17.27n, 4.17.41–42n, 4.17.46n, 4.17.65n, 4.17.68n

Pole, Reginald (cardinal), xxv–xxvi, xxxviii n43

Poliziano (Angelo Ambrogini), xxxvi n30; *In Scabiem*, 4.22.25n

Polyphemus. *See* Cyclops

Pomona, 4.6.1, 4.6.1–2n

Pomponazzi, Pietro, xxii

Pontano, Giovanni Gioviano, 3.13.6n

    *De Amore Coniugali*: **2.8**, 4.2.18n; **2.17**, 4.2.16n; **2.19**, 4.2.18n

    *Eclogues*, 4.15.16n

    *Eridanus*, 3.16.1n, 4.5.9–10n

    *Lyra*, 4.17.9n

484

## · INDEX TO FLAMINIO ·

*Parthenopeus: 1.4*, 3.7.4n; *1.11*,
  4.2.19n
*Tumuli*, 4.16.28–30n
*Urania*, 4.25.16–18n
Poverty (personified), 3.1.7n
Propertius, 3.1–4.25n
  *Elegies* (refs. as in Loeb text):
    *1.16*, 3.7.4n; *1.17*, 4.10.17–
    20n; *1.20*, 4.7.5n; *2.6*,
    3.6.7n; *2.15*, 4.17.89–90n,
    4.19.21n; *2.16*, 4.5.14n; *2.19*,
    4.12.5–6n; *2.20*, 3.12.9–10n;
    *2.28*, 3.12.9–10n; *2.32*,
    4.16.53n; *3.2*, 4.15.7–14n; *3.3*,
    4.5.25–26n; *3.4*, 4.5.40n;
    *3.18*, 4.12.5–6n; *4.4*, 4.18.7–
    8n; *4.5*, 3.28.1–2n; *4.7*,
    4.8.3–4 and 11–12n
Proserpina. *See* Persephone
Prudentius, 4.5.1n
Pylades, 4.12.5, 4.12.5–6n

Raphael (painter), 4.7.9n
Rhea, identified with Cybele,
  4.17.65n
rival girl, unsuccessful tempting
  by, 3.16n, 3.16.5–12, 3.17.7–8,
  3.17.8n
Rota, Bernardino, 3.3.1n

Saints Fabiano and Sebastiano,
  Abbey of, xxv, xxxviii n41
San Colombano, Priory of, xxv,
  xxxviii n41, 4.1.2n, 4.1.16n
Sannazaro, Jacopo, xxi, xxxvi n30;
  *Arcadia*, 4.21n; *De Partu
  Virginis*, 4.17.36n; *Eclogues*,

4.17.97n; *Elegies*, 3.9.1–4n,
  4.2.13–14n, 4.5.69n, 4.18.5–
  6n
San Prospero, Priory of (F.'s coun-
  try house), xxv; called *ager*,
  3.1.7, 3.1.7n; called *villula*,
  3.2.5, 3.2.5n
Saturn (god), 4.3.15–16n
satyrs, 4.1–25n, 4.4.1, 4.5.31,
  4.17.99
Sauli, Stefano, xxii, xxiv, 3.1–3.29n,
  3.10.2n, 3.12.9–10n, 4.1.2n,
  4.25.6–8n
Seneca, 4.18.5–6n
Septimilla, xxii, xxxvi n30
Sermione, 4.1.1, 4.1.2n, 4.1.16n
Serravalle, xx, xxiv, 3.1–3.29n,
  3.6.10n
Sessa, xxv, 4.1.25n
shut-out lover (*exclusus amator*),
  3.7, 3.7n, 3.7.4n, 3.8, 3.8n
silent ones (= the dead), 4.17.27,
  4.17.27n
Silius Italicus, *Punica: 1*, 4.21.16n;
  *3*, 4.3.5n, 4.17.39n; *4*, 4.17.93–
  94n; *7*, 3.8.3n; *10*, 3.8.3n
Silvanus, 3.1.1, 3.1.1n
singing matches, rustic, 3.22n,
  3.26n, 3.27n
Sleep (personified), xxiii, 3.8.3n
Spring (personified), 4.22.43–46,
  4.22.43n, 4.22.45n
Statius: *Achilleid*, 3.8.3n; *Silvae*, *2*,
  3.6.7n; *4*, 3.4.1n; *Thebaid*, *7*,
  4.7.9n; *10*, 3.8.3n
Strozzi, Lodovico, 4.1.2n
Strozzi, Tito Vespasiano, 3.19.5n

485

### · INDEX TO FLAMINIO ·

Styx/Stygian, 4.3.20, 4.8.6,
4.17.32, 4.17.32n
Sun (personified), 4.3.4; (meta-
phorically), 4.21.17
syphilis, xix, xxxvii n33, 4.1–25n
Syrinx, 4.17.61, 4.17.61n

Taburno (mountain), 4.1.5, 4.1.5n,
4.15.12, 4.15.12–13n, 4.16.3,
4.16.25, 4.17.20 (and "great
father" in 4.17.21), 4.20.2
Tagus (river), 4.16.10, 4.16.10n
Tartarus, 4.22.12, 4.22.12n
Tebaldeo, Antonio, 3.10.2n
Tegea/Tegean, 4.5.25–26n, 4.5.26
Terence, 4.25.1n; *Heautontimoru-
menos*, 4.14.4n
Tethys (= sea), 4.22.32, 4.22.32n
Thalia (a Muse), 4.17.12, 4.17.12n
Theocritus, 4.25.1n; "the Old
Sicilian," 4.17.12, 4.17.12n
*Idylls: 1*, 3.18.25–26n; *2*, 3.15.2n;
*5*, 3.17.1n; *7*, 3.19.5n; *8*,
4.2.25n; *11*, 4.17.12n; *15*,
3.18.7–8n
Theseus, 4.12.5–6n
Thestylis, 3.15.2, 3.15.2n, 3.16.1,
3.16.9, 3.17.1, 3.18.5, 3.18.25–
26n
Thrace/Thracian, 4.17.25
Thyrsis, 3.18.1, 3.18.23–24n,
3.18.24, 3.18.25–26n
Tibullus, 3.1–4.25n
*Elegies: 1.1*, 4.2.17n, 4.17.89–
90n, 4.18.5–6n; *1.2*, 3.7.4n,
3.14.1–2n, 4.2.17n; *1.5*,
4.17.11n, 4.17.46n; *1.7*,

4.4.6n; *2.2*, 3.8.3n; *2.4*,
4.10.17–20n; *2.5*, 4.10.7n;
*2.6*, 3.9.1–4n
[Tibullus], *Elegies, 3.10*, 3.12.9–10n
Tisiphone (a Fury), 4.17.29–30n,
4.17.36, 4.17.36n
Tithonus, 4.17.70
Titian, 3.1.7n
Tolomei, Claudio, 3.5n
tombs, inscriptions on, 4.10.17–
20n
Torre, Fernando della, xxxiv n24
Torre, Francesco della, xix, 4.25.1,
4.25.1n; his uncle Raimondo,
4.25.1n
Torre, Marcantonio della, 4.7.9n
Trent, Council of, xxvi
Troyes, Simon de, 3.6n
Turks, 3.10.2n

Urania (Muse of astronomy),
4.25.6–8n, 4.25.13n, 4.25.16,
4.25.16–18n

Valdés, Juan de, xxv, 4.1–25n
Valerius Flaccus, 3.12.9–10n,
4.17.27n
Varchi, Benedetto, 4.29.3n
Venantius, 4.25.16–18n
Venus, xxxvi n31, 3.1.7n, 3.5.6,
3.8.5, 3.9.1, 3.9.1–4n, 3.12.2,
3.13.6, 3.14.11, 3.16.7, 3.18.21–
22n, 3.25.5, 4.5.9–10n,
4.22.38n; called the Cyprian
goddess, 4.16.42, 4.16.42n;
called Cytherea, 3.14.3,
3.28.1, 3.28.1–2n, 4.8.9,

486

## · INDEX TO FLAMINIO ·

4.23.3; cf. "Cytherean bird"
of Cupid, 4.17.39, 4.17.39n
Venus (planet). *See* evening star;
morning star
Vergil, 4.20.11n; called *Menalcas*,
4.17.9, 4.17.9n; seen as Cory-
don, lover of Alexis, 4.17.97n
*Aeneid: 1*, 4.3.11n, 4.3.17n,
4.18.12n, 4.22.13n, 4.22.14n;
*2*, 3.20.7n; *3*, 3.14.5–6n,
3.14.13n, 3.16.7n, 3.20.5–6n,
4.3.5n, 4.5.76–77n, 4.17.87n,
4.22.13n, 4.22.14n; *4*, 3.11.5–
6n, 3.14.12n, 4.5.29n, 4.6.3n,
4.16.25–26n; *5*, 3.7.2n,
3.11.5–6n, 4.10.17–20n,
4.16.13n; *6*, 3.1.7n, 4.2.15n,
4.3.5n, 4.5.1n, 4.5.76–77n,
4.8.9–10n, 4.8.16n, 4.10.17–
20n, 4.17.92n, 4.22.13n,
4.23.4n, 4.23.7n; *7*, 3.6.7n,
3.9.1–4n, 4.15.12–18n,
4.22.14n; *8*, 3.1.7n, 3.8.3n,
4.22.13n; *9*, xxi, 3.4.1n,
3.11.5–6n; *10*, 4.17.93–94n;
*11*, 3.11.5–6n, 4.5.25–26n,
4.8.16n, 4.17.63–64n,
4.17.92n, 4.22.13n; *12*, 3.8.1n,
3.27n, 4.5.8n, 4.6.14n,
4.14.4n, 4.18.7–8n, 4.18.12n
*Eclogues*, 3.10.2n, 4.17.6n,
4.25.1n; *1*, 3.19.5n, 4.17.9n; *2*,
3.15.2n, 3.24.5–6n, 4.5.24n,
4.15.16n, 4.17.19–20n,
4.17.97n; *3*, 3.16.5 and 8n,
3.17.1n, 3.22n, 4.5.15n,
4.22.24n; *4*, 4.17.67n; *5*,

3.4.1n, 3.16.5 and 8n, 3.17.8n,
3.27.3n, 4.16.19n, 4.16.48–
49n, 4.18.12n; *7*, 3.16.5 and
8n, 3.17.1n, 3.26n, 4.2.25n,
4.5.15n, 4.17.11n, 4.17.97n; *8*,
3.3.8n, 3.18.7–8n, 3.18.25–
26n, 3.18.27n, 3.24.1–4n,
4.5.23n, 4.5.28n; *9*, 3.9.1–4n,
3.19.5n, 3.22.1n, 3.26n,
4.22.1–3n; *10*, 3.9.1–4n,
3.16.5 and 8n, 4.16.53n
*Georgics: 1*, 3.11.5–6n, 3.19.2n,
3.23.2n, 4.2.15n, 4.17.6n; *2*,
3.5.4n, 3.11.5–6n, 3.20.5–6n,
4.16.10n, 4.16.48–49n,
4.17.53n, 4.25.6–8n; *4*,
3.4.4n, 3.10.7–8n, 3.11.5–6n,
3.20.1n, 3.20.5–6n, 4.2.5n,
4.2.15n, 4.5.41–42n,
4.16.34n, 4.22.24n
[Vergil]: *Ciris*, 4.5.19n; *Culex*,
3.21.2n, 4.3.11n, 4.16.19n,
4.16.53n
Verino, Ugolino, 4.12.5–6n,
4.22.14n
Volpi, Gaetano, xxxiv n25

wayfarer, imagined (or passing
shepherd, milkmaid, etc.),
4.9.1, 4.10.17, 4.10.17–20n,
4.11.1, 4.15.1, 4.15.1n

Zanchi, Basilio, xxxiv n24
Zephyr (west wind), 3.5.3, 3.10.6;
also = *Favonius*, 3.22.1, 4.1.17,
4.16.11
Zeus, 3.8n, 4.2.1n

487

*Publication of this volume has been made possible by*

The Packard Humanities Institute
The Lila Wallace–Reader's Digest Endowment Fund
The Andrew W. Mellon Scholarly Publications Fund
The ITRL Publications Fund